A Companion to Western Legal Traditions

Legal History Library

VOLUME 65

The titles published in this series are listed at *brill.com/lhl*

A Companion to Western Legal Traditions

From Antiquity to the Twentieth Century

Edited by

Aniceto Masferrer, Cornelis Hendrik (Remco) van Rhee,
Seán P. Donlan and Cornelis Heesters

BRILL | NIJHOFF

LEIDEN | BOSTON

Cover illustration: A close-up angle of the Parthenon in Athens, Greece, Clark Van Der Beken, Unsplash

Library of Congress Cataloging-in-Publication Data

Names: Masferrer, Aniceto, editor. | Rhee, Cornelis Hendrik (Remco) van, editor. | Donlan, Seán Patrick, editor. | Heesters, Cornelis, editor.
Title: A companion to Western legal traditions : from antiquity to the twentieth century / edited by Aniceto Masferrer, Cornelis Hendrik (Remco) van Rhee, Seán P. Donlan, and Cornelis Heesters.
Description: Leiden ; Boston : Brill/Nijhoff, 2024. | Series: Legal history library, 1874–1493 ; volume 65 | Includes bibliographical references and index.
Identifiers: LCCN 2023045798 (print) | LCCN 2023045799 (ebook) | ISBN 9789004687219 (hardback) | ISBN 9789004687240 (paperback) | ISBN 9789004687257 (ebook)
Subjects: LCSH: Law–History. | Law, Ancient.
Classification: LCC K150 .C66 2024 (print) | LCC K150 (ebook) | DDC 340.09182/1–dc23/eng/20231002
LC record available at https://lccn.loc.gov/2023045798
LC ebook record available at https://lccn.loc.gov/2023045799

Typeface for the Latin, Greek, and Cyrillic scripts: “Brill”. See and download: brill.com/brill-typeface.

ISSN 1874-1793
ISBN 978-90-04-68721-9 (hardback)
ISBN 978-90-04-68724-0 (paperback)
ISBN 978-90-04-68725-7 (e-book)
DOI 10.1163/9789004687257

This book is printed on acid-free paper and produced in a sustainable manner.

Contents

Contributors

Seán Patrick Donlan
Professor of Law, Thompson Rivers University, Canada.

Stephan Dusil
Professor of Civil Law, Germanic Legal History, Contemporary Legal History and Ecclesiastical Law, University of Tübingen, Germany.

Adolfo Giuliani
Ministry for Education, University and Research, Rome, Italy, formerly at Max Planck Institute for Legal History and Legal Theory, Frankfurt am Main, Germany.

Jan Hallebeek
Professor emeritus of Legal History, Vrije Universiteit Amsterdam, Netherlands.

Jean-Louis Halpérin
Professor of Legal History, École normale supérieure – PSL Paris, France.

Cornelis Heesters
MA, LLM, independent researcher, writer, editor, and translator living in Baltimore, USA.

Dirk Heirbaut
Professor of Legal History and Roman law, Ghent University, Belgium.

Bernd Kannowski
Professor of Civil Law and Legal History, University of Bayreuth, Germany.

Aniceto Masferrer
Professor of Legal History, University of Valencia, Spain.

Olivier Moréteau
Russell B. Long Eminent Scholars Chair, Justice Pike Hall Distinguished Professorship, Louisiana State University, Baton Rouge, Louisiana, USA.

Agustín Parise
Associate Professor of Law, Maastricht University, Netherlands.

Heikki Pihlajamäki
Professor of Comparative Legal History, University of Helsinki, Finland.

Cornelis Hendrik (Remco) van Rhee
Professor of European Legal History, Maastricht University, Netherlands.

Gerald Schwedler
Professor of Medieval History, Christian-Albrechts Universität Kiel, Germany.

Jacques Vanderlinden†
Professor emeritus of Legal History, Free University of Brussels, Belgium.

Western Legal Traditions: An Introduction

Aniceto Masferrer, Cornelis Hendrik (Remco) van Rhee, Seán P. Donlan and Cornelis Heesters

The present volume provides materials for an historical and comparative introduction to the Western legal traditions, selected, translated and introduced by a group of leading European and North American legal historians. The volume's chapters can be used individually or jointly. It is not a traditional textbook providing the views of individual authors, but offers a variety of views. It is aimed at stimulating discussion and further research in areas of Western legal history that are of particular interest to its users and, consequently, an ideal instrument for university courses in legal history. Serious university courses should contain a range of views.

The title of the casebook needs some explanation where it refers to 'Western legal traditions'. First we should consider the phrase 'legal traditions'. One definition is offered by J.H. Merryman, who states that a legal tradition is:

> a set of deeply rooted, historically conditioned attitudes about the nature of law, about the role of law in the society and the polity, about the proper organization and operation of a legal system, and about the way law is or should be made, applied, studied, perfected, and taught. The legal tradition relates the legal system to the culture of which it is a partial expression. It puts the legal system into a cultural perspective.[1]

We are aware of the fact that other definitions are possible, and have not imposed on the authors in this volume a particular version. We start with Merryman's definition as an opening bid, rather than a final destination. The book was conceived with "legal tradition" as an open-textured concept, resisting the call to narrow nationalism but giving some guidance about the legal and socio-legal characteristics of the objects studied.

Secondly, we need to consider the meaning of *Western* legal traditions. The legal traditions discussed in the present volume find their origin in Europe and North America, and it is these territories which we define as 'Western' in the present volume. In traditional legal historical and comparative literature, the

1 J.H. Merryman, The Civil Law Tradition. An Introduction to the Legal Systems of Western Europe and Latin America (2nd ed.), Stanford, Stanford University Press, 1985, 2.

 | DOI:10.1163/9789004687257_002

main 'Western' legal traditions are commonly referred to as the civil law and common law traditions, but this distinction is problematic in itself. Some of the materials provided in this volume may serve as the starting point for the re-evaluation of this and similar distinctions.

The influence of the Western legal traditions may be found globally. This is not only due to colonialism but also to the voluntary adoption of Western legal ideas and institutions in several jurisdictions, two particularly powerful examples being Japan and China.

In the present volume, priority is given to 'external' rather than 'internal' legal history. 'External legal history' covers the intellectual and institutional context (historical, societal) in which the law developed. Essential themes include the interplay of the *iura propria* and *iura communia*, legal institutions, the legal profession, legal science, the sources of law, and the political and social context, especially the growth of the state. In addition, some attention is paid to 'internal legal history', i.e. the history of the rules of substantive and procedural law. The areas of law treated include what we now refer to as commercial law, criminal law, private or civil law, procedural law, and public or constitutional law. The volume focuses on both common and divergent legal solutions, concepts and principles that exemplify the Western legal traditions. These may favour the dominant legal traditions of Europe, but are not necessarily limited to them.

The volume combines (i) central, original narrative and (ii) collected extracts. Existing learned or scholarly writings, sometimes unavailable in English, play a significant role in the text. Extracts are added where a primary or secondary source (i) expresses ideas in a useful, comprehensive, and concise manner, (ii) expands on the original text, or (iii) illustrates particular points.

The volume contains seven chapters. Apart from an introduction, a summary and conclusion, and sections with literature cited and further reading, each chapter consists of three main sections entitled 'Creation', 'Actors', and 'Application'. 'Creation' is devoted to the formal and material sources of the law, 'Actors' to the individuals and office holders in charge of the management or development – intentional or accidental – of the law, and 'Application' to the law in practice, each for the particular period of the chapter. The respective chapter authors have subdivided these main sections as they felt appropriate for their respective periods, and therefore further subdivisions are not necessarily uniform.

The book is modular in the sense that the chapters can be used individually. Although they will have significant overlapping themes and threads, none is dependent on information provided in another. The chapters are not meant to offer an exhaustive overview of the developments of the law and legal institutions in the periods discussed (if this is possible at all), but contain materials on subject-matter the authors found appropriate for their respective periods. Since all authors are specialists in the period allotted to them, their choice also reflects the current state of research, the 'state of the art', in the various areas discussed. The chapters provide a framework for further study and aim at stimulating such study. The 'further reading' section in each chapter provides the necessary assistance for further research.

Chapter 1 covers Antiquity which, for the purposes of the volume, starts in 753 BC, the year of the mythical foundation of Rome, and ends in 565 AD, with the death of the Emperor Justinian I. In actual fact, however, the chapter starts later since our knowledge of Roman legal history only begins around 450 BC with the 'Law of the Twelve Tables'. The emphasis is on classical Roman Law and what we call here 'Justinianic Law'. Classical Roman Law is the law from the period of the reign of Octavianus, the emperor Augustus, in 27 BC until approximately 300 AD. Justinianic Law coincides with the reign of the Byzantine emperor Justinian I, from 527 until 565 AD. The latter period is crucial since it witnessed the codification – the redaction and revision – of Roman Law, giving rise to what later came to be called the *Corpus iuris civilis*, the 'body of [Roman] civil law'. It was the *Corpus iuris* through which later generations of lawyers would become acquainted with Roman law since most other sources did not survive. Although traces of Roman law were present in the West even after the Fall of the Western Empire in 476 AD, the rediscovery in Italy of the two main parts of the *Corpus iuris*, the *Digest* and the *Codex* at the end of the 11th century, brought about a true revival of Roman legal scholarship. Chapter 1 also discusses internal legal history, especially where it focuses on the Roman laws of property and obligations. The latter included a wide variety of legal relationships between individuals.

Chapter 2 discusses the early medieval period, from 500 until 1100. There is potentially an overlap with Chapter 1, but this overlap is avoided by concentrating especially (but not solely) on the role of Roman law in Western Europe in the early medieval period. The emphasis is on the emerging political powers in the West, especially the new 'Germanic' kingdoms (i.e., those migrants who settled in the former territories of the Western Roman Empire) and the Church, as well as the law they produced. The year 500 is chosen as the starting point since it is around this year that several political events took place that gave birth to new conceptions and applications of the law. The period around 500 also witnessed the establishment of the various Germanic kingdoms in Western and Central Europe. Terminating Chapter 2 around 1100 is justified since the High Middle Ages gave rise to new approaches to legal matters: the introduction of the scholastic method, the rediscovery of the Roman law *in toto*, and the creation of the first universities. The chapter discusses, amongst other things, the law of the Germanic peoples that established themselves in the West, the role of rulers like Charlemagne, the role of the Church, Roman vulgar law, the Barbarian codes, feudal law and canon law. The early medieval period is characterized by decentralization, diversity, polycentrism and a pluralism of legal systems, ethnicities and authorities. There were a multitude of players, all enacting legal rules partly based on Roman law, on Germanic ideas, and on religious beliefs. The resulting legal systems overlapped each other and exercised a sometimes weak, sometimes strong influence on each other. This diversity of legal systems is based on the emergence of a great number of new political entities and the lack of a central power of the sort that will become prominent in the modern era. It was a time in history without lawyers, but with a multitude of legal source materials.

Chapter 3 is devoted to the High and Late Middle Ages. It starts around 1100 since this period forms a watershed moment in European history, a moment that is even more important than the year 1500. Indeed, according to the authors of the Chapter, the period around 1100 was as transformative as the revolutionary period around 1800. Law in this period, like political power, was concerned with privilege, not social equality. There was a bewildering variety of legal rules. The age also witnessed a true revival of Roman law, or of a Roman law as perceived by contemporary perspectives. The scholarly study of law gave rise to the creation of a *ius commune* – strictly speaking, a common law – which formed a true legal toolbox for lawyers or legal actors all over Europe. The period also witnessed attempts to record customary law and saw its subsequent approval (homologation) or disapproval by the ruler. It witnessed the spread of law faculties. In these, Roman and Canon law became the object of scholarly study by so-called 'glossators' and 'commentators', a long-standing division of two diverse, chronologically successive, streams of legal scholarship. The influence of these 'learned laws', the laws studied in the universities, could also be witnessed in England and was instrumental in the genesis of England's laws. The powers of the Pope and the Emperor were subject to debate, and cities were on the rise. The period witnessed the creation of early constitutions and parliaments, as well as the rise of professional lawyers and hierarchical court systems. The chapter ends around 1500 when the Reformation not only ended the relative unity of Western Christianity, but also brought about important changes in politics and law.

In Chapter 4 the starting point is the year 1500 even though to legal history that year may be less relevant than in other areas. A look at the texts, arguments and authorities that jurists used around 1500 shows the persistence of medieval material even though a school of interpreters came into being that today we call 'legal humanism'. The approach of the humanists was, however, not typical of the legal profession. In general, legal practitioners had little sense for the past, feeling they belonged to a temporal continuum shared with older generations of jurists. Authors who wrote centuries earlier, could still be used as a source of arguments and opinions, and their names were cited next to contemporary work. If we look at legal practice or the methods of rationalising the law, we find the recurrence of opinions and arguments produced centuries before. This continuity was insured by largely unchanged methods of legal education, deeply rooted in medieval scholasticism, and consequently, by unchanged patterns of argument and modes of reasoning. In such a setting, tradition was immensely more powerful than in today's world.

Chapter 5 focuses on the period 1650–1775. The start of this period, i.e. the middle of the seventeenth century, can, for several reasons, be seen as a turning point in legal history across Europe. Indeed, in 1648, the pan-European Thirty Years War (and the Eighty Years War between Spain and the Dutch Republic) came to an end with the various treaties of Westphalia. These treaties brought about a weakening of the remnants of the medieval Holy Roman Empire. They are often described as the beginning of the modern international community of independent states, although this view is not uncontested. It is the time of the rise of absolutist rulers, notably Louis XIV in France, and early scholarly treatises on the structure of modern society and the legitimacy of modern government (e.g., social contract theory) like *Leviathan* by the Englishman Thomas Hobbes. The subsequent eighteenth century can be seen as a transitional stage between the medieval polity and the true modern state. In Chapter 5 it is stated that the period 1650–1775 witnessed the transition from decentralized legal systems based on plural legal sources in pre-modern states into centralized legal systems, which were the expression of the legislative state. It is the period of so-called Enlightenment when attempts were made to introduce general statutes for the whole territory of the state, and ultimately at codification of the laws. Criminal law was humanised under the influence of legal thinkers such as Cesare Beccaria. The period witnessed the birth of the modern state with the introduction of specific rules governing public administration, Montesquieu's argument for the primacy of public law and the separation of powers (at least as he understood it), administrative centralization and legislative rationalization. There was an increased intervention by the legislative and judicial authorities in domains like procedural law, commercial law, tort law, the law of contract, and criminal law. And the end of the period witnessed the first few years of the American Revolution which formed one of the bases of the major changes in law and society which would follow in the

West in the period 1776–1900. This period also witnessed the further diffusion of Western laws in other parts of the world.

The period 1776–1900 is the subject of Chapter 6. The Chapter focuses on the revolutionary age of the second half of the eighteenth century and its pervasive consequences for law and society in the period to follow. It also discusses the nineteenth century which, from the legislative perspective, may be qualified as a true codification period, in the sense of modern, binding general laws. Obviously, the French Revolution served as the watershed between the *ancien régime* and the modern nation state. The Revolution gave rise to the first European constitution which served as a basic law promulgating, or purporting to recognize and protect, modern fundamental rights. This period saw the rise of modern constitutionalism, i.e. the promulgation of written constitutions aimed at limiting the powers of the state while at the same time increasing these powers. Keywords or phrases in the chapter are the rule of law, the principle of legality, legislative supremacy, the separation of powers, and fundamental rights such as equality before the law. The nineteenth century further witnessed the rise of the unitary nation state with national codifications, even though some of these codifications were 'received' or 'borrowed' from abroad. Across continental Europe, judges were required to administer justice based on these codes and to provide explicit reasons, rooted in positive law, for their judgments, altering the use of jurisprudence (judicial decisions) as a legal source. Legal scholarship and legal education were also in a parallel state of flux, and legal positivism dominated the legal landscape during much of the nineteenth century. It gave rise to intellectual or institutional developments, or excesses, such as the so-called Exegetical School and the Jurisprudence of Concepts. Whether the codes also meant a break with the past is a matter of discussion. What is clear, however, is that the role of some of the traditional sources of law such as custom and natural law changed. In addition, changes can be observed in the legal profession with the creation of bar associations and enhanced professionalisation. Furthermore, developments in the overseas colonies will be highlighted.

The final Chapter of this volume (Chapter 7) is largely devoted to the twentieth century. In this period, the exclusive law-making powers of the state were challenged. Supranational organisations were created and started to legislate alongside the state. Examples are the Council of Europe and the European Communities and later the European Union. These developments triggered, at least to a certain degree, a de-codification of the law since supra-national rules did not easily find their place in national codes. Often a process of recodification was needed in order to achieve incorporation of these rules. Therefore, the twentieth century may be described as an era of compilation, consolidation, and recodification. The twentieth century also witnessed the further spread of the Western legal traditions, not only due to colonialism but also to economic globalization. Decolonisation did not change this as globalization created a need for the international harmonisation of the laws. As a result, comparative legal scholarship came to occupy a prominent position in the study of the law. Model laws and restatements were drafted, giving rise to what came to be qualified as 'soft law'. Legal scholarship witnessed an enormous growth, facilitated by the democratization of legal education and new types of law schools (e.g. European Law Schools). Legal positivism and natural law became the subject of intense debates, partially due to the horrors of the Second World War and the way one should deal with these. And private law was constitutionalized, a movement that could first be witnessed in some relatively new democratic states such as Ireland (*Meckel v. Córas Iompair Éireann* [1973] IR 121) and South Africa.

CHAPTER 1

Antiquity (753 BC–565 AD)

Jan Hallebeek

1 Introduction

Nothing exerted more influence on the development of law in the western world than the rediscovery of the legal heritage of Rome in northern Italy at the end of the eleventh century. From then until the threshold of the codification era (roughly the nineteenth and twentieth centuries), the *Corpus iuris civilis* – a compilation of Roman law promulgated by the Emperor Justinian (ca. 482–565 AD) in the sixth century AD – played a decisive role in the formation of a common legal culture in continental Europe. Except for the Bible, no other book has been as important to law and society in western Europe as this ancient legal text. Its indelible mark on private law has lasted to this very day, so it is only fitting to start this volume on western legal traditions with a chapter devoted to Roman law.[1]

> *Peter Stein, Roman Law in European history (12th ed.), Cambridge, Cambridge University Press, 2013, 1*
>
> When we think of the legacy of classical antiquity, we think first of Greek art, Greek drama and Greek philosophy; when we turn to what we owe to Rome, what come to mind are probably Roman roads and Roman law. The Greeks speculated a great deal about the nature of law and about its place in society but the actual laws of the various Greek states were not highly developed in the sense that there was little science of law. The Romans, on the other hand, did not give much attention to the theory of law; their philosophy of law was largely borrowed from the Greeks. What interested them were the rules governing an individual's property and what he could make another person to do for him by legal proceedings. Indeed the detailed rules of Roman law were developed by professional jurists and became highly sophisticated. The very technical superiority of its reasoning, which has made it so attractive to professional lawyers

1 This first chapter follows the format observed in the other chapters despite the fact that presenting the Roman materials in this uniform arrangement may sometimes be problematic. All translations from primary and secondary sources are the author's.

 | DOI:10.1163/9789004687257_003

> through the ages, has meant that Roman law is not readily accessible to the layman. Inevitably its merits have a less obvious appeal than art or roads. Yet over the centuries it has played an important role in the creation of the idea of a common European culture.

The *Corpus iuris civilis* was in essence the culmination of a thousand-year history stretching from the mid-fifth century BC Law of the Twelve Tables until the time of Justinian himself. Janus, the Roman god of time, has two faces: one looking backward into the past, the other looking forward into the future. The *Corpus iuris* is sometimes described as Janus-faced because it looks backwards, as it comprises the final stage of the development of Roman law in Antiquity and, at the same time, forwards, as the starting point for European legal scholarship from the twelfth century onwards. In this chapter, we will confine ourselves to the Roman law of Antiquity, which was not the only law in the western world at the time, but has been the most important building block in the continental tradition of private law and legal scholarship.

To get a handle on the long time-period covering the development of Roman law, historians traditionally distinguish five historical stages. First, there is the early, archaic period from the foundation of Rome until ca. 300 BC; second, the formative period of pre-classical law, ca. 300–27 BC; third, the period of classical law, 27 BC–ca. 300 AD; fourth, the period of post-classical or vulgar law, ca. 300 AD until the time of Justinian; and finally, the Justinianic law in the sixth century AD. The use of terms like 'pre-classical' and 'vulgar' are the product of a particular view of the importance of classical Roman law. The term 'classical Roman law' for the Roman jurisprudence, and specifically the jurists' legal replies, of the first until the third centuries AD, was only introduced in the eighteenth century.

In this chapter, the emphasis will be on classical and Justinianic law. To the classical period we owe the old *ius*, i.e., the classical jurists' replies, often seen as a milestone in Roman legal scholarship. Justinian's era is vital because it gave birth to the *Corpus iuris civilis*, which later served as the basis of European legal scholarship. Even though Roman law in the western legal tradition was primarily handed down in its Justinianic form, we will also pay attention to the historical development preceding the compilation of the *Corpus iuris*, especially in the classical law. In many law schools, Roman law is still taught today by focusing on the interpretation of the texts of the Digest in their historical context using, for example, interpolation criticism and palingenesis, and not by studying these texts as provisions of a code of law from the sixth century AD.

2 Creation

Classical Roman law was characterised by a stratification into two bodies; the *ius civile* (literally 'civil law') and *ius honorarium* (literally 'honorary law' or 'law made in office'). This distinction goes back to the pre-classical period. The *ius civile* had existed from time immemorial and consisted of statutes and customs. The *ius honorarium* had a different origin: in the fourth century BC, the office of *praetor* was introduced, and in the second century BC, that of the *aediles curules*. These magistrates were appointed for one year and were entitled to promulgate an edict containing remedies for litigation for the period they were in office. They could adopt (parts of) the edict of their predecessor and remove or add certain remedies. Since new remedies recognized and *de facto* created new claims, the edicts became a source of substantive law. This law, created by magistrates, was called *ius honorarium*. Although it was sometimes also referred to as praetorian law, this is a less accurate description as it only includes the law created by the *praetor* and not the *aediles curules*. The *ius honorarium* added to and corrected the *ius civile*.

> *Wolfgang Kunkel and Martin Schermaier, Römische Rechtsgeschichte* (*14th ed.*), *Cologne etc., Böhlau, 2012, 104*
> The effects of all these law-creating factors are reflected in the structure of the Roman legal order. From the time the magistrates' jurisdiction took control of its development, Roman law was no longer a homogeneous body of materials, but a coexistence and accumulation of various layers of law with a clearly defined nature of their own. When classical legal scholarship took off, it already encountered, apart from the *ius civile*, a highly developed *ius honorarium*. The *ius civile* was rigorous and rigid in its principles, but in many details brought up to date by more recent legislation and borrowings from honorary law. The *ius honorarium* was progressive, free and developing continuously. The relationship between the two was comparable to that in English law between the Common law and Equity, emerging from the practice of the Chancery. Classical legal scholarship adopted the distinction between *ius civile* and *ius honorarium* as an established fact. However, because of the many entanglements between both layers of law and since they developed simultaneously, this gradually wiped out their mutual borderlines. As a consequence, at the turn of the second to the third century, the late classical jurists were probably the last people, who still clearly had in mind the structural distinction between civil law and honorary law.

In the classical period, the magistrates gradually lost their role in creating new law. Edicts were no longer promulgated and, in the post-classical era, legal proceedings were exclusively chaired by imperial judges so magistrates no longer played a role. Nevertheless, the distinction between *ius civile* and *ius honorarium* survived and became part of Justinianic law as a way of indicating the origin of various legal norms. The *ius civile* included statutes and supplementary rulings such as custom, decisions of the Senate, plebiscites, the replies of jurists, and constitutions of the Emperors. The *ius honorarium* consisted of the edicts of the magistrates. This is explained in the following two texts from the *Corpus iuris civilis*. The first is taken from the Institutes of Justinian. The second is a fragment of the late classical jurist Papinian († 212 AD), included in Justinian's Digest.

> *Inst. 2.1.7*
> Also the edicts of the praetors have a considerable force of law. We usually call these *ius honorarium*, because persons with an honorary office, i.e., the magistrates, gave authority to this law. Also the *aediles curules* promulgated an edict for certain cases, and that edict is also part of the *ius honorarium*.[2]

> *D. 1.1.7 Papinian, Definitions, Book II*
> (pr) *Ius civile* results from statutes, plebiscites, decisions of the Senate, decrees of the Emperors, and the authority of the jurists.
> (1) Praetorian law is what the praetors in view of the public interest have introduced to support, supply or correct the *ius civile*, which is also termed *ius honorarium*, so called after the honorary office of the praetors.[3]

2 Inst. 1.2.7 Praetorum quoque edicta non modicam iuris optinent auctoritatem. haec etiam ius honorarium solemus appellare, quod qui honorem gerunt, id est magistratus, auctoritatem huic iuri dederunt. proponebant et aediles curules edictum de quibusdam casibus, quod edictum iuris honorarii portio est.

3 D. 1.1.7 *Papinianus libro secundo definitionum* (pr) Ius autem civile est, quod ex legibus, plebis scites, Senates consultis, decretis principum, auctoritate prudentium venit. (1) Ius praetorium est, quod praetores introduxerunt adiuvandi vel supplendi vel corrigenda iuris civilis gratia propter utilitatem publicam, quod et honorarium dicitur ad honorem praetorum sic nominatum.

2.1 *Political Organization and Law*

Over the course of its history, Rome had various forms of government. The oldest one was the Monarchy which existed from the foundation of Rome until 509 BC. According to Roman writers, especially Livy († 17 AD), the seventh Roman king, Tarquinius Superbus (534–509 BC), was driven out of power around 509 BC in a nonviolent revolution. The Monarchy was followed by the Roman Republic, from 509 BC until 27 BC, and subsequently the Roman Empire. The latter era is subdivided into two periods, the Principate (27 BC until 284 AD) and the Dominate (284 AD until 565 AD).

During the Monarchy, Rome was still a relatively small settlement. The main public bodies were the king, who had various duties and powers; the Senate, the king's advisory body; and the *comitia curiata*, a public assembly which could vote on statutes proposed by the king. A feature of the Monarchy and the early Republic was the subdivision of the population into two social classes: the upper class 'patricians', and the socially weaker 'plebeians'.

In the Republic, Roman influence expanded considerably and from the fourth century BC onwards Rome conquered and ruled major parts of the Mediterranean. During this era, Rome's political structure was shaped by the Senate, the magistrates, and the public assemblies. The former had already existed under the Monarchy and was an important political body. Public assembly decisions concerning statutes and the appointment of magistrates needed the Senate's approval, it had to be consulted in important political matters, and it was responsible for foreign policy. However, the Republican Senate increased in power. According to the *lex Publilia Philonis* (339 BC), statutes could only be put to a vote in public assemblies after the Senate's approval, and the *lex Maenia* (third century BC) said elections of magistrates required Senate approval.

There were various magistrates with divergent political powers in the Republic. The offices were characterised by the principles of annuity and duality: magistrates held their office for one year and most offices were held by two magistrates with equal powers. The superior magistrates were the consul, the praetor, the *decemvir* and the censor, and the inferior ones were the *quaestor* and the tribune of the people, assisted by two *aediles*. The office of the praetor and that of the *aediles curules* were the most important for the development of the law, and we will discuss their significance below. A number of changes to these offices occurred under the Republic. The office of the praetor was introduced in the fourth century BC, and from 242 BC onwards there were two praetors: one for litigation between Roman citizens (*praetor urbanus*) and one for litigation where one or both parties were not Roman citizens (*praetor peregrinus*). The *leges Liciniae Sextiae* (367 BC) also introduced two new *aediles* called *aediles curules*, who later acquired authority over the administration of justice in conflicts related to the sale of slaves and cattle on the market.

There were also a number of public assemblies, of which four were particularly important. At the end of the Monarchy, two new public assemblies were added to the existing *comitia curiata*, namely the *comitia centuriata* and the *comitia tributa*. All three remained in existence during the Republic, but the *comitia curiata* ceased to function properly in the fourth century BC. The most important of these public bodies was the *comitia centuriata*, an assembly composed of the more prosperous citizens which was competent to elect the superior magistrates and vote on statutes. The *comitia tributa*, composed of less prosperous citizens, elected the inferior magistrates and could decide on statutes of minor political importance. From 471 BC the plebeians also gathered in an assembly called the *concilium plebis*. Decisions of the *concilium plebis*, so-called 'plebiscites', were initially only in force for the plebeians themselves, but after the *lex Hortensia* (287 BC) they had binding force for the entire population. Over the course of time, as the Roman empire expanded, the number of patricians fell in proportion to the population as a whole, leading to a gradual decline in the differences between the various public assemblies, including the *concilium plebis*.

At the end of the first century BC, radical political changes took place in Rome. In 27 BC Octavian (63 BC-14 AD), an adoptive son of the murdered Julius Caesar (ca. 100-44 BC), seized power. The Republic turned into an Empire. In 27 BC, the Senate awarded Octavian the name 'Augustus', meaning literally 'the venerable'. Moreover, the Senate and the public assemblies granted Octavian a series of rights which made him the Roman Empire's absolute ruler.

During the first period of the Empire – the Principate – Rome culminated its expansion: around 130 AD, even the larger part of what is now the United Kingdom was occupied by Rome. Initially, the old bodies and offices such as the Senate, the magistrates, and the public assemblies remained intact, and the Senate formally retained many of its traditional competences. Only after the death of Marcus Aurelius (121–180AD), did the Emperors start to ignore the Senate. Imperial civil servants who derived their competences not from their own office, but as delegated by the Emperor took over certain tasks of the old magistrates. The most important of these civil servants were the praetorian prefect and the urban prefect: the former had judicial competence throughout the Empire, and the latter had jurisdiction in the city of Rome and its surroundings. For some time, public assemblies remained in existence, but only until their functions had been transferred to the Emperor once and for all.

Max Kaser, Römische Rechtsgeschichte, Göttingen, Vandenhoeck & Ruprecht, 1967, 111–112
In order to realize their comprehensive tasks in all areas of political life, Augustus and his successors created a massive administrative body that, over time, developed into a new state organ alongside those inherited from the Republic. These institutions partly originated from the private sphere of the *Princeps*, but with the progressive process of consolidation of the Principate they became recognized as state institutions. The imperial administration was superior to the republican administration from the outset as it was tailored to the purposes of the imperial rule, while the institutions of the Republic continued to wrestle with their restrictions because of their origin in a city-state, which was ruled by a triad of the Senate, People and Magistrate. Since, as we have seen, the duties of the *Princeps* far surpass those left to the republican institutions in terms of political importance, it is understandable that the imperial administration, more and more, pushed the republican administration back. Although we should not understand the Principate's administration as the diarchy of Emperor and Senate, the coexistence of the old and new administrative institutions resulted in a peculiar dualism between what, following its constitutional core, we can call the 'domain of the Senate' and the newly created 'domain of the Emperor'. The former consisted primarily of the magistrates surviving from the Republic accountable to the Senate, the treasury (*aerarium populi Romani*) managed by the Senate and the provinces administered by the Senate. On the other hand, the imperial officials, the *fiscus Caesaris* and the imperial provinces belonged to the domain of the Emperor. But this distinction can only be explained by the fact that a partially outdated past merged into a new, nascent form of government. Therefore, it remains limited to the areas mentioned, in which the duties are divided between the Emperor and the Senate. This formal dualism must not hide the fact that the Emperor, by virtue of his superior force, was also able to, widely, intervene in the Senate's domain.

Under the reign of Emperor Diocletian (ca. 243–316 AD) the Empire turned from Principate to Dominate. Diocletian introduced administrative reforms: he became an absolute monarch, appointed three co-Emperors and laid the foundation of a hierarchically structured body of civil servants.

Max Kaser, Römische Rechtsgeschichte, Göttingen, Vandenhoeck & Ruprecht, 1967, 206
When Diocletian, after a decades-long succession of weak rulers, re-established a strong rule, he renounced the restrictions of the past

> and established a complete and undisguised absolute Monarchy. Constantine, however, gives it the shape of an oriental autocracy. The Emperor is no longer the 'first citizen' but 'Lord and God' (*dominus et deus*), a title that had been claimed by Domitian and Aurelian (270–275). His power is unlimited, the entire realm and all citizens are subjected to his free will. The Emperor is, always and everywhere, a God during his lifetime and enjoys divine veneration, as has been the case for the great kings of the Orient since ancient times and is now also owed to the rulers of new Persia, the rival for supremacy in the east and model for the imperial dignity. Even the reinterpretation of the Emperor's divinity into a mere likeness to God, as required by Christianity, does not deprive the Emperor of its splendor. The plenitude of power and the distance from regular mortals are expressed in the oriental clothing, the gold-embroidered purple robe as well as in the diadem, the headband set with pearls, also in the Persian-ceremonial rites and the adoration which anyone, approaching the Emperor, must show by 'prostration in a dog-like manner' (*Proskynesis*) and 'kissing the robe' (*adoratio*). Everything concerning the Emperor is sacred (*sacrum*), from his bedroom to his laws and finances. The Emperor and the state are one, court and state administration are indivisible. The private property of the Emperor (*patrimonium*) and the state property (which is called *res privata*!) are only distinguished for administrative purposes. The Emperor delegates all powers in the state.

From the reign of Emperor Constantine (ca. 280–337 AD) onwards, there were two or three Emperors (*Augusti*) at the same time. At the end of the fourth century AD, the Empire was officially divided into western and eastern parts. Rome was initially the capital of the western part and also, after 404 AD, Ravenna. The capital of the eastern part was Constantinople, named after Constantine, who founded the city in 330 AD on the former site of Byzantium (this is why the eastern part is also called the Byzantine Empire). Justinian's court was in Constantinople, and it was there in the sixth century AD that he compiled the Roman law of Antiquity in the *Corpus iuris civilis*.

2.2 *Natural Law and Natural Rights*

The Roman jurists were familiar with the notion of *ius naturale* or natural law. The term was used by the Roman orator and politician Cicero (106-43 BC), and although it originally came from Greek philosophy, the Romans made the concept their own. The idea of norms which transcend positive law goes back to

Aristotle's philosophy (384-322 BC). Cicero taught that there was a rational, immutable, universal, and divine law as far as the main principles of justice are concerned. Cicero and the Republican jurists used *ius naturale* in their legal scholarship in a similar way to the concept of *ius gentium* or law of nations. They viewed these legal concepts as generally acknowledged, found in all nations, and as equitable principles. In the Institutes of Gaius (ca. 110–180 AD), the two terms, 'natural law' and 'law of nations', are used without clear distinction (see also Gai. D. 41.1.1).

> *Gai. 1.1* (*ius civile and ius naturale*)
> All nations, governed by statutes and customs, partly apply their own law and partly that [law] common to all men. Because the law every nation establishes for itself, is its own law and is termed *ius civile*, being the proper law of the nation (*civitas*). However, what natural reason establishes for all men and what is similarly preserved by all nations, is termed *ius gentium*, being the law that all peoples apply. Accordingly, the people of Rome partly apply their own law, partly that common to all men. Which institutions belong to what category, we will deal with in the appropriate places.[4]

However, the Roman jurist Ulpian (ca. 170–228 AD), later jurists, and the compilers of Justinian's Institutes, distinguished *ius naturale* and *ius gentium*. This was necessary because they held that slavery was introduced by *ius gentium*, whereas according to *ius naturale* men were born free.

> *D. 1.1.4 Ulpian, Institutes, Book I*
> Also manumissions belong to *ius gentium*. The word manumission is derived from 'allowance to go (*missio*) out of the hand (*manus*)', i.e., the granting of freedom. Because as long as someone is in slavery, he is subordinate to another's hand and authority; manumission discharges him from that dominion. These institutions have their origin in *ius gentium*, because according to *ius naturale* all are born free and manumission

4 Gai. 1 (*De iure civili et naturali*). (1) Omnes populi qui legibus et moribus reguntur, partim suo proprio, partim communi omnium hominum iure utuntur; nam quod quisque populus ipse sibi ius constituit, id ipsius proprium est vocaturque ius civile, quasi ius proprium civitatis; quod vero naturalis ratio inter omnes homines constituit, id apud omnes populos peraeque custoditur vocaturque ius gentium, quasi quo iure omnes gentes utuntur. Populus itaque Romanus partim suo proprio, partim communi omnium hominum iure utitur. Quae singula qualia sint, suis locis proponemus.

> was not known, because slavery was unknown. But after *ius gentium* had introduced slavery, the favor of manumission followed. And although with a single and natural law designation we are called 'men' according to *ius gentium*, three categories came into existence: free men and their opposites, slaves and a third category of freedmen, i.e., those who are no longer slaves.[5]

Accordingly, Ulpian distinguished three categories of precepts of private law: *ius civile, ius naturale* and *ius gentium*. Subsequently, he defined what should be understood by *ius naturale* and by *ius gentium*.

> *D. 1.1.1 Ulpian, Institutes, Book 1*
> (pr) Who wants to concentrate on law (*ius*), should first know where the term 'law' (*ius*) derives from. It is so called after justice (*iustitia*), because as Celsus elegantly defines it, law (*ius*) is the skill of the good and equitable.
> (1) One could rightly call us priests, because we practice justice and we preach the consciousness of what is good and equitable, thereby drawing a line between equity and iniquity and distinguishing between permissible and illicit, desiring to educate good people, not only by fear for punishments, but also by attractive rewards, thereby aiming at, if I am not mistaken, the true philosophy not the false one.
> (2) This passion displays itself in two fields, the public and the private. Public law deals with the Roman state, and private law deals with the well-being of individuals. After all, some things have a public interest, some things a private. Public law is related to sacral law, the priests and the magistrates. Private law has three parts because it comprises either natural precepts or those from the nations or civil ones.

5 D. 1.1.4 *Ulpianus libro primo institutionum* Manumissiones quoque iuris gentium sunt. Est autem manumissio de manu missio, id est datio libertatis: nam quamdiu quis in servitute est, manui et potestati suppositus est, manumissus liberatur potestate. Quae res a iure gentium originem sumpsit, utpote cum iure naturali omnes liberi nascerentur nec esset nota manumissio, cum servitus esset incognita: sed posteaquam iure gentium servitus invasit, secutum est beneficium manumissionis. Et cum uno naturali nomine homines appellaremur, iure gentium tria genera esse coeperunt: liberi et his contrarium servi et tertium genus liberti, id est hi qui desierant esse servi.

> (3) *Ius naturale* is what nature has taught all animals; because that law is not the proper law of the human race, but that of all animals, which are born on the land or in the sea, and it is also common to the birds. From this follows the association between male and female, what we call marriage, which results in producing children and hence education. Certainly, we see that also other animals, even wild ones, are supposed to be aware of this law.
> (4) *Ius gentium* is what the nations of mankind apply. That this law deviates from the *ius naturale*, is easy to see, because the former is common to all animals, the latter only to men among each other.[6]

Whereas the *ius gentium* now appears as positive law, although based on a kind of universal consent and not restricted to one specific nation, the *ius naturale* becomes the ideal of justice. It was normative for the work of the jurists and contained general principles which were not yet completely elaborated in the rules of positive law and general rules of law. They were not ready to be applied in practice, but reflected a kind of ideal.

> *D. 1.1.10 Ulpian, Rules of law, Book II*
> (pr) Justice is the firm and stable intention to assign everyone his due.
> (1) These are the precepts of law: to live virtuously, not to injure another, and to give everyone his due.

---

6 D. 1.1.1 *Ulpianus libro primo institutionum* Iuri operam daturum prius nosse oportet, unde nomen iuris descendat. est autem a iustitia appellatum: nam, ut eleganter celsus definit, ius est ars boni et aequi. (1) Cuius merito quis nos sacerdotes appellet: iustitiam namque colimus et boni et aequi notitiam profitemur, aequum ab iniquo separantes, licitum ab illicito discernentes, bonos non solum metu poenarum, verum etiam praemiorum quoque exhortatione efficere cupientes, veram nisi fallor philosophiam, non simulatam affectantes. (2) Huius studii duae sunt positiones, publicum et privatum. Publicum ius est quod ad statum rei Romanae spectat, privatum quod ad singulorum utilitatem: sunt enim quaedam publice utilia, quaedam privatim.Publicum ius in sacris, in sacerdotibus, in magistratibus constitit. Privatum ius tripertitum est: collectum etenim est ex naturalibus praeceptis aut gentium aut civilibus. (3) Ius naturale est, quod natura omnia animalia docuit: nam ius istud non humani generis proprium, sed omnium animalium, quae in terra, quae in mari nascuntur, avium quoque commune est. Hinc descendit maris atque feminae coniunctio, quam nos matrimonium appellamus, hinc liberorum procreatio, hinc educatio: videmus etenim cetera quoque animalia, feras etiam istius iuris peritia censeri. (4) Ius gentium est, quo gentes humanae utuntur. Quod a naturali recedere facile intellegere licet, quia illud omnibus animalibus, hoc solis hominibus inter se commune sit.

(2) Jurisprudence is the understanding of divine and human matters, the knowledge of just and unjust.[7]

D. 50.17.10 Paul, Commentary on the civil law, Book III
According to nature the advantages of each thing fall to the one who will endure the disadvantages.[8]

D. 50.17.206 Pomponius, Various annotations, Book IX
According to natural law it is equitable that nobody is enriched at the expense of or injury to another.[9]

As a Roman legal concept, the term 'natural' is often contrasted with 'civil'. Legal concepts and institutions defined by specific provisions in Roman statutes were considered 'civil', those which were not were called 'natural'. Thus, there were natural and civil ways of acquiring ownership (Gai. 2.65 ff. and Gai. D. 41.1.1 ff.). *Naturalis cognatio* was based on the biological relationship between a mother and her children, *civilis cognatio* on the relationships in family law. Similarly, natural possession was the factual holding of a thing, whilst civil possession was the holding of a thing with a title of acquisition. The *obligatio naturalis* was the mere bond between debtor and creditor, whereas the *obligatio civilis* was the bond which could be legally enforced. Natural goods were all the things that people could enjoy, whereas civil goods were individual assets (D. 50.16.49).

2.3 *Custom*

Custom was a source of law in Roman law from the beginning of its history. The earliest Roman law was primarily determined by custom, which was explained in unclear instances by a council of *pontifices*, public 'priests' with several powers. The Romans held that the binding force of custom was based on *usus,* i.e., the uninterrupted observance of a rule, and *opinio necessitatis,* i.e., the

7 D. 1.1.10 *Ulpianus libro secundo regularum* Iustitia est constans et perpetua voluntas ius suum cuique tribuendi. (1) Iuris praecepta sunt haec: honeste vivere, alterum non laedere, suum cuique tribuere. (2) Iuris prudentia est divinarum atque humanarum rerum notitia, iusti atque iniusti scientia.

8 D. 50.17.10 *Paulus libro tertio ad Sabinum* Secundum naturam est commoda cuiusque rei eum sequi, quem sequentur incommoda.

9 D. 50.17.206 *Pomponius libro nono ex variis lectionibus* Iure naturae aequum est neminem cum alterius detrimento et iniuria fieri locupletiorem.

consciousness that this, indeed, was the appropriate norm. In his *Enchiridium*, a didactical work, the classical jurist Pomponius (2nd century AD), wrote the following about the role of custom in the early period of Rome.

> *D. 1.2.2.1 Pomponius, Enchiridium*
> Certainly, in the initial period of our state, the people started first to act without a distinct statute and without a distinct law, and all was governed by the hand of the kings.[10]

According to some Roman authors, such as Plutarch († 120 AD), Roman kings promulgated statutes, the so-called *leges regiae*. Nowadays, however, historians believe that these laws did not actually exist. The first important Roman statute dates from later, in the early days of the Republic, i.e., the Law of the Twelve Tables (ca. 450 BC). These days this statute is believed to consist mainly of older customary rules. Whatever the case may be, in the second century AD Gaius mentioned various legal institutions based on custom which were enshrined in the Law of the Twelve Tables (Gai. 4. 26–27).

Under the Republic, custom was also handed down in the form of the so-called *mos maiorum*, literally 'the custom of the ancestors'. Under these customs a *pater familias* was not to abuse the paternal authority he had over his wife by virtue of his marital power (*in manu*), over his children and grandchildren by virtue of his paternal control (*potestas*), or over the slaves he owned (*dominium*). Abuse of private property was also seen as contrary to the custom of the ancestors. However, violations were not punished by criminal or civil sanctions, but through the intervention of the *censor*, a magistrate watching over good morals, who could proceed at his own discretion. It was not until the Empire that the function of the *censor* was, to a large extent, taken over by imperial officers. By that time, violations of the *mos maiorum* were subsumed under criminal prosecution, especially when public interest was at stake. In this way, many customary rules turned into legal rules.

Cicero still considered custom a source of law. In the period of classical law, however, custom played no effective role in legal practice – although a number of classical jurists refer to custom, such as Salvius Julianus or Julian (ca. 110-ca. 170 AD) and Ulpian.

10 D. 1.2.2.1 *Pomponius libro singulari enchiridii* Et quidem initio civitatis nostrae populus sine lege certa, sine iure certo primum agere instituit omniaque manu a regibus gubernabantur.

> *D. 1.3.32.1 Julian, Digest, Book 84*
> A deeply rooted custom is rightly regarded as a statute and we call this law established by custom, because the statutes obligate us for no other reason than that they are acknowledged as such by the people's decision. The things that the people approved of without any writing will obligate everyone all the more, because what difference does it make whether a nation expresses its will through voting or through the things itself or its own acts? Accordingly, it is quite rightly accepted that statutes are not only abrogated by the vote of the lawgiver, but also by desuetude, based on the tacit consent of all.[11]

> *D. 1.3.33 Ulpian, The office of proconsul, Book 1*
> Things which do not have their origin in writing are in view of a long-standing custom usually observed as law and statute.[12]

According to some scholars, however, these texts would have been elaborated in post-classical times, and the idea that custom can be a source of law would only have gained acceptance at the very end of the classical period, for example, by the jurist Hermogenian (end of third century AD) and in imperial constitutions.

> *D. 1.3.35 Hermogenian, Summary of the law, Book 1*
> Also, what is approved of through a long-standing custom and has been observed for many years, will, as a tacit consent of the citizens, be upheld as a provision no less than written rules of law.[13]

> *C. 8.52(53).2 Emperor Constantine to Proculus*
> The authority of custom and long-standing use is not insignificant, but their importance is not so solemn, that they will prevail over reason

11 D. 1.3.32.1 *Iulianus libro LXXXIIII digestorum* Inveterata consuetudo pro lege non immerito custoditur, et hoc est ius quod dicitur moribus constitutum. Nam cum ipsae leges nulla alia ex causa nos teneant, quam quod iudicio populi receptae sunt, merito et ea, quae sine ullo scripto populus probavit, tenebunt omnes: nam quid interest suffragio populus voluntatem suam declaret an rebus ipsis et factis? Quare rectissime etiam illud receptum est, ut leges non solum suffragio legis latoris, sed etiam tacito consensu omnium per desuetudinem abrogentur.

12 D. 1.3.33 *Ulpianus libro primo de officio proconsulis* Diuturna consuetudine pro iure et lege in his quae non ex scripto descendunt observari solet.

13 D. 1.3.35 *Hermogenianus libro primo iuris epitomarum* Sed et ea, quae longa consuetudine comprobata sunt ac per annos plurimos observata, velut tacita civium conventio non minus quam ea quae scripta sunt iura servantur.

> and statute. *Given the 24th of April during the fifth consulate of Emperor Constantine and the consulate of co-ruler Licinius* [319].[14]

The text of D. 1.3.32.1, allowing certain rules of law to fall in disuse, seems to contradict the text of C. 8.52(53).2, which denies the prevalence of statutes over custom. The glossators harmonized these texts with a historical explanation: in Julian's days the people could still issue statutes and, therefore, also abrogate statutes through desuetude. However, by Constantine's time all legislative authority was vested in the Emperor.

2.4 *Judicial Decisions*

In Rome, litigation resulted in judicial decisions. These decisions were only occasionally compiled, and none of these compilations were preserved as a whole. In classical and Justinianic law, case law as we know it from later times and other jurisdictions, i.e., judicial decisions as a source of law, did not exist. However, there were other texts from legal practice with a case-based character comparable to judicial decisions, such as the *responsa* of the classical jurists. Justinian selected from the latter while compiling the Digest.

In the late Republic and the classical period there was no state judiciary. A magistrate – the *praetor* – was in charge of and organized civil litigation, but the 'judge' who eventually pronounced the judgment held no official office, and the *praetor* did not collect their decisions. During the classical period, the so-called 'formulary' procedure was the most common method of civil litigation. A private *iudex unus* or a tribunal of *recuperatores* pronounced their verdict, or *sententia*. It contained the opinion of the judge to whose decision parties had submitted themselves. Neither the *sententia* itself, nor its announcement (*pronunciatio*) required any formalities. It appears that these verdicts were usually not collected, although some contemporary scholars think otherwise. The jurists, who were the experts on the law and played an important role in the background of all stages of the procedure, sometimes collected their replies (*responsa*), including a summary of the case, the decision of the judge and sometimes the abstract rule of law that was applied. Some jurists even included the names of the parties in their collections.

---

14 C. 8.52(53).2 *Imperator Constantinus A. ad Proculum* Consuetudinis ususque longaevi non vilis auctoritas est, verum non usque adeo sui valitura momento, ut aut rationem vincat aut legem. *D. VIII k. Mai. Constantino A. V et Licinio C. conss.*

Cicero, De oratore, 2.141–142

A general question regarding what conforms with the law does not require persons' names, but the reason for the decision and the sources of the arguments. In this respect, even our jurists hinder us and deter us from understanding the law. Because I see in the volumes of Cato and Brutus that they always record by name what legal advice is given to a particular man or woman; I think this makes us believe that any reason for consulting or for doubting what conforms with the law emerges from the persons involved, not from the substance of the case. Accordingly, when one realizes there are countless persons, one is discouraged to understand the law, probe the law, and they lose the hope of ever mastering it.[15]

We suspect that compilations of *responsa* and judicial decisions were made by republican jurists such as Cato Licinianus († ca. 152 BC), Quintus Mucius Scaevola († ca. 87 BC), C. Aquilius Gallus († 44 BC), and Alfenus Varus (first century BC). The sources of the *ius civile* provided the structure for these writings, although Servius Sulpicius Rufus († 43 BC) also supposedly made a compilation modeled after the praetorian edict's sequence of actions. All these works were lost, and only some minor fragments are now known via quotations from later jurists.

These replies or opinions turned into a genuine source of law, which was certainly promoted by the so-called *ius respondendi* introduced at the beginning of the classical period, when Augustus granted the right to reply on the authority of the Emperor to some jurists. Previously, jurists had given their advice merely on their own authority. In a fragment in the Digest, again taken from the *Enchiridium* of Pomponius, the following was said about the introduction of the *ius respondendi*.

D. 1.2.2.48–49 Pomponius, Enchiridium

... Massurius Sabinus belonged to the equestrian order and was the first to hold the *ius respondendi*. It was later given as a privilege, but Emperor Tiberius had granted it to him as a right. Before Augustus's time, as is

15 Perpetui iuris et universi generis quaestio non hominum nomina, sed rationem dicendi et argumentorum fontes desiderat. In quo etiam isti nos iuris consulti impediunt a discendoque deterrent; video enim in Catonis et in Bruti libris nominatim fere referri, quid alicui de iure viro aut mulieri responderit; credo, ut putaremus in hominibus, non in re consultationis aut dubitationis causam aliquam fuisse; ut, quod homines innumerabiles essent, debilitati a iure cognoscendo voluntatem discendi simul cum spe perdiscendi abiceremus.

> well known, the *ius respondendi* was not granted by the *Principes*, but exercised by the jurists relying on their own education for the benefit of those asking for advice. And certainly, they did not produce sealed advice, but most of the time, they themselves wrote to the judges, or their help was requested by those seeking advice. The divine resembling Augustus was the first to rule that one could reply under his authority so that the reply would have more legal authority, and from that time on, this privilege was requested. For this reason, he was called the virtuous *princeps*. Consequently, when praetors sought his permission for them to reply, the virtuous *princeps* Hadrian declared in a rescript that it was customary for this right to be granted rather than requested. Accordingly, should someone have sufficient self-confidence for this (task), he would look forward to such a person to prepare for the role to give advice in the service of the people.[16]

It is not known whether the *ius respondendi* was granted frequently or only to a selected number of jurists. Nor is it known how long this practice was observed – at the beginning of the first century AD and later, or even until the middle of the second century. We do know that Emperor Tiberius (42 BC-37 AD) granted the *ius respondendi* to Sabinus and to Sabinus' successor Cassius, and probably also to Proculus and his successors. Furthermore, Javolenus Priscus (ca. 80-ca. 180 AD), belonging to the School of the Proculians, also had the *ius respondendi*.

In the post-classical era, collections of *responsa* remained sources of law. Attempts were made to compile the law as laid down in the classical jurists' replies. The development of this law, termed *ius*, had come to an end, but the *responsa* collections of individual jurists were still being used and elaborated. Although *responsa* were not judicial decrees, they served as guidelines for legal practice. They had a case-based nature, as they responded to concrete cases,

16 D. 1.2.2 *Pomponius libro singulari Enchiridii* 48. ... Massurius Sabinus in equestri ordine fuit et publice primus respondit: posteaque hoc coepit beneficium dari, a Tiberio Caesare hoc tamen illi concessum erat. 49. Et, ut obiter sciamus, ante tempora Augusti publice respondendi ius non a principibus dabatur, sed qui fiduciam studiorum suorum habebant, consulentibus respondebant: neque responsa utique signata dabant, sed plerumque iudicibus ipsi scribebant, aut testabantur qui illos consulebant. primus divus Augustus, ut maior iuris auctoritas haberetur, constituit, ut ex auctoritate eius responderent: et ex illo tempore peti hoc pro beneficio coepit. et ideo optimus princeps Hadrianus, cum ab eo viri praetorii peterent, ut sibi liceret respondere, rescripsit eis hoc non peti, sed praestari solere et ideo, si quis fiduciam sui haberet, delectari se populo ad respondendum se praepararet.

and sometimes even gave insight into the reasons for the decision (*rationes decidendi*). In many respects, they are similar to the case law of later times. The Digest contains a compilation of this *ius* (*vetus*) or classical jurisprudence, but in doing so turned them into legislation, as the Digest was itself promulgated with the force of law.

The development of classical jurisprudence came to an end after the third century AD, but the significance of imperial law considerably increased. Emperor Hadrian (76–138 AD) instituted the practice that citizens could request the Emperor's opinion in debated legal questions. He no longer granted the jurists the *ius respondendi*, but had replies in which an authoritative response was given to a legal question submitted for judgment issued in his own name. These replies were called 'rescripts', and Hadrian had two chanceries producing them. The rescripts did not contain the verdict itself, but they were decisive for the outcome of the proceedings. From then on, the replies of the jurists had to compete with those of the Emperor.

By now, the formulary procedure was increasingly superseded by the *cognitio* procedure. At first, imperial rescripts may have been issued in the context of litigation *per formulas*, but at a later stage they became part of the new procedural law. In this *cognitio* procedure, the verdict was no longer the *sententia* of a *iudex privatus* to whom parties had submitted, but consisted in a decree on behalf of the state pronouncing the resolution of the dispute which conformed with the law (*iudicatum*). The verdict was not subject to many formalities, but it had to be in writing and ought to be read aloud in the parties' presence.[17] Judgments were rendered by inferior judges, who were now imperial officers. Appeal judgments were pronounced by the Emperor himself. These verdicts were genuine judicial decrees, called *decreta*. Occasionally, such verdicts were compiled, as those of Emperor Septimius Severus (145–211 AD), edited by the jurist Julius Paulus (first half third century AD). Traces of the latter's work *Decretorum Libri Tres* were preserved in the Digest. All these texts produced by the Emperor and his chanceries, both rescripts and decrees were considered to have the force of law.

> *Wolfgang Kunkel and Martin Schermaier, Römische Rechtsgeschichte (14th ed.), Cologne etc., Böhlau, 2012, 171*
> Alongside the rescripts, the imperial *decreta* also gained considerable significance as a source of law. Unlike the former, genuine judicial verdicts, they were issued after an oral hearing in the imperial court … For the

17 C. 7.44.2pr, C. 7.44.3.1, C. 12.21.8.2 and C. 12.19.12.2.

> further development of Roman law, the practice of the imperial court was of fundamental importance, especially when according to the legal rules in force, other courts had no competency to comply with a reasonable request of one of the parties, whereas from the plenitude of power of the *Princeps*, who was above the law, the relief of an innovative decision could be expected. If there has ever been a truly 'royal' judge in the context of a highly developed legal culture, it must have been the Roman *Princeps*. This is especially true in those decades of the second century AD, when personalities of the caliber of Hadrian, Antoninus Pius, and Marcus Aurelius, counseled by the greatest jurists of Antiquity (and yet not infrequently adopting a way of their own in their decisions) pronounced their judgments with great care and serious concern for truth and justice. Imperial decrees, which were of importance for the development of law, were frequently cited in the classical jurists' writings.

The general statutes (edicts) and instructions for officials (mandates) issued by the Emperor, as well as his rescripts and decrees, constituted the sources of imperial law, called generically 'constitutions'. From the third century AD, legal developments were based on these constitutions. Imperial laws, also called *leges*, were the counterpart of the *ius vetus*, i.e., the jurisprudence of the classical jurists, which had come to a standstill. During the Dominate, the edicts became the most important category of constitutions, whereas the decrees more or less disappeared, since the Emperors left decisions on appeal to their officers. Before Justinian, no serious attempts were made to compile the entire jurisprudence of the classical jurists, but there were certainly attempts to compile the entire imperial law. The *Codex Gregorianus* (291 AD) and the *Codex Hermogenianus* (295 AD) were private collections. The *Codex Theodosianus* (438 AD), which came into being after the Empire was permanently split into a western and an eastern part, was an official collection of constitutions promulgated with the force of law, i.e. legislation.

2.5 *Doctrine, Including Legal Science and Legal Study*

Legal scholarship emerged in the second century BC. By that time, a group of prominent citizens had managed to acquire considerable legal expertise. Some scholars even suggest that this is when a legal profession came into being. According to Cicero (*De oratore* 1.48.212), the jurists applied themselves to (i) the drafting of legal texts (*cavere*), such as *formulae*, contracts and wills, (ii) pleading in litigation (*agere*) and (iii) giving expert advice (*responsa*) on current legal problems (*respondere*) to both the parties and the *praetor* or judge. This advice was sometimes summarized in compilations which only sometimes stated the rule or principle the advice was based on. In general, the Roman jurists involved in legal practice did not focus on theoretical constructions or on a legal system composed of abstract concepts. This attitude comes through in a statement of the classical jurist Javolenus incorporated in the final title of the Digest.

> *D. 50.17.202 Javolenus, Letters, Book XI*
> Every definition in civil law is risky; there are not many things which cannot be overturned.[18]

In the declining days of the Roman Republic, two opposing legal schools came into being. The Digest contains a fragment from the *Enchiridium* of Pomponius stating the following.

> *D. 1.2.2.47–48 Pomponius, Enchiridium*
> After him (that is Tubero) Ateius Capito, a follower of Ofilius, and Antistius Labeo, who had listened to all jurists but was educated by Trebatius, acquired great authority. Of these two men, Ateius became consul. Labeo did not want to become one when Augustus offered him the consulate, whereby he would become a *consul suffectus*. He was first and foremost engaged in investigating the law. He planned his working year so that he could spend six months in Rome with his students; the other six months, he withdrew from the public and concentrated on writing books. Accordingly, he left 400 scrolls, most of them still in circulation. These two jurists stood at the threshold of divergent schools because Ateius Capito stuck to what was handed down, whereas Labeo, who was also educated in other disciplines, by his genius and confidence in his own knowledge, started to adopt all kinds of innovations. Massurius Sabinus, who succeeded Ateius Capito, and Nerva, who succeeded Labeo, further deepened the, by that time, existing differences of opinion. Nerva was on friendly terms with the Emperor.[19]

---

18 D. 50.17.202 *Iavolenus libro undecimo epistularum* Omnis definitio in iure civili periculosa est: parum est enim, ut non subverti posset.

19 D. 1.2.2 *Pomponius libro singulari Enchiridii* 47. Post hunc maximae auctoritatis fuerunt Ateius Capito, qui Ofilium secutus est, et Antistius Labeo, qui omnes hos audivit, institutus est autem a Trebatio. ex his Ateius consul fuit: Labeo noluit, cum offerretur ei ab Augusto consulatus, quo suffectus fieret, honorem suscipere, sed plurimum studiis operam dedit: et totum annum ita diviserat, ut Romae sex mensibus cum studiosis esset, sex mensibus secederet et conscribendis libris operam daret. itaque reliquit quadringenta volumina, ex quibus plurima inter manus versantur. hi duo primum veluti diversas sectas

Thus, Capito (ca. 30 BC-22 AD) and Labeo were the founding fathers of the two schools of jurists. Capito stuck to traditional legal scholarship. His successors were Sabinus and Cassius († ca. 69 AD) and the school of the Sabinians was named after Sabinus. Labeo, on the other hand, was an innovator. Nerva and Proculus succeeded him, and the school was later referred to as the Proculians. Until the second century AD, these schools defended divergent opinions on numerous legal issues. Most of these controversies emerged in the first half of the first century AD, when Cassius was in charge of the Sabinians, and Proculus led the Proculians. Traces of these controversies can be found in the Digest.

From the beginning of the Roman state, legal training had been informal. However, this changed when the demand for public servants with a legal education drastically increased under the Principate. In the second century AD, there was already a school of law in Rome, referred to in the fourth century *Fragmenta Vaticana.*

> *Fragmenta Vaticana 204*
> Item. And thus those who are in Rome, particularly for the study of the law of Rome, should be exempted as long as they stay in Rome because of the law and are occupied with their studies; and this is what Antoninus Pius wrote in a rescript to Cerealis on the service for taxes and petitions.[20]

In this period, didactic works such as the Institutes of Gaius and the *Enchiridium* of Sextus Pomponius were composed.

In the third century AD, a school of law was founded in Berytus (present-day Beirut) and in the fourth century, further schools were established in Carthage, Alexandria, Caesarea, and Athens. The law school of Constantinople followed in 425 AD. These schools of law were in possession of a vast library of legal materials. During the Dominate, the law schools in the Eastern Empire used the Institutes of Gaius as their textbook, supplemented by the commentaries of classical jurists on the *ius civile* and the Edict. The *responsa* (legal replies) of Paul and Papinian and the imperial constitutions also received some attention.

fecerunt: nam Ateius Capito in his, quae ei tradita fuerant, perseverabat, Labeo ingenii qualitate et fiducia doctrinae, qui et ceteris operis sapientiae operam dederat, plurima innovare instituit. 48. Et ita Ateio Capitoni Massurius Sabinus successit, Labeoni Nerva, qui adhuc eas dissensiones auxerunt. hic etiam Nerva Caesari familiarissimus fuit.

20 FV 204 Item. Proinde qui studiorum causa Romae sunt praecipue civilium, debent excusari, quamdiu iuris causa Romae agunt studii cura distracti; et ita ... imperator Antoninus Aug. Cereali a censibus et a libellis rescripsit.

Lectures consisted of reading texts from legal works, explaining these texts, and comparing them with others.

2.6 *Legislation Preceding the Corpus Iuris Civilis*

We have already mentioned the legislative competencies of the various public assemblies in enacting statutes. These statutes were accepted on the recommendation of a magistrate (*leges rogatae*) or promulgated by the decision of an assembly (*leges datae*). One of the oldest Roman statutes was the Law of the Twelve Tables, dating from ca. 450 BC. The complete text was lost and only reconstructed in the early modern period. The provisions of this statute show little coherence. They belong to various areas of the law: public criminal law, private delicts, family law, law of succession, property, law of neighbors, procedural law, etc. We have also seen that decisions of the assembly of plebeians (*concilium plebis*), taken on the recommendation of a tribune, the so-called 'plebiscites', were originally only binding for the plebeians themselves. However, in 287 BC the *lex Hortensia* declared these plebiscites to have force of law in general. From that time, they were increasingly called *leges*. A famous example is the *lex Aquilia* from 286 BC, dealing with extra-contractual damage to property. The Senate also played a part in legislative procedure. From the time of the early Republic, decisions of the public assemblies concerning statutes needed the Senate's approval. In 339 BC, this rule changed. Approval of the Senate was now required *before* a statute was brought to the public assemblies. From 287 BC on, this also applied to plebiscites. By the end of the Republic, the Senate's decisions, the so-called *Senatus Consulta*, were factually considered a direct source of law.

During the Principate, the Emperor's role in lawmaking increased considerably. Augustus and Claudius (10 BC–54 AD) promulgated many statutes in their capacity as tribunes of the plebs. Until the third century AD, the Emperors also exerted their influence on the Senate's decisions. These decisions were prepared by public servants and announced in the Senate on behalf of the Emperor before the Senate confirmed the proposal. Moreover, the Emperors increasingly produced legislation of their own, i.e., general statutes (edicts) and instructions for public servants (mandates). The capacity to do so was derived from their powers as magistrates.

During the Dominate, imperial constitutions supplanted practically all other forms of legislation. Edicts, mostly in the form of a letter addressed to the praetorian prefect, were the most important. As mentioned above, there were also various compilations of constitutions. They were comparable to records of case law since rescripts and decrees were directly related to litigation.

The official compilation of constitutions promulgated with force of law in 438 AD by the Emperors Theodosius II (401–450 AD) and Valentianus III (419–455 AD), i.e. the *Codex Theodosianus*, can be seen as legislation, albeit not in the sense of the nineteenth-century codes of law. Just like the later Digest and *Codex Justinianus*, it was composed of existing materials based on cases. It lacked the system which the nineteenth-century codes inherited from the northern European Schools of Natural Law and which, in a certain sense, had its roots in Justinian's Institutes. The *Codex Theodosianus* contained constitutions issued between 311 AD and 437 AD, primarily collected from the archives of Constantinople, Rome, and Ravenna, which were still valid. However, the validity of these constitutions was still restricted to the part of the Empire for which they had been issued. It was only in the course of the fifth century AD that they were interpreted as more generally applicable.

There was also a need for a compilation of the *ius vetus*, i.e., the jurisprudence of the classical period. This *ius* was developed within the context of the praetorian edict, the formulary procedure, and the advisory practice of the jurists. However, the development of praetorian law came to a standstill. From the middle of the first century AD, new remedies were no longer adopted in the edict. In the second century AD, by order of Emperor Hadrian, the edict was to be settled as an immutable *Edictum Perpetuum*, no longer susceptible to alterations or adaptations. This was achieved between 135 and 138 AD by the jurist Julian. At the end of the classical period, the formulary procedure was gradually superseded by the *cognitio* procedure, and in 342 AD, the former was abolished. The rescripts of the Emperors had taken the place of the jurists' *responsa*, and the jurists themselves were absorbed into the anonymity of the imperial chanceries. Nevertheless, the classical *responsa*, although by now a poorly organized quantity, were still relevant for legal practice. The same Emperors who promulgated the *Codex Theodosianus* did not manage to compile the *ius*, but they did succeed in establishing a certain order by means of the *lex citandi* of 426 AD. This statute declared that five classical jurists were considered to have issued *responsa* with binding force: Gaius, Paul, Papinian, Ulpian, and Modestinus.

> *Herbert Hausmaninger and Walter Selb, Römisches Privatrecht (9th ed.), Vienna, Böhlau, 2001, 49–50*
> Post-classical legal scholarship was no longer able to cope with the wealth of classical legal writings and controversies. In particular, the contradictions between the late classical authorities confused the practitioners. For this reason, Emperor Constantine in 321 abrogated the *notae* (critical remarks) of Paul and Ulpian on the *quaestiones* (legal questions) and

responsa (legal advice) of Papinian (the so-called Invalidation Statute). In the so-called Statute of Citations of 426 Theodosius II and Valentianus III established a standard list of classical works that should be accepted as authoritative in court. This statute designated five, predominantly late-classical jurists as authorities (Papinian, Paul, Gaius, Ulpian, Modestinus) and their works as legally binding. Other jurists could only be quoted if they were referred to by the five authorities. In the event of differences of opinion among the five lawyers, the majority should be decisive. In the event of a tie, Papinian should decide. On the one hand, the Statute of Citations reflects a clear simplification of the legal culture compared to the classical period's creativity. However, on the other hand, it represents a genuine attempt to revive classical legal literature amid a highly vulgarized legal practice.

2.7 *The Corpus Iuris Civilis*

The term *Corpus iuris civilis* (literally 'the body of secular law'), which goes back to the Middle Ages, is used as the common designation for the extensive project of law-making completed in the sixth century AD under the Emperor Justinian. Unlike the codes of the nineteenth century, the *Corpus iuris civilis* consists of compilations and elaborations on existing legal texts. Many of these texts have a case-based character and the way they are ordered is different from the structure of the modern-day law codes.

At the end of the fifth century AD, the Western Empire was invaded and occupied by various Germanic tribes. In 476 AD, the last Emperor of the Western Empire, Romulus Augustulus († after 507 AD) was deposed.

In the sixth century, Emperor Justinian ruled the Eastern Empire. He resided in Constantinople and considered himself ruler of the entire Roman Empire because, after all, the Eastern Emperor had a share of state-authority over the Western Empire. He therefore saw it as his responsibility to recapture the Western Empire and intended to restore the unity of Rome in many respects and revive its former glory. The new Empire had to have one religion and one code of law. That one religion had to be Christianity, which with the famous edict *Cunctos populos* (380 AD) of Theodosius the Great (347–395 AD), had become the state religion for the entire Empire. In later times, Justinian adopted this edict as a provision in his *Codex* (C. 1.1.1). One Empire and one religion went hand in hand with one unified code of law.

As shown above, the desire to arrange classical jurisprudence and imperial constitutions existed long before the days of Justinian. Justinian was the first, and last, Emperor to codify all parts of Roman law. He was able to do this thanks to the existence of eastern law schools which could provide the necessary expertise, legal sources and literature. The *Codex* was a compilation of the imperial law of the *leges*, first promulgated in 529 AD (*Codex Vetus*), and replaced in 534 AD by an adapted and enlarged version, known as *Codex repetitae praelectionis* or *Codex Justinianus*. The old *ius*, i.e., the replies of the classical jurists derived from writings elaborated in post-classical times, were compiled in the Digest and promulgated in 533 AD. A new didactic work, also called *Institutiones,* which replaced Gaius's textbook was promulgated in 533 AD. Constitutions issued by Justinian after 534 AD, the so-called 'Novels', which were primarily written in Greek, were strictly speaking not part of the project. There are only private collections of these constitutions, sometimes in Latin translation. In the Middle Ages, one of these became part of the *Corpus iuris civilis*.

Justinian left the selection and elaboration of the source materials to committees. Many of their members, later termed 'compilers', taught at the law schools or were practitioners. However, the most important of these compilers, Tribonian († 546 AD), was a member of the imperial council (*consistorium principis*) and later Justinian's minister (*quaestor sacri palatii*). Both the commission in charge of compiling the *Codex* and the one compiling the Digest were ordered by Justinian to alter the texts if necessary, and to eliminate contradictions. This can be read in the introductory constitutions to the Digest, i.e., *Tanta/Δέδωκεν*.

> *Tanta § 10*
> ... Only the following was done by us: if something in the provisions of the ancient jurists appeared to be superfluous, incomplete, or less desirable, this was, as far as necessary, supplemented or shortened and adapted to the correct rules. And as regards similar and conflicting provisions: these are all replaced by what seemed the most correct and in doing so all provisions were granted the same authority. Accordingly, all that is written here emanates from us and is in conformity with our will.[21]

These alterations are called 'interpolations'. The fact that Justinian explicitly ordered the compilers to delete some outdated or obsolete legal concepts and

21 *Tanta § 10* ... hoc tantummodo a nobis effecto, ut, si quid in legibus eorum vel supervacuum vel imperfectum aut minus idoneum visum est, vel adiectionem vel deminutionem necessariam accipiat et rectissimis tradatur regulis. Et in multis similibus vel contrariis quod rectius habere apparebat, hoc pro aliis omnibus positum est unaque omnibus auctoritate indulta, ut quidquid ibi scriptum est, hoc nostrum appareat et ex nostra voluntate compositum.

institutions can also be gleaned from the following text from the *Codex*. It abolished an important distinction in classical law between the *res manicipi*, the economically more valuable things like slaves, cattle, and land which had to be transferred by a formal procedure, and the *res nec mancipi*, which could be transferred by merely granting possession.

> *C. 7.31.1.5 Emperor Justinian to praetorian prefect Johannes*
> Because it is undoubtedly outdated to distinguish things into *res mancipi* and *res nec mancipi* and this justly should be lifted, both movable and immovable things should belong to the same category without pointless ambiguities and distinctions. *Given 18 October at Constantinople after the consulate of Lampadius and Orestes* [531].[22]

The compilers of the Digest not only adapted the classical replies to the changed circumstances, but they selected some fragments, moved them from their original context, and arranged them among other fragments to which they originally had no connection at all. Their new placement sometimes provided the texts – as happened with the constitutions from the *Codex* – with a new context that gave them a different color.

The compilers did not always succeed in smoothing over the contradictions. Sometimes an inconsistency (*antinomia*) eluded them. Interpolating and editing itself resulted in new inconsistencies when the outcome of the process was insufficiently considered. Unfortunately, almost all writings dating from the classical period were lost after the *Corpus iuris* was completed.

2.8 *Corpus Iuris: the Digest or Pandects*

In 530 AD, Tribonian was ordered to establish a committee to codify the *ius vetus*, the classical jurists' jurisprudence. The compilation was called the Digest ('anthology') or Pandects (the 'all-embracing'). The name Digest was in honour of the classical jurist Julian who had written a Digest containing 90 books.

The Digest contains fragments derived from 200 works of 39 jurists. The oldest was from Quintus Mucius Scaevola († 82 BC), the youngest from Hermogenian (around 300 AD). By far the largest part came from the jurists mentioned in the Statute of Citations (426 AD), but the texts originated from widely different works, which had been elaborated in post-classical times. Some

22 C. 7.31.1.5 *Imp. Iustinianus A. Iohanni pp.* Cum etiam res dividi mancipi et nec mancipi sane antiquum est et merito antiquari oportet, sit et rebus et locis omnibus similis ordo, inutilibus ambiguitatibus et differentiis sublatis. *D. xv k. Nov. Constantinopoli post consulatum Lampadii et Orestis vv. cc.* [531].

were didactical in nature, such as the Institutes of Gaius and the *Enchiridium* of Pomponius. Others were commentaries on the three books on the *ius civile* (statutory law) of the early-classical jurist Sabinus (*Iuris civilis libri III*), which had enormous authority throughout the classical period. Extensive commentaries on the praetor's edict from late classical jurists like Ulpian and Paul were also included, as were the *responsa* collections. All these works, except perhaps the more didactical works, had a case-based character. Every fragment (*lex*) in the Digest started with an inscription stating its origin, i.e., the jurist's name and the work it came from.

> *David Johnston, Roman Law in Context, Cambridge, Cambridge University Press, 1999, 16*
> *Loss of Context and Palingenesia*
> A major difficulty in using the Digest is that it consists entirely of excerpts from jurists' works. The excerpts are arranged in books and titles. This means that some caution is needed in the use of evidence, since what appears now under one heading in the Digest may originally have been said by a jurist in connection with something quite different.
>
> Here some help is at hand. Because the compilers of the Digest give the source of each fragment, it is sometimes possible to be fairly sure what the original context of the excerpt was. That is true in particular of the main commentaries, those on the edict or on the civil law. There were many such commentaries, and a comparison of their surviving fragments indicates that they were typically lemmatic in form: that is they followed the order of the work on which they were commenting and dealt with each word or topic in turn. If a fragment from the Digest can be located in a particular book of such a commentary, it follows at least that it is possible to limit the range of possible words or topics with which it may have been concerned; and sometimes the actual word or topic may be identifiable with reasonable certainty.
>
> The fundamental work of retrieving the original context of fragments, usually known as 'palingenesia', was carried out late last century by Otto Lenel and published in his great *Palingenesia iuris civilis* in 1889. Lenel's work is not without flaws but, although corrections have been suggested, it remains an extraordinary achievement and has never been superseded. It is therefore the starting point for trying to identify what the true subject of the excerpts in the Digest actually is

It is remarkable that compiling the Digest only took three years. In 1818, the German jurist Friedrich Bluhme (1797–1874) proposed a theory to explain this: the so-called *Massentheorie* (theory of different 'masses' or collections of texts). Bluhme had discovered that within every title of the Digest, there is a specific structure, existing in three or four 'masses' of texts. The first is composed of fragments, derived from commentaries on Sabinus' *Iuris civilis libri III*. The second contains fragments from commentaries on the *Edictum Perpetuum*, while the third has fragments from case-based replies of, amongst others, Papinian, Q. Cervidius Scaevola (ca. 180 AD) and Paul. According to Bluhme, the compilers had formed three subcommittees, each working on one of the 'masses' i.e., the Sabinus-mass, the Edict-mass, and the Papinian-mass. When they found other materials, these could be placed at the end of each Digest title, resulting in a fourth mass, the so-called 'Appendix-mass'.

The Digest consists of 50 books subdivided into titles, each with its own subject matter – an exception being the books 30, 31, and 32, which together form one title (on bequests and *fidei commissa*) without any subdivision. For the purpose of legal education, the Digest was split into seven sections (*partes*). The last three sections were not given a specific name.

pars 1 (book I–IV) or *τὰ πρῶτα* (the beginning)
pars 2 (book V–XI) or *de iudiciis* (proceedings)
pars 3 (book XII–XIX) or *de rebus* (property, patrimony)
pars 4 (book XX–XXVII) or *umbilicum* (middle)
pars 5 (book XXVIII–XXXVI)
pars 6 (book XXXVII–XLIV)
pars 7 (book XLV–L)

In the introductory constitution *Omnem* to the Digest, Justinian ruled (in §§ 2–6) that first year students should study the Institutes and *pars* one of the Digest, second and third years were to study *pars* two and *pars* three, and in the third year texts of Papinian were also studied. The fourth year was meant for self-study of (parts of) *pars* four and *pars* five, and in the fifth year the entire *Codex* was taught. The sections (*partes*) six and seven were meant to be consulted when practicing.

Traditionally a first year student was called a *dupondius*, named after a bronze coin no longer in use. Justinian considered the term meaningless and ridiculous and ruled that first year students would henceforth be called 'Justinianic recruits' (*Justiniani novi*). Third year students were called 'papinianists' (*papinianistae*), fourth-year students *λυταί* (case solvers) and fifth year students *πρόλυται* (advanced case solvers).

With the constitution *Tanta*/*Δέδωκεν* of 16 December 533 AD, the Digest received the force of law as an imperial constitution. It became effective on

30 December 533 AD. In §§ 21 and 22 of *Tanta/Δέδωκεν*, Justinian prohibited the addition of commentaries to the Digest or the use of abbreviations when it was copied. The oldest surviving manuscript of the Digest, possibly dating from the days of Justinian, is the two-volume *Codex Florentinus* or *littera Florentina*. The name is derived from the city of Florence, where it is kept in the *Biblioteca Medicea Laurenziana*. However, until 1406 it was kept in Pisa, so it is also referred to as the *littera Pisana*. The text of the Digest in the medieval *Corpus iuris*, the so-called 'Vulgate', deviated somewhat from the *Codex Florentinus*. This text version was called *littera Bononiensis* after the city of Bologna, where Roman law was taught from the early twelfth century onwards.

2.9 *Corpus Iuris: the Institutes or Elementa*

The Institutes of Justinian were modelled after an older textbook i.e., the Institutes of the classical jurist Gaius, who must have lived in the second century AD. Although these Institutes were still used in the eastern law schools, we barely know anything about Gaius and the text of Gaius' Institutes went lost and was only recovered in 1816. This does, however, not restrain some Romanists from forming an image of him. In a fictitious interview, Gaius says the following about his textbook.

> *J.E. Spruit Gesprek met Gaius, jurist in Klein-Azië, Antwerp, Maklu, 2000, 21–22*
>
> *We have been talking for some time about your textbook now, but what is the title?*
>
> *Institutiones*. Not very imaginative, to be sure. In this respect, I think I am not any better than all those other jurists: sharp people, a proper understanding of what is good and fair, a good sense of balance in human relationships, keen analytical ability, empathy for the demands of life in society and for the care that is appropriate in our interactions. But imaginative? Forget about it! Did you ever consider the titles of some famous legal writings? 'Replies', 'Legal questions', 'Treatises', 'Digest', 'Opinions', 'Provisions'. That does not excite anyone! So I might as well ask you: what is wrong with 'Institutes'? Is it not the obvious title for an introductory textbook? Yes, my old friend Pomponius named his small manual highly originally *Enchiridium*, but he was also a somewhat eccentric fellow; we should, once in a while, be able to say that in private.
>
> *Indeed, a traditional title, but yet for non traditional material.*
>
> You could look at it that way. We are much less creative in inventing titles for our works than in solving legal problems. However, I do claim that this nondescript or, at least, neutral title of the book covers an innovative

> structure of the material it incorporates: the subdivision of the traditional private law, into the law of persons and family law, patrimonial law – under that rubric I discuss property law, the law of succession and the law of obligations – and procedural law, is entirely new. The entire work of four scrolls is based on the new structure. And another thing: I treated the *ius civile* and the *ius honorarium* as the coherent interconnected whole, which they gradually started to become. That is quite novel! And what do you make of my view on contract and delict as unique and equal sources of obligations?

Apart from Gaius' Institutes, materials from the elementary writings of the classical jurists, parts of the already finished Digest, and imperial constitutions promulgated after 529 AD and from the *Codex Vetus* were used. Unlike in the Digest and *Codex,* references to sources were omitted. Gaius had divided the legal materials into three parts (the law of persons, patrimonial law, and procedural law) and arranged them over four books. This set up was, roughly, adopted in the Institutes of Justinian:

Book I	sources of law, law of persons, family law
Book II	law of property, law of succession
Book III	law of succession (sequel), olaw of contracts
Book IV	law of delicts, procedural law

The Institutes were intended for first year students – 'the youth eager for the law' (*cupida legum iuventus*) as the opening line of the preface puts it. With the constitution *Tanta/Δέδωκεν* the Institutes acquired the force of law as an imperial constitution at the same time as the Digest became effective. The Justinianic Institutes were taught at the eastern law schools.

2.10 *Corpus Iuris: the Codex*

The first version of the *Codex*, compiled by order of Justinian, the *Codex Vetus*, was promulgated in 529 AD. It was quickly outdated. While compiling the Digest, the commission discovered numerous contradictions between the various jurists' replies and as a result the rules could be unclear. This prompted Justinian to issue no less than 50 new constitutions to reconcile these differences, going back to the era of classical law. When the Digest was completed, the *Codex* was made to conform to the Digest, and new constitutions had to be included. This work, done by a small committee, resulted in a new version of the *Codex*, the so-called *Codex repetitae praelectionis*, also known as *Codex Justinianus*. Only this text survived in later days. It contains various types of constitutions: rescripts, decrees, edicts and mandates. The compilation consists of twelve books, just like the Twelve Tables. It is subdivided into titles, each dealing with a particular subject matter, and within these titles, the constitutions are listed with reference to their origin (i.e., the various Emperor[s]). Like in the *Codex Theodosianus* the constitutions are recorded in their chronological order, but it differs from the former in that constitutions of Emperors preceding Constantine were included, such as those of Diocletian. The arrangement of the subject matter is approximately as follows:

Book I	ecclesiastical law, sources of law, the chancery
Book II–VIII	private law
Book IX	criminal law
Book X–XII	fiscal and administrative law

The *Codex repetitae praelectionis* was promulgated by the constitution *Cordi* of 16 November 534 AD and came into effect on 29 December of the same year. From that point onwards, it was forbidden to quote the *Codex Vetus*. However, the introductory constitutions lacked a provision giving the compilation as a whole force of law, as *Tanta*/*Δέδωκεν* did for the Digest. On the contrary, from the constitution *Haec* § 2 it appears that we should not consider the original constitutions abrogated. If there was a contradiction between two constitutions, the younger rule was to prevail over the older one, under the principle *lex posterior derogat legi priori* (D. 1.4.4).

2.11 *The Novels*

With the promulgation of the Digest, Institutes and *Codex*, the great codification project of Justinian was concluded. Nevertheless, Justinian continued to issue new constitutions until he died in 565 AD. Private collections of these 'Novels' or *novellae constitutiones*, were compiled. The oldest one was the *Epitome Juliani*, containing 134 Novels, made in the sixth century AD by someone named Julian. Another one was the *Authenticum*, also dating from the sixth century AD, and containing 98 Novels, all translated from Greek into Latin. Finally, the most complete collection dates from the end of the sixth century AD, the so-called *collectio Graeca*, of 168 Novels.

To identify the texts from the *Corpus iuris* referred to in the secondary literature, one has to understand the internationally standardized way of quoting the Digest, Institutes, and *Codex*. For these works, the abbreviations D. (previously ff.), Inst. and C, are used, followed by the book's number and the number of the title within the book. For the Digest and *Codex* this is followed by a third number indicating the fragment within the title. Longer fragments in the Digest and *Codex* are subdivided into paragraphs. In the case of the Institutes, the third number indicates the paragraph within the title. The subdivision into paragraphs is of medieval origin. The first paragraph is always pr (*principium*). The second paragraph is number one. In the older literature, the titles are referred to by the first Latin words of their headings. The fragments within the titles are referred to by their initial words. References to texts within the same part of the *Corpus iuris* are made by using indications as *supra* (above) or *infra* (below). To refer to fragments within a title, i (one), ii (two), *penult.* (second to last), *ult.* (last) are used.

2.12 *Diffusion of Laws and Legal Institutions*

There has been an enormous diffusion of Roman law and Roman legal rules, concepts, and principles. In the East, Justinian's codification was the starting point for Byzantine law. The *Corpus iuris* itself was replaced in the ninth century AD by a Greek version, the so-called Basilica (*τὰ βασιλικά νόμιμα*). This Basilica again was the primary source for the book of law composed around 1350 by Constantine Harmenopoulos (1320-ca. 1385), a judge from Thessaloniki. This work, entitled Hexabiblos (*ἡ Ἑξάβιβλος*), remained the main handbook for legal practice, including after the Ottoman Empire conquered Constantinople. From 1835 until 1946, it served as the Code of Law of the Kingdom of Greece.

The majority of the *Corpus iuris* was lost in the West. However, parts of the *Codex Theodosianus* survived in the *Lex romana visigothorum*, promulgated in 506 AD by king Alaric II († 507 AD) of the Visigoths. Some rules and concepts of Roman law were also preserved in the Etymologies of Isidore of Seville († 636 AD) and the so-called *Leges barbarorum.*

The 'second life' of Roman law started at the beginning of the twelfth century when the more or less 'complete' text of the *Corpus iuris* was available again. At first, at the law school in Bologna, Roman law was primarily a subject for scholarly reflection. The Church also applied it as a subsidiary source of law at an early stage, and it was the foundation of early legislative projects such as the *Liber Augustalis* (1231) in Sicily and the *Siete Partidas* (1251–1265) in Castile. In southern Europe, Roman law developed into a *ius commune,* a general body of law, used to interpret, supplement, or even partially replace indigenous legal standards. This 'reception' spread to northern Europe, except for England and Scandinavia, promoted by academic jurists with jurisdiction in superior courts, and by the establishment of universities disseminating legal scholarship. Although early modern humanist jurists were interested in classical law, the *Corpus iuris* itself, i.e., Roman law in its Justinianic form, shaped the *ius commune* for many centuries in continental Europe.

Today, the 'second life' of Roman law continues only in jurisdictions where a code of civil law has not replaced it as a source of law. This includes systems where Roman-Dutch law is still in force, such as those of South Africa and Sri Lanka, and the jurisdictions of some areas in Europe where *ius commune* still functions as a subsidiary law, such as Scotland, Jersey, Guernsey, San Marino, and Andorra.

For most other civil law jurisdictions, the 'second life' of the Roman law came to an end with the introduction of civil law codes and the *Corpus iuris civilis* can no longer be invoked as a source of law. However, this does not mean that Roman law has no relevance in understanding and interpreting those codes. To some extent, this can be seen as a continuation of the pre-codified law and some speak of a 'third life' of Roman law. The Roman heritage lived on in discourse on legal concepts and principles.

> *Hendrik Kooiker, Lex scripta abrogata. De derde renaissance van het Romeinse recht, Nijmegen, Ars Aequi Libri, 1996, 507–508*
> Although when the law was codified, there was a renewed focus on Roman law, this period sometimes is in danger of being somewhat neglected because legal historians are inclined to see the process of codifying as the start of a new era, while present-day practitioners see this period as a start-up phase of little interest. In this twilight zone, however, some significant developments took place. Several of our current fundamental legal doctrines emerged: an open or more restricted system of interpretation, an open or more restricted system of remedies (unjustified enrichment), an open or more restricted system of real rights, a causal or abstract system for transfer of ownership, and the position of a good faith third possessor. We can often find the key to understanding developments which resulted in our current civil law in this period.
>
> All in all, instead of speaking about the death of Roman law because of codification, it would be better to speak of a third birth of Roman law, prompted by the codification process. Regarding the function of Roman law as a tool of interpretation and as a source for supplementing substantive law (*raison écrite*) in the creation of a *système d'application* of codified law, it was specifically case law and the French commentators

on the *Code civil* in the first half of the nineteenth century who promoted this continuity and revival of Roman law. Because of their case-based approach and by continuously using and referring to Roman law, these authors collected materials for construing the bridge that connected the former un-codified law with that of the Codes. By so doing, they made it possible, even today, when following the path of the development of the law, to cross the border river of the codification process between new and former law effortlessly.

Questions

1. Which are the main differences in the political organization of Rome between the period of the Principate (534–509 BC) and that of the Dominate (284 AD until 565 AD)?
2. What is meant by the statement that classical Roman law was characterised by a stratification into *ius civile* (civil law) and *ius honorarium* (honorary law)?
3. Legal concepts and institutions are sometimes labelled as 'natural' in contrast to their 'civil' counterparts. What is the meaning of the designation 'natural'?
4. In which way can the replies of the classical Roman jurists be considered to have functioned as a source of law?
5. The *lex citandi* (426 AD) and the *Codex Theodosianus* (438 AD) are sometimes described as precursors of Justinian's project of law-making. To what extent is that correct?
6. How did the *Corpus iuris civilis* eventually achieve to influence the development of law and legal thought in Western Europe?

3 Actors

It is important to keep in mind that the actors in Roman law cannot always be compared to those of later periods in the western legal tradition. For example, the formation and development of law during the Republican period and early classical Roman law was far more influenced by magistrates than judges, the private opinions of jurists were more important than case law, and there was no equivalent to the legislator and judiciary as they came to be understood later. The role of legislative bodies and the legislative activities of the Roman Emperors has already been discussed. We have also mentioned magistrates' and jurists' role, but their contribution to the legal order deserves some more attention.

3.1 *Magistrates*

The *pontifices* (singular: *pontifex*), played an important role in the oldest form of civil litigation: the *legis actio* procedure. Although they were not experts like the later jurists, these *pontifices* had some knowledge of the law and they were competent to decide whether parties could institute civil proceedings. They continued in this role some hundred years after the Law of the Twelve Tables came into being.

> *D. 1.2.2.6 Pomponius, Enchiridium*
> Subsequently, around the same time, actions were established enabling men to institute proceedings. In order to prevent people from bringing these actions at their own discretion, it was decided that they would be of an immutable and formal nature: this part of the law was called *legis actiones* i.e., actions based on statute. Consequently, almost simultaneously, three kinds of law emerged. After promulgation of the Law of the Twelve Tables, this resulted in the *ius civile* and the formation of *legis actiones*. Both the expertise to interpret and grant such actions to litigants rested with a council of *pontifices*. Every year one of the council was appointed to supervise litigation between private individuals. And for approximately one hundred years, the people observed this custom.[23]

Later, the office of praetor was instituted (in 367 BC) and the praetor took over the task of the *pontifices* in litigation. The praetor (and even later, the *curulian aedils* as well) were in charge of civil litigation – for the aedils in particular, litigation related to market trade. Like the praetors, the latter promulgated an edict listing the legal remedies available during their term of office. Holding the office of praetor was, for many, just a stage in their political career, and they often lacked specific expertise in legal matters, implying that they commonly had to rely on the replies of jurists. Both in the ancient *legis actio* procedure (largely abrogated in 17 BC) and in the later formulary procedure, the praetor was in charge of the first stage of the trial (the phase *in iure*) but did not pass

23 D. 1.2.2.6 *Pomponius libro singulari enchiridii* Deinde ex his legibus eodem tempore fere actiones compositae sunt, quibus inter se homines disceptarent: quas actiones ne populus prout vellet institueret certas solemnesque esse voluerunt: et appellatur haec pars iuris legis actiones, id est legitimae actiones. Et ita eodem paene tempore tria haec iura nata sunt: lege duodecim tabularum ex his fluere coepit ius civile, ex isdem legis actiones compositae sunt. Omnium tamen harum et interpretandi scientia et actiones apud collegium pontificum erant, ex quibus constituebatur, quis quoquo anno praeesset privatis. Et fere populus annis prope centum hac consuetudine usus est.

judgment. In the provinces, the role of the praetor was performed by the provincial governor (*praeses provinciae*).

3.2 *Jurists*

As stated above, in the second century BC, a distinct group of prominent citizens had emerged with specific expertise in legal matters. This resulted in a class of jurists, who, according the Cicero (*De oratore* 1.48.212), applied themselves to the drafting of legal texts (*cavere*), pleading in litigation (*agere*) and giving expert advice (*responsa*).

> *James Gordley, The Jurists. A critical history, Oxford, Oxford University Press, 2013, 2*
> Although Rome was perfected during the classical period, as Schulz observed, '[t]he heroic age of creative genius and daring pioneers was not the Empire, but the late Republic.' It was then that the jurists first appeared and assumed a unique position in Roman society that they kept throughout the classical period. We know little about the first jurists. The only surviving description of them is in a few lines written by the classical jurist Pomponius about 130–140 AD. He said that the civil law was 'founded' by M. Manilius, M. Junius Brutus, and P. Mucius Scaevola, all of whom lived in the late second century BC. In the following generation, the first commentary on civil law was written by Q. Mucius Scaevola. Only fragments of their writings survive. Yet, by the end of the Republic, the jurists had identified the concepts that became the foundations of western private law. They had developed a unique method for analyzing and refining these concepts that the classical jurists perfected.

As seen above, at the beginning of the classical era, some jurists were granted the *ius respondendi*, but in the second century AD this was no longer the practice: Emperor Hadrian issued replies in his own name as a response to legal problems submitted to him. The most important late classical jurists, whose works were copiously used for Justinian's Digest, were praetorian prefects (a senior officer, commander of the imperial guard) or members of the Senate or the imperial council, such as Papinian, Paul, Ulpian, and Modestinus. Papinian († 212 AD) was head of one of the imperial chanceries and starting in 203 AD, praetorian prefect. He compiled case-based replies (*Quaestiones* and *Responsa*). Paul was also head of one of the imperial chanceries. Under Emperor Alexander Severus (208–235 AD), he was a praetorian prefect and member of the imperial council. He wrote important commentaries on the Edict and the *ius civile* as summarized by Sabinus. Ulpian, a student of

Papinian, was also praetorian prefect and wrote, just like Paul, commentaries on the Edict and on Sabinus and, in addition, collections of legal replies. One-third of the Digest texts come from Ulpian, one fifth from his Commentary on the Edict. Modestinus was a student of Ulpian and worked at the end of the third century AD. By that time, the jurists were vanishing into the anonymity of the imperial chanceries or the imperial council. The following fragment deals with the interaction between magistrates and jurists.

> *James Gordley, The Jurists. A critical history, Oxford, Oxford University Press, 2013, 6–7*
> Moreover, ... in Rome, the promulgation of law by state authority was a matter of 'continuous day-to-day adjustment'. Legislation was rare because it was regarded as 'cumbrous'. A praetor could change his edict as he saw fit. The bulk of it would track the edict of his predecessor and the changes would be made with the advice of the jurists. The jurists could not revise the law except by working th[r]ough the praetor. The praetor, whatever his prominence and political acumen, was likely to listen. He was not an expert and he knew that any enduring change would need the approval of future praetors, who would receive the advice of jurists. Indeed, enduring change depended on the praetors and the jurists making the sort of changes that would be preserved because they commended themselves to other praetors and jurists. Consequently, while the task of the jurists was to explain the *ius civile* as promulgated by the state authority, it was, at the same time, to determine what state authority should say. The task was ongoing. The jurists explained what the law should be, not occasionally, when suggestions were made for law reform, but continuously, as part of their normal work.

In recent decades, there has been a renewed focus on the possibility of explaining texts from classical Roman jurists from a rhetorical perspective. The idea that, from the end of the Republic, there must have been a close connection between law and politics on the one hand, and rhetoric on the other has become more widely accepted. The Roman jurists were not theorists merely engaged in 'legal scholarship'. The Digest has a case-based nature, which indicates that the jurists' main occupation was *respondere*, i.e., to issue replies (*responsa*) to actual legal questions. In the late Republic and early Principate, citizens used to approach a jurist for advice when facing a legal problem. Cicero refers explicitly to this practice in *De Oratore* (1.239–240). The jurists used rhetorical principles in their replies. Therefore, there must have been a connection between legal practice and rhetoric.

Rhetoric had gradually penetrated legal practice. In the second century BC, Rome conquered Greece. At the same time, Rome was conquered by Greek rhetoric, as the poet Horace (65-8 BC) writes in his *Epistulae* (II.156–157). The upper class of Roman society engaged Greek teachers to instruct their sons in rhetoric with an eye on their political careers. Cicero's *De Oratore* (55 BC) was the first monograph on rhetoric. In it, Cicero maintained that the ideal orator or rhetorician should be a prudent man, capable of speaking splendidly and having an extensive knowledge at his disposal about law and history. Another work of Cicero on rhetoric was the *Topica* (45-44 BC). A later rhetorician, Quintilian (ca. 40-ca. 100 AD), wrote a systematic treatise on rhetoric, the *Institutio Oratoria* (ca. 95 AD). In this work, he discussed how to construct a plea, which figures of speech one can use, and gave practical examples.

> *Olga E. Tellegen, Roman Law and Rhetoric, Revue belge de philologie et d'histoire 84/1 (2006), Antiquité – Oudheid, 75*
> In Roman rhetoric, judicial oratory definitely occupied a leading position. However, this was not only used in the criminal courts and, for private law cases, in the courts of the *centumviri*, but also in that of the *unus iudex*. The introduction of the formulary procedure removed the traditional limitations and created a need for interpreting existing formulae and making new ones. The art of oratory offered the means of doing so effectively. Cicero, in his *De oratore*, makes Crassus say that, in Rome, knowledge of civil law was considered as much more important than in Greece, because there men of the lowest social station acted as assistants to orators in trials, whereas in Rome the most eminent and distinguished appeared in this capacity. This difference may also explain why it was Roman law and not Greek law that has conquered the Western World. Still, it was Greek rhetoric that made Roman law strong enough to do so.

3.3 *Judges*

In the ancient *legis actio* procedure and the formulary procedure, the verdict was commonly pronounced by one judge (*iudex unus*), i.e., a citizen appointed by the magistrate (formerly the *pontifex*) and the parties to judge the case. This took place in the second stage of the trial, the phase *apud iudicem*, where a legal advisor could assist the judge. Appeal was impossible since the parties had agreed to submit themselves to the judgment of the *iudex unus*. In formulary procedure cases where the general interest was at stake, the praetor could also appoint a tribunal of three citizens to act as judges: the so-called *recuperatores*. Although this method of civil litigation was largely abolished in 17 BC, two ancient judicial tribunals from the old *legis actio* proceedings continued to exist: the *centumviri* (hundred men) for disputes concerning the inheritance of extensive estates, and the *decemviri* (ten men) for manumission trials. In the *cognitio* procedure, judgment was by imperial officers. In the provinces, it was now the provincial governor (*praeses provinciae*) who acted in major civil cases as judge of first instance, or as judge of appeal in minor cases where the municipal magistrate had pronounced judgment.

In public criminal litigation, verdicts were handed down by magistrates or by tribunals of adjudicators who belonged to the senatorial or equestrian order. In the *cognitio* procedure which emerged in the classical era, their role was supplanted by imperial officers. In the provinces, criminal justice belonged to the competence of the provincial governor.

The *iudex unus* was no legal expert and sometimes made mistakes. This can be seen in some texts in the Digest, where the jurists speak about the judge's ignorance.

> *D. 21.2.51pr Ulpian, Commentary on the Edict, Book LXXX*
> If through stupidity or mistake of the judge, the buyer of something lost the suit, we deny that the plaintiff should bear the loss. What difference does it make whether the suit is lost through the judge's greed or foolishness? Because the harm done to the buyer should not affect the plaintiff.[24]

> *D. 24.3.17.2 Paul, Commentary on the civil law, Book VII*
> If, in a trial concerning a dowry, the judge blunders because of ignorance of the law and rules against the husband for the whole, Neratius and Sabinus say that he should bring the exception of fraud (*exceptio doli*) and will be protected.[25]

3.4 *Parties*

In Roman civil litigation, there were some restrictions on who was eligible to be a plaintiff or defendant. Women were not *sui iuris* and therefore were subjected to their father's or husband's power, and slaves could not be party to a

24 D. 21.2.51pr *Ulpianus libro octogesimo ad edictum* Si per imprudentiam iudicis aut errorem emptor rei victus est, negamus auctoris damnum esse debere: aut quid refert, sordibus iudicis an stultitia res perierit? Iniuria enim, quae fit emptori, auctorem non debet contingere.

25 D. 24.3.17.2 *Paulus libro septimo ad Sabinum* Si in iudicio dotis iudex ignorantia iuris lapsus condemnaverit maritum in solidum, Neratius Sabinus doli exceptione eum uti oportere aiunt eaque tutum fore.

trial. In some cases, juveniles (*impuberes*) and women who were *sui iuris* (i.e., not under the control of another) needed their tutor's authority, and the mentally ill needed that of their curator, in order to become eligible.

The formulary procedure primarily endorsed and affirmed existing social relationships. The plaintiff had to appear together with the defendant before the praetor. However, there was no coercion from the authorities' side to compel the defendant to appear and, thereby, enable the plaintiff to sue. The latter was left to his own devices. Accordingly, it was much easier for the socially stronger party to sue a socially weaker party than the other way around. In the *cognitio* procedure, by contrast, it was quite different, since the court summoned the defendant at the plaintiff's request.

> *John M. Kelly, Roman Litigation, Oxford, Clarendon Press, 1966, 14*
> The result of the foregoing considerations is that Roman litigation in the republican and classical periods was devoid of the sanction of state power which modern English litigation enjoys, and that the only physical sanction of Roman litigation in these periods consisted in such force as the plaintiff was able to muster in order to overbear the actual or possible resistance of a weaker defendant. If, therefore, the only sanction of any kind supporting a system of litigation were to consist in the plaintiff's own strength, we would be driven to conclude that this system must have functioned with the utmost irregularity, since the tendency would be for potential plaintiffs who were weaker than their prospective adversaries to refrain from instituting a useless proceeding. Only those would emerge as plaintiffs who were stronger than, or at least as strong as, the defendants; only those would appear as defendants who were weaker than, or at least no less weak than the plaintiffs.

Questions

1. Why is it difficult to compare the actors in Roman law with those in later periods of the western legal tradition?
2. What was the role of the praetor in the formulary procedure?
3. Which were according to Cicero the principal occupations of the jurists in his days?
4. Some classical jurists received from the Emperor the *ius respondendi*. What did this right entail and how did it affect the jurists' replies?
5. Were there during the era of classical Roman law any restrictions as regards access to court?

4 Application

So far, we have primarily focused on the 'external' legal history of Antiquity, i.e., the general features of Roman law, the way it functioned in a wider social and political context, and its sources. The final part of this chapter will briefly address 'internal' legal history and say something about actual rules, institutions, and Roman law doctrine, both procedural and substantive. Given this volume's scope and structure, this 'internal' history can only provide an outline of the various areas of law and no detailed treatment. However, we will delve a little deeper into the substantive law of property and the law of obligations during the classical era and the time of Justinian. This will enable the reader to understand some case-based texts from the *Corpus iuris civilis*, specifically the Digest, dealing with actual questions regarding ownership, contract, and delict.

Many texts from the Digest have a case-based character. Most of the time, the description of a distinct case is followed by the jurist's opinion, responding to one or more questions raised by the case. However, the problem itself and the *ratio decidendi* underlying the reply are rarely given. To understand the text, one should break it down in various segments, starting with the facts (Who is involved? What is their position from the perspective of the law of obligations and the law of property? What is the chronology of the facts?). Subsequently, the facts combined with the reply suggest the question posed to the jurist (who wanted to know what?). Third, we can map out the jurist's answer to the question. It is seldom a straightforward yes or no, and most of the time it includes a sophisticated and balanced reply distinguishing various relevant circumstances. The fourth and most challenging thing is to put the reply in broader context. How can the reply be explained and justified from the perspective of what we know about Roman law? The difficulty here is that the jurists did not apply general legal rules to the facts of the case in order to reach their decision by a kind of syllogism. However, replies in comparable cases sometimes reveal a common understanding of the law and the existence of implied common legal principles. So, there is often a legal context which makes it possible to discover a legal justification for the reply.

4.1 *Civil Litigation*

During its long history, Roman law knew three kinds of civil procedure. The oldest one, the *legis actio* procedure, was largely abrogated in 17 BC. The formulary procedure, which came into being in the Republican era, was the most commonly used type of litigation during the classical period. These proceedings had two stages. First, the phase *in iure*, where the *praetor* investigated whether the edict contained an action with a *formula* suitable for the claim in the case under dispute. The *praetor* could also adjust the words of the *formula* (*actio utilis*) or create a new *formula* tailored to the facts of the case and independent of the edict (*actio in factum*). The main distinction was between actions aimed at protecting proprietary rights, which could be maintained against anyone (*actiones in rem*), and actions aimed at protecting the plaintiff's right against one specific debtor (*actiones in personam*). The phase *in iure* was concluded by joinder of issue (*litis contestatio*), an agreement between the *praetor* and the parties in which the judge was assigned and the procedural steps were laid out (*formulae* of remedies, containing instructions for the judge). In the second stage of the trial, the phase *apud iudicem*, proof had to be presented, and the advocates could plead the plaintiff and the defendant's case. Finally, the *iudex*, a citizen called to judge the case, pronounced his judgment orally in the presence of the parties. There was no appeal from the verdict of the *iudex* since the parties had agreed to submit themselves to his decision. Some details concerning the formulary procedure only became known in the nineteenth century, when the Institutes of Gaius were discovered, such as the rule that the *iudex* could only order the defendant to pay an amount of money and not order specific performance (*comdemnatio pecuniaria*).

> *Gai.* IV.48
> However, the condemnation of all *formulae*, containing a condemnation, is aimed at a monetary assessment. Accordingly, also when we claim an object, for example, a plot of land, a slave, a garment, gold or silver, the *iudex* does not condemn the one sued to hand over the thing itself, as usual in olden times, but after assessment of the object, he condemns him to pay an amount of money.[26]

At the end of the Republican era, new forms of civil procedure emerged in the provinces, known as *cognitio extraordinaria*. At the beginning of the first century AD, this kind of litigation was also introduced in Italy and Rome. In the third century AD, it became the common type of civil procedure and managed to banish the formulary procedure into the background. In 342 AD, the

26 Gai. IV.48 Omnium autem formularum, quae condemnationem habent, ad pecuniariam aestimationem condemnatio concepta est. itaque et si corpus aliquod petamus, uelut fundum, hominem, uestem, aurum, argentum, iudex non ipsam rem condemnat eum, cum quo actum est, sicut olim fieri solebat, sed aestimata re pecuniam eum condemnat.

formulary procedure was prohibited, and the *cognitio* procedure remained. There are significant differences between the two types of civil litigation. Under the new procedure, an imperial officer was in charge of the proceedings and acted as judge. An appeal to a higher court or the Emperor was possible. Judgments to perform acts other than paying money were allowed, and the verdict had to be recorded in writing. During the later Empire, this procedure was only slightly altered: from that time on the defendant had to be summoned by the court, and the plaintiff had to submit a request to that effect. The plaintiff's claim could be adjusted during the procedure, and the judge was bound to certain precepts for evaluating the evidence produced.

By the time of Justinian, the judiciary had developed into a hierarchical system. For minor claims, one could call on the municipal authorities, and for major claims on the provincial governors. From the latter's verdict, an appeal was possible to the vicar (administrator) of the diocese (an administrative level between the province and the praetorian prefect). The decision of the vicar could be appealed to the Emperor. Parties could also decide to submit their case to the bishop, and his decision was binding and final. This procedure, called *episcopalis audientia*, was officially recognized by Emperor Constantine.

4.2 *Criminal Procedure*

In public criminal law, it was traditionally the *comitia centuriata* that did the sentencing in more serious crimes; minor cases fell within the jurisdiction of the magistrates. From 200 BC, the *tresviri capitales* (lower magistrates) dealt with crimes of violence and arson by slaves and foreigners. In 149 BC, new judicial bodies were established for specific crimes: the *quaestio de repetundis* for extortion by officials, and the *quaestiones perpetuae*, i.e. tribunals of jurors led by the praetors. From the days of dictator Sulla (138-78 BC), there were six such courts for criminal justice, each with its own competence. At the beginning of the classical period, criminal justice by the *tresviri capitales* was taken over by imperial officials, and two more *quaestiones* were added to the existing six.

In the Republic, the procedure was adversarial. Every reputable citizen was competent to denounce someone before the *praetor*. Subsequently, the latter would appoint, by lot, a jury to judge the case. In cases where the complainant could furnish proof of his accusation, this would greatly benefit him. Every crime had a fixed penalty, and he received, for example, part of the confiscated assets of the accused. However, if he did not provide proof, he could be sentenced as if he himself had committed the alleged crime. If there was no competent court (*quaestio*), it was impossible to denounce the wrongdoer.

In the course of the first century AD, almost all *quaestiones* disappeared. Criminal justice was henceforth dealt with by the *cognitio* procedure for criminal matters. The competent authorities were: prefects (the urban prefect for Rome and the area of a hundred miles around Rome, and the praetorian prefect for the other territories in Italy); the Senate (for crimes committed by members of its own class); and as the highest court, the Emperor, possibly with his advisory council. In the imperial provinces, criminal justice was in the hands of the imperial delegate, and in the senatorial provinces in the hands of the governor. There was no appeal from the prefects' sentences, since their judicial competences were delegated by the Emperor. The new criminal procedure was inquisitorial. A complaint lodged by a private complainant was no longer required, except in the so-called *crimina publica*. It was now the state which prosecuted the wrongdoer. The accused could only be sentenced when it was established that he had committed the crime. An appeal was not possible in case of a confession, or a conviction for acts of violence and murder. Punishments were no longer fixed but left to the judge's discretion and based on the circumstances, and capital punishment was allowed only in cases of a confession or similar evidence. Penalties were more severe during the time of the Empire than during the Republic: for the *humiliores* or lower orders of society (ordinary citizens and slaves) it was commonly forced labor, corporal punishment or sentence of death, and for the *honestiores* or privileged orders usually exile, monetary fines or confiscation of assets. The most peculiar punishment of Roman law, which existed until the second century AD, was the *culleus*.

> *D. 48.9.9pr Modestinus, Pandects, Book XII*
> According to the customs of our ancestors, the following punishment is determined for parricide. The parricide is flogged with twigs of red dogwood and sewed into a leather bag (*culleus*) together with a dog, a domesticated cock, a viper, and a monkey; subsequently, the bag is thrown into deep-sea i.e., when the sea is close by. If not, he is, according to a constitution of the idolized Hadrian, left to the mercy of the wild beasts.[27]

27 D. 48.9.9pr *Modestinus libro duodecimo pandectarum* Poena parricidii more maiorum haec instituta est, ut parricida virgis sanguineis verberatus deinde culleo insuatur cum cane, gallo gallinaceo et vipera et simia: deinde in mare profundum culleus iactatur. hoc ita, si mare proximum sit: alioquin bestiis obicitur secundum divi Hadriani constitutionem.

4.3 *Substantive Private Law*

Substantive private law covers many areas. As far as the law of persons and the law of succession is concerned, we will confine ourselves to some basic ideas. However, for the law of property and the law of obligations, we will delve more deeply into the Roman provisions and, by way of illustration, show some case material from the Digest.

In Roman law, not every human being is considered the subject of rights or able to perform legal acts. One's legal position depends on whether one is free or a slave (*status libertatis*), under the power of another, or 'of one's own right' (*status familiae*), a Roman citizen, or foreigner (*status civitatis*). Those who were not under the power of another (*sui iuris*), such as a *pater familias*, were entitled to their own assets. Children under paternal control (*alieni iuris*) were only entitled to certain things, such as the assets a son acquired as a soldier (*peculium castrense*), or as a civil servant (*peculium quasi castrense*), or the things received from their mother's inheritance (*bona materna*), or from outsiders (*bona adventicia*). Nevertheless, a *pater familias* could grant his slaves and children under paternal control certain assets, which enabled them to engage in economic activities. The *pater familias* retained the right to this property, the so-called *peculium*. Only those who were *sui iuris* or had assets of their own and were of age (25) had full legal capacity. If they had not yet reached this age, they needed their tutor (if they were no longer infants, until they reached maturity) or their curator (until they became of age) to perform valid legal acts. Some people required the assistance of their curator their entire life. However, this does not mean that contracts entered into by slaves and sons under paternal control were without legal consequences. As a general rule, these contracts resulted in limited liability for the master or father, unless they had issued an order (*iussum*) to enter into the contract, which would result in full liability. In general, the master or father was liable in cases of non-performance for the amount he was enriched, or for the amount of the *peculium*. Also, (private) delicts of slaves resulted in a limited liability for their master. However, to avoid payment of the fine, the master could surrender the slave to the plaintiff (*noxae deditio*). In classical law, this also applied to delicts by children under paternal control.

In 212 AD Emperor Antoninus Caracalla (188–217 AD) granted civil rights to all inhabitants of the Roman Empire, under the so-called *Constitutio Antoniniana*. This implied that the *status civitatis* lost much of its relevance and that the 'foreigners' (*peregrini*) as a category ceased to exist. For the rest, Roman historians nowadays tend to think that the *Constitutio Antoniniana* had only limited legal effect on the Empire.

In Roman law, there were two grounds for being entitled to, or as the Roman sources say, 'being called' to an inheritance (*vocari ad hereditatem*). The first is as the heir in a will (*ex testamento*), the second is on the basis of statutory rules in the absence of a (valid) will (*ab intestato*). The two bases are mutually exclusive. Apart from some exceptions, the heir succeeds the testator in his patrimony and all his rights and duties. The heir's remedy to claim the inheritance is called *hereditatis petitio*. A last will has to be put in writing (on paper, parchment, or wax tablet), signed by witnesses, and can be invalidated by a later will. The intestate law of succession distinguishes various categories of persons who could successively 'be called' to the inheritance. If there is nobody who belongs to the first category, those belonging to the second category can 'be called', etc. In a will, the testator could lay down that a specific part of his assets be allocated to someone who was not an heir. The heir had to pay out these assets, called a 'legate' or 'bequest', to the beneficiary or legatee. In classical law, there were various types of legates. One could disinherit relatives, but if there was no sound reason to do so the next of kin, especially the children, remained entitled to a certain part of the inheritance (a statutory share). If this share was not recognized, the will could be nullified.

4.4 *Substantive Private Law: Law of Property*

The Roman right of ownership was indivisible in the sense that it did not recognize multiple titles to a thing, each with its own nature. Neither did title to land provide legal and/or military rights and obligations as it did under feudal land tenure in the Middle Ages. On the other hand, co-ownership did exist, as well as restricted rights that burdened the owner's use. Ownership and restricted rights to property formed a closed system. Only certain types were recognized, and people were not free to create others. These real rights had in common that they could, in principle, be enforced against anyone: similar to absolute rights. The remedies to protect these rights were called *actiones in rem*. In classical times, the *formula* of each specific *actio in rem* could be found in the praetor's edict. Mere possession was not regarded as a right, but it did have legal implications. It could be protected against infringement by interdicts (possessory remedies) provided the proper requirements were met, and it could lead to ownership through prescription. The law of property was limited to material objects and rights to them. There was no concept of an absolute right to a claim, and creditors could not transfer claims.

The Roman jurists distinguished two ways to acquire ownership: through the civil law (transfer and prescription) and the natural law (accession, specification, occupation, etc.). In later Roman sources, the main distinction became that of original and derivative acquisition of ownership. In the case of original acquisition, the right was not derived from a legal predecessor, such as in the natural law modes of acquiring ownership and long-term prescription of immovables. In the case of derivative acquisition, the right was derived from a predecessor, i.e., the former owner, for example, through transfer of ownership and acquisitive prescription of movables. Prescription was necessary when ownership was not acquired through the transfer of possession. This could be due to the fact that the transferor lacked the authority to transfer the object. In classical law, it could also be because the prescribed formal way of transfer (*mancipatio*) was not followed. The goal of prescription was to avoid a situation where it was not clear who held the title to things. An owner who had lost possession of his property had a certain amount of time to assert rightful ownership of his property. If he refrained from doing so, the factual possessor could become entitled. During the prescription period, the possessor had limited legal protection, i.e., not against the one entitled, but against third parties.

To illustrate this outline of Roman property law, we will present some cases from the Digest. They show something of the substantive law of property, the case-based character of the texts, and how the Digest was compiled. The texts can be considered from at least two perspectives: as replies of jurists from the classical law era, and as provisions of imperial legislation from the sixth century AD. To fully understand the texts, it may be necessary to consult one or more of the introductory textbooks on Roman private law mentioned in the bibliography below.

Case 1: The Seller Lacking Authority Who Later Became Owner

D. 21.3.1pr. Ulpian, Commentary on the Edict, Book LXXVI

Marcellus writes that, if you have sold another man's plot of land, and later, when it has become yours, you claim it back, your claim is rightfully barred by this exception.[28]

Notes

(1) The facts of the case are the following. The 'you character' sold another man's plot of land and also conveyed it (he granted the buyer possession). Since he was not the owner, the recipient did not become the

28 D. 21.3.1pr. *Ulpianus libro septuagesimo sexto ad edictum* Marcellus scribit, si alienum fundum vendideris et tuum postea factum petas, hac exceptione recte repellendum.

owner. In Roman law, it is impossible to transfer a right one does not have oneself (*nemo plus iuris transferre potest quam ipse habet*). That the plot of land was actually conveyed follows from the fact that it was reclaimed. Subsequently, the seller became entitled to the land. How this occurred is not mentioned. He could, for example, have become the owner by inheriting the land.

(2) The case raises the question of whether the buyer who holds possession of the land is protected against the seller's claim as the owner of the land.

(3) According to the reply of the jurist (originally Marcellus, but quoted here by Ulpian) the owner's claim can be blocked by an exception (defense). In Justinianic law, this exception is the defense that the plaintiff has sold and conveyed to the defendant the object he now claims from him. This follows from the fact that the Digest compilers listed this fragment in a title dealing with such a defense, in Latin called the *exceptio rei venditae et traditae*.

(4) The *ratio decidendi* must have been that the sale is valid. The authority to transfer ownership is not a requirement for a contract of sale. Sale is a contract which merely requires consent between the parties in relation to the object and the price. The seller is obligated to grant the buyer possession, and he has done so in the case under dispute. Normally, ownership would have passed (at least in Justinianic law), but the 'seller' was not the owner in this case. However, after conveyance had taken place, he became owner of the plot and is now, as the owner, entitled to claim the object he owns from the possessor. The remedy to achieve that is based on a property right, and is called *rei vindicatio*. In classical law, the term refers to a certain *formula* of the action in the praetor's edict. In Justinianic law, it just indicates the plaintiff's claim. In general, every owner can use this remedy against any possessor who refuses to hand over the object. However, in this case the *rei vindicatio* can be blocked by the possessor's defense: he can object that the plaintiff himself sold and conveyed the object which he now reclaims. After all, his lack of authority to alienate was the reason why the buyer did not acquire ownership at the moment of conveyance.

Case 2: The Donation by Letter

D. 6.1.77 Ulpian, Commentary on the Edict, Book XVII
A woman had donated by letter a plot of land to a man who was not her husband and leased from him the same plot of land. It can be argued that he has an *actio in rem*, as if he acquired possession through her as through a lessee.

Moreover, it was mentioned that he was on the land when the letter was sent. That very circumstance suffices for the transfer of possession, even if no lease took place.[29]

Notes

(1) The facts of the case are the following. A woman donates a plot of land to a man. The donation is valid since she is not the man's wife (a donation between spouses is void in Roman law). In classical law, a donation was the granting of a benefit without any quid pro quo. In Justinianic law, it is an act that obligates granting the benefit. The donation was communicated by letter, and the man was situated on the plot of land when the letter was sent. At the same time, both parties entered into a lease contract for the same plot of land – the man as lessor and the woman as lessee.

(2) The case raises the question of whether the man now has a proprietary claim to the land. The answer depends on the question of whether he acquired possession or not. If so, he has a claim; if not, he has no claim. Roman law has a traditionalistic (not a consensualistic) system of transfer. Ownership is transferred not by the mere sale or donation, but through conveyance.

(3) According to the reply of the jurist Ulpian the man has acquired possession through the woman as his lessee or by the fact that he was on the plot of land at the time the letter was sent. One of these suffices. Since he has possession, he has an *actio in rem*. In classical law this would have been the *actio Publiciana*, since ownership of Italic land (non-provincial land) could not be transferred by the mere granting of possession. Accordingly, the man acquired possession and not ownership. However, being a possessor who can acquire ownership through prescription, he has a remedy, which presumes him to be the owner: the *actio Publiciana*. In Justinianic law, ownership of immovables can be transferred by granting possession. The man is the owner, and his *actio in rem* is the *rei vindicatio*.

(4) The *ratio decidendi* must have been that apparently, the man could have acquired possession in two ways:

29 D. 6.1.77 *Ulpianus libro septimo decimo ad edictum* Quaedam mulier fundum non marito donavit per epistulam et eundem fundum ab eo conduxit: posse defendi in rem ei competere, quasi per ipsam adquisierit possessionem veluti per colonam. proponebatur, quod etiam in eo agro qui donabatur fuisset, cum epistula emitteretur: quae res sufficiebat ad traditam possessionem, licet conductio non intervenisset.

(a) Through the lease contract, where the woman has taken the position of a holder (*detentor*). She no longer has the will to exercise factual power herself but hands it to another. She has gone from being the possessor of the land to the holder of the land for the lessor, who can now be considered the possessor. This is a transfer of possession, called *traditio per constitutum possessorium*. Being on the plot of land is not necessary.

(b) By being on the plot of land, the man became possessor. He was present on the plot of land when he became aware that the woman permitted him to take possession of the plot. Subsequently, the man started to hold the land as his own (possession). This is corporeal acquisition of possession. A lease contract is not necessary.

Case 3: The Rented Slave

D. 18.6.17(16) Javolenus, Elaboration of Cassius, Book VII

The buyer of a slave had requested to hire him [i.e., the slave] until he paid the price. He is not able to acquire anything through this slave, because a slave who is in possession of the seller by means of letting, is not considered to be conveyed. The risk of the slave is for the buyer, at least as long as there is no malicious intent from the side of the seller.[30]

Notes

(1) The facts of the case are the following. Two people entered into a contract of sale. This contract only requires the consent of the parties concerning object and price. The obligations resulting from the sale can be enforced by remedies (in classical law: actions from the edict) controlled by good faith. This implies that the judge has extensive discretionary power and can consider any other agreement the parties consented to in relation to the sale of the slave. Apparently, the seller and buyer had agreed that the slave sold would not be conveyed before the entire selling price was paid. Given this agreement, the seller had

30 D. 18.6.17(16) *Iavolenus libro septimo ex Cassio* Servi emptor si eum conductum rogavit, donec pretium solveret, nihil per eum servum adquirere poterit, quoniam non videtur traditus is, cuius possessio per locationem retinetur a venditore. periculum eius servi ad emptorem pertinet, quod tamen sine dolo venditoris intervenerit.

requested to hire the slave and so it was decided. The slave was now factually held by the buyer and at the latter's disposal.

(2) The construction chosen by the parties causes various problems. Who is the possessor of the slave? This is relevant as to the question who acquires possession (and through possession ownership) of the goods the slave will receive, for example, after buying these goods. The seller of the slave or the buyer? Moreover, would the seller be liable, if he would no longer be capable of conveying the slave before the selling price is paid? In which situations would he be liable for breach of contract? In which cases should the buyer still have to pay the full price?

(3) According to the reply of the jurist Javolenus it is the buyer who will acquire possession (and ownership) through the slave, and the seller is only liable for non-performance if he cannot deliver the slave due to his own malicious intent. In all other cases, he has to pay the full price.

(4) The *ratio decidendi* must have been that the slave is handed over based on a lease, not based on sale. The lessee's factual power is that of a holder; he cannot be considered to have factual power with the intention of exercising this power for himself (possession); instead, he holds the slave for the seller, who through the lease, remains in possession. Accordingly, the slave is not yet conveyed. Conveyance (*traditio*) will take place after the entire selling price has been paid. In such a case, handing over the goods is superfluous because possession is transferred by the mere change of the intention of seller and buyer. The seller abandons his intention to have possession, and the buyer starts holding the slave as if he were his own (*brevi manu traditio*). By so doing, in Justinianic law the buyer will become owner; in classical law he will only become possessor, because ownership of slaves, just like that of immovables (*res mancipi*), cannot be transferred by mere delivery. With regard to the situation that the seller can no longer convey the slave to the buyer, the Digest sometimes indicates that the seller is liable if the object sold perishes before conveyance due to the seller's malicious intent (*dolus*) or his negligence (*culpa*); in classical law even if the object sold was stolen through no fault of the seller (*custodia*). In this case of the rented slave, however, the seller's liability appears to be reduced to situations of malicious intent. If the seller is not liable, the buyer has to pay the full price, also a commonly adopted rule in the Digest (*periculum est emptoris*), but in the case in dispute this covers many more situations than normally would be the case. The deviation from the common pattern can be explained by the fact that it is not the seller who has the slave at his disposal, as will be the normal situation

before conveyance, but the buyer himself. He is in a better position than the seller to influence the well-being of the slave and enhance the likelihood that proper performance remains possible.

Case 4: The Ignorant Heir

D. 41.3.43pr Papinian, Questions, Book XXII

The heir of someone who in good faith had bought something, shall not acquire through prescription (*usucapio*), if he knows it is another man's property, at least if possession is transferred to him. Continuation of prescription, however, is not obstructed by the heir's knowledge.[31]

Notes

(1) The facts of the case are the following. Someone buys something in good faith, i.e., he thinks the seller has the authority to transfer ownership. In fact, this is not the case. The sale is nevertheless valid since consent between parties suffices. Subsequently, the buyer dies. By contrast, his heir knows that the seller was not the owner of the thing he sold.

(2) The case raises the question of whether the heir, despite his knowledge, can acquire ownership of the object through prescription. The Latin term used for prescription, *usucapio*, refers to a prescription of movables, which requires three years of possession. In classical law, it was one year. Another requirement is that of good faith (*bona fides*). Good faith is absent when the possessor knows at the moment he acquires possession that the seller has no authority to transfer ownership.

(3) According to the reply of the jurist Papinian a distinction has to be drawn. The heir will not acquire ownership when possession is transferred to him, but he can continue the prescription. This reply may seem obscure and needs to be explained more fully. In the first situation, the testator had bought something, but no conveyance had taken place, and subsequently, he died. Now the testator was no longer there; the heir took his place and was entitled to delivery as a buyer. But since he knows that the seller has no authority to transfer ownership of the object sold, he is in bad faith when delivery takes place and possession

31 D. 41.3.43pr *Papinianus libro vicensimo secundo quaestionum* Heres eius, qui bona fide rem emit, usu non capiet sciens alienum, si modo ipsi possessio tradita sit: continuatio vero non impedietur heredis scientia.

is acquired. Accordingly, no prescription will take place. In the second case, however, the testator had bought in good faith, and the merchandise was also conveyed to him. Since the testator was in good faith, prescription started to run. Before the required period of three years had lapsed, he died. Since the testator was a possessor/non-owner who was engaged in becoming owner through prescription, the heir took over this position. Accordingly, he became the object's possessor, but the prescription, which had started with the testator, could now be continued despite the heir's bad faith.

(4) The *ratio decidendi* must have been that, if after conveyance had taken place, the testator would have discovered that the seller had no authority to transfer ownership, the acquisitive prescription would nevertheless have continued. This principle is expressed in the maxim *mala fides superveniens non nocet* (subsequent bad faith does not harm). There is a strong similarity between the situation where a buyer, after delivery, discovers the seller was a non-owner, and the situation where a buyer's position in good faith is taken over by his heir who knows the seller was a non-owner.

4.5 *Substantive Private Law: Law of Obligations*

The law of property, with its *actiones in rem*, protects either one's entitlement or a restricted right to a material thing. The law of obligations protects the legal relationship between two persons, which obligates one to a performance to which the other is entitled. In Roman law, the remedies for this purpose were called *actiones in personam*. Gaius was probably the first to outline the many different sources of obligations, in his Institutes, where he made a distinction between contract and delict. Later, in Justinian's Institutes, four classes were distinguished: contracts, quasi-contracts, delicts, and quasi-delicts. The contracts and delicts were a limited and defined set of agreements or wrongs which resulted in one or more obligations. Accordingly, parties were not free to create a binding agreement that was not recognized by law, and each contract and delict was governed by its own specific provisions. Both Gaius' and Justinian's Institutes distinguished four categories of 'nominate' contracts based on how they were formed. Delicts had different legal consequences: fines claimed by and paid to the injured party, sometimes including damages, and sometimes separate from them. The law of delict also contained a strong retributive element for crimes, a function nowadays frequently superseded by public criminal law.

Case 5: The Broken Measuring Implements

D. 19.2.13.8 Ulpian, Commentary on the Edict, Book XXXII

Someone had rented measuring implements, which by order of the magistrate were broken. If they were indeed inaccurate, Sabinus distinguished two situations: the lessee was aware of it or not. If he knew, there is an action based on letting. If not, there is no action. However, if the measuring implements were accurate, the lessor is only liable if it was his fault that the aedile broke them. And Labeo and Mela say the same.[32]

Notes

(1) The facts of the case are as follows. Someone rented measuring implements (rods or scales). A lease (*locatio conductio*) is a consensual contract, so mere consent between the parties is sufficient and results in obligations. The lessor has to grant the lessee the use of what is rented. The lessee has to pay the rent and make sure he returns the rented objects in good condition. The measuring implements were broken by order of the magistrate – in this case, the aedile – supervising the marketplace. The reason was probably that the implements were inaccurate, or at least that the aedile was under the impression that they were. Consequently, the lessee is incapable of restoring the measuring implements (in good condition) to the lessor.

(2) The case raises the question of whether the lessee is liable for damages towards the lessor.

(3) According to the reply of the jurist Ulpian, referring here to the older jurists Sabinus, Labeo, and Mela, four different situations can be distinguished, and four corresponding solutions are presented. (i) If the implements were inaccurate and the lessee knew this, he is liable. (ii) If the implements were inaccurate and the lessee did not know this, he is not liable. (iii) If the implements were accurate and it was the lessee's fault that they were broken, he is liable. (iv) If the implements were accurate and it was not the lessee's fault that they were broken, he is not liable.

(4) The *ratio decidendi* must have been that someone knowingly using inaccurate measuring implements on the market knows he runs the risk that the market police (the aedile) will take action. If he is not

32 D. 19.2.13.8 *Ulpianus libro trigesimo secundo ad edictum* Si quis mensuras conduxerit easque magistratus frangi iusserit, si quidem iniquae fuerunt, Sabinus distinguit, utrum scit conductor an non: si scit, esse ex locato actionem, si minus, non. quod si aequae sunt, ita demum eum teneri, si culpa eius id fecit aedilis. et ita Labeo et Mela scribunt.

aware of the fact that the implements are inaccurate, he is not at fault. Someone using accurate measuring implements but nevertheless creating the impression that they are inaccurate (by measuring off less fabric than he says to sell, for example) is at fault, but if he gave no cause for breaking the (accurate) implements, he is not at fault.

Case 6: The Golden Dish

D. 12.1.11pr Ulpian, Commentary on the Edict, Book XXVI
You asked me to lend you money. Because I had no money, I gave you a golden dish or a gold nugget, so that you can sell it and use the money of the sale. If you sold the thing, I think a loan of money is established. But if through no fault of yours you lost the dish or the nugget before it was sold, I wonder whether you or I will suffer the loss. I think Nerva drew an appropriate distinction, maintaining that it is relevant whether the dish was for sale or not. If I wanted to sell the dish, I suffer the loss, as in the case where I gave it to someone else to sell it. But if I had no intention to sell, but the sole ground for the sale was that you could use the money of the sale, then you will suffer the loss, especially when I did not stipulate any interest.[33]

Notes

(1) The facts of the case are the following. The 'you-character' approaches the 'I-character' with the request for a loan of money. The 'I-character' has no ready money and hands over a golden object to be sold. Before any sale takes place, the object is lost without the fault of the 'you-character'.

(2) The case raises the question of whether the 'you-character' is liable to the 'I-character'.

(3) According to the reply of the jurist Ulpian, referring to a distinction previously drawn by Nerva, he is not liable if the 'you-character' wanted to sell the object. He is liable, however, if the 'you-character' did not want to sell the object.

---

33 D. 12.1.11pr *Ulpianus libro vicensimo sexto ad edictum* Rogasti me, ut tibi pecuniam crederem: ego cum non haberem, lancem tibi dedi vel massam auri, ut eam venderes et nummis490 utereris. si vendideris, puto mutuam pecuniam factam. quod si lancem vel massam sine tua culpa perdideris prius quam venderes, utrum mihi an tibi perierit, quaestionis est. mihi videtur Nervae distinctio verissima existimantis multum interesse, venalem habui hanc lancem vel massam nec ne, ut, si venalem habui, mihi perierit, quemadmodum si alii dedissem vendendam: quod si non fui proposito hoc ut venderem, sed haec causa fuit vendendi, ut tu utereris, tibi eam perisse, et maxime si sine usuris credidi.

(4) The *ratio decidendi* must have been that in Roman law, a money loan is a form of *mutuum*, a contract where fungible goods (not only money but also gold, silver, wine, grain, oil, etc.) are lent. This agreement is a real contract and so cannot be entered into by mere consent. The fungible things lent have to be handed over. Only then do the contract and the obligation to restore (as much as received from the same generic goods) arise. If the golden dish is sold, and the 'you-character' has received the selling price, there can be no doubt. The selling price (money, coins) is in his hands now and can be considered the amount lent out by the 'I-character'. In that case, there is an obligation to pay back the same amount. The 'you-character' cannot avoid liability, since the sort of thing (money) cannot vanish (*genus non perit*). In the case under dispute, however, the object is lost before it is sold. The liability of the 'you-character' now depends to a larger extent on the qualification of the legal relationship between the parties. What kind of contract was there before the sale had taken place, and the 'you-character' received the sale price? The reply maintains that this should be determined by whether or not the 'I-character' wanted to sell the golden object, but why this fact is so important is not explained. The underlying reasoning could have been that if the 'you-character' wanted to sell, the agreement between 'I' and 'you' is one of mandate (*mandatum*). The *mandatarius* is requested to do something (sell the dish) in the interest of the mandator (the 'I-character'). In that case, the 'you-character' did not acquire ownership of the dish (the 'I' remains possessor and owner) and is only liable when the object is lost through his fault. If the 'I-character' did not want to sell the dish, the agreement may have been a *mutuum*-contract from the very beginning: selling the dish is not in the interest of the 'I-character'. Moreover, the golden dish can be seen as a specific object (manufactured by a craftsman), but under these circumstances ('I' did not want to sell) also as a fungible good (just a quantity of gold). Thus, when the dish was handed over, the parties entered into a contract of *mutuum*. The 'you-character' acquired possession and ownership of the dish as a certain quantity of fungible goods (gold). His obligation is to pay back as much money (coins were also made of gold) as he received. This obligation will continue to exist when the dish perishes. It is not the dish that should be restored but as much gold or as many coins as handed over to the recipient. The last line, 'especially when I did not stipulate any interest', only indicates a situation in which the 'I-character', to an even greater extent, lacked any interest in the agreement with the 'you-character'. This remark does not

contribute substantially to the argument: according to some, it would be an interpolation.

Case 7: The Twice-purchased Merchandise

D. 21.2.29pr Pomponius, Commentary on the ius civile, Book XI
I have the thing you sold me, although it was another man's property, bought for a second time from the owner. Celsus the younger said that the reply of Nerva, that you can claim from me the selling price with the remedy of sale, as if I am not prevented from retaining the merchandise, is unjust, because this is not in conformity with good faith and because I retain the merchandise by virtue of a different title.[34]

Notes

(1) The facts of the case are the following. The 'I-character' bought something from the 'you-character', but the latter had no authority to sell. The contract is nevertheless valid. Conveyance takes place because the seller transferred possession to the 'I-character' (this follows from the seller's argument that he performed what he was obligated to). The buyer acquired possession, not ownership (*nemo plus iuris transferre potest quam ipse habet*), through the conveyance. The buyer had not yet paid the sale price (this follows from the fact that the question is brought up whether the selling price has to be paid). Subsequently, the buyer was faced with the fact that someone else was the owner and that this owner was capable of evicting (he could claim the object from the buyer/possessor by bringing a *rei vindicatio*). To avoid this, the buyer proposed the owner to sell it to him. Apparently he attached more value in retaining possession than giving it up. The latter would have enabled him to bar the seller's claim for the selling price and even to sue the seller for consequential damages. The offer to the owner is accepted, and a second sale is concluded, this time with the real owner.

(2) The case raises the question of whether the buyer is now liable towards the first seller for the sale price. In Roman law, a seller is obligated to provide the buyer with undisturbed possession. The seller argues that

34 D. 21.2.29pr *Pomponius libro undecimo ad Sabinum* Si rem, quam mihi alienam vendideras, a domino redemerim, falsum esse quod Nerva respondisset posse te a me pretium consequi ex vendito agentem, quasi habere mihi rem liceret, Celsus filius aiebat, quia nec bonae fidei conveniret et ego ex alia causa rem haberem.

he has done so: he transferred possession, and the buyer retained it. The argument was apparently in conformity with an old response from the jurist Nerva. The *ratio decidendi* could have been that if the 'you-character' did not accept the solution the law offered (hand over the merchandise to the owner and refuse to pay the sale price to the seller) but bought the same thing for a second time, he ran the risk of not being protected against a claim by the first seller for the sale price.

(3) According to the reply of the jurist Pomponius, quoting Celsus the younger, who, in turn, referred to the old reply from Nerva but rejected it, the claim for the sale price should be dismissed or blocked.

(4) The *ratio decidendi*, which can be found in the last line, is that the seller's argument that the buyer is not prevented from retaining the merchandise is not in accordance with good faith. The seller had no authority to sell. If the buyer had not purchased the object for a second time, the seller would have had no ground for claiming the sale price and would even have been liable for eviction. The fact that the buyer can retain the merchandise is not due to the first contract of sale, but to the second one with the genuine owner, which is termed by Pomponius 'a different title'.

Case 8: The Barber and the Soccer Players

D. 9.2.11pr Ulpian, Commentary on the Edict, Book XVIII

Mela writes likewise: if some people would play with a ball and one of them would kick the ball quite forcefully against the hand of a barber and accordingly, through a plunge of the razor, the throat was cut of the slave the barber was shaving, then the one at fault is liable under the *lex Aquilia*. Proculus maintains the barber is at fault. And this is clearly so, when the barber was shaving at a place where usually ball games take place or traffic is heavy; then he rightfully can be blamed, although also this reasoning is plausible: if someone puts himself in the hands of a barber who put his shaving chair in a dangerous spot, he has to blame himself.[35]

Notes

(1) The facts of the case are the following. People play a ball game. One of them kicks the ball. The ball hits the hand of a barber, holding a razor. The razor cuts the throat of a slave who was being shaved by the barber. The slave dies.

35 D. 9.2.11pr *Ulpianus libro octavo decimo ad edictum* Item Mela scribit, si, cum pila quidam luderent, vehementius quis pila percussa in tonsoris manus eam deiecerit et sic servi,

(2) The case raises the question of who is liable under the *lex Aquilia* for the death of the slave. The *lex Aquilia* is a statute dealing with damage (to things). According to chapter one of this statute, the owner of a slave can claim a fine from the one who killed his slave, amounting to the sum of the highest value of the slave in the past year. This fine includes the loss caused by the killing. If the defendant denies liability, the fine is doubled.

(3) In Ulpian's reply, there are various opinions. Two older opinions contradict each other: Mela taught that the ballplayer at fault is liable, Proculus that the barber is liable. The third opinion is that of Ulpian himself. He stated only that where the shaving took place on a dangerous spot, two different positions could be justified. One can blame the barber and make him liable, or one can blame the slave, which excludes, apparently, the barber's liability.

(4) The *ratio decidendi* must have been that there should be a clear connection between 'who is to blame' and 'who is liable'. According to Roman law, the *lex Aquilia* requires negligence (*culpa*) from the side of the wrongdoer to render him liable. One could argue that it is negligent to shave at a dangerous spot. On the other hand, if the injured party himself (the slave) can be blamed, the wrongdoer (the barber) is discharged from liability. The underlying reasoning is not given here. Does the slave's negligence exclude the barber's negligence? Is the slave's act of having himself shaved the ultimate cause that resulted in the loss (his death)? It is clear that this is an 'all-or-nothing approach': the barber is liable or not and, if he is liable it is for the full amount of the fine. It is also clear that the late slave's negligent behavior can be ascribed to his master when suing the barber.

Case 9: The Knocked-Out Eye

D. 9.2.5.3 Ulpian, Commentary on the Edict, Book XVIII

A cobbler ... hit with his last a student, a freeborn son under paternal control, who did not perform correctly what he had demonstrated, in such a way that the boy lost an eye. Accordingly, maintains Julian, there is no *actio iniuriarum*,

quem tonsor habebat, gula sit praecisa adiecto cultello: in quocumque eorum culpa sit, eum lege Aquilia teneri. Proculus in tonsore esse culpam: et sane si ibi tondebat, ubi ex consuetudine ludebatur vel ubi transitus frequens erat, est quod ei imputetur: quamvis nec illud male dicatur, si in loco periculoso sellam habenti tonsori se quis commiserit, ipsum de se queri debere.

because the blow was not dealt with the intention to injure, but as admonition and for instruction. He doubts whether an action based on the education contract is possible, since a teacher may chastise moderately. But I do not doubt that proceedings can be brought, based on the *lex Aquilia*.

D. 9.2.6 Paul, Commentary on the Edict, Book XXII.
Because a far too rough act implies negligence.

D. 9.2.7pr Ulpian, Commentary on the Edict, Book XVIII
With this action, he says, the father can claim the loss of his son's income due to the deficient eye and the expenses incurred for the recovery.[36]

Notes

(1) The facts of the case are the following. A father entered into a contract of apprenticeship (*locatio conductio*) with a cobbler. The cobbler is obligated to train the father's son to be a cobbler. The cobbler demonstrated something the boy had to imitate. The boy did not perform very well. The cobbler hit the boy with the last. As a consequence, the boy lost an eye.

(2) The case raises the question of whether the cobbler is liable. Which action can the father bring against him? What can he claim?

(3) According to the reply of the jurists – the compilers connected three fragments from divergent writings: one from Ulpian, referring to Julian; one from Paul; and another one from Ulpian – the father can bring no action for injury or contractual damages, but he can bring a remedy for damage to property (based on the *lex Aquilia*), although in this case only for the loss of income and medical expenses.

(4) The *ratio decidendi* must have been that claiming a fine for the injury is not possible, since the intention to injure (*animus iniuriandi*) is lacking. Claiming damages based on the contract of apprenticeship is not possible either, because a teacher may castigate his students. Bringing a claim for the property damage is allowed. However, this is by no means

36 D. 9.2.5.3 *Ulpianus libro octavo decimo ad edictum* ... sutor ... puero discenti ingenuo filio familias, parum bene facienti quod demonstraverit, forma calcei cervicem percussit, ut oculus puero perfunderetur. dicit igitur Iulianus iniuriarum quidem actionem non competere, quia non faciendae iniuriae causa percusserit, sed monendi et docendi causa: an ex locato, dubitat, quia levis dumtaxat castigatio concessa est docenti: sed lege Aquilia posse agi non dubito. D. 9.2.6 *Paulus libro vicensimo secundo ad edictum* praeceptoris enim nimia saevitia culpae asignatur. D. 9.2.7pr *Ulpianus libro octavo decimo ad edictum* Qua actione patrem consecuturum ait, quod minus ex operis filii sui propter vitiatum oculum sit habiturus, et impendiae, quae pro eius curatione fecerit.

obvious, since the *lex Aquilia* does not cover injuries to free men, but only to slaves and animals. Probably the *actio* was granted here by analogy (*actio utilis*). Since it is not possible to assess the value of the boy (in a case of an injured slave, the wrongdoer would be sentenced to the value of the slave in the nearest thirty days), the remedy is now focused on something else: loss of income and medical expenses. There are hardly any texts in the Digest that describe this unusual application of the *lex Aquilia*.

Case 10: The 'Borrowed' Donkey

D. 47.2.52.20 Ulpian, Commentary on the Edict, Book XXXVII

If someone took away my donkey and brought it to his mares for the sole purpose that they would breed, he is not liable because of theft (*furtum*), unless he also intended to commit theft. The same I wrote back to my student Herennius Modestinus, who consulted me from Dalmatia about stallions to which someone for the same purpose had put his mares. He is only liable if he had the intention to commit theft; if not, one should bring an *actio in factum*.[37]

Notes

(1) The facts of the case are the following. Someone takes away my donkey, not in order to take possession of the animal, but just to use it for a short period (namely so that it breeds his mares).

(2) The question the case evokes is whether this person is now liable for theft. If so, the owner of the donkey can claim a fine (*poena*).

(3) According to the reply of the jurist Ulpian, referring to a similar case, he is only liable if he acted intending to commit theft.

(4) The *ratio decidendi* must have been that, given the analogy with the earlier case in Dalmatia (the case was the other way around: the stallions were not brought to the mares, but the mares brought to the stallions) the theft (*furtum*) under dispute cannot be the wrongful taking away of possession of the donkey. However, it must be in the donkey's wrongful use (in later dogmatics a *furtum usus*, theft of the use, like 'joyriding'). One can only commit theft with the intention to steal, which in this

37 D. 47.2.52.20 *Ulpianus libro trigensimo septimo ad Edictum* Si quis asinum meum coegisset et in equas suas της γονης dumtaxat χαριν admisisset, furti non tenetur, nisi furandi quoque animum habuit. quod et Herennio Modestino studioso meo de Dalmatia consulenti rescripsi circa equos, quibus eiusdem rei gratia subiecisse quis equas suas proponebatur, furti ita demum teneri, si furandi animo id fecisset, si minus, in factum agendum.

case means if one knew that using the donkey would be against the will of its owner. Thus, for example, if it was common practice to use each other's animals, or the owner had consented to a similar use of his donkey several times in the past, one would not have had the intention to commit a theft by bringing the donkey to the mares. The final remark on the *actio in factum* is considered by many to be an interpolation.

Case 11: Waving the Red Rag

D. 47.2.50.4 Ulpian, Commentary on the Edict, Book XXXVII

Against the one who by waving a red rag made cattle run away so that it fell into the hands of thieves, an action for theft can be brought, if he did so with malicious intent. But also if he acted not with the intention to commit theft, such dangerous play should not remain unpunished. Therefore, Labeo wrote, an *actio in factum* should be given.

D. 47.2.51 Gaius, Commentary on the Provincial Edict, Book XIII

Because also when they would have fallen into an abyss, a remedy would have been given in view of damage to property, as if it were based on the *lex Aquilia*.[38]

Notes

(1) The facts of the case are the following. Someone waved a red rag, which made cattle run away. The cattle fell in the hands of thieves.

(2) The case raises the question which remedy the owner of the cattle can bring against the one who waved the red rag.

(3) According to the reply of the jurists – the compilers connected a fragment of Ulpian (referring to an older opinion of Labeo) with a fragment of Gaius – a distinction is drawn. If the waving took place intending to commit theft (apparently the person waving was assisting the thieves), the person waving is liable as one of the thieves. If the waving was just some kind of mischief, there is no liability based on theft, but the waver is nevertheless liable under an *actio in factum*, which is in classical law an action with a *formula* the praetor tailored to the facts of the case. In

38 D. 47.2.50.4 *Ulpianus libro trigensimo septimo ad edictum* Cum eo, qui pannum rubrum ostendit fugavitque pecus, ut in fures incideret, si quidem dolo malo id fecerit, furti actio est: sed et si non furti faciendi causa hoc fecit, non debet impunitus esse lusus tam perniciosus: id circo Labeo scribit in factum dandam actionem. D. 47.2.51 *Gaius libro tertio decimo ad edictum provinciale* Nam et si praecipitata sint pecora, utilis actio damni iniuriae quasi ex lege Aquilia dabitur.

Justinianic law, it is any claim acknowledged in the *Corpus iuris* under such a term, most of the time granted by analogy or for reasons of equity.

(4) The *ratio decidendi* for the first part of the text must have been that an associate of the thieves is seen as equally liable under the action for theft as the thieves themselves, an opinion which can be found in many other texts in the Digest. But what is the character of the *actio in factum*, given in the case of dangerous play? The words 'should not remain unpunished' point into the direction of a remedy for a delict. But what specific delict would the dangerous play without intention to steal imply? The short fragment from Gaius, introduced as an argument, points to the answer, at least for Justinianic law: when dangerous play causes the cattle's death, there is a remedy modeled after the *actio legis Aquiliae*. This apparently should also apply in the case of dangerous play which caused the cattle to disappear.

4.6 *Substantive Commercial Law*

Most institutions and concepts of commercial law were developed on the basis of Roman law, in which only a few scattered building blocks of this law were present, or the medieval customary *lex mercatoria*. Legal personality (of non-human entities), one of the pillars of today's corporate law, was still in its infancy in the Roman law of Antiquity and retained a public law nature. Membership of professional associations was, for example, compulsory and hereditary. Companies took the form of a *societas*, which is basically an agreement that binds the partners to a contract and regulates their mutual relationships and liability towards third parties. This did not create a legal personality. It was, however, possible to restrict the investor's liability. One could enter into a contract of partnership (*societas*) with a manager of the company (*institor*) and make an agreement to what extent one would be liable financially for the commercial activities of this manager. In such a case, parties could hold each other liable internally based on the contract (*actio pro socio*), while the investor's liability to third parties was limited. He could, from the second century BC onwards, be sued directly. The third party could bring his contractual claim in the shape of an *actio institoria*, but this had an upper limit. In the *Corpus iuris civilis* only the contract of *societas* is present, but from the Theodosian Code we know that various types of other partnerships (*corpora*) must have existed.

We do not find very much on financing of commercial activities in the *Corpus iuris* either. However, bankers' archives from Antiquity have revealed much more information in this respect. In the Digest (D. 13.5) we do find the origin of the use of 'bank notes' in financial transactions, the *pecunia constituta*.

Creditor and debtor can roll an existing debt in an instrument (*constitutum*), and the debt is thereby recognized as indisputable, and the day of payment fixed. Instead of cashing the *constitutum* oneself, the holder could use it as currency or offer it to a bank in return for cash (coins). If the debtor appeared to be insolvent on the day of payment, the holder had legal recourse against the one who gave him the *constitutum*.

Related to trade, and specifically to sea transport, there are also some institutions of Greek origin. The *fenus nauticum* was the financing of a carriage by sea. In the case of shipwreck, the money did not have to be paid back. The person granting the credit could stipulate a substantial interest as a kind of insurance premium: in Justinianic law, up to twelve percent. When cargo was jettisoned overboard, the Romans followed the Greek *lex Rhodia de iactu*: the loss had to be apportioned among the owners of the preserved cargo.

4.7 *Substantive Criminal Law*

Rome did not have extensive public criminal law from its beginning. The state only prosecuted *crimina publica,* i.e., serious crimes that caused social unrest or endangered the state's interests, such as lèse-majesté and parricide. Smaller offences affecting only fellow citizens were addressed through private law. They resulted in an enforceable obligation of the wrongdoer to pay the victim a fine (apart from or including damages). Above, we saw various examples of such offences: theft (*furtum*), injury (*iniuria*) and damage to property (*damnum iniuria datum, lex Aquilia*). We also saw that public criminal justice was in the hands of tribunals, the *quaestiones*, with each authorized for a specific crime: murder and poisoning, forgery of instruments, lèse-majesté, electoral bribery, extortion by officials in the provinces, and misappropriation of state funds. In the first century AD, some more *quaestiones* were introduced: for adultery and matchmaking, and for speculation leading to an increase in food prices. Imperial constitutions further expanded substantive criminal law. Numerous criminal law provisions were introduced in the late Dominate, including those concerning corrupt provincial governors, decurions refusing to perform their fiscal duties, men who repudiated their wives, and anyone deviating from the doctrines of orthodox Christianity. The nature of the punishments is discussed above.

4.8 *Public Law*

As mentioned above, in 212 AD, the *Constitutio Antoniniana* of Emperor Antoninus Caracalla granted citizenship to all free men in the Roman realm; and the same rights as Roman women had to all free women. However, this does not imply that the state acknowledged something comparable to our civil and human rights. The legal sources do show that during the classical period, there was an increase in private law protection of all human beings, including slaves, that is to say, certain safeguards against violation of physical integrity. However, it is not clear whether these safeguards also had to be observed by the civil authorities, i.e., the Emperors and their officers. Moreover, even in its latest and most 'humane' stage, Roman law was still characterized more by the absence of equal liberties and rights for all human beings than by the acknowledgment of such rights. Since slavery was still an established institution, and prisoners of war could be enslaved, there was no human freedom for everyone. There was no freedom of religion since Christianity was imposed as the state religion and, just as in earlier times with pagan cults, had a mandatory character. And there was nothing like legal equality for all. For example, in private law, things such as *status personae*, *status familiae*, and even age and gender remained determinative factors for someone's capacity to have rights and obligations or participate in legal intercourse.

4.9 *Informal Justice*

When someone exercises his right by force and takes possession of something he owns, i.e., without appealing to a judge or the strong arm of the law, this can be seen as taking the law in one's own hands, but it is not theft or robbery. Nor is this the case when one is convinced one is entitled to the thing, but in fact, is not. In such cases, the malicious intent (*dolus malus*) required for theft is lacking. Nevertheless, in several imperial constitutions, the oldest issued by Marcus Aurelius, to exercise one's own rights in a forceful way is regarded as an offence. The owner of a plot of land who expels the possessor or the lessee by force commits 'assault and battery' (*violentia*, see C. 9.12.7). He has to return the possession, and if he is the owner, he will lose ownership. If he is not the owner, he has to pay the value of the object to the victim (C. 8.4.7, Inst. 4.2.1). The creditor who takes, under his own authority, possession of pledged items by seizing them from the debtor who has not settled his debts, forfeits his right of pledge (see D. 48.7.7).

Questions

1. Many texts from the Digest have a case-based character. How could these texts be relevant for other cases?
2. Which were the main differences between the criminal justice dealt with by the *quaestiones* (in the time of the Republic) and that of the *cognitio*-procedure (from the first century AD onwards)?

3. Which were the three kinds of civil procedure that Roman law knew over time? Which were their main characteristics?
4. Which were the various sources of obligations in Roman Law?
5. Could a slave or child under paternal control validly enter into a contract?
6. What was the difference between original and derivative acquisition of ownership?
7. Is there any connection between institutions and concepts of Roman law and today's commercial law?

5 Summary and Epilogue

This chapter presents a concise outline of the development of Roman law from the time of the Law of the Twelve Tables until the death of Justinian, with an emphasis on the classical period and the time of Justinian, and on the law of property and the law of obligations. Of course, not all of the intricacies of Roman law can be discussed, not even for the few subjects that are treated in more detail. This chapter is meant as a first introduction to Roman law, hoping to inspire further study. It should also be noted that Roman law was not the only type of law in the western world in Antiquity.

As stated above, we confined ourselves to Roman law, its history, sources, and some of its institutions because Roman law was a major force in shaping the later tradition of civil law in continental Europe. Through the survival of parts of the Theodosian Code in the *Lex Romana visigothorum*, there was an almost uninterrupted tradition of Roman law concepts and rules in parts of southern Europe. Through a rediscovery of the Digest and *Codex* at the end of the eleventh century, and a revival of the study of the *Corpus iuris civilis* in law schools and universities, knowledge of Roman law was revived in the medieval world. Teaching and studying Roman law was perhaps, at first, a purely academic occupation, but it soon gained enormous significance for legal practice. At an early stage, it was used by the canonists as an additional source of law and, together with canon law, spread all over Europe. From the south, Roman law gradually conquered the continent. It spread through universities and the superior courts of law, which, staffed with academic lawyers, not only followed the romano-canonical procedure but if necessary also substantive Roman law. Sometimes it took away the disadvantages of indigenous law, i.e., the incompatibility of divergent customs and the irrationality of the ordeals. Sometimes Roman Law was received eclectically (at will), sometimes *in complexu* (in its entirety). However, reception took place everywhere within the sphere of influence of the universities and the superior courts.

We have to be aware of the fact that the civilian tradition of continental Europe was based on Roman law in its Justinianic form, i.e., Roman law as we find it in the *Corpus iuris civilis*. The humanist jurists in the sixteenth century developed an interest in the earlier classical law and removed interpolations from the Digest to reconstruct the original context. However, they did not manage to set aside the mainstream tradition based on the *Corpus iuris* itself. The Institutes of Gaius were only discovered in 1816 and neo-humanist Romanists started their investigations only after the German *Bürgerliches Gesetzbuch* was promulgated (in 1900) and, as a consequence, the *Corpus iuris* itself had lost its status as a source of law. The emphasis on classical law in this chapter is, therefore, somewhat misleading. Classical law helps us understand the developments which eventually led to the *Corpus iuris.* However, one needs to keep in mind that in the tradition of legal scholarship and the civilian tradition on the continent, the legal provisions of the Justinianic texts have always been the starting point for legal doctrine and practice. They were not merely historical sources. This is particularly relevant since many of the elementary textbooks on Roman law, including those mentioned below, are part of the neo-humanist tradition and present classical Roman law as *the* Roman law.[39]

Further Reading

English Translations of Roman Law Sources

English translations are available of almost all sources mentioned above. The main pre-Justinianic sources are the Institutes of Gaius and the Codex Theodosianus. The Institutes of Gaius have been translated several times, such as: James Muirhead, The Institutes of Gaius and Rules of Ulpian, Edinburgh, Clark, 1904; Francis de Zulueta, The Institutes of Gaius I: Text with critical notes and translation, Oxford, Clarendon Press, 1946 (and many reprints); and William M. Gordon & Olivia F. Robinson, The Institutes of Gaius translated with an Introduction, London, Duckworth, 1988. The Codex Theodosianus was translated as: Clyde Pharr, The Theodosian Code and Novels and the Sirmondian Constitutions, Princeton, Princeton University Press, 1952.

39 I thank Laurens Winkel (Erasmus University Rotterdam) and Paul du Plessis (University of Edinburgh) for their advice and help and Frances M. Gilligan (Vrije Universiteit Amsterdam) for advice and correcting the English.

The only complete English translation of the entire Corpus iuris civilis is Samuel P. Scott, The Civil Law I-XVII, Cincinatti, The Central Trust Company, 1932, reprinted several times (https://constitution.org/2-Authors/sps/sps.htm; accessed in September 2022). There are also translations of parts of the Corpus iuris. The Institutes were translated several times: Thomas Collett Sanders, The Institutes of Justinian, London, Longmans Green, 1922; John B. Moyle, The Institutes of Justinian (5th ed.), Oxford, Clarendon Press, 1955; Joseph A.C. Thomas, The Institutes of Justinian, Cape Town, Jutta, 1975; Robert W. Lee, The Elements of Roman law with a Translation of the Institutes of Justinian (4th ed.), London, Sweet and Maxwell, 1986; Peter B.H. Birks & Grant McLeod, Justinian's Institutes, New York, Cornell University Press, 1987. There are many translations of parts of the Digest. A complete translation is: Alan Watson, The Digest of Justinian I-IV, Philadelphia, University of Pennsylvania Press, 1985. For the Codex and Novels there are, besides the Scott translation, also 'The Annotated Justinian Code' of Fred H. Blume (http://www.uwyo.edu/lawlib/blume-justinian; accessed in September 2022) and the recent translation: Bruce W. Frier (ed.), The Codex of Justinian. A new annotated translation, with parallel Latin and Greek text, Cambridge, Cambridge University Press, 2016.

Introductory Literature to Roman Law in English

Bauman, Richard A. Lawyers in Roman Republican Politics. A Study of Roman Jurists in their Political Setting, 316–82 BC, Munich, Beck, 1983.

Borkowski, Andrew and Paul J. du Plessis. Textbook on Roman Law (6th ed.), Oxford, Oxford University Press, 2020.

Buckland, William W. and Peter Stein. A Textbook of Roman Law from Augustus to Justinian (3rd ed.), Cambridge, Cambridge University Press, 1966.

Crook, John A. Law and Life in Rome, 90 BC-AD 212, New York, Cornell University Press, 1967.

Frier, Bruce W. The Rise of the Roman Jurists, Princeton, Princeton University Press, 1985.

Honoré, Tony. Emperors and Lawyers (2nd ed.), Oxford, Clarendon Press, 1994.

Honoré, Tony. Justinian's Digest; Character and Compilation, Oxford, Oxford University Press, 2010.

Johnston, David. Roman Law in Context, Cambridge, Cambridge University Press, 1999.

Jones, Arnold H.M. The Criminal Courts of the Roman Republic and Principate, Oxford, Blackwell, 1972.

Nicholas, Barry. An Introduction to Roman Law, Oxford, Clarendon Press, 1975.

Schulz, Fritz. History of Roman Legal Science, Oxford, Clarendon Press, 1946.

Schulz, Fritz. Classical Roman Law, Oxford, Clarendon Press, 1969.

Stein, Peter. Roman Law in European History (12th ed.), Cambridge, Cambridge University Press, 2013.

Strachan-Davidson, James L. Problems of Roman Criminal Law I-II, Oxford, Clarendon Press, 1912 (reprint Amsterdam: Rodopi 1969).
Tellegen-Couperus, Olga E. A Short History of Roman Law, London etc., Routledge, 1993.
Thomas, Joseph A.C. Textbook of Roman Law, New York, North-Holland Publishing Company, 1976.
Watson, Alan. Law Making in the Roman Republic, Oxford, Clarendon Press, 1974.
Watson, Alan. Rome of the XII Tables, Princeton, Princeton University Press, 1975.

CHAPTER 2

Early Middle Ages (500–1100)

Stephan Dusil, Bernd Kannowski and Gerald Schwedler

1 Introduction[1]

The legal culture of the Early Middle Ages is characterized by a great diversity of norms and customs, parallel legal systems, and different ethnicities and authorities. New political entities emerged due to the shift of political power and the decline of the Western Roman Empire. This led to the creation of a patchwork of legal approaches and procedures. The focus of this chapter about the Early Middle Ages is these emerging political powers, especially the new kingdoms and the Church, as well as the law they produced.

There is a reason why the period starting in 500 and ending around 1100 can be seen as a distinct historical era. Around the year 500, several political events took place that gave birth to new conceptions and applications of the law. There was the establishment of the Germanic kingdoms in the territory of the former Roman Empire: the Visigothic Kingdom on the Iberian Peninsula, the kingdom(s) of the Franks in the Roman provinces of Gallia, and Vandal kingdoms on the Italian Peninsula as well as in Northern Africa, among others. They became stable societies with monarchical political regimes (such as kings). In the Eastern Empire with Constantinople at its center, administrative and legal reforms were taking place that ultimately led to the promulgation of the later so-called *Corpus iuris civilis*, a compilation of ancient Roman law.

The period of the Early Middle Ages ended roughly around 1100 when a new approach to legal matters emerged. Scholars began to employ the scholastic method. Roman law was rediscovered *in toto* and was taught at proto-universities such as Bologna. These developments brought about a new level of sophistication in legal thought. Therefore, in terms of legal history, both of these developments justify using the years 500 to 1100 as the demarcation.

Roman culture and Roman law shaped the Early Middle Ages. The emerging new powers – such as the Visigothic kingdom – encountered the elaborate

1 Stephan Dusil dealt with canon law, Bernd Kannowski with Germanic tribal law, and Gerald Schwedler with Roman Law and Byzantine Law. The Introduction and Summary are collaborative work. We would like to thank Marie Jäcker (Kiel), Tapio Bronner and Luise Keinath (both Tübingen), Maximilian Mayer and Oskar Walther (both Bayreuth) for their help.

 | DOI:10.1163/9789004687257_004

Roman law of Antiquity. They could have ignored Roman law, but in practice they often used it. Recent research has emphasized that the new Post-Roman powers adopted a certain 'Roman-ness' in the legal codes, laws, and customs they used to resolve conflicts. 'Roman-ness' is a new term in medieval studies, used to indicate an orientation towards the Roman Empire and its laws and legal culture. Elsewhere it has been called 'being Roman after Rome'.[2] First we will explain how Roman law was used and how it influenced early medieval Germanic and canon law.

Germanic law is much more difficult to define than Roman and canon law. It can best be understood when it is contrasted with Roman law. Roman law was, in general, learned and supra-regional. The opposite was true for Germanic law, which was neither, and incorporated regional particularities. This, however, is a recent interpretation of Germanic law. In 1947, Paul Koschaker argued in his popular book *Europa und das römische Recht* that the Germanic heritage was one of two major pillars of the law of Europe.[3] Koschaker argued based on the development of the English Common Law, where he assumed that 'the roots of Anglo-American law are purely Germanic' because England remained almost untouched by the reception of Roman law. According to Koschaker, the origin of English law was thus to be found in the Germanic peoples who populated the island before and even after the Norman Conquest. This led him to speak of Germanic law as a globally effective legal system ('Weltgermanismus'). Even though today's scholars consider this view mistaken, Koschaker's conception was extremely influential for a long time.

An important source of Germanic law were the rules drafted by different local peoples such as the *Lex Salica* which reflects the customs of the Franks. These were – unlike those of the Anglo-Saxon or the Slavic peoples – drafted exclusively in Latin. The notion of the Germanic peoples as one unified group is mainly the product of the ideas of ancient authors such as Caesar (d. 44 BC) and Tacitus (d. around 120), but also of the growing awareness of a unique national heritage since the age of humanism (which started roughly around the year 1500). Germanic tribes replaced the Romans as the rulers over Europe, although their reign was usually short-lived. Charlemagne (d. 814), however, succeeded in subjugating the different tribes to form one empire subject to

2 Rosamond McKitterick, Being Roman after Rome, Early medieval Europe 22 (2014), 387. On 'Roman-ness', see recently: Walter Pohl et al. (eds), Transformations of Romanness. Early Medieval Regions and Identities (Millenium Studies in the culture and history of the first millenium C.E. 71), Berlin, de Gruyter, 2018.

3 Paul Koschaker, Europa und das römische Recht (1st ed.), Munich and Berlin, Biederstein, 1947, 140.

some supra-regional legislation ('capitularies'). Germanic *Leges* have some characteristics in common such as orality, the great importance of court practice, and compensation in the event of violent conflicts.

Another important institution, besides the Roman and Germanic law that connected Antiquity to the Early Middle Ages, is the Church. It developed into both a social and religious organization and a political player. In Church history, the year 313 is an important milestone. In that year the Emperor Constantine I (d. 337) stopped the persecution of Christians in the Roman Empire and legalized Christianity as one religion amongst others. Before then, Christians had often been violently oppressed, as their monotheism meant they refused to worship the Emperor. After it became formally tolerated, Christianity gained influence in the Empire, and especially at the Imperial Court. Constantine I, a pagan Emperor, was even baptized on his deathbed. One of his successors, Theodosius I (347–395), elevated Christianity to the state religion in 380. Henceforth it was the only accepted religion in the Roman Empire and pagan traditions were suppressed.

Christianity fulfilled a unifying function in the fragmented Roman Empire. In addition, it also grew in local and regional political significance. The bishops, for example, were often the head of their bishopric and dealt with secular matters. The bishop's court was competent to deal with matters of private law when a clerical party was involved. The Church also created its own legal material and procedural rules, collected them in canonical collections and penitentiaries, and applied them in court. Roman law (for instance, the snippet-collection of the Theodosian Code) inspired the content and structure of these canonical collections. The phrase *ecclesia vivit lege romana* – 'the Church lives according to Roman law' – really captures the position of the Church as an intermediary between Antiquity and the Middle Ages, the authority of written Roman law, and the emerging amalgam of Roman, tribal Germanic and canon law.[4]

Older research presented the transformation of Antiquity into the (Early) Middle Ages as a narrative of the 'Decline and Fall of the Roman Empire'. This implied that it was a process of regression from a highly developed to an unsophisticated, 'barbarian' culture. In recent research, this grand narrative has been revised. The emerging kingdoms are no longer seen as destructive or anti-imperial organizations, but as institutions partly based on Roman culture

4 Cf. Liber Papiensis, Lud. 53 (55), Alfred Boretius (ed.) (MGH LL 4), Hannover, Hahn, 1868, 539 = Lombarda III, 1, 38, ibid. 634, cf., 539.

and partly on their own, non-Roman culture, thus adopting a certain Roman identity ('Roman-ness').

Researchers of Roman law saw the change in how Roman law was created, transmitted, and used as a step backward. The name Ludwig Mitteis (1859–1921) is paramount in this context. He studied Eastern Roman law between the third and the sixth century and coined the term 'Roman vulgar law', suggesting that the evolution of law was parallel to that of the post-Roman languages. He drew an analogy to the transformation of Latin into the vernacular French, Spanish, Italian etc., via the intermediate forms of vulgar Latin. Ernst Levy (1881–1968) applied this concept to Western Roman law. He reflected on the evolution of the concept 'Roman vulgar law' in his fundamental study *West Roman Vulgar Law* in 1951.

> *Ernst Levy, West Roman Vulgar Law. The Law of Property (Memoirs of the American Philosophical Society 29), Philadelphia, American Philosophical Society, 1951, 2*
>
> It ['Roman vulgar law'] was taken over into Roman legal science by Ludwig Mitteis who distinguished it from peregrine law, to which his own research was devoted. According to Brunner, vulgar law is the law applied in the practice of the Roman provinces of that period, presenting itself as an evolution, or, if one prefers, a degeneration of pure Roman law, and contrary to the theory of the written law. This statement contains essential elements. ... Vulgar law grows inordinately, out of the practice, at times assisted by a doctrine which consciously or unconsciously misinterprets the old sources. So it comes to be contrasted with the official law such as is laid down during this period by the emperors in their *constitutiones*.

The strength of this explanatory model lies in the fact that university scholars in the twentieth century could use it as a base for their national legal systems and argue that Roman vulgar law transmitted Roman law.[5]

In 1919, Fritz Kern formulated another important explanatory model for the creation, perception and significance of law in the Middle Ages. In his foundational and famous essay, he alluded to the 'good old law' of the Middle Ages ('the law is old – the law is good'). The article was translated into many languages and has been frequently reprinted. However, the conception of medieval law

5 D. Liebs, Roman Vulgar Law in Late Antiquity, in B. Sirks (ed.), Aspects of Law in Late Antiquity, Dedicated to A.M. Honoré, Oxford, All Souls, 2008, 35–53.

as a traditional and immutable order that even the legislator could not change is today not widely accepted anymore.

Fritz Kern, Kingship and Law in the Middle Ages, Studies by Fritz Kern, Oxford, Basil Blackwell, 1948, 149
For us law needs only one attribute in order to give it validity; it must, directly or indirectly, be sanctioned by the State. But in the Middle Ages, different attributes altogether were essential; mediaeval law must be 'old' law and must be 'good' law. Mediaeval law could dispense with the sanction of the State, but not with the two qualities of Age and Goodness, which, as we shall see, were considered to be one and the same thing. If law were not old and good law, it was not law at all, even though it were formally enacted by the State.

[on Age] § 1. Law is Old. Age has at all times been important for subjective rights, especially for rights of possession, and in certain circumstances, prescription can have the force of law. But for the validity of objective law, Age, in the present era of enacted law, is of no account. For us, law, from the time of its promulgation to that of its repeal, is neither old nor new, but simply exists. In the Middle Ages, it was a different matter altogether; Age was then the most important quality even of objective law. Law was in fact custom. Immemorial usage, testified to by the memory of the oldest and most credible people; the *leges patrum*, sometimes but not necessarily proven by external aids to memory, such as charters, boundaries, law-books, or anything else that outlived human beings: this was objective law. And if any particular subjective right was in dispute, the fact that it was in harmony with an ancient custom had much the same importance as would be given today to the fact that it was derived from a valid law of the State.

[on 'good'] Not the State, but 'God is the source of all law'. Law is a part of the world-order; it is unchangeable. It can be twisted and falsified, but then it restores itself, and at last confounds the evil-doer who meddled with it. If anyone, a member of the folk, or even the highest authority in the State, made a 'law' which conflicted with a good old custom, and this custom were proved beyond doubt by the evidence of venerable witnesses or by the production of a royal charter, then the newly-made law was no law, but a wrong; not *usus*, but *abusus*. In such a case, it was the duty of every lawful man, of those in authority as well as the common man, to restore the good old law.

This classical work on the medieval concept of law has been severely criticized. First, the terminology 'old' and 'good' is of late medieval origin and can not easily be predated to the Early Middle Ages. Second, Kern's concept presupposes the validity of rules that did not depend on whether those rules were actually complied with. This notion has been questioned, as early medieval law is now thought to consist of 'rights' of individuals rather than 'law'. These rights had to be enforced in each conflict; thus, they were not 'law' in a modern sense of binding general rules. Third, Kern's concept has never been true for canon law, since a crucial part of early medieval law was always based on rules made by popes and councils.

In contrast to the research on Roman law and the Barbarian codes, the study of canon law did not undergo such a fundamental historiographical change. The creation of canonical collections starting in the fourth century and the Church's evolution towards becoming a 'global' player did not fit with a narrative of decline and decay. Furthermore, as the Church had always claimed the right to make and implement new rules, ideas such as Kern's did not make inroads here.

In conclusion, older concepts such as a decline, or ideas of 'good' and 'old', have lost ground in recent years as ways to explain the Early Middle Ages. The older view has now been replaced by an understanding of the Early Middle Ages that is based on decentralization, diversity, poly-centrism, and a parallelism of legal systems, ethnicities and authorities. These terms refer to a multitude of players, all enacting legal rules partly based on Roman law, on Germanic ideas and on religious beliefs. These legal systems overlapped each other and exercised a – sometimes weak, sometimes strong – influence on each other. This parallelism of legal systems is based on the emergence of a great number of new political entities and the lack of a central power. These peculiarities help to describe the 'Early Middle Ages', the period we will discuss in the following sections.

Questions

1. What is the meaning of 'Roman-ness'?
2. Why and how is the idea of the decline and fall of the Roman Empire criticised in current research?
3. The term 'diversity' is used to describe the legal systems in the Early Middle Ages. Do you think this term is appropriate?

2 Creation

Early Medieval Law had different sources, legislators, and traditions. Legal historians often distinguish between (vulgar) Roman law, Germanic law, canon law, and Byzantine law to categorize the different sources. These were parallel legal systems that, at the same time, overlapped. A legislator – such as the Visigothic king Alaric – issued rules for the Visigothic population (thus creating 'Germanic law') as well as orders for the Roman population (thus creating 'Roman vulgar law'). It is, therefore, not surprising that Roman legal concepts influenced codes of Germanic law. In addition to this mixture, ecclesiastical matters were dealt with by the Church as well as by secular rulers. Scholars use the term 'hybridization' to describe the amalgam of different rules in the Early Middle Ages. Nevertheless, this Chapter's presentation follows the established distinctions between (vulgar) Roman law, Germanic law, canon law, and Byzantine law.

2.1 *Roman (Vulgar) Law*

In the effort to cope with the enormous number of high-quality texts, their interpretation, and the institutional application of Roman law, the post-Roman legal culture tried to creatively adapt, reduce and prevent the loss of the ancient heritage rather than create new rules. There were many good, well-developed texts, but there were also many imprecise and even contradictory texts. These texts had to be shortened and condensed. At the same time, legal institutions were adapted to new needs. Some examples can illustrate the process of hybridization in the creation of the law. An example is the way the kings of the Visigoth realm adapted Roman law. After the Visigoth dominion was stabilized with Toledo and Toulouse as its centers of power in the fifth century, its territory included the Iberian Peninsula and important parts of Gaul, i.e., southern France (where diverse ethnic and political units had to be integrated). Its most impressive achievement was the creation of a new code of law for the Roman population of the kingdom, the *Lex Romana Visigothorum*, while at the same time, the Visigoth people used the code produced for them, the *Lex Visigothorum*.

The Visigothic king Alaric II (484–507) and his codification project, today called *Breviarium Alarici* or *Lex Romana Visigothorum*, were part of the process of creating the Roman vulgar Law. Alaric was a successful warlord and an important political player in the post-imperial struggles. He betrayed Syagrius, the last Gallic military commander of a Roman rump state in northern Gaul. Alaric did not provide Syargius shelter, instead he delivered him to the Franks. In 502, he met the king of the Franks, Clovis, in person. Being an

Arian (a Christian group which differed in the answers to theological questions from the RomanCatholic Church), Alaric tried to accommodate his empire's Catholic population by supporting Catholic bishops. His project of creating a uniform law, in the beginning of the year 506, must be seen as an effort to bring about general unification. It took place with the consent of the bishops and high provincials and by convening a Catholic Gallic council in Agde in the same year.

Together with its 'epitomizations' (abbreviated versions), the *Breviarium Alarici* has been handed down in over 100 handwritten versions. It is the most widespread and comprehensive Roman *corpus* of the Early Middle Ages. Alaric commissioned Roman jurists to compile an anthology of Roman law who chose many different significant legal texts available to them. First, they used the *Codex Theodosianus*. Additionally, they used various collections of imperial laws issued after the *Codex Theodosianus* was compiled, the so-called post-Theodosian *novellas*. They also used multiple other works that were the product of Roman legal culture, e.g., the so-called *Responsum* of Aemilius Papinianus. The goal of the new code was to establish an authoritative text for the use of his Roman subjects. The code was completed in 506 and then handed over to a council of bishops and nobles held at Aduris (Aire in Gascony) for approval. Finally, it was promulgated under the direction of Gojarich, the *comes palatii*, the highest office in the administration of the imperial court. He sent a certified copy to each count (*comes*) in the realm. These copies were accompanied by a *commonitorium* or proclamation, which explained the exclusive character of the work. It prohibited the use of any other law or legal form.

The name *Breviarium Alarici* or *Breviarium* did not appear before the sixteenth century, when it became common. The *commonitorium* describes it as: *Codex de Theodosiani legibus atque sententiis juris vel diversis libris electus* or 'Volume compiled from Theodosian laws and legal sentences and various books'. This title indicates the difficulties in creating law in post-Roman societies. In the preamble, king Alaric addresses his audience as follows.

> *Preamble of the Breviarium Alarici* or *Lex Romana Visigothorum* (*transl. by Gerald Schwedler*)
> For the benefit of our peoples and with God's favor, we have decided to turn to this undertaking, namely that we correct that which appears unjust in the laws, after a sensible discussion, so that through the counsel of priests and the great ones, all ambiguity of the old law and the Roman laws now shines in the light of better understanding, and nothing is left ambiguous so that now the everyday complaints of the most diverse disputants can be settled. Having clarified all these points and compiled

> them based on a selection by many legal scholars in clear a book, the approval of the venerable bishops and the elected representatives of our provinces confirmed all that was written out or compiled to provide a clearer interpretation. And therefore, in accordance with the signed book to be kept in our treasury, a book for the business to be done shall be sent to you out of our clemency, so that all the cases that arise may be decided based on this book; for we desire that nothing else, either in law or in justice, shall be cited in cases of dispute, except what is recorded in an orderly manner in this book, which, as we commanded, was received by the honorable man (*vir spectabilis*) Anianus himself. Therefore, it is advisable for you to take care that no other law or legal formula may be brought forward or heard before your court. If it is determined that it may have happened, you should know that the death penalty for him, and the confiscation of your goods, is imminent. We order this decree to be added to all the books we have sent out, so that all may be kept in discipline and order by our determination and that the punishment may be binding.[6]

Although the *Breviarium Alarici* comes close to a codification in the modern sense of a comprehensive regulation of a large area of law, there is a major difference. The compilers had such an extreme veneration for the Roman formulations that they rarely modified them. The jurists in charge of the project of emperor Justinian in Constantinople, some twenty-five years later, changed the text and structure much more. The legal experts at the court of Alaric only changed a few but significant details. First, they omitted regulations that were

6 Lex Romana Visigothorum sive Breviarium Alaricianum, Auctoritas Alarici regis, Gustav Haenel (ed.), Leipzig, Teubner, 1848, p. 3: Utilitates populi nostri propitia divinitate tractantes hoc quoque, quod in legibus videbatur iniquum, meliori deliberatione corrigimus, ut omnis legum Romanarum et antiqui iuris obscuritas, adhibitis sacerdotibus ac nobilibus viris, in lucem intelligentiae melioris deducta resplendeat, et nihil habeatur ambiguum, unde se diuturna aut diversa iurgantium impugnet objectio. Quibus omnibus enucleatis atque in unum librum prudentium electione collectis, haec quae excerpta sunt, vel clariori interpretatione composita, venerabilium Episcoporum vel electorum provincialium nostrorum roboravit adsensus. Et ideo subscriptum librum, qui in tabulis habetur collectus, Goiarico comiti pro distringendis negotiis nostra iussit clementia destinari, ut iuxta eius seriem universa causarum sopiatur intentio: nec aliud cuilibet aut de legibus aut de iure liceat in disceptationem proponere, nisi quod directi libri et subscripti viri spectabilis Aniani manu, sicut iussimus, ordo complectitur. Providere ergo te convenit, ut in foro tuo nulla alia lex neque iuris formula proferri vel recipi praesumatur. Quod si factum fortasse constiterit, aut ad periculum capitis lui, aut ad dispendium tuarum noveris facultatum. Hanc vero praeceptionem directis libris iussimus cohaerere, ut universos ordinationis nostrae et disciplina teneat et poena constringat.

unpleasant reminders of previous imperial rule. Where possible, imperial authorizations and institutions were adapted. For example, all parts of the law that touched upon the status of free women in danger of losing their freedom through connubial connection with a foreign slave were omitted. Military law, administrative law and some articles of criminal law and procedure were also fundamentally changed through omissions and adaptations.

The *Breviarium Alarici* demonstrates the difficulties of creating law in the post-Roman period. The introductory *commonitorium* shows the paradoxical situation. To create binding law within the kingdom, neither the king's authority, the consensus of the bishops and nobles of his reign, nor of the jurists at his court seemed to be enough to replace the immense mass of Roman legal texts used in local courts – texts that gave an advantage to the party with the resources to make use of this complicated law. This 'shadow-existence' of ancient Roman law within the post-imperial kingdoms strongly influenced the legal thinking of the centuries to come. Under the headings of 'compilations' and 'excerpts' from Roman law, new law was created without changing the language of the old laws.

2.2 *Germanic Law*

The situation was different for Germanic law. The *Lex Salica* is a good example. The *Lex Salica* is perhaps the one Germanic tribal law that is almost entirely free from Roman influences. Here we can find legal ideas that can be contrasted with Roman ones. It forms a Germanic counterpart of, and has nothing to do with Roman law. The peculiarity of Germanic legislation comes to the fore in the prologue of the *Lex Salica*. We are not confronted – as for instance, in the *Leges Visigothorum* – with a collection of royal laws strongly characterized by Roman and Christian features. The *Lex Salica* is characterized by consensus ('it was decided and agreed among the Franks and their notables') between wise men ('from among many men four were chosen who were named: Wisogast, Arogast, Salegast, and Widogast ... These men, meeting together in three different courts and discussing the causes of all disputes, gave judgment in each case in the following fashion'). Underneath all this lies the idea that these wise men did not create the law, but only discovered that which had always been there and would be there forever: law which was considered fixed and, in principle, immutable. All it takes to identify eternal law is possession of the necessary wisdom. This is how, according to the prologue, all of the individual cases listed in the *Lex Salica* were decided: not by a judge who decided complicated legal questions, but by a group of men with legal wisdom called *Rachinburgen* (in later medieval sources 'jurors'), who sit where justice is administered (*in mallobergo*). They were obligated to declare the Salic law when asked.

It is readily apparent that the *Lex Salica* was made for a warrior society. Many articles deal with killing and injuries. The wrongdoer, if he was a free man, was usually allowed to settle the matter by paying a sum of money (*compositio*). On the other hand, if he was not a free man, he could be punished with corporal punishment or death. The amount of money depended on the value of the injured party. If a free Franc was killed, the law mentions 200 shillings. For a foreigner or a Roman, only about one-third of this sum was required. It is unknown whether the amount of money was related to the right of revenge, i.e., if it had any practical significance. However, we do know that the amounts of money exchanged to buy off revenge are confirmed by archaeological evidence. The value of Franconian grave goods for persons of different social status correspond approximately to the amounts of money provided by the *Lex Salica* for these people.

> *The Laws of the Salian Franks ['Lex Salica', 507/511], Philadelphia, University of Pennsylvania Press, 1991, 59 (Prologue, transl. by Katherine Fischer Drew)*
> 1. With the aid of God, it was decided and agreed among the Franks and their notables in order that peace be established among themselves, that all increase of litigation be curtailed so that just as the Franks stand out from other peoples living around them by the strength of their arms so also they shall excell them in the authority of their laws. Thus they [the Franks] will provide an end to criminal actions according to the nature of the cause.
> 2. Therefore from among many men four were chosen who were named as follows: Wisogast, Arogast, Salegast, and Widogast from places beyond the Rhine named Botheim, Saleheim, and Widoheim. These men, meeting together in three different courts and discussing the causes of all disputes, gave judgment in each case in the following fashion.[7]

7 Lex Salica, Karl August Eckhardt (ed.) (MGH LL nat. Germ. 4,2), Hannover, Hahn, 1969, 3s.: § 1 Gens Francorum inclita, auctorem Deo condita, fortis in arma, firma pace fetera, profunda in consilio, corporea nobilis, incolumna candore, forma egregia, audax, uelox et aspera, [nuper] ad catholicam fidem conuersa, emunis ab heresa; dum adhuc [ritu] teneretur barbaro, inspirante Deo, inquerens scienciae clauem, iuxta morem suorum qualitatem desiderans iusticiam, costodiens pietatem.
§ 2 Dictauerunt Salicam legem per proceris ipsius gentes, qui tunc tempore eiusdem aderant rectores, electi de pluribus uiris quattuor his nominibus: UUisogastis, Bodogastis, Salegastis et UUidogastis in loca cognominancia Salechagme, Bodochagme, UUidochagmi, qui per tres

The system of feudal tenure is key to understanding fundamental aspects of medieval legal and constitutional history. Remnants of it are still present in modern European law, e.g., in the English common law. In it, all land belongs (theoretically, it must be said, even today) to the Crown, which can grant 'freehold'. This concept dates back to Norman times. After victory at the Battle of Hastings (1066), William the Conqueror (1027/28-1087), introduced a feudal system which did not allow the keeper of land (the so-called 'tenant') to alienate the fief from his 'landlord'. There were different types of such fiefdoms, each with different (mutual) obligations. With the abolition of the feudal system, all fiefs became 'fee simple' (from 'fief simple'), whereby 'simple' means that no duties are associated with ownership. Another term for 'fee simple' is 'freehold', which we refer to today as 'ownership (of land)'.

The Holy Roman Empire, until its demise in 1806, was constitutionally based on feudal rights.[8] The system of feudal tenure is – just like Roman and canon law – a European phenomenon. This is also reflected in the *Glossa Ordinaria* by Accursius. This famous medieval author treats Longobard feudal law (the *Libri Feudorum*) in the same scholarly manner as he treats Roman law (the *Corpus iuris civilis*). In the system of feudal tenure, the feudal lord had the duty to ensure the protection and maintenance of the vassal, whereas the vassal, in return, owed obedience and several services (primarily military support).

For decades the well-known study of the system of feudal tenure by the Belgian historian François Louis Ganshof (*Qu'est-ce que la 'féodalité'?*) reflected the state of the research. This study is in fundamental respects, still valid today. In the following passage, Ganshof discusses terminological issues. In doing so, he emphasizes the European dimension and the old Germanic origins of the system of feudal tenure, the so-called *Lehenswesen*.

> *François-Louis Ganshof, Feudalism, New York and London, Longmans, Green, 1952, 96–97*
>
> The property element in feudal relationships was still in the 'classical' period the same as it had been under the Carolingians, at any rate if one reduces it to its essential element – a tenement granted freely by a lord to his vassal in order to procure the latter the maintenance which was his

mallus conuenientes, omnes causarum origines sollicite discuciendo tractantis de singulis iudicium decreuerunt hoc modo.

8 In the General Territorial Laws for the Prussian States of 1794 (Allgemeines Landrecht für die Preußischen Staaten), the right of feudal ownership is still regulated in detail, I 18 §§ 1–819 ALR ('Vom Lehne').

due and to provide him with the means of furnishing his lord with the services required by his contract of vassalage.

In the tenth century a new word appeared to describe the tenement of the vassal: *fevum, feudum* or *feodum*. The earliest examples of the use of the word in this sense date from the end of the ninth century, and it became more frequent in the tenth. They come from the south of France, but it seems that the term appeared almost as early in Italy. The word itself is older, and no doubt of Frankish origin (apparently **fehu-ôd*); it was related to the German *Vieh*, meaning cattle, and in early times, and indeed still in the ninth century, it was applied to movable property in general. With its new meaning of 'benefice' the word rapidly spread in France and Italy, and soon began to penetrate parts of Western Germany (Lotharingia). By the second half of the eleventh century it was in general use, but had not yet been accepted as a technical term; a charter of Hainault of 1087 refers to 'a benefice that in vulgar parlance is called a fief' (*beneficium quod vulgo dicitur feodum*). In the twelfth century, the word began to be current in Germany beyond the Rhine, and by the thirteenth century it had driven out its rivals. In the form *fevum* it was dominant in the south of France and in the western part of the kingdom of Burgundy-Arles along the Rhône. The French equivalent was *fief* or *fieffe*, the Provencal *feu*, the English *fief* or *fee*. In German it was translated by *Lehen*, or *leen* in Dutch.

The research on feudalism seemed to be finished until Susan Reynolds' monograph *Fiefs and Vassals*[9] sparked controversy and debate. Reynolds put forward the thesis that feudalism with vassals was an invention of the learned lawyers in the sixteenth to eighteenth centuries. This raises the question of whether constitutional history and the history of feudalism can be equated to and understood as a formative element of the structure of the medieval state. According to Reynolds, it is questionable whether an element *in rem* on the one hand (a fiefdom) and a personal element associated with it (subordination of one free person to another) ever existed. Reynolds' theory was sharply attacked for her research method and her choice of sources.[10] However, Reynolds' view has

9 Susan Reynolds, Fiefs and Vassals. The Medieval Evidence Reinterpreted, Oxford, Oxford University Press, 1994.

10 To give just one example: Kurt-Ulrich Jäschke, book review of Susan Reynolds, Fiefs and Vassals. The medieval evidence reinterpreted, Zeitschrift der Savigny-Stiftung für Rechtsgeschichte: Germanistische Abteilung 116 (1999), 525: 'I would like to turn the reproach of scholarly dishonesty suggested by Oexele … into the objection 'dangerous work economy''.

been well received in recent literature,[11] which leaves the matter open-ended, so that room for further research remains.

As feudal law sources are fundamental to medieval law, a significant shift in favor of vassals deserves particular attention. When the Carolingian ruler Charles the Bald (823–877) was about to set out on an Italian campaign, he first promulgated the Capitulary of Quierzy (Picardy) on 14 June 877. It contained his instructions for the empire's administration in his absence, and in case of the eventuality that he did not return from the campaign. A large part of it consists of directions to his son Louis the Stammerer, as is the case in the passage quoted here. However, another part of them proved to be important to the history of European Constitutional Law, especially regarding the inheritability of feudal tenures. This was reinforced in the centuries that followed. It strengthened the vassal's position since the feudal lord could no longer dispose of his fief at will following the latter's death.

> *Capitulary of Quierzy (877) (transl. by Bernd Kannowski)*
> *The Political Testament of Charles the Bald; The Inheritability of Feudal Tenures*
> Suppose a count (back) in the empire should die while his son travels in our party. In that case, our son – together with our other loyal subjects– is to choose (someone) from amongst those who were intimates of and stood close to the count, who together with the principal officials of the county and the bishop, whose bishopric lies within the county, will administer the county until such time as we are informed of the death, and we can appoint the deceased's son, who is traveling with us, to his office. If he, however, should have a young(er) son, then the latter should administer the county together with the principal officials of the county and the bishop, whose bishopric lies within the county, until news of the count's death has reached us and with our assent his son has been appointed to take over as count. Should he, however, have no son, then our son shall, together with our other loyal subjects, choose someone to administer the county alongside the principal officials and the local bishop until such time as our command changes this. For this reason, the man who was administering the county shall not be angered if we then

11 To name just a few: Jürgen Dendorfer and Roman Deutinger, Das Lehnswesen im Hochmittelalter, Ostfildern, Thorbecke, 2010; Steffen Patzold, Das Lehnswesen im Spiegel historiographischer Quellen des 12. und 13. Jahrhunderts, in Karl-Heinz Spieß (ed.), Ausbildung und Verbreitung des Lehnswesens im Reich und in Italien im 12. und 13. Jahrhundert, Ostfildern, Thorbecke, 2013, 269–306.

hand over the county as is our right to someone other than the man who has been administering it up to that point. The same will also be the case with all our vassals.[12]

2.3 *Canon Law*

The third group of legal materials discussed in this chapter is canon law, the Church law's internal ecclesiastical rules. One can distinguish five ways in which legal rules for the Church were made, namely 'state legislation' in Church matters, inner-ecclesiastical rules (papal decretals and conciliar decisions), forgeries and the realignment of older rules. All these will be discussed below.

First, Roman Emperors exerted a substantial influence on matters of the Christian faith. For instance, Constantine I convened the Christian bishops in Nicaea in 325. He presided over this council of bishops that decided matters of faith and Church discipline. Another prime example of the close connection between state and Christianity is the Theodosian Code of 438, whose sixteenth book addresses religious matters. The Theodosian Code deals, for example, with heterodoxies, privileges of bishops, clerics, and monks, and also prohibits the repetition of baptism. The following excerpts illustrate this; the first grants privileges to the minor orders (the lower church ministers), the latter enforces Christianity by destroying pagan sanctuaries.

> *The Theodosian Code. And Novels. And the Sirmondian Constitutions. A Translation with Commentary, Glossary, and Bibliography, Princeton, Princeton University Press, 1952 (transl. by Clyde Pharr, Theresa Sherrer Davidson, and Mary Brown Pharr)*
> 16.2.24 We direct that priests, deacons, subdeacons, exorcists, lectors, doorkeepers, and likewise all persons who are of the first rank in the

---

12 Capitularia regum Francorum, Georg Heinrich Pertz (ed.) (MGH LL 1), Hannover, Hahn, 1835, 542: 3. Si comes de isto regno obierit cuius filius nosbiscum sit, filius noster cum ceteris fidelibus nostris ordinet de his qui eidem comiti plus familiares propinquiores fuerunt, qui cum ministerialibus ipsius comitatus, et cum episcopo in cuius parochia fuerit ipse comitatus, ipsum comitatum praevideant, usque dum nobis renuntietur, ut filium illius qui nobiscum erit, de honoribus illius honoremus. Si autem filium parvulum habuerit, isdem filius eius cum ministerialibus ipsius comitatus et cum episcopo in cuius parochia consistit, eundem comitatum praevideant, donec obitus praefati comitis ad notitiam nostram perveniat, et ipse filius eius per nostram concessionem de illius honoribus honoretur. Si vero filium non habuerit, filius noster cum ceteris fidelibus nostris ordinet, qui cum ministerialibus ipsius comitatus et cum episcopo proprio ipsum comitatum praevideat, donec iussio nostra inde fiat. Et pro hoc ille non irascatur qui illum comitatum praeviderit, si eundem comitatum alteri, cui nobis placuerit, dederimus quam illi qui eum eatenus praevidit. Similiter et de vassallis nostris faciendum est.

Church shall be exempt from the compulsory public services that are incumbent on persons.
16.10.16 If there should be any temples in the country districts, they shall be torn down without disturbance or tumult. For when they are torn down and removed, the material basis for all superstition will be destroyed.[13]

The fact that Roman Emperors considered themselves responsible for religious matters is in line with their previous position as highest priests in pagan times. Consequently, and this is typical of Late Antiquity and the Early Middle Ages in general, the idea of a separation of Church and state is unknown. Secular rules often dealt with business that one would later describe as internal ecclesiastical matters.

The involvement of secular authorities in internal ecclesiastical matters is a recurring phenomenon in the Early Middle Ages. It was not only the Roman Emperors, but also the Carolingian rulers who meddled in the affairs of the Church they sought to protect. A prime example of this development is the *Admonitio Generalis*, the 'General Admonition', a capitulary issued by the Frankish King and later Emperor Charlemagne (747/8–814) in 789. To restructure his Kingdom, Charlemagne tried to establish a disciplined and well-organized Church whose bishops, monks and clerics were in charge of educational matters. They were, for instance, obligated to establish (monastic or cathedral) schools to educate young boys. Often, these capitularies oscillate between protection and paternalism. The following excerpt from the *Admonitio Generalis* illustrates the attempts of Charlemagne to establish a law-abiding, uniform clergy by harking back to older (conciliar and secular) decisions.

Admonitio Generalis, in P.D. King, Charlemagne, Translated Sources, Lambrigg, King, 1987, 211 and 218
13: To bishops: Further, in the same council [of Antioch, c. 20], and also in that of Chalcedon [c. 19]: that the bishops of a province are to meet together in council twice a year with their metropolitan [archbishop] to deal with the affairs of the Church.

13 CTh. 16.2.24 Presbyteros diaconos subdiaconos adque exorcistas et lectores, ostiarios etiam et omnes perinde, qui primi sunt, personalium munerum expertes esse praecipimus. 16.10.16. Si qua in agris templa sunt, sine turba ac tumultu diruantur. His enim deiectis atque sublatis omnis superstitioni materia consumetur.

> 80: To all the clergy: That they are to learn the Roman chant thoroughly and that it is to be employed throughout the office, night and day, in the correct form, in conformity with what our father of blessed memory, king Pippin, strove to bring to pass when he abolished the Gallican chant for the sake of unanimity with the apostolic see and the peaceful harmony of God's holy Church.[14]

A close relationship between secular and ecclesiastical powers is common in the Early Middle Ages; it was only around 1100 when both powers were separated – at least partly – from each other in the 'Investiture Controversy'. Before this separation took place, the Church made rules more or less autonomously. Two different forms of this internal ecclesiastical rule-making can be distinguished: by conciliar legislation and papal decretals.

Second, a common way to deal with challenges and establish new rules was to adopt conciliar decisions. A council is a meeting of bishops, often also attended by abbots and other religious leaders, where matters of faith, church discipline, and other issues were decided. Councils could be held on all levels within the Church: at the local (within a bishopric), regional (within an archbishopric) or ecumenical level. The latter councils decided on matters for the whole Church. Among the universal councils are the Council of Nicaea I (325), Constantinople I (381), Ephesus (431), Chalcedon (451), Constantinople II (553), Constantinople III (680), and Nicaea II (787). The Council of Chalcedon in 451, for instance, was attended by roughly 400 participants who convened to discuss theological questions, but who also provided rules on legal jurisdiction. They promoted the settlement of disputes within a bishopric, if possible; otherwise, higher courts would make a decision. The goal was to avoid biased judges and to guarantee fair judgments.

> *The Acts of the Council of Chalcedon, translated with introduction and notes, vol. 3 (= Translated Texts for Historians 45), Liverpool, Liverpool University Press, 2005, 97 (transl. by Richard Price and Michael Gaddis)*
> 9. If any cleric has a suit against a cleric, he is not to leave his own bishop and have recourse to civil courts, but is first to argue the case before his

14 MGH Capit. I [Capitularia regum Francorum], Alfred Boretius (ed.), Hannover, Hahnsche Buchhandlung, 1883, Nr. 22: c. 13 Episcopis. Item in eodem concilio necnon et in calcidonense, ut provinciales episcopi cum suo metropolitano bis in anno propter causas ecclesiae concilia celebrent. c. 80 Omni clero. Ut cantum Romanum pleniter discant, et ordinabiliter per nocturnale vel gradale officium peragatur, secundum quod beatae memoriae genitor noster Pippinus rex decertavit ut fieret, quando Gallicanum tulit ob unanimitatem apostolicae sedis et sanctae Dei aeclesiae pacificam concordiam.

> own bishop, or at least with the consent of the bishop himself let justice be done before whomever both parties choose. If anyone infringes this, he is to be subject to the canonical penalties. If a cleric has a suit against his own, or another, bishop, he is to plead his cause before the council of the province. If a bishop or cleric is in dispute with the metropolitan of the same province, he is to have recourse to the exarch of the diocese or to the see of imperial Constantinople and plead his case there.[15]

Third, a further and very important form of lawmaking were papal decretals (*litterae decretales*). A decretal was a papal letter in which the Pope answered a legal question. The first extant decretal is from Pope Siricius (384–99). Pope Damasus, the predecessor of Siricius, was addressed by a Spanish bishop, Himerius of Tarragona. The latter needed urgent advice on the reintegration of the Arians in the Catholic Church. The Arians were a group of Christians whose view on the nature of Christ as the son of God differed from the teachings of the Catholic faith. Pope Siricius urged the addressee, Himerius, to disseminate his decisions in the adjacent provinces, since they should be known and followed by all bishops. Although Siricius just answered the question of one bishop, he tried to make his decision a general rule. This 'rule-making' beyond the single case is typical of decretals that, in this regard, resemble precedents in modern common law.

> *Prefaces to Canon law Books in Latin Christianity. Selected Translations, 500–1245, New Haven, London, Yale University Press, 1998, 37, 45–46 (transl. by Robert Somerville and Bruce C. Brasington)*
> [385 AD, cc. 2, 20] [Pope] Siricius to Himerius, bishop of Tarragona
> 1. On the first page of your letter, therefore, you indicated that multitudes who were baptized by the impious Arians were hastening to the Catholic faith, and that certain of our brothers wished to baptize these same people

15 Conciliorum oecumenicorum generaliumque decreta, 1: The oecumenical councils from Nicaea I to Nicaea II (325–787), Josepho Alberigo et al. (eds), Turnhout, Brepols, 2006, 142: IX. Si quis clericus adversus clericum habet negotium, non deserat episcopum proprium et ad saecularia percurrat iudicia, sed prius actio ventiletur apud episcopum proprium vel certe consilio eiusdem episcopi apud quos utraeque partes voluerint, iudicium continebunt. Si quis autem praeterierit nec fecerit, canonicis correctionibus subiacebit. Quodsi clericus habet causam contra episcopum proprium vel adversus alterum, apud synodum provinciae metropolitanum episcopus vel clericus habet querellam, petat aut primatem dioceseos aut sedem regiae urbis Constantinopolitanae et apud ipsum iudicetur.

again. This is not allowed, since both the Apostle forbids and the canons oppose doing it; and after the Council of Rimini was annulled, the general decrees sent to the provinces by my predecessor of venerable memory Liberius prohibit it. We unite these people, and the Novatianists and other heretics, to the assembly of Catholics, just as it was constituted in the synod, solely through invocation of the sevenfold Spirit by imposition of the bishop's hand. Indeed, all the East and the West preserves this practice, and it is also inappropriate henceforth for you to deviate from that path, if you do not wish to be separated from our company by synodal sentence.

post 15. We explicated, I believe, dearest brother, all the things which were set forth as being at issue, and we provided adequate replies, in my opinion, to the individual cases which you referred to the Roman Church, just as to the head of your body, through our son the priest Bassianus. Now, brother, we incite your spirit more and more for observing the canons and adhering to the constituted decretals, so that you make known to all our fellow bishops, and not only those situated in your region, what we wrote back in response to your questions. But these things which were set forth by us in salubrious fashion should even be sent by escort of your letter to all the Carthaginians, Baeticians, Lusitanians, and Gallicians, and those who border you in neighboring provinces on either side. And although there is freedom for no priest of the Lord to be ignorant of the statutes of the apostolic see and the venerable decrees of the canons, it can, nevertheless, be helpful, and because of the antiquity of your see, beloved, exceedingly glorious for you, if those things of a general sort which were written to you by name are brought to the attention of all our brothers through your cooperative solicitude, so that the things which were salubriously established by us, not haphazardly, but prudently, with very great care and deliberation, might remain inviolate, and that in the future access to all excuses should be blocked, which according to us cannot be available now to anyone.[16]

16 Klaus Zechiel-Eckes, Die erste Dekretale. Der Brief Papst Siricius' an Bischof Himerius von Tarragona vom Jahr 385 (JK 255). Aus dem Nachlass mit Ergänzungen hrsg. v. Detlev Jasper, Hannover, Hahnsche Buchhandlung, 2013 (MGH, Studien und Texte 55), 84–6, 112–116: 1. Prima itaque paginae tuae fronte signasti baptizatos ab impiis Arianis plurimos ad fidem catholicam festinare et quosdam de fratribus nostris eosdem denuo baptizare velle.

Fourth, conciliar decisions and papal letters are the two main forms of 'rule-making' in the Early Church. Nonetheless, one may also count forgeries among the common early medieval forms of establishing new rules. What is a forgery? A forgery is a text that pretends to be from a certain author, although it is not. A famous example of a forgery is the pseudo-Isidorian Decretals from the mid-9th century, attributed to a fictitious collector called Isidor Mercator. However, this collector never existed. The mastermind of the forgery, perhaps Paschasius Radbertus from the monastery Corbie in France, intended to strengthen the position of the bishops and protect them against secular powers in the late Carolingian Empire. To this end, he wrote, among other texts, a collection of forged letters attributed to the first popes. In these letters, he created procedural rules to impede trials against bishops and allowed bishops to appeal to the bishop of Rome, the Pope. The forgeries were created when the Church was under (secular) pressure. To defend the Church, the forgers invented rules and ascribed them to popes, to give their invented rules the 'authority' to make them binding for all. For this reason, even forgeries may count among the common forms of rule-making in the Early Middle Ages. The following excerpt highlights the importance of the early medieval pseudo-Isidorian Decretals.

Quod non licet, cum hoc fieri et apostolus vetet et canones contradicant, et post cassatum Ariminense concilium missa ad provincias a venerandae memoriae prodecessore meo Liberio generalia decreta prohibeant. Quos nos cum Novatianis aliisque hereticis, sicut est in synodo constitutum, per invocationem solam septiformis spiritus episcopalis manus inpositione catholicorum conventui sociamus, quod etiam totus oriens occidensque custodit. A quo tramite vos quoque posthac minime convenit deviare, si non vultis a nostro collegio synodali sententia separari. post 15. Explicuimus, ut arbitror, frater karissime, universa, quae digesta sunt in querellam, et ad singulas causas, de quibus per filium nostrum Bassianum presbiterum ad Romanam ecclesiam, utpote ad caput tui corporis, retulisti, sufficientia, quantum opinor, responsa reddidimus. Nunc fraternitatis tuae animum ad servandos canones et tenenda decretalia constituta magis ac magis incitamus, ut haec, quae ad tua consulta rescripsimus, in omnium coepiscoporum nostrorum perferri facias notionem, et non solum eorum, qui in tua sunt diocesi constituti, sed etiam ad universos Carthaginienses ac Baeticos, Lusitanos atque Gallicos vel eos, qui vicinis tibi conlimitant hinc inde provinciis, haec, quae a nobis sunt salubri ordinatione disposita, sub litterarum tuarum prosecutione mittantur. Et quamquam statuta sedis apostolicae vel canonum venerabilia definita nulli sacerdotum domini ignorare sit liberum, utilius tamen et pro antiquitate sacerdotii tui dilectioni tuae esse admodum poterit gloriosum, si ea, quae ad te speciali nomine generaliter scripta sunt, per unanimitatis tuae sollicitudinem in universorum fratrum nostrorum notitiam perferantur, quatenus et quae a nobis non inconsulte, sed provide sub nimia cautela et deliberatione sunt salubriter constituta, intemerata permaneant, et omnibus in posterum excusationibus aditus, qui iam nulli apud nos patere poterit, obstruatur.

Detlev Jasper and Horst Fuhrmann, Papal Letters in the Early Middle Ages (History of Medieval Canon Law), Washington DC*, The Catholic University of America Press, 2001, 142–143 (The Pseudo-Isidorian Forgeries)*

They [the forgers] concerned themselves with far more than ecclesiastical jurisdiction; they wrote about the liturgy, the sacraments, and marital law, further sketching an image of the 'vita primitiva' ['simple life'], which has been called a 'vision of a Church in a golden age'. This vision, however, was not simply a product of imagination, since it built on what had already been discovered. The very breadth of the Pseudo-Isidorian Decretals was one reason for their success; it is the most extensive collection of canon law arranged in a historical, chronological order. A significant goal of the forgeries was to protect suffragan bishops [bishops of a diocese] from intervention by the metropolitans [the higher archbishop], the provincial synods, or the secular power. Trial procedure and the possibility of deposing bishops, who themselves are heaped with panegyric and flattering titles ('oculi [domini]', 'columnae', 'summi sacerdotes', 'servi dei', 'throni dei', 'dii', 'sancti' ['eyes of God', 'columns', 'highest priests', 'servants of God', 'throne of God', 'Gods', 'Saints']), are rendered immeasurably difficult. For example, no layman, no subject, no alien or freedman, no one who is an enemy of the bishop, no one infamous, could accuse the bishop, particularly not before a secular court. If such an accusation occurred, the accused is to regain full possession of all rights, and if the accused, who can reject suspect judges, makes no confession, then 72 witnesses are needed to condemn him, and at any moment of the trial … he can appeal to the primate or the pope. In order to strengthen the position of the bishops, the 'chorepiscopi' [lower bishops; disappeared in the High Middle Ages], conceived as rivals, were suppressed to the status of priests. Metropolitans, who were supposed to make their decisions together with their fellow bishops in their province, were limited by Pseudo-Isidore's establishment of a new superior authority for primates or patriarchs.

In keeping with the distribution of the ancient *Notitia provinciarum* [a register of provinces and cities in Africa], the chief city (metropolis) of the 'first (prima) province' should also be the place of residence of the primate or patriarch. In Pseudo-Isidore, the growth of papal power served to protect the position of bishops. Indeed, it was not the pope but the bishops who were called the 'keys' of the Church – according to an understanding of Cyprian – and for whose invulnerability all were to cooperate. The Lord had granted to them the power of binding and loosing. Accusations against them were no longer to be handled by provincial

> and national synods. Cases that touched upon their prerogatives were called 'causae maiores' and reserved to the pope who alone had the right to confirm the decisions of the councils. Papal rights were stressed when used to defend the suffragan bishops.

Fifth, the authoritative texts from councils, popes, and forgeries were collected and handed down in canonical collections. The term 'canonical' is derived from 'canon', meaning 'rule'. These collections were assembled by bishops, monks and other erudite clerics. As the Church did not 'officially' approve them, they are often described as private. Some collectors chose a chronological order of the texts they excerpted; others went for a thematic order. Some, for instance, elaborated on clergy, some on procedural rules and others on sacraments. By determining the topics and their order, by choosing texts, excerpting and shortening them, by headlining them with a rubric, they gave a new interpretation to older texts. This realignment of older canons was called 'secondary rule-making' to distinguish the original, primary rules from the new interpretation in the collections.

> *Andreas Thier, Dynamische Schriftlichkeit. Zur Normbildung in den vorgratianischen Kanonessammlungen, Zeitschrift der Savigny-Stiftung für Rechtsgeschichte. Kanonistische Abteilung 93 (2007), 1–7 (transl. by Stephan Dusil and Robert Getz)*
> The collections of ecclesiastical legal texts known as canonical collections played a decisive role in the process of the formation of ecclesiastical law between Late Antiquity and the rise of papal decretal law in the twelfth century. These collections, which can be understood as repositories of texts, started to emerge in the fourth century when collections such as the *Canones apostolorum* (fourth century) or the *Corpus Canonum Africano-Romanum* (around 420) were compiled. These historical-chronological collections (though commonly ordered thematically) encompassed both texts of councils and popes but, in many cases, also excerpts taken from the Bible, patristic literature, or secular laws. Of special significance were texts from Late Antiquity, since church fathers such as Tertullian and Cyprian, popes like Innocent I (402–417) and Gelasius I (492–496), and councils such as the First Council of Nicaea (325) and the African synods shaped rules and concepts that were widely received because of their foundational nature and the authority of their authors. This reception was enabled by the transmission of those texts in canonical collections, which probably formed the most important repository of ecclesiastical legal concepts up to the twelfth century. In brief, it was canonical

collections where ecclesiastical legal concepts were first condensed into a concrete written form. These characteristics point to the often discussed relation between normativity and writing in the Early Middle Ages; in historical discourse, this topic has been especially discussed in connection with the question long referred to under the catch-phrase 'pragmatic literacy' (*pragmatische Schriftlichkeit*). And indeed, the canonical collections also formed an integral part of ecclesiastical rule-making and rule application. For instance, the recital of older canons and decretals was embedded in the synodal liturgy at least of the Early Middle Ages and made the use of canonical collections indispensable. ...

The significance of canonical collections, however, cannot be reduced to the mere preservation of ecclesiastical legal texts. The example of the ninth-century Pseudo-Isidorian decretals in particular makes clear that canonical collections were purposefully augmented with apocryphal or spurious texts to establish specific normative statements (in the case of Pseudo-Isidor in order to protect bishops against metropolitans and laypeople). Even apart from the repeatedly analyzed phenomenon of rule-making by forgery, it can often be observed that legal texts gathered in canonical collections were reworked to serve specific legal purposes: This is true not only in the case of abbreviation, but also of rubrication of a canon resulting in a different focus on the legal content of a canon. Putting originally independently transmitted canons in a certain order was also a way to alter their initial intention. At the same time, these modifications often led to new arrangements of canons, in which texts thus assembled were used as proofs of the assertions of the individual title rubrics. This phenomen may be called 'secondary rule-making', and should be distinguished from the canons themselves which constitute the primary rules. The process of 'secondary rule-making' can be observed especially in the thematically ordered canonical collections that developed into the main type of collection by the end of the ninth century. Later the Decretum of Gratian, compiled between 1125 and 1145, created a new kind of legal analysis and prepared the ground for new rule-making.

2.4 *Byzantine Law*

After periods of unrest, Justinian (482–565), emperor of the Eastern Empire, succeeded in reconquering the territories of North Africa, Italy and small parts of Spain occupied by the Vandals, Goths, Suebs, etc. Part of his military and political strategy was to try to unify his Empire into a legal entity, with the Roman Empire's glory days in mind. He pursued the goal of a comprehensive codification. His ambition was based on the fact that the classical Latin legal literature was read and understood better in the eastern than in the western parts of the Empire. The law schools of Constantinople and Beirut were the most important centers of learning in the eastern Empire of late Antiquity. These schools contributed to the flourishing of jurisprudence. The practice in the East was not only to use the elementary writings, with their wealth of casuistry, but also to draw on the classical Roman compilations and commentaries. Justinian tried to use this project as a strategy to renew the Roman empire. The so-called *Corpus iuris civilis* was the last and most complex code of law written in Latin. Although the 'Code' is discussed in-depth in the first chapter, it is important to refer to it in the context of the later legal tradition and its medieval 'Nachleben' (afterlife).

The Code of Justinianic law was first referred to as *Corpus iuris civilis* in 1583 in the complete edition of the Justinianic legislation by Dionysius Gothofredus (Denis Godefroy). Standard editions of it are still the ones by Theodor Mommsen and Paul Krueger (Berlin 1888–1895).

The *Corpus Iuris Civilis* consists of four parts. However in the Early Middle Ages it was accessible mostly in *epitomae* (abbreviations), i.e., versions or fragments.

The next text illustrates how the continuation or revitalization of classical Roman law took place. The approach of Justinian's jurists can especially be seen in the subtle explanation on how the new collection was to be used.

> *C. 1.17.1.7 Constitutio Deo auctore (transl. by Gerald Schwedler)*
> But we also want you to direct your efforts towards this: If you find something in the old books that is not well regulated, or something superfluous or imperfect, then you should supplement that which is imperfect by eliminating superfluous lengths, and in general present the whole work in a well-ordered and beautiful manner as good as possible.
>
> You should pay not less attention to this: If you find anything in the old popular laws and emperor's constitutions, which the old jurists included in their books, not correctly understood, you should also improve and bring into a well-formed order that which appears to be true and the best, and that which has been written from the beginning, as it were, what has been selected by you and taken up there: and no one should dare to attack this text as false by a comparison with an old work.[17]

17 C. 1.17.1.7 Sed et hoc studiosum vobis esse volumus, ut, si quid in veteribus non bene positum libris inveniatis vel aliquod superfluum vel minus perfectum, super vacua longitudine semota et quod imperfectum est repleatis et omne opus moderatum et quam pulcherrimum ostendatis. hoc etiam nihilo minus observando, ut, si aliquid in veteribus

The *Corpus iuris civilis* shows how law was 'created' by selecting pre-existing legal texts for a post-Roman society in the Eastern empire. The same procedure of revising and adapting Roman law was carried out in the case of Alaric's Breviary only a little more than two decades before, though under different circumstances. All laws and paragraphs that had to do with imperial rule or Roman-ness were preserved in the *Corpus iuris civilis*; but in the *Breviarium Alarici*, they hindered the authority of Alaric and were, therefore, eliminated. The creation of law in this post-imperial period was a process of omission and re-form(ul)ation.

2.5 *Summary*

In the Early Middle Ages, legal rules were part of different *corpora* of law, namely Roman (vulgar) law, Germanic (tribal) law, and canon law. These various bodies of law were distinct, but they also overlapped: Alaric, as shown above, promulgated a code of law for the 'Barbarian', Germanic population of his realm as well as for the Roman people. Besides, Roman legal principles shaped the law of the Church ('the Church lives according to Roman law'). The term 'hybridization' describes the mixture of these different fields quite well. Canon law is a prime example of this amalgam. Another concept that characterizes the Early Middle Ages is 'decentralization', as it refers to a plethora of rule-makers after the decline of the centralized Roman Empire. Secular kings and lords, popes and bishops, abbots and many other rulers issued rules and norms. 'Decentralization', however, also points to a second phenomenon: even the popes did not yet have the power to impose rules for the whole of Christendom in general, but tried to make a specific decision binding by circulating it amongst the ecclesiastical stakeholders (e.g., Pope Siricius). Finally, there was a great diversity of processes that led to new rules: the rulers made the new codes of Roman (or Germanic) law with the assistance of legally trained jurists; whereas conciliar decisions were based on the consent of the bishops, a powerful group within the Church. And with regard to the process of creating new rules, one can also note a striking variety: the wording of rules was partly new (for example, in canon law), partly a reformulation or amendment of older texts (for example, in Roman law). Because of this, rule-making in the Early Middle Ages has a hybrid and decentralized character and was based on various procedural forms.

---

legibus vel constitutionibus, quas antiqui in suis libris posuerunt, non recte scriptum inveniatis, et hoc reformetis et ordini moderato tradatis: ut hoc videatur esse verum et optimum et quasi ab initio scriptum quod a vobis electum et ibi positum fuerit, et nemo ex comparatione veteris voluminis quasi vitiosam scripturam arguere audeat.

Questions

1. What legal sources can be distinguished in the Early Middle Ages?
2. To what extent do different legal systems overlap? What is meant by 'hybridization'?
3. Was the main objective of post-Roman legal culture to create new law?
4. To what extent is the Lex Salica influenced by Roman and Christian ideas? Is the Lex Salica aimed at the creation of new law?
5. Describe the system of feudal tenure. What are its main characteristics?
6. What different methods of law-making can be distinguished in canon law?

3 Transmission

This variety of sources of law was transmitted in different forms: partly by charters, partly by parchment *codices*, often preserved in libraries of monasteries or cathedral schools. These are just some examples of the various material objects which helped transmit rules. However, the transmission should not only be understood in material terms (transmission of *codices*) but also in a figurative sense, namely as the transmission from the older generations to the younger ones. This section will address both aspects of the term transmission.

3.1 *Roman Vulgar Law*

Roman law was transmitted in a variety of ways. Law schools, or at least centers of legal knowledge, existed in Gaul and the Iberian Peninsula. Copies of the Code and interpretations were accessible in ruling cities and various libraries. Marseille was one of the last important places where Roman law was studied. Many fragments of copied texts, excerpts still extant today, demonstrate the high standard of Roman jurisprudence at that time. But during the following decades, a decline of Roman legal practice ensued. The number of experts and manuscripts decreased, and legal material was transmitted by other means and in different formats.

A specific type of Roman legal thought resulted in so-called *formulae*. These texts were anthologies of frequently needed standard forms for charters, letters and all sorts of legal material, organized to be used by scribes and notaries and adapted for particular cases. The *formulae marculfi*, named after the compiler Markulf, show the persistence of Roman legal thought in Salic law. The *formulae andecavenses*, named after Angers, where they were compiled, are based on a Visigothic compilation of Roman law. Alf Uddholm dates the *marculfi* prior to 690, Karl Zeumer dates the *formulae andecavense* prior to 676. Despite their pragmatic and almost unsophisticated appearance, they are invaluable sources for understanding the role of Roman legal thought in post-Roman civic life. One of the most telling formulae, the first formula of Angers, provides an insight into the early medieval professional procedure of a court session held in Angers. Note that the editor introduced the letters XY, AB etc. to distinguish the many anonymous persons and to make it easier to understand the text.

Formulae Andecavenses 1 (*transl. by Gerald Schwedler*)
In the fourth year of the reign of our King Childebert, and it happened in that month and on that day when, as usual, the *curia publica* of the town of Angers had settled on the *forum*, that *vir magnificus* XY and *prosecutor* said there: 'I ask you, praiseworthy *defensor* AB, *curator* CD and commander of the soldiers (*magister militum*) EF and the rest of the *curia publica*, that you order to open the public books because I have something to investigate in the files'.

The *defensor* and at the same time the head and the whole *curia publica* said: 'The public books shall be open for you; examine what you wish'.

Through this document, the latter urges me to obey the order, because there must be a *prosecutor* to refer to the municipal files: that order which I have made for my dearest husband to stand up for all his legal claims both in the *pagus* (region) and in the palace or in any other place, and my inheritance, which according to the law falls or is to fall to him from my parents' own property, or which must be returned to him in a very just manner, to stand up against his parents and against any man, to sue and to fight in court with full knowledge of this order which I have made for my dearest husband.

The *curia* said to the man: 'The commission you say you have is for the *vir venerabilis* GH, deacon and scribe to accept'.

The *prosecutor* said to him: 'I wish and demand that you prove before the whole assembly if this commission as you have come to know it, is according to the law, so that you command that the morning gift I hold in my hands be read out in the public assembly'.

But the assembly said, 'The morning gift which you say you have in your hands is to be given to GH, deacon and scribe of the city of Angers, to read it to us'. After he received the morning gift, he read to us: ...[18]

18 MGH Formulae Merowingici et Karolini aevi, Karl Zeumer (ed.), Berlin, Hahn, 1887, 4: Annum quarto regnum domni nostri Childeberto reges, quod fecit minsus ille, dies tantus, cum iuxta consuetudinem Andicavis civetate curia puplica resedere in foro, ibi quae vir magnificus illi prosecutor dixit: 'Rogo te, vir laudabilis illi defensor, illi curator, illi

It should be noted that in the fragment above, Latin legal terms are used anachronistically:

curia publica	public court
forum	court
vir magnificus	honorary title
prosecutor	prosecutor
defensor	defender
curator	keeper of the public books
magister militum	master of the soliders (highest army rank)
pagus	a territory/region
gesta municipalia	public books

This form is, in fact, the protocol for a public insinuation (transcription of an act in the public registers) of a mandate. After the mandate was written, the *cession* followed, that is, the official transfer into the *gesta municipalia*, the public books of Angers.[19] Embedded in the protocol are two documents presented for this purpose before the assembly on the civic *forum*. The Latin is very difficult to translate, as it has many colloquial and post-Roman words – often called 'vulgar' Latin – which is also the reason this law is called 'vulgar Roman law'. Not only do we encounter unexpected versions of words (*annum*

magister militum, vel reliquam curia puplica, utique coticis puplici patere iobeatis, qua habeo, quid apud acta prosequere debiam'. Deffensor, principalis simul et omnis curia puplica dixerunt: 'Patent tibi cotecis puplici; prosequere que optas'. 'Oboedire illa per mandato suo pagina mihi iniuncxit, ut prosecutor exsistere deberit, qualiter mandatum, quam in dulcissimo iocali e meo illo fici pro omnis causacionis suas, tam in paco quam et in palacio seu in qualibet loca, accidere faciat, illas porciones meas, quem ex alote parentum meorum aei legibus obvenit vel obvenire debit, aut iustissime aei est reddebetum, aecontra parentis suis vel contra cuiuslibet hominem accidere vel admallare seu et liticare facias, inspecto illo mandato, quem in dulcissemo iocali meo illo fici, gestis municipalibus adlegare debeam'. Curia viro dixerunt: 'Mandato, quem tibi habere dicis, accipiat vir venerabilis illi diaconus et amanuensis'. Illi prosecutor dixit: 'Rogo domno meis omnibus puplicis, ut sicut mandatum istum legebus cognovistis esse factum, ut dotem, quem per manebus tenio, vobis presentibus in foro puplico iobeatis recitare'. Curia vero dixerunt: 'Dotem, quem te dicis per manibus retenire, illi diaconus et amanuensis Andecavis civetate nobis presentibus accipiat relegendum'. Quo accepto dixit.

19 Cf. for research and an alternative translation A. Rio, The formularies of Angers and Marculf, Liverpool, Liverpool University Press, 2008, 42–43.

stands for *anno*, *regnum* instead of *regno* and *reges* for *regis*),[20] but there are also unconnected sentences, and missing verbs or changes in subject. It is also very likely to contain legal and political anachronisms, although this is difficult to prove as it is not possible to date this form precisely. It is dated the 'fourth year of the reign of Childebert', but it is uncertain which Childebert is meant: Childebert I (511–558), Childebert II (575–596), or Childebert III (694–711)? There is no case where the *magister militum* (master of the soldiers) mentioned in the form from the Merovingian era, corresponds to an actual ancient top-level commander. So the transmission of formulaic terms from Roman law into a Frankish cultural environment does not necessarily mean that they described social reality. However, the dialogue put forward in the first form of Angers shows that there was a fair amount of 'living Roman law', which transitioned from the classical into the Frankish context. The hybrid character of law made it possible, and even attractive, to absorb the Roman nomenclature into a Frankish legal culture. Even though the Roman system of courts of law, public administration, and central means of execution was no longer fully functional, the usage of outdated terms – not unusual for jurists – gave stability and comfort in times of political unrest, at least in Angers.

3.2 *Germanic Tribal Law*

'Transmission' refers to the physical distribution of legal knowledge in the broad sense of the word and the development of law through scholarly thought. The latter includes legal education and issues of interpretation and analogy. These two are probably the closest to what we understand by 'legal scholarship' that can be found with the ancient Germanic peoples.

Franz Wieacker is the author of a highly regarded study, the *Privatrechtsgeschichte der Neuzeit* (History of Private Law). Wieacker's book has been translated into English, Portuguese, Italian, Russian and Chinese. In this work, he argues that the training of lawyers in the period up to about 1100 was part of the general curriculum of subjects taught (*trivium, artes liberales*). At least in the West, specialized training for lawyers apparently did not exist. Wieacker discusses the fragmentation of the world once united under Roman rule and the advantages and disadvantages it entailed. He argues that the end of the Roman Empire gave rise to a more true-to-life and emotional law at the expense of a mature and elaborated system of law. The training of lawyers

20 Formulae Andecavenses 1, MGH Formulae Merowingici et Karolini aevi, Karl Zeumer (ed.), Berlin, Hahn, 1886, 4: 'Annum quarto regnum domni nostri Childeberto reges'.

was very practical, and clerics as well as scholars played an important role in a largely illiterate world. This was a period poor in legal sources that had to work with Germanic content expressed in Latin culture and language. Wieacker also emphasizes the independence of the individual Germanic tribes and peoples, particularly the special role of the northern tribes.

> *Franz Wieacker, A History of Private Law in Europe. With particular reference to Germany (translated by Tony Weir and with a foreword by Reinhard Zimmermann), Oxford, Clarendon Press, 1995, 15–18, 21–24*
> If the *imperium* of the late ancient world was a creation of Roman power, its cultural ideals rested primarily on Greek education and the concept of *Paideia*.[21] This survived in schools throughout the Hellenized Roman empire: elementary instruction consisted of the *trivium* of Grammar, Logic (Dialectic), and Rhetoric, which together with the higher disciplines of Arithmetic, Geometry, Music, and Astronomy formed the *artes liberales*. Grammar helped elicit the meaning of written texts, Rhetoric enabled one to speak in an orderly manner, and Dialectic promoted the art of discussion and logical argumentation in theology, philosophy, and law. That the training of lawyers took place in the *trivium* and in a school of rhetoric and dialectic is another crucial fact of legal history in the Early Middle Ages; no specialized law schools, as far as we know, existed outside the Byzantine East. …
>
> The unitary society of those who had been subject to, and often exploited by, the bureaucratic and centralized Byzantine Empire was now broken up into a large number of regional groupings, held together not by imperial organization but by the Church, by a new attitude to law, and in the upper echelons by a sense of common descent. Law was thereby rejuvenated, but at a price. A mature and sophisticated legal culture where power was used for rational purposes was replaced by one in which law was a spontaneous expression of life and feeling; in place of a unitary order there was a profusion of personal and group laws; and as often happens on the collapse of great powers, order and legal security were lost. …

---

21 *Paideia* (Greek for 'upbringing', 'education') is a key term for understanding ancient culture and a central concept of values. It stands on the one hand for intellectual and ethical education and training as a process and on the other for education as a result of the educational process. It thus refers not only to schooling for children, but also to a man's turning towards the perfection of his thinking and himself.

The *legal systems* of the Early Middle Ages bespeak the remarkable tension between this new vitality and the civilization of antiquity, or what remained of it. Where the law was in writing it rested on the remnants of Roman imperial law, on the Romanized laws of the Germanic peoples, the tribal laws written down at the instance of the Franks, on capitularies and on the law used by the Church; all of these were drafted and applied by literati and clerics. In the background was a new unwritten legal culture which found expression in land holdings and succession, feudal and service relationships, in clan, fellowships, and groups, in word and sign, in complaint, court, and judgement; but whenever any of it had to be put in writing, in ordinance, deed, or protocol, resort to the language of late antiquity was unavoidable, and it was hard to bypass the trained literati and clerics or to eschew the legal terminology of vulgar law. This means that for our knowledge of these unwritten legal systems we have to rely on secondary sources, on ecclesiastical historians and chroniclers, on deeds, genealogies, and inventories of the great, on documents, signatures, lists of holdings, rent rolls, books of the dead, and so on. Only at the start of the High Middle Ages does the rich law hitherto unwritten break out in an astonishing profusion of vernacular writings, from the Spanish *fueros* and the *Ordinamenti* of Italy to the law books of Germany and Scandinavia; the same happened with poetry, too, both being rendered possible by the increase among the population of literacy learnt from the old traditions of clerical education. …

It was different for those Germans (like the Old Saxons, the Frisians, and the North Germans) who had never been on imperial territory or those who had destroyed Roman civilization before they settled down (the Alemanni and Bavarians in Southern Germany, and in Britain the Angles, Saxons, and Jutes). The Anglo-Saxons were able to keep their statutes (and their poetry) in their own language, thanks to the open-mindedness and tolerance of their clerics, even after the missionaries landed. In Germany itself it was only through church missionaries that the tribes were exposed to the culture of the ancient world, and the old Saxons only when forcibly incorporated into the Carolingian Empire. It took longer for Roman ideas of state and law to have any effect on the North Germans who had a distinctive legal culture of their own. These differences also had a long-term effect, and traces of it are still discernible in German, English, and Scandinavian law. …

There is very little documentary evidence for the continuance, interruption, and rebirth of Roman law in the Early Middle Ages, but the following facts are fairly well established. The *Lex Romana Visigothorum*

> and its glosses and extracts continued to be observed in large parts of romanized territory even outside the Visigoth Empire (which reached as far as the Loire before 507); the late ancient practice of putting transactions, gifts, and wills into writing was dominant enough to reach even into southern Germany; and all statutes and other legal writings, from the Eurician Code of the Visigoths to the capitularies of Carolingian times, adhered to the style and terminology of Roman vulgar law. This is all due to the monopoly of literacy enjoyed by the clerk in late antiquity and by the *clericus* who succeeded him, even where the actual substance recorded was unquestionably Germanic, as in the tribal laws and the law books of the Lombards. *Legal scholarship* in the Early Middle Ages was elementary, never going beyond school-learning in mode of expression and the understanding of simple logical relationships – the *trivium* which had formed the basic training of legal officials from Constantine onwards. In the Early Middle Ages, the transmission and drafting of written law continued to be in the hands of ecclesiastical educators. Such as it was – and the quality of church education varied a great deal – this education was available only in schools attached to a monastery or to a royal chapel run by a cleric, and eventually also in cathedral schools. Thus there was no specialist training in law, only general education for the cleric; this was, however, a preparation for secular administration as well as for pastoral and ecclesiastical duties, for not all the students in monastic schools took holy orders. Occasional references to the study of law or statutes in Merovingian or Carolingian times relate to such schools, which had some interest in practical legal tasks and in the documentation of legal proceedings, as is shown by the Formulary Book of Marculf the Monk.
>
> What is clear is that in the early Middle Ages the West had no system of instruction which concentrated *exclusively* on the explication of secular statutory texts or on the methodical treatment of legal problems. The functions later to be performed by the *studium civile* were executed by the *trivium*, involving schooling in deeds and drafting and *also* explaining legal texts. In fact, the *studium* of Bologna emerged directly from this form of liberal arts education, with which it maintained its links even in its prime.

'Transmission' in a broader sense clearly refers to more than mere 'legal education'. Besides, we cannot really discover how legal training was carried out, and legal expertise was acquired in the Franconian Empire. Cathedrals and monasteries played a central role in propagating and particularly in codifying the Germanic *leges*. This was also the place where an intellectual engagement with the laws of the Germanic tribes developed. In his fundamental textbook on German legal history, Kroeschell describes monasteries as institutions of legal education.

> *K. Kroeschell, Deutsche Rechtsgeschichte 1. Bis 1250 (13th ed.), Cologne, Weimar, Vienna, Böhlau, 2008, 97–98 (transl. by Bernd Kannowski)*
> This manifold contact with legal life caused the monasteries also to be interested in secular legal texts. The fact that the book catalog of the St. Gallen Monastery, which dates from Carolingian times, already lists several legal manuscripts is surely primarily based on the practical requirements of the monastery to inform themselves about Alemannic and Franconian law. At the same time, an academic interest developed, which was eventually applied to the monastery school's teaching. It seems that we owe the fact that these texts that record tribal law have been passed down to the latter interest. Except for the fragments of the *Codex Euricianus* and the oldest manuscript, the *Edictum Rothari*, all manuscripts preserved today originate from Carolingian times at the earliest. This also applies to those manuscripts which reproduce the Precarolingian versions of the texts. The monastic scriptoriums continued to produce manuscripts of the *leges* into the 11th century – a time in which they had become almost unknown outside of the monastery walls. They seem to have been used for monastic tuition. Therefore, it comes as no surprise that we encounter a profound reflection on questions of German legal life in the writings of the highly educated head of the monastic school of St. Gallen, Notker the German, from around the year 1000. It seems that Fulda was a center of academic study of the law in the Carolingian time itself. It is from there that the Old High German translation of the *Lex Salica*, of which a fragment has been preserved, seems to originate. It can also be assumed that it was there that the learned monk Lupus, who later became abbot of the Ferrières Monastery, produced the large manuscript for Duke Eberhard of Friuli, a son in law of Louis the Pious. The remarkable document attempts the systematic restructuring of both the *Lex Salica* and Lombard law in general.

There are various possible explanations for the counter-intuitive fact that clerics were the most efficient transmitters of secular law. It was, certainly, not only because of the higher developed culture of the written word nor the better-developed library infrastructure. Various incidents make it clear that they needed to be knowledgeable in matters of secular law to be able to resist secular political aspirations and territorial claims. Many saw secular law and canon law as complementary, and therefore they were often transmitted in the same contexts, if not in the same manuscripts.

> *Notker Teutonicus, De Arte Rhetorica, in Karl Kroeschell, Deutsche Rechtsgeschichte 1. Bis 1250 (13th ed.), Cologne, Weimar, Vienna, Böhlau, 2008, 104 (transl. by Bernd Kannowski)*
> *On legal disputes. Literal and actual meaning*
> Legal disputes are controversies that arise about laws. For example, in accordance with Alemannic law, someone was offered twelve shillings for the wrongful loss of a horse. The original owner declined to accept, claiming that this was a disgraceful compensation for such a valuable animal. Thereupon the other replied that he had thereby complied with the law and, for this reason, the other could not decline to accept the recompense dictated by the law, unless he wanted to unhinge the law itself. The other said, no evil originated from the law, and it was not created to harm, but to serve the benefit of all. And whilst the Gospel, which no Christian law can contradict, contains the rule, that one should reimburse fourfold what one has taken wrongfully, you, who have deceived me, do not even want to reimburse me that of which you have defrauded me? Buy me such a horse with the money if you can. This will be the only reason which can convince me that I have to accept and value what you offer. He who makes a law can surely only want to determine the penalty or the method as to how a horse, ox, or donkey should be compensated so that the victim does not have to spend more money than he receives to purchase a new one.
>
> This legal dispute is called 'Literal and Actual meaning' because one part is based on the lawmakers' text and the other part contradicts the text, which is the intention of the lawmakers, as it is based on how the meaning is construed.
>
> Cicero provides a famous example from Greek history of this type of legal dispute: The ruler of Thebes Epaminondas who, when he exercised sovereignty for just one year, did not follow the letter of the law and did not transfer his power over the army to his successor on the fixed date, but retained it for himself for the benefit of the state. Although it was against the text, it was justified with the meaning intended by the lawmaker.[22]

22 *Paul Piper (ed.), Die Schriften Notkers und seiner Schule, vol. 1, Freiburg i. Br. – Tübingen, J.C.B. Mohr, 1882, 656–657:* De statibus legalibus. Scriptum et sententia. Status legales sunt contraversiae de legibus orte. Ut pro equo iniuste ablato quidam reddere voluit XII solidos secundum legem Alamannorum. Repetitor hos recusavit suscipere dicens. Vile

The text that we will discuss below is from the *Liber Papiensis* (Latin for 'Pavian Book'), also called the *Liber Legis Langobardorum* ('Book of the Law of the Lombards'). It is a collection of the laws the Lombard kings passed between 643 and 755, the laws of the Carolingians from 774 to 887, as well as those of later Ottonian and Salian rulers. The *Liber Papiensis* was written in the first half of the eleventh century in Pavia, then the capital of the Lombard Empire. The collection is closely connected to the law school of Pavia. The case presented is an example of litigation where a party is deliberately trying to circumvent the applicable law.

The case deals with a raid conducted by militant women and can be seen as a rare example of a type of academic interpretation of Germanic law. The passage shows that it was known to all that such an attack was prohibited if conducted by men. The planners gave considerable thought to figuring out a way to circumvent the law. To do so, they sent their (free and unfree) women to conduct the raid since the law only prohibited raids conducted by men.

Liutprand considers a new statute necessary because the case could not be solved by simply applying the old law, as can be seen from the extremely brief explanation given. It appears that the court initially considered treating the case under the laws of Liutprand's predecessor Rothari, either as an armed robbery (*arschild*) or as a peasant uprising. However, the assembly concluded that neither of these could decide the case, 'because this is what men do, not women'. Unlike men, women were not considered fit for warfare (*non possunt faidam levare*). This distinction makes it impossible to apply the principles from the cases already decided. Using a kind of analogy (*adsimilare*), which was, in principle, available and later used in the interpretation of Roman and Canon law, was of no help in this case. The approach of comparing it to

sibi precium offerre pro equo preciosissimo. At ille satis fecisse se ait secundum iustitiam legis, nec eum posse statutum legis recusare, nisi velit ipsam legem dissolvere. De lege inquit nihil umquam incommodi venit, nec ad hoc data est ut noceat, sed omnium utilitatibus consulat. Et dum evangelium cui nulla lex Christiana contradicit, si quid aliquem defraudavi reddo quadruplum, dicat quomodo tu, qui fraudem fecisti, nec tantum pro eo, quod fraudasti restituere cogitas? Eme talem tanto si potes. Ea sola ratio est, que suadeat mihi, quod offers, suscripiendum esse et tam carum estimare. Eo pacto, qui legem dedit, credendus est scribere de solutione damni, et aliquem modum de restituendo equo ponere vel bove vel asino, quo eum non deberet quisquam carius emere. Iste status vocatur scriptum et sententia, quia alius legislatoris scripto nititur; alius scriptum interpretando, de sententia, i. voluntate scriptoris, scripto contradicit. Cicero huius status nobile dedit exemplum de Greca historia, quomodo Epaminondas dux Thebanorum, dum annuam potestatem haberet, successori suo statuto tempore exercitum secundum scriptum legis non reddidit, sed pro utilitate rei publice diutius aliquantum secum retinuit, seque contra scriptum sententia scriptoris rationabiliter defendit.

previously decided cases is closer to the contemporary Anglo-Saxon legal culture ('case law') than to the legal culture of continental Europe, shaped by the reception of learned law.

Despite the gap in his own set of rules, Luitprand did not freely create law. He applied a norm from another Germanic law, albeit without disclosing it. Luitprand adopted a provision from the *Lex Visigothorum*. This law punishes those who expect not to be punished because they commit acts not covered by the law, by being shaved bare and public whipping.[23] Under Lombard law, shaving (*decalvatio*) someone as a penalty was unusual. This indicates that there was a connection between the Germanic *Leges* of that time. By applying a law from another Germanic people, this law became equally valid as a source of law for the Lombards.[24]

The text originates in Northern Italy. Consequently, the original academic work on the text was probably done by the Lombards in their *Liber Papiensis*, or possibly even before that at the law school of Pavia.

> *A case from the Liber Papiensis: King Liutprand († 744) and the Women Raiders (transl. by Bernd Kannowski)*
> Laws of King Liutprand 141.3: We have been told that some cunning and wickedly devious men, while they did not dare to enter a village or house of another man in a brave or violent way by themselves because they feared that composition set for it in the old law [Rothair 279], had their women gather together, as many as they had, both free and unfree, and sent them upon men of lesser fortitude. And that they seized the men of

23 Lex Visigothorum VI, 4, 5, Samuel Parsons Scott (transl.), The Visigothic Code (Forum Judicum), Boston, The Boston Book Company, 1910, reprinted Littleton (Colorado), Fred B. Rothman & Co, 1982, 215: He who Violates the Law by Inflicting Injury upon Another, shall undergo the same Punishment which he Himself Inflicted. It is no less a fault to be ignorant of the laws than, knowing them, to commit crimes. Wherefore, whoever, up to this time, or hereafter, has perpetrated, or shall perpetrate, any act forbidden by law, and shall either declare that he was ignorant of the law, or shall plot to carry out any act that shall entire to the injury or danger of anyone, alleging, at the same time, that such act is not prohibited by law, and that for this reason he cannot be held liable for its commission, and should such person be convicted, he shall at once undergo the same dangers, ignominy, tortures, suffering, or pecuniary loss, which he inflicted, or attempted to inflict, upon another, shall receive, in addition, a hundred lashes in public, and shall be scalped, as a mark of perpetual infamy.
Cf. Harald Siems, 'Adsimilare'. Die Analogie als Wegbereiterin zur mittelalterlichen Rechtswissenschaft, in Klaus Herbers (ed.), Europa an der Wende vom 11. zum 12. Jahrhundert, Stuttgart, Franz Steiner, 2001, 143–170, in particular 163 et seq.

24 Ibid.

that place, and inflicted wounds on them, and did other evil in a violent manner, more cruelly than men do.

Since this has come before us, and these less strong men, seeking vengeance for the violence against them, complained. So by way of precaution we add to the edict that if from now on women dare to do this at any place, then we first of all stipulate, that if they suffer any injury or disgrace or wounds or brutality or death there, those, who in self-defence did in any way harm to them or caused destruction, shall pay no composition to the women themselves or to their men or legal guardians. Furthermore, the public official, who has been established at that place, shall seize these women, and he shall shave their heads and drive them through the neighbouring villages of that place, so that the rest of the women do not dare to commit such evil. And if the women on this occasion inflict wounds to or behave brutally towards any man, their husbands shall pay composition for the inflicted wounds or the women's brutal behaviour according to the provisions of this edict.

But therefore, we have stipulated this in account of both the discipline as well as the composition because we cannot equate the gathering of women either with armed forces [arschild, Rothair 19; Liutprand 35, 134] or with a peasants revolt [Rothair 280; Liutprand 134] because those are deeds that men do, not women: Therefore it shall be done regarding these women just as we have stipulated above. However, if a woman simply brings any disgrace upon her, and bears death or wounds or brutality, justice shall be done to her just as our predecessor King Rothair decided and ordered [Rothair 378].[25]

25 Georg Heinrich Pertz (ed.), MGH LL 4, Hannover, Hahn, 1868, 170–171, 141 III: Relatum est nobis, quod aliqui hominis perfidi et in malitia astuti, dum per se non presumpsessent mano forti aut violento ordinem intrare in vicum aut in casam alienam, timentes illam conpositionem que in antiquo edicto posita est, fecerunt collegere mulieres suas, quascumque habuerunt, liberas et ancillas, et miserunt eas super homines, qui minore habebant virtute, et adprehendentes hominis de ipso loco, et plagas fecerunt, et reliqua mala violento ordine plus crudeliter quam viri exercuerunt. Dum autem hoc ad nos pervenissit, et ipsi homines pro sua violentia, qui minus potebant, interpellabant: ita prospeximus in hoc edicto adfigere, ut si amodo mulieres hoc facere in qualecumque locum presumpserit, primum omnium decernimus, ut si aliqua iniuria aut obprobrium, aut plagas aut feritas, aut mortem ibi acceperint, nihil ad ipsas mulieres aut ad viros aut ad mundoald earum conponant illi, qui se defendendum eis aliqua fecerint lesionem aut internicionem. Insuper et publicus, in quo loco factum fuerit, conprehendat ipsas mulieres, et faciati eas decalvare et frustaren per vicos vicinantes ipsius loci, ut de cetero mulieres tale malitia facere non presumant. Et si in ipsa causa feritas aut plagas fecerint ipsae mulieres cuicumque homini, mariti earum conponant ipsas plagas aut feritas, quas ipsae fecerunt,

3.3 *Canon Law*

Monasteries not only transmitted secular legal texts but also, of course, had an interest in canon law materials. Libraries of monasteries and episcopal seats preserved manuscripts with canonical collections and kept them available for users, who often annotated them with glosses. Some readers also compiled new collections based on older materials. The following excerpt elaborates on the educational background of some authors.

John J. Contreni, The Carolingian Renaissance: Education and Literary Culture, in Rosamond McKitterick (ed.), The New Cambridge Medieval History, vol. 2, c. 700–900, Cambridge, Cambridge University Press, 1995, 749–750

The evidence for the *learning* of the law in contrast to the abundant evidence for its practise is sparse. A diploma of 751 from Pippin III mentions *legis doctores*; 'masters of the law' participated in a mid-ninth-century dispute involving Fleury. But were these teachers or simply experienced practitioners? The evidence of manuscripts and of texts suggests that law was indeed studied at the schools, at least in those schools that had the legal resources and special interest in the subject. Isidore of Seville's *De Legibus* from the *Etymologiae*, useful for its handy précis of legal terminology, was copied into manuscripts of legal texts. The texts themselves were glossed, epitomised and made the subjects of *interpretationes*. Bishops throughout the Carolingian realms compiled digests of capitularies and canons for the use of their priests, implying thereby that parish clergy possessed the basic skills to read, understand and apply ecclesiastical law, although Bishop Sigemund of Meaux had doubts on this score. The modest church libraries of the Bavarian priests, Egino and Baldric, contained among their titles books of 'canons' which the priests undoubtedly used in the performance of their pastoral duties. The clearest evidence for a learned tradition of legal studies once again comes from those who wrote the most – the great ecclesiastics and scholars of the Carolingian world. Alcuin and Theodulf of Orléans were locked in a bitter struggle over the law of sanctuary that required Charlemagne's intervention. It was a

secundum edicti tinore. Hoc autem ideo prospeximus tam de disciplina quam de conpositione, quia non potuimus mulierum collectionem ad arschild consimilare, neque ad seditionem rusticanorum, quia istas causas viri faciunt, nam non mulieres: ideoque sic de ipsis mulieribus faciat, sicut supra statuimus. Si quidem simpliciter in scandalum qualiscumque mulier cucurrerit, et mortem aut plagam aut feritam ibi susceperit, sic ei faciat iustitiam, sicut decessor noster Rothari rex instituit et iudicavit.

palace chaplain and abbot, Ansegisus of St Wandrille, who compiled the first systematic and widely copied collection of Carolingian capitularies. Archbishop Magnus of Sens (801–18) presented Charlemagne with a compilation of *notae iuris*, a specialised collection of legal abbreviations, for the use of the royal chancery. The bishops of Lyons put together an exceptional collection of law-books, some of which undoubtedly served as sources for the collection compiled *ex lege et canone* by Florus (d. *c.* 860), the prolific deacon of that city. Archbishop Hincmar of Rheims possessed formidable knowledge of Roman and church law and presented the younger Hincmar with a canon law collection as well as a copy of the decretals of Gelasius on the day of his ordination to the bishopric of Laon. Lupus of Ferrières copied one of Eberhard of Friuli's law-books and was probably the legal expert the abbey of St Denis called in to defend its claims against Fleury.

3.4 *Summary*

In conclusion, the topic of the transmission of legal texts is complicated as the surviving historical sources from the period only provide evidence of moments of continuity, co-existence and mutual influence of the three different legal spheres. Parchment codices containing Roman law, Germanic law and canon law mostly survived in the libraries of monasteries and cathedral schools. The Church offered the best conditions for materials from the Early Middle Ages to survive. Ecclesiastical libraries offered great access for those interested in the content of these manuscripts. Learned clerks studied these materials closely and often annotated or excerpted them, producing new manuscripts with copies of older texts.

The transmission of texts requires three steps, writing, preserving and using them. It is not surprising that the use of the texts was important for church institutions. It was a vital tool to organize and defend the Church with legal weapons in a political and military world where the benign influence of the Gospel alone would not suffice. When studying old library inventories from the Middle Ages, one can clearly see that between one-third and one-half of the books on the shelves contained legal texts. They were necessary as in a context where law-making authority was contested, it was useful to have an array of legal arguments and formulations at hand when needed. That is the reason why so many legal texts were copied and preserved.

Questions

1. What were the different methods of the transmission of law in the Early Middle Ages?

2. To what extent and in what manner are Roman legal terms used in early medieval legal texts? What does this teach us about the character of the law at that time?
3. How were lawyers trained in Western Europe before c. 1100? Can early-medieval lawyers be compared with modern lawyers?
4. How come that clerics and their institutions were efficient transmitters of secular law in the Early Middle Ages?
5. What can you say about the character and content of the collection of laws in use at the School of Pavia?

4 Actors

The Early Middle Ages is characterized by a great diversity of institutions, forms, procedures and actors involved in law-making. There were many such actors: Germanic rulers such as king Alaric, popes like Siricius, bishops, monks and lords. They all created rules, applied norms and settled conflicts. This section gives an overview of the different actors involved.

4.1 *Roman Vulgar Law*

Instead of beginning this section with some of the chief actors such as emperors or other high-ranking officials, we will start with an almost anonymous group of actors, members of a 'lost population', i.e., the last Romans in Northern Europe. These Roman actors can be traced to Eastern Bavaria and the so-called Rottachgauer fragment they produced. This fragment may be considered the most prominent example of the intentional application of Roman law in the Bavarian context of the Early Middle Ages. It is preserved as a copy in the inventory of the property of the bishop of Passau (*Passauer Traditionskodex*).

> *Max Heuwieser (ed.), Die Traditionen des Hochstifts Passau, München, Beck, 1930, Nr. 1, 1–2 (transl. by Gerald Schwedler)*
> The price, the seller set for the buyer, was accepted under these circumstances, and they transferred the aforementioned cleared forest land to the buyer. To protect the ownership of the property, the buyer asked for an insurance from the seller. They gave credible praise and spoke as follows: Should any of the latter or any of the outside persons wish to vote against this deed, then the sellers undertake that they will return double the money to the buyer, and the deed shall continue in force after this certification has become valid. Negotiated in the village of Fonalva on the day of the Consul. And they asked the people present as witnesses: Signature

> by own hand from Mairan, Dominic and the Dominicans who made this deed. Signature by own hand of Floritius the Provost as witnesses. Signature by own hand of soldier Vigilius as witnesses. I, Quartinus, have written this.[26]

The fragment is later than the fifth century, yet the form that is used dates from that time, as is clear from the mentioned offices and specific terminology used. It likely came from the Romanesque population present in Bavaria in the eighth century. The cultural autonomy is highlighted even more if one dates the document later to a time when other Roman communities had long merged with Germanic society. In search of the actors (rule-makers), their backgrounds, and importance in civic life, Franz-Rainer Erkens compared the document's legal concepts to other regions with a sizable Roman population such as the former province of Raetia in today's Switzerland.

> *Franz-Rainer Erkens, Actum in vico fonaluae die consule, Das Rottachgau-Fragment und die romanische Kontinuität am Unterlauf des Inns, in Uwe Ludwig and Thomas Schilp (eds), Nomen et fraternitas: Festschrift für Dieter Geuenich zum 65. Geburtstag, Berlin, W. de Gruyter, 2008, 502 (transl. by Gerald Schwedler)*
>
> Ultimately, the document could have been written any time between the late 6th and the first third of the 8th century. However, if the document was drawn up in the area of the Agilolfing dukedom, it is quite unlikely that it was written later because then, the document would have been probably more strongly influenced by the culture of the second half of the 8th century. The document would probably have the features of the Bavarian documents, which were quite distinct in the second half of the 8th century. For example, it would not have been called a *stipulatione interposita* in the stipulation formula, but rather, as was customary (with the exception of nine Freising documents) in Bavaria in the 8th and 9th centuries, but also in the Rhaetian area, would have been referred to as a

26 Die Traditionen des Hochstifts Passau, Max Heuwieser (ed.), München, Beck, 1930, n. 1, 1–2: Quantum praecium vinditoris ad emptoris de presente acceperunt et rememoratum runcum tradiderunt emptori demenio in perpetuo possidendi emptor fidem querit vinditoris fide spondiderunt et sic dixerunt: sed de proximis aut de extraneis personis contra hunc strumentum refregare voluerit, tunc se spondiderunt vinditores emptori dupla pecunia esse reddituri et pagina vero strumenti in suam permaneat firmitatem stipulatione interposita. Actum in vico fonaluae die consule. Et testes de presente rogaverunt: Signum manus Mairani, Dominici et Dominicantes que strumentum fecerunt. Signum manus Floriti prepositi testes. Signum manus Uigili milites testes. Ego Quartinus qui escripsi.

> *stipulatione subnexa*. However, what remains striking is the erratic peculiarity of the fragment. It not only does not fit into the landscape of the Bavarian charters and, despite all the common features, also shows clear differences from the formulae of the Raetian charters. These include not only, as already mentioned, the phrase *stipulatione interposita*, but also the unambiguous Roman formulation: *Emptor fidem querit, venditoris fide spondiderunt*, which is not found in any Raetian sales document from before 850. Moreover, the fragment did not at all influence the Passau charters of the 8th and 9th centuries. None of the cited phrases can be found in the charters of the Passau church (reduced by losses, of course) during the period mentioned (while the *poena dupli*, for example, appears in as many as 23 of the transfers of property (*traditio*) of the Mondsee monastery and is also known in Rhaetia – although not in sales documents).

The traces the Roman actors left in early medieval Eastern Bavaria indicate that they had a distinct and, therefore, recognizable way of 'doing Romanness': instead of the expected formula *stipulatione subnexa* they apply the formula *stipulatione interposita*. Members of the Roman population organized themselves to address legal matters such as the buying and selling of land. They even established an institution as a substitute for public authority, the unspecified person of the provost who, in some way, must have had some relation to the duke of Bavaria. It was peculiar that they used the outdated title 'soldier/ milites' for witnesses as, after the collapse of the Roman army, the persons carrying weapons were, at most, legionaries. It must have been an honorary title used by the remnant of the Roman population in the former Roman provinces along the Danube. However, as hybrid legal cultures are not stable over time, a process of assimilation and adaption led to the decline of the importance of Roman law in legal life.

4.2 *Germanic Tribal Law*

Compared to Roman vulgar Law, it is much easier to name the actors involved in law-making in Germanic law, despite the fact that the notion of law-making played a less prominent role in Germanic law than, for example, in ancient Roman law. The making of new laws (*novas leges condere*) was not typically done by Germanic rulers and legislators known by name. This is rather an exception. Because of the lack of written records, we know very little about them, as is true for almost all people of this time. However, some legislators are known and deserve to be mentioned. In chronological order, they are two

Lombard rulers from the territory of present-day Italy, namely Rothari and Liutprand, and, above all, Charlemagne.

Rothari (around 606–652) was elected king of the Lombards by the nobles in 636. He owes his fame – just like many other rulers – to the extremely successful military expansion he achieved. In domestic matters, Rothari was concerned with securing his power and stability. Thus, at the beginning of his reign, he had many of his aristocratic Lombard enemies killed.

Important for legal history is the *Edictum Rothari* from 643. Rothari had the law of the Lombards, which before then had 'only been handed down by memory and use' (*cadarfida*), collected and written down by a 'notary' named Ansoald. Before starting this undertaking, Rothari had obtained the people's assembly's consent to write down the law in the form of an ancient ritual (*gairethinx*). Although the *Edictum Rothari* came into being later than other Germanic legal codes such as the Visigothic *Codex Euricianus* (around 475), the Ostrogothic *Edictum Theoderici* (around 500), and the *Lex Burgundionum* (around 510), it showed little influence of the Roman legal tradition. Similar to other *Leges*, the *Edictum Rothari* was written in Latin, but contained untranslatable legal terms from the Lombard language. Since legislation was considered a feature of a powerful and well-organized empire in the Roman sense, the *Edictum Rothari* can be understood as a message to the Byzantine Empire that the Lombards were not merely a horde of barbarians but that, to the contrary, they had established a serious and enduring state in Italy.

Liutprand († 744) was King of the Lombards from 712 to 744. During his long reign, he sought to consolidate his empire internally and emerged as a legislator and promoter of the Church. He expanded royal power and used the weakening of the position of the Byzantine Empire in Italy to enlarge his territory. Under his reign, the Lombard Empire reached the height of its power. Liutprand legislated through annual statutes and held popular assemblies to confirm his laws. It made Lombard popular law extremely broad and gave it the character of case law.[27] Liutprand's law (*Lex Liutprandi*) often had religious content, for example, when it prohibited and sanctioned apostasy, sorcery or the worship of trees and springs. It also dealt with the hierarchy of offices and the prohibition of violence to resolve conflicts. Provisions on marriage and inheritance law brought Liutprand closer to Roman law than Rothari.

27 See above: A case from the Liber Papiensis: King Liutprand († 744) and the Women Raiders.

Charlemagne (747/748–814) is known as a legendary ruler and a legislator with supreme authority in the Middle Ages. Important collections of laws, such as the 'Sachsenspiegel' from the beginning of the thirteenth century, have been connected to his reign. But to what can Charlemagne's fame as a medieval lawmaker be attributed? He created a regionally uniform system of laws by way of so-called 'capitularies'. These applied to all people within a certain territory (territorial law, therefore, as opposed to personal law, which applies to someone who belongs to a certain group, as in Germanic tribal law). Charlemagne attempted to maintain his rule of his large realm via the so-called king's messengers, the '*missi*'. The following example is taken from a capitulary in which cross-tribal applicability ('territorial theory') is particularly apparent. The *Capitulare legibus additum* were – as the Latin name suggests – added to the tribal laws of the individual Germanic tribes ('Leges', such as the *Lex Salica*). Therefore, they were supposed to apply to everyone, irrespective of his or her origin. The source indicates that the life of a clergyman is deemed particularly valuable and Church sanctuary and the authority of the courts are discussed. Furthermore, there is evidence that the *Lex Salica* enjoyed a certain measure of fame and importance.

> *Capitulare legibus additum* [*803 AD*] (*transl. by Bernd Kannowski*)
> These are the capitularies, which Charlemagne, the great emperor, in his wisdom, commanded to be written down and placed under the other capitularies.
> (1) About the killing of clergy: If someone has killed a subdeacon, he is to forfeit 300 shillings; he who kills a deacon, is to forfeit 400; he who kills a priest, 600; he who kills a bishop, 900; he who kills a monk, will be sentenced to 400 shillings.
> (3) If someone has taken sanctuary in a church, he shall have peace in the courtyard of this church, and he should not be required to enter the church, and nobody should dare to remove him violently; instead, he should be permitted to confess what he has done, and he should be led from there to public examination at the hand of an honest men.
> (4) If someone should dare to assist a man in evil intrigue, who wrongly appears in court against another man who is accused before the judge or the count and cannot deny, he should be sentenced to 15 shillings.
> (9) All debts, which one must forfeit to the king, should one pay with shillings of twelve Pfennigs, with the exception of peace money that is recorded in the Lex Salica; this should be forfeited with the same shilling, with which the rest of the penance is paid.

(10) If someone should dare to bring a decided case before the court anew and is convicted by witnesses, he should forfeit 15 shillings or he should receive 15 strokes from the jury, who decided the case before.[28]

The Church played a prominent role in the reorganization and consolidation of Charlemagne's realm. In the *Capitulare legibus additum* he supported church institutions by granting them the right of asylum and (limited) immunity. Yet it was clear that he did not want these ecclesiastical units to interfere with secular legal procedure: in Chapter 3 he states that churches were safe spaces, but only for a limited time. Wrongdoers were supposed to make their confessions and then face secular judges. The *Capitulare legibus additum* also delineates the range of judicial actions within various legal systems. While Chapter 3 formulates that ecclesiastical judges are not competent in criminal cases but only secular judges (public examination), Chapter 10 regulates possible appeals.

4.3 *Canon Law*

There were many different law-makers in canon law. At each level of the Church, men were engaged in legal affairs: settling disputes, making new rules and reordering older rules in new canonical collections. The bishop of Rome, the pope, was the most venerated bishop of the Western Church and in charge of matters that applied to the whole Church. On a regional level, bishops tried to enforce discipline among the clergy and the people so that they would lead a faithful, Christian, life. Abbots led their monasteries and resolved quarrels

28 *MGH Capit. I [Capitularia regum Francorum], Alfred Boretius (ed.), Hannover, Hahnsche Buchhandlung, 1883, Nr. 39, 113–114:* Haec sunt capitula quae domnus Karolus magnus imperator iussit scribere in consilio suo et iussit eas ponere inter alias leges.

1. De homicidiis clericorum. Si quis subdiaconum occiderit, CCC solidos componat; qui diaconum, CCCC; qui presbiterum, DC; qui episcopum, DCCCC solidos componat; qui monachum, CCCC solidis culpabilis iudicetur.

3. Si quis ad ecclesiam confugium fecerit, in atrio ipsius ecclesiae pacem habeat, nec sit ei necesse ecclesiam ingredi, et nullus eum inde per vim abstrahere praesumat; sed liceat ei confiteri quod fecit et inde per manus bonorum hominum ad discussionem in publico perducatur.

4. Si quis hominem in iudicio iniuste contra alio altercantem adiuvare per malum ingenium praesumpserit atque inde coram iudicibus vel comite increpatus fuerit et negare non potuerit, solidis XV culpabilis iudicetur.

9. Omnia debita quae ad partem regis solvere debent, solidis duodecim denariorum solvant, excepto freda quae in lege Saliga scripta est; illa eodem solido quo caeterae compositiones solvi debent componatur.

10. Si quis causam iudicatam repetere in mallo praesumpserit ibique testibus convictus fuerit, aut quindecim solidos componat, aut quindecim ictus ab scabinis qui causam prius iudicaverunt accipiat.

among the brethren and the surrounding peasants. To react to the needs of their time, popes, bishops and abbots made new rules. The letter of Pope Siricius is a prime example of papal law-making (see see p. 94–5); the following texts illustrate episcopal attempts to impose new rules and to harmonize existing ones. The first text stems from a Carolingian bishop, Theodulf (ninth century), the second from an Ottonian, Burchard (eleventh century). Theodulf (d. 821) was a writer and poet and, as bishop of Orléans (France), engaged in the administration of his diocese. He worried about the conditions in his diocese, for example, the state of the churches (see below c. 8) and admonished the clergy to lead a disciplined life (without drunkenness, avoiding taverns and women) and to teach the children entrusted to their care (c. 20).

> *Theodulf of Orléans, 1. Capitulary*
> *George E. McCracken and Allen Cabaniss, Early Medieval Theology (The Library of Christian Classics 9), London, SCM Press, 1957, 382, 384, 387*
> Theodulph to our brothers and fellow presbyters, the priests of the diocese of Orléans. …
> 8. We frequently see in churches harvested crops and hay piled up, and for this reason we wish it to be thoroughly observed that nothing should be stored in a church except ecclesiastical vestments and holy vessels and books, lest by chance if businesses are being carried on other than should be, we may hear from the Lord, 'My house shall be called a house of prayer, but you have made it a brigands' cave'.
> 20. Let the presbyters keep schools in the villages and hamlets, and if any of the faithful desires to entrust his small children to them to be taught their letters, let them not refuse to receive and teach them, but let them teach them with the greatest love, noticing what is written: 'They, however, who shall be learned shall shine as the splendor of the firmament, and they who instruct many to righteousness shall shine as the stars forever and ever'. When, therefore, they teach them, let them demand no fee for this instruction, nor take anything from them, except what the parents shall offer them freely through zeal of love.[29]

29 Theodulf of Orléans, 1. Capitulary, preface, cc. 8 and 20, Peter Brommer (ed.), MGH capit. episc. 1, Hannover, Hahnsche Buchhandlung, 1984, 73–142: Theodulfus fratribus et compresbyteris nostris Aurelianensis parrochiae sacerdotibus in domino salutem. … c. 8 Videmus crebro in ecclesiis messes et fenum congeri. Unde volumus, ut hoc penitus observetur, ut nihil in ecclesia praeter vestimenta ecclesiastica et vasa sancta et libri recondantur, ne forte, si alia ibi, quam oportet, negotia exerceantur, a domino audiamus: Domus mea domus orationis vocabitur, vos autem fecistis eam speluncam latronum. c. 20 Presbyteri per villas et vicos scolas habeant. Et si quilibet fidelium suos parvulos

Two hundred years later, Burchard, the bishop of Worms (1000–25), also tried to improve the administration of his diocese and the clergy's education. He stumbled over a plethora of canons, often contradicting each other, often missing details. He complained in the preface to his collection that even the most erudite scholar would have had difficulties in applying these canons. To tackle these issues, Burchard compiled his 'Book of Decretals' (*Liber Decretorum*), a famous and widely used compilation of canon law of pre-Gratian times. What did Burchard consider a problem, and how did he tackle it?

> *Burchard of Worms, Liber Decretorum, Preface*
> *Robert Somerville and Bruce C. Brasington (ed.), Prefaces to Canon law Books in Latin Christianity. Selected Translations, 500–1245, New Haven, London, Yale University Press, 1998, 99–100*
> For a long time now, intimate and most dear brother [the addressee of the dedicatory letter], in person you frequently urged that with a careful mind I should compile into one corpus from various useful things – from the statements of the holy Fathers, from the canons, and from diverse penitentials – a little book for the work of our fellow priests. And for this reason especially: because in our diocese the laws of the canons and the judgments for those doing penance are confused, varied, and disordered … Whence it frequently happens that for those fleeing to the remedy of penance, both on account of the confusion of the books and also the ignorance of the priests, help in no way is at hand. Why is this? I believe that it happens especially because the canons do not prescribe for each and every offense the gravity of the sin and the amount of time for doing penance carefully, clearly, and fully enough in order to tell for individual cases how each sin should be corrected, but, rather, they state that it ought to be left to the judgment of an understanding priest. Wherefore, because this cannot be done except by the wise and those learned in divine law, you, beloved, requested that I deliver this little book.[30]

---

ad discendas litteras eis commendare vult, eos suscipere et docere non rennuant, sed cum summa caritate eos doceant attendentes illud, quod scriptum est: Qui autem docti fuerint, fulgebunt quasi splendor firmamenti. Et quia iustitiam erudiunt multos, fulgebunt quasi stellae in perpetuas aeternitates. Cum ergo eos docent, nihil ab eis pretii pro hac re exigant nec aliquid ab eis accipiant excepto, quod eis parentes caritatis studio sua voluntate obtulerint.

30 Burchard of Worms, Liber Decretorum, preface, Gérard Fransen (ed.), in Gérard Fransen and Theo Kölzer, Burchard von Worms. Decretorum Libri XX. Ergänzter Neudruck der Editio Princeps Köln 1548, Aalen, Scientia, 1992, 99–100: Multis iam sępe diebus familiaritas tua, frater carissime, praesens nobis hortando suggessit, quatenus libellum ex

4.4 *Byzantine Law*

To illustrate a similar variety of law-makers in Byzantine law, it is possible to refer to a constitution issued by emperor Romanos II between 959 and 963. The constitution itself deals with the *prostimon*, a penalty for the breach of a contract.

> *Marie Theres Fögen, Legislation in Byzantium: A Political and a Bureaucratic Technique, in Angeliki E. Laiou and Dieter Simon (eds), Law and Society in Byzantium: Ninth-Twelfth Centuries, Washington D.C., Dumbarton Oaks Research Library and Collection: Distributed by Harvard University Press, 1994, 61–62*
>
> In Zachariae's edition, the constitution is headed by the words: Νεαρὰ νομοθεσία τοῦ αὐτοῦ ἦν, ὑπηγόρευσε συμεὼν πατρίκιος καὶ πρωτασηκρῆτις, περὶ προστίμων. 'New legislation of the same emperor (i.e., Romanos), which the *patrikios* and *protasektaris* Symeon formulated, about (contractual) penalties'.
>
> It is not surprising that it was not the emperor himself who composed the Novel. Emperors usually have more important things to do and are, perhaps with the peculiar exception of Leo the Wise, Byzantine emperor from 886 to 912, hardly able and willing to waste their time formulating nicely polished laws. So, it is not the fact that the emperor did not compose the Novel himself that is noteworthy, but, rather, that the heading of this Novel mentions the name of the real author. ... If in the tenth century we get to know remarkably often the names of the functionaries who composed the imperial laws, in the eleventh century we find such a case only once. Instead, we are now informed with an almost equally remarkable frequency of the persons or institutions who *stimulated* the emperors to issue laws. In eight cases the petitioners or reporters, usually persons with some official rank and public office, are mentioned by name, in other seven cases we are told that an anonymous official,

---

variis utilitatibus ad opus conpresbyterorum nostrorum tam ex diversis poenitentialibus vigilanti animo corpus in unum colligerem ob id maxime, quia canonum iura et iudicia poenitentium in nostra diocesi sic sunt confusa ... Unde fit plerumque, ut confugientibus ad remedium poenitentiae tam pro librorum confusione quam etiam presbyterorum ignorantia nullatenus valeat subveniri. Cur hoc? Inde aestimo evenire maxime, quia mensuram temporis et modum delicti in agenda poenitentia non satis attente et aperte et perfecte praefigunt canones pro unoquoque crimine, ut de singulis dicant qualiter unumquodque emendandum sit, sed magis in arbitrio sacerdotis intellegentis relinquendum statuunt. Quapropter quia hoc nisi a sapientibus et legis divinę eruditis fieri nequit, rogavit me dilectio tua, ut hunc libellum breviter collectum.

> or the clergy or the imperial court had asked the emperor for a rescript, and five laws – either confirmative or dispositive – are directed to the patriarch and the synod. That means the emperors seldom acted alone, nor did they take the initiative as a rule; more often they were invited or requested to issue laws.
>
> The first information we derived from our 'leading' Novel on contractual penalties – that it was formulated by the functionary Symeon – may thus be cautiously generalized: imperial legislation was representatively and frequently provoked by imperial officials and some other persons who referred topical legal questions to the emperor, who in his turn entrusted, at least in the tenth century, the composition of his legislation to identifiable officials. In short, bureaucracy was working for bureaucracy, the higher staff for the lower staff.

The analysis of Fögen shows the various actors that interacted in the process of making and adapting law. Only a few rulers saw law-making as a central feature of their government and became active in it themselves. The ones who did quickly earned a reputation of being wise, learned, or even that of being a philosopher-king.

4.5 *Summary*

It is difficult to sketch the ideal types of the various lawmakers of the Early Middle Ages: it is challenging to give a systematic account of all legislative and legal activities, and they are much easier to detect under the Roman Emperors. The judicial offices were not clearly defined because of the many other offices that existed. Courts were convened by the king, bishops, counts, provosts and even peasants. In sum, actors ranged from pope to *populus*. Often, parties were not forced to engage legal experts but could use extrajudicial resources ranging from absence, corruption and blackmail to the use of the sword. As we saw with the Salian law, military and violent solutions were common, and legal procedures were often bypassed.

Questions

1. In which manner did the instability of the political system support the application of Roman, Germanic and Canon law?
2. Legal actors operating in a hybrid legal culture will encounter certain difficulties. Can you name some of them?
3. How do differences in terms of authority and financing affect the work of legal actors?

4. Competing law-making processes can be distinguished in the early medieval period. Discuss some of them.
5. What methods of extrajudicial conflict resolution were popular in the early medieval period?

5 Application

The issue of the application of the law raises the question of the relationship between societal strategies of conflict resolution and the rule of law. Our discussion will highlight the many nuances in the binding force of the various laws and law courts in different ethnic, religious and social contexts. The Early Middle Ages were a period in which law was applied based on a specific person (application *ad hominem*) and a specific situation (application *ad hoc*). Individuals were more closely connected to small and medium-sized groups than a particular territory, which made the territorial application of the law impossible. Verdicts were based more on the facts of the case than on complex laws. Above all, the application of the law was – more often than not – frustrated by inapropriate political interference from a monarch, or because it was ignored by those who were to follow it. At first glance, however, the examples of the application of rules in the Early Middle Ages are widespread, namely from treason to self-help and compositions, and from the crime of lèse-majesté to repentance. This chapter aims at identifying some common themes, among which is certainly the gap between 'law in action' and 'law in the books'.

Additionally, this chapter highlights the striking similarity between quite disparate sources, namely the *leges* and penitentials (texts prescribing a certain penance for sins), as both contain lists providing the reader with the appropriate consequence for a certain type of misbehavior. In particular, there are strong examples from Germanic and canon law, namely the Germanic *rachinburgen*, wise men, who acted as arbiters, and the evolution of ecclesiastical courts. The evolution of both institutes demonstrates a development from a 'private' to a 'public' form of reaction to misbehavior.

5.1 *Roman Vulgar Law*

Evidence for the application of Roman legal rules and concepts in the Early Middle Ages can be found in the existence of normative texts (procedural law) – these are rare in this period – and by the analysis of the reception of legal procedures in narrative sources. This is especially true for Roman vulgar law. The application of these complex legal texts did not meet the needs of the population. Neither was it possible to pursue claims through different stages of appeal nor to have the problem resolved when the laws were contradictory. In addition, it was not clear if judges basing their verdicts on Roman law were able to enforce acceptance of their decisions. It is, therefore, important to analyze the application of the law from a broader historical perspective.

A good example to demonstrate the application of Roman law in the later contexts are the laws against traitors in late Antiquity. We will explore how the draconian laws against the *crimen laesae maiestatis* formulated in late Antiquity were transformed and applied in the post-imperial world. The severity of the law was a product of the enormous political tensions during the reign of the emperors Arcadius and Honorius at the end of the fourth century. The relevant regulations on how to deal with high treason were enacted under the title *Lex Quisquis* on 4 September 397.

It should be noted that as often in Roman law, jurists used the first word of a law as a name for the whole law. As the law begins with the words *Quisquis cum militibus*, the jurists called it *Lex Quisquis*.

The regulations of the *Lex Quisquis* are part of the two large Roman legal collections, in the *Codex Theodosianus* (put into effect by Theodosius II in 438) as Cod. Th. IX,14,3, and in the Codex Justinianus (issued by Justinian in 529/534) as C. 9.8.5. Strangely enough, the title in the *Codex Theodosianus* was not inserted to deal with high treason, but subsumed under the title for manslaughter, 'To the Cornelian Law on Daggers' (*Ad Legem Corneliam de Sicariis*).

> *C. 9.8.5 Lex Quisquis (Arcadius and Honorius, 397 AD)*
> *The Codex of Justinian: A New Annotated Translation, with Parallel Latin and Greek Text Based on a Translation by Justice Fred H. Blume, Cambridge, Cambridge University Press, 2016, 2298–2299 (transl. by Timothy Kearley)*
> Emperors ARCADIUS and HONORIUS Augusti to Eutychianus, Praetorian Prefect. Whoever forms a criminal organization together with soldiers, civilians, even barbarians, or offers to others or takes an oath that binds the group together, or plots the murder even of *viri illustres* (honourable men) who participate in Our deliberations and Council, (and) of senators too, since they are a part of Our government, and, finally of anyone at all working in the imperial service, shall himself, to be sure, inasmuch as he is guilty of treason (*maiestas*), be executed with the sword, and all of his property shall be confiscated by Our Treasury. For the laws (*iura*) have required that the intention to commit such a wicked act be punished with the same rigor as its actual commission.
>
> 1. But to his sons We grant the remission of a death sentence through a special act of clemency, since they, in whom precedents of parental, meaning inherited, criminality are a source of fear, ought (in principle) to

> be punished through execution, as was their father. They shall (however) be denied the right of inheritance or succession to the property of their mother, their grandparents, as well as all their close relatives. They shall take nothing left to them in the wills of non-relatives. They shall ever be needy and poor. They shall forever be accompanied by their father's legal infamy (*infamia*), so that they shall never be admitted to political offices or any oaths of loyalty at all. Finally, they shall be such that for them, as they languish in a permanent state of need, death shall be a consolation and life a punishment.[31]

The offence of high treason, and the potential to use it as a tool to wipe out opposition and enemies of the state, also existed in post-Roman communities. In his book called 'Histories', the bishop and historian Gregory of Tours used the term *crimen laese maiestatis* five times and *reus maiestatis* once.[32] He reserves the uses of the word *maiestas* exclusively for God or Jesus. This is an indication that the meaning of specific words originating in Antiquity was shifting. While authors of the sixth century ascribed *maiestas* to Jesus, the terminus technicus *crimen laese maiestatis* was applied to treason.

A very interesting application of the term *crimen* (*laese*) *maiestatis* can be found at the court of Charlemagne in the ninth century. We can actually track the moment the term re-entered legal discourse after it had been used in the texts of Gregory of Tours. It was introduced in a polemical context when one of the members of the court of Charlemagne wrote a text to justify why the legitimate ruler of Bavaria, Duke Tassilo III, had to meet such a dramatic end: Tassilo was summoned before Charlemagne in Ingelheim in 788 and accused of many

31 C. 9.8.5 Imperatores Arcadius, Honorius. Quisquis cum militibus vel privatis, barbaris etiam scelestam inierit factionem aut factionis ipsius susceperit sacramenta vel dederit, de nece etiam virorum illustrium qui consiliis et consistorio nostro intersunt, senatorum etiam (nam et ipsi pars corporis nostri sunt), cuiuslibet postremo qui nobis militat cogitarit (eadem enim severitate voluntatem sceleris qua effectum puniri iura voluerunt), ipse quidem utpote maiestatis reus gladio feriatur, bonis eius omnibus fisco nostro addictis: 1. Filii vero eius, quibus vitam imperatoria specialiter lenitate concedimus (paterno enim deberent perire supplicio, in quibus paterni, hoc est hereditarii, criminis exempla metuentur), a materna vel avita, omnium etiam proximorum hereditate ac successione habeantur alieni, testamentis extraneorum nihil capiant, sint perpetuo egentes et pauperes, infamia eos paterna semper comitetur, ad nullos umquam honores, nulla prorsus sacramenta perveniant, sint postremo tales, ut his perpetua egestate sordentibus sit et mors solacio et vita supplicio.

32 Gregor von Tours, Decem libri historiarum, Bruno Krusch and Wilhelm Levison (eds), Hannover, Hahn, 1951 (MGH SS rer. Mer. 1, 12), Hist. V,25 p. 232; Hist. VI,37, p. 309, Hist. IX,13, p. 427, Hist. IX,14, p. 428, Hist. X,19, p. 512f., Hist. V,25, p. 232; Hist. V,27, p. 233.

crimes, documented in an account of the trial in the Royal Frankish Annals. Written only a little after 788, one version does not use the term *crimen laese maiestatis*. However, a later version of the Royal Frankish Annals, written after 814, clearly did. Tassilo was accused of the *crimen maiestatis* and *crimen laesae maiestatis*.

> *Annales Einhardi, F. Kurze (ed.), Hannover, Hahn, 1950, 81 (transl. by Gerald Schwedler)*
> In the year DCCCLXXVIII. As the king decreed in the same village a general assembly and ordered duke Tassilo and other vassals to that named assembly; and he, as was ordered, came to the presence of the king, was accused by the Bavarians of the *crimen maiestatis*. [list of various allegations] Of these he did not start to refute a single one, but was – with the consent of all – convicted guilty and sentenced to death due to lèse-majesté.[33]

Why is there no mention of the fact that Tassilo had been accused of the *crimen laese maiestatis* in the first version of around 788? Why does it appear in the second version after 814? What happened in the meantime? On Christmas Day in the year 800 (25 December 800), Charlemagne was crowned Emperor in Rome. He assumed the title and rights of imperial *maiestas*. From then on, the crime of *laese maiestatis* could be committed against him. Later kings (also those who did not wear the imperial crown) also demanded protection against this crime originating in Roman law. It was incorporated in the Golden Bull (1356), and it also covered the Electors. The Electors or *Kurfürsten* were the seven princes of the Holy Roman Empire who had a right to vote in the election of the future emperor: the archbishops of Mainz, Cologne, and Trier as well as the king of Bohemia, the duke of Saxony, the count palatine of the Rhine and the margrave of Brandenburg. The immunity and protection of today's heads of state and members of parliament is nothing but a distant echo of the severe Roman legislation on *laese maiestatis*.

The Carolingian application – or, so to speak, the revival – of the crime of *laese maiestatis* and its adaptation to new political realities reintroduced the crime and the applicable penalties. Probationary torture, death by the sword or the systematic confiscation of the perpetrator's property, as well as the fact

33 Annales Einhardi, F. Kurze (ed.), Hannover, Hahn, 1950, 81: [Anno] DCCLXXXVIII. Cum in eadem villa generalem populi sui rex conventum fieri decrevisset ac Tassilonem ducem sicut et ceteros vassos suos in eodem conventu adesse iussisset atque ille, ut ei fuerat imperatum, ad regis praesentiam pervenisset, crimine maiestatis a Baioariis accusatus est.

that a whole family could be held liable for a crime of a single person, became characteristic features of later legal practices. The reintroduction of the penalties for the *crimen laese maiestatis* also shows that the revival of Roman law did not necessarily mean the that the law became more humane.

5.2 *Germanic Law*[34]

Rothari (ca. 606–652) reigned as king over the Lombards in what today is Italy (636–652). To protect the empire's internal security, he enacted a written collection of laws after obtaining the consent of the nobility in 643, the so-called *Edictum Rothari*. One passage reads:

> Of brawls and wound fines: if they occur amongst free men, they will be atoned in the way described below, and the feud, that is, the enmity, will cease.[35]

Then follow thirty sentences which establish a penalty for knocked out eyes or teeth, hacked off noses or ears, and for many other injuries. The list concludes with the exhortation that:

> In the case of all the blows and stab wounds described above, which occur amongst free men, we have prescribed higher penalties than the former ones for the reason that feud, that is enmity, shall be abandoned after the receipt of the penalty mentioned above, and no evil intention shall remain. Instead, the matter shall cease, and friendship shall prevail.[36]

This brings to light an aspiration that runs like a golden thread through Germanic tribal laws: the desire to replace self-help in the form of long and bloody feuds with peaceful reconciliation through the payment of fines. The

---

34 For this see also above 'A case from the Liber Papiensis: King Liutprand († 744) and the Women Raiders'.

35 Edictus Langobadorum, Georg Heinrich Pertz (ed.), MGH LL 4, Hannover, Hahn, 1868, 20: 45. De feritas et conpositionis plagarum, quae inter hominis liberûs eveniunt, per hoc tinorem, sicut subter adnexum est conponatur, cessante faida hoc est inimicitia.

36 Edictus Langobadorum, Georg Heinrich Pertz (ed.), MGH LL 4, Hannover, Hahn, 1868, 23: 74. In omnis istas plagas aut feritas superius scriptas, quae inter hominis liberos evenerint, ideo maiorem conpositionem posuimus quam antiqui nostri, ut faida, quod est inimicitia, post accepta suprascripta conpositione postponatur, et amplius non requiratur, nec dolus teneatur, sed sit sibi causa finita, amicitia manentem. Et si contigerit de ipsas plagas intra anni spatium qui plagatus est mori, tunc ille qui eum plagavit conponat, qualiter in angargathungi, id est secundum qualitatem personae.

long catalogues of penalties that were created for this purpose shaped the tribal laws for a long time. They reflect the rough and tumble, even violent, day-to-day life of militant peasant people. They undoubtedly reflect the violent reality of Germanic life when they announce that the plundering of a burial mound incurs a fine or that the test to determine the seriousness of a wound is to throw fragments of bone over a path against a shield to see whether they make a loud noise. It is certain that with the decline of the Roman Empire, there was a gradual breakdown of the administration and justice. This caused an increase in self-help. However, what the Germanic laws say about feud and penance deserves particular attention. It provides us some insight into the development of the law of the Germanic tribes that settled on the soil of the former empire.

The purpose of the fine is to compensate the injured party and to open the door to reconciliation. The compensation is determined based on the stolen object's value or the severity of the inflicted wound. The penance for manslaughter ('Wergeld') is fixed according to the dead man's social rank. The text cited from the *Edictum Rothari* shows that the kings that made laws also occasionally adjusted the fines; in doing so, they probably drew on Roman rules for compensation. In the majority of cases, however, the fines are not the creation of the lawmakers. Instead, they are the codification of penances negotiated in countless penance proceedings between feuding groups or families, between the perpetrator and the injured party and his or her supporters. It is reasonable to assume that one usually sought the help of experienced arbiters, who had frequently acted as an arbiter or in an advisory capacity in similar cases. These – one may call them legally trained – men were consulted for the first codification of the penances, and the catalogues of penances were based on their responses. That this happened is particularly clear in the older prologue of the *Lex Salica*.

It appears that fines were agreed upon and paid even when there were no proper courts. Some parts of the Germanic laws still seem to reflect this older state of affairs. The Franconian *rachineburgii* could be arbiters who, as 'Rechenbürgen', determined the fine and weighed whether the penance was sufficient. The number of shillings, in which the fines were expressed in the codified laws, only seem to have been used to determine the value of the penalty. The real fines were 'paid' by surrendering cattle or horses, precious weapons or hunting falcons, and even by ceding land. To evaluate and decide these issues required legally trained men, but not an actual court. One may have attempted to settle disputes and arrange the payment of fines in early times at the 'Thing Assemblies'. These sacred meetings took place under the protection of the gods and provided a safe space for a meeting of feuding groups. This procedure certainly opened the way for the influence of royal authority. It was not until the Early Middle Ages, influenced by Roman law, that legal scholars who helped the parties come to a judgment in the case, installed a judge who opened and conducted the proceedings and announced the verdict at the end. This started the division between judges and jurors which dominated the entire Middle Ages until the scholarly law gained ground. The nineteenth century sought to reclaim this division in an effort to guarantee that the people played a role in decision making.

The modest authority of courts in the Middle Ages provides more evidence that their origins lie in the arbitration procedure. Phrases like 'the perpetrator owes the determined fine' or 'he is to be sentenced to' keep recurring in the catalog of penances. They only mean that for a crime of that type, a particular fine applies. However, the obligation to pay the fine itself is not founded in the judgment but requires a contract or at least a vow on the perpetrator's part. And for a long time, the difficult problem remained how to get the perpetrator make that vow and actually be able to enforce it. That the judgment itself originally did not create the obligation to pay is clear from the fact that the judgment was often made before it was determined whether the defendant had really committed the crime for which the penance was claimed. So the term judgment seems to have had two possible meanings: first, that the defendant should either prove that he was not guilty of what he was accused of; or, second, if he could not prove his innocence, that a fine applied.[37]

> *Leges Alamannorum* [*8th c.*] (*transl. by Bernd Kannowski*)
> § 1. A man beating another man in anger shall pay one shilling. This is called bruise by the Alemanni.
> § 2. However, if he spills blood onto the ground he shall pay one and a half shilling.
> § 3. However, if the brainpan becomes visible because of the beating and [the brainpan] is hurt, he shall pay three shillings.
> § 4. However, for ripping a bone fragment out of the head wound which clinks on a shield when thrown over a public road 24 feet wide, a man shall pay six shillings.
> § 5. However, if the doctor looses it [the bone fragment] and cannot show it, he shall provide two witnesses who saw him [the wrongdoer] ripping a

37 See below: Two-tongued judgement. K. Kroeschell, Deutsche Rechtsgeschichte I. Bis 1250 (13th ed.), Cologne, Weimar, Vienna, Böhlau, 2008, 35–37.

bone fragment out of that wound, or the doctor shall prove the fact that he [the wrongdoer] had ripped a bone fragment out of that wound.
§ 6. However, if the brainpan is broken open, making the brain appear so that the doctor can touch it with a feather or a cloth, a man shall pay twelve shillings.
§ 7. However, if occasionally the brain leaks out of the wound and the doctor has to bandage it with a remedy or a silk cloth and he can heal it and this is proven, it is to be paid with 40 shillings.
§ 8. If a man cuts off another mans ear and the other man does not become deaf, he shall pay twelve shillings.
§ 9. However, if he cuts it off completely making him deaf, he shall pay 40 shillings.
§ 10. However, if he cuts off half the ear he shall pay 6 shillings. This is called notch by the Alemanni.[38]

In a world without the effective authority of the state, there was much more violence than there is today. It resulted in a high number of violent deaths in the Early Middle Ages. In the late sixth century – a period of which there are very few sources indeed – bishop Gregory of Tours (d. 593) tells us about violent conflicts in the French (then Franconian) city of Tours. It becomes clear that the parties involved saw the court only as one possible avenue to enforce their legal claims. Another option was to take the law into their own hands through

38 *Karl Lehmann, Karl August Eckhardt (eds) (MGH LL nat. Germ. 5,1,), Hannover, Hahn, 1966, LVII, 116 -118, Art. 57:*
1. Si quis alium per iram percusserit, quod Alamanni "pulislac" dicunt, cum uno solido conponat.
2. Si autem sanguinem fuderit, sic ut terra tangat, conponat solido uno et semis.
3. Si enim percusserit eum, ut testa appareat et radatur, eum 3 solidis conponat.
4. Si autem de capite ossum fractum de plaga tullerit, ita ut super publica via lata 24 pedis in scuto sonaverit ille ossus, cum 6 solidis conponat.
5. Si autem ipsum perdit medicus et non potest eum praesentare, tunc duos testes adhibeat, qui hoc vidissent, quod de illa plaga ossus tullisset, aut ille medicus hoc conprobet, quod verum fuisset, quod de ipsa plaga ossus tullisset.
6. Si autem testa trescapulata fuerit, ita ut cervella appareant, ut medicus cum pinna aut cum fanone cervella tetigit, cum 12 solidis conponat.
7. Si autem ex ipsa plaga cervella exierunt, sicut solet contingere, ut medicus cum medicamento aut cum sirico stuppavit, et postea sanavit, et hoc probatum est, quod verum sit, cum 40 solidis conponat.
8. Si quis aliquis aurem alterius absciderit et non exsurdaverit, 12 solidos conponat.
9. Si autem sic absciderit profundo et eum exsurdaverit, 40 solidos conponat.
10. Si enim medietatem aurem absciderit, quod 'scardi' Alamanni dicunt, cum sex solidis conponat.

self-help. This was inevitable in a world without a state monopoly on the use of force. This solution was accepted by the community, at least under certain conditions. Because of this it is even possible to say that there was a right to wage feuds, which only disappeared at the beginning of the modern age.

Gregory of Tours, The History of the Franks [6th c.]. Transl. with an introd. by Lewis Thorpe, Harmondsworth etc., London, Penguin, 1974, 428–429. Excerpt from Book VII (transl. by Lewis Thorpe)

A most serious civil discord now arose between the citizens of Tours. When Sichar, the Son of John, was enjoying himself in the village of Manthelan, as part of the Christmas festivities, with Austregesil and a number of other local folk, the village priest sent one of his servants to invite some of the men to come and have a drink in his house. When the servant arrived, one of the men who were invited drew his sword and hit him. He fell down dead. Sichar was a personal friend of the priest. As soon as he heard that the priest's servant had been killed, he seized his weapons and went to the church to wait for Austregesil. When Austregesil was informed of this, he snatched up his own weapons and went to look for Sichar. A pitched battle ensued. In the end a number of people slipped away on both sides, and Sichar was brought safely out by some of the clerics. He sought refuge in the country estate where he lived. In the priest's house he left behind four of his servants who had been wounded, together with some money and some of his effects. Once Sichar had fled, Austregesil launched a second attack, killed the four servants, and stole the gold and silver with the other things. The two parties were called up before a tribunal of citizens. Their verdict was that Austregesil, who had committed murder, killed Sichar's servants and removed his goods without having any right to them, was guilty in the eyes of the law. A few days after the case had been tried, Sichar heard that the goods which Austregesil had stolen were now in the hands of a man called Auno, Auno's son, and his brother Eberulf. Sichar thereupon dismissed the tribunal from his mind as if it had never been, sought the help of a certain Audinus and started an affray by attacking those three in the middle of the night with a gang of armed men. He broke into the house where they were sleeping, murdered Auno, his son and his brother, killed their servants and stole not only all their portable property but also their herds.[39]

39 Gregory of Tours, Historiae VII, 47: Bruno Krusch and Wilhelm Levison (eds), Gregorii episcopi Turonensis. Libri historiarum X, MGH Scriptores rerum Merovingicarum 1.1 (rev. ed.), Hannover, Hahn, 1884, 366–367: Gravia tunc inter Toronicos cives bella civilia

The case of Sichar has been the topic of scholarly debate for at least 200 years.[40] French scholars emphasized the illegitimate nature of Sichar's act as part of a sequence of ever escalating conflicts that were finally prosecuted by the Franconian king Childebert II, who rendered his verdict (expropriation and exile). However, German scholars argued that Sichar's reaction was the first example of a legal institution called 'feud' (*Fehde*), based on individual liberties, lack of central authority and the need for local conflict resolution. The 'feud' of Sichar is a good example of conflicts and the various options of conflict resolution within a hybrid community of Franks and Gallo-Romans. It shows that legal institutions such as feud are the subject of an ongoing scholarly debate. After a close reading of the historiographical sources (with the difficulties of translation and interpretation it entails), a final consensus has still not been reached, even after 200 years of research.

The spoken word was a formative element of medieval law. In an oral context, the form an action takes and its execution, and the rituals of law, have a greater importance than in a legal culture based on writing. Therefore, the law of the Middle Ages is, in essence, procedural law. How a decision is arrived at is more important than what the final decision is. Customs do not play a subordinate role to written legal rules; custom itself constitutes the law (the law *is* custom, not merely based *on* custom). Due to the absence of the stability inherent

surrexerunt. Nam Sicharius, Iohannis quondam filius, dum ad natalis dominici solemnia apud Montalomaginsim vicum cum Austrighyselo reliquosque pagenses caelebraret, presbiter loci misit puerum ad aliquorum hominum invitationem, ut ad domum eius bibendi gratia venire deberint. Veniente vero puero, unus ex his qui invitabantur, extracto gladio, eum ferire non metuit. Qui statim cecidit et mortuus est. Quod cum Sicharius audisset, qui amicitias cum presbitero retinebat, quod scilicet puer eius fuerit interfectus, arrepta arma ad eclesiam petit, Austrighyselum opperiens. Ille autem haec audiens, adpraehenso armorum apparatu, contra eum diregit. Mistisque omnibus, cum se pars utraque conliderit, Sicharius inter clericos ereptus, ad villam suam effugit, relictis in domo presbiteri cum argento et vestimentis quattuor pueris sauciatis. Quo fugiente, Austrighyselus iterum inruens, interfectis pueris, aurum argentumque cum reliquis rebus abstulit. Dehinc cum in iudicio civium convenissent et praeceptum esset, ut Austrighyselus, qui homicida erat et, interfectis pueris, res sine audientia diripuerat, censura legali condempnaretur, inito placito, paucis infra diebus sicharius audiens, quod res, quas Austrighyselus direpuerat, cum Aunone et filio adque eius fratre Eberulfo retinerentur, postposito placito, coniunctus Audino, mota seditione, cum armatis viris inruit super eos nocte, elisumque hospicium, in quo dormiebant, patrem cum fratre et filio interemit resque eorum com pecoribus, interfectisque servis, abduxit.

40 Carsten Bernoth, Die Fehde des Sichar. Die Geschichte einer Erzählung in der deutschsprachigen und frankophonen rechtshistorischen und historischen Literatur unter besonderer Berücksichtigung der Auseinandersetzungen des 19. Jahrhunderts (= Rheinische Schriften zur Rechtsgeschichte 10), Nomos, Baden-Baden, 2008.

in the written word, an oral culture cannot establish the same precise norms as written law. Law can only be whatever the community decides it is through its continuing legal traditions. Law is whatever is valid in any given court.

Whether we can really speak of 'law' when dealing with these notional norms that grew out of local customs, morality or religion depends on whether the community actually prosecuted breaches of these rules and described them in language consistent with the commission of a crime. One has to keep in mind that judges did not enjoy the same position as they do today. They were not qualified legal experts deciding the case. The judge merely directed the proceedings and sought the final adjudication from the community affected by the court's decision. The judge established what the final judgment was, but he did not render it. In this respect, the parties were part of the court and did not stand *before* the court. Jürgen Weitzel has dealt with these phenomena in his important work on the subject "Dinggenossenschaft und Recht" (1985). In an article about court procedures in the Early Middle Ages, he summarizes some of his results as follows:

> *Jürgen Weitzel, 'Gerichtsverfahren', in Johannes Hoops et al. (eds), Reallexikon der germanischen Altertumskunde XI, Berlin, De Gruyter, 1997, 164–165 (transl. by Bernd Kannowski)*
>
> Overall, one has the impression of, in essence, surprisingly standardized legal procedures, whose regional features do not stand in the way of the adoption of West Franconian practices in the East in the 8th and 9th centuries. Franconian court procedures were clearly more rational and, therefore, more likely to accept the practice of the exchange of pertinent arguments than were those of the High Middle Ages. Older 'Germanic' based theories, probably under the influence of northern formalism, have underestimated the Roman influence. This becomes clear principally in the crucial area of the presentation of evidence. Nowhere do we read that in Franconian court proceedings the case would have had to be presented in a formal way [by the plaintiff] and be denied 'word for word' by the defendant or that a trial would have been lost as a result of a faux pas in either speech or gesture. Besides, older scholars did not accept any kind of formalism, either in their hypothetical 'prehistoric' tribal courts or in the Franconian royal courts, because there (it was claimed) decisions would have been made purely on the grounds of fairness. The distinction between procedures based strictly on law and those based on fairness is, however, unsound. This has been proven to be wrong for the Franconian royal courts, and it is, therefore, reasonable to assume that court actions, in general, did aspire to standardized procedures but only

adopted a strictly formal modus operandi in special cases, in particular of oath-taking and other ways of presenting evidence, as well as vows. Furthermore, many formal procedures are only known to us from normative texts, but not from original sources giving clear information about court practice.

A highly mysterious passage of the *Lex Salica*, interpretation of which is controversial among scholars, concerns the so-called 'earth cast'.

The Laws of the Salian Franks ['Lex Salica'], Philadelphia, University of Pennsylvania Press, 1991, 121–122 (transl. by Katherine Fischer)
Art. 58. Concerning the Chrenecruda (i.e., involving the kin in the payment of composition for homicide)
1. If anyone kills a man and, having given up all his property, he still does not have enough to pay the total composition, let him offer twelve oath-helpers [who will support his oath] that neither above the earth nor below the earth does he have more property than he has already given.
2. Afterwards he should enter his house and in his hand collect dust from its four corners, and then he should stand on the duropello, that is, on the threshold, looking into the house, and then with his left hand he should throw the earth over his shoulders onto him who is his nearest relative.
3. If his mother and brother have already paid [and the composition is still not fully paid], then he should throw the earth over the sister of his mother or her children. If there are none of these, then he should throw the earth over three from the maternal kin and three of the paternal kin who are next most nearly related.
3. If the father or mother or brother have already paid for him [and the composition is still not fully paid], then he should throw the earth over the sister of his mother or her children; but if there are none of these, [he should throw the earth] over those three from the paternal and maternal kin who are next most nearly related.
4. And afterwards without a shirt and barefoot, with a stick in hand, he should go jump over his fence [i.e., abandon his house?] and those three from the maternal side shall pay half of whatever is the value of the composition or the judgment set; and those others who come from the paternal side should do the same [i.e., pay the other half].

5. If any of these does not have that with which to pay his full share, let him who is poor throw the chrenecruda[41] over him who has more so that he pays the entire judgment.
6. If he does not have that with which to pay the entire judgment [if he does not have that with which to pay the judgment or make full composition], then he who has the man who committed the homicide in his surety (*sub sua fide*) should present him in court, and after presenting him in four courts, he may remove (*tollant*) his surety. And if no one exercises the surety for him by paying the composition, that is, does not pay that which would redeem him, then he shall make composition with his life [i.e., become a slave to the party to whom the composition is owed].
6a. At the present time, if a man does not have enough of his own property to pay or defend himself from the law, it is fitting that everything be done from the beginning as set out above.[42]

---

41 'Earth cast', explained in more detail below.

42 Pactus Legis Salicae, Karl August Eckhardt (ed.) (MGH LL nat. Germ. 4,1), Hannover, Hahn, 1962, LVIII, 218–221:
§ 1. Si quis hominem occiderit et, tota facultate data, non habuerit, unde ⟨conponat, ut⟩ totam legem impleat, XII iuratores donet, quod nec super terram nec subtus terram plus de facultate non habeat, quam iam donauit.
§ 2. Et postea sic debet in casa sua intrare et de quatuor angulos terrae [puluerem] in pugno colligere ⟨debet⟩, et sic postea in duropello, hoc est in limitare, stare debet, intus in casa respiciens, et sic de sinistra manu de illa terra trans scapulas suas iactare super illum, quem proximiorem parentem habet.
§ 3. Quod si iam pro illo et mater et frater solserunt, tunc super sororem matris aut super suos filios debet de illa terra iactare. ⟨Quod si ille non fuerit, de(bet) illa terra iacta(re)⟩, id est super tres de generatione matris ⟨et super tres de generatione patris⟩, qui proximiores sunt.
[§ 3. Quod si iam pater aut mater seu frater pro ipso soluerunt, tunc super sororem matris aut super eius filios debet illam terram iactare; quod si isti non fuerunt, super tres de generatione patris et matris, qui proximiores sunt.]
§ 4. Et sic postea in camisa discinctus ⟨et⟩ discalci⟨at⟩us, palo in manu ⟨sua⟩, sepe sallire debet, ut pro medietate, quantum de conpositione diger est aut quantum lex addicat, et illi tres soluant [de materna generatione]; hoc et illi alii, qui de paterna generatione ueniunt, similiter facere debent.
§ 5. Si quis uero de illis quicumque pauperior fuerit, ut non habeat, unde integrum debitum soluat, quicumque de illis plus [alio] habet, [exsoluat et] iterum super illum chrenecruda ille, qui pauperior est, iactet, ut ille totam legem ⟨per⟩soluat.
§ 6. Quod si uero nec ipse habuerit, unde totam legem ⟨per⟩soluat,
[§ 6. Quod si hic etiam non habet, ut legem soluat et totam legem componat,] tunc illum, qui homicidium fecit, ⟨ille⟩ qui eum sub ⟨sua⟩ fide habet, in mallo praesentare debet, et sic postea eum per quatuor mallos ad suam fidem tollant. Et si eum in conpositione

The text is taken from the *Lex Salica* (Salian Law), which dates from 507 to 511. It is part of the law code of a Germanic tribe, namely that of the Salian Franks (hence the name 'Lex Salica'). The historical records of specific Germanic peoples' laws are referred to as 'leges' by some researchers. The use of the Latin expression suggests that the texts frequently reflected a mixed legal culture composed of Roman and Germanic elements. The background of these laws is puzzling, particularly as it can hardly be assumed that written culture played a large role in the lives of the people of those days or even that they had any real familiarity with reading and writing in the proper sense of the words. Perhaps, the best explanation is that at a time characterized by regional instability and ubiquitous violence, the young Germanic imperial rulers wanted to model themselves after Roman examples. They regarded written codification of their laws as a means for establishing stability and a national identity.

The *Lex Salica*, in fact, is one of those 'Leges' where the influence of Roman law is very difficult to discern. It stands out from other Germanic codes because of the number of extant copies – over sixty manuscripts. The *Lex Salica* is also barely influenced by the Christian belief system.

The passage reproduced here is concerned with a perplexing and clearly ancient phenomenon – the so-called 'earth cast'. The *Lex Salica* is written in Latin – as are all the other Germanic codes from Continental Europe – although Frankish words are inserted on occasion to refer to judicial phenomena for which there was no appropriate Latin equivalent ('Malberg Glosses'). Thus the unknown author of the *Lex Salica* calls the ceremonial earth casting 'Crenecruda' when dealing with the following case.

One man has killed another and, as a result, has to live in fear that the relatives of the victim will revenge the killing. In Salian Law – as in other Germanic tribal codes – such a vendetta could be avoided by paying the relatives a fixed sum of money corresponding to the current valuation of the life of the deceased. The value of each individual (for the purpose of compensation – 'Wer(e)gild') is listed in comprehensive catalogues in all the tribal codes, including the *Lex Salica*. The next step is the so-called 'system of compositions',[43] applied when the perpetrator is not in a financial position to raise the money he owes. In a formal, quasi-magical ritual, as detailed in the text, he must now gather earth

nullus ad fidem tulerit, hoc est ut eum redemat de ⟨hoc⟩, quod non persolsit, ⟨tunc⟩ de sua uita conponat.

[§ 6a. At praesentibus temporibus, si de suis propriis rebus non habuerit, unde tran(s)soluere aut se de lege defensare possit, omnis caussa superius comprehensa ad caput suum pertinet obseruare.]

43 From the Latin 'compositio', meaning 'reparation' or 'damages' in this context.

from his house and, standing on his own front step, throw it over his shoulder at designated family members who are lined up behind him. After that, he must jump lightly dressed, shoeless and bearing a stick over his own fence. There are various interpretations of the significance of all this. According to some, all the perpetrator's possessions, particularly his land, are thereby transferred to his relatives. For others, this signifies that the perpetrator's person is thus transferred to his kin, who are now, on the one hand, obligated to pay on his behalf, but who, on the other hand, equally may well hand him over to his pursuers without any consequences for themselves. The duty to pay is transferred on a next-of-kin basis, but insolvent relatives can pass on the earth cast to the next in line.

All this may be understood as a kind of 'Westfranconian insolvency proceeding'. It begins with a form of 'oath of disclosure' by the person who committed the killing. If the money necessary to compensate the victim is not raised in this way, it becomes possible to involve more distant relatives in the proceedings. This can be done by way of a 'public summoning' but without recourse to the earth cast. A person has to be found who will guarantee that the culprit will appear at the next four court sessions. This will provide his more distant relatives with the opportunity to raise the necessary money and pay it to the deceased's relatives. If this happens, the perpetrator is thereby released and the vendetta against him withdrawn. If by the fourth court session the necessary sum of money has still not been raised, then, finally, nothing stands in the way of the perpetrator's having to face the full enactment of the terms of the blood feud.

As detailed at the beginning of the text, the culprit must have his inability to pay testified to by twelve supporting 'oath helpers'. These 'oath helpers' are not our material witnesses. Consequently, they are not claiming in their statements that the perpetrator is in fact insolvent based on their own knowledge. They have not actively investigated whether the perpetrator can in fact not pay. They are simply supporting him in his oath. However, the 'oath helpers' are putting their own good name and reputation at risk when they state that the perpetrator is not committing perjury. In doing so, they are giving expression to their conviction that the perpetrator's moral integrity is such that they cannot imagine that he would commit perjury ('attestation of good character').

One characteristic of Germanic law which is commonly contrasted with Roman and the learned laws was the acceptance of judicial duels. Before the Germanic peoples' encounter with Rome, conflicts had been settled by arbitration or in a contest with winners and losers, i.e., by judicial duel. A legal concept based on 'ideas of justice' was unknown. As strange as this may seem to us today, originally, law and physical strength went hand in hand. The superordinate term 'justice' only developed later.[44] This is reminiscent of the right to wage feuds that we have previously encountered in the story told by bishop Gregory of Tours. In this case, too, it is necessary to find a solution for a conflict. In the bishop's story, the solution could be legal, but other methods were just as feasible and theoretically possible. From a modern vantage point, it is remarkable that one can either roll the dice or ask the judge for a decision. Both routes, however, could lead to a binding decision. And the more mysterious the provisions of the law, the closer these two approaches were. The following text shows how a legal question was decided at the highest level by a duel.

> *Day of Hearing of Otto I the Great in Steele near Essen in the year 938 (transl. by Bernd Kannowski)*
> An argument arose about diverging laws, since some claimed that grandchildren are not to be considered sons and hence may not share their grandfather's heritage with their sons in case of an eventual premature demise of their father. Therefore, the king ordered a gathering of the people near the village called Steele, where it was decided that this argument should be examined and decided by the arbitrators. However, the king heeded better advice and, not wanting the noble and the elderly to be treated disrespectfully, ordered that paid combatants should settle this dispute. The party in favor of including the grandchildren was victorious, and it was decided once and for all that they should share the heritage equally with their uncles.[45]

---

44 Clausdieter Schott, Traditionelle Formen der Konfliktlösung in der Lex Burgundionum, in La giustizia nell' alto medioevo (secoli V–VIII), Spoleto, Centro italiano di studi sull'alto Medioevo, 1995, 945, 958; František Graus, Die Gewalt bei den Anfängen des Feudalismus und die Gefangenenbefreiung der merowingischen Hagiographie, Jahrbuch für Wirtschaftsgeschichte 1 (1961), 63.

45 *Die Sachsengeschichte des Widukind von Korvei, H.E. Lohmann, Paul Hirsch (eds) (MGH SS rer. Germ. 60), Hannover, Hahn, 1935, 73:* De legum quoque varietate facta est et contentio, fueruntque qui dicerent, quia filii filiorum non deberent computari inter filios hereditatemque legitime cum filiis sortiri, si forte patres eorum obissent avis superstitibus. Unde exiit edictum a rege, ut universalis populi conventio fieret apud villam quae dicitur Stela; factumque est, ut causa inter arbitros iudicaretur debere examinari. Rex autem meliori consilio usus noluit viros nobiles ac senes populi inhoneste tractari, sed magis rem inter gladiatores discerni iussit. Vicit igitur pars, qui filios filiorum computabant inter filios, et firmatum est, ut aequaliter cum patruis hereditatem dividerent pacto sempiterno.

5.3 *Canon Law*

The application of canon law in the Early Middle Ages is quite difficult to assess. We have a substantial number of normative texts addressing questions of behavior, but few that provide a glimpse of the application of these texts in practice. For one, judgments were seldom transmitted, and – as most cases were orally decided – records are scarce. The example of the French bishop Saffaracus who was convicted, deposed and sent to a monastery by the Parisian Council in 552 is an exceptional case. Even though we know about his deposition and condemnation, we remain in the dark about the reasons for this verdict. It is important to note that fellow bishops heard and decided the case of Saffaracus. In general, bishops were important stakeholders in the application of the law, including in judging fellow bishops and presiding over trials in their own diocese. It is impossible to underestimate the importance of bishops for resolving disputes in this era. It was the responsibility of bishops to judge cases in which they were competent: matters of private law in which Church personnel (a priest, deacon, acolyte or a layman working in a monastery) were involved (jurisdiction *ratione personae*). A Church court also dealt with sins, as bishops, priests and monks tried to correct Christians' behaviour and impose penance on sinners (jurisdiction *ratione materiae*). A specific group of normative texts, the penitentiaries, tariffs with penance, and procedural rules, offer a glimpse of the sinners, their sinful behavior and the penances imposed before 1100. They provide us with some insight into the application of canon law. These sources present catalogues of sins and the appropriate consequences and procedures to follow. They are counted as canon 'law', although they deal with spiritual welfare, at least at first glance. Nonetheless, penitentials may be bound together with canonical collections in one book, and penitential provisions may even be mixed with canons so that they have a normative character and can be considered as binding.

The following text stems from a book by Regino, the abbot of the monastery in Prüm (diocese of Trier, Germany), who authored a bipartite treatise on the administration of a diocese and on hearing confessions at the beginning of the tenth century. This treatise underscores the bishop's function as an itinerant judge travelling in his diocese, checking churches and their interior, supporting the Christian faithful and correcting sinful behavior. To this end, he relied on the help of locals who were familiar with wrongdoers and sins in the local community. He asked seven of these local men to swear an oath on the relics of saints and report any misbehavior. To remind them of all kinds of possible improper behavior, he presented a long list of sins, starting with homicide and bodily harm and ending with sexual deviance. This jury of seven men identified sinners, thereby implicating members of their local parish. Thus, they fulfilled a function similar to a modern public prosecutor today identifying wrongful behavior; the jury, however, did not decide a case (like a modern jury).

Regino of Prüm, Libri duo de synodalibus causis, c. 2.2. – c. 2.5 F.G.A. Wasserschleben, Reginonis abbatis Prumiensis libri duo de synodalibus causis et disciplinis ecclesiasticis, Leipzig, Engelmann, 1840 (reprint Graz, Akad. Dr.- u. Verl.-Anst., 1964), 206–209 (transl. by Stephan Dusil and Rob Getz)

2.2. *About the jury* If the bishop sits in judgment in a synodal court, after having given an appropriate address, he shall summon seven men of the people of this parish – or more or less, as it seems appropriate to him. Those men must be respected, honored, and veracious. He shall have relics of the saints brought forward and bind each of these men with the following oath.

2.3. *The synodal oath* Until this time and hereafter, whatever you know or have heard or shall learn later, that has been done or shall be done in this parish against the will of God and right Christianity, if it happens during your lifetime, so that it comes to your knowledge in any way, if you know or if it has been made known to you that it pertains to the synodal court and to the ministry of the bishop: This you shall not conceal, either for love, or fear, or for recompense, or for kinship, from the archbishop of Trier or his proxy, whom he has ordered to inquire into it, whenever he questions you about it. So help you God, and these relics of the Saints. The others shall swear in this way: This oath, which this man has sworn concerning the synodal court, that you will keep it, insofar as you have knowledge, or have heard, or shall come to learn, from this day henceforth. So help you God.

2.4 *After the oath has been taken, the bishop shall address the jurors* Brethren, be careful to fulfill your vows to the Lord because you have sworn not to a human being, but to God, your creator. We, who are his servants, do not aspire to your worldly possessions but seek the salvation of your souls. Beware lest you conceal anything, and the sin of another becomes your damnation.

2.5 *After this, the bishop shall ask them in order*

1. In this parish, is there a manslayer who intentionally killed a person, out of cupidity or rapacity, or by accident, or unwillingly, or being forced?

Or as vengeance for his kinsmen, which we call feud, or in war, or commanded by his master, or is there someone who killed his own slave?
2. Does there live any parricide or fratricide here who murdered his father, his mother, his sister, his brother, his uncle, or another relative?
3. Is there someone who killed a priest or a deacon or any cleric, or deprived him of a limb?
4. Is there a man or woman here who smothered his or her child by lying on it or suffocated it by the weight of the garments? And when did this happen: prior or after baptism? Or did a weak child die due to the negligence of one parent without being baptized?
5. Is there a man or woman who caused a woman to miscarry, or is there a woman who miscarried by her own will and procured an abortion?[46]

---

46 F.G.A. Wasserschleben, Reginonis abbatis Prumiensis libri duo de synodalibus causis et disciplinis ecclesiasticis, Leipzig, Engelmann, 1840 (reprint Graz, Akad. Dr.- u. Verl.-Anst., 1964), 206-209.
2.2 De iuratoribus synodi. Episcopus in synodo residens, post congruam allocutionem septem ex plebe ipsius parochiae vel eo amplius aut minus, prout viderit expedire, maturiores, honestiores atque veraciores viros in medio debet evocare, et, allatis sanctorum pignoribus, unumquemque illorum tali sacramento constringat. 2.3 Iusiurandum synodale. A modo in antea, quidquid nosti aut audisti, aut postmodum inquisiturus es, quod contra Dei voluntatem et rectam Christianitatem in ista parochia factum est, aut futurum erit, si in diebus tuis evenerit, tantum ut ad tuam cognitionem quocunque modo perveniat, si scis aut tibi indicatum fuerit, synodalem causam esse, et ad ministerium episcopi pertinere, quod tu nec propter amorem, nec propter timorem, nec propter praemium, nec propter parentelam ullatenus celare debeas archiepiscopo de Treveris aut eius misso, cui hoc inquirere iusserit, quandocunque te ex hoc interrogavit. Sic te Deus adiuvet et istae sanctorum reliquiae. Reliqui ita iurent: Istud sacramentum, quod iste iuravit de synodali causa, quod tu illud observabis, in quantum sapis aut audisti, aut ab hac die in antea inquisiturus es. Sic te Deus adiuvet. 2.4 Post datum sacramentum iuratores episcopus alloquatur: Videte, fratres, ut Domino reddatis iuramenta vestra; non enim homini iurastis, sed Deo creatori vestro. Nos autem, qui eius ministri sumus, non terrenam substantiam vestram concupiscimus, sed salutem animarum vestrarum requirimus. Cavete, ne aliquid abscondatis, et ex alterius peccato vestra fiat damnatio. 2.5 Post hac ita per ordinem interroget: 1. Est in hac parochia homicida, qui hominem aut spontanea voluntate aut cupiditatis aut rapacitatis causa, aut casu, aut nolens et coactus, aut pro vindicta parentum, quod faidam dicimus, aut in bello, aut iussu domini, aut proprium servum occiderit? 2. Est aliquis parricida aut fratricida, qui patrem, matrem, sororem, fratrem, avunculum aut aliquem parentem interfecerit? 3. Est aliquis, qui presbyterum aut diaconum aut aliquem clericorum occiderit, vel aliquo membro detruncaverit? 4. Est aliquis vel aliqua, qui infantem proprium oppresserit, vel vestimentorum pondere suffocaverit? Et, si hoc factum est, ante baptismum aut post baptismum, aut si infans infirmatus per negligentiam parentis absque baptismo obierit? 5. Est aliquis vel aliqua, qui alterius partum excusserit, vel, si ipsa femina propria voluntate suum partum excusserit, et abortivum fecerit?

The denunciation of sinners comes at the end of a centuries-long development. In Late Antiquity, penance was performed publicly within a parish and mostly at the end of life, as penance was done once in a lifetime. Public penance included the – temporary – exclusion from the community, or – in the case of clerics – deposition. This ancient practice of public penance lost ground around 600 when Irish monks did missionary work on the continent. Columbanus (540– 615), the founder of the monasteries in Luxeuil (France) and Bobbio (Italy), is a prime example of such a missionary. He – and other Irish monks – not only preached the Gospels to (half-)pagan European society and heard confessions, but they also brought with them a different understanding of penance. This new understanding included a private, secret confession. Consequently, the penitent was not excluded from the community but had to follow the penance the confessor had imposed. Long catalogues provided the confessor with the appropriate punishments for the sins. This form of penance is also called 'tariffed penance'. The term 'tariffed penance' refers to the notion that the priest consulted his books to impose the right penance – not too short, not too long, not too rigid, not too light. These catalogues often made distinctions based on the circumstances of the transgression and, of course, intention. Murder carried out for revenge was more serious than homicide based on negligence; and the penance imposed by the Church to reconcile the sinner with God, accordingly more severe. These catalogues were presumably drafted as a guideline for confessors and helped achieve greater uniformity in the imposed penances.

The following text comes from such a penitential. It was ascribed to a renowned and widely venerated author, the Venerable Bede (672/3–735), a Benedictine monk, although he never authored this penitential. The penitential presumably stems from the eighth century (now often called *Paenitentiale additivum Pseudo-Bedae-Egberti*). It is intriguing for different reasons. First, it shows a nuanced understanding of homicide, as the intention of the wrongdoer was crucial for the imposed penance. Second, it provides insight into the protected rights, persons and their value. Third, this catalog resembles the catalogues of the *leges* – in the Early Middle Ages, it was obviously not yet possible to formulate rules in a more general way, but it was possible to list specific cases.

Paenitentiale additivum Pseudo-Bedae-Egberti, also know as Liber de remediis peccatorum, cc. 2.1–2.11
Medieval Handbooks of Penance. A translation of the principal libri poenitentiales and selections from related documents, New York, Columbia

University Press, 1938, reprint New York, Columbia University Press, 1990, 224–225 (transl. by John T. McNeill / Helena M. Gamer, slightly revised)
Of [man]slaughter
1. He who slays a monk or a cleric shall lay aside his weapons and serve God or do penance for seven years.
2. He who slays a layman with malice aforethought or for the possession of his inheritance, four years.
3. He who slays to avenge a brother, one year and in the two following years the three forty-day periods and the appointed days.
4. He who slays through sudden anger and a quarrel, three years.
5. He who slays by accident, one year.
6. He who slays in public warfare, forty days.
7. He who slays at the command of his master, if he is a slave, forty days; he who, being a freeman, at the command of his superior slays an innocent person, one year and for the two years following, the three forty-day periods and the appointed days.
8. He who by a wound in a quarrel renders a man weak or maimed shall pay for the physician and the fine for the scar and make compensation for his work while he is recovering and do penance for half a year. If indeed he has not the means, he shall make good these things in an entire year of penance.
9. He who rises up to strike a man, intending to kill him, shall do penance for three weeks; if he is a cleric, three months.
10. But if he has wounded him, forty days; if he is a cleric, a whole year; but he shall also pay to the person injured, according to the severity of the wound; even if the law does not require it, he shall pay him whom he has injured, lest the injured cause scandal.
11. A mother who kills her child before the fortieth day shall do penance for one year, if after the fortieth day, three years of penance. If it is after the child has become alive, [she shall do penance] as a murderess. But it makes a great difference whether a poor woman does it on account of the difficulty of supporting [the child] or a harlot for the sake of concealing her wickedness.[47]

47 Bruno Albers (ed.), Wann sind die Beda-Egbert'schen Bussbücher verfasst worden, und wer ist ihr Verfasser?, in Archiv für katholisches Kirchenrecht 81 (1901), 404:
[De occisione]

Church officials were very much opposed to these penitentials, as they often contained contradictory provisions. 'The mistakes are known, the authors unknown' (*quorum certi errores, incerti auctores*) was a frequent complaint about these books. In 829, the Council of Paris even condemned penitentials and demanded that they be burned. This order, however, was not successful. Since Carolingian times, public (ancient) and secret (Irish) penance existed alongside each other (also known as the 'Carolingian dichotomy'). Public penance was imposed on public transgressions which caused scandal (*scandalum*; a prime example was the public penance of King Louis the Pious in 822); secret penance in all other cases. Regino's treatise reflects this dichotomy to some extent, as the sinners were publicly denounced, but penance was imposed in secret. It, therefore, had 'public' and 'private' elements. The fact that the bishop visited his diocese also indicates a new understanding of this office, with more of a focus on taking care of all the souls committed to him. The bishop's public investigation is accompanied by a public ceremony of submission and the later readmission to the community. This practice seemed to support the idea that the penance helped to settle disputes within a local community. The fact that a murderer, who was denounced and convicted, underwent penance and was later readmitted to the parish may have appeased the victim's family and the feelings of the community as a whole. In this regard, penance is more reminiscent of a criminal procedure with a punishment than of an inner conversion to God.

---

1. Qui hocciderit monachum aut clericum armo relinquat et deo serviat vel VII annos peniteat.
2. Qui laicum odii meditatione vel possidendi hereditatis eius annos IIII.
3. Qui pro vindicta fratris annum I et in sequentibus duobus III XLmas ac legitimas ferias.
4. Qui per iram subitam et rixam III annos.
5. Qui casu annum I.
6. Qui in bello publico dies XL.
7. Qui jubento domino suo, servus dies XL; qui liber jubente majore suo innocentem annum I et sequentes II XLmas et legitimas ferias.
8. Qui per rixa, ictu debilem vel deformem hominem redidit, impensas in medicos et macule precium et opus ejus donec sanetur restituat, et dimidium annum peniteat. Si vero non habet unde restituat haec, anno integro.
9. Qui ad feriandum hominem surrexit volens eum occidere III septimanas peniteat. Si clericus fuerit III menses.
10. Qui et si vulneraverit dies XL, si clericus annum totum; sed et pecuniam pro modo vulneris licet, licet lex non commendat, cui inflixit, tribuat, ne lesus scandalizet.
11. Mulier partum suum ante dies XL sponte perdens annum I peniteat si vero post XL dies III annos. Si vero postquam animatus fuerit, quasi homicida; des distat multum, utrum pauper culpa pre difficultate nutriendi an fornicari causa sui sceleris celandi faciat.

The Church, however, was not only competent in the area of sin, but also in matters of sexuality and marriage. Many articles in these penitentiaries are dedicated to sexual (mis)behavior. The so-called penitential of Theodore (late seventh century) offers a glimpse of the sexual practices of the day, especially of that era's contempt for homosexuality (c. 5). Although the catalogues are casuistic in character, their canons are not always consistent: the relation between c. 2 and c. 3 and the imposed penance (ten to fifteen years) remains unclear, at least to a modern historian. In this regard, the penitentiaries did not always succeed in 'harmonizing' contradictory rules.

> *Penitential of Theodore (late 7th century).*
> *Medieval Handbooks of Penance, New York, Columbia University Press, 1938, reprint New York, Columbia University Press, 1990, 185 (transl. by John T. McNeill and Helena M. Gamer)*
> *Of Fornication*
> 1. If anyone commits fornication with a virgin he shall do penance for one year. If with a married woman, he shall do penance for four years, two of these entire, and in the other two during the three forty-day periods and three days a week.
> 2. He judged that he who often commits fornication with a man or with a beast should do penance for ten years.
> 3. Another judgment is that he who is joined to beasts shall do penance for fifteen years.
> 4. He who after his twentieth year defiles himself with a male shall do penance for fifteen years.
> 5. Sodomites shall do penance for seven years, and the effeminate man as an adulteress.[48]

The next excerpt reveals the strict sexual morals in the Early Middle Ages, limiting the amount of time per year intercourse was allowed and the imposition of harsh restrictions even on married couples. The following canons can be

48 F.W.A.H. Wasserschleben, Die Bussordnungen der abendländischen Kirche, nebst einer rechtsgeschichtlichen Einleitung, Halle, Ch. Graeger, 1851, 185:
De fornicatione
§ 1. Si quis fornicaverit cum virgine I anno poeniteat, si cum marita, IV annos, duos integros, duos alios in tribus XLmis et III dies in ebdomada poeniteat.
§ 2. Qui saepe cum masculo aut cum pecode fornicate, X annos ut poeniteret judicavit.
§ 3. Item aliud. Qui cum pecoribus coiret. XV annos poeniteat.
§ 4. Qui coiret cum masculo post XX annum XV annos poeniteat.
§ 5. Si masculus cum masculo fornicate, X ann. poeniteat.

understood as marriage law *avant la lettre*, as a clearly defined body of marriage law of the Church (encompassing the requirements for a consensual marriage and its annulment) did not exist before 1150. The final provisions indicate that marriages arranged by the families of the bride and groom were quite common. However, at least a rudimentary form of free choice is granted to the bridal couple, as they had a right to veto.

Penitential of Theodore (late 7th century).
Medieval Handbooks of Penance, New York, Columbia University Press, 1938, reprint New York, Columbia University Press, 1990, 208–211 (transl. by John T. McNeill and Helena M. Gamer)
Of Matters Relating to Marriage
1. Those who are married shall abstain from intercourse for three nights before they communicate.
2. A man shall abstain from his wife for forty days before Easter, until the week of Easter. ...
3. When she has conceived a woman ought to abstain from her husband for three months before the birth, and afterward in the time of purgation, that is, for forty days and nights, whether she has borne a male or a female child.
5. If the wife of anyone commits fornication, he may put her away and take another, that is, if a man puts away his wife on account of fornication, if she was his first, he is permitted to take another; but if she wishes to do penance for her sins, she may take another husband after five years.
6. A woman may not put away her husband, even if he is a fornicator, unless, perchance, for [the purpose of his entering] a monastery.
30. A husband who sleeps with his wife shall wash himself before he goes into a church.
31. A husband ought not to see his wife nude.
34. Parents may not give a betrothed girl to another man unless she flatly refuses [to marry the original suitor]; but she may go to a monastery if she wishes.
35. But if she who is betrothed refuses to live with the man to whom she is betrothed, the money which he gave for her shall be paid back to him, and a third part shall be added; if, however, it is he that refuses, he shall lose the money which he gave for her.

> 36. But a girl of seventeen [also transmitted: 16, 14, 13] years has the power of her own body.[49]

James A. Brundage summarized the rigid sexual morals of the Church in the following excerpt.

> *James A. Brundage, Law, Sex, and Christian Society in Medieval Europe, Chicago, London, The University of Chicago Press, 1987, 173–175*
>
> The work of Regino of Prüm typifies the common teaching of the Western Church concerning proper sexual behavior at the beginning of the tenth century. Churchmen had reached agreement by this period that only married persons should have sex and that they should do so primarily in order to conceive children. The Church stood the sexual teaching of the Manichaeans and Gnostic sects on its head. The Manichaeans had taught that sex for pleasure was acceptable, but they abominated procreation. The rejection of pleasure as a legitimate purpose of sex depended in turn upon the dichotomy between body and soul, flesh and spirit, that is fundamental to late ancient and medieval Christian belief. This antagonism between the carnal and spiritual impulses of a man, a notion that early Christians absorbed from Greek philosophy, likewise received prominent emphasis in the penitentials, which were concerned, as we

---

49 F.W.A.H. Wasserschleben, Die Bussordnungen der abendländischen Kirche, nebst einer rechtsgeschichtlichen Einleitung, Halle, Ch. Graeger, 1851, 213–217:
De questionibus conjugiorum
§ 1. Qui in matrimonio sunt, III noctes se abstineant a conjunction antequam communicant.
§ 2. Vir abstineat se ab uxore sua XL diebus ante pascha usque in octavas paschae.
§ 3. Mulier tres menses debet se abstinere a viro suo quando concepit, ante partum et post tempore purgationis, hoc est XL diebus et noctibus, sive masculum sive feminam genuerit.
§ 5. Si cujus uxor fornicaverit, licet dimittere eam et aliam accipere, hoc est, si vir dimiserit uxorem suam propter fornicationem, si prima fuerit, licitum est, ut aliam accipiat uxorem, illa vero, si voluerit poenitere peccata sua, post V annos alium virum accipiat.
§ 6. Mulieri non licet virum dimittere licet sit fornicator, nisi forte pro monasterio.
§ 30. Maritus qui cum uxore sua dormierit, lavet se antequam intret in ecclesiam.
§ 31. Maritus quoque non debet uxorem suam nudam videre.
§ 34. Puellam disponsatam non licet parentibus dare alteri viro, nisi illa omnio resistat, tamen ad monasterium licet ire, si voluerit.
§ 35. Illa autem disponsata, si non vult habitare cum eo viro, cui est disponsata, reddatur ei pecunia, quam pro ipsa dedit, et tertia pars addatur, si autem ille noluerit, perdat pecuniam, quam pro illa dedit.
§ 36. Puella autem XIV annorum sui corporis potestatem habet.

have seen, with ritual purity and the need to cleanse oneself from sexual defilement as a condition for participation in the sacred mysteries of the Church. The aversion to sex that had become a central feature of Christian thought by the tenth century reflected a further characteristic of the early medieval Church: the ascendency of the monastic ideal and the presumption that ascetic virtues represented the highest form of Christian life. By the tenth century, monks, who were bound to a rule of complete sexual abstinence, had imposed on Europe's married population rules of periodic continence that made marriage more sexually frustrating than celibacy. At the same time, influential figures in this period increasingly favored imposing celibacy upon the secular clergy as well as monks. Although marriage was not generally prohibited to clerics in the tenth century, authorities often exhorted clerics in the West to cast their wives, concubines, and children out of their homes and to embrace a celibate virtue that few secular clerics seem to have desired. The wives, consorts, and children of priests were as much the targets of this pressure as the priests. The penitentials, as we have seen, gave central prominence to sexual offenses; in so doing they implicitly told both confessor and penitent that sexual purity was the key element in Christian morality. The penitentials also reinforced the belief that there was a hierarchy of sexual offenses and subtly propounded a slightly different ordering of that hierarchy than appears in the writings of earlier Church authorities. Whereas earlier writers paid only scant attention to masturbation and homosexual practices, the penitentials often prescribed stern penances for homosexual activities and slight ones for masturbation. The implicit message was that homosexuality was amongst the most heinous offenses in the catalogue of sins. Solitary masturbation, by contrast, ranked as the least serious sexual indulgence. The reordered emphases on masturbatory and homosexual activities that surfaced in the penitentials mirrored the experience and concerns of the monastic in an environment in which most penitential writers received their spiritual and intellectual formation. Their handbooks ensured that monastic beliefs about these types of sexual behavior would be imparted, both directly and indirectly, to the laity. The penitentials also fostered the emergence of a distinctively ecclesiastical view of marriage. The clerical model of marriage promoted the concept that marriage was a lifelong commitment; accordingly, this paradigm restricted divorce, prohibited remarriage following divorce, and discouraged second marriages following the death of a first spouse.

At the end of this section, it is worth reflecting on the role of the bishops one more time. They acted as judges, which is the first indication of how canonical rules in the Early Middle Ages were applied. Nonetheless, it remains unknown how exactly they applied canonical rules. The importance of rules, however, is underscored by the Westgothic rules on how to hold a council (*ordo de concilio celebrando*) according to which a book with canons should be brought in the middle of the assembly (*codex canonum in medio proferens*) and the procedural rules should be read aloud. Evidently, written rules on procedure were important to the Church. This significance is illustrated by a short introductory text written by the French bishop Yves of Chartres (c. 1040–1115), in which he provides a glimpse of the harmonization of rules around 1100, and thus of the application of rules in an episcopal court. James Brundage examined the harmonization of the rules by Yves.

> *James A. Brundage, Medieval Canon Law, London, New York, Longman, 1995, 38–39*
> An even more important contribution than his canonical collections to the development of systematic canon law was the prologue that appears in numerous manuscripts of Ivo's *Panormia*. In the prologue he sketched out a much more sophisticated canonical methodology than appears in the work of any of his predecessors. Ivo's prologue set forth rules for the interpretation of canonical texts that became central to the work of later canonists, and especially to the work of Gratian. Canonists found Ivo's prologue immensely valuable as a guide for resolving the discrepancies that they often encountered between contradictory ecclesiastical laws. Faced with such conflicts Ivo advised canonists to examine the context in which the canons had been adopted. Such an examination might reveal that the apparently conflicting canons had addressed different problems or separate aspects of a single problem. In that case the canonist might be able to resolve apparent discrepancies by showing that the canons did not in fact conflict at all. Ivo also cautioned canonists to test the authenticity of their sources in order to eliminate forged or interpolated texts that might conflict with authentic canonical rules. In addition, Ivo declared that when canonists interpreted the law, they must take account of the hierarchy of jurisdictions within the church. The basic principle here was that canons that originated with higher authorities took precedence over canons adopted by lesser authorities. Thus, if the canons of a general council conflicted with the canons of a provincial council or a diocesan synod, the general council's enactments overrode those of the lesser body. Further, Ivo warned canonists that they must be alert to

> the distinctions between variable laws and invariable laws and between general and particular canons. Variable laws might be subject to dispensation by an appropriate authority, while invariable laws were not. The application of particular canons was limited to specific regions or situations or classes of persons, whereas general laws applied across the board to all Christians.

The techniques employed by Ives and the distinction between variable and invariable rules allowed a flexible application of rules. Previously existing contradictions – also bemoaned by Burchard of Worms – could easily be resolved. This theory of harmonization prefigures the methodology employed by Gratian and others in the twelfth century, pointing the way to a new era of learned, erudite jurisprudence.

5.4 *Summary*

At first glance, the examples of the application of rules in the Early Middle Ages seem extremely diverse. It is difficult to see the relationship between treason and the crime of lèse-majesté, earth cast, self-help, compositions and the inner conversion to God. Nonetheless, some common themes can be identified. First, our knowledge of the application of rules is quite limited, as judgments and records are not transmitted and, presumably, were not even produced in an oral society. Therefore, our knowledge is based on written rules of procedure, but whether the 'law in action' reflects the 'law in the books' remains unclear. We are on more solid ground when we have narrative texts from which we learn how a court procedure took place. However, these texts are mostly about politically significant procedures of royal courts and not the day-to-day business of local courts.

Second, there is a striking similarity between sources as disparate as the *leges* and the penitentials. Both contain lists with the appropriate consequences for misbehavior. The *leges* provided suggestions for the just amount of animals, weapons or land to compensate the violation of someone's rights; the penitentials offered a list of just penances for sins to achieve an inner conversion. In the Early Middle Ages, laws were primarily catalogues containing extensive lists of misbehavior (distinctions were made according to intent, infringed object, etc.), not general rules.

Third, issues arising from the misbehavior of members of a community were settled even before courts were established. The Germanic *rachinburgen,* wise men, acting as arbiters, were of supreme importance and considered competent to resolve conflicts before the existence of formalized courts. These courts changed the character of the conflicts. They transformed a private dispute between parties into a public one that demanded a public solution, known to the community. This last point is related to a fourth one. The practice of penance offers an insight into the transition from a 'private' to a 'public' conflict and its solution. The bishop urged a jury to denounce members of their community and after an examination, a penance was imposed. The penitents were publicly expelled from common life and only later, after having done their penance, readmitted to the parish and the community. The 'bilateral' and secret penance between the penitent and the priest hearing the confession is changed into an official investigation carried out by a bishop. In a similar vein, the *rachinburgen* as arbiters are replaced by a court. These transformations suggest that courts were becoming part of the established social order and with them an 'official' way to settle misbehavior and crimes. Thus a third actor entered the scene – which evolved, in the long run, into the state, with the exclusive competence to investigate and to punish.

Questions

1. How did Roman legislation on traitors affect later legal development?
2. Which were the advantages of the ill-defined competences of different judicial fora in the early-medieval period?
3. How was 'self help' in dispute resolution conceived in the early-medieval period?
4. What were the decisive (legal and extra-legal) factors that led to the creation of rules of procedure in dispute resolution in the early medieval period?
5. Which role did the 'invention of penance' play in the development of punishment in the early-medieval period?

6 Main Characteristics

In the final part of this chapter we will focus on some of the main characteristics of the law in the Early Middle Ages. Roman law in the Early Middle Ages was a law in the process of transition and transformation. Even though it originated in Antiquity, in a society that was socially and economically very different, it shaped the Early Middle Ages. Roman law was part of Roman-ness, from a perceived superior culture inspiring imitation by rule-makers. Alaric's collection of Roman vulgar law and his subtle but important changes are just one example. And although, even today, Roman law is seen as the golden standard of complex, systematized law developed in a highly sophisticated society, it was too complex for medieval societies in the centuries that followed the demise of the Roman Empire. It was not transferred to the next historical epoch in its pure form but was transformed. Roman law collapsed precisely because it was such a complex system: the breakdown of legal institutions, disappearance of appellate institutions, corrupt judges, etc., led to a situation in which whole parts of the society stopped functioning in the way described in the concise language of late classical jurists such as Ulpian.

Ancient law lost its applicability to different institutions and was only 'allowed' in parts of the new *regna,* and then mainly in the area of procedural law. Because of its close connection to political power, it changed drastically. Despite all this, Roman legal thought with its specific terminology, distinctions and practices outlived the empire for centuries. The original meanings and procedural forms turned into empty shells filled with new meaning. The Bavarian charter from the eighth or ninth century mentioned above, for instance, illustrates this transition: the transfer of real property was documented in classical terms and with the Roman ceremonies of a long bygone era. To the people back then, there somehow seemed to be some magic in the anachronistic words used in the charter. There was no reason to invoke the title of the *magister militum* (master of the soldiers), which had not been used for decades, if not centuries, other than to recall the 'good old times' of Roman law and Roman rule. Besides, jurists often embellished decisions with ponderous and grave formulations.

With regard to Germanic law, the following text mentions several important issues.

> *Bernd Kannowski, Rechtsbegriffe im Mittelalter. Stand der Diskussion, in Albrecht Cordes and Bernd Kannowski (eds), Rechtsbegriffe im Mittelalter, Frankfurt am Main etc., P. Lang, 2002, 5–6, 8–9, 12 (transl. by Bernd Kannowski)*
>
> Law as the right procedure: Medieval law is characterized by orality, which brings about its own set of rules. The form of an action, its execution, and the legal ritual have a much higher status than in a written legal culture. In connection to this, the scholarly community is in agreement that Medieval law is, in its essence, procedural law. The manner in which a decision is reached is more important than the content of the decision ('Form is the oldest norm'). ... Law is what is applied in court. ...
>
> Legal custom: The tradition of the ancestors, a practice unchallenged for a long time, and usage are decisive sources of medieval law. They so determine medieval law's character that the term 'customary law' does not suffice. Habit did not merely play a secondary role besides a written legal system, but it constitutes the law as a whole ('legal custom'). In an

> oral culture, norms cannot be laid down with the same precision as in written law. They cannot be fixed in writing. Law can then only be what the community keeps alive through constant legal practice.
>
> Openness of law: Custom is the basis of medieval law. These customs are connected to complex medieval legal thought that avoids the use of sharply defined concepts. Because of this, for the legal historian, the only appropriate form of presentation might lie in simply juxtaposing different strands of thought. Hermann Krause spoke of an 'openness of law' in the time of the Saxon and Salian rulers: It is by no means closed off to extra-legal influences; Christian values, in particular, cannot be separated from legal ones. Krause's view is confirmed in an often quoted verse from the high Middle Ages, which says that nobody is as sublime as the law, because God is truly a just judge (*Nieman ist so hier, sô daz reht zware, wan got is ze ware, ein rehtir rihtaere* ...). ...
>
> Violent resolution of 'legal disputes': As is well known, there was no all-powerful state in the Middle Ages that could claim a monopoly on the use of force. This leads to another feature of medieval law that is foreign to our time. Since the authorities could neither provide a consistent set of instruments for conflict resolution nor consistently claim to be in charge of this area of the law, there was room for legally permitted, private use of force and the recognition of its results. ...
>
> Legal rituals as a means of communication in conflict: ... The ritual is rooted in the religious sphere ('rite') and denotes an action of legal significance staged in public. According to the *Edictus Rothari* the terms 'ritual' and 'law' are difficult to separate: A condition for the validity of new law should be that it is affirmed according to the rite of the Longobard people. In various works, Gerd Althoff has discussed how the exercise of power was staged as a ritual in the Middle Ages. He traces how Carolingian rulers used to seal the conclusion of alliances by a public demonstration of friendship (*amicitia*) and emphasizes the great importance of the *deditio* as a *forme fixe* of public submission.

Canon law has always been written law. Rules were made at different levels of the Church: the Roman pontiff, as well as minor abbots, tried to impose rules on their subjects to organize the Church better, solve conflicts and care for the souls of all Christians.

However, the Early Middle Ages' main characteristics are not revealed by a summary of the features of the different bodies of law. The essence of the Early Middle Ages only reveals itself by comparing these laws. Then, its diversity, its polycentrism, and the parallelism of different legal systems is revealed.

This chapter highlights the parallel systems that overlapped each other; for example, Roman and Germanic law, but also Roman and canon law. Rulers like Charlemagne considered themselves competent in secular and ecclesiastical matters. The itinerant episcopal court described by Regino provided a cure for the transgression of religious commandments and had a secular function in pacifying disputes between parties.

Law in the Early Middle Ages was also diverse, because different institutions, procedures and courts existed at the same time; it offered a wide variety of possibilities for settling conflicts. Their competences were not clearly defined, which in turn caused new conflicts. In addition, law in the Early Middle Ages was polycentric, it varied from area to area, it had different rule-makers and enforcers.

Finally, a certain tension is inherent in the law of the Early Middle Ages. Codes of Roman law transmitted the elaborate legal system of Antiquity, whereas Germanic law was often shaped by rural traditions. The written law of the Church stood in contrast to the predominantly oral traditions of Germanic law. The – still humble – attempts of late Carolingian bishops to officially investigate the violations of ecclesiastical commandments and other rights can be contrasted with a procedural system based on the accusation of parties. And while the bishops discussed issues about which passions flared and made rules based on mutual consent, Emperor Otto the Great still paid combatants to answer a legal question. The elements mentioned above seem to stem from different periods, but they are all part of the Early Middle Ages. Even if the following saying may hold true for many different historical periods, it is especially true for the Early Middle Ages: they are characterized by the contemporaneousness of what is not contemporary.

But what were the Early Middle Ages clearly *not*? They were not yet a time of lawyers, legally trained men that read normative texts, interpreted them, and applied them to actual cases. In this regard, the Early Middle Age's legal culture can better be seen as 'law without lawyers'.[50]

Questions

1. The legal system in the Early Middle Ages was not always functioning smoothly, but knew tensions between its different parts. Explain.
2. Antiquity and the Early Middle Ages are considered to be two different periods in history. Do you agree with this opinion, also where it concerns the law?

50 James A. Brundage, The Medieval Origins of the Legal Profession. Canonists, Civilians, and Courts, Chicago, University of Chicago Press, 2008, 46.

Further Reading

Barbier, Josiane. Archives oubliées du haut Moyen Âge. Les gesta municipalia en Gaule franque (VIe-IXe siècle), Paris, Honoré Champion, 2014.

Barnwell, P.S. Emperors, Jurists and Kings: Law and custom in the late Roman and early Medieval West, Past and Present 168 (2000), 6–29.

Brundage, James A. Law, Sex, and Christian Society in Medieval Europe, Chicago, Chicago University Press, 1987.

Brundage, James A. and Melodie H. Eichbauer. Medieval Canon Law (2nd ed.), Abington, Routledge, Taylor & Francis Group, 2023.

Brundage, James A. The Medieval Origins of the Legal Profession. Canonists, Civilians, and Courts, Chicago, University of Chicago Press, 2008.

Brunner, Heinrich. Zur Rechtsgeschichte der römischen und germanischen Urkunde, Berlin, Weidmannsche Buchhandlung, 1880.

Collins, Roger. Law, Culture and Regionalism in Early Medieval Spain, Hampshire, Variorum [Aldershot], Hampshire, 1992.

Faulkner, Thomas. Law and Authority in the Early Middle Ages, Cambridge, Cambridge University Press, 2016.

Firey, Abigail. (ed.), A new History of Penance (Brill's Companions to the Christian Tradition 14), Leiden, Brill, 2008.

Fögen, Marie Theres. Römische Rechtsgeschichte. Über Ursprung und Evolution eines sozialen Systems, Rechtsgeschichte – Legal History 2002, 14–19.

Jasper, Detlev and Horst Fuhrmann. Papal Letters in the Early Middle Ages, Washington DC, Catholic University of America Press, 2000.

King, P.D. Law and Society in the Visigothic Kingdom, Cambridge, Cambridge University Press, 2006.

Kunkel, Wolfgang. Römische Rechtsgeschichte, Köln, Böhlau, 1956 (14th ed. with M.J. Schermeier, 2005).

Levy, Ernst. Pauli Sententiae: a Palingenesia of the Opening Titles as a Specimen of Research in West Roman Vulgar Law, Ithaca, Cornell University Press, 1945.

Levy, Ernst. West Roman Vulgar Law. The Law of Property, Philadelphia, American Philosophical Society, 1951.

Levy, Ernst. Weströmisches Vulgarrecht. Das Obligationenrecht, Weimar, Böhlaus Nachfolger, 1956.

Liebs, Detlef. Römische Jurisprudenz in Gallien (Freiburger Rechtsgeschichtliche Abhandlungen. Neue Folge, 38), Berlin, Duncker und Humblot, 2002.

Liebs, Detlef. Die pseudopaulinischen Sentenzen. Versuch einer neuen Palingenesie, Zeitschrift der Savigny-Stiftung für Rechtsgeschichte, Romanistische Abteilung 112 (1995), 151–170.

Liebs, Detlef. Roman Vulgar Law in Late Antiquity, in B. Sirks (ed.), Aspects of law in Late Antiquity dedicated to A. M. Honoré, Oxford, Oxford University Press, 2008, 35–53.

Lupoi, Maurizio. The Origins of the European Legal Order, Cambridge, Cambridge University Press, 2000.

Manlio, Bellomo. The Common Legal Past of Europe, 1000–1800, Washington DC, The Catholic University of America Press, 1995.

McKitterick, Rosamund. The Carolingians and the Written Word, Cambridge, Cambridge University Press, 1989.

Meens, Rob. Penance in Medieval Europe 600–1200, Cambridge, Cambridge University Press, 2014.

Mitteis, Ludwig. Reichsrecht und Volksrecht in den östlichen Provinzen des römischen Kaiserreichs mit Beiträgen zur Kenntnis des griechischen Rechts und der spätrömischen Rechtsentwicklung, Leipzig, R.G. Teubner, 1891.

Rainer, J. Michael. Das Römische Recht in Europa. Von Justinian zum BGB (2nd ed.), Wien, Manzsche Verlags- und Universitätsbuchhandlung, 2020.

Rio, Alice. Formulae, Legal Practice and the Settlement of Disputes in the Frankish Kingdoms: the formulary of Angers, in Per Andersen, Mia Münster-Swendsen and Helle Vogt (eds), Law before Gratian: Law in Western Europe, c. 500–1100, København, DJØF, 2007, 21–34.

Rio, Alice. Legal Practice and the Written Word in the Early Middle Ages: Frankish formulae, c. 500–1000, Cambridge, Cambridge University Press, 2009.

Rio, Alice. The formularies of Angers and Marculf: Two Merovingian Legal Handbooks, Liverpool, Liverpool University Press, 2008.

Rouche, Michel and Bruno Dumézil. Le Bréviaire d'Alaric. Aux origines du Code Civil, Paris, Presses de l'Université de Paris-Sorbonne, 2008.

Shoemaker, Karl. Germanic Law, in Heikki Pihlajamäki, Markus D. Dubber and Mark Godfrey (eds), The Oxford Handbook of European Legal History, Oxford, Oxford University Press, 2018, 249–61.

Stein, Peter. Roman Law in European History, Cambridge, Cambridge University Press (12th ed.), 2013.

Vinogradoff, Paul. Roman Law in Medieval Europe (3rd ed.), Oxford, Oxford University Press, 1961.

Weitzel, Jürgen. Dinggenossenschaft und Recht. Untersuchungen zum Rechtsverständnis im fränkisch-deutschen Mittelalter (Quellen und Forschungen zur höchsten Gerichtsbarkeit im Alten Reich 15/1 and 15/2), Köln-Wien, Böhlau, 1985.

Wieacker, Franz. Vulgarrecht und Vulgarismus. Alte und neue Probleme und Diskussionen, in Studi in onore di A. Biscardi I, Milan, Istituto Editoriale Cisalpino-La Goliardica, 1982, 33–51.

Wormland, Patrick. Æthelred the lawmaker, in David Hill (ed.), Ethelred the Unready: Papers from the Millenary Conference, Oxford, British Archaeological Reports, 1978.

Wormland, Patrick. The Leges Barbarorum: Law and Ethnicity in the Post-Roman West, in Hans-Werner Goetz, Jörg Jarnut and Walter Pohl (eds), Regna and Gentes: the Relationship between Late Antique and Early Medieval Peoples and Kingdoms in the Transformation of the Roman World, Leiden, Boston, Brill, 2003, 21–53.

Wormland, Patrick. Legal Culture in the Early Medieval West: Law as Text, Image and Experience, London, Hambledon Press, 1999.

Wormland, Patrick. The First Code of English Law, Canterbury, Canterbury Commemoration Society, 2005 (Reprinted 2010).

Wormland, Patrick. The Making of English Law: King Alfred to the Twelfth Century, vol. 1: Legislation and Its Limits, Oxford, Blackwell Publishers, 2001.

CHAPTER 3

High and Late Middle Ages (1100–1500)

Dirk Heirbaut and Heikki Pihlajamäki

1 Introduction

Traditionally, the era from about 500 until about 1500 in Western Europe is called the 'Middle Ages', but it is more accurate to make a distinction between the 'early' and 'late' Middle Ages. The period around 1100 was a watershed moment in European history, even more important than 1500 and as transformative as the revolutionary period around 1800. Higher agricultural productivity made population growth possible, which in turn led to the rise of cities and the increase of trade and industry. Society became progressively more complex. Economic growth required specialization, and this caused the rise of new social groups in addition to the three traditional groups of fighters, labourers, and those who pray. Cultural developments meant a more literate society: reading and writing spread, and more people were educated as higher institutes of learning and the universities were established. The Church was at the vanguard of reform: during the so-called 'Gregorian reform' in the eleventh century, the popes had taken control to root out a plethora of abuses. They became such capable administrators that they could challenge the power of the king of Germany, who, as emperor, claimed supremacy in the West (the East of the old Roman Empire survived as Byzantium and, though Christian, did not recognize the pope's authority). By the first half of the thirteenth century, the popes were victorious, but they soon had to deal with other monarchs and princes all over Europe whose power had grown and who followed their lead on administrative practices. The Church itself also ran into internal trouble, as believers started to notice that bureaucratic efficiency had replaced religious zeal.

2 Creation

The transformation of Western society around 1100 had a profound impact on the world of law. Growing social differentiation resulted in enormous legal diversity, but the goal of the law was privilege, not equality. Groups and individuals did not seek merely to have the same 'rights' as others; they fought

 | DOI:10.1163/9789004687257_005

for more 'rights'. As a consequence, there were stark differences in legal status between noblemen and commoners, freemen and serfs, townsmen and country folk, clerics, merchants, and others, etcetera. Even within those groups, everyone constantly jockeyed for a better position, and privileges obtained were jealously protected against outsiders.

> *J. Davis, Medieval Market Morality. Life, Law and Ethics in the English Marketplace, 1200–1500, Cambridge, Cambridge University Press, 2012, 152–153*
> A burgess normally had the benefits of burgage tenure, jurisdictional rights and trading privileges, though this differed from borough to borough. In smaller seigneurial ('mesne') boroughs, there might be only a few nominal rights that accorded a town the title of 'borough', such as burgage tenure or exemption from paying tolls in the town's market. The further up the burghal scale, particularly in royal boroughs, the greater the liberties and autonomy that burgesses enjoyed. The basic privileges within a royal chartered borough contained some, or all, of the following: burgage tenure; the right to farm taxes and tolls; the right to their own jurisdiction in their own borough court; a Merchant Guild; the right to retail freely; exemption from tolls, both within the borough and elsewhere; and the right to share in bargains.

Some people even received individual privileges. In other words, instead of one law for all, there was a bewildering variety of legal rules. Some differences in legal position were based on landholding and the status of the land one held in freehold (allod) or tenure, but sometimes legal status and landholding were unrelated. Tenure was divided into feudal and non-feudal tenure, which was then subdivided into an enormous variety of categories. Finally, there were also differences in legal rules based on geographic location: they usually applied to a city or lordship, not to a larger territory like a kingdom. Even in today's modern states this medieval regionalism still exerts so much influence that is difficult to impose modern administrative divisions on it, as illustrated by this Norwegian author.

> *O. Bukve, Towards a New Regionalism in Norway, in I. Sagan and H. Halkier (eds), Regionalism Contested. Institution, Society and Governance, Aldershot, Variorum, 2005, 124–125*
> In Norway, the Sami territory in the North is the most obvious candidate to a region of this type. One can also still find historic and cultural divisions between the regions which date back to the Age of the Vikings, when they

> had their own territorial organisation, laws and courts. Until the 13th century, Norway was united only by the reign of a king who had to be elected at each of the regional assemblies of the 'free' men. Norwegians still see themselves as *vestlendingar* (Western Norwegians, corresponding to the *Gularingslag* from the Medieval Ages), *trønderar* (corresponding to the *Frostatingslag* or *Trøndelag* – a medieval name still used),[1] *nordlendingar* (from Northern Norway, the old Hăløygaland), *aust-lendingar* (from Eastern Norway, corresponding to the old *Eidsivating* and *Borgarting*) and *sørlendingar* (from Southern Norway or Agder). The spoken dialects are so different that Norwegians usually recognize the regional origin of a person by their speech. In Western Norway, a huge part of the population also uses a different written language, the New Norwegian (*nynorsk* as opposed to the dominating *bokmål* – literally 'book language'). Recent language research shows that there is a standardisation of spoken language. But this standardisation is within each region, and does not tend towards a national tongue. Polls indicate that the identification with the old regions (*landsdel* in Norwegian) is stronger among Norwegians than the identification with one's county. Local identities also surpass county identities. An interesting question is how cultural distinctions of the kind mentioned are used in the debate on the new regionalisation and to what degree they have any convincing power.

The bewildering variety of laws did not address the needs of the increasingly complex society of the Middle Ages. When it was looking for a way to organize its control over a vast territory, the Church turned to Roman law. As a result, the *Corpus iuris civilis* was revived in the late eleventh century and both provided the legal structure for the reorganization of the Church and a model for secular princes. As Roman law, together with the heavily Romanized law of the Church (hence Romano-canon instead of just canon law), was studied at the universities, a scholarly body of law called 'learned law' came into existence. It was considered the common law of Europe, the *ius commune*, and separate from the many local laws, the *iura propria*. However, this terminology, although it originated in the later Middle Ages, did not accurately reflect reality: there was no wholesale adoption of Roman law.

First, the *ius commune* was never a uniform body of legal rules in force over all of Europe. It was referred to as 'common' because learned European jurists shared the same legal toolbox, i.e. shared language, terminology, leading

1 For the region in the middle of Norway.

books, etc. Second, there were geographical differences. The situation in the Mediterranean region in the south was different from the north. The south already had Roman law, even though it was a vulgar version and not a 'learned' one. Switching to the *ius commune* only amounted to an upgrade of their existing system of law. The north, in contrast, had so-called 'Germanic' legal customs. There, the introduction of the *ius commune* would have meant a significant change from those customs to an entirely new set of laws. Therefore, a more complete reception of Roman law in this period only occurred in the Mediterranean. Elsewhere, the reception of the *ius commune* was limited to canon law, which not only governed internal matters in the Church but also defined fundamental aspects of life, like marriage.

This chapter is about the differences and conflicts between local customary law and the *ius commune*. In most instances, we will discuss them separately for clarity's sake. In reality, the lines between them were blurred because many legal practitioners did not care about the origin of legal rules. To them, the bewildering variety of legal solutions available from fragmented customary law and the many disputes amongst legal scholars were a godsend. It meant that, whatever side they were on, they could always find legal arguments to support their position. Because the law was so complex, it was more often the cause of conflicts rather than a remedy for them. R.C. van Caenegem argues that law was so important for medieval people that they were willing to fight for and over it.

> *R.C. van Caenegem, Law in the Medieval World, Tijdschrift voor Rechtsgeschiedenis 1981, 17–19*
>
> Medieval society had law – there was too much of it, if anything – and greatly cared for it … The Law was not only a reality, it was considered very important. The 'importance' of something to some people is by definition a matter of subjective, personal appraisal and therefore difficult to assess in objective terms, let alone in figures or statistics. Nevertheless, it is obvious to anyone acquainted with the general history of the Middle Ages that the observation and the restoration of the good old law or its defense and improvement were the occasion of numerous initiatives and a good deal of conflict and strife. We all know that the Gregorian reformers at the time of the Investiture Struggle ransacked their libraries in search of texts that would prove the validity of papal claims to independence from and even superiority over emperors and kings: they wanted to prove that what they fought for and tried to restore was the true legal position. The imperial party was also looking for authoritative texts, but its task was more difficult, since lay authority over the Church and such institutions

as the 'Reichskirche' were based on custom rather than written edicts, and custom by its very nature is not easy to prove. Besides, Gregory VII had some sharp things to say about 'custom not turning wrong into right' and about Christ not having said 'I am custom' but 'I am truth'. So real was the concern for the correct legal position that we hear of an abbot of Monte Cassino who resorted in 1083 to an ordeal to discover who, the pope or the emperor, was right on the Investiture issue – it is ironic that the ordeal ended in favour of the imperial party.

If we descend from the lofty heights of popes and emperors to the middle strata of knights and burgesses, we again meet the appeal to the Law in countless conflicts and endeavours. The barons and knights who won the battle for Magna Carta were fighting for the restoration of the traditional laws, which had been perverted by the king's arbitrary rule: Magna Carta is a legal, not a philosophical document, it contains no resounding proclamation of universal principles, but very precise and detailed rules, rooted in everyday feudal life. The same respect for the Law appears as soon as the Flemish towns enter the historic scene. In 1127 the burgesses of Bruges obtained from the new count of Flanders the authority to improve and correct their customary laws. And when, a year later, the burgesses of Ghent revolted against the same new count, they reproached him with numerous injustitiae and proclaimed that he had reigned as a tyrant, against the Law, and had therefore forfeited the country. Henceforth, and in the course of the numerous and dramatic revolts of which Ghent was the theatre, the defence of the Law against the innovations introduced by evermore absolutist monarchs was a historic 'Leitmotiv': it outlived the Middle Ages, for the first demand of the Calvinist republic of Ghent, in revolt against Philip II in 1577, was the restoration of the old urban constitution which had been abolished by the king's father, the Emperor Charles V.

The picture is not different when we analyse the motives of the numerous peasant revolts: the respect of the masses for the law is obvious and their constant complaint is that the powerful and the rich have violated the established legal order and created a reign of illegality and oppression.

It took some time for theories to solve conflicts of law to develop. The most important theory articulated was that the *iura propria* had priority over the *ius commune*, a clear sign that the impact of the latter should not be overestimated (however, see also below).

2.1 *Customary Law*

Customary law dominated the early Middle Ages, and even when, at the end of the eleventh century, the *ius commune* arrived on the scene as a competitor, custom remained an important source of law. Outside the Mediterranean area (and even there to some degree) customs, considered legally binding, provided the framework for the daily life of ordinary people. What the nature of a custom is has been intensely debated among legal historians, with no agreed definition of 'customary law', but they do agree that customary law is different from law as we know it today. The fact that it is different from our understanding of law means that it is not always easy for us to distinguish mere practices from actual legal rules, or to determine the scope of these rules, as the following text on the *laudatio parentum*, the approval of relatives (in this case for gifts of land to cloisters) shows.

> *S.D. White, Custom, Kinship and Gifts to Saints. The Laudatio Parentum in Western France, 1050–1150, Chapel Hill, University of North Carolina Press, 1988, 40–41*
>
> Studies of the *laudatio parentum* can provide general conclusions about eleventh- and twelfth-century land tenure, kinship, and social development only after historians have established the legal or normative status of this practice. How the *laudatio* is interpreted depends largely on whether the people who secured it or gave it were following a legal rule, discharging a religious duty, following custom, taking a practical precaution, or simply behaving in a way that falls into a statistical pattern. Even if we do not treat the *laudatio* as 'the product of obedience' to any kind of rule, we need to know how medieval people viewed the practice. It has proved difficult, however, to determine whether the *laudatio* was essential to the legal validity of gifts to saints or to identify the exact legal, moral, religious, or social consequences of failures to make gifts in this way. These problems are hard to solve not only because the available evidence is open to different interpretations, but also because the question of whether the *laudatio* was a mere prudential practice or a legal institution ... is a useful one to ask only if we make certain debatable assumptions about gifts to saints and about earlier medieval law.
>
> Moreover, even if a custom or legal rule required that some gifts be made with the approval of certain relatives, its scope still has to be delineated. Did it apply to all transfers of land? Or were there circumstances in which individuals could make valid gifts without the *laudatio*? Perhaps the rule applied only to inherited, as opposed to acquired, property, whereas gifts of property acquired through a donor's wife, mother,

> or other female relative were subject to special restraints. But neither of these hypotheses has been confirmed. While an individual's power to alienate real property may have depended on his own status, the status of his donee – the recipient of the gift – or the nature and origin of the property alienated, no one has demonstrated that the gifts of great nobles, for example, were not governed by the same customs as the gifts of less powerful people.
>
> To answer these questions, we also need to gain an understanding of the normative context in which the *laudatio parentum* was practiced. If a rule or custom required that gifts to saints be made with the consent of relatives, did it form part of a system of real property law? Or did it instead regulate social exchanges in which the establishment or reaffirmation of social relationships was at least as important as the transfer of land? In other words, did the rule dictate how farmland, mills, vineyards, or other forms of landed property – along with power over serfs – were to be transferred from one person to another? Or did it regulate the actions of participants in more complex social transactions that entailed more than the transfer of land? Was the rule or custom primarily concerned with things or with people? Or is this distinction an unhelpful one to make for this period? At the same time, we must also determine whether the gifts that eleventh- and twelfth-century landholders so often made to monks and saints were ones that they were obliged to make and that their kin had a duty to support or whether the making and approving of such gifts were matters of purely personal choice or preference. Were a donor's relatives completely free to approve or not to approve his gift? Was their consent something that had to be extracted from them, because in giving it, they suffered a loss? Or did relatives have an active interest in approving gifts to saints? If gifts to saints were simply land transactions governed by a code of legal rules that were distinguished from mere customs or religious norms, then we should be able to determine whether a rule requiring the *laudatio* formed part of this code. If, however, we reject this way of looking at gifts to saints, then the normative status of the *laudatio* becomes more problematic and difficult to establish.

Before customs were written down, they were extremely flexible and adaptable (contrary to the natural assumption that customs are rigid and immutable). One characteristic of customary law is that it reflects social changes. Legal customs are stable if the society that adheres to them remains stable, as was the case during the early Middle Ages. However, the later Middle Ages were more dynamic, and customary rules could change as often as every generation.

This was possible because no one could present a legal text showing that the law had once been different. Instead, the content of the custom was based on memory, a very unreliable tool. Changing a custom could be as easy as claiming that others misunderstood or misremembered the law.

Who was responsible for these changes? The traditional answer is that the people spontaneously created their own customs. There are many problems with this argument. First of all, some customs started as legislation, but the legislative origin was soon forgotten when people liked the new rule. What made customary law popular was not its creation, but the acceptance by the people. This also holds for customs originating in the courts. Most customary legal rules started as judgments, of which the people approved. Once stripped of the facts of the case and reduced to its essence, the judgment could be condensed into a legal rule. The role of the judges was then quickly forgotten. It is, therefore, difficult to identify the creators of much of customary law because, whereas the names of legislators and professors have been recorded for posterity, those of the leading judges of customary law have not. Furthermore, the typical court of customary law did not consist of a single judge: the judgment was a collective act. Nevertheless, it is possible to identify some of the leading judges who made customary law in the late Middle Ages.

> *Dirk Heirbaut, The Spokesmen in Medieval Courts: The Unknown Leading Judges of the Customary Law and Makers of the First Continental Law Reports, in P. Brand and J. Getzler (eds), Judges and Judging in the History of the Common Law and Civil Law: From Antiquity to Modern Times, Cambridge, Cambridge University press, 2012, 193–195*
>
> The *Lois des pairs dou castel de Lille* contains a hodgepodge of legal rules and case law from the feudal court of the count of Flanders in the castellany of Lille … The *Lois de Lille* show how the collective judgement of the Lille judges came to be reached. As in other Flemish courts, the proceedings consisted of a series of questions by the court's president, the lord or his representative, who asked the court to judge, on the one hand, and of answers by the judges, on the other. Other texts give us the impression that the judges answered their president collectively, which may have been possible for simple questions, where a rote formula could be used (for example, as to whether the sun had risen, so that the court could start its activities), but when legal and factual issues were more complex this would have led to chaos, because some judges would have contradicted the others. One can only imagine what a cacophony of shouts and brawls would have resulted from any more-or-less complicated question put by the court's president. Moreover, not everyone sitting in a court was an

expert, so that some judges would have remained silent. For this reason and also to avoid confusion, in Lille one of the judges who was more of an expert than the others, acted as a spokesman for his fellows and, after he had spoken, they followed suit ... That all the judges did so, was only possible because they had first withdrawn to debate the matter and reach agreement. During this discussion, the later spokesman came to the fore and he can be seen as the intellectual author of the court's judgement. This means that the spokesmen were the leading judges and, as such, the real creators of customary law in the Lille area. The usual terminology of 'judgement by peers' is somewhat misleading here. In the feudal hierarchy the judges may have been the peers of the parties, but their spokesman was first among these peers and, literally, a leading judge.

2.2 *The Corpus Iuris Civilis and the University*

Customary law came under increasing pressure as legal scholarship started to flourish. This revival of legal studies was due to the birth of the universities and to the intense interest in ancient Roman culture at that time. Towards the end of the eleventh century, Roman law texts were discovered in the cities of northern Italy and began to circulate in different manuscript versions. In the wake of this, students soon began hiring the services of knowledgeable teachers and forming partnerships with them. One of the first and the best known of these teachers was Irnerius, who began teaching in Bologna in the late 1080s. During the twelfth century, the university (*universitas*) of Bologna gained preeminence as the foremost teaching institution in the field of law, but Bologna was by no means the only European city to establish an early university: significant law faculties were also established in Salamanca (1218), Montpellier (1260), Oxford (1096), and Cambridge (1209).

The emerging legal scholarship at the universities was based on the study of Roman law, which had come down from late Antiquity and was rediscovered in the late eleventh century. A preoccupation with Roman law, instead of the local legal order, typified legal science for many centuries: it often strikes the modern observer as odd that it was taught at the medieval universities, but local laws were not.

The Roman law that became the principal object of research and study at the universities was not just any Roman law. It was the *Corpus iuris civilis* compiled by the Byzantine Emperor Justinian I in the 530s, and, for the first medieval legal scholars, that was the only source of information on ancient Roman law, as the vast legal literature of the classical period of Roman law (ca. 1–250 AD) had been lost and destroyed. The *Corpus iuris* was not 'found' as one complete volume but was discovered piecemeal, and it took time to put the compilation together. The *Digestum vetus* ('the old Digest') was found first, around the 1080s. The parts discovered after that were put together into one work, the so-called *Vulgata* version of the Digest, in the early twelfth century. It was not until the 1150s that the only known full manuscript of the Digest, the *Littera* or *Codex Florentina* emerged in Pisa.

> *Robert Feenstra, Law, in Richard Jenkyns (ed.), The Legacy of Rome: A New Appraisal, Oxford, Oxford University Press, 1992, 403–404*
> In the twelfth century there was a revival of jurisprudence which was closely linked to the full accessibility of the *Corpus iuris civilis.* In the preceding period only portions of Justinian's Code, his Institutes and the *Epitome Juliani* (the abridged Latin version of the Novels) were known. ... The reappearance of the Digest, about 1070, was the turning point.
> ... The complete text of the Digest is extant in a sixth-century manuscript. ... It is certain that it was in Pisa in the twelfth century ... In 1406 the Florentines carried it off as war booty from Pisa .... To modern scholars it is known as the *codex Florentinus* (F) ... All extant copies of the Digest (with the exception of one ninth-century fragment) are derived from it. ... [T]hese so-called vulgate manuscripts, constituting the *littera Bononiensis,* go back to a single lost archetype, the *codex secundus* (S), which was itself an emended copy of F. The emendations of S show in general such critical and philological insights that its origin must be placed in the last third of the eleventh century. This is the period in which the beginnings of the Bolognese School are usually put.

2.3 *The Glossators and the Commentators of the Roman Law*

The first scholars of Roman law came to be known as glossators, a name based on the scholarly methods they used. Even before the birth of the medieval universities, 'glossing' had been a common practice in a variety of scholarly pursuits: for example, it was employed by philosophers and theologians. The method entailed writing comments (*glossa*) on the margins of an authoritative text (marginal gloss) or between the lines of a manuscript (interlinear gloss). The extent of the glosses varied from just a couple of words to substantial explanations. Glosses varied in form and content, and several types of legal literature developed based on individual glosses. As Peter Stein explains:

> *Peter Stein, Roman Law in European History (12th ed.), Cambridge, Cambridge University Press, 2013, 46–47*
> The Bolognese glossators did not tamper with the order of the texts approved by Justinian. They supplied cross-references to all the texts

> which dealt with a particular topic, explaining differences and marshalling the arguments for and against a particular result. Their familiarity with the texts as a whole is indicated by the fact that they could cite every fragment in the Corpus iuris by its first words. No later generation of Roman law scholars has had a closer familiarity with the texts. They used all the techniques of dialectic to squeeze the correct meaning from a text. For them every text, indeed every separate clause in every text, having been approved by the Emperor Justinian, had equal authority.
>
> Various types of legal literature developed out of the glosses on individual texts. Summaries of the content of particular titles of the Digest or Code evolved into *summae* of the content of a whole part of the Corpus iuris, especially the Code and the Institutes. An *apparatus* was a collection of glosses covering the material contained in a particular title in a fuller manner than in a *summa.* A particular favourite for this treatment was the last title of the Digest, 50.17, *de diversis regulis iuris antiqui,* which contained over two hundred 'rules', many in the form of general maxims. The glossators delighted in *distinctiones*, elaborate classifications with many divisions and sub-divisions, sometimes illustrated by diagrammatic tables. There were collections of opposing views on particular points (*dissensiones dominorum*) and collections of *quaestiones*, disputed points, with arguments for each view set out with its supporting texts and usually a *solutio.* Whatever the form, however, everything they wrote revolved around Justinian's texts in all their complex entirety. The glossators worked in an incremental way, each generation imposing a new layer on that laid down by its predecessors.

The Justinianic *Corpus* consisted of materials from a period covering roughly one thousand years. When Justinian's compilers put these texts together, they sometimes changed them to fit Byzantine legal policy or to make them fit in with the whole. Nevertheless, inconsistencies and contradictions remained and needed to be explained and reconciled if the *Corpus iuris* was to become authoritative. Over time, however, it became authoritative in the same way as the Bible was to the theologians or Aristotle's writings to the philosophers. The glossators' method was typical of medieval scholasticism and was shared by other medieval disciplines. They did not slavishly follow the Roman sources but created innovations based on them. A typical example is the statutory theory of proof and the inquisitorial criminal procedure, which profoundly altered the way criminal behaviour has been defined and approached ever since.

The effort of the glossators to construct a legal text free of contradictions was not some strange and exotic enterprise. It was very similar to the way modern legal scholars work; their primary task is to explain the sometimes heterogeneous legal sources, from different historical periods and different circumstances, as a logical and coherent whole. This approach is especially typical for continental legal scholarship.

Irnerius, already mentioned above, is generally considered one of the founders of the school of glossators. Whether he really was the first one or just one of the most important early glossators is not known. More than a hundred years later, Odofredus, an Italian legal scholar, described Irnerius as follows: 'When the books of law were brought from Ravenna [to Bologna], he began to study them by himself, and by studying to teach the Laws, and he was a man of the greatest renown, a true *lucerna iuris* (lantern of the law)'.

Because their focus was on explaining the *Corpus iuris civilis*, the glossators of Roman law did not extend their scholarly activities to local legal sources. However, this did not mean that they were completely detached from the practical legal matters of their day. A prime example of the glossators' involvement in practical issues is related to the Diet of Roncaglia (1158), where Emperor Fredrick II asked the Bolognese law professors Martinus, Bulgarus, Hugo and Jacobus – the famous 'Four Doctors' – for counsel. It is the first known case of legal scholars actively participating in governmental affairs, and it shows how much respect learned law was gaining in twelfth-century Italy. Another great glossator was Azo, who became known for his *Summae*, textbooks with comments, of the Codex and the Institutions. According to the contemporaries, *Chi non ha Azzo non vada al palazzo* (roughly translated, 'who does not understand Azo, should not go to the court room').

The number of glosses kept accumulating over time. Towards the end of the twelfth century, glosses were sometimes gathered together in separate volumes, but they were also routinely copied into the authoritative texts. The culmination of this development was the *Glossa ordinaria* of Accursius, containing roughly 100 000 glosses. With the work of Accursius, glossing had come to its end. Bellomo describes the importance of Accursius in the following way:

> *Manlio Bellomo, The Common Legal Past of Europe, 1000–1800, Washington, The Catholic University of America Press, 1995, 172–173*
>
> Toward the mid-thirteenth century, the *Magna glossa* was universally accepted as an essential and standard accompaniment to the texts of Justinian. Some manuscripts that contained only the laws of Justinian (and had sufficiently empty margins) were used to copy the glosses of Accursius's *apparatus* next to the laws to which they pertained. On

occasion the *apparatus* of Azo or Hugolinus or anonymous networks of glosses were erased by the usual technique of scraping the margins of the parchment leaf, and the freed space was used to transcribe portions of the *Magna glossa* instead (which is why such reworked manuscripts are called palimpsests, from the Greek for 'rescraped'). When new *codices* were made, Justinian's laws were always accompanied by the *Magna glossa*, often copied in the same hand. In this manner the laws lent some of their sacrality to the *apparatus*, and in their reflected glory Accursius's *Glossa* became as untouchable as the laws themselves.

From the mid-thirteenth century on, the diffusion of the *Magna glossa* in Europe reached impressive proportions. It became such a common custom of the schools to accompany the *libri legales* with Accursius's *Magna glossa* that it came to be called *Glossa ordinaria*.

We can find copies of Accursius's *Glossa ordinaria* in all regions of Christian Europe – on the Iberian Peninsula, where one of Accursius's sons, Guglielmo (Guillelmus Accursii), went to teach civil law, in France, especially in the *pays de droit écrit*,[2] where we find the same Guillelmus Accursii, in Germany in monasteries and the libraries of cathedral chapters and collegial churches, in what is now Switzerland, and in many other European lands.

2.4 *The Commentators*

There is no clear-cut dividing line between the glossators and the school which came after them: the 'commentators'. The *glossa ordinaria* remained influential for a long time after glossing as a scholarly method had been replaced by what we think of as a modern approach to legal scholarship. This approach was a response to the growing need to deal with the emerging bodies of city, customary, and feudal law, which exerted an increasing influence on the practical life of thirteenth-century Italy and France. Another reason for the methodological reorientation was that 150 years of glossing the authoritative texts of Roman law had drained the school of glossators of their innovative impetus. If legal scholarship was to retain its position as a significant social force, something new was needed. The commentator school developed a method which helped legal scholarship to stay relevant – and legal scholars to hold on to their influential and powerful positions.

2 *Pays de droit écrit* means 'the land of written law'. The term refers to those parts of France – central and southern – in which the *ius commune* came to prevail in the Middle Ages. The northern part is often call *pays de droit coutumier* or the land of customary law.

The commentators were much more practically-minded than the glossators. The *Corpus iuris civilis* remained an authoritative source for them, but they thought it was important to pay attention to other bodies of law as well. From the thirteenth century onward, town laws, feudal law, commercial law, and royal law had gained importance in different parts of Europe, as will be discussed in more detail below. At the same time, in many parts of Europe customary law started to be written down. European law was now clearly polycentric, as many different – sometimes competing – power-centres produced legal norms. This caused practical problems: the different bodies of law often conflicted – local laws with each other, or with civil law, or civil law with canon law.

To be able to deal with this multitude of laws, the commentators of the thirteenth century developed a theory of legal circles (*Rechtskreistheorie*). According to this theory, courts of law were to apply, first and foremost, the local law, followed by the law of the larger polity. If a suitable legal norm was not found, the court would then have recourse to 'the common law of Europe' (the *ius commune* – not to be confused with English common law). The *ius commune* was a combination of the two universal bodies of law; Roman and Canon, both taught in and studied at universities, influencing and complementing each other. Although the *ius commune* was not the primary source of law, but the one of last resort, certain factors made it extremely important in practice.

First, the *ius commune* directly influenced the contents of the other bodies of law. Legal professionals were often in charge of writing royal and town laws, and of collecting and screening the customary law. They obviously used their *ius commune* training when doing this, and hence the *ius commune* inevitably affected the contents of the other laws. Second, the doctrine of *fundata intentio* advised the courts to apply *ius commune* whenever the applicability of a competing body of law was uncertain – which it quite often was. Third, and relatedly, the doctrine of *iura novit curia* ('the court knows the law') applied only to *ius commune* and the *lex fori*, the local law of the tribunal. Parties to lawsuits had to prove the content of other laws they wished to refer to. These three points together significantly reinforced the position of *ius commune*.

The commentators continued the use of *summae*, the same literary genre as their predecessors had produced. A good example of the way commentators worked is the most famous of them: Bartolus de Saxoferrato (ca.1313–1357). Here, Bartolus approached conflicts of laws concerning a custom of Venice:

> *Peter Stein, Roman Law in European History (12th ed.), Cambridge, Cambridge University Press, 2013, 72*
>
> Bartolus confronted the issue of a conflict between civil law and local law in a discussion of a custom of Venice. This custom accorded validity

to a will if it had three witnesses, which was directly contradictory of the Roman rule that required a minimum of five witnesses (C.6.23.31). Bartolus sought the reason for holding a local custom to be void, if it conflicted with imperial law, and concluded that it must be that it was thereby presumed to be a bad custom. The Roman emperors, however, are known to have allowed conflicting local customs to exist by way of privilege. It follows that it must have been possible to rebut the presumption that a conflicting custom is necessarily a bad custom. Justinian's law could only invalidate customs already in existence in his time. It is possible to prove that a later custom is good, even if it conflicts with Justinian's law. The Venetians knew their own needs best. If they thought it unreasonable to expect five merchants to interrupt their business activities in order to witness a will, a rule according validity to a will with only three witnesses should be valid or else testators' last wishes would be frustrated. In this way Bartolus used Roman arguments to stand Justinian's rule on its head.

One of the commentator's essential working methods was to reconcile conflicting laws (hence the term consiliators sometimes used for the school). Bartolus managed to establish the rule that the local statutes had to be interpreted according to the rules of the *ius commune* and, as far as possible, in such a way that *ius commune* be violated as little as possible.

After Bartolus, his student Baldus dominated the scene of legal science during the second half of the fourteenth century. Baldus perfected the art of judicial opinion (*consilium*), of which he wrote a breath-taking amount of approximately 30 000. The involvement of the commentators in the practical legal life is shown in these expert opinions, delivered to courts of law and parties to lawsuits at request and in exchange for monetary compensation (hence the term commentators).

2.5 *The Canonists*

Not all glossators and commentators were experts in Roman law. From early on, some lawyers specialized in ecclesiastical law. The development of canon law as a discipline distinct from theology and civil law was not a given. However, from the late eleventh century onward, as the administration of the Roman-Catholic Church increasingly became the subject of legislation, there was a growing need to train specialists in canon law. An important milestone in this development was Gratian's Decrete (*Decretum Gratiani*), a textbook of canon law, which took its final form in the late 1140s. The author of the Decrete compiled the existing sources of canon law from the time of the Church Fathers until his own, and made the first attempt to present them as a coherent whole. The work came to be used widely as an authoritative textbook in canon law teaching, much like the *Corpus iuris* in Roman law, retaining its formal authority until 1918. Gratian's Decrete gave the impetus for the school of the 'Decretists', who soon took on the task of commenting on the Decrete. Their work was foundational in many ways. For instance, the genre of *ordines iudiciarii* (handbooks of legal procedure), fundamental to the creation of Roman-canon law of procedure, was a creation of the decretist school.

Another reason why canon law scholarship became so significant was that canon law, unlike civil law, was growing. During its 'golden age', in the twelfth and the thirteenth centuries, it grew with such speed that it was sometimes difficult even for judges and practitioners to keep abreast of the latest developments. Canon law poured out from the Papal Chancery in Rome in the form of decretals or papal letters, most of which were solutions to individual legal cases; however, some were written with a broader scope of application in mind, and even the individual solutions often included norms which came to be applied in other cases as well. Another important source of new canon law were the decisions of the church councils, most notably the Third Lateran Council of 1179 and the Fourth Lateran Council of 1215, which together produced hundreds of laws. In the late twelfth and early thirteenth century, five important collections of church laws (*Compilatio prima, secunda, tertia, quarta* and *quinta*) were issued, culminating in Pope Gregory IX's *Liber Extra*. The *Liber Extra* remained the basic collection of ecclesiastical law until the *Code of Canon Law* was issued in 1918. Despite *Liber Extra*'s paramount position, several other collections were also issued in the Middle Ages. It is sufficient here to mention the *Liber sextus* (1298) and the *Constitutiones Clementinae* (1318).

Canonists intensively glossed all of the compilations and commented upon them. The *Liber Extra* gave rise to a school of canonists often called 'decretalists' (from the other name of Gregory IX's compilation, *Decretales Gregorii IX*).

Civil and canon law also had a significant impact on each other, but it is not easy to determine which branch of legal scholarship actually led the way for legal development in the high and late Middle Ages. Harold Berman describes the relationship of the two bodies of law as follows.

> *Harold J. Berman, Law and Revolution: The Formation of the Western Legal Tradition, Cambridge Mass., Harvard University Press, 1983, 204–205*
> It is sometimes said that the new system of canon law was an 'offspring' of the Roman law of Justinian, and that 'the great codifications that make up the *Corpus Juris Canonici* were patterned on those that make up the *Corpus Juris Civilis*'. At the very least, such statements require the

modification that it was not the Roman law of sixth-century Byzantium, but the revivified and transformed *Romanist* law of eleventh- and twelfth-century Christendom, to which the parentage of canon law must be traced. Yet even with this modification, the idea that canon law was somehow modeled on Roman law involves serious misconceptions. The canonists used Roman law abundantly – as Roman law was understood in their time – just as they used Biblical law, and just as they used Germanic law; they used them all as sources. Thus one may speak, in a qualified sense, of the 'romano-canonical' legal system. Also the canonists shared with the Romanists of their day the same basic theories concerning the nature and functions of law and the same basic methods of analysis and synthesis of opposites – theories and methods which were as much borrowed from them by the Romanists as by them from the Romanists. Indeed, not only theories and methods but also many specific legal concepts and institutions were taken over into contemporary Roman legal science from the new science of canon law.

The comparison of Roman law and canon law in the late eleventh, the twelfth, and the thirteenth centuries is confounded by the fact that canon law was the positive law of the church, while Roman law was not the positive law of any specific polity in the West. Roman law was, of course, the positive law of the Roman Empire in Byzantium; but that was not Roman law as the Western Romanists understood it – it was not the *corpus juris Romani*. In the West, Justinian's Roman law was considered to be an ideal law, a written embodiment of reason, *ratio scripta*, whose principles ought to govern all legal regulation everywhere, both in the church and in the secular polities. Jurists turned to Justinian's text as they turned to the Mosaic law and as they later turned to Aristotle, as sources of positive law. It is true that from the time of Charlemagne, Western emperors claimed succession to the authority of the ancient Roman emperors; and with the discovery of the Justinianic texts, the Western emperors relied upon them – as did the popes – for support. But the 'Holy Roman Empire of the German Nation' was governed by the laws laid down by Western emperors, which were superimposed on tribal (clan), local, feudal, urban, mercantile, ecclesiastical, and other particular laws. Rules and concepts and institutions of Roman law only became the positive law of the Western Empire, just as they only became the positive law of the Western Church, if they were expressly incorporated into that positive law by legislations or juristic interpretation. Roman law was called 'a handmaiden of canon law': it could equally have been called a handmaiden of imperial law and a handmaiden of the positive law of the emerging secular kingdoms and

> city-states. It was, however, always a handmaiden; those scholars err who suppose that Western jurists believed that the Eastern Roman Empire of Justinian somehow continued to exist in the West as a political reality.
>
> Perhaps the most significant difference between Roman law and canon law in the West was the fact that Roman law, with certain rare exceptions, was treated as finished, immutable, to be reinterpreted but not to be changed. Canon law, by contrast, although also handed down from the past, was not finished, it was continually being remade. It had a quality of organic development, of conscious growth over generations and centuries. This gave it a somewhat disorderly character, which has perhaps made it less appealing than Roman law as an intellectual discipline, but surely more interesting from both a moral and a political point of view. For its 'disorderliness' as a science was a necessary part of its dynamic quality as a system – its movement from past to future. The existence of such a time dimension is an essential attribute of modern Western legal systems.

The canonists were innovators in many sectors of the law. The institutional side of Church reform has already been mentioned and will be treated in more detail below. The Catholic Church, 'the first modern state' as Harold Berman put it, organized its judicial system in a hierarchical fashion. This enabled the Papal curia in Rome to control, at least in theory, the judicial functioning of the Church in all corners of Europe.

2.6 *Resistance?*

The victory of the common law of Europe or *ius commune* was far from total. As we will see below, customary law actively reacted to the rise of this new competitor and several bodies of law, including feudal, English, and commercial law, managed to keep some independence from it. However, none of them managed to completely escape its influence.

2.7 *English Common Law*

During the Middle Ages, the influence of Roman law was mainly a Mediterranean phenomenon, as northern Europe proved much less receptive. Strange as it may sound, the main exception to this was England. To avoid confusion with modern usage, we will not call English law 'the common law'. There were many common laws in Europe, and, of course, there was also the *ius commune*. Even if one distinguishes the common law of England from the others, the problem remains that English law consisted of different parts of which the common law of England was just one element. However, it later acquired so much prestige that that part of English law gave its name to the whole.

English law did not develop independently from the European continent during the Middle Ages. The oldest element of today's English law is the aforementioned common law. It developed after the conquest of England by William Duke of Normandy in 1066. William, a ruthless ruler, and his successors as kings of England centralized and strengthened already considerable royal power. His great-grandson Henry II expanded the role of his *curia regis* (royal court) as a tribunal by issuing writs, i.e., written orders to royal officials, so that cases had to be brought to the royal court and not to some local tribunal. Confronted with parties from all over England, the judges of the royal court developed a law common to the whole country, hence the name 'common law'. However, these judges were themselves Normans, not Englishmen, and the raw material for their new law was the customary feudal law of their homeland. The English common law is not a home-grown product, and its oldest part is an immigrant from France. For a long time, this remained audible in the common law, because it used a bastardized French, the so-called 'Law French', until the seventeenth century. Moreover, during the Middle Ages the dominance of French was so great that it wiped out almost all of the original English legal terms, as Frederick Pollock and Frederic William Maitland describe eloquently.

> *Frederick Pollock and Frederic William Maitland, The History of English Law before the Time of Edward I, Cambridge, Cambridge University Press, 1898, 83–85*
>
> But, though throughout the Middle Ages some Latin could be written by most men who could write at all, and the lord of a manor would still have his accounts as well as his court rolls made up in Latin, still only the learned could speak Latin readily, and it could not become the language of oral pleading or of debate. Here was a field in which French and English might strive for the mastery. There could for a long while be no doubt as to which of these two tongues would be spoken in and about the king's court. The king spoke French, his barons French, his prelates French, and even when barons and prelates were beginning to think of themselves as Englishmen, some new wave of foreign influence would break over the court; the new French queen brings with her a new swarm of Frenchmen. And 'the king's court' was not then a term with several meanings; the language of courtiers and courtliness was of necessity the language of business, discussion, pleading. All this might well have happened, however, and yet the English language, which was in the future to

be the language even of courtiers, might have retained its stock of old and its power of engendering new legal terms. A French-speaking royal tribunal might have been merely superimposed upon an English substructure. But here what is perhaps the main theme of our legal history decides the fate of words. Slowly but surely justice done in the king's name by men who are the king's servants becomes the most important kind of justice, reaches into the remotest corners of the land, grasps the small affairs of small folk as well as the great affairs of earls and barons. This is no immediate and no necessary effect of the Norman Conquest. It would never have come about if the nobles who helped William to conquer England could have had their way; William himself can hardly have dared to hope for it. The destiny of our legal language was not irrevocably determined until Henry of Anjou was king.

If we must choose one moment of time as fatal, we ought to choose 1166 rather than 1066, the year of the assize of novel disseisin rather than the year of the battle of Hastings. Then it was that the decree went forth which gave to every man dispossessed of his freehold a remedy to be sought in a royal court, a French-speaking court. Thenceforward the ultimate triumph of French law terms was secure. In all legal matters the French element, the royal element, was the modern, the enlightened, the improving element. The English stock of words is stricken with barrenness, the French stock can grow. The things of the law which have English names are things that are obsolete or obsolescent, sake and soke, wer and wite: – already men hardly know what these words mean. It is difficult for us to believe that in the local courts, the suitors, who were for the most part peasants, pleaded their causes and rendered their judgments in French; still from the thirteenth century we get books of precedents for pleadings in manorial courts which are written in French, while we look in vain for any similar books written in English. We may suspect that if the villagers themselves did not use French when they assailed each other in the village courts, their pleaders used it for them, and before the end of the thirteenth century the professional pleader might already be found practising before a petty tribunal and speaking the language of Westminster Hall. Then in 1362 a statute, itself written in French, declared that as the French tongue was but little understood, all pleas should be 'pleaded, shown, defended, answered, debated and judged' in the English tongue. But this came too late. It could not break the Westminster lawyers of their settled habit of thinking about law and writing about law in French, and when slowly French gave way before English even as the language of law reports and legal text-books, the English to which

> it yielded was an English in which every cardinal word was of French origin. How far this process had gone at the end of the thirteenth century we may learn from Robert of Gloucester's historical poem. He sets himself to translate into English verse the Constitutions of Clarendon, and in so doing he uses the terms which we now write as custom, grant, lay fee, service, pleading, assize, judgment, traitor, chattels, felon, patron, advowson, court, plea, purchase, amendment, hold in chief, bailiff, homage, confirm, appeal, debt. Down to the end of the Middle Ages a few Old English terms perdured which, at least as technical terms, we have since lost: English 'domes-men' might still 'deem dooms in a moot hall'; but the number of such terms was small and the blight of archaism was on them.

The judges from the royal court soon formed three distinct common law courts: the Court of Exchequer, the Court of Common pleas, and the King's Bench. Initially, royal legislation and writs gave guidance to the judges sitting on these courts. However, the English barons resented the loss of money and influence the rise of common law courts caused. At the end of the thirteenth century, they made the king promise to only issue new writs by analogy with existing ones. This meant that the common law judges were left to their own devices and henceforth had to base their decisions on their own precedents. Eventually, those precedents acquired so much importance in the common law that the term became synonymous with judge-made law. These precedents took the law in a new direction, and over time moved the common law ever further from its Norman French (and thus continental) origins without ever fully getting rid of them.

From the time of the conquest, another continental influence contributed to the development of law in England: the *ius commune*. Canon law and its courts remained important throughout the Middle Ages, but Roman law also had more of an impact here than anywhere else in Northern Europe. In part, this was because of the teaching of Roman law at Oxford and Cambridge from the late twelfth century on. Even earlier, in the late eleventh century – when the *ius commune* was still in its infancy even in Italy – England was unique in that it had already come into contact with it. The Normans are best known for their conquest of England, but around the same time, they also took control of Sicily and Southern Italy and established a kingdom there. Because of the links between the Normans in the South, their homeland, and England, the Norman clergy in Normandy and England were more acquainted with Roman law than clergy elsewhere in Northern Europe. This made the English aware early on of the need for and the usefulness of writing down the common law. These first redactions of the common law borrowed from the nascent *ius commune*. The first book of English law, ascribed to Ranulf de Glanvill, appeared as early as the end of the twelfth century. The next book, in all likelihood written by Henry de Bracton, followed in the thirteenth century. Its high quality is due to the incorporation of Roman law. Ironically, as a consequence, Roman law lost much of its influence in England. English practitioners felt they had enough Roman law in Bracton so that they did not need the professors of the *ius commune.* Through Bracton, Roman law continued to exert its influence on later authors, e.g., Littleton and Fortescue, in the fifteenth century. John Baker, following Frederick Maitland, in an early edition of his leading textbook, described how England could escape the 'disease' of the *ius commune* by being inoculated at an early date (in the latest editions of the book this passage has been changed).

> *John Baker, An Introduction to English Legal History, London, Butterworth, 2002, 28*
>
> And, with few outward signs of struggle, the common law withstood two waves of Romanist influence which swept across the Continent. The rediscovery of Justinian's Digest, and the consequent explosion of Roman legal studies in the universities of the twelfth and thirteenth centuries, made Roman Civil law the common currency of European lawyers, including the doctors of law at Oxford and Cambridge. Early royal judges were in touch with that new learning, and may have injected some of it into the early chaos; but the effect was prophylactic, and served to immunise English law against fatal infection later. Compared with the rest of Europe, England and its system of government and law were precocious. The scheme of writs described in Glanvill and the attendant procedure and terminology, the developed notion of pleas of the Crown with all the machinery for the discovery and trial of criminals, the existence of central and itinerant royal courts capable of subjecting the whole nation to the kings' law and government: all these things were in being before the university law schools were founded. And so, 'while the other nations of Western Europe were beginning to adopt as their own the ultimate results of Roman legal history, England was unconsciously reproducing that history; it was developing a formulary system which in the ages that were coming would be the strongest bulwark against Romanism and sever our English law from all her sisters'.
>
> The second wave of Romanism struck at the end of the Middle Ages, when Renaissance humanism drove out older methods of proof from continental courts and encouraged the application of rational legal principles based on the Civil law. But once again England had anticipated the rest of Europe without recourse to scholastic learning. Through the

> process called 'pleading' the common lawyers had built their own elaborate and rational system of law around the writs which governed the business of the royal courts. England's lawyers had their own law schools, located not in the universities but between London and Westminster Hall, where the chief study was not classical texts but writs and pleading and feudal land law. Not that England in any way escaped the rapid social and legal changes of the Renaissance period; but the common-law system was sufficiently adaptable to accommodate them without importing foreign ideas.

A third strand of medieval English law was also an offshoot of the *ius commune*. At the end of the thirteenth century, the barons of England stopped the king from issuing new types of writs, but they could not prevent Englishmen from presenting new cases to the king personally instead of to his common law courts. The king soon delegated the task of rendering judgment to his chancellor. The latter had broad discretion to rule based on what his conscience dictated, so his decisions were ad hoc. However, even then he needed some sources of inspiration, and because he was a clergyman, trained in theology and the *ius commune*, he turned to the latter, not to the common law of England. In the end, the chancellor's court of conscience became a court autonomous from the other English courts which developed a new body of law based on its own precedents, called 'equity'. This evolution moved it away from its original connection with the *ius commune*. However, although the latter's influence diminished, it never disappeared. In short, English law never developed in a bubble of its own. One sizable branch of it, the common law of England, was French in origin and borrowed from the *ius commune*, the other, equity, was also inextricably linked to the *ius commune*.

2.8 *Feudal Law*

Feudalism was one of the most original creations of the Middle Ages, but the term itself has meant many things, as F.-L. Ganshof, one of its leading historians, explains.

> *F.-L. Ganshof, Feudalism, London, Longman, 1952, xv–xvii*
> The word feudalism (Germ. Lehnswesen or Feudalismus; Fr. féodalité) is one to which many different meanings have been attached. During the French Revolution, it was virtually adopted as a generic description covering the many abuses of the Ancien Régime, and it is still in popular use in this sense today. Even if this quite illegitimate extension of its meaning be ignored, there exist many attempts at its analysis and definition which

do not seem to be very closely related to one another. But if we limit ourselves to essentials and are prepared to overlook the subtle nuances of meaning which scholars, and particularly legal scholars, delight in, it will be found that the word is used by historians in two more or less distinct senses.

Feudalism may be conceived of as a form of society possessing well-marked features which can be defined without difficulty. They may be summarized as follows: a development pushed to extremes of the element of personal dependence in society, with a specialized military class occupying the higher levels in the social scale; an extreme subdivision of the rights of real property; a graded system of rights over land created by this subdivision and corresponding, in broad outline to the grades of personal dependence just referred to; and a dispersal of political authority amongst a hierarchy of persons who exercise in their own interest powers normally attributed to the State and which are often, in fact, derived from its break-up.

This type of society, whether one calls it feudalism or the feudal regime, was that of western Europe in the tenth, eleventh and twelfth centuries. It came into existence in France, Germany, the kingdom of Burgundy-Arles and Italy, all of them states deriving from the Carolingian empire, and in other countries – England, certain of the Christian kingdoms of Spain, the Latin principalities of the Near East – which passed under their influence. In other places and at other times, types of society have existed which show many analogies with the feudalism which one finds in France, Germany, the kingdom of Burgundy-Arles and Italy during the Middle Ages, so that scholars have been led to speak of 'feudalism' in ancient Egypt, in India, in the Arab world, in the Turkish empire, in Russia, in Japan, and elsewhere. In making these comparisons, historians have sometimes drawn parallels which a closer examination of the sources has failed to justify, though in some instances, as in that of Japan, the parallelism is very close.

Professor Calmette and the late Marc Bloch, in writing on feudalism in this sense, preferred to speak of 'feudal society'. Such a practice, if it were generally accepted, would have the advantage of allowing one to use the word 'feudalism' only in the second sense that can be attached to it.

In this second sense of the word, 'feudalism' may be regarded as a body of institutions creating and regulating the obligations of obedience and service – mainly military service – on the part of a free man (the vassal) towards another free man (the lord), and the obligations of protection and maintenance on the part of the lord with regard to his vassal. The obligation of maintenance had usually as one of its effects the grant by the lord to his vassal of a unit of real property known as a fief. This sense of the word feudalism is obviously more restricted and more technical than the other. We can perhaps regard it as the legal sense of the word, while the first use covers mainly the social and political senses.

These two meanings of the word feudalism are not unrelated to each other, since the society which we have described above is known as feudal because in it the fief, if not the corner-stone, was at least the most important element in the graded system of rights over land which this type of society involved.

Feudalism in its narrow sense, meaning the system of feudal and vassal institutions, was also, and to an even greater degree than feudalism in its broad sense, proper to the states born of the break-up of the Carolingian empire and the countries influenced by them.

Feudalism, in the strict sense of lords, fiefs and vassals, was most of all a phenomenon of the higher classes. It could be found all over Europe with common terminology, rituals, and rules. As such, it was another 'European' law like the *ius commune,* while the manorial rules only applicable to peasants were of local importance. However, the differences between the regional varieties of feudalism were so large that its common elements, at times, were empty forms that could be filled with very different content. This made it possible to have feudalism even without its typical male primogeniture, which awarded all, or the largest part, of the feudal succession to the eldest son. Moreover, feudalism was established at different times and places in history. Its origins can be traced back to the Carolingian empire, but even in the pioneering regions where a mature feudalism first broke through, it did not appear until around the year 1000, and it did not develop in other parts of Europe until the twelfth century, or even later. This meant that regional versions of feudalism in Europe could vary enormously, and that 'feudalism' as a concept is only a later creation, as Susan Reynolds states.

S. Reynolds, Fiefs and Vassals. The Medieval Evidence Reinterpreted, Oxford, Oxford University Press, 1994, 1–3

FEUDALISM, to any members of the general public who ever refer to it, stands for almost any hierarchical and oppressive system. ... Medieval historians may dislike this ... but they are not on the whole much more precise in their use of the words feudal and feudalism. ... A good many medievalists have, however, continued to maintain that, whatever the difficulties of describing medieval society in general as feudal, there is a

> narrow, technical, more precise sense to feudalism which retains its utility. ...
>
> This book is concerned only with feudalism in its supposedly more precise sense. Its object is to establish how far vassalage and the fief, as they are generally understood, constituted institutions which are definable, comprehensible, and helpful to the understanding of medieval history. My argument will be that in so far as they are definable and comprehensible they are not helpful. ... Fiefs and vassalage, as they are generally defined by medieval historians today, are post-medieval constructs ... Historians often refer to both fiefs and vassals when neither word is in their sources.

Feudalism was so pervasive in medieval society that the *ius commune* already took account of it in the twelfth century. The glossators made a collection of the feudal customs of Northern Italy, the *Libri feudorum* (books on fiefs), the importance of which was so significant that it was the only sizable text which the glossators integrated into the *Corpus iuris civilis*. They studied it like the rest of the *Corpus*, adding glosses, writing commentaries, etc. Thus, the *ius commune* included not only Roman and canon, but also feudal, law. The learned feudal law of the *Libri feudorum* displaced or amended indigenous feudal law in some parts of Europe, mainly in the Mediterranean, whereas elsewhere it was ignored by local feudal law. In England, feudal law was enormously influential as it provided the basic elements for the creation of the common law of England, and traces of feudalism are still visible in today's English law. A term like 'fee simple', for example, is feudal in origin ('fee' is derived from 'fief').

For some of its most important functions, like providing knights to a lord or binding nobles to a king or prince, feudalism became outdated, in some places as early as the thirteenth century. Nevertheless, as a mechanism for structuring the holding of land, it survived the entire Middle Ages. In England, it mostly disappeared in the seventeenth century. France abolished feudalism at the start of its revolution in 1789, and also abolished it in territories they annexed or controlled during the revolutionary and Napoleonic periods, like Belgium. In Germany, its last vestiges disappeared in 1900. Scotland only said farewell to feudalism in 2004. The last hold-out of feudalism in Europe, the isle of Sark, relented a few years later. A British newspaper provided its readers with a report on the capitulation of this last bastion, which shows that in those areas where it still existed feudalism could rule daily life and create problems for modern people.

The Independent, October 26th, 2006
John Michael Beaumont makes an unusual despot. In his standard-issue pensioner's outfit – cosy crewneck jumper, blue work trousers, grey leather-look shoes – the 79-year-old ex-aircraft engineer looks much like any other septuagenarian. He drinks tea. He tends his garden. He potters. Kim Jong Il he most certainly is not. However benign, though, Beaumont is an old-fashioned sort of dictator – the hereditary overlord of the last independent feudal state in the world.

As Seigneur of Sark, an island three miles long and one mile wide, 25 miles from the French coast, Beaumont's position is an enviable one. Since 1565, when Elizabeth I granted the island to the nobleman Hellier de Carteret in return for his protection against pirates, the Seigneurs have ruled this rock. And, in return for the £1.79 Beaumont pays annually to the British Crown to keep the island 'in perpetuity', the Seigneur holds the privilege of granting the Sarkees permission to buy and sell their houses; and he is also entitled to collect a treizieme – one-thirteenth of every land transaction.

But not for long. Beaumont's days of occupying his unique position are numbered. Earlier this month, the self-governing island, which falls under the protectorate of the British crown, voted by a majority of 234 to 184 to usher in universal suffrage for its population of 610. No longer will the island's 40 landowners, or 'tenants' as they are confusingly known, sit on Sark's government – the 'Chief Pleas'. Nor will Beaumont retain his treizieme, or his right of veto.

Next year, the adult population of the island will go to the polls for the first time with one vote each and elect 28 new members of the 'Chief Pleas'. Sark will be a democracy …

An islander who feels he has been wronged or assaulted in some way can drop to one knee, throw his hat to the ground, recite the Lord's Prayer in Norman French and then say: 'Haro, haro, haro! A mon aide mon Prince, on me fait tort!' (Help me, my prince, someone does me wrong). The assailant must immediately cease what he is doing, while a formal complaint is made to the island's Greffe (court). It would have been wonderful to see Dermot use the 'Haro', but it was unlikely; the custom was last enacted in Sark in 1970, during a dispute over a garden wall …

The Seigneur, for instance, is accorded some pretty odd privileges denied to all other Sarkees – the right to keep an unspayed bitch (he doesn't); the right to keep pigeons (he does); and the right to keep the flotsam and jetsam that washes up on the island (he wouldn't want to).

In retrospect, the writing was on the wall for Sark's ancient system of government when the Barclay brothers, the Telegraph Group's billionaire

> owners, paid £2.33m for the neighbouring island of Brecqhou in 1993. Brecqhou falls under the jurisdiction of Sark, and as such they were forced to pay their treizieme – £179,230 – straight into Beaumont's pocket.
>
> Of further irritation to the Barclays – who are believed to have set foot on Sark only once – was the law of primogeniture, meaning that property must pass whole and undivided into the hands of the eldest male heir. This, they argued, ran contrary to the European Convention on Human Rights. They mounted a formal challenge, both to Brecqhou's status as part of Sark (they lost), and to primogeniture (they won, and Sark has since changed that law so that the eldest female can inherit).

2.9 *Commercial Law*

The early Middle Ages had no need for commercial law because the economy was too simple. However, the growth of the European economy from the eleventh century onward led to the rise of rules and customs for trade, the sources of which were extremely varied. For example, international fairs, most of all those of the Champagne region, contributed to the development of new legal mechanisms like bills of exchange. Another important source was maritime law, which can, in turn, be divided into a Mediterranean and a northern European 'family'. The former was created by Italian and Spanish trading towns, like Pisa, Genova, Venice, Barcelona, and Valencia, on the basis of an older Byzantine text. It was further developed by specific commercial courts, like the 'Consulate of the Sea' in Barcelona. Northern European maritime law started with the twelfth century 'Rolls of Oleron', which contained the judgments of a maritime court on Oleron, an island on the French Atlantic seacoast. The main texts based on this work were the Water law of Damme, a major trading hub near Bruges, and the Sea Law of Wisby, a city on the island of Gotland in the Baltic Sea.

The new rules and customs of trade served the needs and desires of merchants, and as a result they deviated from the rest of the law in many ways. Trust in other merchants made it possible to get rid of complex formalities. A fair and swift settlement of disputes was preferred over a rigid adherence to the formal dictates of law. Moreover, the general idea was that the merchant was a professional who was familiar with market practices and needed no special rules to protect him.

The exact nature of the rules and customs of trade law has been debated. According to an older theory, Europe, since the eleventh century, had a *lex mercatoria* (commercial law), a coherent body of legal rules distinct from the *ius commune*, which aspired to be European-wide in scope, not merely local. Merchants had to develop their own common law, as the professors from the universities were not interested in adapting Roman law to commercial practice, even though this would have been possible. Moreover, canon law was actually hostile towards trade, given its prohibition on usury, which excluded charging not just usurious interest but any interest at all. In these circumstances, the logical step for merchants was to create their own law, which had to be as European-wide as their business was. However, there were large differences in the rules and customs of trade within Europe and there was even diversity within the smaller Mediterranean and northern 'families'. The former was shaped by the *ius commune*. In places where specialized commercial courts or great books of commercial law were absent, the existence of commercial law as an autonomous body of law with a distinct identity was even less likely. In short, when talking about the Middle Ages, it is better to avoid using the term *lex mercatoria* and to stick to the more neutral expression 'rules and customs of trade'. The researcher looking for a common European *lex mercatoria* will not find it. As Albrecht Cordes explains:

> *Albrecht Cordes, The Search for a Medieval Lex Mercatoria, Oxford University Comparative Law Forum 5 (2003) (available at* ouclf.iuscomp.org*; accessed in June 2022)*
>
> [I]n the Middle Ages, the term 'Lex mercatoria' is used in the context of advantages and privileges granted to merchants in the field of civil litigation. This is quite different from the modern sense of a system of substantive trade law that cannot be traced back any further than to the seventeenth century. In this sense, Lex mercatoria formed part of an English dispute about court competence in which the merchants argued that the Lex mercatoria was an integral part of the English Ius Commune, i.e. the common law. Contrary to this, in contemporary Germany, trade law was not viewed as part of continental common law (in Germany: 'Ius commune – Gemeines Recht'), but as a specific legal system based upon privileges, a Ius singulare. Therefore the sources on the continent refer to 'Ius mercatorum' instead of 'Lex mercatoria': a set of subjective rights, of privileges, with the merchants as the bearers of special rights, instead of a system of law with 'mercantile' as its description. Investigating the history of the term Lex mercatoria thus leads to a clear result: Lex mercatoria is not a term of European or international, but of English law. In English law, it stands for certain privileges in thirteenth-century legal procedure, maybe even for a separate system of judicial procedure. Until the seventeenth century, the term Lex mercatoria does not gain any meaning beyond that.

This outcome leads to another question: if the use of 'Lex mercatoria' in the sense of a body of substantive trade law can not be traced back to the Middle Ages, did a widespread, cross-border legal system of this kind nevertheless exist, perhaps under another name or without any denotation at all – a system which may well have served as an example to the modern international trade law? Has there been a Lex mercatoria *avant la lettre*? The Lex mercatoria has occasionally been called a universal trade law but this is not very convincing. Only two areas of medieval law could claim to be universal (in the eurocentric sense of the word of before 1492): canon law and imperial law, the law of the catholic church and the law of the Roman Emperor. From the late eleventh century, both were treated scholarly at Bologna and other northern Italian and French universities. As for the sphere of trade law, opinions differ greatly. It is even discussed whether a body of objective rules of law could have existed at all before 1100. Be that as it may, there is a consensus concerning one point: a theoretical concept of a substantive law of trade did not come into existence before the beginning of the twelfth century. On the continent, the famous foundation charter of the market of Freiburg im Breisgau, located at the foot of the Black Forest, most likely from the year 1120, may well be one of the earliest examples for the term 'Ius mercatorum' to be used in the sense of a body of law.

2.10 *Customary Law Fights Back*

Compared to the *ius commune*, customary law was inferior because it had no European ambitions, no great books of professors, no support of the Church etc. To survive, it had to become more unified, written, and academic. The easiest way to do this was to switch to the *ius commune*. The Mediterranean region had already opted for this in the Middle Ages, but in Northern Europe the change came later, starting with the establishment in 1495 of the *Reichskammergericht* (Imperial Chamber Court) as the supreme court of the Holy Roman Empire.

The greatest weakness of customary law was its fragmentation and particularism. Unification was hard to achieve as it went against vested interests, and movements in the later Middle Ages in support of greater political unification did not always result in legal unification. Local populations were more willing to give up their rulers than their law. In this context, central authorities could only take gradual steps. The increase in appeal procedures and the establishment of central courts of appeal contributed to the process of greater legal unification, as judges in appeal courts were less likely to respect local customs and more inclined to impose their own rules – not because of any hostility towards the customary law as such, but because of its enormous variety. The higher or central court just could not know all the customary law. Central courts, appearing on the scene later, were a double-edged sword for customary law; at times, they strengthened it by unifying the law (e.g., the English common law); at others they weakened it by introducing Roman law.

Unification at the lower level was sometimes the result of happenstance. For example, when a person sat on two local courts and shared with his colleagues a new solution he had encountered in the other court. This process could be more formal if a smaller court with less experience and expertise asked for advice of a knowledgeable and larger, or at least more prestigious, court. Over time the latter's advice evolved into a binding judgment on the other court, which came to be seen as subordinate. Paradoxically, the founding of new cities sometimes also contributed to legal unification. An easy way for the founder to make the new town attractive was to give it the law of an older, well-established city, which led to different families of city laws. The best known and most influential was the city law of Magdeburg, which spread from Germany all over Eastern and Central Europe.

> *Heiner Lück, Aspects of the Transfer of the Saxon-Magdeburg Law to Central and Eastern Europe, Rechtsgeschichte 2014, 85*
> For decades, scholars have been preoccupied with the spread of two important historical legal documents from the German Middle Ages to regions in Central and Eastern Europe: *Sachsenspiegel* (lit. 'Saxon Mirror'), a legal code of the German Middle Ages which had an enduring effect on German law for many centuries and *Magdeburger Recht* (Magdeburg Law), a set of town privileges developed under the reign of Otto I. (936–973) and his successors. The relevance of these documents today, and the curiosity they have sparked, extend far beyond the academic environs. There has been a general revival of the interest in the common origins of European statehoods and legal orders, and more so in the context of the integration of a couple of Central and Eastern European countries into the European Union in 2004 …
>
> Before we ask if the Magdeburg Law had any impact on the identity of cities and towns, we first need to identify factors that play a significant role in the evolution of cities and towns. The factors defining the identity of cities evolved parallel to the development of cities and the formation of their internal organization in the Middle Ages. The external elements we should list here include: market square, town hall, the building of the municipal court or the seat of the Bench, city walls, municipal seal, the city's coat of arms, specific municipal books, precious privileges which had been granted to the city, as well as a statue of a knight in armour (the

> so-called 'Roland') or another symbolic figure of that kind, and, of course, the city's main church. All of these elements have developed a specific external form due to their links with Magdeburg Law, and all of them, collectively considered, represent a specific type of a municipal liberty. The liberty in question was also in some way rooted in the Magdeburg Law that contained a set of norms regulating the co-existence of political and social groups. These common features of the family of cities functioning under Magdeburg Law have maintained their power until the present day ...
>
> Many cities and towns in Eastern Europe continue to remind us about the fact that they used to be linked by a common system of town law. No matter how different all the specific legal cases of these cities might in fact have been, they used to belong to the same family functioning under the common trademark of 'Magdeburg Law' – and indeed, they still belong to that family today.

Unification could also be the result of the work of private persons who had started to record the law. At first, judges and lawyers (or those wanting to become judges or lawyers) only took notes on small slips of parchment for their own use or the instruction of others. As systemization was not a priority for them, they kept these notes in bags. The next step to bring more structure to the law was the composition of books in which an author tried to look at the law as a whole. Most of the time, the author was a practitioner who had not studied law at a university. As a consequence, the systematization of the law remained modest, and analysis and commentary were lacking. The best authors looked beyond their own local law and tried to offer an account of the customs of a broader region, which made them very influential, e.g., Jean Boutillier in Northern France and the Low Countries or Jacques d'Ableiges for Paris and the neighbouring regions. The most successful treatise was the *Saxon Mirror* by Eike von Repgow. It became the model for other works on customary law in Germany and its influence stretched from the Netherlands and Northern Germany to Eastern and Central Europe. In some parts of Germany, it survived as subsidiary law until the German civil code of 1900. However, the *Saxon Mirror* was exceptional. In reality, the importance of most authors of customary law was rather limited in their own time, as the translator of one of them admits.

> *F. Akehurst, The Coutumes of Philippe de Beaumanoir, Philadelphia, University of Pennsylvania Press, 1992, xiii–xiv*
>
> The esteem in which modern scholars hold Philippe de Beaumanoir's Coutumes de Beauvaisis is evidenced in such descriptions as admirable,

significant, most important, the best, 'l'oeuvre juridique la plus originale et la plus remarquable du moyen âge francais', and so forth; indeed it is hard to find any disparaging remarks about it (I have found none). It is all the more surprising, therefore, that no translation of it has been published up to now, except in Japanese. Only three printed editions have been produced of the original Old French version, in 1690, in 1842, and in 1899–1900 (reprinted in 1970). The present translation therefore fills a very real need.

It is all the more important to stress from the outset that Beaumanoir's treatise is limited both in place and time: it deals only with the customs of the Beauvais region (or to be more precise, the county of Clermont), and it was valid in its entirety perhaps only for the two or three years during which it was being written, ending in 1283. Customs described in the Coutumes de Beauvaisis cannot be assumed to have been in force in any other region, or at any other time (although they may have been). While many customs were identical in several adjoining castellanies, others were different in a province as close as Normandy, where for example the royal writs introduced by the Angevin monarchs were still in force in Beaumanoir's time, yet totally unknown in Clermont. What the Coutumes offer us is not the common law of France, but the customs of a small region. They also provide the incalculably valuable testimony of an important public official who was familiar with the laws, who had meditated on their worth and cohesiveness, and who left on his book the stamp of a personality which today's readers cannot but find attractive and surprisingly modern. It has become unfashionable in literary studies to look for 'the author behind the work'. The reader who does not sense the man Philippe de Beaumanoir behind this book is missing one of the greatest pleasures it holds.

Features of the Coutumes de Beauvaisis which have won for it the accolades quoted above include comprehensiveness, clarity, and independence. The comprehensiveness may be an illusion, since there remain questions to which Beaumanoir provides no answers: the actual course of the procedure, the rhythm of cases, the formality of the proceedings – much that an observer of 1283 could see for himself – all remain rather obscure. Yet Beaumanoir does cover much more law than other custumals, which seem preoccupied with property, its ownership and change of ownership. The law is clearer, also, in Beaumanoir, for he gives definitions which non-specialists of his own time could probably understand fairly readily, many of which are still transparent to us today. And for Beaumanoir, the living law is the customs, as seen applied in cases that he

> recounts, rather than the law of Rome which, in spite of its growing prestige, is sometimes hard to reconcile with the customs of the time. Other custumals take pains to cite the Roman law most like the custom under discussion, but Beaumanoir never does this, and it is easy to imagine that the customs he describes have gradually grown up and evolved, that they somehow reflect the will of the people. This is probably a delusion, and scholars have discovered many influences of Roman and Canon law; but the customs of Beauvais hang together, and the modern reader can learn a considerable amount about the society of Clermont and its county just by reading Beaumanoir. He often gives his defense of a custom, usually based on reasonableness or, as he says, the fact that 'it would be a bad thing' if the law were otherwise.
>
> While Beaumanoir's law is thus at once limited and broad, allegedly merely remembered but in fact logically defensible and defended, it can often be used to explain some actual or literary event or procedure elsewhere and at a different time. Nowadays Beaumanoir is frequently cited as an authority, even for events which occurred decades before his time. This recourse to Beauvais law can be dangerous, since the law is not always and everywhere the same; but even if the law is not available to us for the region where an event occurred, the fact that the event would have been (un)lawful in Beauvais allows us to guess that it was also (un) lawful where it did occur.

The notes taken in court also contributed to the development of chronological or systematic collections of case law. This development was complex, as in some places some forms of judicial decisions began to exert authority. That authority itself varied: sometimes it was formal and associated with the forum in which the case was decided, sometimes informal, drawing on assumptions or claims that the decision was rational. Famous examples of this are the decisions of the Rota, the highest court of the Church, or the English Year Books.

Official registrations of customary law remained limited at first. Most of the time, charters only contained fragments of local or regional customs, though more elaborate city and land laws do appear. In Sweden, this even resulted in a land law and a city law for the whole country. In France, the king systematically registered the customs of the French cities and regions and promulgated them as law. In the Low Countries, the dukes of Burgundy followed the example of their French cousins. This process of homologations started in the fifteenth century and continued throughout the first part of the early modern era, forming a bulwark against Roman law. When circa 1500, many other parts of Northern Europe switched to the *ius commune*, Northern France and the Southern Low Countries remained staunchly loyal to their own customs. Roman law was more successful in the Northern Low Countries where, before they became independent from the Habsburg successors to the dukes of Burgundy, homologation had not yet started. Homologated customs, as defined by R.C. van Caenegem, stand between custom and legislation.

> *R.C. van Caenegem, An Historical Introduction to Private Law, Cambridge, Cambridge University Press, 1992, 36*
> There was also an increasing tendency to set customs down in writing. At first sight, this is a contradiction in terms, because the qualities *par excellence* of custom are the adaptability, flexibility and fluidity with which it arises and disappears. Once a customary rule has been reduced to writing, however, the written version takes on a life of its own and a certain performance; the writing fixes the text and restricts all further modification. These effects had already been felt in private compilations made on the initiative of practitioners, and the official compilation of customs followed by their promulgation with the force of law completed the development. The end product of this operation, known as the recording or 'homologation' of customs, is a hybrid source of law. On the one hand, the written customs are customary law. That is how they are presented, and the fact that they were compiled on the basis of statements by witnesses who had experience of local usages confirms their customary origin. On the other hand, the collected texts were promulgated after revision by the central authorities and the courts were then bound to apply them to the exclusion of all other contrary custom. Since it is rare (as history shows) for a promulgated version to be adapted or modified later, the established text resembles a statute even more. The homologated customs therefore represent a transitional phase between the true customs spontaneously formed and developed in the early Middle Ages and the true legislation of the following period.

Whether the authorities or private authors wrote texts of customary law, the written redactions soon started to exhibit Roman law influence, with some works of the later Middle Ages claiming to describe local customs closer in substance to treatises of Roman law. Such works were not always popular, and for a real blending of customary and local law all over Europe one has to wait for the early modern era. Writing not only allowed the learned law to slip in, it also changed the nature of customary law. As long as it was oral, it could go with the flow and constantly adapt itself to new challenges. The written text, however, fixed the custom, so that it became harder to change. Judges of local courts could no longer do as pleased them, because the authorities and scholars could check what they were doing using written texts. On the other hand, writing also facilitated schooling. Apprentice lawyers and judges took notes in court, and copied the notes from their predecessors. Once more systematic works appeared, instruction was their main beneficiary. Formal schooling in customary law remained limited. Only in England did a fully-fledged alternative to the law faculties of the universities arise. An embryonic law school already existed in the second half of the thirteenth century. In the fourteenth century, the Inns of Court and the Inns of Chancery appeared and trained so many English lawyers and judges that they could later be called the 'third university of England'. P. Brand sketches their origins and importance.

> *P. Brand, Legal Education in England before the Inns of Court, in J. Bush and A. Wijffels (eds), Learning the Law. Teaching and the Transmission of Law in England, 1150–1900, London, Hambledon Press, 1999, 82–83*
>
> What is known about legal education during the reigns of Edward I and Edward II is largely, though not exclusively, derived from written remains deposited by the teaching and learning process. This means that we know quite a lot about how students were educated, and we can see that this was through a mixture of lectures, learning exercises, private reading and practical experience. We know much less about how legal education was organised. We can be fairly certain that as yet there were no 'inns of court' in London where law was taught or law students lived. Had such institutions existed there would surely be at least a passing reference to them in surviving sources. But how much did legal education owe to official sponsorship or initiative? The Common Bench clearly went out of its way to accommodate its apprentices in a crib from 1291 onwards and its justices helped to educate them through helpful remarks. It may also be significant that although most law teachers of the period are stubbornly anonymous, those whose identities are known include Gilbert of Thornton (a serjeant of the Common Bench) and Ralph de Hengham (the Chief Justice of King's Bench). It seems likely that the Common Bench exercised some kind of quality control over those it admitted to practise in the court as its serjeants and this may have taken the form of some kind of examination which tested the knowledge acquired by the would-be serjeant during his period as an apprentice. But there is no reason to believe that the Common Bench went so far as to take control of legal education, whether in 1292 or at

some other time; nor even that it exercised any kind of direct quality control over those who practised as professional attorneys in the court. Even in the case of future serjeants, education was gained partly through direct experience as an attorney and private reading. Thus it looks as though legal education in this period was partly a matter of private initiative and partly a matter of official encouragement.

At first sight, at least, it seems puzzling that from the last quarter of the thirteenth century law was studied and taught in England in two quite separate institutions: in the two universities, where it was canon law and Roman law that were being studied, and in the law 'school' that was closely connected with the king's courts at Westminster and was soon to be transmuted into the inns of court, where it was the common law that was being studied. There are, indeed, some signs that this was by no means an inevitable development: Glanvill may have been intended as the foundation for a course in English law, to be studied side by side with Roman and canon law at the university of Oxford; Bracton may have been the product of a short-lived law school that genuinely integrated the study of the common law and Roman and canon law. Even at the end of the thirteenth century it was by no means rare for the elite of the legal profession to have at least a grounding in the learned legal tradition as well as a thorough knowledge of the common law. But it would have been difficult to change the Oxbridge syllabus to incorporate any substantial coverage of the common law. Any dilution of the existing syllabus in Roman and canon law ran the danger of producing graduates who were inadequately trained for what the system was set up to produce, trained canon lawyers. It was therefore left up to what seems to have been a combination of private enterprise and official sponsorship, and encouragement from the courts themselves, to create an educational system for the training of common lawyers in and around the courts. The London law school had a number of major advantages, anyway, over any putative law school for training common lawyers at either Oxford or Cambridge. It allowed its students to support themselves while studying through work as attorneys and they had privileged access to the courts and to their leading personnel and were kept au courant with the latest decisions, something which neither Oxford nor Cambridge could offer.

The longer-term consequences of the establishment of a separate non-university London law school were very significant for English legal education, indeed for the development of the common law as whole. The system of separate legal education for common lawyers created during the reign of Edward I, but modified and further developed in the fourteenth century, remained the basic system for educating common lawyers till the mid seventeenth century. It was then to be another two centuries before the common law itself came to be regularly taught in an English university. It was in large part the separation of the teaching of the common law from university legal education that made the common law so resistant to the influence of Roman law which elsewhere in Western Europe exercised a powerful influence over the development of national legal systems. One consequence of this was to make English judges and lawyers resistant to abstract thought and theoretical speculation: they had not been trained to think about law in that kind of way and saw no need to do so. The common law tradition of legal education produced tough and sharp thinkers, but not generally speculative ones. The consequences are perhaps still with us.

Questions

1. When did the *ius commune* emerge? What was its relationship to the local laws (*iura propria*)?
2. In what ways did customary law develop and change? Give examples.
3. What were the similarities and differences between glossators and commentators?
4. The influence of the *ius commune* was not the same everywhere in Europe. Can you describe the differences between the regions?
5. What makes it difficult to identify precisely what feudalism and feudal law are? What about identifying the *lex mercatoria*?

3 Actors

3.1 *The Pope and the Secular Princes*

From the eleventh century onwards, law developed into one of the main tools for organizing European polities. Judicial and legislative powers became, at least a significant, if not the central element, of political power. Sovereignty in the high and late Middle Ages was not absolute: it was dispersed and multilayered. As a consequence, law was produced on many levels and medieval law became polycentric. The most important law-making secular authorities were the emperor and kings, princes, and other lords.

As for the ecclesiastical authorities, the power to make new law resided in the pope, but synods also produced local canon law. A decisive landmark was the year 1075, when Pope Gregory VII issued his famous *Dictatus papae*, Dictates of the Pope, claiming legal supremacy over all lords, both ecclesiastic and secular. This development paved the way for what Harold Berman has called 'the first modern Western state'.

> *Harold J. Berman, Law and Revolution: The Formation of the Western Legal Tradition, Cambridge Mass., Harvard University Press, 1983, 113–114*
> After Gregory VII, however, the church took on most of the distinctive characteristics of the modern state. It claimed to be an independent, hierarchical, public authority. Its head, the pope, had the right to legislate, and in fact Pope Gregory's successors issued a steady stream of new laws, sometimes by their own authority, sometimes with the aid of church councils summoned by them. The church also executed its laws through an administrative hierarchy, through which the pope ruled as a modern sovereign ruler through his or her representatives. Further, the church interpreted its laws, and applied them, through a judicial hierarchy culminating in the papal curia in Rome. Thus the church exercised the legislative, administrative, and judicial powers of modern state. In addition, it adhered to a rational system of jurisprudence, the canon law. It imposed taxes on its subjects in the form of tithes and other levies. Through baptismal and death certificates it kept what was in effect a kind of civil register. Baptism conferred a kind of citizenship, which was further maintained by the requirement – formalized in 1215 – that every Christian confess his or her sins and take Holy Communion at least once a year at Easter. One could be deprived of citizenship, in effect, by excommunication. Occasionally, the church even raised armies.

The highest secular lord was the emperor. Legal arguments were used to boost his imperial powers, just as legal arguments were advanced in favour of the pope's universal power. The power struggle between them is an important thread in the political history of the twelfth and thirteenth centuries. The emperor was, from the twelfth century onwards, considered *legibus solutus*, unbound by laws, and above all kings. This was true in principle, although in practice large regions of Europe, such as England, Spain, France, and Scandinavia, were outside the imperial domain. Legal theory came to also consider the kings in these regions *legibus solutus*.

> *Kenneth Pennington, The Prince and the Law, 1200–1600: Sovereignty and Rights in the Western Legal Tradition, Berkeley, University of California Press, 1993, 32–35*
> The jurists began to give general definitions of the emperor's authority in a series of aphoristic glosses at the beginning of the thirteenth century.

Somewhat surprisingly, the canon, rather than the Roman lawyers, wrote the first catalogues of imperial powers and prerogatives. We have already seen that the civilians were not inspired by *Bene a Zenone* or other texts of Justinian's codification to expatiate on the authority of the emperor. However, when the canonists glossed *Venerabilem*, Pope Innocent III's famous decretal regulating imperial elections, they gathered together the emperor's prerogatives. Johannes Teutonicus, a German canonist, began this canonistic tradition in his gloss to *Venerabilem*: The emperor is over all kings ... and all nations are under him ... for he is the lord of the world ... even the Jews are under him ... and all provinces are under him ... unless they can show themselves to be exempt ... none of the kings can have prescribed an exemption, since prescription has no place in this ... A kingdom cannot have been exempted from imperial authority, since it would be without a head ... and that would be monstrous. Rather all must give the emperor tribute, unless they are exempt ... All things are in the power of the emperor.

Johannes quarried Roman and canon law for a set of milestones marking imperial prerogatives. We should note, however, that this list of privileges and prerogatives is similar to the *Dictatus papae* and does not define the emperor's relationship to the law or to the rights of his subjects.

Johannes's gloss to *Venerabilem* was not his last word on the omnipotence of the emperor. He repeated the substance of this gloss in his Ordinary Gloss to the Decretum. In the printed edition, his gloss to the Decretum declared that 'the kings of Spain are not under the emperor, for they have plucked their kingdom out of their enemies' jaws'. The manuscripts prove, however, that this sentence was a later addition.

In other glosses, Johannes added elements to his eulogy of the emperor. He taught that those who deny that they are under Roman rule cannot own anything. Further, the emperor shall crown all kings. If one did not recognize the Roman emperor as the prince of the whole world, one could not claim hereditary rights or other rights that private persons have under Roman law. His glosses to the Decretum were read and taught in the schools for centuries; his gloss to *Venerabilem* was copied word for word by Bernardus Parmensis into his Ordinary Gloss on the Decretals of Gregory IX. Much later in the thirteenth century, Guilielmus Durantis included the substance of Johannes's gloss in his great textbook on procedure. Consequently, the canonists' glosses became embedded in the textbooks and would play a major role in the polemics of the fourteenth century defending imperial prerogatives.

Historians, particularly German historians, have been keenly interested in the emperor's title, 'dominus mundi', because it adumbrates a unitary theory of a Germanic empire that was one of the great myths of medieval and early modern Europe. Like all myths of real power, it was deeply buried in the consciousness of men like Frederick Barbarossa, and long after the empire was no longer a political force in Western Europe its sometimes baleful influence still captured the imaginations of many in the twentieth century. Other historians, mainly French and Italian, have concentrated on the equally interesting question of when a juridical theory first appeared granting independence from imperial rule to European national states.

Sidney Woolf took a third position. He noted that Bartolus never used the maxim 'a king is emperor in his own kingdom' and consigned this omission to Bartolus's being much more concerned with the Italian cities than with kingdoms. Woolf's observation can be expanded. Because most early jurists were not notably concerned to explore the relationship between emperor and kings, the debate over origins and meaning has been quite acrimonious – and slightly beside the point.

The debate has had the salutary effect, however, of clarifying the historical roots of the maxim, 'Rex imperator in regno suo est'. Although historians have argued about the maxim's French or Italian origins and its exact meaning, there is no doubt that jurists used it to reconcile the difference between the political realities in thirteenth-century Europe and the ideal description of the emperor in their texts. English canonists, Alanus and Ricardus Anglicus, and a Spaniard, Vincentinus Hispanus, articulated unambiguous statements of royal independence from the emperor in the early thirteenth century. Azo cited a version of the maxim in a question he wrote (ca. 1200). By the middle of the thirteenth century the maxim had become a commonplace.

However, as Kenneth Pennington has demonstrated, legal scholars not only attempted to define the emperor's powers but to limit them as well. Being 'unbound by laws' did not mean that the emperor could do whatever he wished, and legal scholars developed the idea at the same time as the law professors argued for limitations on his absolute power (*absoluta potestas*). Pennington writes the following about the Italian commentator Andrea de Isernia.

> *Kenneth Pennington, The Prince and the Law, 1200–1600: Sovereignty and Rights in the Western Legal Tradition, Berkeley, University of California Press, 1993, 112–113*
> Andrea de Isernia's commentary (ca. 1315) to *Super feudis* discussed ecclesiastical and secular 'potestas absoluta'. The pope possessed absolute and ordained power and exercised absolute power outside the order of the legal system. But he may not act without cause. The prince also may not confiscate the private property of his subjects without cause, because dominium is protected by natural law. If the prince acts without cause, he exercises his absolute, not his ordained, authority. Even though no one may judge him when he resorts to his 'potestas absoluta', he still sins against God, just as he sins when he imposes a new tax without cause. By distinguishing between the proper and the improper use of absolute power, Andrea fitted 'potestas absoluta' into the earlier paradigm. The prince's power is not enhanced by absolute power; rather, it is another term for 'legibus solutus' or 'plenitudo potestatis'. The prince may act; his act may be legally binding; but he may fall into sin for it. His absolute power does not justify an unjust act.

The emperor and the kings were, however, not the only lords of medieval Europe. The dissolution of the Carolingian empire had left many regional princes and local lords in charge, who acted as if they were kings, as the following example shows.

> *Thomas Bisson, The Crisis of the Twelfth Century, Princeton, Princeton University Press, 2009, 142–143*
> As in Anjou so in Flanders the counts were mighty lord-princes. Their power was conspicuously regalian, coming down to them through Charlemagne's great-granddaughter Judith and first consolidated in programmatically Carolingian terms as early as the reign of Arnulf I (918–65). The later counts who will concern us here retained close ties with the kings of France, including Charles the Good (1119–27), who was the son of King Knut II of Denmark, and who seems to have been the candidate of some to succeed Henry V as emperor in 1125. As in Barcelona and Anjou possession of the county was disrupted in the third quarter of the eleventh century, when the succession of minor sons to Baldwin VI tempted the latter's brother Robert to usurp power in scandalous violence. Robert I ('the Frisian' 1071–93) soon justified himself; 'he held Flanders in great peace and was of great power', one recalled in the twelfth century, expelling 'all pillagers and thieves from his own land, so that in no region could be found greater peace and security than in his'. Threatened in the times

of Robert II (1087–1111), an illustrious crusader, and Baldwin VII and badly shaken by the murder of Charles the Good on 2 March 1127, the comital peace was restored in an exemplary princely regime thereafter.

The acts of these counts, bestowing powers, immunities, protection, and justice, were to be commemorated. Their diplomas and charters, which survive in swelling numbers after about 1050, were remarkably imposing. Diversely written by scribes in the religious houses that preserved them, they represent the count's power, 'by God's grace', as that of a *principatus* or *comitatus* or *monarchia* or *regnum*; the count is variously styled *marchio*, *princeps*, *consul*, as well as *comes*. 'What the contumacy of the wicked contrives let the princely power crush', ran the *arenga* to a diploma of 1090 for the church of Phalempin, and this sentiment was characteristic. One approached these lord-counts in deference, petitioned them humbly, thereby confirming an image of condescending grace cultivated by monastic scribes schooled in the theocratic culture of Saint-Omer, Arras, and Ghent. The counts doubtless shared the clerical sense that they dominated officially.

3.2 *Countervailing Powers*

The modern state was born during the high Middle Ages. There was, however, a fundamental difference between a medieval and an early modern prince. Both had to manage the practical limitations of their power, like, e.g., the slow means of communication available to them. Legally, however, the early modern prince was no longer bound by the law, whereas autonomous cities, constitutional texts, parliaments, and privileged groups had imposed limits on the power of his medieval predecessor. However, the contrast is less sharp than it seems because medieval tradition sometimes survived or resurfaced during the early modern era.

Autonomous cities were particular to certain parts of Europe, depending on the power of the prince and the degree of urbanization. At one end of the extreme, there were the big cities of northern Italy which, in the late Middle Ages, no longer had to deal with a king. At the other end were the English cities, which did not have the power to resist a mighty monarch. Flanders was a special case because it had the second-largest concentration of big cities, after northern Italy, and powerful princes in the count of Flanders and the king of France. The situation was in flux and changed over the centuries. The growing power of the Capetian monarchy meant that even France's most powerful city, Paris, lost its hopes of autonomy, whereas the breakdown of the Holy Roman Empire meant that some German cities could go their own way. The autonomy of the cities sometimes implied the subjugation of the surrounding countryside, which may have preferred a faraway prince as lord over the neighbouring burgesses. David Nicholas stresses that the conflict between lord and burghers shaped a city's institutions, even after it had been granted liberties.

> *David Nicholas, Urban Europe, 1100–1700, New York, Red Globe Press, 2003, 95*
> But liberties are relative. Town lords always played an important role. Their rights usually included confirming newly elected members of the city council, even if they were chosen by the sworn association or by the previous council, or joining with the town government in choosing electors who would present a slate of nominees. Virtually all town lords could nullify the choice of an individual by refusing to install him. Lords held large amounts of land in all the cities, and rent was an important income for them as for townspeople. Their officials were the oldest urban elites, dominating the early councils and rarely yielding complete power to merchants.
>
> Lords also collected tolls and fees, including in most places a substantial payment in return for giving the town such rights as issuing statutes and collecting taxes. Some charters gave control of the town walls to the city government, but many lords retained this right, and control of the gates gave them important leverage over the town. The lord had a representative in the town, variously called the bailiff, advocate or burgrave, who aided in law enforcement, handled criminal cases and supervised the mint.

Constitutions and parliaments cropped up everywhere in Europe. The terminology is somewhat misleading because today's constitutions and parliaments are not the same as their medieval ancestors. Modern constitutions contain articles on the structure of the government and the rights of its citizens – medieval constitutions focused on the latter. Their primary goal was to limit the power of the ruler by protecting the rights of the people he ruled. In a certain sense, privileges for individual cities, groups, or persons can be seen as constitutional texts because they restrained the power of the prince. In order to get a sense of the constitutional situation, it is better to focus on texts applicable to the whole country, because on a more local level, more rights for one group often just meant less for another. Despite its reputation, England's 1215 Magna Carta (Great Charter) was not the oldest constitution in this sense, as the Decreta of the Cortes of León of 1188 had been approved almost twenty five years earlier. In addition, the *fueros* (charters) already appear in the Spanish kingdoms in the twelfth century. The granting of a charter gave a settlement and its inhabitants the right to town privileges under the overlord regime. People who lived in chartered towns were burghers, as opposed to peasants who lived in rural areas or villages dominated by lords who exerted patrimonial or jurisdictional faculties. Towns were considered, then, 'free' (*Stadtluft macht frei*, in German; *City air makes you free*), in the sense that they were not submitted to the overlord regime, and enjoyed privileges, rights and exemptions. Moreover, at the time, Magna Carta was not a document that provided a guarantee of the rights of the king's subjects in general. The barons were the main beneficiaries of some of the changes in feudal law, and even of the articles protecting the rights of freemen, given that many peasants were still serfs. However, Magna Carta's power as a symbol that the king was bound by law soon eclipsed its limited practical importance. Thus, what was a failure in 1215 soon became one of legal history's most famous texts. J.C. Holt captures the appeal of Magna Carta through the ages.

> *J.C. Holt, Magna Carta, Cambridge, Cambridge University Press, 1992, 1–2*
> In 1215 Magna Carta was a failure. It was intended as a peace and it provoked war. It pretended to state customary law and it promoted disagreement and contention. It was legally valid for no more than three months, and even within that period its terms were never properly executed. Yet it was revived in the re-issues of 1216, 1217 and 1225. The last version became law, to be confirmed and interpreted in Parliament and enforced in the courts of law. Three of its chapters still stand on the English Statute Book. These embody, with some slight and occasional amendments, four of the original provisions of 1215. No other English legal enactment has enjoyed such long life. Some of these measures survived because they seemed to have a specific value. Until 1970, for example, the prohibition of fish-weirs in cap. 23 still sought to preserve navigation on the Thames and other rivers. Some survived because they were harmless confirmations of rights and privileges conveyed by other instruments. Hence the Charter still declares that the English church shall be free and still confirms, but does not define, the privileges of the city of London and other towns and boroughs. But the other surviving clause states deeper principles and less restricted privileges. At the other extreme from the fish-weirs of cap. 23 there stands cap. 29, which lays down that no free man is to be imprisoned, dispossessed, outlawed, exiled or damaged without lawful judgement of his peers or by the law of the land. Cap. 29 owes its continued existence to the pietas of legislators and lawyers, for it is not now essential or often even relevant to the liberty of the individual. But this pietas is in turn a product of the long struggles in which men appealed to this principle against authority. Individual freedom can be justified by many methods. There is no logical reason for including Magna Carta among

> them. That something survives from 1215 is a reflection of the continuous development of English law and administration. Magna Carta has been preserved not as a museum piece, but as part of the common law of England, to be defended, maintained or repealed as the needs and functions of the law required. That so much of what survives is now concerned with individual liberty is a reflection of the quality of the original act of 1215. It was adaptable. This was its greatest and most important characteristic.

Charters like Magna Carta are a snapshot of the power relations at a particular moment. What a prince gave to his subjects one day, he or his successor could just as easily take away the next, depending on the circumstances. Even though later convention looks to a single document cited as the source of inspiration for a country's 'constitutional tradition', the latter was frequently based on a whole series of different texts (for example, the so-called 'Joyous Entries' in the duchy of Brabant, which at times were anything but that for its prince). The real importance of these texts depended on the social and political situation. For an example we can turn to a comparison between Magna Carta and its Hungarian counterpart by T. Ertman.

> *T. Ertman, Birth of the Leviathan. Building States and Regimes in Medieval and Early Modern Europe, Cambridge, Cambridge University Press, 1997, 271–273*
>
> In the manner of their contemporaries in Latin Europe and Germany, some well-connected counts then attempted to convert their offices, and the income attached to them, into heritable private property. This move would have placed the free royal knights (*servientes regales*) and the dependent castle soldiers (*iobagiones castri*), the lesser landowners of the country, at the mercy of aristocratic families. In response to such a threat, these two groups revolted against their royal master with the support of dissident aristocrats.
>
> In the aftermath of his disastrous participation in the Fifth Crusade of 1217–18, Andrew was forced in 1222 to concede the Golden Bull, Hungary's Magna Carta. While the Golden Bull is sometimes characterized as the bill of rights of the Hungarian nobility, this description is misleading. It was above all the rights of the *servientes* and *iobagiones castri* that were confirmed and strengthened in this document, while those of the office-holding aristocracy were in fact curtailed. Thus the Golden Bull forbade hereditary grants of the office of count, reaffirmed the royal claim to two-thirds of the county's income, insisted on the king's right to remove

> incompetent or exploitative officials at will and banned the cumulation of offices. At the same time, it protected the property of *servientes* and *iobagiones* from the depredations of both rulers and aristocrats and shielded their persons from arrest without due process of law, while also exempting them from extraordinary taxes and releasing them from the obligation to serve in military campaigns abroad unless paid. Finally, the Golden Bull obliged the king to hold a national assembly once a year on St. Stephen's Day at which *servientes* had the right to appear with their grievances. While this document does indeed exhibit many parallels with the nearly contemporaneous Magna Carta, the differences between the two are more telling. In England, the barons appeared at Runnymede as spokesmen for the entire 'community of the realm', concerned to constrain the actions of a monarch whose greatest source of strength lay in the fact that he had at his disposal a powerful, independent administrative and financial apparatus built up over the previous century. In Hungary, by contrast, the king lacked such an apparatus. He thus came to rely ever more heavily on the aristocratic officeholders who occupied key positions in a minimal state infrastructure which had hardly expanded, due to the lack of a sustained geopolitical stimulus, since its creation by St. Stephen 200 years earlier. This alliance between ruler and aristocracy provoked a counter-reaction from the knightly classes of the kingdom, whose aspiration was above all to secure the same rights as their aristocratic superiors. In England, Magna Carta set in motion a dynamic in which the power of the Crown was counterbalanced by a 'community of the realm' which became progressively more inclusive – first encompassing all barons, then all free men, and finally all royal subjects. In Hungary, on the other hand, the Golden Bull paved the way for a unification of the aristocracy and lesser fighting men into a single, equally privileged noble class against which a weak Hungarian monarch – and an even weaker peasantry – proved incapable of defending themselves. When a sustained geopolitical stimulus finally did come to affect Hungary in the late 1400s, it was too late for this stimulus to benefit the Crown, as had been the case in England during the 1100s. Rather, as will be seen below, the continuous threat posed by the Turks served only to strengthen the nobility still further.

Constitutionalism went hand in hand with the development of parliamentarianism. The medieval parliament was different from its modern descendants. Today's parliaments are legislatures. Medieval parliaments served another purpose: they afforded the prince a chance to meet with the representatives of the land and discuss his financial needs with them. These discussions (Latin: *parliamentum*) gave their name to the institution. The ideal outcome for the prince was that his subjects granted him the right to levy a tax, so that, at least for the moment, his coffers would be filled. In the meantime, his subjects had another agenda; they tried to use their prince's financial problems to obtain concessions ranging from constitutional decrees to more powers for parliament. Their success varied considerably and depended on the prince's ability to find other sources of funding. Parliaments tried to hamstring these efforts by not agreeing to permanent taxes and by jealously guarding the principle that there would be no taxation without their consent. 'No taxation without representation' may have been a very popular slogan at the beginning of the American Revolution, but it was a medieval idea. A quote from the *Corpus iuris,* although the original context had nothing to do with parliaments, expressed the justification of their existence in the Middle Ages: *quod omnes tangit ab omnibus approbari debet* (what concerns all should be approved by all).

The first medieval parliament of which we can be certain appeared in the Spanish kingdom of Léon at the end of the twelfth century, and its Decreta of 1188 is the oldest documentary manifestation of the European parliamentary system, as J. Keane reports.

> *J. Keane, The Life and Death of Democracy, London, Simon & Schuster, 2009, 169, 173, 175–176*
>
> Contrary to some old-fashioned, devoutly British accounts, which … suppose, arrogantly, that parliamentary institutions were 'incomparably the greatest gift of the English people to the civilization of the world', parliaments were in fact an invention of what is today northern Spain.
>
> It was in … Léon, in March 1188 – a full generation before King John's Magna Carta of 1215 – that Alfonso IX convened the first ever cortes. …
>
> The king promised that from here on he would consult and accept the advice of the bishops, nobles and 'good men' of the towns in matters of war and peace, pacts and treaties. … The participants together agreed that property and security of residence were inviolable. They accepted that judicial proceedings and the laws they produced would be respected; and that the king's realm would be guided wherever possible by the general laws inherited from earlier times. … And it was agreed by the participants that there would be future assemblies of the king and the three estates. Both the substance and method of agreement heralded a new way of governing. It was based on the path-breaking principle that who got what, when and how could be best decided by talk.

After 1188, parliaments sprouted up all over Europe. The most common way to organize these medieval parliaments, already visible in 1188, was a division into three chambers, one for each estate: the clergy, the nobility, and the cities (the so-called third estate). Some, however, had four chambers, with the peasantry having its own estate. Others had only two, as was the case in England, with the lay and ecclesiastical barons in the House of Lords and the smaller landowners and the burgesses in the House of Commons. There were even some with only one chamber, as in Flanders, where the influence of the cities overshadowed everyone else. All these differences revolve around one common element: power. Those sitting in parliament were either those who had the power to make others pay taxes (the clergy and the nobility) or the power to decide themselves what they would pay (the cities). Within this common European pattern many variations existed, so that every parliament could claim that it was exceptional, as J.R. Maddicott does for the English parliament.

> *J.R. Maddicott, The Origins of the English Parliament 924–1327, Oxford, Oxford University Press, 2010, 452–453*
> There were many points of contrast between the English parliament and other continental assemblies. In no other state was general taxation so closely tied to assembly consent as in England. ... In no other state was the nobility so strictly subject to taxes, with all the scope thus provided for political association with other taxpayers and for an abiding interest in the parliaments and processes through which taxes were granted. In no other state were assembly representatives drawn predominantly from the rural gentry, creating the potential ... for a landed alliance between magnates and gentry hard to detect in continental societies. And in no other state did a national assembly come to embody so close an enmeshment of central authority and local action. ... Private petitions, common petitions, the participation of the commons in tax grants, the public proclamation of statutes and political decrees ... all testify to a degree of integration between local aspirations and royal government which is difficult to identify in any continental state. We may freely acknowledge the evolution of parliament to have been part of a general European pattern. All the same, we need not baulk at the notion of English exceptionalism.

Privileged groups, in particular the clergy and nobility, constituted another limit on the prince's power. They are often seen as relics of the older world of the early Middle Ages which did not belong in the new cities, constitutions, and parliaments. However, the old and the new were closely linked. Many parliaments would not have existed without the participation of the nobility and the clergy, and many constitutions and autonomous cities were only possible thanks to the support of nobles and clergymen. Some of the new institutions stemmed from feudal law: parliaments, for example, evolved from the obligation of the feudal landholder to provide counsel in his lord's court. By inviting others to attend some of their meetings, parliaments came into existence. The Spanish word for parliament, 'cortes', reminds us of this.

3.3 *Servants of Power: the Medieval Legal Professions*

The roots of the modern legal profession can, in many ways, be traced back to the twelfth century. At that time, canon lawyers started to become a professional group. From the late eleventh century onwards, the administration of the Church had become increasingly subject to legislation, and canon law courts had to master increasingly complex law. By the mid-thirteenth century, popes and bishops, even though they formally held judicial power, could no longer manage the increased volume of judicial business themselves and routinely delegated the disposition of legal cases to legal professionals. Indeed, receiving legal training became so valuable that it often helped to attain high clerical positions and many popes were jurists. A similar change was taking place in the civil government, as cities and princes began to hire the services of legal professionals. James A. Brundage describes the professionalization of Church courts as follows.

> *James A. Brundage, The Medieval Origins of the Legal Profession: Canonists, Civilians, and Courts, Chicago and London, The University of Chicago Press, 2008, 375*
>
> Professionalization of ecclesiastical judges advanced gradually over the course of the thirteenth century. Around 1217, while Johannes Teutonicus was putting the finishing touches to his ordinary gloss on Gratian's Decretum, he equivocated on the question of whether ecclesiastical judges must have formal legal training or not. 'It can be argued', he wrote, 'that no one can be a judge, especially an ecclesiastical judge, unless he is learned in the law'. He then went on in the usual scholastic fashion to consider the opposing view and cited in its support a constitution in which Justinian had declared that soldiers who lacked a scintilla of formal legal education could nonetheless serve as military judges. Johannes concluded by adopting a compromise position: 'A modest amount of learning' he concluded, 'is quite enough for a judge, just as it is for a prelate'.
>
> Twenty years later attitudes were changing. A reforming council at Tours in 1236, for example, decreed that officials appointed to preside

> over bishops' courts in that province must have studied law for at least five years or have the equivalent in practical experience through dealing with legal matters and procedure in the courts. The next year in a legatine council at London, Cardinal Otto da Tenengo demanded that judges who handled marriage cases and other weighty matters have legal training, although he failed to specify how extensive that training ought to be. Other authorities began to voice similar sentiments during the decades that followed. By the 1270s, Hostiensis could maintain that the law now presumed that judges were legally trained.

It was not only the ecclesiastical judiciary who required academic training. The complexity of the law also incentivized wealthy parties to hire the legal services of jurists to protect their interests. By the mid-thirteenth century, it became possible for lawyers to make a living representing clients in either canon law courts or secular tribunals. The lawyers were typically further divided into different subcategories.

> *James A. Brundage, The Medieval Origins of the Legal Profession: Canonists, Civilians, and Courts, Chicago and London, The University of Chicago Press, 2008, 203–204*
>
> Legal theory distinguished sharply between the functions of advocates and those of proctors. Both could be described as lawyers and both performed essential legal services, but procedural writers insisted that they filled separate and distinct duties in litigation. Advocates were skilled legal experts intimately familiar with the fine points and technicalities of the law, adept at legal analysis, and persuasive argument. Proctors, by contrast, were the law's men of affairs, experienced in the practical details of the operations of courts, adroit at smoothing over difficulties, men who knew what the judges liked and (perhaps more important) what they disliked, who mastered every detail of each client's case and had all the relevant facts at their fingertips. Since the tasks that advocates and proctors performed called for different skills, they were trained differently, received different levels of compensation, and came from different socio-economic backgrounds.

Nowadays, notaries form an important subcategory of the legal profession everywhere in the West except for the common law countries and Scandinavia. The origins of the notary as a legal profession date to the same period when legally trained professionals started to populate the judicial benches of both the Church and secular tribunals. The profession of notary already existed in late imperial Rome, but it was only towards the thirteenth century that increasing numbers of notaries begin to have legal training of some sort. Many of them remained in the lower echelons of the professional hierarchy, but some were able to make a handsome living from their practice.

The timeframe used above is based on Northern Italy, Southern France, and North-Eastern Spain. The development of the Roman-canon procedure, which is intimately linked to the rise of the legal profession, occurred first in these regions. A similar development took place later in other parts of Europe, as universities were founded in Germany and the Netherlands. In Scandinavia and Russia, the influence of legal scholarship was much less direct, and a legal profession did not develop there during the Middle Ages.

Questions

1. To which extent were the medieval cities autonomous or 'free'?
2. How was parliamentarianism and constitutionalism understood in the Middle Ages? How is it different from the way we understand it now?
3. What Roman-law principle was used to justify the rise of parliaments in Europe?
4. Is there any connection between the rise of the cities and the emergence of parliaments?
5. When did the law as a profession emerge in Europe? What kind of careers became possible? Give examples.

4 Application

4.1 *The Judicial System*

Modern Western judicial systems are hierarchical, based on a system of lower courts, appellate courts, and supreme courts. The basic idea is the same everywhere, even though the details vary from place to place. On the one hand, citizens have a right to have their case reviewed if they are unhappy with the decision of the forum of first instance. On the other hand, the hierarchical judiciary guarantees, or at least contributes to, the uniformity of judicial decisions. The origins of this kind of judicial system can be traced, as has been said, to the medieval Catholic Church.

The Church's administrative and judicial systems were restructured into a hierarchy as a result of the Gregorian Reform and primarily based on the Dictates of Gregory VII (1075). At the top of the hierarchy stood the pope himself as the supreme judge who enjoyed a 'plenitude of authority and power' (*plenitudo auctoritatis et potestatis*). Some popes with legal training (such as

Innocentius III and Innocentius IV) actively participated in legal decision-making. However, because of the increasing caseload arriving at Rome from Western Christendom, papal judicial power had to be organized more permanently and a court system evolved piece by piece. By the fourteenth century, it consisted of two main parts. The Rota Romana, the papal supreme court, was in charge of appeals in both civil and criminal cases (*forum externum*). The Grand Penitentiary took care of the absolutions and dispensations in *casus reservatae*, or cases reserved for the pope, as well as of the appeals from penances ordered by lower instances (*forum internum*). The Grand Penitentiary is described in the literature as follows.

> *Kirsi Salonen, The Penitentiary as a Well of Grace in the Late Middle Ages. The Example of the Province of Uppsala, 1448–1527, Helsinki, Academia Scientiarum Fennica, 2001, 48–49*
> The Penitentiary, *Poenitentieria Apostolica*, was one of the papal offices within the curia. It has been described as one of the papal tribunals and sometimes it has been called 'the Supreme Court of the papal curia in matters of conscience'. This is partly correct, because several severe violations of the regulations of canon law were handled in this papal office, but this gives only a partial picture of the wide faculty of the Penitentiary.
>
> It is actually wrong to call the Penitentiary 'a court' because it did not hold any trials and sentence people who turned to it because of the crimes they had committed. It only examined on the basis of the supplications, what had happened in a criminal case and afterwards gave absolution to the supplicant, who humbly and with repentance asked for it. 'A court in the matters of conscience' is also partly an unsatisfactory description because some of the matters handled in the Penitentiary did not have anything to do with a bad conscience. The absolutions given by the Penitentiary because of some violation of the regulations of canon law were of course matters of conscience, but the Penitentiary also had the faculty to grant dispensations which did not concern violations of the regulations of canon law or matters of conscience. The Penitentiary also had the faculty to grant special licenses in matters which often concerned the practicing of religion and letters of declarations of innocence for persons who were unjustly accused of a crime whose handling was reserved to the papal authority. If the accused person could be, according to the extenuating regulations of canon law, considered innocent of the crime, the Penitentiary could declare him not guilty. In these cases the supplicant did not need absolution or dispensation, but a letter declared him free from all accusations.

Below the papal courts stood the archbishop's court, which received appeals from the bishop's courts. The lowest judicial instance, thus, as far as regular ecclesiastical jurisdiction (*forum externum*) is concerned, was the bishop's court. Just as the pope's entourage, so also the amount of staff members at the bishops' courts grew from the late eleventh century onwards. The key staff member in judicial affairs was called the 'official' (*officialis*), a legal professional entrusted with presiding the bishop's court. In addition to the learned judge, other legal or semi-legal office-holders were appointed as seal-bearers, notaries and clerks. The bishop's court typically had its own host of advocates and proctors, whose activities the bishop's court supervised. An important feature of it was the papal delegate. In addition to exercising his judicial power in Rome, popes frequently sent judges-delegate to different locations to inspect and decide cases on the pope's behalf and with his authority.

It is important to stress that the construction of a hierarchical court system would not have been possible without the development of the learned law. The old system of proofs based on ordeals was not set up for appeals, as God's decisions, obviously, could not be appealed. Furthermore, the old substantive law based on legal customs and consensual decision-making by lay judges was also not suited to a hierarchical system of appeals. Such a system was only possible if questions of law were solved based on positive, largely written, law, and if questions of fact were also amenable to legal reasoning. The medieval, post-Gregorian, canon law developed to address both of these issues.

Secular rulers began to imitate the hierarchical judicial system of the Church in the thirteenth century. The first example is the Parlement of Paris, established in the early fourteenth century. Its jurisdiction covered all of France until other parliaments were founded from the fifteenth century onwards. Particularly noteworthy are the Great Council of Malines and the Imperial Chamber Court of the Holy German Empire, both from the fifteenth century. It was typical for all of these courts to be staffed largely by university-educated legal professionals capable of dealing with the growing intricacies of the 'learned law' of the *ius commune*. J.H. Shennan describes the rise of non-nobles in the Parlement of Paris.

> *J.H. Shennan, The Parlement of Paris, Ithaca, New York, Cornell University Press, 1968, 110–111*
>
> Originally the king's counsellors had been great barons and prelates, and indeed the Parlement never altogether lost its ancient lineage: thus it remained the sole tribunal before which cases involving peers could be decided and the only one upon whose benches peers and royal princes sat by right. From the very beginning of the court's history, however, a

> growing number of qualified counsellors, the *magistri*, who were experts in the law, sat among the traditional royal advisers. These new men did not at first come from a particular social background. Some were clerics, others members of the lesser nobility, others again of non-noble origin. Until the middle of the fifteenth century the majority of these *magistri* were clerics – monks, archdeacons and, more rarely, bishops – but from that time onwards, laymen predominated. They were recruited increasingly from a non-noble background. In 1340, twenty-five out of twenty-nine counsellors in the Grand' Chambre[3] were members of the lesser nobility; nineteen years later only one in five could claim that status, and by the beginning of the fifteenth century their appearance was exceptional.

High courts in the style of Rota Romana or Parlement of Paris were established everywhere in the Middle Ages. Even where they were not, the local courts often experienced a similar process of professionalization. This was especially typical for Italy.

> *Chris Wickham, Courts and Conflict in Twelfth-Century Tuscany, Oxford, Oxford University Press, 2003, 50–51*
> By the end of the century, Lucchese *iudices* were going more often to Bologna ...
>
> One of the ... examples concerns Uberto *iudex*, who appears as a plaintiff in a case about the inheritance of land in March 1196. It emerges in the arguments he had with Forese, advocate for the defendants, the cathedral canons, that Uberto had finally (*inregressibiliter*) returned from Bologna in January 1191, 'as a *iudex* and *causidicus*'; by 1192 or 1195 he had become a *consul querimoniarum*. This is a clear career pattern, and apparently a new one: Uberto came back with Bolognese qualifications and moved straight into the Lucchese judicial hierarchy. He came back with continuing Romanist interests, too: Forese in a bizarre counter-claim to Uberto's plea demanded a copy of the *Summa Placentini* back from Uberto, worth 40s., which he had borrowed from a canon, *magister* Armanno. Uberto rebutted this, stating that he had returned it, and that Armanno had subsequently lent it to another *iudex*, Ubaldo. Placentinus' *Summa codicis*, a well-known Romanist survey of the 1170s, was evidently much in demand

3 The *Grand Chambre* was the central court of the Parlement of Paris.

> in Lucca. … Readers like these were not part of a city culture entirely interested in separating itself off from outside influences.

Outside the Mediterranean region, university-trained lawyers came very late, if at all, to the many local courts of customary law, which had their own experts, the so-called spokesmen (see above).

4.2 *Criminal Law*

In no other field of law is the divide between the early and late Middle Ages more visible than in criminal law. The most profound change took place in the area of evidence. The old system of ordeals came under increasing criticism, and at the start of the thirteenth century, the Church even forbade the priests to cooperate in trials by fire and water. This left lawmen all over Europe with the task of finding alternatives, with options varying from juries to inquisitions by the court. The learned law provided an elaborate law of evidence. Ideally, one had to get a spontaneous confession from the accused, as this would leave no doubt about his guilt. Also, two witnesses equalled a confession. However, in most cases there was neither a confession nor witnesses, so the judge could resort to torture, although as J. Whitman shows, it would be wrong to think that judges could arbitrarily apply it to obtain a confession.

> *J.Q. Whitman, The Origins of Reasonable Doubt. Theological Roots of the Criminal Trial, Newhaven, Yale University Press, 2008, 100*
> So the inquisitorial court was obliged to induce at least two witnesses to talk, if possible. Of course, the testimony of two unimpeachably trustworthy eyewitnesses was rarely available. Some offenses were witnessed by only one person, or none. But even where eyewitnesses existed – as they might well have in cases of heresy or feud killings, for example – it was unlikely that they would willingly testify. To be sure, as we shall see shortly, the new canon procedure called for such witnesses to be compelled. But even the theoretical possibility of compulsory testimony did not guarantee that full proof would always be attained. So what was to be done if full proof was impossible? It was only in cases in which full proof was lacking that Continental law called for judicial torture.
>
> Torture could not be ordered in all cases. Persons of high social standing – members of the nobility and the like – could not be tortured at all. Even with regard to lower-status persons, moreover, judges were forbidden to order torture unless there were 'half-full proof' – 'semiplena probatio', proof that was the equivalent of the testimony of a single eyewitness. A confession extracted by torture also had to be repeated

voluntarily in court. This last limitation is one that John Langbein is surely right to regard as 'feeble'. Nevertheless, taken together, these restrictions do show that the application of torture was never a matter of wholly uncircumscribed discretion. Continental law treated the decision to torture as weighty and troubling.

4.3 *Private Law*

The learned law of the universities had to grapple with a difficult problem. The Roman law text, the *Corpus iuris*, had to be adapted to a medieval society which was in many ways radically different from Antiquity. The biggest problem was land ownership, the cornerstone of medieval society. Medieval concepts of landholding, which understood ownership as divided and multiple, were not compatible with Roman law: in the medieval conception, several people could have a legal claim to a piece of real estate, but Roman law could only allow for one owner. The glossators solved this contradiction by giving all of the stakeholders a right of ownership and then, subsequently, distinguishing different types of ownership. The most important distinction divided property into *dominium directum* and *dominium utile*. The latter belonged to the person who exploited the land, the former to his lord. This theory of *duplex dominium* (double ownership) resembled customary law in which both the lord and his tenant had seisin, but with very different competences. As such *duplex dominium* was extremely flexible and, therefore, successful.

Dirk Heirbaut, Feudal law: The Real Ius Commune of Property in Europe, or: Should We Reintroduce Duplex Dominium?, European Review of Private Law 2003, 313–314

The theory of duplex dominium was an empty box, but that was exactly the reason for its success. Duplex dominium only meant that the lord and his man were both owners of the fief, though with different rights in it. What these rights really were, was less important, and thus duplex dominium could be used to describe very diverse relationships. The theory was so flexible that duplex dominium could become a multiplex dominium, since a man could, in his turn, enfeoff a third with the whole or part of what he had received from his lord. Thus, the man became a new lord, and a new man was created, resulting in three owners, the overlord and his man, the lord, having dominium directum, and the vassal at the bottom having dominium utile. Neither was the duplex dominium limited to fiefs, as the same words could also be used to describe other kinds of tenure, the lord having dominium directum, and his tenant, whatever his name might have been, having dominium utile. Even today scholars can find no better theory for grasping the rights in land in the Middle Ages and the Early Modern Period. For example, when one explains customary feudal law one could do worse than use the glossators' terminology, even though the practitioners of the system one studies did not use it. The theory of duplex dominium may have been a theory, but it was and is uniquely qualified for describing the complex realities of property in the old Europe.

Duplex dominium was, if all is considered, a very simple theory, but its implications were far-reaching. It changed the background of the old property law. The dangers and pitfalls of misunderstanding the old property law are great, if one disregards the context of divided property. Take for example Bartolus' definition of property as the right to have the complete disposition of a corporeal thing, unless the law forbids this. At first sight, this definition is akin to the one given in the 1804 French Code civil in art. 544: 'La propriété est le droit de jouir et disposer des choses de la manière la plus absolue, pourvu qu'on n'en fasse pas un usage prohibé par les lois ou par les règlements'. However, for the authors of article 544 only one type of property could exist, whereas Bartolus wrote his definition for a world which knew, at least, dominium utile and dominium directum. Thus, 'complete disposition' for both the Code civil and Bartolus did not mean that an owner could disregard the rights of his neighbours or legal rules, but for Bartolus there was a third limitation, that no longer existed in 1804: the rights of lords and tenants. These same rights could also radically change the outlook of other rights than ownership, like usufruct. In the system of the Code civil, the presence of a usufruct reduces the rights of the owner, who has only a 'bare property', as he can no longer use or enjoy his own thing. However, at the end of the usufruct the owner's rights revive, he has, once again, full property. This is not necessarily true in a system of duplex dominium. The end of the usufruct, the life estate, does not always mean a return to full property for the owner, as there may still be lords or tenants whose rights have to be taken into account.

5 Summary

The effect of the rise of the *ius commune* on legal practice varied in Europe from region to region. Learned law influenced the way the courts functioned earlier in Southern Europe (Italy, Southern France, and parts of Spain) than other parts of Europe (Northern and Eastern Europe). In other areas, such as

England, Scandinavia, and Russia, it exerted little influence. It is good to bear in mind that the experience of *ius commune* was far from uniform.

The Kingdom of Sicily provides a good example of how learned law shaped early legal practice and the judiciary. Frederick II, the Emperor of the Holy Roman Empire and the King of Sicily promulgated a legal code called the Constitutions of Melfi (sometimes called *Liber Augustalis*) for Sicily in 1231. The new law, some say, contributed to turning Sicily into the first modern state. Among other things, Frederick's objective was to organize his judiciary and administration hierarchically. The great changes that the Constitutions of Melfi brought with it cannot be understood without the influence of legal professionals and learned law. David Abulafia describes the effects of the Constitutions of Melfi as follows.

> *David Abulafia, Frederick II: A Medieval Emperor, London, Allan Lane, 1988, 202–203*
> The *Constitutions of Melfi,* containing over two hundred laws and proclamations, have been hailed by historians as the clearest evidence of Frederick's wish to make of Sicily a 'model state', well-ordered, centralized, efficient, in which all rights and obligations are subject to the ruler's whim or will ... Such an interpretation of the *Constitutions of Melfi* is, however, based on wishful thinking. Whatever the degree of influence upon Frederick of the great Roman law-codes, of the contemporary canon lawyers, and of the newly fashionable philosophy of Aristotle, his legislation does not mark the coming of a new Justinian. The laws were not issued on the scale of the Roman codes; they did not seek to encompass the whole of human experience, but rather to deal with problems specific to a kingdom in urgent need of reconstruction. Nor were the laws profoundly original. They formed a practical combination of themes from Roman, canonist and feudal sources; elements of German common law, where thought most practical, were thrown in alongside the inveterate customs of the south Italians.

Learned law and legal professionals exerted much less influence on the medieval Scandinavian legal culture than they did in Sicily. Practically the only learned lawyers in Scandinavia were in the service of the Catholic Church. They did succeed in influencing the contents of statutory laws to a certain extent. However, in the circumstances it was impossible to adopt the *ius commune* with all its finesses in Scandinavia. For the legal profession to grow, economic resources have to be available, with which administrations (princes and cities) and private parties can hire the services of lawyers. If such resources are non-existent, a legal profession cannot emerge. In the meantime, there was a movement toward the centralization of political power in Scandinavia, but it occurred very differently: by way of peace legislation, which was no longer the most modern layer of law elsewhere. Mia Korpiola describes medieval Swedish law.

Mia Korpiola, 'The People of Sweden Shall Have Peace': Peace Legislation and Royal Power in Later Medieval Sweden, in Anthony Musson (ed.), Expectations of the Law in the Middle Ages, Woodbridge, Boydell Press, 2001, 37, 50–51

On the Continent, the church-initiated, late-tenth-century peace movement, 'the peace of God', became a generation later 'a truce of God' (*treuga Dei*). These movements had sought to limit warfare by stopping all violence at certain times, while taking certain institutions and persons into special ecclesiastical protection. Although these ecclesiastical peace movements had some limited success, from the twelfth century kings and territorial rulers took up the peace keeping mantle, building on the existing tradition. This in turn proved to be a successful method of increasing their authority.

The ripples of the Continental ecclesiastical peace movements, linked with the increasing power of princes and kings, reached Scandinavia via Germany. …

Peace legislation was the first step towards all-Swedish law: outlawry ceased to be only local as the offender no longer enjoyed peace anywhere in the realm. When in the late thirteenth and early fourteenth centuries the local legal customs were written down as provincial laws, the royal peace legislation was incorporated into them as sections pertaining to the so-called *edsöre* crimes. Through their incorporation into the laws of king Magnus Eriksson around 1350, peace legislation became uniform and universal.

The growth of peace legislation marked the beginning of the kings' activity as legislators, and increasing numbers of statutes started to be issued toward the end of the thirteenth century. This happened simultaneously with the expansion of the royal jurisdictional powers and the introduction of Continental lese-majesty and treason doctrine to Sweden. This was no coincidence but a slow and winding campaign to increase the royal powers within the judicial field. No longer regional chieftains, the Swedish kings expanded their authority within the framework of an elective monarchy by limiting violence, homicide and kin-revenge. In these respects the medieval Swedish realm followed the European development, though with some delay.

Questions

1. Explain how hierarchical judicial systems emerged in medieval Europe.
2. What were the main elements of the "new" criminal law in the Middle Ages?
3. In what way does medieval law remind us of modern law? In which sense does medieval law seem exotic to the modern person?
4. In modern law, written statutory law is the most important legal source. How would you describe the medieval system of legal sources?
5. Law never develops in a vacuum but is always connected to the social, economic and political reality. Which contextual factors shaped the development of medieval law and how?

Further Reading

Ascheri, Mario. The Laws of Late Medieval Italy (1000–1500). Foundations for a European Legal System, Leiden, Brill, 2013.

Bellomo, Manlio. The Common Legal Past of Europe, 1000–1800, Washington, The Catholic University of America Press, 1995.

Brundage, James A. Medieval Canon Law, London, Longman, 1995.

Hartmann, Wilfried and Kenneth Pennington (eds), The History of Medieval Canon Law in the Classical Period, 1140–1234, Washington, The Catholic University of America Press, 2008.

Haskins, Charles Homer. The Renaissance of the Twelfth Century, Cambridge Mass., Harvard University Press, 1982 (first ed. 1927).

Helmholz, Richard H. The Spirit of Classical Canon Law, Athens GA, The University of Georgia Press, 2010.

Radding, Charles M. The Origins of Medieval Jurisprudence: Pavia and Bologna 850–1150, New Haven, Yale University Press, 1988.

Stein, Peter. Roman Law in European History (12th ed.), Cambridge, Cambridge University Press, 2013.

van Caenegem, R. An Historical Introduction to Private Law, Cambridge, Cambridge University Press, 1992.

CHAPTER 4

Early-Modernity (1500–1650)

Adolfo Giuliani

1 Introduction: Main Features of the Period 1500–1650

Since the nineteenth century, the period around 1500 has been taken as the point of separation between old and new: the temporal line marking the passage from the medieval to the modern. During the sixteenth century, the world changed abruptly, with major impact on spiritual and material life. It was a period of many new beginnings. Columbus' arrival in America (1492) opened a new phase for European monarchies who wished to expand to World Empires: as the *conquistador* Hernán Cortés wrote back from Mexico in 1524, '[soon] there would be nothing more left to Your Excellency to do in order to become the ruler of the world'.[1] The Protestant reformation divided the medieval unity of Christian Europe in a Catholic South and a Protestant North, and ushered in an age of individualism. Constantinople's fall to the Ottomans (1453) brought an end to the Christian Roman Empire and restricted 'the West' to Europe. New science, and especially the printing press, facilitated dissemination of knowledge, but at the same time displaced traditional oral culture based on memory.

When we turn to legal history, however, that temporal line is less visible. Even a superficial look at the texts, arguments and authorities that jurists used around 1500 shows the persistence of medieval material, which continued to be cited throughout this period. It is true that a school of interpreters came into being that today we call 'legal humanism'. They translated into the legal field the humanist concern for language and shed new light on legal texts, investing them with philological rigor. This attitude, however, was not typical of the legal profession. In general, legal practitioners had little sense for the past, feeling they belonged to a temporal continuum shared with older generations of jurists. Authors who wrote centuries earlier could be drawn on for arguments and opinions, and their names cited next to contemporary work. If we look at legal practice or the methods of rationalising the law, we find the recurrence

1 See P. De Gayangos (ed.), Cartas y Relaciones de Hernán Cortés al Emperador Carlos v, Paris, s.n., 1866, 308.

 | DOI:10.1163/9789004687257_006

of opinions and arguments produced centuries before. For example, the standard procedural reference manual used in legal practice, Guillaume Durand's *Speculum iudiciale*, was written in 1260–76 and was still in use in the seventeenth century. The contemporaries of René Descartes and Thomas Hobbes still worked with intellectual material written four centuries before. This continuity was insured by largely unchanged methods of legal education, deeply rooted in medieval scholasticism, and consequently, by unchanged patterns of argument and modes of reasoning. In such a setting, tradition was immensely more powerful than in today's legal world.

Jurists, equipped with their peculiar culture and methods, were a specific professional class which did not passively reflect society but contributed to its development. If the twelfth-century rediscovery of Roman law texts marked the beginning of a long phase called *ius commune*, those jurists could operate by rationalist methods of thinking, dissecting the text, and structuring the material in precise taxonomies taught in universities (known as 'Aristotelian Scholasticism') by which jurists could extract new norms from ancient texts. Scholasticism (from 'schola': school) was a methodological approach to scholarship based on a concern of explaining Faith in terms of Reason. Its most immediate feature was the concern with structure: this is visible, for instance, in structuring the written text in a hierarchy of titles, numbers, and paragraphs on a page – a feature we can still observe in modern legal texts. But its veritable importance would not be appreciated without realizing that University education, monopolized by Scholasticism, offered a curriculum based on a canon of Aristotelian texts (known as the *Organon*: the 'instrument') that remained in use until the seventeenth-century. At its heart was the pedagogical idea that knowledge can be mastered by working on a fixed canon of texts, to be conquered gradually in order to eventually reach a coherent and organic view of human knowledge, although there is an important observation to be made about this structure.

Merio Scattola, Dialectics, Topology and Philosophy in Early Modern Times, in M. Dascal and H. Chang (eds), Traditions of Controversy, Amsterdam, John Benjamins Pub. Co., 2007, 184

> … [T]he arguments are not disposed in a logical order, in the descending stairway of the deduction, but are grouped within a dialectical disposition. It is impossible to link together all pieces of human knowledge in a descending deductive chain (*per modum conclusionis*). They must be compared together in order to understand which among them is compatible with all others. In general, since every one of them is proved to be true, each element or argument of practical knowledge must be

> compatible with each other element. But this relationship is not evident immediately and must be searched for, and this search is a typical dialectical duty. The tradition is often full of arguments that are apparently opposite.

To this purpose, university teaching and even more importantly, pre-university education based on liberal arts, transmitted a methodology based on dialectics that made pupils skilled in using distinctions, definitions and disputations and provided them a general grounding in dialectical reasoning. One of the major features of this approach was the understanding that legal rules address specific cases that cannot be separated from the circumstances. The idea of a general rule that applies without reference to specific conditions would have seemed difficult to imagine. In their mind, legal rules and generally statements needed to be refined through a process that tested, in their parlance, the 'yes and no' or, Latin, 'sic et non' (Petrus Abelardus, 1079–1142) of their competing arguments. They reasoned in terms not of first principles but of questions.

> *Merio Scattola, Dialectics, Topology and Philosophy in Early Modern Times, in M. Dascal and H. Chang (eds), Traditions of Controversy, Amsterdam, John Benjamins Pub. Co., 2007, 184*
>
> The duty of the dialectic discussion [was] to demonstrate that this opposition is only in appearance and that the one argument is part of the other one, if only we understand it in the right way. The weaker argument must be therefore a specification, an exception, and a subordinate case of the stronger one.
>
> In the 16th century this dialectical approach is particularly evident in the tradition of the catholic Scholastic, which to some extent inherited from the medieval Scholastic not only the discussed matters, but also the way of discussing them. So the works of Francisco de Vitoria, Domingo de Soto or Diego de Covarrubias, which oft are commentaries on the *Summa theologiae* by Thomas Aquinas, repeated closely the scheme of the medieval *quaestio*.

The working language was Latin, an international medium of communication that was not related to Roman literary models and that was constantly updated with new philosophical terms, sometimes very abstract. It was precisely those two features of Scholastic Latin – its inelegance and abstraction – that made it the target of the most virulent attacks from sixteenth-century legal humanism.

This intellectual tradition evolved, including a reformulation in the sixteenth century (known as 'Second-Scholaticism'), to finally decline during a deep intellectual, political and spiritual crisis that affected Europe around 1650 – the end of the period covered by this chapter. By then, the treatises of Westphalia (1648) had symbolically recognized a community of sovereign and territorial nation-states strengthened by the effective end of claims to universal jurisdiction from the Papacy and the Holy Roman Empire. Now, individuals felt a stronger allegiance to the nation state they belonged to than to an Empire or Church. Identity was to be found in national history, language, and in that body of territorial rules (*ius patrium* or *ius municipale*) which bound the individual to the state.

Questions

1. Why is the year 1500 traditionally taken as a point of change in history?
2. What was legal culture like in the sixteenth century? How was it similar or different to the preceding period from c. 1100- c. 1500 described in the previous chapter?
3. The text above argues that jurists lived in a 'long now' and did not distinguish the date of origin of different legal authorities. What might be the advantages and disadvantages of this approach?

2 Creation

The question of how legal rules come into being is relatively simple to answer in modern law. However, for *ius commune* jurists it was more complicated. One of the main features of the period under discussion was the presence of plural normative orders in a dialectical relationship between common and particular laws, usually indicated as *ius commune*. Today we explain the 'creation' of legal rules as a technical process by which specific state organs produce legal statements and use particular procedures to draw a clean-cut line between law and non-law. But *ius commune* jurists had difficulty in defining 'law' (*jus*). Of course, legal rules come into being all the time: they are continuously produced, interpreted, observed and reversed. But the crucial point here is that they believed human societies were ruled primarily by an unwritten constitution rooted in nature, customs and memory, which could not be transcended. In their mind, law was an undefined entity which kept societies together, and it was visible in the many settings to which human communities belonged: it could be found in nature, in the Bible, in the law of nations, in customs, and in the rulings of a prince. The prospect of a law-maker who acted simply using sovereign power, as a modern legislator does, made them suspicious.

> *T. Herzog, A Short History of European Law: The Last Two and a Half Millennia (3rd ed.), Cambridge Mass., Harvard University Press, 2019, 4*
> Today we might take for granted that law is something that is created and can be changed, but … this vision is a relatively recent invention. For many centuries, law was said to exist because it simply did, because it was spontaneously created by the community or because God had handed it down. Even if these perceptions were untrue, in the sense that law was always made by someone somewhere, the fact that people believed them was of great significance to how they viewed, interpreted, or obeyed the law, to whom they listened and why.

In its proper sense, the idea of 'creating' law belongs to nineteenth-century legal systems focused on legislation. In such a setting, the only creator is the state legislator, and the only normative form is state-law. Other corollaries are the separation of powers, a body of judges bureaucratically structured, that the law is a given that the judge receives and applies as an entity formed externally. Primacy is thus given to the law laid down by state authority, and the natural consequence is the disregard and even exclusion of other sources like custom, doctrine, and legal theory. In this context, the idea of creating law is quite simple and uncontroversial. However, before the nineteenth century, legal systems in the Western Legal Tradition tended to be more normatively complicated, with many sources of law instead of just one.

2.1 *Multi-normativity: a Lecture Delivered in 1573*

To understand the complicated picture of *ius commune* legal thinking, we need to consider that one of its primary features was the belief in a plurality of normative orders. Each of them had a different nature and effects and implied a range of applications involving different individuals in different ways.

> *S.P. Donlan and D. Heirbaut, A Patchwork of Accommodations: Reflections on European Legal Hybridity and Jurisdictional Complexity, in S.P. Donlan and D. Heirbaut (eds), The Laws' Many Bodies: Studies in Legal Hybridity and Jurisdictional Complexity, c1600–1900, Berlin, Duncker & Humblot, 2015, 11*
> At least until the nineteenth century, Europe was a landscape of multiple – often transnational, or pre-national and trans-territorial – legal traditions coexisting in the same geographical space and at the same time, though often affecting different individuals. Law was multi- or polycentric, with disparate and nested competing centres of power and

> persuasion. Jurisdictional complexity was the norm, a complex mix of local and larger laws; the former contributed much to the substance and subsequent success of the latter common laws. Legal orders of the pre-modern past only rarely expected to govern their rivals without a contest. The ability to legislate or adjudicate authoritatively was disputed for centuries. Local power and practical considerations saw different institutions dominate different times and places. Especially before the nineteenth century, 'law' and 'non-law' were not easily distinguished. The boundaries between official and unofficial norms (informal and non-institutionalized) were especially porous. These 'legalities' 'are not produced in formal legal settings alone'; instead: 'They are social products, generated in the course of virtually any repetitive practice of wide acceptance within a specific locale, call the result rule, custom, tradition, folkway or pastime, popular belief or protest'.

Explaining how these plural and overlapping normative orders worked would be impossible without considering the role played by juristic interpretation. The canons of interpretation applied by jurists were taught as a part of their legal education and went back to medieval jurisprudence, but they were constantly refined by doctrinal discussions and legal practice. Let us turn to one of their lectures.

In the year 1573, in a classroom at the Faculty of Law at Perouse, central Italy, the inaugural lecture was entrusted to the canonist Giovanni Paolo Lancellotti (1522–1590). At the time, he was perhaps the greatest canonist of his age, and had made a name for himself as the author of a teaching manual which reorganized canon law sources into the systematic structure of Justinian's *Institutes*. As we will see, the reorganization of material into a more 'rational' structure was a key legal development in this period. The topic chosen for this lecture was 'the diversity of laws'. From the title (On the Comparison of Pontifical and Imperial Law: *De comparatione iuris pontificii et caesarei*) we learn that the subject involved an early form of comparative law, discussing the interrelation between five normative orders: natural law, the law of nations, Roman common law, canon common law, and local statutes.

> *Giovanni Lancellotti, De comparatione iuris pontificii et caesarei et vtriusque interpraetandi ratione, Perugia, Ex typographia Valentis Panitij & Sociorum, 1573, 71 (transl. by Adolfo Giuliani)*
> The individual, because of whom all the laws of the world have been instituted and enacted, can be considered in five different ways.

(i) Firstly, the individual can be considered just in his particular genre, namely, as an animal and a sensitive creature, in other words, lacking reason.
(ii) He can be considered as belonging to a species, namely, as a human being and thus featuring reason;
(iii) as a subject of the Roman Empire;
(iv) as a subject of the Roman Church; or
(v) as a citizen of a particular city, as for example Bologna or Perouse.

Now, different kinds of laws can be used according to the way the person is considered. When he is considered in his own genre, namely, not as a human and rational creature but as an animal and sensitive creature, he makes use of that law we call natural, which nature taught all animals.[2]

But when the individual is considered in his own species – as a human being – he makes use of the law that we call the law of nations (*ius gentium*) since it is common to all peoples,[3] from which we are induced to keep trust, not to break agreements, to obey and venerate God, homeland and parents,[4] which nature did not deliver to any other animal, only to humans.

When the individual is considered as a subject of the Roman Empire, he makes use of the civil law of the Romans (*ius civile Romanorum*) which today we call *ius commune*.[5]

When the individual is considered subject of the Roman Church, he makes use of the Pontifical or canon law.

When he is regarded as a citizen of a particular city e.g. Bologna or Perouse, he makes use of the particular statutes of Bologna, Perouse or another city or location.

The text presented by Lancellotti was perfect for teaching: it was clear, simple, and illustrated with citations to well-known Roman laws. It was also particularly suited for an opening lecture as it answered the question: 'How many kinds of laws are there?' This was a transparent reference to the idea that any exposition must begin with a table of laws: a clear example is the opening of the Digest[6] and of the Institutes,[7] from which most of his references were

2 Inst. 1.2pr (Ulp.).
3 l. omnes populi (= D. 1.1.9 and Inst. 1.2.1), Inst. 2.1.11.
4 D. 2.14.1, D. 13.5.1, D. 1.1.3.
5 Inst. 1.2.1 (= D. 1.1.9); C. 1.1.
6 D. 1.1 De iustitia et iure.
7 Inst. 1.2 De iure naturali et gentium et civili.

drawn. A similar concern with 'mapping' laws by a clear structure can also be detected in a variety of treatises, sometimes accompanied by metaphorical and visual symbols. For instance, Guillaume Durand's standard judicial procedure manual mentioned above begins by illustrating six normative orders with the image of the six wings of seraphims.

However, the most important lessons to be drawn from this picture of law are its implications. The first is that individuals inhabit a plurality of normative orders simultaneously. Life involves different contexts, each ruled by its own normativity, and it is unthinkable that one law – even the universal orders of Roman or canon law – can entirely dominate them. Second, those normative orders are overlapping, placed next to one another (not stacked up hierarchically): they govern at the same time and in the same place, each deriving from a distinct source and regulating a particular aspect of life. Third, at the heart of this construction are real human beings, part of specific communities and circumstances.

This view can be contrasted with the abstraction of natural law writing, which beginning from the seventeenth century presents a theory of human action based on the belief in a rational essence of the human mind.

> *M. Scattola, Models in History of Natural Law, Ius Commune. Zeitschrift für Europäische Rechtsgeschichte 28 (2001), 137–138*
>
> The main effect of the theory of human action developed by modern natural law is that the force of reason is the only actual constraining power in moral and juridical behaviour. Human beings act as moral subjects because they are led by logical consistency and honour it as the most important quality of their essence. Why does an individual obey the law of nature? Because he is rationally persuaded. Why does he respect the life of the other human beings and not commit murder or hurt them? He recognises himself as a rational essence and acknowledges a first principle as the starting point of any other deduction. From this empty idea he gains a chain of inferences, at the end of which he realizes that homicide is against the first principle, against his own good as a human being and incongruent with his rational nature. This contradiction involves a prohibition, and therefore the subject of natural law will not act against the life and preservation of other human beings.
>
> This simple example shows that the compelling power of modern natural law consists in a truly internal constraint, which flows from the rational essence of the human being. Reason has in this sense only an *individual dimension*, as in the whole deduction of the natural law no external authority is admitted and no external intervention takes place.

> Natural law is constructed within the individual, in a small personal world, which is completely and perfectly isolated from the outside. The subject of natural right could be alone, he could be the last man on this earth: he would nevertheless be able to synthetise natural law. He needs other human beings only as objects of his rights and duties and as a necessary environment made of equal men; but he does not need them as source of right. The only recognised authority capable of producing right and law is *individuated* reason: every human being believes only his own particular intellect and obeys only it. There is no other possibility to convince him than by appealing to the promptings of his own reason.

The final point to be gathered from Lancellotti's lecture is that legal practice, busy with questions about multi-normative orders, operates with 'comparative' knowledge. Judges need to be especially aware of such comparative approach, as we can see in sixteenth-century France.

> *Alain Wijffels, 'Ius commune', Comparative Law and Public Governance, in Maurice Adams and Dirk Heirbaut (eds), The Method and Culture of Comparative Law. Essays in Honour of Mark Van Hoecke, Oxford and Portland, Hart, 2014, 151–152*
> Whatever meaning is given to any notion of common law – whether *ius commune* or any other form of common law – it always necessarily implies legal pluralism: there is no point in styling a set of principles and norms as 'common' unless there is some diversity of principles and norms for which the common set has been worked out. A common law always aims at transcending and to some degree controlling the various laws within its ambit. That process requires the common law to elaborate notions and principles which enable it to assemble the different ('particular') laws into a homogeneous structure. The process of homogenisation, however, can only be effective if the proper nature and purpose of any particular law is not exaggeratedly distorted. This was achieved in the medieval *ius commune* tradition by working out concepts and principles which were sufficiently abstract to allow some leeway in their application, so that its users had a reasonable degree of discretion to apply policy considerations which made it possible to take into account the interests at stake and to deal with conflicts of interests.
>
> For most historical common law models, the purpose was not to compare different particular legal systems, though occasionally such a comparison could nonetheless occur. One of the best-known examples is that of the early-modern *droit commun coutumier* in France, which different

> authors tried to achieve through different means; for some, the method consisted in drawing common or comparable features from individual customs, an approach which necessitated a comparison between different customs within the realm. Sixteenth-century French legal literature shows how those comparative experiments could still be carried out along different lines: some authors would propose general principles or rules of law which were deemed to form a common core of law shared by various customs within the realm; others would draw converging principles from the most elaborate written custom of the realm, *viz* the custom of Paris, which could, moreover, benefit from a substantial and well-documented case law (in particular of the Paris Parlement); however, any somewhat sophisticated comparative approach by such authors would inevitably also borrow concepts and principles from the *ius commune* tradition.

It was important for jurists in practice, as well as those teaching and working in the universities, to be aware of the different normative orders and their mutual interactions. This is true also today when we consider how they did (or did not) fit into the broad Western Legal Tradition.

2.2 *Ius Commune Crisis*

So far, we have considered a lecture on the sources of law delivered in 1573, wherein the lecturer presented a view of plural normative orders as components of a unified whole in accordance with patterns of thought from medieval jurisprudence. This is not to say, however, that the writings of the sixteenth and seventeenth century can be adequately seen as a continuation and development of those existing strands of thought. The material and spiritual outlook changed and had an impact on how law was viewed. One consequence was that the idea of united legal orders did not survive early seventeenth-century shifts in legal scholarship, and those different normative orders drifted apart under the influence of their own internal reasoning.

One striking symbol of this change was a new attitude towards the ancient image of 'sources of law'. The image from Roman texts visually illustrating the normative 'flow' from the XII Tables as the ultimate source of authority resurfaced in sixteenth-century explanations of the origin of legal rules, but in a new sense. When some treatises spoke of the 'sources of law' (*fontes iuris*) they reformulated the creative process. By analogy with geometry and other physical sciences, these jurists said that it originated from a few key elements; they wanted to describe a small number of first principles from which the whole body of laws could be deduced. The French humanist François Douaren

(1509–59) thought that law begins with axioms and propositions, 'just as geometry with points, lines, surfaces'.[8]

This approach was one of the main characteristics of seventeenth-century writings.

> *Merio Scattola, Scientia Iuris and Ius Naturae: The Jurisprudence of the Holy Roman Empire in the Seventeenth and Eighteenth Centuries, in E. Pattaro, D. Canale, P. Grossi, H. Hofmann and P. Riley (eds), A Treatise of Legal Philosophy and General Jurisprudence, Dordrecht, Springer, 2009, 8*
> The idea that the whole complex of the laws in a country should derive from one principle, that it should build a coherent system, that it should be organised into a deductive connection, that we can go from a superior point to an inferior one by means of a single uninterrupted inference. ... Of course, principles of law and system were not new. But the idea that law should adopt the structure of a theory was a product of the late seventeenth century and could be developed only on the basis of a Cartesian methodology.

This idea suggested new ways of thinking about law as an object of pure and rational speculation, coherently structured as a system. The fluid sources of law of the *ius commune* period were solidified into an orderly hierarchy dominated by the state-legislator, who progressively monopolized the process of law-making.

2.3 *Natural Law*

Medieval people tended to think that the important norms in their community had their foundation in nature, which included humans and animals, as we saw in Lancellotti's lecture. In the seventeenth-century, however, we find another account of natural law. Jurists increasingly favored the methods of the mathematical and natural sciences of the early-seventeenth century. Such methodologies were sometimes followed as a model to establish universal rules of conduct or universal laws. Hugo Grotius, for example, wrote:

> *Hugo Grotius, De jure belli ac pacis (1625), Aalen, Scientia Verlag, 1993, Prolegomena XXXIX (transl. by Robert Feenstra)*
> I have been concerned to base my proofs regarding natural law on notions so evident that no one could deny them without committing violence

8 F. Douaren, Opera Omnia, Lyon, Rouillius, 1558, 1:1.

upon themselves. In fact the principles of such a form of law ... are manifest and evident in and of themselves.

And such principles are binding, Grotius added, 'even if we should concede (*etiamsi daremus*) that, which cannot be conceded without the utmost wickedness, there is no God, or that the affairs of men are of no concern to Him'.[9]

T. Herzog, A Short History of European Law: The Last Two and a Half Millennia (3rd ed.), Cambridge Mass., Harvard University Press, 2019, 160
Grotius cited the work of previous authors, as well as many sacred and Roman texts, but he also appealed to commonsense conclusions based on a reasonable analysis of the situations he examined. These conclusions, he argued, were so natural that they could be understood by all, Europeans and non-Europeans, lawyers and nonlawyers alike. Rather than having been systematized from existing laws and regulations, Roman law included, they could be deduced by observing society and nature and employing reason. Rather than being complex, they would be simple and straightforward.

Let us examine this shift from the medieval to the modern idea of natural law.

Merio Scattola, Models in History of Natural Law, Ius Commune. Zeitschrift für Europäische Rechtsgeschichte 28 (2001), 91–92, 100–102, 104
Natural law theories gave the modern state a rational theoretical frame for the first time in the seventeenth century. However the idea of a natural law is much older. Aristotle for instance divided the justice of the city into what is right by nature (*toè fusikoèn diékaion*) and what is right by a particular law of the city (*toè nomikoèn diékaion*). Cicero recognized the existence of a *ius naturae* that is not produced by human opinion, but is present in the human soul by some kind of natural force. This natural law concerns religion, the respect for family and country, friendship, the impulse to revenge injuries, the acknowledgment of authorities and ranks within a human society and the search for truth. It is based upon a 'heavenly', universal, eternal and unchangeable law, which corresponds to the rational order of the world and to the will of the gods who govern all things. ...

9 Hugo Grotius, De jure belli ac pacis (1625), R. Feenstra (ed.), Aalen, Scientia, 1993, Prolegomena, 39 and 11.

The first parts of the *Digestum* and of the *Institutiones* bear the titles *De iustitia et iure* (D.1.1 and Inst.1.1) and *De iure naturali, gentium et civili* (Inst.1.2) and contain some indications about the general features and the essence of natural law. The jurisprudence of the late sixteenth and early seventeenth centuries engaged itself in a continuous elaboration of the statements collected under those titles, partly in great commentaries on the whole of the *Corpus iuris civilis*, partly in specific literary genres such as the dissertation *De iustitia et iure*, the treatise *De arte iuris* and the introduction to the study of law.

This tradition achieved important results in the definition of natural law. The starting point was the opinion of Ulpian, who defined *ius naturale* as that set of behaviours that are common to human beings and animals. A main difficulty of this point of view is that it assumes that humans and animals take part in one community of right, but nobody can oblige himself by law with an animal nor an animal can contract by law an obligation with a human being.

The commentators solved the problem by resuming the medieval distinction between *ius primaevum* and *secundarium*. Both *ius naturae* and *ius gentium* were divided into a primary and a secondary part so that at the end there were four kinds of law: *ius naturae primaevum et secundarium* and *ius gentium primaevum et secundarium*. The 'primary natural law' was excluded from the description of natural right because it concerns only the instinctive actions of animals. On the other end, the 'secondary law of nations' was in the same way ignored as containing all the agreements between nations made by human decision. The commentators turned their attention to the 'secondary natural law' and the 'primary law of nations', which are exactly alike: they contain all the rules that arise from the use of natural reason and therefore are recognized by all human beings in every time. This distinction in three classes, which was achieved by the humanistic jurisprudence during the sixteenth century, is discussed also in the treatises of the early seventeenth century and offered a conceptual frame to Grotius and to the doctrine of natural law after him. …

In the Roman tradition natural law did not constitute in any sense a system, nor did it include universal principles; rather it was a *summa* or a conglomerate of different rights. In the same sense Thomas Aquinas and the whole medieval Scholasticism identified the *lex naturae* with a number of clear prescriptions and statements known by all human beings, particularly with the Ten Commandments. …

> In modern teaching of the *ius naturae et gentium* of the seventeenth and eighteenth centuries law falls primarily into positive and natural law. *Ius naturae* does not offer any practical rules to decide the cases of ordinary life or those of the law courts. In fact, it is conceived as a part of practical philosophy and as a science, which acts only as theoretical foundation according to reason. Its principles are realized by private and public law, which produce general rules suitable for all political societies. Both *ius gentium* and *ius civile* are subjects of the *ius naturae*. The former, which applies to political society the natural laws originally intended for individuals in the condition of nature, considers every commonwealth as an individual acting in the state of nature. The latter is contained both in the *ius privatum*, which describes mankind in the condition of nature, and in the *ius publicum*, insofar as this concerns the relationships between individuals. In both cases, civil law appears as a set of practical prescriptions deduced from the general principles of natural law.

Natural law, therefore, was given primacy within a new structure of legal norms. Rather than seeing normative orders as coordinated units, the jurists of this period wanted to understand them as a top-down hierarchy, and in terms which paved the way to the fundamental postulates to create the new legal systems of the modern period.

2.4 *The Law of Nations: Ius Gentium*

A step below natural law we find the law of nations (*ius gentium*). Lancellotti presented this normative order as common to all peoples, including for example principles requiring people to keep trust, not to break agreements, to obey and venerate God, homeland and parents.

Europe's expansion on a global scale and the encounter with non-European peoples led jurists to rethink their basic categories, including the law of nations. A major breakthrough of the group of theologian-jurists today referred to as the 'Second Scholastics' was to revise Roman law by investing those texts with moral philosophy. They did this in order to create a flexible normative body that could offer solutions to new moral problems arising from changed social settings. The Dominican Francisco de Vitoria (1483–1546) had a major role in reformulating the medieval understanding of the law of nations in the context of the overseas expansion and clarifying the legal framework to explain the relations between Europeans and native Americans.

> *T. Herzog, A Short History of European Law: The Last Two and a Half Millennia (3rd ed.), Cambridge Mass., Harvard University Press, 2019, 158–59*
> [Vitoria] suggested that, in their conditions as humans, both Spaniards and the native inhabitants of the New World formed legitimately organized societies and both were therefore under obedience to natural law. This natural law, which he called the law of nations (*ius gentium*), was universal. It could apply to all human communities whether their members knew about it or not, consented or not, inhabited Europe or not, were Christian or not.
>
> Rather than local law being applied to foreigners as was the case in Rome, Vitoria imagined the law of nations as an instrument defining relations between polities and among their members. This new law of nations ruled among sovereign entities rather than individuals. A precursor of today's international law, it was mainly concerned with the activities of public powers, not private individuals. Its ultimate justification was that it expressed norms Europeans considered natural and thus universally valid. That is, instead of recognizing that these norms were anchored in tradition, place, religion, or system, these norms were decontextualized and made to appear absolute.

Colonisation of new places, especially in the Americas, generated a need for a new understanding of law which facilitated and made sense of colonial powers' extending their legal regimes into those new territories. We can draw parallels with the Romans encountering similar challenges in governing their Empire hundreds of years before, which stimulated them to consider the role of the *ius gentium*, too. The concept of a law common to all peoples was, as with the Romans, attractive because it did not require that the governing powers identify the legal rights of those governed under the particular law reserved for, e.g., citizens.

2.5 *Ius Commune*

A step below the *ius gentium*, or law of nations, is Roman law (*ius civile Romanorum*). Lancellotti tells us that in his time Roman law was called *ius commune* (common law). To understand this, we need to make three observations. First, the adjective *commune* qualifies a mode of being of *jus*: a legal rule that is applied to a class of individuals or situations is 'common'. In Lancellotti's text, several normative orders were qualified *commune*. Beginning at the top, we first find natural law, which is common to all animated beings (humans and animals); then the law of nations (*ius gentium*) which is common to all humans globally; a step below is Roman law which is common to the citizens of the Roman Empire; then is Pontifical law, which is common to the citizens of the Papal State, located in central Italy; and, finally, the city statute, which is common to the citizens of a particular city. In cities, Roman law functioned as *ius commune* by dictating general provisions which could be derogated from on specific matters by local rules (city statutes or *iura propria*), but generally, if we compare Roman law to natural law or the law of nations, we will find that Roman law was applied to a restricted number of individuals, making it a 'particular' rather than a general law.

Second, the *ius commune* (common law) performs its function in a dynamic structure which is open to the possibility that in some circumstances a 'particular' rule can be applied to some individuals or situations only. There is a good example in the Roman testament of soldiers.

> *D. 29.1.11pr Ulpian, Commentary on the Edict, Book* XLV, *Testamentum militis*
> Those sentenced to capital punishment for a military crime are permitted to make a testament only in respect of their property acquired on military service; but the question arises whether [they may do so] by military law or common law ['utrum iure militari an iure communi']. However, the preferable view is that they should make their testament by military law. Since the right of making a testament is conferred upon him as a soldier, it will follow that he ought to make his testament by military law.[10]

Whilst Roman rules dictated formalities that were required in order to constitute a valid testament, particular rules established an informal regime for the testament made by soldiers during wartime.

Finally, the *ius commune* cannot be separated from a *ius particulare* with which it is in a constant process of negotiation: understood in this sense, the *ius commune* is a relational idea. With this background in mind, some legal historians use the term *ius commune* to indicate the whole structure comprising plural normative orders united by a mutual relationship. Inextricably linked to this context was the view of Roman law as the main example of a *ius commune*, until it was abrogated by nineteenth-century codifications.

---

10 D 29.1.11pr *Ulpianus libro quadraginta quinto ad edictum* Ex militari delicto capite damnatis testamentum facere licet super bonis dumtaxat castrensibus: sed utrum iure militari an iure communi, quaeritur. Magis autem est, ut iure militari eis testandum sit: nam cum ei quasi militi tribuatur ius testandi, consequens erit dicere iure militari ei testandum.

Alain Wijffels, 'Ius commune', Comparative Law and Public Governance, in Maurice Adams and Dirk Heirbaut (eds), The Method and Culture of Comparative Law. Essays in Honour of Mark Van Hoecke, Oxford and Portland, Hart, 2014, 148–150

When the phrase *ius commune* was used by late-medieval scholars (whether in their academic work or in the course of their consultations on behalf of authorities or private parties involved in specific controversies), it served almost invariably as a concept which enabled the author to deal with a particular law. This could be in order to solve a conflict of laws, to determine whether a specific customary or statutory rule was applicable in a particular situation, and also in order to construe a customary or statutory rule. In addition, though it was by no means in all cases the main purpose of bringing in the concept of *ius commune*, it would justify the actual application of a rule of Roman or canon law, and in such a case all the doctrinal issues and controversies which could be associated with that rule would inevitably be brought into the argument, adducing even more textual and doctrinal authorities from Roman and canon law scholarship. …

The distinctions are blurred even more by present-day references to *ius commune* as an undifferentiated historical category supposed to entail a body of law (mainly Roman law) throughout (continental) Europe previous to the era of national codifications. Especially when supporters of a greater legal integration within the EU use the phrase, the pre-nineteenth-century *ius commune* is sometimes presented either as the roots of the present-day European legal systems (having somehow survived under the layer of national codifications during the nineteenth and twentieth centuries) or as a more abstract reminder that, before the legal systems of the nation-states were established as national legal systems, the various European countries had shared a common legal system, or at least a common legal culture. One way or the other, the historical reference simply serves as a stepping stone to forward the notion of European law as a 'new *ius commune*'. It is a typical example of how a historical category is being used largely out of context. As a historical notion of reference, *ius commune* not only has, as has already been pointed out, different meanings (some going back to medieval and early modern law, some as constructs of different historiographic approaches), but, even when one considers *ius commune* as a body of positive (and mostly substantive) legal rules, most authors still overlook the essential transformations *ius commune* underwent when, over the centuries, it was cast in different moulds of thinking, each time producing a distinctive brand of legal

> methods. Although, each time, more or less the same textual sources, mainly drawn from Justinian's compilations, were recycled, the outcome was a new framework of legal thinking. Each time, the theoretical and practical relationship between Roman–canon law and particular laws was redefined.

This serves as a good reminder that when we are using the same term *ius commune*, the meaning of that term changes when we look at how it was deployed in different historical periods.

2.6 *Canon Law*

At Roman law's side we find the other 'universal' normative body: canon law. Canon law can be briefly described as the body of precepts (called '*canones*') issued directly or indirectly by an ecclesiastical authority. It existed in a dualism of jurisdictions at the heart of the Western Legal Tradition: on the one hand, there was canon law and the ecclesiastical structures, and on the other, secular law and public power. Harold Berman was notable for his claim that canon law was the first true Western legal system.

> *R. H. Helmholz, Harold Berman's Accomplishment as a Legal Historian, Emory Law Journal 42 (1993), 483*
>
> ... the primacy of the canon law was recognized as an accurate assessment by a majority of the reviewers. The controversial assertions – that the canon law was the first Western legal system, that other kinds of European law grew either from or in reaction to it, and that it is to religious law that we owe many of our basic ideas of law – went down quite well.

Canon law evolved hand in hand with Roman law; for example, dioceses (districts under the pastoral care of a bishop) were organised according to Roman administrative structures. Christian ethics influenced Roman law, and juristic concepts were used in the service of theology, shaping ecclesiology, rules of faith, liturgy and discipline.

> *J. Gaudemet, La formation du droit seculier et du droit de l'eglise aux* IV *et* V *siecles, Paris, Sirey, 1979, 230*
>
> Roman law allowed the Christian community to organise itself as a society. This service will continue for centuries. It will turn the Catholic church, as it were, into the most authentic heir to the Roman Empire.

This dualism of political power and religion is at the heart of Harold Berman's influential account of the Western Legal Tradition.[11] His thesis focuses on the 'revolutionary' impact of the period 1050–1200, which he presents as the juncture that produced the deepest transformations in Western law. The bishops of Rome claimed control over the Church, and their newly acquired autonomy from secular powers transformed the legal world. It reformulated legal thinking, giving rise to coherent bodies of laws and legal studies whose major fruit was the learned legal science of canon and civil law. It is therefore from religion and canon law that the Western Legal Tradition found its beginning. This argument then expanded by including the dissemination of canon law on a European scale that included English law. By turning to canon law, Berman broadened legal-historical studies to the interplay between the religious and secular component of the law, giving life to the most fruitful stream of research.

2.7 *Diffusion of Canon Law in England*

The sweeping and destructive power of Martin Luther's criticism against the Roman Catholic Church is shown in his burning some fundamental books of canon law in Wittemberg (1520), including the *Decretals* and the *Summa Angelica*. He meant to attack the Church's role as a spiritual guide, its law-making powers, and its claims to general legal authority.

The *Decretals* are one of the major sources of canon law. Originating from papal decisions on specific matters particularly between the 13th and 14th centuries and structured in collections, those works were the standard canon law texts used both in legal education and legal practice. There were some attempts to supplement and update the standard collections of decretals.

The *Summa Angelica* (1st ed. 1476), named after its author Angelo Carletti (d. 1495), was a major work on cases of conscience. Such writings had a sweeping impact in the early-modern period. Individuals often sought advice on concrete moral questions (contracts, avarice, frauds, usury, sex), which were solved looking at principles located between ethics and law and according to a methodology focused on specific cases ('casuism'). Such works had an immense influence in shaping social life and in disseminating juristic practices.

---

11 Harold J. Berman, Law and Revolution I: The Formation of the Western Legal Tradition, Cambridge Mass., Harvard University Press, 1997 and Id., Law and Revolution II: The Impact of the Protestant Reformations on the Western Legal Tradition, Cambridge Mass, Harvard University Press, 2003.

However, despite of the symbolic value of Luther's gesture, it would be highly misleading to imagine total estrangement between the Protestant north and the Catholic south in Europe. Much of the writings on canon and Roman law in southern Europe continued to circulate and to be printed in northern countries (without dedication pages referring to the Pope, of course). These texts also made their way to England and by conscious or unconscious borrowings, influenced aspects of English common law.

> *R.H. Helmholz, Continental Law and Common Law: Historical Strangers or Companions?, Duke Law Journal 1990, 1214–1215*
> England was assertively Protestant in religion and had cut the ties that once connected it with the Roman Church. Moreover, common lawyers were self-conscious of the special role their law played in defining the rights and liberties of Englishmen. This was the age of Sir Edward Coke, the great English lawyer who (with Blackstone) probably did as much as any single individual to shape the common law. ... The question, then, is whether English lawyers in this time of growing sophistication and constitutional struggle made any use of or drew any inspiration from the *fontes* of the civil law.

If we turn to cases discussed at that time we see that English lawyers used continental sources. A good example is the Case of Mixt Monies (1605) , in which we find these lawyers using arguments from Roman law to frame the question of royal power and specifically the Crown's right to alter the coinage.

> *R.H. Helmholz, Continental Law and Common Law: Historical Strangers or Companions?, Duke Law Journal 1990, 1214–1215*
> Invoked in the course of argument and decision were texts from the Roman law Digest, and also opinions of Baldus de Ubaldis (d. 1400), Carolus Molinaeus (d. 1566), Jean Bodin (d. 1596), Covarruvias, and (most frequently) Renerus Budelius (d. 1597), the author of a standard civilian work on the subject of coinage. Of course, Continental texts and opinions were not the only authorities cited in these cases – far from it. No one would argue that the civil law dominated such litigation. But [such] cases are not alone in employing authority drawn from civilian treatises, and they are quite incompatible with a depiction of common lawyers as ignorant and uncaring of any but domestic law.

Looking at broader European legal history, we can clearly see that ecclesiastical courts served as a bridge between England and the continent.

2.8 *Custom*

Any description of medieval and early-modern normativity must mention customs. Their importance in medieval life has led some legal historians to claim that medieval law was essentially customary in origin. However, their juridical nature is still debated: customs belong to a conceptually indeterminate area placed between uses, habits and general social behaviour, and official law. To understand this requires some consideration of where norms come from. There are two major approaches to this question. The first explains that social facts emerge spontaneously amongst a people and turn into rules. The second argues that only when such facts are captured in writing do they achieve consistency and upgrade social behaviour into official law.

> *Paolo Grossi, A History of European Law, Hoboken, John Wiley & Sons, 2010, 10–11 (transl. by Laurence Hooper)*
>
> What is custom? … an action repeated over time in the context of a community, whether small or large. The action is repeated because the members of that community perceive some positive value in it. And the philosophers are therefore correct to define it as a normative action: one which, by some peculiar quality, begins to be repeated over a long period of time and becomes the norm.
>
> Since it is an action at root, custom conserves two necessary underlying characteristics. Firstly custom originates from below, from things and from the Earth, from which it cannot be separated; it sticks to the Earth like a serpent and faithfully reproduces the geological, agricultural, economic and ethical structures of the surrounding reality. Secondly, custom originates from the concrete, even if thereafter its significance may be extended by analogy; it therefore carries with it the unavoidable traces of the concrete reality which it seeks to govern with its laws.
>
> But custom is never a solitary behaviour; quite the contrary, it cannot exist without the collective repetition of the action whence it springs. This shows us a further characteristic of custom: it expresses the identity of a group, of a collective – usually a small one at the time the custom is formed, but which can grow far broader with the passage of time. …
>
> Every region has its own customs; every region forms its own customary laws and moulds them to its purposes. Since custom does not lend its weight to artificial and arbitrary actions but rather to deeper values and convictions, it represents the superficial flourishing of the most profound cultural roots of a given region.

However important the social role of custom, the variation of different rules in different places did not sit well with the new desire to rationalise the law into coherent structures. Control over customs, particularly control over how they were adapted into the structured legal order, was also an issue of political power. The control of custom through solidification or codification by sovereign law-makers was a part of a general trend towards legal systems centred on a single source of legal normativity instead of a plurality.

> *T. Herzog, A Short History of European Law: The Last Two and a Half Millennia (3rd ed.), Cambridge Mass., Harvard University Press, 2019, 130*
> By reducing customs to written texts, [French] kings aspired to control the local normative order and indeed change it. Royal commissioners who engaged in this task understood what was at stake. They constantly imposed their opinion on locals as to how norms should be identified and written down, what should be added and what subtracted. Royal officials also favored the unification of various customary regimes and selected those customs that should be applicable everywhere in the kingdom. The writing down of customs, royal jurists hoped, would also stop their evolution by fixing them conclusively. No longer would customs change, no longer would negotiations be possible. Most importantly, the local norms that became royal law after they were written down would no longer depend on the community. Instead, they would obtain their validity and would be legitimized and obeyed because the king had so willed.
>
> In the long run, rather than being an instrument for preservation, the writing down of customary law was a means to introduce change. … In the aftermath of its official recording, local law would no longer depend on the community. It would instead be imposed on locals by outsiders who would tell them what their own customs dictated. Paradoxically, the one point on which both humanists and kings converged was the hope that customary law would replace the *ius commune*. … But the hope that customs would replace the *ius commune* were frustrated. Not only did *ius commune* survive the fifteenth and sixteenth century crisis, but the writing down of customs manifested its hegemonic presence.

Although the process of committing customs to writing changed their legal nature, and sometimes their substantive content, even this was insufficient to displace the role of the *ius commune* at the heart of the legal order. Instead, written descriptions of custom became a part of a broader legal culture centred on written texts instead of oral arguments.

2.9 *The Printing Press and the Law*

A great deal of attention has recently been paid to the printing revolution between the fifteenth and sixteenth centuries. The change of *medium* impacted legal thinking, as the printed page afforded a new range of reasoning operations involving legal texts. But we would have an incomplete idea of this evolution without considering the material dimension of the printing revolution, made of a flood of printed texts that became available to legal study and legal practice.

M.A.P. Fratoni, Printing the Law in the 15th Century. With a Focus on Corpus iuris civilis and the Works of Bartolus de Saxoferrato, in C. Dondi (ed.), Printing R-Evolution and Society 1450–1500. Fifty Years that Changed Europe, Venice, Ca' Foscari, 2020, 68–71

The editions of legal texts are a very important sector of 15th-century book production; the category is second only to Theology. With about 4,500 editions, it represents 15% of known surviving output.

Two main groups of texts form the category:

a. the compilations of Civil and Canon law with their medieval supplements and the exegetical works of the jurists: (1) the *Corpus iuris civilis*, the Justinian compilation (Roman law), the law of the Empire; (2) the *Corpus iuris canonici*, the law of the Church; (3) commentaries, treatises, and works written by the jurists for teaching purposes or in the course of their professional activity, such as *consilia* (the texts of the *ius commune*).
b. Collections of local rules, such as statutes, regulations, customs (the texts of the *iura propria*) but also the acts promulgated by the superior authorities as part of their daily activity. The numerous papal bulls issued for the granting of indulgences are found in this group, making canon law the largest group of contemporary texts, as well as among the earliest kind of texts, to appear in print.

The production, distribution and transmission of texts was characterised by a direct and strong link with the social, intellectual and cultural environment of the universities. The rediscovery and arrangement of the texts of the law were at the very origin of the university as an institution: 'We all know that the teaching of the law was not only the earliest one; it was also the first one to be raised to the level of a university school, during the phase of renewal of the texts and practice'.

University teaching in law (and medicine, philosophy and theology) featured an efficient distribution of books, known as the 'pecia' system. The legal texts needed by students and teachers were produced

> on demand by some University officers (*stationarii*). They entrusted to scribes the faithful reproduction of 'exemplars', namely, the official texts previously checked and approved by the academic authorities. To speed up the reproduction, the exemplar was divided in sections ('peciae') and given to a group of scribes who worked at the same time. …
>
> During the course of the sixteenth century, the first critical editions of various parts of the *corpora iuris*, and of a number of works of medieval authors, were prepared, which strengthened the search for the best manuscripts, such as the oldest ones or the autographs.

Printing was indeed a key component in the evolution of legal thinking. It is crucial to specify, however, that such changes occurred gradually as a result of the progressive expansion of printed texts in a professional environment in which they coexisted with handwritten material; we see printers and scribes reciprocally imitating each other in the visual appearance of their texts: on one hand printers produced texts set out in a font that imitated the flourishing style of humanist handwriting ('italic', first used by the Venetian printer Aldus Manutius in 1500); on the other, scribes produced perfect handwritten copies of printed pages. It may be added that legal archives are repleted with sixteenth- and seventeenth-century material used in legal practice made of a compound of handwritten and printed texts. Nevertheless, the introduction of the printing press marked the beginning of a new phase.

How did the printing press influence the law? One of the consequences is in introducing new forms of legal reasoning. When a legal rule is captured in a printed text, it acquires a degree of stability, and can be generalised and elaborated intellectually. Such rule disregards differences and circumstances, suggests conceptual maps and principles that can be set out in systems. There is no true consistency without a printed text.

Once legal information is stored on the printed page, traditional argumentative methods based on memory become obsolete, and the collective elaboration of the discipline turns from a memory-based to a text-based methodology. This perspective explains the eclipse of a range of educational methods based on rhetorical learning aimed at educating and developing memory (e.g. commonplaces and maxims) and the spread of other criteria to store and retrieve information.

This change is also perceptible in legal works. Justinian's *Corpus Juris* was a difficult text to be managed for its lack of a clear structure. One of the traditional purposes of legal education was a close reading of the singular laws ('lectura') which were then analysed and memorized as they were located in the original text. To possess a strong memory was one of the chief qualities of a jurist. But in the sixteenth-century we see a shift from the original structure to be found in Justinian's compilation (called *ordo legalis*), unchallenged by Glossators and Commentators and followed in teaching, interpretation and practice, to explore other ordering methods. One of them was to attract simple topics under broader headings (*ratione materiae*); some jurists also explored alternative ordering methods: alphabetic, topics, indexed by word and others. The traditional structure went out of fashion. Those new arrangements reflected new ways of thinking about the law.

The jurists' frame of reference turned away from the shared assumptions of the profession ("common learning") to printed sources. This contributed to a dissolution of the scholarly community tied to one particular place in favour of standardisation and the production of a fixed canon and doctrine of precedent. Printing sources produced standards that became the doctrinal orthodoxy.

Turning to another perspective, legal texts are also battlefields between two state powers: the legislator who creates texts and the judges who interpret and apply them. The printing press impacted on this power struggle, too. On one hand, the rise of printing went hand in hand with the creation of professional Supreme Courts in the sixteenth century (for instance, Senates, *Parléments*, *Rotae*) and the circulation of printed decisions contributed to the prestige of judicial bodies by enabling them to treat like cases alike across time. On the other hand, the concentration of power in the sovereign-legislator enabled the control of legal information and the institution of bureaucratic judicial bodies.

> *D. Ibbetson, Legal Printing and Legal Doctrine', Irish Jurist 35 (2000), 345–347*
> The printing of law books, beginning in the late fifteenth century, brought about an immediate change to the nature of English law, moving it from an oral culture to an essentially written one. Where fifteenth century lawyers based their arguments on the common learning of the profession, their counterparts in the sixteenth century based their arguments on printed sources. Most notable among these were the Year Books, the reports of arguments and decisions in the Kings' courts dating from the fourteenth century onwards, and their successors, the so-called nominate reports which began to be printed in the second half of the sixteenth century. The Year Books were printed and reprinted many times and we may be sure that every lawyer arguing in court would have possessed a set. It is very likely that every serious student learning the Common law would have had a set too. It was not simply that printing made the Year Books more widely available; it also allowed the production of a standardised text. This had many ramifications. Standardisation

and consistent pagination made it possible to produce indexes. These might be the simple head-word references which we think of as indexes today, or they might be more substantial Abridgements, collections of abbreviated reports culled from the Year Books and re-arranged under alphabetical headings with cross-references between categories. This latter form in particular enabled lawyers to track down relevant cases from the Year Books. No longer were they dependent on the fallibility of human memory. Arguments based on vague, hand-waving references to 'our books' were gradually replaced by references to specific cases within those books. The books themselves became the source of legal authority. …

This primacy of the written text generated paradoxical changes in legal doctrine. Most obviously, it gave a fixedness to legal rules that had not existed previously. Once a decision was reported, it became part of the legal canon; and from the beginning of the seventeenth century we can see the stirrings of what would later come to be referred to as the doctrine of precedent. On the other hand it freed up legal doctrine, allowing it to develop in order to fit changing needs and circumstances. Lawyers were no longer constrained by the common learning of the Inns of Courts. Abstract, principled arguments going against current orthodoxy could be justified by reference to reported cases. Orthodoxy might be 'proved' to be wrong.

The changes introduced by the arrival of printing were undoubtedly significant in shaping the Common law mentality, but they did not bring about any real discontinuity from the old ways of doing things. English lawyers still thought in terms of the forms of action just as they had done in the Middle Ages, and still framed their arguments in terms of the old law found in the Year Books. It was not until the eighteenth century that really radical changes in legal thinking began to occur, as there began to be printed treatises imposing a degree of order on areas of the law. Such works had existed earlier, works such as John Cowell's *Institutiones Iuris Anglicani*, Francis Bacon's *Maxims of the Law* or Henry Finch's *Nomotechnia*. Although these had some measure of popularity in their time, they were either too general or too abstract to have any real influence on the law. The only honourable exception was Littleton's *Tenures* especially with the commentary of Sir Edward Coke, which had revealed the general principles of the law of real property. In the eighteenth century, for the first time, England was given a general legal textbook worthy of the name, in the shape of Blackstone's *Commentaries*; and a host of other writers mapped out individual areas of the law. These writers made use of legal ideas which were not tied to the mediaeval legal categories: ideas of contract rather than rules of debt, covenant and account, ideas of negligence rather than rules of trespass and case. The Common law provided no direct source for such ideas, at least no source that could be called upon as authority in court. Unless they were to be generated by lawyers' own speculations they had to be imported from outside, from sources independent of the Common law. In reality, that meant from Roman law or from the northern Natural law school of the seventeenth and eighteenth centuries. These ideas were taken up by legal writers, passed off as English law, and picked up from there by judges and advocates. Legal publishing hence took on a crucial role in the formulation of legal doctrine at this pivotal point in the history of English law.

Questions

1. What are the different meanings of *ius commune* in the period under discussion?
2. Today's legal systems have unquestionably brought some advantages, but questions recurrently arise when formally valid legal rules conflict with higher values (for example, human rights). Did *ius commune* as a multinormative system deal with this issue more satisfactorily?
3. How did the sixteenth- and seventeenth-century definitions of natural law differ from their medieval predecessors? What was the impact of printing on the law?
4. How might changes to the physical presentation of a legal text reflect changes in, or impact on, legal reasoning?

3 Actors

Legal systems cannot be adequately explained by focusing only on written norms. Every legal system includes a class of professionals who know the law (*jurisperitus*, *jurisconsultus*, barrister, *rabbi*, *mufti*, *kadı*) and in turn determine the features of that specific legal system. Legal science is inaccessible to lay people: legal texts are obscure and extracting solutions requires specific skills acquired by study and experience. Legal professionals are the guardians of legal science, and self-aware of their role in authoritative interpretation of the intellectually sophisticated knowledge they keep and refine. They are not, however, creators, but mediators, whose specific task is to work out new rules from extant law. The creative process of extracting new rules from existing texts was called interpretation (*interpretatio*) until the late sixteenth century when, following the rise of sovereign-legislators, the meaning of the term changed in order to refer to the process of inquiry into the will of the legislator.

Broadly, there are actors whose role is to lay down general laws (legislators), others who conceptualise and clarify existing rules (professors), and some others who apply them to the disputed facts (judges). These roles can change over time: there have been legislators limited by superior norms and absolute creators; judges who actively created new law and others who mechanically applied it; professors who created new general rules from texts, and others who merely explained them. These actors also have social influence and standing, and the balance of power amongst them can change: some historical periods are characterised by the prevalence of professors, others of legislators, and others yet of judges. Legal systems are the result of their interaction, symbiotic relations and inevitable tensions.

3.1 *A Closed Professional Class*

The jurists of this period were not only the contributors to the collective elaboration of legal science, but also members of a specific social class with identifiable traits. Firstly, they were united by a common education: the law degree was conferred as a result of highly formalised education, and academic training followed a standard curriculum based on a time-honoured and fixed Roman law framework based on rhetorical-dialectical scholastic skills. Secondly, they shared a social status: the legal profession conferred a nobility believed to be a degree above family origin although twenty-years of academic work was required to achieve this, according to Bartolus. Thirdly, the legal profession was highly remunerative: in the early sixteenth century, a law professor holding a chair at Wittenberg earned 250–300 florins per year, to be compared to the sum of about 8 florins needed by a student for a year of university study.[12] However, university jurists' status declined from the early seventeenth century: professional Supreme Courts absorbed and nurtured a new breed of legal professionals equally competent in both doctrine and practice. Court decisions, rather than academic texts, became 'jurisprudence'.

Although the primary role of legal science and of learned jurists is perhaps the most recognisable trait of the Western legal tradition, it should be noted that jurists constantly negotiated their position against their direct competitors: sovereign-legislators. In England, Sir Edward Coke (1552–1634), then Chief Justice, recounted a dialogue he had with King James I, explaining that the

12 Johann August Roderich von Stintzing, Geschichte der deutschen Rechtswissenschaft I, München, R. Oldenbourg, 1880, p. 266.

law used an artificial and specialist reasoning which was inaccessible to the outsider and the untrained, even if they were highly educated in other ways.

> *Edward Coke, The English Reports, 77, King's Bench Division, VI, containing Coke, parts 5 to 13, Edinburgh and London, W. Green & Sons and Stevens & Sons, 1907, 1343*
>
> A controversy of land between parties was heard by the King, and sentence given, which was repealed by this, that it did not belong to the common law: then the King said, that he thought the law was founded upon reason, and that he and others had reason, as well as the Judges: to which it was answered by me, that true it was, that God had endowed His Majesty with excellent science, and great endowments of nature; but His Majesty was not learned in the laws of his realm of England, and causes which concern the life, or inheritance, or goods, or fortunes of his subjects, are not to be decided by natural reason but by the artificial reason and judgement of law, which law is an act which requires long study and experience, before that a man can attain to the cognisance of it: that the law was the golden met-wand and measure to try the causes of the subjects; and which protected His Majesty in safety and peace: with which the King was greatly offended, and said that then he should be under the law, which was treason to affirm, as he said; to which I said, that Bracton saith, *quod Rex non debet esse sub homine, sed sub Deo et lege* ('the King ought not be subject to man, but to God and to the law').

Other writers imagined new societies with no legal professionals at all. For example Thomas More, who was later to be Lord Chancellor of England (1529–32), conceived an imaginary state which rejected both legal professionals and most law in his *Utopia* (1516).

> *Edward Berry, Thomas More and the Legal Imagination, Studies in Philology 106/3 (2009), 331*
>
> The Utopians have very few laws, and they look with dismay at the 'almost innumerable books of laws and commentaries' used in other countries, finding it unfair to bind people to laws that are 'either too numerous to be read through or too obscure to be understood by anyone'. In Utopia the simplicity and clarity of the laws make it possible for each man to become an 'expert in law' and, with the assistance of the judge, to 'plead his own cause'. The Utopians, indeed, 'absolutely banish from their country all lawyers, who cleverly manipulate cases and cunningly argue legal points'.

If so, although norms of behaviour are a constant feature of human settings, the same cannot be said of professional legal science (*jurisprudentia*). Normativity is indeed present in all human communities, but the specific legal science that grows from the texts studied in lecture halls and elaborated by interpreters comes later and is tied to the existence of authoritative texts.

During the sixteenth century, the sovereign-lawgiver acquired a prominent position in Western legal systems. The rise of this figure was accompanied by an influential literature on theories of sovereignty that offered the view of a structure of public power in which individuals owed their duties not to a multiplicity of jurisdictional authorities, either ecclesiastical or civil, but to one singular centre of authority, the state (*état, stato, Staat*), which they indicated as the highest form of authority in civil government. Such theories mark the beginning of a new phase in the history of political thought in which the idea of public power is expounded in purely abstract terms. In such structure the sovereign is legislator, and the legislator is sovereign. This idea received a first notable statement by the French jurist Jean Bodin (1530–96) in his *Republic* (1576), a work that had an immediate currency in Europe, England included.

> *Jean Bodin, Six Books of the Commonwealth, Oxford, Basil Blackwell, 1955, 157 (transl. by M. J. Tooley)*
> Book I, Chapter X: The True Attributes of Sovereignty
> Before going any further, one must consider what is meant by law. The word law signifies the right command of that person, or those persons, who have absolute authority over all the rest without exception, saving only the law-giver himself, whether the command touches all subjects in general or only some in particular. To put it another way, the law is the rightful command of the sovereign touching all his subjects in general, or matters of general application. …
>
> The first attribute of the sovereign prince therefore is the power to make law binding on all his subjects in general and on each in particular. But to avoid any ambiguity one must add that he does so without the consent of any superior, equal, or inferior being necessary. If the prince can only make law with the consent of a superior he is a subject; if of an equal he shares his sovereignty; if of an inferior, whether it be a council of magnates or the people, it is not he who is sovereign.

This change also engendered a rapidly growing body of regional and national laws (called *ius hodiernum* or *ius modernum*) which included statutes, princely law, collections of judicial decisions, ordinances, and local legislation generally addressed to the functioning of central and peripheral institutions. Each local legislature stressed its own identity through its laws (*iura hispanica, danica, gallica, italica, germanica*), without denying a shared horizon of reference through the intellectual framework of Roman law.

3.2 *Schools of Interpretation*

At the heart of the continental tradition are Roman texts. But texts require jurists to work with them, to extract new legal rules, clarify obscure passages, rephrase them for understanding, or reorganise them systematically. There have been different schools of interpretation debating how to go about this since the medieval era. Two schools are often considered central to the period considered in this chapter, and as encapsulating early modern jurisprudence: 'bartolism' and 'legal humanism'.

The sixteenth century philological and historical approach to the study of legal texts gave rise, particularly in France in the course of the sixteenth century, to a new school of legal studies today designated as legal humanism, and then known as *mos gallicus* (*iura docendi*), in reference to a new a teaching method opposed to the traditional or Bartolist approach also known as *mos italicus*.

> *P.J. du Plessis and J. Cairns, Reassessing of Legal Humanism and Its Claims: Petere Fontes?, Edinburgh Studies in Law, Edinburgh, Edinburgh University Press, 2016, 109*
> … early humanist jurists such as Guillaume Budé (1467–1540) in France, Ulrich Zasius (1461–1536) in Germany, and Andrea Alciati (1492–1550) in France and Italy, turned away from the dominant Scholastic natural law and natural rights discourse of the late-medieval and early modern periods (wherein these categories are central), and turned instead to discussions of the cultivation of civic virtues, civic utility, and procedures for securing the common good.

3.3 *Bartolists or Mos Italicus*

Bartolus and the followers of the *mos Italicus* are sometimes described as unoriginal practitioners. Bartolism (or *mos italicus*) was essentially a methodology for the production of new norms. The jurist could wrap a Roman text in the Scholastic dialectical apparatus and thus produce new law. For a simple example we turn to a text from Justinian's *Institutions* (535 A.D.).

> *Inst.* 2.1.12
> Wild beasts, birds, fish and all animals, which live either in the sea, the air, or the earth, so soon as they are taken by anyone, immediately become by the law of nations the property of the captor.[13]

Beginning from this text, medieval jurists produced a new norm. They reformulated the statement generalising the provision and extracted the general rule that ownerless things became the property of the first occupant. Such dialectical methodology was part of the basic teaching in legal education embedded in Scholasticism, which students summarized in a mnemonical verse.

> *Matteo Gribaldi Moffa, De methodo ac ratione studendi, Lyon, A. Vincentium, 1541, I, c. XIV, 95*
> I introduce the problem, I analyze it, I summarize it, and I frame the case, I read through the text, I set my arguments, I remark on other points, and I discuss objections.[14]

Working out the text, there was no place for historical or philological considerations, in fact, this treatment downgraded the Roman text to a mere starting point for the production of further norms, and even implied that the authority for those norms stemmed not from the text but from the doctors interpreting them. But in that normative system their interpretive creations had authority and were accepted by the courts as learned opinions. These jurists were not just interpreters, but actual creators of law.

3.4 *Legal Humanism or Mos Gallicus*

Another major approach was detectable in France: legal humanism (*mos Gallicus*). Expanding on the humanist movement that in the fifteenth-century aimed to bring back to life philosophical and literary texts from the Greek and Latin tradition and reconstruct them with sophisticated philological skills, some jurists transferred those historical concerns to the law. Beginning from a deeply held concern for the historical and philological value of the Roman texts, some major jurists such as Guillaume Budé (1467–1540), Ulrich Zasius (1461–1536), and Jacques Cujas (Cujacius, 1522–1590) wanted to reconstruct what they believed was the law as it was practised at the time of ancient Rome. In their mind, the compilation of Justinian was a legacy that needed to be approached with the philological veneration due to an ancient

13 Inst 2.1.12 Ferae igitur bestiae & volucres & pisces, & omnia animalia quae in coelo & terra nascuntur, simul atque ab aliquo capta fuerint, iure gentium statim illius esse incipient.

14 Praemitto, scindo, summo, casumque figuro, perlego, do causas, connoto et obiicio.

historical object. They detested Bartolists and harshly criticised their lack of historical sense, their clumsy Latin and their convoluted dialectical methods. One of them was François Rabelais (1494–1553) who invested Commentators (the school of Bartolus) and Glossators (the school of Accursius) with some superbly violent remarks.

> *F. Rabelais, Gargantua and Pantagruel, New York, Everyman's Library, 1994, Ch. 2.v (transl. by Thomas Urquhart and Pierre Le Motteux)*
> … the books of the civil law were like unto a wonderfully precious, royal, and triumphant robe of cloth of gold edged with dirt; for in the world are no goodlier books to be seen, more ornate, nor more eloquent than the texts of the Pandects, but the bordering of them, that is to say, the gloss of Accursius, is so scurvy, vile, base, and unsavoury, that it is nothing but filthiness and villainy.

There is another and even more important legacy that legal humanists received from classical authors. This is the concern with precise proportions and the search for a correct method that some jurists – particularly François Douaren (Duarenus, 1509–1559), François de Connan (Connanus, 1508–1551) and Hugues Doneau (Donellus, 1527–1591) – applied to the legal field to reshape the legal material. They said that 'law is architectural' to imply that the legal material must be shaped according to precise systematic design; they imagined that law could be more logical and scientific, more similar to mathematics. Those authors have been at the inception of considering their discipline as a coherent system of law.

Several approaches to the Roman text were under way in sixteenth-century Europe, and the *mos Gallicus* developed by French humanists using historico-philological methods was particularly influential.

> *Douglas Osler, Images of Legal Humanism, Surfaces 9 (2001) (no pagination)*
> The general term 'humanism' has two distinct meanings. In its modern usage humanism refers vaguely to a philosophy which lays emphasis on the material welfare of mankind in this world, and is thus often contrasted to the religious outlook. In its second meaning humanism refers specifically to the study of antiquity in the period of the Renaissance. Legal humanism is used exclusively in the latter context and refers to a particular direction in the study of Roman law.
>
> The first manifestations of legal humanism can be detected in fifteenth century Italy, but it is not until the second half of the sixteenth century that the first major school is active in France. In other words, legal

humanism flourishes some two centuries after the beginnings of humanism in Italy in the persons of Petrarch and Boccaccio. To compound this general disorientation in historical periodisation, the two most famous names in medieval jurisprudence, Bartolus de Saxoferrato (1314–57) and his pupil Baldus de Ubaldis (1327–1400) were contemporaries of Petrarch and Boccaccio. …

Certainly, some further sources of Roman law were discovered in the sixteenth century, but the master source, the *Corpus Iuris Civilis* of Justinian, had by then been in active use for half a millennium. The Renaissance 'discovery' of classical antiquity in the legal sphere thus primarily lay not in the bringing to light of new physical remains, as manuscripts of lost literary works or long-buried sculptures, but in a new orientation in the treatment of legal texts which had been known for centuries.

In 1755 the German scholar Ioannes Fridericus Jugler captured the essence of legal humanism in the following definition: 'Legal humanism is the study of Roman law in close conjunction with philosophy, antiquities, the Greek and Latin languages, the art of textual criticism, Roman history and literature'. (He does not use the expression legal humanism, but rather the Latin synonym used in previous centuries, *jurisprudentia elegantior*.) Legal humanism thus signifies the investigation of Roman law, using philological and historical methods, as part of the historical study of antiquity, and may be contrasted with the pragmatic, unhistorical application of Roman law to the conditions of contemporary Europe.

In the sixteenth century the legal humanists developed a series of sophisticated techniques for the historical reconstruction of classical Roman jurisprudence. … the humanists sought to 'deconstruct' [the Corpus Juris Civilis] in an effort to retrieve the original sources. Through textual criticism the humanists sought both to cleanse the text of scribal errors and also to retrieve those elements which had been omitted in the Middle Ages as of no interest. In particular, through the restoration of the 'inscriptions' of the Digest fragments (which identified the works from which they were derived), the humanists were able to reconstruct the works of the classical jurists. Through historical and linguistic analysis they sought to detect the 'interpolations' of Tribonian, the changes silently introduced into the classical texts by Justinian's compilers to bring the law up to date. It was the humanists, too, who first brought to light some of the classical juristic texts which have been transmitted to us outside the *Corpus Iuris*. They began also the discovery and editing of Byzantine legal sources, the legal tradition carried on in the Greek-speaking Eastern Empire until the fall of Constantinople in 1453. …

> In the sixteenth century a new era in legal history begins, the era of legal humanism. The new humanist method was inititiated by Andreas Alciatus (1492–1550), who carried it from Italy to France. Between the years 1529 and 1533 Alciatus taught at Bourges, the university which was to become the great citadel of legal humanism. Hence the humanist method was to be named the French method or *mos gallicus*, as opposed to the *mos italicus*, for in Italy in the sixteenth century the medieval method of Bartolus and Baldus was to remain dominant. Legal humanism was thus a Northern affair, always tainted with Protestantism; clear analogies could be drawn between the Protestant rejection of the authoritative character of the Latin Vulgate of the Bible and the humanist challenge to the traditional text of the *Corpus Iuris*. Both used critical, historical and philological methods, including a knowledge of Greek.

Summarising, it may be said that legal humanism, beginning from the humanist concern for language, spread its efforts in three main directions. First, because language has a history, some of them (Alciato, Budeus, Cujas) wanted to bring back the legal texts to the Roman times in which they had been first created; second, because language is inseparable from society, some others (Hotman, Loysel) thought that proper legal rules cannot be separated from specific geographical communities and promoted their written setting; and third, because language has a precise syntax, another stream (Douaren, Doneau) reengineered the legal material according to a precise systematic structure. One important question, however, regards its impact on legal practice.

> *P. Stein, Legal Humanism and Legal Science, Tijdschrift voor Rechtsgeschiedenis 54 (1986), 297*
>
> It is tempting to assume that all this ferment of activity must have had immediate repercussions on the practice of the law. Yet the impact of these movements was barely perceptible in the contemporary work of the courts or the notaries' offices. This was not because the practitioners were unaware of the challenge that humanism was offering them. It was rather that they found it irrelevant or even unhelpful. … Any jurist who practised needed to know the contemporary law, and where that was not local custom or feudal law, it was not Roman law but *ius commune*, the law adapted from the *Corpus Iuris* by the Commentators. It was all very well to know the prehistory of a rule of the *ius commune*, but what was needed was a precise rule of authority which a hard-pressed judge would respect – and such rules could still be found in the writings of Bartolus and his more recent successors. So in practice, the *mos italicus* continued,

> and indeed even acquired its own apologists and theorists, who in the sixteenth century built up the notion of the *communis opinio doctorum*. If the agreement of the main Commentators could be identified on any doctrine, it was said, that opinion had an authority greater than any text of the *Corpus Iuris*. Only from the commentaries could the *communis opinio* be gleaned. So the demand for their works remained constant through the century. The presses, not just of Venice, but those of Paris and Lyons too, poured out reprints of Bartolus and Baldus and the more recent masters of the *mos italicus*. ... Thus the scholar could be a humanist but the practitioner had to be a Bartolist. ... The conclusion must be that whereas those who professed the civil law in the universities, with some exceptions, largely adopted the humanists' methods and ideas, the law recognized in the practitioners' offices and in the courts showed little sign of its impact.

3.5 *Late-Scholastics*

Traditional accounts often focus exclusively on the Bartolist and legal humanist schools described above. There was, however, another influential presence: the school of jurists-theologians that flourished in sixteenth-century Spain – sometimes called *novissimi Hispani*. The distinctiveness of this Spanish juristic school was due to the interplay of two factors. The first was a dialogue with late Scholastic theological speculation, which unquestionably constituted the most influential think-tank of the time. In spite of bold statements about their incompetence as jurists (Alberico Gentili, 1552–1608: 'Theologians, be silent outside your field!'),[15] as we turn to the writings of influential authors such as Francisco de Vitoria (1483 or 1486–1546), Domingo de Soto (1494–1560), Luis de Molina (1535–1600) and Francisco Suárez (1548–1617) we find a refined understanding of the traditional *ius commune* literature. In fact, for them theology was a broad discipline that straddled on the cusp between moral philosophy and law, as Domingo de Soto wrote.

> *Domingo de Soto, De iustitia et iure, Venice, Minimam Societatem, 1594, Prologo (no page numbers) (transl. by A. Giuliani)*
> Nobody should criticise the fact that theologians deal with such [juristic] questions, which seems closer to those treated by jurists, given that canon law has emerged from the interiors of Theology as well as civil law from those of Ethics. As a result, it is proper to the theologian to adapt the

15 A. Gentili, De iure belli libri tres, 1598, I.12: Silete theology in munere alieno.

> provisions of canon law to the norms of the Gospels; and to the philosopher to accomodate civil law to the principles of philosophy.

The second factor was their concern with the *ius particulare*, which provided Spanish jurists with basic material that in their mind constituted the starting point of further theoretical speculation.

Moreover, unlike legal humanists, they were profoundly concerned with an explanation of jurisprudence in terms of moral philosophy. One of their major achievements was to reformulate in an original way some general categories of private law, beginning with contract.

> *J. Gordley, The Philosophical Foundations of Modern Contract Doctrine, Oxford, Oxford University Press, 1991, 4*
> In the sixteenth and seventeenth century, Spanish theologians and jurists attempted to synthesize the Roman texts with the moral theology of Thomas Aquinas. The fundamental concepts and doctrines of private law with which we are familiar are a simplification of the synthesis they achieved. … They built a system of doctrines Thomistic and Aristotelian in ground plan and Roman in much of its detail. They gave Roman law a systematic doctrinal organization which had previously lacked. In the works of Molina and Lessius, the synthesis became so complete that these works can be described with equal accuracy as treatises on Aristotelian and Thomistic moral philosophy annotated to moral law, or as treatises on Roman law in which the particular rules are organized and presented as illustrations of Thomistic and Aristotelian principles.

Given this background, Spanish jurist-theologians constituted an independent tradition, and they were perceived as such in early-modern Europe. Recurring citations of their works are noticeable until the mid-seventeenth century among the German jurists of the *Usus modernus*. We can, therefore, argue that they exerted an influence at a European level which lasted until the mid-seventeenth century, following the political decline of the Spanish kingdom and its religious fervour.

3.6 *Schools of Interpretation beyond the Roman Law Tradition*

Jurists performed a fundamental function in working out new legal rules from Roman texts, and their university training equipped them with a range of skills for doing so. Recent research has shown that such methods were known also in the contemporary Jewish and Muslim legal traditions, enabling a web of interactions between them and the Western Legal Tradition.

The *shari'a* shows normative forms comparable to the civilian *communis opinio* (*ijma*) and to analogy (*qiyas*).

> *P. Owsia, Sources of law under English, French, Islamic and Iranian law. A Comparative Review of Legal Techniques, Arab Law Quarterly 6 (1991), 53, 60*
>
> The classical common language is a familiar Greek: Aristotelian logic. It is supplemented by affiliated symbiotic disciplines such as grammar and letters. Methodological differences between the systems under review are not due to variant conception of basic methodological rules, but lie in the respective selectiveness and measure of application. The basic approach to interpretation may differ from one legal system to another, depending on the respective essential features of each system as stated under the previous heading, but the technical rules of interpretation show common conceptual traits. ...
>
> ... [the] process known as *Tanqīh al-manāt* (or *-milāk*), used in Shīah law for circumventing the prohibition of applying a straight analogy for the extension of an existing particular rule to a similar instance, closely resembles, in its analytical stage and for its aim, the English technique of arriving at the *ratio decidendi* of a case in the process of *distinguishing*. Both methods are used for the adaptation of the law to a new situation and, as such, both are motivated by some pre-conception to perfect the law. When the *manat*, the *rationale*, of a Shīah existing rule, or the *ratio decidendi* of an existing English case, is determined and formulated, Shīah and English law then in theory differ but in functional terms arrive at similar conclusions. While English law has in principle no problem in applying the rule thus obtained directly to the new case through analogy, Shīah law extends the rule thus extracted to the new instance in the guise of syllogism (*qiyās*, in logical sense). This process involves, in the final analysis, an analogical extension at the initial point of consideration and for the end result ... This again shows that when a strict law persists through an evolutionary process, forces of development keep the technical appearance intact but change the contents within the limits of the fundamental postulates.

If we turn to Jewish law, we find other argumentative methods with Aristotelian origins. Some Muslim and Jewish authors like Avicenna, Averroé, and Maimonides produced commentaries on Aristotle which also had an impact on European scholasticism. David Daube and other scholars have shown this in relation to Moses Maimonides' (1135/8-1204). His major work, *Dux seu Director dubitantium aut perplexorum*, shows the rich web of cultural connections in which scholasticism was embedded.

> *D. Daube, Rabbinic Methods of Interpretation and Hellenistic Rhetoric, Hebrew Union College Annual 22 (1949), 240*
> Rabbinic methods of interpretation derive from Hellenistic rhetoric. Hellenistic rhetoric is at the bottom both of fundamental ideas, presuppositions from which the Rabbis proceeded and of the major details of application, the manner in which these ideas were translated into practice.

The Aristotelian corpus had a role in shaping three legal traditions – Roman, Jewish and Muslim – which, working beyond the printed page, created new law from a broad and potentially unlimited text.

Questions

1. Some sixteenth-century utopian projects imagined societies without jurists. What would the advantages and disadvantages of this be for law?
2. Why were Bartolists and Legal Humanists at odds?
3. Do you think that the closed nature of the legal profession hampered or furthered innovation in legal science? Explain.
4. Were the developments in the Western Legal Tradition during this period truly 'Western', or are they more accurately described as 'global'?

4 Application

After having described the main normative orders and the legal actors who contributed to their creation and interpretation, we now turn to the sector in which those norms were applied to settle disputes. If it were possible to summarise the main character of judicial procedure in the period 1500–1650, it would be the 'intellectualization of legal practice'. There was, for instance, a growing concern with impartiality, the professionalization of the judiciary, a search for coherent judicial decisions in time and space, the introduction of proof-based reasoning standards, and the careful setting out of a principled procedure based on a strict separation between the issues of fact and of law. The outcome of this intense concern with upgrading procedure to an intellectual sophistication was that, following a stream of treatises on evidence and legal reasoning that flooded the libraries of the late-sixteenth-century, it helped to bring about a revolution as regards the basic principles of decision making.

These factors converged in an institution which arose almost synchronically in European territories from the early-sixteenth century: Supreme Courts. Their development can be seen as marking the end of a distinct phase in the development of European law as well as the beginning of another (more familiar) one.

A.M. Godfrey and C.H. (Remco) van Rhee, Introduction, in A.M. Godfrey and C.H. (Remco) van Rhee (eds), Central Courts in Early Modern Europe and the Americas (Comparative Studies in Continental and Anglo-American Legal History 34), Berlin, Duncker & Humblot, 2020, 12–13

The development of central courts in European legal history can be seen as a crucial part of the transition from the medieval to the modern state, reflecting the disintegration of a medieval model of governance based on the general competence of royal councils, and the way that central judicial bodies originally associated with royal councils were coming to function autonomously from government. It also reflected a strengthening of the very idea of central authority within individual 'states' in the late medieval and early modern periods. This affected the role of representative assemblies, central administration, bureaucracy and government, law making, methods of raising revenue, and the financing of diplomacy and war. In the work of historians, this has led to an emphasis on the fourteenth and fifteenth centuries in particular as a 'transitional period' when the medieval state gradually gave way to the modern. The development of central courts is a feature of this transition. It is also important for the investigation of many other questions, including the role of central courts in importing the influence of the 'learned laws' (Roman and canon law) into the judicial development of municipal law (local or national) in the early modern period.

Why such courts developed is a crucial question which requires wider attention in its own right. Was enhancement in the provision of central justice a response to demand from litigants, or was it a refashioning of judicial institutions to better embody contemporary perceptions of how authority should be exercised in a state, especially the authority of a sovereign ruler? The circumstances of individual states are likely to vary significantly, but an understanding of the nature of judicial development and the specific form jurisdictional change took may help illuminate the range of possible answers.

Supreme Courts announce the end of an era in the development of judicial procedure and point to an intellectually sophisticated and altogether more centralised and bureaucratic model which has remained with us ever since. This has come to be embodied in a number of basic ideas, such as the judge's obligation to apply principles of reasoning. It is no coincidence that, by the mid-sixteenth century, the goddess of justice Themis, to express the new concern for impartiality, began to be represented blindfolded. The same characterization is true in the evolution of judicial procedure in the English common law.

> *David Ibbetson, Common Law and Ius Commune, Selden Society Lecture, London, Selden Society, 2001, 4–5*
> We should stress that the *primary* thrust of the early modern developments was not so much the adoption of a version of Roman law as the intellectualisation of legal practice. Looked at this way, England was no different in spirit from the rest of Europe. The early sixteenth century marked a real intellectual revivication of Common law thinking, against the background of the highly developed if over-complex system which had been built in Westminster Hall and the Inns of Court in the fourteenth and fifteenth centuries. In continental Europe, the development of printing brought about the transformation from an oral to a written legal culture, with a consequent change in the whole nature of legal reasoning. So too in England. No longer were advocates constrained to argue within the terms of reference of generally accepted ideas; they were free to put forward unorthodox arguments so long as these could be grounded in the ever-increasing bulk of tracts, commentaries, and decisions. Nor was there any gulf between England and continental Europe in the type of literature that mattered: English common lawyers were as happy to rely on treatise literature as their continental counterparts were, and continental lawyers were as willing as the English to reason from case-law. Throughout Europe there was an increased concern with legal rationality; English litigants were as concerned as their continental counterparts that their disputes should be resolved by consistent procedures according to known criteria. Throughout Europe there was a growth in the professionalisation of the law. England, like some parts of continental Europe, was already highly professionalised in the upper echelons of legal practice, but it shared in the general trend towards trained lawyers taking control of the courts lower down in the hierarchy. At this *intellectual* level, England was a mainstream participant in the European legal revival.

This process also had a significant effect on legal education and the possession of university qualifications deemed to be necessary for a professional jurist.

> *D. Ibbetson, English Law and the European Ius Commune, 1450–1650, Cambridge Yearbook of European Legal Studies 8 (2005), 118*
> Central to this movement was a rapid shift towards seeing a university degree as an essential qualification for practice, at least in the highest national courts. When the *Reichskammergericht* was set up in Germany in 1495 it was explicitly laid down that at least half of the members of the court should hold a university degree in law. In exactly the same year it was laid down in Castille that advocates must have a university degree; and in practice by 1520 it was normal for them to have not simply a bachelor's degree but a doctorate. Four years later in Paris, in 1499, there was introduced a formal examination in Roman law which had to be passed before a man would be permitted to practise in the Parlement. Unsurprisingly, as rules of this type were introduced around Europe, there was a very rapid rise in the number of graduates in Law emerging from the universities.

Whilst this intellectualization was a general European trend, the training process and approach to legal texts differed for the common law.

> *J.H. Baker, English Law and the Renaissance, The Cambridge Law Journal 44 (1985), 51*
> What changed most was not the law as a body of principles, but the learned treatment of legal disputes by the doctors of law who advised and adjudicated in real cases. Courts which had been governed by laymen were replaced by courts composed of professional lawyers, who naturally used the materials available to them in their texts and glosses when arguing and deciding cases. Now, was that process any different in kind from the process whereby common lawyers took questions from the laymen on the jury (or the burgesses in the portman-moot) and argued about them in the king's courts? Their learning was not that of Rome and Bologna, but of Holborn and the Temple; yet the process of increasing sophistication is present in both systems at the same period. The difficulties in pursuing this question are appalling because of the gulf which has existed between the work of English legal historians and that of their continental counterparts. So different are their training and traditions that comparison seems virtually impossible. Civilians and canonists are taught to revere texts before judicial decisions, and their legal history is

largely a study of texts, their authors and commentators, and the relationship between them. Cases are of interest only as showing how texts were used in dealing with real problems. Common lawyers, by contrast, have few texts, and work largely from the reports and records of real cases arising before the royal courts. Such texts as they have are usually assumed to reflect the jurisprudence of the courts, or else to be speculative works of doubtful scientific value. The magnitude of these differences between historians can hardly be exaggerated. But the extent to which those differences represent the historical reality of the fourteenth, fifteenth and sixteenth centuries has also been exaggerated, on both sides of the channel.

4.1 *Styles of Judicial Decision*

The paramount importance of intellectual sophistication of procedure also helps to explain the turn in doctrinal writings toward strict technical rules to regulate the decision-making process. As Filippo Ranieri shows, this concern had a European dimension.

Filippo Ranieri, Styles of Judicial Decision in European History: Divergent Models or Common Traditions?, in R. Jacob (ed.), Judge and Judgment in European Legal Traditions, Comparative History Studies 17, Paris, LGDJ, *1996, 181, 190–191*

The separation between a decision and its motivation is not characteristic only of the Common Law tradition, as some comparatists have sometimes claimed, but it is also detectable in the judicial practice of continental Europe. We will focus on two instances.

The procedure before the Roman Rota constitutes the most ancient model. At the heart of a collegiate court, a judge (*ponens*) is in charge to conduct the proceeding. The dispute is analyzed point by point by the judge in agreement with the parties. The college then proceeds to vote on each point of controversy or *dubia* presented by the judge (*ponens*), and each judge issues an opinion. The ponens then gathers the *dubia* and opinions in the so-called *decisio*, which in turn does not include the reasons but rather constitutes a declaration (*declaratio*) addressed to the parties and refers precisely to their arguments (*dubia*). In the words of the authors of the time, a *decisio* was defined as a compilation of the advice of the auditors (*compilatio consiliorum dominorum auditorum*), which is reminiscent of the written record (report) of the opinions issued by common law judges.

It is interesting to note that traces of this pedagogical literature can be found in German legal works as early as the sixteenth century. Berger cites more than twenty such works published during the seventeenth and eighteenth centuries. Strict rules of logic and syntax in the construction and formulation of such a trial report are thus transmitted. The construction thus suggested (the rules of which will be taken up in the Prussian general ordinance on judicial institutions of 1781) is found in certain rules still taught today in German legal education. An account of the trial at the Imperial Chamber of Spire in the sixteenth century was usually structured according to this template:

- Issue of fact (*species facti*)
- Account of procedural phases (*historia processus*)
- Reproduction of the parties' written acts (*extractus actium*)
- Advisory opinion (*votum*)
- Decision.

Beginning from the sixteenth and seventeenth centuries the Parliament of Paris followed a similar procedure accompanied by similar educational writings. In the first edition of the *Procédure civile* by Eustache Nicolas Pigeau (1787), several detailed chapters are focused on the rules about the preparation and articulation of a report to be drawn for each proceeding. If we look at German educational works of the time, we find similar instructions. The report of a judge of the French Parliament usually followed this model:

- Issues of fact (in chronological order), which corresponds to the *species facti*;
- Summary of the procedure, which corresponds to the *historia processus*;
- Summary of the written acts that bring together the claims of the parties;
- Advisory opinion (*votum*).

As we have tried to show, the judicial activities in continental Europe of the sixteenth to the eighteenth centuries tended to be structured in the proceeding and decision according to strict technical rules. The very elaborate drafting technique of a *votum*, a sort of advice, in which the various points of law and fact are discussed in a rational order to arrive at the decision, is at the centre of these rules. It is important to note that such binding forms were common to the European tradition of the *ius commune*, although such common tradition today seems to be forgotten.

4.2 *Merchant Law*

Another factor in sixteenth-century procedural innovation was the relaxation and, in some specific instances, abandonment, of formalism. Courts responded in many ways to the demands arising from new kinds of litigation and a deep anxiety about lengthy proceedings (*lites immortales*). One of the most vital sources in promoting innovative procedural solutions was mercantile law – which, from the perspective of the general development of procedure, may be said to have played the part of the Trojan horse.

K.W. Nörr, Procedure in Mercantile Matters: Some Comparative Aspects, in Vito Piergiovanni (ed.), The Courts and the Development of Commercial Law, Berlin, Duncker & Humblot, 1987, 195

Whatever mercantile law means, it contains special and often unwritten rules which the law-court had to be confronted with. This was no problem in case of mercantile courts with merchants as judges, as in the *arti* of medieval Italy, in the period of the *consules mercantiae*. Often the merchants were not alone, many statutes provided that a *iurisperitus* had to join to the *apices iuris* but was free to judge according to *negotii veritatem*, that is to the circumstances of the case in question. Through the *facti veritas* the usages of the merchants entered the court, but they were shaped in conformity with the technics of the *ius commune*. In ordinary courts with professional judges the mercantile customs like other customs had to be pleaded and proved. This was a widespread rule throughout Europe whereas the way of showing them, of course, varied. In the west, for instance, we find the device of the inquisition *par turbe*; it was used in the Netherlands until the eighteenth century.

In medieval England mercantile matters were handled by a variety of local courts; the merchants in the town or the port acted as suitors and gave the pertinent judgements. … In the view of the law as administered in Westminster the law merchant originally was no law, but a matter of fact, therefore to be proved. But later, during the seventeenth century, the maxim turned up that the law merchant is part of the law of the land. … The result, anyway, as practised by Holt and Mansfield, was the distinction between the general and better known customs, of which the courts took judicial notice, and the special and particular customs, which had to be pleaded. In the latter case merchants were chosen in order to explain their uses and customs, either as members of the jury or as authorities within an informal inquiry. This was the way how the common law courts were shaping the commercial law. We find a striking parallel in the continental *ius commune* and especially in the approach of the Rota Genuensis. Customs which were notorious and general, need not be alleged and proved, and the judge took notice *etiam per solam famam* (also by reputation only), whereas other customs or stiles of the merchants had to be proved; they were usually attested by an opinion (*parere*) of merchants or of *iurisconsulti, procuratores* and *practicantes*, as a decision of the Rota reads.

The concurrence of the general and the mercantile law could lead to tensions with practical results in a lawsuit. In Italy and Germany the legal literature developed certain rules for the relation between the common and the particular law, above all the statutes, but these rules, the *dottrina degli statuti*, were not distinctive of mercantile matters. In England the situation was different. There was no theory on the limits of operation, on the province of the common law, and so the lines had to be drawn as required. Thus the Statute of the Staple ordered the judges to apply the law merchant and not the common law, and in the well-known case of the carrier who broke bulk, the Chancellor in the Star Chamber in favour of an alien merchant advanced the law of nature, '*que est appelle par ascunz ley marchaunt, que est ley universalle par tout le monde*' ('which by some is called law merchant, which is a universal law for everyone') against an inconvenient rule of the common law. In this case the legitimation of the mercantile law in face of the common law was touched upon, a question which was to be discussed in a wider context since the seventeenth century. …

A good example of the mercantile procedure with romano-canonical background outside Italy is to be found in the Edict Charles IX's which created the court of the *juge et consuls des marchands* in Paris in 1563. The measures were similar all over Europe: suits should be settled within a fixed period, summonses secured by efficient pressure, delays cut down in every stage of proceedings, exceptions and proof restricted, and the execution quickened and sharpened; in addition, sometimes the attorney or advocate is excluded, and the suspensive effect of appeal removed. … There was nothing more desirable for the merchants than a prompt execution when they had won their case. …

Thus on the continent and in England the traditional legal forms were used, but to the same purpose, and the results were remarkably similar, tailored to the needs of the merchants, and directed by public interest in a swift and smooth traffic and trade.

4.3 *Applying the Ius Commune in Latin America*

It is well known how Columbus' arrival in America in 1492 began a new economic and imperial phase on a world scale. It must be pointed out, however, that those developments not only had political and cultural impact, but also influenced the law. This was true at both a theoretical level, where questions of natural rights were framed in terms that overturned traditional categories, and in the practices related to the application and interaction of the *ius commune* with the local normativities of the native peoples of America.

> *Damian A. Gonzales Escudero, Beyond Ius Commune: The Creation of Local Native Customary Law in Colonial Peru (16th-17th Centuries), in Damian Gonzales Escudero (ed.), Introduction to Peruvian Legal History, Lima, Pontificia Universidad Católica del Perú, 2023, 1–2*
>
> The arrival of the conquistadors not only meant the mobilisation and settlement of the European population in the conquered territories, but also the arrival of their forms of social organisation, which included their law. The historiography has been extensive in studying the colonial encounter and its development in the years that followed. In the field of legal history, it has been approached since the early decades of the 20th century by authors who considered that a new law was born, different from the law applied in Spain: The *Derecho Indiano.* …
>
> Authors such as Hespanha and Herzog look at local forms of normativity and justice. Within this perspective, it is possible to understand the importance of local dynamics in the exercise of power, as well as to appreciate the functioning and interrelation of the colonisers' Law, the European *Ius Commune*, with local normativities. …
>
> As a colonial enterprise … the legal categories through which space was classified and controlled were fundamental in establishing social hierarchies and power relations between the colonisers and the colonised. Categories born within the *ius commune* and Iberian normativity such as *dominio*, possession, census, *estancia*, community, among others, were the spatial idiomatic repertoire that Europeans used to classify the conquered space. In the same way, they were used to determine the kind of access to land that both natives and colonisers would have. …
>
> … The repertoires of legal categories of European law, then, were strategically integrated into native normativity within the contexts of negotiation and dispute that arose in the process of settling colonial power … The integration of the categories of *ius commune* resulted, in practice, in the construction of legal arguments in which the elements of indigenous normativities were clothed with this vocabulary.

Seen from America, the *ius commune* brought by colonisers interacted with native normativities, producing hybrid forms of judicial administration. They were operated by a plurality of legal actors, and the law they applied reflected a complicated normative network made of social networks and local communal uses. In this environment, the purely legal was integrated by a broader range of social and even theological normativities.

Questions

1. In which instances is the 'intellectualization of legal practice' detectable in procedure?
2. In what ways has merchant law been a factor of innovation in procedure?

5 Conclusion

In the period 1500–1650, some processes profoundly transformed all sides of the intellectual, spiritual and material life of the individual: the discovery of America, colonial expansion, the Lutheran reformation, the Council of Trent, and the introduction of the printing press. Jurists faced new questions raised by a radically changed world. Some wrote a bold 'today' at the beginning of their discussions, forcefully declaring their distance from previous interpretations of Roman texts that they deemed out of touch with their own world. This evolution involved modifications in the style and range of sources cited, in the shades of meaning projected onto old words (*ius, actio, dominium, natura, status*), in the arrangement of legal materials, and the modification of styles of argument. By 1650, we see jurists shedding another and original light on often unchanged legal materials. It would be difficult to imagine a conversation between a jurist from this time and another who operated two generations before: whilst they shared a knowledge of the same fundamental legal texts, their style of reasoning and the assumptions they projected onto those texts were immeasurably different: they would be speaking from two different worlds.

Let us summarise the main features of the period around 1650:

i) The mid-seventeenth century saw the demise of Aristotelianism. We noted at the beginning that the formative phase for our period was in the twelfth century, not only because of the rediscovery of Justinian's monumental compilation, but also through the introduction of characteristic reasoning methods used to extract new rules from those old texts. Thinking by *quaestiones*, *maximae*, *genus* and *species*, and structuring knowledge by *loci communes* were the typical working tools of this phase. However, that intellectual framework crumbled under the new philosophies based on first principles announced by Hobbes, Leibniz, Descartes and other writers; they made their anti-Aristotelianism one of the most visible features of their projects.

(ii) Legal thinking therefore reformulated its premises according to a philosophy of first principles which explained legal rules in terms of Reason. Legal minds were captivated by the prospect of a logical law that could be derived from a set of philosophical principles and expanded by deduction to cover all cases. In the background was the outspoken demise of Scholastic Aristotelianism, one of the most radical turns in the European intellectual tradition. It is arguable that this demise determined the sharp divide between the new and the old, and it contributed to an attitude stubbornly hostile to the *ancien régime*.

(iii) One of the leading premises in legal thinking was the thrust toward an idea of public power expressed in abstract terms, indicated as *état*, *stato*, *Staat*, state, and designed in a progressively unified sovereignty, paradigmatically expressed in the well-known writings of Jean Bodin and Thomas Hobbes.

(iv) Large sectors of the legal profession were deeply concerned with a yearning for legal certainty. From the mid-sixteenth century they insistently demanded the coherent reformulation of legal rules in a systematic design. Clarity of expression and systematic exposition of normative material was claimed early by Franciscus Connanus and Hugo Donellus, and continued to have influence after this period.

(v) Finally, the concern after 1650 was about texts: a deep and obsessive interest in law as a written text and legal authority operating through formally enacted texts. New judicial institutions were designed in compliance with new textual standards: coherent, precise and typographically exact texts. One of the features of those newly designed institutions was a strict control of normative information. Roman legal texts were progressively transformed into reliable and unambiguous texts until they were able to be directly used without interpretative assistance.

Questions

1. How would you summarise the legal developments described in this chapter?
2. What are the connections between the rise of nation-states and the centralisation of legal information in this period?

Further Reading

Baker, J.H. An Introduction to English Legal History (5th ed.), Oxford, Oxford University Press, 2019.

Bellomo, Manlio. The Common Legal Past of Europe, 1000–1800, Washington D.C., The Catholic University of America Press, 1995.

Blair, Ann. Too Much to Know: Managing Scholarly Information before the Modern Age, New Haven, Yale University Press, 2011.

Borah, Woodrow. Justice by Insurance: the General Indian Court of Colonial Mexico and the Legal Aides of the Half-Real, Berkeley, University of California Press, 1983.

Bossy, John (ed.), Disputes and Settlements: Law and Human Relations in the West, Cambridge, Cambridge University Press, 1983.

Coing, Helmut. Europäisches Privatrecht, 2 vols, München, C.H.Beck, 1985–89.

Dawson, John Philip. The Oracles of the Law, New York, Legal Classics Library, 1994.

Domingo, Rafael and Javier Martínez-Torrón (eds.), Great Christian Jurists in Spanish America, Cambridge, Cambridge University Press, 2018.

Donahue, Charles. The Civil Law in England, The Yale Law Journal 84 (1974), 167–181.

Donahue, Charles. Why the History of Canon law is Not Written, Selden Society Lectures 1984, London, Selden Society, 1986.

Duve, T., C. Birr and J. Egio Garcia, The School of Salamanca: a Case of Global Knowledge Production, Dordrecht, Brill Nijhoff, 2021.

Elliott, John Huxtable. Europe Divided, 1559–1598, Malden, Blackwell, 2007.

Elliott, John Huxtable. The Old World and the New, 1492–1650, Cambridge, Cambridge University Press, 1992.

Franklin, Julian H. Jean Bodin and the Sixteenth-Century Revolution in the Methodology of Law and History, Westport Conn., Greenwood Press, 1977.

van Gelderen, Martin. The Political Thought of the Dutch Revolt, 1555–1590. Ideas in Context, Cambridge, Cambridge University Press, 1992.

Glenn, Patrick. Legal Traditions of the World, Oxford, Oxford University Press, 2010.

Gordley, James. The Philosophical Foundations of Modern Contract Doctrine, Oxford, Clarendon Press, 1991.

Gordley, James. The Jurists: a Critical History, Oxford, Oxford University Press, 2013.

Hanke, Lewis. The Spanish Struggle for Justice in the Conquest of America, Philadelphia, University of Pennsylvania Press, 1949.

Helmholz, Richard H. (ed.), Canon Law in Protestant Lands, Berlin, Duncker & Humblot, 1992.

Helmholz, Richard H. Roman Canon Law in Reformation England, Cambridge Studies in English Legal History, Cambridge, Cambridge University Press, 1990.

Helmholz, Richard H. Canon Law and English Common Law, London, Selden Society, 1983.

Herzog, Tamar. Defining Nations: Immigrants and Citizens in Early Modern Spain and Spanish America, New Haven, Yale University Press, 2003.

Ibbetson, David. Comparative Legal History: a Methodology, in A. Musson and C. Stebbings (eds), Making Legal History: Approaches and Methodologies, Cambridge, Cambridge University Press, 2012.

Kuehn, Thomas. Law, Family and Women: Toward a Legal Anthropology of Renaissance Italy, Chicago, The University of Chicago Press, 1994.

Le Bras, Gabriel (ed.), Histoire du droit et des institutions de l'Eglise en Occident, Paris, Cujas, 1971.

Leijenhorst, Cees. The Mechanisation of Aristotelianism. The Late Aristotelian Setting of Thomas Hobbes' Natural Philosophy, Leiden, Brill, 2002.

Lesaffer, Randall. Peace Treaties and International Law in European History: from the Late Middle Ages to World War One, Cambridge, Cambridge University Press, 2004.

Maclean, Ian. Interpretation and Meaning in the Renaissance: the Case of Law. Ideas in context, Cambridge, Cambridge University Press, 1992.

Mirow, M.C. Latin American Law: a History of Private Law and Institutions in Spanish America, Austin, University of Texas Press, 2004.

Mohnhaupt, Heinz. Lex Certa'and 'Ius Certum': the Search for Legal Certainty and Security, in Michael Stolleis and Lorraine Daston (eds), Natural Law and Laws of Nature in Early Modern Europe, London, Routledge, 2016, 85–100.

Muldoon, James. The Americas in the Spanish World Order: the Justification for Conquest in the Seventeenth Century, Philadelphia, University of Pennsylvania Press, 1994.

Novoa, Mauricio. The Protector of Indians in the Royal Audiencia of Lima: History, Careers, and Legal Culture, 1575–1775, Leiden, Brill Nijhoff, 2016.

Osterhammel, Jürgen. The Transformation of the World: a Global History of the Nineteenth Century, Princeton, Princeton University Press, 2014.

Pagden, Anthony. The Fall of Natural Man: the American Indian and the Origins of Comparative Ethnology, Cambridge, Cambridge University Press, 1986.

Pagden, Anthony. European Encounters with the New World: from Renaissance to Romanticism, New Haven, Yale University Press, 1993.

Parry, J.H. The Spanish Seaborne Empire, New York, Alfred A. Knopf, 1966.

Pennington, Kenneth. The Prince and the Law. Sovereignty and Rights in the Western Legal Tradition, Berkeley, University of California Press, 1993.

Pérez-Perdomo, Rogelio. Latin American Lawyers: a Historical Introduction, Stanford, Stanford University Press, 2006.

Prodi, Paolo. The Papal Prince: One Body and Two Souls. The Papal Monarchy in Early Modern Europe, transl. Susan Haskins, Cambridge, Cambridge University Press, 1987.

Prosperi, Adriano. Justice Blindfolded: the Historical Course of an Image, Leiden, Brill, 2008.

Rowan, Steven. Ulrich Zasius: a Jurist in the German Renaissance, 1461–1535, Ius Commune, Sonderhefte 31, Frankfurt am Main, Klostermann, 1987.

Skinner, Quentin and Martin van Gelderen (eds), Republicanism: a Shared European Heritage, Volume I: Republicanism and Constitutionalism in Early Modern Europe, Cambridge, Cambridge University Press, 2002.

Skinner, Quentin. The Foundations of Modern Political Thought, 2 vols, Cambridge, Cambridge university Press, 1978.

Tierney, Brian. Hierarchy, Consent, and the 'Western Tradition', Political Theory 15 (1987), 646–652.

Tierney, Brian. The Idea of Natural Rights: Studies on Natural Rights, Natural Law, and Church Law, 1150–1625, Grand Rapids Mich., Wm. B. Eerdmans Publishing Co., 1997.

Wiesner-Hanks, Merry. Early Modern Europe, 1450–1789, Vol. 2, Cambridge, Cambridge University Press, 2006.

CHAPTER 5

New Legal Dynamics and the Emergence of Modern States (1650–1775)

Jean-Louis Halpérin

1 Introduction

The middle of the seventeenth century can, for several reasons, be seen as a turning point in the legal history of many European countries. In 1648, the Thirty Years' War came officially to an end with the treaties of Westphalia signed at Osnabrück and Münster. The provisions in the peace treaties further weakened the remnants of the Holy Roman Empire by reaffirming the ancient rights, liberties and privileges of the German Electors, princes, and states (*status* in Latin). The idea of a *ius territoriale*, or *Landeshoheit* in German, was one of territorial superiority that did not give rise to absolute sovereignty (*iura maiestatis*). However, since the treaties recognized the exclusive sovereignty over a territory of a state, they are often interpreted as the beginning of the modern international community of independent states. International law referred to it later as 'Westphalian sovereignty' or 'state sovereignty'.

The formal recognition of the independence of the Swiss cantons from the Holy Roman Empire and of the Netherlands (the United Provinces or Dutch Republic) from Spain reinforced the idea of a Western world divided into separate states, each with its own territorial integrity, its own political regime (monarchy or republic) and its own religious identity (according to the principle *cuius regio, eius religio*, meaning that the religion of the ruler dictated the religion of the ruled).

During this period, the kingdom of France, which had been ruled by Louis XIV since 1643, saw its first revolt from the judges, i.e. the members of the Paris *Parlement*, and the nobility. This led to a series of civil wars called *Fronde* (1648–1653), which the king won. After the death of Cardinal Mazarin, his chief minister, the king decided to abolish the office of chief minister and take the reins himself. This opened the gate to absolute power based on the kings' divine right, a power exercised by the longest-reigning monarch in European history until 1715. In 1661, Frederick III of Denmark seemed to take the same path by forcing the nobility to recognize him as a hereditary king.

 | DOI:10.1163/9789004687257_007

It is telling that 1651 was the year of the publication of Hobbes' *Leviathan*, whose famous frontispiece (drawn by the Parisian printmaker Abraham Bosse) represented a giant figure composed of three hundred small persons. This striking image of the emerging Leviathan foreshadows the rise of the (pre-)modern state.

Historians have used the concept of the 'modern state' to distinguish the ancient polities from our contemporary western conception of the state as a moral person. That is to say, an entity separate from the physical person of the sovereign, in which the public powers are concentrated and which monopolizes the legitimate exercise of violence in its territory.[1] This 'modern state' is not purely a creation of the revolutionary movements originating in America and in France at the end of the eighteenth century. In a certain sense, the transfer of sovereignty from the British crown to the United States of America or from the French king to the French nation, presupposed that the rudiments of the modern states already existed. Some of the (medieval) roots of the modern state can be found in the increased influence of law and legislation due to the revival of Roman law. In addition, in some places, the state apparatus was built up in the sixteenth century because of the political consequences of the Reformation. Finally, there was the development of standing armies, and the taxes they required, which, for example in France and Spain, led to the growth of the system of venal offices (offices sold by the state to raise money) for civil servants.

In the period under discussion, decisive steps were taken to pave the way for the ultimate triumph of the modern states in the whole of Europe. Even though there was a general trend in that direction, its spread throughout Europe was unequal. Often the 'French model' was imitated, including the building of royal palaces that were copies of Versailles. This was especially done by princes, who obtained the title of king, like Frederick I, the Brandenburg Elector who became King of Prussia in 1701, or Victor Amadeus II, the duke of Savoy, who was recognized as King of Sicily in 1713, and afterwards as King of Sardinia. But there were enormous differences between the most centralized and powerful states on the one hand and the myriad of small polities in Italy, the Holy Roman Empire and the declining kingdom of Poland (which disappeared at the end of the eighteenth century) on the other. In some countries, the prince and the 'estates' (*Stände* in German territories) continued their assemblies on a regular

1 Gianfranco Poggi, The Development of the Modern State, Stanford, Stanford University Press, 1978, and from the same author, The State: Its Nature, Development and Prospects, Stanford, Stanford University Press, 1990; Christopher Pierson, The Modern State, London, Routledge, 1996 and 2004.

basis. In contrast, other meetings were 'suspended', and some others only gathered for protocol ceremonies (like the 'General Estates' in France from 1614 until 1789, or the Spanish *Cortes* during the eighteenth century). With all these variations, the eighteenth century can be seen as a transitional stage between the medieval polity and the true modern state. The traditional legal position of monarchies, purportedly based on an 'ancient constitution' and their close links with the religious authorities (both in the Protestant and Catholic states) was a conservative influence which resulted in a more 'moderate' exercise of power rather than a revolutionary change of the system of government.

The influence and necessity of 'absolutism' as a stage in the development of the modern state is a subject of debate.[2] It is possible to identify some trends that led towards absolutism: the decline of deliberative assemblies of estates, the development of a standing army or navy, the rise of a centralized bureaucracy under the leadership of a council selected by the monarch, the growth of the national tax system or the increased intervention of the state in the economy through mercantilist policies. But, even in France, where this movement was strong, it remained an aspiration – an unreachable goal – and its influence was limited by opposing forces. One such force was the nobility, which had not completely disappeared, and the royal officers who bought their offices and associated patrimonial rights. Another was the weakness of the armed forces inside the kingdom: only a few thousand soldiers were left to maintain public order. This 'model' of absolutism was beyond the reach of many other European states. Besides, it had to compete with other political models like the English state (characterized by the strength of the Parliament after the Glorious Revolution) and the 'enlightened despotism' in Prussia, Austria, Russia, and Portugal during the eighteenth century. It is, therefore, far from clear that the 'absolutist state' was a necessary stage in the development of the modern state. However, what did occur in this period was that a sizable fiscal-military state with a vast bureaucracy developed. In England, for example, the size of the army and navy forces tripled between 1688 and 1783.[3]

It is even more challenging to discover the relationship between these political changes, which were often much less important in practice than in theoretical discussions, and the evolution of the law. What were the transformations in western legal traditions between 1650 and 1775 that made the rise of the 'modern state' possible? The modern state is generally associated with an increasingly centralized and strict system of 'law and order' which

2 Perry Anderson, Lineages of the Absolutist State, London, Random House Incorporated, 1974.

3 John Brewer, The Sinews of Power. War, Money and the English State 1688–1783, Cambridge Mass., Harvard University Press, 1990.

was the product of two developments. On the one hand, the increased legislative power of sovereigns like the monarch, and prince, and also parliaments and assemblies. On the other hand, the decline of sources of law based on tradition or authorities other than the state like customary, divine, canon, and Roman law. The authority of these latter sources was based on the transmission of Roman jurisprudence which was thought of as the law of reason (*ratio scripta*).[4] The modern state did not see law as an expression of reason. The Latin quote that Hobbes used in Leviathan '*(167) Auctoritas, non veritas legem facit*' (the authority, and not the truth, makes the law), captures succinctly the new idea of the sovereign legislative power as the central, primary source of the legal order.

The period 1650–1775 witnessed the transition from decentralized legal systems based on plural legal sources in pre-modern states into centralized legal systems, which were the expression of the 'legislative' state. The concept of a 'decentralized legal system' has several aspects. First, decentralized legal systems are characterized by a decentralized process of law-making based upon custom. Second, they have 'individual norms' created by the discretionary decisions of courts in litigation between individuals, as opposed to a centralized system with its vast array of legislative rules. Third, in a decentralized system, local laws are different from region to region, while in a centralized legal system, the norms are enforceable throughout the entire state. During the second half of the seventeenth century and the eighteenth century, there was a distinct movement toward progressive centralization. However, it had different characteristics from one state to another. There was a uniform law in England from the Middle Ages, whereas France or Spain had to develop a robust centralized bureaucracy to curtail the 'freedoms' of the diverse provinces.[5] A feature of the period between 1650 and 1775 was a decline of customary rules in favour of statutory laws. Judges had to, more and more, apply general norms, and there was a trend toward a unified, statewide law in the largest European countries.

4 Cf. Aniceto Masferrer and Juan A. Obarrio, The *Ius Commune* as the *ratio scripta* in the Civil Law Tradition: A Comparative Approach to the Spanish Case, in Olivier Moréteau et al. (eds), Comparative Legal History, Cheltenham, Edward Elgar Publishing, 2019, 212–241.

5 Hans Kelsen, Pure Theory of Law, transl. Max Knight, Berkeley, University of California Press, 1967, 228, 251, 315.

2 Creation

With the emergence of modern states in the period 1650–1775, there was a noticeable increase in the development of legal sources designed for an entire territory controlled by a sovereign. This included general statutes connected with ambitious legislative goals, and sometimes plans for codification, rationalized precedents available through new kinds of law reports, and writings in the vernacular, which promoted the development of a national doctrine. However, these beginnings of what Paolo Grossi has called 'legal absolutism' (a catchphrase used to characterize the monopolization of the law-creating processes by the state, including private law) were merged with old conceptions concerning the relationship between common laws, including the *ius commune*, and *iura propria* and new theories of universal natural law or natural rights. This dialectic between common and particular laws becomes a feature of the law from 1650 to 1789. Hobbes' *Leviathan* successfully incorporated this conception of law as a set of rules ordered by the Sovereign in the traditional structure of judge-made law.

> *T. Hobbes, Leviathan, London, Penguin Books, 1985, 311–313, 321–322 and 326*
> By Civil Lawes, I understand that men are therefore bound to observe, because they are Members, not of this Commonwealth in particular, but of a Commonwealth. For the knowledge of particular Lawes belongeth to them, that professe the study of the Lawes of their severall Countries; but the knowledge of the Civill Law in generall, to any man …
>
> Which considered, I define Civill Law in this manner. Civill Law is, to every Subject, those Rules which the Commonwealth hath Commanded him, by Word, Writing, or other sufficient Sign of the Will, to make use of, for the Distinction of Right, and Wrong; that is to say, of what is contrary, and what is not contrary to the Rule …
>
> The Legislator in all Commonwealths, is only the Soveraign, be he one Man, as in a Monarchy, or one Assembly of men, as in a Democracy, or Aristocracy. For the Legislator, is he that maketh the Law … For the same reason, none can abrogate a Law made, but the Soveraign; because a Law is not abrogated, but by another Law, that forbideth it to be put in execution.
>
> The Soveraign of a Commonwealth, be it an Assembly, or one Man, is not subject to Civill Lawes. For having power to make, and repeale Lawes, he may when he pleaseth, free himselfe from that subjection, by repealing those Lawes that trouble him, and making of new; and consequently he was free before …

When Long Use obtaineth the authority of a Law, it is not the Length of Time that maketh the authority, but the Will of the Soveraign signified by his silence ... And our Lawyers account no Customes Law, but such as are reasonable, and that evill Customes are to be abolished: But the Judgement of what is reasonable, and what is to be abolished, belongeth to him that maketh the Law, which is the Soveraign Assembly, or Monarch ...

The Legislator known; and the Lawes, either by writing, or by the light of Nature, sufficiently published; there wanteth yet another very materiall circumstance to make them obligatory. For it is not the Letter, but the Intendment, or Meaning; that is to say the authentique Interpretation of the Law (which is the sense of the Legislator, in which the nature of the Law consisteth) ... All Laws, written, and unwritten, have need of Interpretation ...

And therefore unlesse there be an Interpreter authorised by the Soveraign, from which the subordinate Judges are not to recede, the Interpreter can be no other than the ordinary Judges, in the same manner, than they are in cases of the unwritten Law; and their sentences are to be taken by them that plead, for Lawes in that particular case; but not to bind other Judges, in like cases to give like judgements.

The case of the Dutch Republic or United Provinces established by the Union of Utrecht, a treaty signed in 1579 between seven provinces that revolted against Spain, is an exception. The Dutch Republic was recognized as a sovereign power independent from Spain and the German Empire in the Westphalian treaties of 1648. It was a loose confederation with no written constitution and a complex equilibrium between the Assembly of the States-General (where each of the seven provinces had one vote) and the Provincial States (notably the most wealthy province of Holland). It shows that an oligarchy of merchants (the regents of the cities) could acquire significant power from 1650 to 1775. However, it was an anomaly in Europe as it was a republic that was not restricted to a small territory, like the Italian cities of Venice or Genoa, and formed a 'decentralized' state without strong legislative powers. John Leslie Price focuses on these characteristics of the Dutch Republic.

J.L. Price, The Dutch Republic in the Seventeenth Century, New York, Palgrave Macmillan, 1998, 63–65

Nevertheless, the final power in effect remained with the states – but not, as might have been expected, with the States General, but with the States of Holland, and it was this body which guaranteed the continuing integrity of the republican system. The States of Holland could be manipulated but not coerced, and their financial strength meant that their consent was essential to the successful government of the Republic.

More fundamental than the uncertainty as to the nature of the Dutch state is the question whether it was a real state at all. Conventionally, the modern state has been associated theoretically with the concept of sovereignty and practically with the strengthening of central government. The Dutch polity had a central government so weak as to be hardly recognizable from this point of view, and the location of sovereignty was so uncertain as to suggest that the term was simply inapplicable. There are both normative and anachronistic assumptions lurking in such criticisms: one form of the modern state is taken as the only viable one, and is used as a criterion by which the Republic can be condemned. Less obviously anachronistic but still radically misleading is to take one form of political thought – that recommending the absolutist and centralizing state – and to judge contemporary polities by its standards. Inevitably, this approach leads to the judgement that all traditional, republican and decentralized systems were inefficient, outdated and – in one way or another – doomed. The Dutch Republic is a fine example of such rather messy systems and was criticized by contemporaries who took the centralized, monarchical state as the norm, and by later commentators who have failed to see how it could possibly have worked.

Certainly, the responsibilities – never mind the powers – of the central government of the Republic were minimal: formal control of relations with other countries, the running of the armed forces, and general oversight of common finances (which were almost exclusively concerned with the armed forces). The provinces were in theory almost completely autonomous, and in practice governed themselves. There was not even a central of law for the Republic as a whole. However, the state held together, despite severe internal strains and constant external pressure, for over two hundred years and only collapsed – along with the most of Europe's *ancien régime* – when faced with the French revolutionary armies.

The Dutch Republic cannot be understood in conventional terms: even contemporaries found it difficult to comprehend. The central authorities of the Republic had such limited powers that one can question whether it was a state at all. Political authority was concentrated at the local and provincial levels, and from there, powers were ceded to the central government. It was unique, even though the Swiss Confederation and the Holy Roman Empire had similar characteristics, mainly because it was a major power, both in Europe and globally.

The example of the Dutch Republic shows that different types of states existed during the period 1650–1775. The Hobbesian absolutist blueprint does not provide for an arrangement with sovereign cities, estates, and princes acting in concert with republican institutions such as the *stadthouder*, a position monopolized by the Princes of Orange in the Dutch Republic. Although there was no 'federal law' in the Republic, the statutes of the East (1602) and the West India Companies (1621) may be considered as such. The High Court or *Hoge Raad*, established in 1582 and located in The Hague, was a court of appeals only for the provinces of Holland and Zeeland. Every other province had its own superior court. Private law was regulated through customary laws (thirteen homologated customs) and Roman-Dutch law, and some of the great ordinances promulgated by the Habsburgs in the sixteenth century remained in force. The municipal governments enacted local laws, an example being Amsterdam's burial laws, which triggered the violently suppressed 'Undertakers Riots' in 1696. Legislative activity in the Netherlands was significant, and it increased during the seventeenth and eighteenth centuries. The colonial empire of the Dutch Republic can be seen as an element pointing to the beginnings of a modern state.

2.1 *Political Organization and Law*

The Peace of Westphalia was a landmark in the historical process establishing the principles of a common 'law of nations' (called *ius gentium, ius publicum Europaeum, droit des gens* or *Völkerrecht*). However, most of the principles of international relations, such as the recognition of privileges for ambassadors, existed before 1648. Others developed within the context of the great peace conferences terminating the wars of Louis XIV, including those giving rise to the 1713 peace treaties of Utrecht. These reinforced Britain's position as the peace arbiter of Europe. Douglas Johnston argues that it is questionable whether the Westphalian Peace was a turning point in the history of international and public law. The absolute right of self-preservation of states in the period between 1650 and 1775 was strengthened as a result of the decline of the German Holy Empire and the advent of national states despite the development of a law of nations based on natural law foundations proposed by Vitoria and Grotius (e.g. Pufendorf's 1672 *De jure naturae et gentium*, Wolff's 1740–1749 *Jus naturae et jus gentium*, Vattel's 1758 *Le droit des gens*, translated in English in 1760),[6] and the recognition of concrete rules on neutrality (especially those on shipping by non-belligerent states in maritime wars).[7]

D. Johnston, The Historical Foundations of World Order, Leiden, Martinus Nijhoff, 2002, 411–412
Although guarantees of peace were not a new feature of European treaty-making, this was the first time they had been written into a system-wide settlement that could be described as an 'international constitution'. The call for the peaceful settlement of disputes and for collective sanctions against aggressors has resonated down the ages since 1648, forming a model for Articles 10, 12 and 16 of the Covenant of the League of Nations, and later for the counterpart provisions of the UN Charter. Yet, by the late 1960's, the Westphalian and Charter conceptions were only two of the several ways of configuring the international order.

To the extent that constitutionalism is a continuous thread in the fabric of European heritage in the history of international law, it was stitched into place at Westphalia. The 'foundationalists' include also many historians who ascribe to the 1648 settlement the origin of the 'balance of power system' of European diplomacy, generously interpreted as intended to protect the weak from the strong, or at least to curb the excessive powers of the strongest.

Revisionists, however, have pointed out that the Peace of Westphalia was not such a clearly cut settlement. On religious issues, the outcome was a compromise between the traditional prerogative of the monarch to choose the country's religion (*cuius regio, eius religio*) and the subject's freedom to practise the faith of his or her own choice. The ruler's traditionally absolute authority over the religious sphere was limited by Article 5(11) of the Osnabrück Treaty, which provided that in changing religion the ruler could not compel his or her subjects to do the same. In Article 5(28) of the same instrument, freedom of worship and religious education was guaranteed to Protestants living in Catholic areas, and *vice versa*. Moreover, the Treaty of Osnabrück granted equality between Catholics and Protestants in most of the organs of the Empire.

6 Cf. Joseph Barthélemy, Les fondateurs du droit international: F. de Vitoria, A. Gentilis, F. Suarez, Grotius, Zouch, Pufendorf, Bynkershoek, Wolf, Wattel, de Martens: leurs œuvres, leurs doctrines, Paris, V. Giard & E. Brière, 1904.

7 Randall Lesaffer, The classical law of nations (1500–1800), in Alexander Orakhelasvill (ed.), Research Handbook on the Theory and History of International Law, Cheltenham, Edward Elgar Publishing, 2011, 433.

Part of the argument that Westphalia was a crucial moment is based on the fact that, for the first time, all members of the Holy Empire – more than 300 altogether – were entitled to enter into alliances with other countries, provided that these were not detrimental to the Empire or contrary to the provisions of the Peace Treaties. In this way, the German principalities were accorded treaty-making capacity which only independent sovereign states, with the absolute sovereignty envisaged by Jean Bodin, possess. However, critics have noted that the old idea of *Landeshoheit* (territorial supremacy) was preserved, and that the conditions attached to the Peace Treaties were incompatible with true sovereignty.

Today, most legal writers do not believe that the Peace of Westphalia created the world's first system of fully independent sovereign states. Despite its political importance (it was a triumph of French diplomacy designed to keep Germany divided), these writers believe that the significance of the Peace is generally overblown.

The legal community amongst European states was not limited to a *ius publicum universale* (a common public law that can be understood as a set of common principles concerning interstate relations). Private law was also a part of it. As a heritage of the seventeenth and eighteenth centuries, lawyers continued to refer to the *ius commune* and, of course, to England's common law, as fundamental law. Patrick Glenn shows that the claim that there are different common laws was not inherently contradictory. What was considered common for diverse territorial legal systems was not an identical set of rules but a set of relationships between various legal sources and a method to resolve conflicts of norms.

> *H.P. Glenn, On Common Laws, Oxford, Oxford University Press, 2007, 42–43*
> Ius commune did ... exist in ... multiple form, as iura communia, and there were vigorous relations not only between the common laws and the particular laws of each of them, but also between the common laws themselves. There were also ... common laws which were free of a territorial base, such as canon law or commercial law ... The common law which received ... the greatest renown was that based on Roman law, in large measure because it was expressed in a common language, Latin, and because it was the only ius commune taught in a manner which transcended the states which were later to emerge. Yet the ius commune was only one example of a common genus of relational common law, which also included the common law, the droit commun coutumier of what we know today as France, the gemeine Recht of what is today Germany, the

derecho común of the *Siete Partidas*, as well as what were recognized as common laws, such as those of Tuscany or the region of Naples.

Blackstone's *Commentaries on the Laws of England* (1765–1769) also show signs of the patterns of systematization of the law in Europe following the model of Justinians's *Institutes* and natural law conceptions. At the same time, they are an expression of growing legal nationalism. John Cairns describes how the institutional model could be combined with the nationalistic ideas of English common lawyers.

> *J.W. Cairns, Blackstone, An English Institutist: Legal Literature and the Rise of the Nation State, Oxford Journal of Legal Studies 4/3 (1984), 358–359*
> The European institutional writers have been recognized as having had a significant role in the movement from the old traditional forms of law to the modern, looking forward to codification. In England, Blackstone is, in a sense, the culmination of one tradition while being also the forerunner of a new ... Blackstone is generally seen as giving a definitive account of the traditional common law just before the massive changes of the next century. It may even plausibly be suggested that Blackstone provoked and facilitated reform through his exposition of English law as an ordered whole...
>
> In the past, Blackstone has been denied the description of institutional writer. This denial seems to have resulted from too great a reliance on the modern Scottish conception of institutional writer as a writer of a particular and special authority. Blackstone seems truly to fit into the institutional category by virtue, first, of the structure and content of the *Commentaries* and, secondly, of the context in which he wrote. Thus, Blackstone wrote in his national language; his *Commentaries* were structured after the pattern of Justinian's *Institutes*; they were comprehensive; they treated the common law as a national law; they attempted to state English law as a united whole; and ... they arose out of the university teaching newly introduced of the national law, expressing the new vision of Europe conceived as consisting of separate nation states with distinct laws.

The possibility of a European legal science based on the same textual foundations as those of the twelfth and thirteenth centuries inspired Helmut Coing's *magnum opus* in the 1980s.[8] It highlighted the idea of a common private law for European civil law countries, and even England. Wilhelm Brauneder, on

8 Helmut Coing, Europäisches Privatrecht I: Älteres Gemeines Recht (1500 bis 1800), München, Beck, 1985.

the other hand, has argued that this European private law never existed, as the Roman law and other sources of the *ius commune* were subsidiary in relation to the various European national laws.[9]

As an aside, a remark about 'international law'. It is not surprising that Thomas Hobbes, the theoretician of legislative sovereignty, was also convinced that a positive *ius gentium* binding on states did not exist.

2.2 *Natural Law and Natural Rights*

One can argue that Grotius unintentionally created the Modern School of Natural Law. Grotius' work was discussed and imitated, forming a key part of the school's development. However, Francisco de Vitoria's influence on Grotius should not be overlooked,[10] nor should the way both authors contributed to early modern political theory and jurisprudence.[11] Samuel Pufendorf (1632–1694), a philosopher influenced by his reading of Grotius and Hobbes, was the first professor of the new chair devoted to natural law in Heidelberg in 1667, before his departure for the University of Lund in Sweden. His main work, *De iure naturae et gentium libri octo* (1672), was summarized and published as a shorter teaching manual titled *De officio hominis et civis iuxta legem naturalem libri duo* (1673). It focused on the duties of man to himself, God, and society. Pufendorf developed, in line with Grotius, self-evident legal principles – rules deduced from human nature. According to Franz Wieacker, Pufendorf was the 'originator of a General Part of the law of obligations' later used in German codes.[12] He gave a central role to contract as the foundation of the whole society, as the basis of any government and as the central means of economic exchanges. After his appointment in 1694 at the new Prussian university of Halle, Christian Thomassius (1655–1728) followed Pufendorf in his attempt to combine the study of natural law with that of public law, based on the territorial sovereignty of the various princes, and private law according to the *Usus modernus pandectarum*.[13]

---

9 Wilhelm Brauneder, Europäisches Privatrecht, aber was its es?, Zeitschrift für Neuere Rechtsgeschichte 1993, 225–235.

10 Federico Puig Peña, La Influencia de Francisco de Vitoria en la obra de Hugo Grocio: los principios del derecho internacional a la luz de la España del siglo XVI, Madrid, Tipografía de archivos, 1934.

11 Diego Panizza, Political Theory and Jurisprudence in Gentili's De Iure Belli: The Great Debate between 'Theological' and 'Humanist' Perspectives from Vitoria to Grotius, IILJ Working Paper No. 2005/15 (https://ssrn.com/abstract=871754 and http://dx.doi.org/10.2139/ssrn.871754; accessed in August 2022).

12 F. Wieacker, A History of Private Law in Europe, Oxford, Clarendon Press, 1996, 246–247.

13 Michael Stolleis, Geschichte des öffentlichen Rechts in Deutschland. Erster Band: Reichspublizistik und Policeywissenschaft, München, Beck, 1988, 282–291.

Natural law combined with the *ius gentium*, the law of nations, was also taught in Halle by Christian Wolff (1679–1754), who tried to subject it to the logic of mathematics (he wanted to formulate it *more geometrico*). K. Haakonssen describes the impact of this approach to natural law in America.

> *K. Haakonssen, From Natural Law to the Rights of Man: A European perspective in American debates, in M.J. Lacey and K. Haakonssen (eds), A Culture of Rights: The Bill of Rights in Philosophy, Politics and Law, 1791 and 1991, Cambridge, Cambridge University Press, 1991, 42–44*
> *The derivative nature of rights and the watering down of contractarianism*
> The Americans broke the connection between traditionalism and the derivative character of rights, and they got rid of the former or at least reduced it significantly. But apparently nobody achieved a radical theory of subjective rights of the sort whose beginnings we encountered in Grotius and Hobbes. Philosophically rights remained, derivative.
>
> This is, of course, not surprising, for Americans drew upon the same natural-law tradition as their British contemporaries; and they shared its development into the broader, conventional moral philosophy outlined earlier ... I have no method of intellectual calibration that allows me to measure the relative significance of the roles played in these wider contexts of natural law, common law, evangelicalism, liberalism, or republicanism, or whatever stripe...
>
> Whatever the exact role of natural law and the associated moral philosophy in the great event in North America in the last third of the eighteenth century, the assumption mentioned seems well founded and is widely documented in the literature. Perhaps the most important point to remember is that this material was, in effect, school-learning. Several important American colleges, following the Scottish and dissenting pattern already discussed, taught a natural law-based moral philosophy as part of the arts curriculum. Apart from general political talk of rights, the theory of rights outlined here was thus the first, and certainly the first systematic, exposition of the topic to which significant parts of the American intelligentsia were exposed while still boys in their teens. It is uncertain and controversial how much direct influence was exerted by the seventeenth-century natural lawyers, especially Pufendorf and Locke. However, whether Americans read the original texts or learned their ideas from textbooks like those of Hutcheson, Rutherforth, Fordyce or Burlamaqui to mention only the few already referred to, the common theoretical framework for teaching and learning was certainly natural-law theory.

It is entirely understandable that having grown up with natural law theory and the moral philosophy associated with it, the Americans found a use for such ideas in their own writings and, eventually, in the documents relating to their independence and constitution.

Natural law was officially taught as a university subject in Germany, Sweden, the Netherlands, Switzerland, and Spain. However, it was not taught in France due to fears of the effect of reflecting on it in an academic context for public law, nor in England, where the number of law professorships was limited. Yet, natural law treatises, in Latin and in French translations were vigorously circulated. Jean Barbeyrac (1674–1744), professor at the Lausanne Academy, was the translator and annotator of Grotius and Pufendorf as well as of the writings of Richard Cumberland (1632–1718). He corresponded about this work with John Locke. Jean-Jacques Burlamaqui (1694–1748), professor at the Geneva Academy, influenced French philosophers like Jean-Jacques Rousseau, especially through his 1747 *Principes du droit naturel*. In England, Blackstone adopted some of the views of the natural law teachers and supported the idea of the absolute rights of man.

2.3 *Custom*

In a large part of continental Europe, the so-called 'municipal law' covered many aspects of private law (family law, succession, property, feudal rights, and in some cases, contract and tort). This law continued as homologated (i.e. approved) customs, applicable locally in a province or a municipality. Geographically, customary law was dominant in Northern France, known as the *pays de droit coutumier*, but not in the Southern provinces which had received Roman law, known as *pays de droit écrit*. Because the sovereign confirmed these local customs and through this homologation made them equal to statutory law, the situation in this part of Europe was comparable to that of the German territories with their *Landrechte*. The latter were published as a statute but contained customary rules. Customary rules were also present in Italy and Hungary. The texts of the *ius commune* and the precedents of England's common law became authoritative through customary practice and their recognition for a long period of time as binding.

> *A. Padoa-Schioppa, Storia del diritto in Europa, Bologna, Il Mulino, 2007, 311, 313–314 (transl. by J.-L. Halpérin)*
>
> In France local laws have specific features that are a product of the history of the country and the presence of a strong monarchy. The difference between the Southern regions (*Pays de droit écrit*) and the Central

and Northern regions (*Pays de droit coutumier*), originated in the Middle Ages, and remained in force until the [French] Revolution ...

At the eve of the Revolution, France counted about 400 local customs and about 65 provincial or regional customs. ...

Because the customary law was written down [in the 16th century] the creative process of the development of customary law came to an end. ...

In Holland customary law was fragmented but the work of Hugo Grotius provided it with a general framework ...

Even 18th century Switzerland, began to rethink its legal system. But significant differences remained. Since a proper reception of the *ius commune* was absent in all cantons, the codification of urban laws varied considerably. Basel, a town with many humanist lawyers, mandated in 1719 to Johann Wettstein the task to compose a new redaction of the urban statutes. His work was inspired by the 1614 statutory model of ... neighbouring Württemberg. It also included many elements of Roman law, in the form of the *usus modernus pandectarum* of the German School. ...

The vast bulk of customary laws were written down in the sixteenth century, and amendments or 'reformations' were very rare after 1650. Examples of such late redactions are the customs of Limburg (1696) and Wodecq in Hainaut (1682 and 1732) in the Low Countries, and also that of Hattonchatel (1784–1788) in French Lorraine. In the period 1650–1789, customary laws were a body of static rules. If they were changed at all, it was through judicial interpretation. They were difficult to reform because the process of altering them involved setting up consultative bodies, which sovereigns did not want to do, as they did not fit the absolutist political environment. For this reason, many customs risked falling into disuse and were replaced by references to Roman law (the *ius commune*). In some places, customs were nationalized through statutory law. An example of this is the German *Landrechte*, which applied to large parts of the country. The development in France was different: the customary law of Paris was used by French lawyers to fill the gaps in other customs. There is also evidence of the decline of customary law in the Netherlands.

A. Cavanna, Storia del diritto moderno in Europa, Milano, A. Giuffrè, 1982, 433–436 (*transl. by J.-L. Halpérin*)

The writing down of customary law, ordered by Charles V [in the Low Countries] in 1531, followed a similar path as in France. Its results were, partially, the same: the modernization and certification of customs that were in force, followed by a reduction of their number and a unification on a regional level. Many local customs were eliminated in favour of a homogenous text for every jurisdiction.

In the 17th century this process of recording customary laws and their approval by the governmental authorities was concluded as follows: of the about one hundred submitted texts, only 88 were homologated (i.e. approved) and considered to be the exhaustive and representative list of the Belgian legal tradition. It is clear that because of this reinforcement and standardization of indigenous law … had the side effect that fewer rules of the *ius commune* were absorbed in the law …

In the Northern Provinces, after the revolt against the Spanish monarchy and the separation from the Southern territories, the sovereign order to write down customs, was disregarded, quasi forgotten, the moment it was issued (1531). … [I]n the central courts of the different provinces … one had to prove the existence of oral customs. In the absence of this proof, the *ius commune* was applied. In the 17th and the 18th centuries, because of these circumstances and the fact that the Romanist tradition was favoured, a particular jurisprudence developed in the Netherlands at the Universities, which led to the formation of a Roman-Dutch law.

In Spain, the Spanish War of Succession at the beginning of the eighteenth century led to the victory of a Bourbon king (Philip V, or Felipe V in Spanish). He was a grandson of the French king Louis XIV. Against this background Aniceto Masferrer analyzes the development of royal absolutism in Spain and the resulting decline of *fueros* as sources of private law in Valencia and Aragon. The term *fueros* originally referred to the marketplace (*forum*), but in medieval Spain it became a municipal franchise conferred on a community by the crown, a nobleman or a bishop. This franchise involved legal incorporation, confirmation of local customs and privileges, and might include rights to taxation or self-government.[14]

A. Masferrer, Spanish Legal Traditions. A Comparative Legal History Outline, Madrid, Dykinson, 2012, 249 and 251–252

As a consequence of Felipe V's victory in Almansa (April 25, 1707) and the reprisal against the military opposition on the Aragón territories, Felipe V decided to abolish the legal systems of these territories. What Felipe IV … unsuccessfully [sought to achieve] through political means, facing

14 See https://www.britannica.com/topic/fuero (accessed in August 2022).

separatist rebellion (1640), the first Bourbon king, Felipe v, [achieved] not by using ordinary political means, but in the context and as a result of war.

The first Decree of *Nueva Planta* was promulgated by Felipe v on 29th June 1707, by which the laws of the kingdom of Valencia and Aragón were abrogated. Later on, subsequent Decrees of *Nueva Planta* were enacted …, affecting both kingdoms …

The main difference between the … Decrees imposed on Valencia and Aragón is remarkable, namely, while Felipe v re-established for Aragón its former *fueros* on private law and legal procedure …, the *Furs* of Valencia were never re-established in such general terms.

In this regard, on 3rd of April, 1711, Felipe v promulgated a Decree for Aragón, by which, among other things, a General Commanding Officer was established as the supreme authority for military, political, economic and governmental matters. Furthermore, a tribunal called *Audiencia* with two chambers was created to settle judicial disputes in private and criminal law matters, being the former established according to the *fueros* of Aragón. Consequently, the civil law chamber could decide lawsuits related to the laws of the kingdom of Aragón, although they turned to the Council of Castile on appeal. In other words, Felipe v eventually allowed Aragón to maintain its proper private law but abolished all public law by imposing Castilian law.

Catalonia was the next territory affected by the Decrees of *Nueva Planta*. More specifically, the new legal regime of Catalonia was established by the Decree of 16th January, 1716, by which a new legal-administrative system was imposed, abolishing and re-establishing in the same Decree the civil law, commercial law, criminal law and procedural law. Furthermore, a new judicial and political body, presided over by a captain general, governed life in Catalonia. …

Felipe v also wanted to make clear that the political constitution of Catalonia, which had not been explicitly abolished, was equally replaced by a new law, that is, by the Castilian one. …

It is true that the civil, commercial, criminal and procedural laws were all maintained, but they were not affirmed through a pact, but rather by the absolute power of the king, being legitimated retroactively: 'by which it is to be understood that they are established anew by this Decree'. This was a concept of absolute power which, while referring to the past, projected itself much more into the future, definitely abolishing the political notion of agreement (*pactismo*).

In the seventeenth and the eighteenth centuries, modern states continued to recognize customs or local laws as *fueros*. These were sources of private law in Aragon, Catalonia, and Valencia. As a consequence of increasing centralization, customs were not only accepted by the king through a 'pact' or homologation, as was the case in the Middle Ages, but truly granted to localities by the absolute power of the relevant state authorities. Thus, the authority of customs was clearly subordinated to general laws, even if the policy of some monarchs (such as Philip V in Spain) mixed absolutism with a cautious attitude towards local particularism. Because of the growing criticism of 'barbaric' customs by French philosophers, and the abuse of feudal power during the Middle Ages, the eighteenth century saw a decline of customary law as a living normative source and the beginning of a process of legislation and codification. However, it was a gradual process influenced by the courts' practices and the way the people used customary law.

2.4 *Case Law*

The use of precedents and the acknowledgment of the authority of judgments is not new in the period 1650 to 1789. Many volumes of case law containing selections of decisions of various courts had been printed in the sixteenth century in almost all European countries. This gave seventeenth- and eighteenth-century lawyers two problems. First, how to determine the reasons or grounds (*rationes decidendi*) for the judgments, as these had either not been provided since the end of the Middle Ages, or, in England, were only very briefly explained. Second, how to select those precedents which would be useful for a large geographical territory.

The following text shows that historians should not have too much confidence in these volumes of case law, since they are full of errors.

> *J.-L. Halpérin, Legal Interpretation in France under the Reign of Louis XVI: A Review of the Gazette des tribunaux, in Yasutomo Morigiwa, Michael Stolleis and Jean-Louis Halpérin (eds), Interpretation of Law in the Age of Enlightenment. From the Rule of the King to the Rule of Law, Dordrecht, Springer, 2011, 29–30*
>
> From … the Middle Ages to … the 16th and 17th centuries, several authors played a vital role in developing private law reports (*recueils d'arrêts*). These include the writings of Jean Le Coq, known as *Johannes Gallus* from 1340 to 1399 and his *Questiones*, which [brought together] the judgments of the *Parlement de Paris*. Other works that should be mentioned here include the *Decisiones Parlamenti Dalphinali* written by Gui Pape (who passed away in 1477) [and] the *Recueil des 74 arrêts du Parlement*

> *de Toulouse*, written by Étienne Aufréri (1458–1511). Law reports [provided] a selection of decision[s] of [a specific] *Parlement*: for example, in Toulouse, the decisions of Maynard were [published] in 1603, d'Olive in 1638, Cambolas in 1659, and Maynard once again in 1705. These volumes were followed by extensive compilations in … alphabetical order: by Louet at the beginning of the 17th century, Bouguier in 1622, Henrys in 1638, Bretonnier in 1718, and Guy Rousseaud de la Combe in 1736. Journals also began to develop during this period, such as the *Journal des principales audiences*, which began under Jean du Fresne in 1648. This journal [consists of] seven volume[s] and [brings together] judgments of the *Parlement de Paris* from 1622 to 1722. Furthermore, the *Journal du Palais* was founded by Gabriel Guéret in 1672 and continued by Claude Blondeau in 1737, and [consists of] two volumes containing judgements from 1660 to 1700. Finally, legal dictionaries saw the light of day. In 1711, Brillon's *Dictionnaire des Arrests* was published in 3 volumes; followed by Denisart's *Collection des decisions nouvelles*, published in 6 volumes between 1754 and 1756. Subsequently Guyot's *Répertoire universel* appeared in 1775. These law reports were written by lawyers and judges with the chief editor usually having been present during the hearing of the particular cases that were reported, and they were vehemently criticized by many authors, including the authors of other reports. This criticism of the law reports was, for the most part, leveled against their numerous faults (especially their old-fashioned style) and many errors in dates, names and facts. However, the real and not seriously discussed problem was with the methodology, which attempted to infer the reasons of the judgment from the pleadings of the lawyers, and those of the winning litigants in particular.

However, between 1650 and 1789, the number of collections of decisions published by lawyers multiplied. This proves that they were considered useful and, at the same time, illustrates a growing reliance on precedent. Even though there was no rigid adherence to precedent, judgments were quoted as authorities in continental Europe and England. In France, this source of law came to be called *jurisprudence des arrêts* to emphasise the difference between the authority of precedents and theoretical legal science (jurisprudence stems from the late Latin *iurisprudentia*, the science of law; the English word is derived from the French). With the development of legal dictionaries from 1774 onwards, during the reign of Louis XIV, such as Guyot's *Répertoire universel*, the *Encyclopédie méthodique* edited by D'Alembert and Diderot and the latter's *Encyclopédie*, Prost de Royer's *Dictionnaire de jurisprudence et des arrêts* and the publication of periodicals such as the *Gazette des tribunaux* from 1775 to 1789, there was a true movement towards 'nationalization' and 'rationalization' of 'jurisprudence'. This development can be compared to the rise of precedents in eighteenth-century England. In England, the lack of official reports was not an obstacle to the development of the authority of precedents, as is shown by David Lieberman.

> *D. Lieberman, The Province of Legislation Determined, Cambridge, Cambridge University Press, 2002, 88–89 and 236–237*
> The published evidence of Mansfield's judicial achievement is contained in a dozen odd volumes of eighteenth-century law reports. These are an important source which deserve greater attention from historians of eighteenth-century social and political ideas. But they also present special problems which warrant no less careful consideration. Throughout the period England still lacked any official system of standard law reporting. Mansfield, as his contemporaries fully recognized, was singularly blessed in the private reporters he attracted, and it is easy to mistake the novelty and distinctiveness of his judicial leadership simply on account of the unmatched quality of the law reports covering his tenure at King's Bench. …
>
> Bentham, however, was hardly alone in making these protests. Michael Foster in the 1760s has condemned 'the indigested things called *Reports of Adjudged Cases*' as 'mere fragments of learning, the rummage of dead men's papers, or the first essays of young authors', which were nothing less than 'the bane and scandal of the law considered as a science *founded on principle*'. Chief Justice Holt confessed his fears that 'scrambling reports' would 'make posterity think ill of his understanding' and Mansfield often overcame troublesome precedents simply by impugning the law reports in which they were found. In a revealing statement in 1782 he claimed that 'the uncertainty of law of evidence' was owing 'to mistaken notes which have turned particular cases into general rules'. Indeed Bentham's own solution to those institutional problems, a systematic program for official law reporting, was, ironically enough, a proposal Blackstone himself had advocated in the *Commentaries* (1 Comm 72).

Even though there was less centralization in some Italian and German jurisdictions and case law had been collected there for a longer period of time, it still became the subject of state intervention as the state tried to control the interpretation of law in individual judgments. The 1723 and 1775 *Leggi e Costituzioni del Regno di Sardegna* (in Piedmont), the 1771 *Codice di Leggi e Costituzioni del ducato di Modena*, and the 1774 *Dispaccio del re di Napoli Ferdinando IV* attempted to reserve the power to state the authentic interpretation of legal texts to the prince. These efforts can be seen as early examples of an approach chosen by the French revolutionary law of 16–24 August 1790 and the 1794 Prussian *Allgemeines Landrecht*. However, one has to be cautious and not assume that the judges were 'automats' mechanically uttering the words of the law. After all, the image of judges as the 'mouth of the law' used in 1748 by Montesquieu in his *Esprit des lois* is ambiguous. It can also mean that statutory laws need to be interpreted and actively given meaning through judicial analysis and decisions.

2.5 *Doctrine, Including Legal Science and Legal Study*

Legal writing in this period largely abandoned the traditional model of the medieval commentators of the *ius commune*. This was even the case where Roman law (and canon law in Catholic countries) continued to be used and commented on alongside the sixteenth- and early seventeenth-century works of learned jurisprudence by Cujas, Doneau, Zoesius, Suárez and Grotius (new editions of his books appeared after 1650). This radical change in the approach to law originated in France during the second half of the sixteenth century. The so-called *mos gallicus* evolved as a result of nationalist demands to favour French law, which was in large part customary law. From 1600 onward, this resulted in advocates and judges developing a legal literature in the vernacular. This trend continued in the period 1650–1789. The most important doctrinal work of this period was *Les lois civiles dans leur ordre naturel* (1689), a systematic presentation of Roman law in its 'natural order' based on Christian ethical and religious principles by the royal advocate-general and member of the *ministère public* in the court of Clermont, Jean Domat (1625–1696). Writers often published their works either in the vernacular or Latin. Grotius, for example, in the first half of the seventeenth century, published his *De iure belli ac pacis* (1625) but also the *Inleidinge tot de Hollandsche Rechtsgeleerdheyd* (1631).

After 1650, the development of a 'practical jurisprudence' in Italy, notably in the books of Cardinal De Luca (1614–1683), combined the vernacular with the use of Latin.

> *M. Bellomo, The Common Legal Past of Europe, 1000–1800, Washington DC, The Catholic University of America Press, 1995, 221–222*
> The first trend to emerge and become consolidated was known as 'practical jurisprudence'. It preceded a second movement, the *Usus modernus Pandectarum*, with which it was in part intertwined ... One major Italian jurist of 'practical jurisprudence' was Giovan Battista de Luca (1613–83),

> born in Venosa but Roman by adoption and a cardinal of the Holy Roman Church in the period of its greatest religious intransigence, expressed by the Counter Reformation and its operational arm, the Holy Inquisition. Giovani Battista de Luca went his own way, however. Above all, in the composition of his works he alternated between the use of the 'vulgar' language (Italian) and Latin, which was already a revolutionary novelty in the official culture of Europe. His most widely read work, *Il Dottor volgare* (written in Italian) was a sober and balanced work that took up the legal problems of civil coexistence and reorganized the 'institutes' of private law. De Luca had two basic guiding principles: one must always be a 'person of good sense' and one must listen to the voice not only of 'reason' but also of 'reasonableness'. All the 'practical' currents in Italian and European jurisprudence merged in De Luca's thought, especially in the monumental collection of jurisprudential 'maxims' that he extrapolated from an immense number of judicial decisions. The work was entitled, significantly, *Theatrum veritatis ac iustitiae* (the Theatre of Truth and Justice) almost as if the author wanted to dramatize truth and justice in a world in search of guidelines for everyday life ...
>
> The second methodological trend, the *Usus modernus Pandectarum*, began in Germany after the 'reception' of Roman law in 1495. The name of this event came from an expression coined considerably later by Samuel Stryk, a jurist who lived from 1640 to 1710 and was a professor at Frankfurt on the Oder and at Hall, a famous work of whose was entitled *Usus modernus Pandectarum* (roughly, 'Romanistic Practice Brought into Line with the Needs of the Times') ... The jurists who proposed an *usus modernus* of Justinian's Pandects praised German jurisprudence for its power of assimilation. They stressed the 'national' character of the new law and pointed to the way that 'German' jurisprudence had adapted to new needs while utilizing the ancient law.

In this period, systematic commentary on the *Corpus iuris* and the search for a rational system of law was associated with new conceptions of natural law. Examples include the great commentaries by Johannes Voet (1647–1713) from the Netherlands, and the German *Usus modernus pandectarum* (with Struve, Huber, Stryk, and Böhmer). At the University of Göttingen in Germany, Hermann Conring (1606–1681) provided historical perspectives and background information on the law (*De origine iuris germanici*, 1643), particularly public law. From 1690, the German professor Samuel Stryk (1640–1710) published his *Usus modernus pandectarum*, which was another attempt to present a modern practice of Roman law in Germany, especially in Brandendurg, and to make a link with natural law theories. All this gave rise to theoretical innovations focusing on basing general insights on Roman sources for use in court, rather than mere casuistry.

Another change occurred with the diffusion of textbooks devoted to 'national' law modeled after Justinian's *Institutes*, a method employed by Grotius and Vinnius. The latter's commentary on the *Institutes*, first published in 1642, went through many editions until the end of the eighteenth century. It was reworked by the German professor Heineccius and heavily used in Spain. Klaus Luig discusses this European phenomenon of writing national Institutes. The prototype for teaching national law was France in 1679, with the appointment of a *professeur de droit français* in each law faculty. In 1713, under the Bourbon king Philip V, Spain followed the French example, and Denmark encouraged textbooks that presented national law according to the plan of Justinian's *Institutes* in 1736. As we have seen, a similar development can be observed in England in the works of Hale, Wood, and Blackstone. The development of a new kind of law teaching in the vernacular and not in Latin was a crucial part of the formation of a body of 'national' scholarship. The question is whether this legal literature was an instrument to consolidate conservative powers (an argument made by Duncan Kennedy about Blackstone's *Commentaries*), or if it became the theoretical foundation for the effort to rationalize legal systems to transform them, i.e., to change the legal practice of the courts.

> *K. Luig, The Institutes of National Law in the Seventeenth and Eighteenth Centuries, Juridical Review 17 (1972), 197–199, 216–217 and 223*
> Finally, during the last stage, at the end of the period of the *usus modernus*, the national legal systems of the European principalities were independently the objects of legal study. The national language replaced the use of Latin in legal literature. Roman law was now no longer the central topic of European legal science. Rather, occupation with the indigenous legal sources of statutory law and decisions of the courts led to the formation of a new branch of legal science …
>
> No concept of Italian law as a set of national laws existed in Italy in the eighteenth century. As can be seen in a comparison with Germany, the reason probably was not only the absence of political unity, but perhaps also the fact that in Italian-speaking countries there existed no indigenous statute and customary law which did not itself rest on a Romanist foundation. Therefore, if parallels are to be traced between developments in Italy and the other European states of the *ancien régime*, only the larger territories like, for instance, Naples and Venice can be considered … To satisfy the need for instruction in Venetian law, the Senate of Venice

> decided in 1765 to establish a course on the *Institutiones iuris civilis* in the building of the Bibliotheca Marciana ... In the kingdom of Naples the *ius neapolitanum* was taught in the University as an independent subject side by side with Roman law from 1736.

Changes in legal education are not very apparent during the period 1650–1800. The universities or the specialized colleges (like the Inns of Court in England) inherited from the past centuries maintained and transmitted the traditional education based on the *ius commune* in continental Europe and the *common law* in England. However, many of these institutions were in decline. Poor quality of education and examinations worsened their reputations over time and the number of students attending them dropped drastically. At the same time, reforms and the creation of new universities (Duisburg in 1654, Modena in 1682, Innsbruck in 1669, Halle in 1794, Dijon in 1723, Fulda in 1734) produced new trends in teaching and learning. A 1679 edict promulgated by Louis XIV sought to control legal education in France by creating a special course of French law devoted to royal legislation and local customs. Richard Mowery Andrews indicates how these new courses would change legal education.

> *R. Mowery Andrews, Law, Magistracy, and Crime in Old Regime Paris, 1735–1789, Vol. 1, Cambridge, Cambridge University Press, 1994, 247–248*
> Two years were required for the baccalaureate in law, and three for the *licence*. In order [for the] study of [the] humanities and philosophy not to be cut short, the minimum age for admission to a law faculty was 17 (although candidates could be exempted from the age requirement by the Crown, for a fee). Attendance at lectures was policed. Students had to sign a register four times a year ... The entire curriculum was directed toward general examinations at the end of the second and third years. The first two years were devoted primarily to the study of Roman law (known as *le droit civil*) and secondarily to canon law. The 1700 edict prescribed the sequence of instruction and the texts. In the first year, they studied Justinian's *Institutes* of Roman Law with a [final] examination. In the second year the texts were [from the] *Code* ..., lessons from the *Digest* and selections from the *Decretals* ... with further examination[s] for the degree of bachelor of law. The third year was devoted principally to the study of French law, with an additional course ... in either Roman or canon law. There was a final, oral examination in French law, and the student also had to present written theses or propositions, and defend them before a faculty jury, at the end of the third year. Instruction and examination in French law were in the vernacular ... The third-year course in

French jurisprudence was the cynosure of legal education. The Crown appointed each professor of French law from among three candidates nominated to the Chancellor by the general advocates and prosecutors of the Parlement of Paris. The candidate had to be licenciate in law and to have served as barrister or magistrate for at least ten years, 'assiduously and successfully' … Professors of French law were allowed with wide latitude in selecting their subject matter. The texts most preferred for intensive exegesis, in the faculty of the University of Paris and elsewhere during the eighteenth century, were the Gallican Concordat of 1516 … the 1695 ordinance of ecclesiastical authority, the comprehensive 1579 Ordinance of Blois, the 1667 Civil Ordinance, the 1670 Criminal Ordinance and the civil ordinances of Chancellor d'Aguesseau … Professors commonly used both the works of major jurists (from Damhoudère [*lege*: Damhouder] and Loysel in the sixteenth century to Pothier, Jousse, Serpillon, and Muyart in the eighteenth) and collections of rulings by Parlements as major sources in explicating French legal statutes and customs. The law faculties did not comprehensively instruct future barristers and magistrates in French positive law, civil, criminal, customary and ecclesiastical. They introduced them to the principles of French jurisprudence through selective analysis of broad themes.

The use of textbooks in the vernacular according to the model of the *Institutes* of Justinian was also a pedagogical tool which helped to unify and nationalize legal cultures. Seán Donlan considers how an Irish law professor, Francis Sullivan (1719–1766), tried to combine the teaching of English law (the law of the conquerors he considered as valid) while trying to preserve the tradition of the old Irish law.

S.P. Donlan, 'All this together make up our Common Law': Legal hybridity in England and Ireland, 1704–1804, in Esin Örücü (ed.), Mixed Legal Systems at new Frontiers, London, Wildy, Simmonds and Hill, 2010, 127–129, 131 and 137
Francis Stoughton Sullivan began lecturing on English law at the University of Dublin in 1761 … The University of Dublin's creation of a Regius Professorship in Feudal and English Law in 1760 placed it at the forefront of legal reform. The chair was second only to that of Oxford and preceded Cambridge lectures by nearly three decades. A Common law barrister, Sullivan was better known as a civilian, and advocate of the Irish law courts whose substance and procedure had much in common with European Civil and Canon law … Indeed, when Sullivan began, Blackstone's *Commentaries* (1765–9) were not yet published.

The Irishman's broad legal training may have suggested that he, rather than Blackstone, was more likely to present English law in a systematic, institutional fashion. Sullivan's assigned text was, in fact, a work of the Dutch civilian, canonist, and feudalist Arnoldi Corvini (Corvinus, c. 1582-?). Corvini's *Ius feudale, per aphorismos strictim explicatum* was, in his opinion, 'the shortest and plainest book' on feudalism. The work was supplemented by the standard sources of Common law pedagogy, including Sir Thomas Littleton's *Tenures*, Coke's *Commentaries* on Littleton, and selections of Coke's *Reports*. While frequently glossed by English jurists, none of these works post-dated the early seventeenth century ... Sullivan did not, however, press English law into civilian forms or adopt even Blackstone's method. Instead he complimented Corvini's treatise with 'an historical method ... more entertaining to beginners, and better adapted to show the reasons for the original law, and of its several subsequent alterations.'...

The process was similar to that which had occurred in Wales in the previous century. It was also consistent with the general, if gradual, movement towards legal unity and the elimination of European legal pluralism. In his lectures at the University of Dublin, Sullivan sang the praises of English law. In his collection and translation of ancient Irish texts, he sought to preserve the tradition that had preceded it in Ireland. In doing this, he dignified the ancient constitutions of both Britain and Ireland.

English and German texts show the role of these changes in legal education. It gave rise to efforts to try and re-formulate the system of the *Institutes*, which was now seen in terms of a logical continuum between those subject to the law (persons), things (rights of property) and ways to transfer rights (obligations) in harmony with natural law theories. So, even in countries where natural and public law were not taught (as in France), legal education was not completely immune from the impact of the Modern School of Natural Law: the *Institutes* written by professors of French law such as François de Boutaric (1672–1733 in Toulouse) or Claude Serres (1695–1768 in Montpellier), preceded the monographs of Robert-Joseph Pothier (1699–1772 in Orléans), such as his well known *Traité des obligations* (1761–1764).

J.W. Cairns, Eighteenth Century Professorial Classification of English Common Law, McGill Law Journal 33 (1987), 226, 229, 236 and 242–243

Sir Robert Chambers has been virtually forgotten ... He was Sir William Blackstone's successor in the Vinerian chair of English law at Oxford, and, on the evidence of his lectures, not an unworthy one. Memory

> of Chambers' tenure of the Vinerian chair was to some extent kept alive by his nephew's publication in 1824 of a part of the lectures as a *Treatise on Estates and Tenures* … With the initiative coming primarily from private individuals, England followed the European trend, with the establishment of university teaching of national law in the middle of the eighteenth century. Perhaps aware of the impending Vinerian bequest, Blackstone started to teach privately in 1752, being elected to the Vinerian professorship in 1758, when Viner's will was made effective. Less well known is the establishment in 1761 in the University of Dublin of a Regius Chair of Feudal and English Law to which F.S. Sullivan was elected … [Chamber's] course commenced with four introductory lectures on: first, the law of nature, the revealed law, and the law of nations and the primary sources of the law of England; second, the origin of feudal government and of Anglo-Saxon government and laws; third, feudal law and its effects on the English constitution and government; and fourth, the general division of the laws of England … In obvious contrast to Blackstone's *Commentaries*, Chamber's lectures lack any specific account of procedure and actions … The eighteenth century's concern with classifying law was of great importance. In all legal systems, but perhaps especially in English law, it was a significant step in the creation of formally rational law. The effects of categorizing activity on the substantive law are hard to specify, but Professor Milsom has argued that Blackstone was important in the emergence of English law as a system of substantive law. In this respect, it is significant that Chambers sought to expound English law without an account of actions. He treated it, insofar as he could, as a system of purely substantive law, in the categories of public law, criminal law, and private law.

According to Franz Wieacker, reforms in German Universities were more extensive. In the universities of Heidelberg, Strasburg, Giessen and Ingolstadt, new statutes were drafted to adapt the teaching of Roman law to practical legal issues and to follow a more systematic method of teaching. The first chairs devoted to *ius patrium*, or later to the law of nations and criminal law, enlarged the curriculum.[15] The Historical School of Law in Göttingen started with lectures given by Johann Stephan Pütter in 1746. It was not until

15 Franz Wieacker, A History of Private Law in Europe, Oxford, Clarendon Press, 1996, 162–163.

1788, forty-two years later, that Gustav Hugo, considered the founder of this school, was appointed. Their goal was to save 'jurisprudence from the clutches of the so-called Natural Law' with its 'infinite arrogance' and its 'shallow philosophy'.[16]

What do we know about the number of law students? In Turin, a 1729 reform inspired by the Enlightenment caused a rise in the number of students. Leiden continued, in contrast with Bologna, to attract foreign students. In Germany, the number of students, estimated at 8,000 in 1620, decreased to 6,000 between 1740 and 1800. These figures seem to be the result of a change in the time it took to finish legal education. It was shortened from a period of up to ten years to a more condensed and standardized period of formation for professional lawyers. As a consequence, an important part of the existing legal literature, with complete commentaries on the learned laws, began to be forgotten and replaced by handbooks that dealt with national legal practice.

2.6 *Legislation*

The recognition of a legislative power embodied, even monopolized, by the sovereign did not originate in the seventeenth and eighteenth centuries. What changed in modern states, particularly in the territories of the most powerful princes of the seventeenth century and the 'enlightened despots' of the eighteenth century, was the intensity and character of the law creating processes through statutes. This sea change happened in England as a result of the Glorious Revolution: while Parliament was in session every year from autumn or January to late spring or early summer between 1688 and 1800, more than 13,600 acts were passed. Many of these were private bills and local acts (these constituted 73%, primarily concerning estates, inheritance, enclosures, and turnpikes). However, the number of general acts also increased and contributed to what, over time, came to be called the *Bloody Code* because of the huge numbers of crimes for which the death penalty could be imposed. As David Liebermann shows, the publication, diffusion and consolidation of numerous statutes took place both in England and on the Continent without parliamentary representation.

16 Nathan Isaacs, The Schools of Jurisprudence: Their Places in History and their Present Alignment, Harvard Law Review, 31/3 (1918), 373–411 (http://www.jstor.com/stable/1327078; accessed in August 2022).

> *D. Lieberman, Codification, Consolidation, and Parliamentary Statute, in John Brewer and Eckhart Hellmuth (eds), Rethinking Leviathan. The Eighteenth-Century State in Britain and Germany, Oxford, Oxford University Press, 371–372 and 377*
> The sweeping criticisms of Coke and Blackstone, moreover, were frequently sustained by those legal scholars who attempted a more systematic review of Parliament's legislative production. In 1766, the distinguished legal antiquarian Daines Barrington published the first detailed history of English legislation in his *Observation on the Ancient Statutes*. Barrington's study ... not only confirmed the common charges against the statute book's chaotic condition and often obsolete subject matter, it also disclosed the many occasions where Parliament has legislated on matters already effectively covered by the common law, or enacted provisions that unintentionally served to weaken the common law. ...
> In ... calling for a 'reformation of the Code of Statutes', Barrington joined a host of other contemporary jurists who likewise urged upon Parliament a programme to rehabilitate English legislation practice. The programme centred on a comprehensive reformulation of English legislation through a systematic consolidation of the existing statute law ... We can title this scheme of reform 'the Baconian science of legislation' ...
> The much-noted 'swelling of the statute book', it appears, was the product of a law-making system in which private, specialist legal counsel was routinely available to those ... seeking legislative measures, and regularly included careful, critical parliamentary scrutiny of proposed bills. What perhaps most distinguished the Hanoverian procedures ... was the manner in which private and public efforts were ... combined in legislative practice.

In many territories traditionally seen as absolute monarchies, the development of statutory law took place after the last meetings of the assemblies of estates: in France, the General Estates were not convened between 1614 and 1789, in Spain, the *Cortes* only had protocol meetings from 1665 onward, and the same evolution took place in Portugal and Brandenburg. All statutory laws in all its different forms varying from general ordinances, mandates, and rescripts to decisions of the Royal Council, emanated from the king and his bureaucratic apparatus. In France, the 'great ordinances' on civil and criminal procedures (1667 and 1670), commerce (1673), and the maritime ordinance (1681) are the first examples of codifications of a limited subject-matter through general statutes which abrogated earlier laws and local regulations. Paolo Grossi analyses these texts as paradigms for 'legal absolutism' developed by modern States.

P. Grossi, A History of European Law, Chichester, Wiley-Blackwell, 2010, 74–77

At the outbreak of the revolution, the complex legal landscape of the [French] nation remains, therefore, substantially unchanged, although there have been some attempts by the kings of the sixteenth and seventeenth centuries to enlarge the portion of the legal sphere under the influence of royal legislative power. The most conspicuous of these attempts is certainly that carried out by Louis XIV and Colbert, via four penetrating declarations: the *Ordonnance civile* of 1667, the *Ordonnance criminelle* of 1670, the *Ordonnance du commerce* of 1673 and the *Ordonnance de la marine* of 1681. The four *ordonnances* constitute a legislative programme without parallel in other monarchies, as is evident if one compares them to the various *recopilaciones* promulgated by the Spanish kings between the sixteenth and the nineteenth centuries …

The first two *ordonnances* are usually known by the name *Code Louis* and the third by the name *Code Savary*. The term *code* here may provoke some misunderstandings and so let me put these documents in their proper historical and legal context straight away. *Code*, like constitution, has a number of meanings and can therefore be used in a number of different ways. The Latin word *codex* originally denoted the material, be it wood or paper, on which a text was written. In legal terminology, the term came to mean a collection which organized a diverse group of laws: here the ancient codes, such as those of Theodosius and Justinian and their many successors in France of the sixteenth to nineteenth centuries.

However, when legal historians talk of the 'age of legal codes', and specifically of the 'Code', they are referring to a moment in the history of legislation characterized by a very particular type of legal source that should not be confused with these earlier experiments which we dub 'codes' for formal reasons because they result from a prince's or a jurist's attempt at a general organization of legal material. The meaning of *code* in the technical language of legal history assumes two preconditions: firstly the great cultural revolutions of the Enlightenment and of the doctrine of natural law; secondly an omnipotent and daring legislator with no compunction towards legal pluralism in the territory under his control, who seeks to bring the entire legal order under the aegis of his legislation. This type of code partakes of the legalistic and legally idolatrous myths of the Enlightenment in order to take on the role of an archetype capable of imbuing certain historically produced documents with a totalizing value. To group the Napoleonic Code … with the *Code Louis* and the Justinian Code because of a superficial verbal resemblance is a form of nominalism that places the cart of terminology before the horse of historical meaning.

None of this changes the fact that Louis XIV's *ordonnances* are a very important quartet of legal-historical sources and deserving of our attention. The first three will be covered here. The fourth, published in 1681, is also interesting but deals mainly with maritime law, although this fact in itself demonstrates that contemporary France was already a major colonial power with trading partners from across the world.

The first two *ordonnances* sought to unify and reform civil and criminal trials. Their reorganization of the judiciary had one precise legal and political aim: to redefine the role of the French parliaments. These had originally begun as judicial bodies, but were now beginning to erode the king's power by claiming the role of representatives of the nation and interprets of its 'fundamental laws'. The *ordonnances* reiterated the subaltern status of all judges, including the parliaments, to the law, which was itself identified as coinciding with the will of the king alone. They moreover contributed to the reduction of the law to a system of legislation. These aims lend the two *ordonnances* their historical and legal significance. Although they limit themselves to ordering pre-existing legal material and do claim to be the exclusive manifestations of the law, they were nonetheless a certain and decisive step forwards on the historical journey towards the Code because they used the French experience of the law, specifically civil and criminal trials. The first two *ordonnances* therefore represented a victory for royal power in its efforts to achieve a sought-after legal monism.

The third Louisian *ordonnance* is somewhat different, both in character and in legal historical importance. This text is aimed squarely at unifying the governance of the law of commerce. This was already a delicate area because it intersected with the economic interests of powerful corporations of merchants.

It would be misrepresenting Colbert's work if I argued that his wish to regulate matters generally left to the everyday customs and practices of merchants represented nothing more than a simple affirmation of power. Instead, the complexity of this very subtle politician's aims is made fully clear if one considers the way in which the central government had the *ordonnance* drawn up. The primary responsibility was given over to professional merchants, the foremost among whom was one Jacques Savary, a man of little learning but who was nonetheless given the great privilege of being the authentic and experienced voice of the mercantile class; Savary came from a family of merchants and had begun trading long before he entered public service: he was, in effect, an expert practitioner.

The resulting legal document, which is relatively concise at merely 122 paragraphs, enacts only very modest technical legislation. However, it gives close attention to the merchant's desire for greater order amongst the key points of commercial law, which had developed alongside the mercantile practices of the medieval and post-medieval periods. The *ordonnance* therefore deals with such issues as commercial legal subjects (merchants, apprentices, mediators), commercial ledgers, business associations, negotiable instruments, insolvency and the commercial courts, where merchants could have their cases heard by unrobed judges who passed reassuringly equitable rulings.

As well as signaling a victory for royal power, the third *ordonnance* represents the consolidation of an alliance that will prove extremely durable. It is no coincidence that it is the merchants who will later help the king to unify the national territory by breaking down the local legal peculiarities that favoured the feudal nobles. The third *ordonnance* may have affirmed the king's status as legislator and sovereign but it also allowed the merchants free rein (albeit with the king's blessing) to draw up their own branch of law, founded on their own customs, that was very much distinct from ordinary civil law.

The law governing matters between private citizens remained untouched by Louis XIV's *ordonnances*. The *coutumes* continued to govern these cases until the winds of revolution swept through. In the first half of the eighteenth century there were three isolated, and yet significant, reforms made by Chancellor d'Aguesseeau on the subjects of gifts and of wills. However, these stick out somewhat against a background of a general absence of legislation.

By way of conclusion, we may note that, thanks to the combined labours of the jurist heirs of historical humanism and a legislator set on asserting his sovereignty, the outlines of a national legal system, an authentic *droit français*, are becoming ever sharper.

The 'enlightened despots' in Prussia and in Austria developed ambitious codification plans influenced by natural law professors. Most of these projects were achieved only after 1789, like the 1794 General Prussian Code (*Allgemeines Landrecht* or ALR). Their effects will be described below.

P. Stein, Roman Law in European History (12th ed.), Cambridge, Cambridge University Press, 2013, 112–113

When Frederick succeeded his father, he resolved to have a code, written in German and based primarily on 'natural reason and the character of the country', with Roman law included only if it fitted in with them. The main draftsman was Carl Gottlieb Svarez, who shared the view of Christian Wolff that the duty of the ruler was to lead his subjects to a perfect, rational life, in which they would be good men as well as good citizens. The Prussian code was therefore to have an educational function and, being addressed to the ordinary man, had to be comprehensive, clear and certain.

The final text of the *Allgemeines Landrecht*, enacted in 1794, is enormous. It is loosely structured on Pufendorf's distinction between man as an individual and man as a member of groups, ranging from the family, through social classes, to the state. It comprises 19,000 articles, dealing not just with private but with public, criminal, feudal, ecclesiastical and commercial laws and purports to govern much that would normally be regarded as unsuitable for legal regulation, such as the intimate relations of husband and wife. Roman influences are noticeable mainly in the sections on property.

In Austria, with its vast rambling provinces, each with its own separate administration and court structure, the need for unification was particularly acute. The Emperor Charles VI sponsored a unified law of intestate successions, which was largely based on Justinian's law. This was put into force in Upper and Lower Austria between 1727 and 1747. Charles's successor, Maria Teresa, wanted a more comprehensive codification. In 1753 she issued a directive to draft a general private law, ignoring the laws of special groups or classes, to be based on the *ius commune*, but using the law of reason to correct or complete it.

The first draft, the *Codex Theresianus* of 1766, was a compromise between the traditional laws of the various provinces, with their differing mixtures of customary and Roman elements. Its 8,367 articles were written in the vernacular but grouped the material of Roman categories. It was attacked both by conservatives, who did not want to lose their provincial privileges and felt that it went too far, and by reformers, who believed that it did not go far enough …

The leading exponent of natural law in Austria was Karl Anton von Martini and he was clear that to jettison Roman law completely was to throw out the baby with the bath-water …

The work of revision of the Theresian draft continued sporadically and twenty years after its publication a simpler version, reduced to a quarter of the original size, was completed and sent to the provincial assemblies and the universities for their observations … Martini was replaced as senior draftsman by Franz von Zeiller, who produced the code of 1,502 articles which finally came into force in 1812.

The era from 1650 to 1775 can best be seen as the 'pre-codification' period. It is, however, necessary to distinguish between the various 'codes' that were promulgated. In Denmark and Norway, the 1683 *Danske Lov* (issued by king Christian V), was the result of seven committees drafting and revising six books on the ordinary courts, religion, temporal offices, the maritime court, estates, inheritances, debts, and penal law. Just like the 1687 *Norske Lov* (also issued by king Christian V and very similar to the *Danske Lov*) it can be considered a 'proto-codification', as it was a compilation of older laws for territories where the influence of Roman law remained limited and the impact of natural law theories absent. The revision of the Swedish Code (*Sveriges Rikes Lag*, 1734) took place within an old tradition of statutory law, but was influenced by German legal science based on Roman and natural law theories. The compilations of statutory laws for the kingdom of Piedmont-Sardinia (the 1723 *Lois et constitutions du roi de Sardaigne*, with new editions in 1729 and 1770), and the Bavarian codes (a criminal code, a judicial code, and a civil code issued between 1752–1756) were still faithful to the Roman law tradition. They were characterized by a vast number of *ius commune* rules which had been in place for a long time in these countries.

> *M. Agren, Domestic Secrets. Women and Property in Sweden, 1600–1857, Chapel Hill, The University of North Carolina Press, 2009, 1600–1857, 25*
> The Swedish legal system was different in many ways from systems in other parts of Europe at the time. For instance, there were usually no notaries who registered property transactions, as in France, since all such matters were taken care of by the primary courts (Stockholm differed in this respect). Nor was there the same array of competing legal traditions and courts as in England, where common law existed alongside ecclesiastical law, manorial law, equity law and statutory law. In Sweden, the ecclesiastical courts lost much of their power after the Reformation, and they were not in charge of the registration of probate inventories and wills. Very few manorial courts existed, and those that did were placed under the supervision of the courts of appeal, as were all other primary courts. There was no special equity court of the sort that existed in England; however the appeal court judges did adduce *aequitas*. As we will see, considerations of what was fair and equitable (*billigt, skäligt*) under the circumstances are likely to have played a significant role not only in the courts of appeal. Statutory law (*kungliga förordningar*) played quite a significant role, mainly because the legal code was becoming increasingly outdated and obscure, especially with respect to economic matters.

> Much of the new eighteenth century credit legislation (which is of great interest in this context) was introduced through statutory law.
>
> The main legal authority was the national legal code, which regulated central aspects of life, such as marriage, inheritance, landed property, relations within villages and hamlets, trade, crime and the relationship between the king and his subjects. It also laid down procedural rules for the courts. The code dated back to c. 1350, when Magnus Erikson was king, but had been slightly revised in 1442, during the reign of Christopher of Bavaria. This was the legal code named after King Christopher that was applied in the courts throughout the seventeenth century and up until 1736, when the new code, ratified by the four estates in 1734, was put into practice.

Contrary to the previous compilations of legislation, the Prussian 1794 ALR and the Austrian codes (1811 ABGB and earlier codes of civil procedure, criminal law, and criminal procedure) were prepared by learned jurists and law professors influenced by the work of the Modern School of Natural Law. These products of enlightened despotism maintained the traditional structure of the societies of the *ancien régime* (*Stände,* such as the clergy, the nobility, and the third estate) and can be considered as transitional codifications before the advent of the Napoleonic codifications, based on the revolutionary principle of equality.

2.7 *Diffusion of Laws and Legal Institutions*

The period 1650–1775 witnessed further Western colonization in the Americas and Asia. The control over the colonies in South America established by the Portuguese and Spanish in the sixteenth century remained unchallenged. The British and the French, however, were involved in a struggle for power in North America. The English established colonies in Virginia and New England in the first half of the sixteenth century and extended their influence from there, from Pennsylvania and New York, which they acquired from the Dutch in 1674, to Carolina, and finally to Georgia. The French acquired Quebec in 1608 and developed it through charter companies. The colony of Canada submitted to French royal control in 1663, until the British victory in 1763. French Louisiana, created in the first half of the seventeenth and the beginning of the eighteenth century, was ceded to Spain in 1763 and returned to France in 1802. In Asia, Spain (Philippines) and Portugal (Goa) found new rivals in the Dutch or, more precisely, the Dutch East India Company (*Vereenigde Oost-Indische Compagnie* or VOC), created in 1602 by the Estates-General of the Netherlands, which also conquered Malacca, the coasts of Ceylon, founded Batavia (present-day Jakarta) and established an outpost at the Cape of Good Hope in 1652. The

French established several posts in India, among them Pondichéry in 1673 and the British colonized Surat in 1612, Madras in 1639, Bombay in 1668, and Calcutta in 1690. The British defeated the French at the end of the Seven Years War (1763), obtaining for their East India Company the right to collect taxes and the administration of Bengal, Bihar, and Orissa in 1765.

All of this had a significant impact on the legal history of the colonized peoples. In the Americas, the Spanish and Portuguese, and later the French and the British, tried to impose their own laws on the natives (who they considered a lawless people) and the colonists emigrating from the mother country. In Asia, the colonial powers often decided to maintain the laws of the natives. In some parts, that meant that Muslim law was used, in other regions, 'Hindu' or customary law.

In America, during the period 1650–1800, the Spanish and the Portuguese continued to impose their own legal system, the 'law of Castile' and the 'law of the Portuguese crown', with some adaptations. Historians refer to the laws used by the Spanish Crown in this period as *Derecho Indiano*.[17] For example, Spanish colonies in South America were organized in territories under a viceroy. This happened first in Mexico and Lima, and later in Bogota in 1717 and in Buenos Aires in 1776. They were subject to royal legislation promulgated for the West Indies. This *Derecho Indiano* was consolidated through a 1680 *Recopilación* in nine volumes devoted principally to public law, including the status of slaves and of Indians and to the *ius commune* as understood in Spain. Roman legal sources thus remained important and were used in local literature and court decisions.[18] Aniceto Masferrer discusses how this compilation was made and how it, in a way, transformed the techniques of codification.

> *A. Masferrer, Spanish Legal Traditions. A Comparative Legal History Outline, Madrid, Dykinson, 242–245*
>
> The need for compilation was greater in America than in Castile because Indian law was composed of a countless number of legal dispositions whose casuistic character made it more difficult to systematize.

17 Francisco Tomás y Valiente, Manual de Historia del derecho Español, Madrid, Tecnos, 1987, 325–345. See also Thomas Duve and Heikki Pihlajamáki (eds), New Horizons in Spanish Colonial Law, Frankfurt am Main, Max Planck Institute for European Legal History, 2015, 1.

18 Juan Javier del Granado and Alejandra Mayagoitia, Roman Law and ratio decidendi in Spanish Colonial Law, 16th through the 19th centuries, in Serge Dauchy, W. Hamilton Bryson and Matthew C. Mirow (eds), Ratio decidendi. Guiding Principles of Judicial Decisions, Vol. 2: 'Foreign' Law, Berlin, Duncker & Humblot, 2010, 107–112.

> Consequently, many attempts were made to collect the laws. The method used differed from one compilation to another: some compilations reproduced the text of the whole legal disposition; others just contained an extract of it, sometimes even modified or rearranged …
>
> León Pinelo, *relator* (rapporteur) of the *Consejo de Indias*, drafted, after working for 12 years, a compilation which was delivered to the *Consejo* in 1636. Consequently, the *Conde de Castrillo*, Governor of the Consejo, thought it convenient publishing it and turning it into the official compilation of Indian laws. However, economic difficulties made its publication impossible. It was drafted like the Castilian *Nueva Recopilación*, and consisted of 9 books, subdivided into titles containing over 10,000 laws, including in each one mention of its author and the date. The complete text was lost, and there remains just a part of its 2nd book, which was promulgated as the *Ordenanzas* of the *Consejo Real de Indias*. …
>
> After León Pinelo's death in 1660, a new committee was appointed in order to draft a compilation of Indian laws. Fernando Jiménez Paniagua, a committee member, was given the already existent elaborated material. The undertaking started in 1661 and concluded in 1680, the king being asked for his approval on April 12, 1680. Carlos II, by an Act of May 18, 1680, sanctioned it, abrogating the legislation not contained in it except '*las Cédulas y Ordonanzas dadas a nuestras Reales Audiencias en lo que no fueren contrarias a las Leyes*'. The committee was ordered to provide two original printed copies, signed by all of the members of the *Consejo*, one of them for the Archives of the *Consejo*, the other for the Archives of Simancas.

In French Canada, the customary law of Paris, with its rules about the seignorial system (French feudalism),[19] was introduced in 1664, as well as some of the royal ordinances of Louis XIV. On the French Caribbean Islands, the regulation of slavery could be found in the 1685 *Code Noir*. This code was the product of Roman sources (for example, slaves were regarded as the property of the planters), influences of Catholicism (slaves should be converted to Christianity and should be considered persons in religious and criminal matters), and royal control. In British North America, where, in principle, British migrants brought their own laws, privileges, and liberties with them, it was not the whole of the common law which was introduced. In proprietary colonies like Pennsylvania,

19 Richard Colebrook Harris, Seigneurial System in Early Canada: A Geographical Study, Quebec, McGill-Queen's University Press, 1984, 3–8 (http://www.jstor.org/stable/j.ctt815gd.5; accessed in August 2022).

the founder of the colony (William Penn) was endowed with the power to make laws (which should not be 'repugnant' or contrary to the laws of England), and he used it to impose Puritan rules of conduct. In Massachusetts, the *Book of the General Laws and Liberties* (1641–1648) was a kind of code of criminal and civil law based on Biblical laws (quoting extracts of the Bible after every article). It was in force until the 1691 Charter decreed that all laws of the colony had to be sent for approval to England.

Because of their different charters, the thirteen American colonies at the end of the eighteenth century had their own institutions and legislative bodies. These charters contained local laws, provisions for juries (though they were not generally used, even in criminal matters), and, in some colonies, for religious tolerance. The common law of England, as well as equity, were adopted. There were also 'slave codes' in nine of these colonies (Massachusetts, Rhode Island, Connecticut, and New Hampshire being the exceptions), following the model of the 1661 slave code of English Barbados.[20]

As far as the Asian colonies are concerned, and especially in the early days of the British Empire in India between 1650 and 1800, a policy preference to leave the natives their own laws led to different results. The policy was started by the Portuguese, followed by the Dutch who ordered that the Tamil customary law in Ceylon in 1707 should be written down, and in Pondichéry by the French who established a local court called *tribunal de la chaudrie* with the duty to respect the local laws of the Gentoos. While implementing British regulations and institutions in Madras, Bombay, and Calcutta, the rural territories (called *mofussil*) were placed under the authority of the administrators and judges of the East India Company. The decision, taken by Governor Warren Hastings in 1772, to let the natives in Bengal keep their own laws meant that it was necessary to know and translate the rules of the Hindu and Muslim communities. As David Ibbetson explains, William Jones, an English jurist who had written an original work on the law of bailments, much influenced by Roman law, was the central figure in the effort of translating and modifying Hindu and Muslim law. Jones's knowledge of oriental languages led him to translate the so-called laws of Manu and to suggest an improbable mix of Hindu or Muslim customary laws with English procedural norms.[21]

20 Sally S. Hadden, The Fragmented Laws of Slavery in the Colonial and Revolutionary Areas, in Michael Grossberg and Christopher Tomlins (eds), The Cambridge History of Law in America, Vol. 1, Cambridge, Cambridge University Press, 2007, 259–264.

21 David Ibbetson, Sir William Jones as Comparative Lawyer, in Alexander Murray (ed.), Sir William Jones, 1746–1794: A commemoration, Oxford, Oxford University Press, 1998, 19–42.

The so-called 'Law of Manu', a treatise on duties (*Dharmasatsra*) written between the 2nd century BC and the 2nd century AD, was considered to be the main source of Hindu Law. The translation distorted the text, and transformed its meaning completely through the use of English legal concepts. Furthermore, English colonizers exaggerated its importance. Western concepts, mainly influenced by the Roman model of Justinian's Code and Digest, remained important, even in the colonial legal systems based on personal laws. For example, the British conception of 'ownership', completely absent in the Hindu tradition (and in the first version of texts proposed by Hindu *pandits*), was introduced in the text of translated Hindu laws. It provided legal certainty for landowners (especially the *zamindars*, the wealthy landowners who had to collect taxes).

The thirteen British colonies in North America were granted a charter by the English king which bestowed on each colony its own legislative power. The colonial assemblies of the different states made 'by-laws', which applied to the colonists. Their statutes supplemented the common law of England that was introduced in North America. According to James Henretta, dozens of statutes were voted during the first years of independence.[22] The great bulk consisted of private bills concerning specific communities and individuals. The new legislation suppressed the remains of feudalism such as primogeniture and entails. It restricted the number of death penalties as in the 1786 Pennsylvania 'criminal code'.

North America adopted much of the common law, but the development of statutory laws in the thirteen colonies resulted in laws specific to each of the colonies.

Questions

1. What does it mean that 'authority', and not 'truth', makes the law? By what change of paradigm is this Hobbesian statement suggested?
2. What is the connection between natural law, natural rights, colonialism, and the foundation of international law?
3. What was the role of legislation and custom from 1650 to 1775?
4. What was the relevance of reason in the Prussian *Allgemeines Landrecht* (1794)?
5. How was the law created in the colonial territories? How did it develop or evolve? What was the 'Derecho Indiano'? And the 1685 *Code Noir*?

---

22 James A. Henretta, Magistrates, Common Law Lawyers, Legislators: The Three Legal Systems of British America, in Michael Grossberg and Christopher Tomlins (eds), The Cambridge History of Law in America, Vol. 1, Cambridge, Cambridge University Press, 2008, 555–592.

3 Actors

3.1 *Judges, Legislators and Jurists*

There was a general trend in this period toward increased state intervention in the legal profession. This was achieved through rules on legal education, qualifications for becoming a lawyer, mandatory registration, the incorporation of lawyers in professional associations, and even direct control of professionals, as they were considered public agents. However, the way it was done was different in every European state and depended on the local situation. The effort was highly centralized in England, less so in France, Spain and the Netherlands. In England, the process of recruitment of judges from experienced barristers was at the discretion of the sovereign. David Lemmings shows how the Inns of Court influenced the barristers' profession in England.

> *David Lemmings, Gentlemen and Barristers, Oxford, Clarendon Press, 1990, 258–259*
>
> The inns of court entered a period of steep decline in the later seventeenth century. This was not so much a result of the loss of their role as academies for educating the gentry: rather it was a consequence of their diminishing function as institutional centres for the training, regulation and accommodation of the English bar itself ... Financial problems and falling rolls also made the inns willing to accept the practical erosion of the formal qualifications prescribed for admission to the bar, so that country gentlemen who had no intention of practising the law were encouraged to acquire the status of barrister, and the 'degree of the utter bar' became less synonymous with the practising bar itself. These qualifications became increasingly irrelevant to the real business of becoming a lawyer, just as the empty forms which survived the parallel decay of readings and moots had no bearing on legal education in a real sense ...
>
> The regime of the inns of court had developed in response to the requirements of medieval England and the lawyers who serviced it. By 1700 at least, the structure of a medieval guild organization was inappropriate to the demands of a society which was experiencing rapid economic change in the context of free market capitalism ... The evidence suggests that the bar experienced an invigorating purge. In 1720 it was leaner, fitter, more professional, and more respected than it had been in 1680. It is surely no coincidence that the bar was now less firmly attached to the inns of court, and to that other feature of the profession's ancient structure, the order of serjeants at law ... Progressively liberated from the restrictions of the inns and the coif, the 1730 bar should have been in a

position to play a full part in the creation of the new world which was opening up before English men and women … Thus, at the time as the bar seemed to be adapting itself to the requirements of a society moving towards industrialization, the profession was equipped to operate as a career open to the talents which might absorb some of the social pressures engendered by that momentous change.

In France, there were still venal offices, but some of the reforms launched in the eighteenth century by enlightened despots were producing results. David A. Bell describes the attempt to establish a 'corps' and 'order of barristers' at the Parisian Bar during the reign of Louis XIV, a decision which was an attempt to assert monarchical power but led to the relative independence of the Parisian legal elite in the eighteenth century, who supported the *Parlement* of Paris in its political struggles.

D.A. Bell, Lawyers and Citizens. The Making of a Political Elite in Old Regime France, Oxford, Oxford University Press, 1994, 50–53, 56 and 58

Sometime in the year 1660, a number of barristers began to assemble regularly … Each claimed to represent one of the thirteen 'benches' of the great hall of the Palais de Justice …

The early activities of the newly constituted 'Order of Barristers' mostly fell into four categories. First, it lobbied the crown to obtain titles of nobility for each successive *bâtonnier*, but met with no success. Second, François de Montholon and his colleagues struggled to compile an accurate list (*rôle*) of those *avocats en parlement* who actually practised law … Third, the Order began to police itself, and to take control over recruitment and disbarment … The fourth, … set of activities concerned a word that has no exact English translation: *préséance*. It … means 'precedence', but in the early modern context it referred to precedence in ceremonial processions, and more generally to codes of etiquette and deference …

The royal ordinance of civil procedure issued in these years [1667] … had another important consequence for the Order. … [I]t ordered Parisian barristers not merely to keep a written list of practising barristers, but to publish it annually under the title of *Tableau des avocats* … In 1707, the Order also asserted its authority … by striking one of his members from the *Tableau*; in other words, disbarring him.

Hannes Siegrist gives an example of an authoritarian reform in Prussia. The development of an independent legal profession was hindered in Germany by the strict controls imposed by the states on all lawyers.

> *H. Siegrist, Advokat, Bürger und Staat. Sozialgeschichte der Rechtsanwälte in Deutschland, Italien und der Schweiz (18.-20. Jh.), Frankfurt am Main, Klostermann, 39–42 (transl. by J.-L. Halpérin)*
> As the Prussian State made the administration of justice more uniform and developed an administrative and judicial apparatus based on the centralized and hierarchical models of the 18th century, it reformed the bar as well. Until then, it had been subject to old court rulings, urban and seigniorial statutes on advocates, and exam regulations from universities. Efforts to regulate and raise the ethical standards and qualifications for lawyers had existed for a long time. What was new was that the norms were now uniform and effectively and consistently applied. All the authorities which dealt with the procurators and advocates, notably noble seigniors, cities, courts, and universities, were excluded from the administration of justice or reduced to be mere organs for the execution of judgments. Unification of advocates by the state was one of the many measures introduced by Friedrich Wilhelm I and his successors to combat particularism and all forms of decentralized authority or patronage. …
>
> Until the beginning of the 18th century, the office of procurator was regulated by a *numerus clausus*. The control of procurators lost its importance when their functions were being taken over by advocates, whose number was [originally] not limited. The balance of power tipped to the advocates. In 1713 the king reduced the number of advocates from 887 to 304, and he decided that the number of licensed advocates would be fixed for every court and city.
>
> In 1781 the king (Friedrich II) decided … to make the advocates civil servants. … When the dispositions of the General Ordinance about Procedure were adapted in 1793, the 1781, radical, experiment was partially abandoned.

A text about the Scandinavian territories reminds us that the legal profession was not very organized in the Nordic countries. The Danish and Swedish codes were produced by a very small group of jurists, supported by royal counsellors.

> *P. Letto-Vanamo, K.Å. Modéer and D. Tamm, History of Expropriation in the Nordic Countries, in Recueils de la Société Jean Bodin, Assistance in Conflict Resolution, Vol. 3, Bruxelles, De Boeck, 281–283*
> A central turning point in the regulation of advocates in Sweden and Finland (until 1809 a part of Sweden) was the founding of the Royal Courts of Appeal, *hovrätt* (in Stockholm in 1614, in Åbo-Turku in 1623 etc.). The Rule of Legal procedure regulating their work was passed in 1615. Legal

> representation was for the first time admitted as a general principle. On the basis of the Rule of 1615 the Courts of Appeal could later regulate the advocates with further procedural statutes. Already in these rules we can find the first attempts to control the advocates.
>
> The Courts of Appeal had a central position in the Swedish court organization and legal life due to the importance of correcting the old deficient legislation by judge made law. For the first time an hierarchic appellate order was created, which was able to control the court system as a whole. The lower courts were compelled to send their record books annually to the *hovrätt* so that the unity of the law could be controlled …
>
> The Courts of Appeal started to give rules eventually leading to the creation of a body of advocates. The idea was to create a body of permanent legal representatives who were first called *procurators* and later advocates. Not everybody could be accepted as a member of this body. Some qualifications were needed. In 1656 a first set of rules were given in a procedural regulation of the Court of Appeal of Stockholm, *Svea Hovrätt*, but probably those were adopted also by the other Courts of Appeal. In order to tract as an advocate before the court a previous permission from the court was needed. The court would try the applicant's qualifications when he had presented his written application with some proof of his knowledge. If he was accepted he swore an oath of admission. Still one could not maintain that a legally trained body of advocates had come into existence. Some advocates might present their University credentials (*testimonium*), for example from the University of Uppsala or Åbo (founded 1640) but even in that case the studies would mainly have been of a general character. Legal studies were still more or less only of a rudimentary character … The 17th century Swedish and Finnish courts' records reveal that the use of legal representatives was at any time quite common even in county courts.

A comparison of different regions brings some common features to light. In England in the middle of the eighteenth century there were about 400 practicing barristers and more than 4,000 attorneys and solicitors. The former were educated at Oxford and Cambridge (50–60%) and/or through apprenticeships as clerks (especially for special pleaders), with the latter receiving only a practical apprenticeship. There was no national organization. The barristers belonged to one of the four Inns of Court; in 1739, a small group of London solicitors formed a *Society of Gentlemen Practisers*. Despite this lack of organization, legal professionals had a monopoly on common law matters adjudicated by the Court of Westminster, whose twelve judges were chosen from among the elite barristers. In France, there were between 5,000 and 6,000 advocates. They were university graduates and in the big cities, they were organized in *orders* according to the Parisian model. They formed the first group of professional lawyers in the kingdom and were considered senior to the approximately 5,000 procurators and 4,000 judges of the ordinary courts (there were also thousands of royal office-holders in administrative and judicial functions). In Naples, with a population of 400,000 souls, the number of advocates reached a maximum of 3,600. In many parts of Italy, Germany, and the Netherlands, the number of professional lawyers was limited to a few dozen or a few hundred, because of an official *numerus clausus*. The Swiss cantons also had a low level of professionalization (except for Geneva); their professional organizations had less than 100 advocates. The defense of litigants was the task of *Richter-Fürsprecher*, members of the court, often men without legal qualifications, who represented the parties. The eighteenth century was a transitional period towards professionalization. There were a great variety of different laws addressing the issue, and in some cases, professionalization was imposed by the state.

Questions

1. In the period 1650–1775 the intervention of the state in the legal profession notably increased. What forms did such intervention take?
2. What was the relationship between lawyers and the monarchical power across Europe?
3. What was the role of lawyers in the public administration of the state?

4 Application

4.1 *Institutions*

The process of creating higher courts continued in the second half of the seventeenth century and during the eighteenth century. It resulted in more unification of the law through state institutions. The level of centralization of these institutions varied between countries. The English Judiciary was concentrated in London. In France, in 1789, there were thirteen *Parlements* (Courts of Appeal) for the whole kingdom. Spain had a variety of *Audiencias*. The situation was even more complicated in federal states such as the Netherlands, where only the provinces of Holland and Zeeland had a common High Court, the *Hoge Raad*, in The Hague. The Holy Roman Empire had the *Reichskammergericht*, which continued to sit in Wetzlar from 1689 to 1806 and dealt with only a small number of cases, as many princes had obtained a *privilegium de non appellando*. Despite attempts to centralize, in practice a plurality of justice systems remained, some of which were under limited state control, and others were partly controlled by a monopoly of professional lawyers. There were also the justices of the peace, whose numbers increased from 3,700 in 1702 to 8,402 in 1761, the courts of requests (with self-elected judges among the local nobility) and borough courts in England, and ecclesiastical and municipal courts across the whole of Europe.

> *S.P. Donlan, 'All this together make up our Common Law': Legal Hybridity in England and Ireland, 1704–1804, in Esin Örücü (ed.), Mixed Legal Systems at New Frontiers, London, Wildy, Simmonds and Hill, 2010, 289*
> There were also England's *iura propria*, its numerous jurisdictions beyond or below the 'superior' courts. If we only use Chambers' account, the courts of justice at mid-century (c 1767–73) included: parliament, the privy council, the lords and the court of the lord high steward, chancery, king's bench, common pleas, exchequer, exchequer chamber (of various sorts), circuit or assize courts, the session of justices of the peace (quarter sessions), county courts, the sheriff's torn court, the manorial courts of leet and baron, the coroner's court, the courts of weights and measures, and the fair courts of piepowder. Even this list is not comprehensive. There existed, too, counties palantine, providing varying levels of legal autonomy, as well as the Isle of Man and the Channel islands. Numerous 'courts of requests' created by statute served as small claims courts, as did a wide variety of borough courts. Many of these were administered in a summary manner by men untrained in the law, common or otherwise. There was considerable discretion and little precedent. Frequently lacking a record of their activities, the equitable 'law' they applied was ephemeral. Here especially, the 'often contradictory systems of normative ordering' that existed could easily trespass on the motivations and decisions of the courts.

Conflicts were also resolved by the Church and smaller courts, as the text written by David Sabean shows for the German village of Neckarhausen in Württemberg. At the end of the eighteenth century, the institutional apparatus of the state had not yet succeeded in controlling all regulatory sanctions through its institutions and courts. Seigniorial, municipal, and Church courts could administer more informal justice than higher courts with fully-fledged jurists under the direct influence of the state legislation.

> *D. Warren Sabean, Property, Production and Family in Neckarhausen, 1700–1870, Cambridge, Cambridge University Press, 1990, 428–429*
> During the eighteenth and part of the nineteenth century, there were two main village courts, the church consistory (*Kirchenkonvent*) and the *Gericht* (court), which sometimes sat as a semi-annual *Ruggericht* (court of complaint) and sometimes in ad hoc sessions to handle matters as they arose. There was a court of higher instance in the town of Nütringen, the *Oberamtsgericht*, but its records are only available from 1801 onward in various miscellaneous volumes …
>
> Discipline was surely the issue for the establishment of the church consistory. The churchman/administrator who was most responsible for founding the institution in 1644, Johann Valentin Andreae, was on the cutting edge of the first pietist movement. Early in the seventeenth century, he argued that new behavior should be institutionalized to match the correct doctrine established by the Reformation … The history of the consistory in Neckarhausen indicates that insofar as family quarrels were concerned, this institution was primarily used by women, and their alliance with the pastor calls for some comment. The reigning ideology viewed the house as ordered and maintained by the *Hausvater*, the *pater familias*, although the hidden agenda had to do with the *Hausvater*'s subjection to civil and religious authority. The pastor heard many a complaint from the wives of the village and during confession and registration for communion received detailed knowledge about the inner life of many of the families of the village. He had the power to summon offenders to the parsonage to offer spiritual advice and issue relevant warnings about behavior. In those instances where his authority was challenged, the consistory was the vehicle for re-establishing it or getting even. Looked at quantitatively, the number of marital cases which came before the consistory was very small, less than one a year … On formal grounds then, most cases appear to have been a collusion between the pastor and wife against the husband …
>
> The ideology of the house was also originally given definition by the fiscal interests of the state … By the eighteenth century, there were clear mechanisms for sorting out rights between siblings, parents and children, and husbands and wives. When women felt threatened by wastrel husbands, they could bring suit in court to have the entire estate inventoried.

In Catholic countries, the role of ecclesiastical courts and, more generally, the power of Church institutions remained important during the seventeenth and eighteenth centuries. In those countries, the Church continued to administer their patrimony, which was significant – often around 10% of the territory. However, monarchs reinforced their control over bishops and ecclesiastical courts. For example, in France, bishops were elected by the king in accordance with the 1516 Concordat. As far as the courts were concerned, the remedy called *appel comme d'abus* allowed royal courts or *Parlements* to review ecclesiastical decisions according to the rules of canon law which were approved in France. In the larger monarchies, there was also a trend to develop the Catholic Church's national character. At the end of Middle Ages, a movement known as *gallicanisme* began in France. It was based on the notion that local customs could trump the regulations of the Church. This idea was reinforced under the reign of Louis XIV and officially imposed by the 1682 *Déclaration des Quatre Articles.* One of its goals was to encourage the independence of the clergy from the Papacy. The following text, written by William James Callahan, is about Spain and shows what happened to the status of the Church in the period 1650–1775.

> *W.J. Callahan, Church, Politics, and Society in Spain, 1750–1874, Cambridge Mass., Harvard University Press, 1985, 3–4, 8–9, 15, 31–34*
> Spanish monarchs had long attempted to control the Church at the expense of Rome, but it was only in the eighteenth century that the 'Catholic Kings' successfully minimized the power of the papacy in Spain. The victory took the form of the Concordat of 1753, which bestowed on the Crown nearly universal patronage over the most important ecclesiastical benefices, a right hitherto shared in an uncomfortable relationship with Rome. Favouritism and influence played their parts in the ecclesiastical patronage of the Bourbons, but during the reign of Charles III the State used its powers to form a clerical establishment that accepted in large the royal vision of the Church's role in the reforming program. …
>
> Enlightened absolutism as it developed after 1750 suffered from internal contradictions. Absolute monarchy pressed forward to centralize power, eliminate the archaic, and devise policies capable of transforming the administration of the State and the economy; but it would not, indeed could not, tamper with a traditional social structure dominated by aristocratic and corporate privilege. In the end, the reforming initiatives of the Bourbons resulted in only a superficial resolution of national problems, but the utilitarian spirit with which the Crown and its bureaucracy approached reform influenced the State's ecclesiastical policies. …
>
> To foreigners visiting Spain for the first time, the number of priests, monks, friars and nuns appeared 'prodigious'. A massive clerical presence was obvious in the major towns. Barcelona alone had a

cathedral, eighty-two churches and chapels, twenty-six religious houses of men, eighteen of women, two oratories, a seminary, a tribunal of the Inquisition, and several smaller foundations. In Valencia 2,610 priests and religious lived in a population of approximately 80,000; in Seville the religious orders were so numerous that they could marshal 1,600 members to participate in the processions of Holy Week and Corpus Christi. But the impression of a nation overrun by priests, friars and nuns is misleading. The census of 1797 showed an ecclesiastical population of 128,778 in a total population of 10,5 million. But recent studies of ecclesiastical demography have noted that this figure includes a certain number of lay employees of the Church, such as sacristans and administrators. An adjusted total of 148,409, or approximately 1,5 percent of the general population, was not excessive; in some Catholic countries the proportion was higher (Note: the kingdom of Naples thus had nearly 50,000 secular priests in a population of approximately 5 million). …

In fact, the 22,000 priests with cure of souls faced their task with often inadequate pastoral training and financial circumstances distinctly inferior to those of bishops and canons. …

One institution still occupied a special place within Church and State, the Inquisition. Founded by Ferdinand and Isabella in 1478, the Council of the Supreme and General Inquisition, although established by papal decree, was in fact a royal body whose head was named by the Crown. Originally created to punish converted Jews and their descendants (*conversos*) suspected of secretly observing their old faith, the Inquisition gradually expanded its activity to include censorship and the punishment of heresy; witchcraft; sorcery; magic; superstitious practices; moral offences, such as bigamy and homosexuality; and immorality among the clergy. The Inquisition of the late fifteenth, sixteenth, and seventeenth centuries went implacably about its work of enforcing orthodoxy and morality … A recent examination of 50,000 cases between 1560 and 1700 shows that only 1 percent of those accused suffered the ultimate penalty; the incidence of execution was far higher in the Inquisition's first twenty years than at any later time. Secrecy coupled with the ability to strike at any moment, confiscate the property of condemned, and destroy careers for even minor offenses conspired to create the pervasive psychology of fear that lay behind the institution's ruthless effectiveness as a guardian of orthodoxy and morality. …

The history of the Inquisition in the eighteenth century has not been widely studied, and for good reasons. After a flurry of activity against *conversos* (often Portuguese merchants who had settled in Spain between

> 1720 and 1730), the cases coming before the Holy Office declined to the lowest levels in its existence. Thus, the Inquisition of Toledo (one of fourteen provincial tribunals) heard an average of 200 cases a year during the middle of the sixteenth century, 30 a year during the early seventeenth century, and only 3 or 4 a year by the end of the eighteenth. Moreover, charges showed a dramatic shift away from the most serious accusations of Judaism and Protestantism toward those focusing on superstition, morality, and erroneous and heretical 'propositions' that fell short of formal heresy. A survey of more than 4,000 cases taken to the Supreme Council during the eighteenth century shows that 43,5 percent dealt with 'propositions' (compared with 19,4 percent in the seventeenth century) and less than 10 percent dealt with Judaism and Protestantism (compared with 48,6 percent in the preceding century). ...
>
> It was, paradoxically, during Bertran's tenure as inquisitor general that the Inquisition aroused itself from its apparent lethargy to strike a spectacular blow reminiscent of the heady days of old. The arrest in a 1776 trial, and subsequent condemnation of a prominent royal official, Pablo de Olavide, on a charge of formal heresy shocked enlightened circles in Spain and Europe. That the former royal governor of the extensive province of Seville and superintendent of one of the king's favourite schemes (the creation of new settlements on the Sierra Morena) should disappear in the prisons of the Inquisition for two years without a trace and should then appear in the peaked cap and smock of the condemned to hear himself sentenced to eight years of confinement to a monastery and the confiscation of his property seemed to herald the beginning of a new age of inquisitorial fanaticism.
>
> Sensational as it was, however, the case did not lead to a general campaign of persecution against the enlightened circles of government and society with whom Olavide was identified. But it did reveal that the Inquisition was still capable of baring its teeth.

It became increasingly difficult – certainly more difficult than in the Middle Ages – for the state to justify the immunity of some citizens or foreigners from the general courts. The situation was, however, not the same everywhere. Some states were in transition from allowing a plurality of courts and laws to exist for their subjects based on their membership of a guild or religious community, to a centralized state where everyone was subjected to the same law. This was the situation in the modern Western states, which became increasingly different from Muslim states such as the Ottoman Empire using the *millet* system. The *millet* were autonomous self-governing religious communities of Christians and Jews under a personal law, with their own community courts. The Jewish communities scattered through Europe show the difficulties, but also the possibilities, for religious minorities in obtaining or maintaining recognition of their jurisdictional institutions in modern states. Their situation was difficult in Europe as they were struggling to achieve recognition as full citizens. In some states, they were allowed to apply Jewish law (whose most authoritative text was, since the middle of the sixteenth century, the *Shulhan Arukh* written by Joseph Karo, a victim of Spanish extradition living in Palestine). However, they could still choose to have their cases heard in the general courts, and cases between Jews and non-Jews were not heard in Jewish courts. Edward Fram discusses the main Jewish courts in Europe in the seventeenth and eighteenth centuries in the following text.

> *E. Fram, Jewish Law from the Shulhan Arukh to the Enlightenment, in N.S. Hecht, B.S. Jackson, S.M. Passamaneck, D. Piattelli and A.M. Rabello (eds), An Introduction to the History and Sources of Jewish Law, Oxford, Clarendon Press, 1996, 360–362*
>
> The extent of Jewish judicial autonomy varied from place to place and often reflected developments in the non-Jewish environment. For example, Jews enjoyed traditional forms of self-government in much of Southern, Central and Western Germany during the early to mid-seventeenth century. As the century progressed, however, the political doctrine of absolutism took hold in the German States and called for the elimination of independent entities within the State. In seventeenth century Venice, too, Jews faced opposition from a Government that was trying to exert its jurisdiction over all its citizens – including members of the Catholic clergy – in civil and criminal matters. Theorists argued that the prince must be recognized as the final authority in all temporal matters. Nevertheless, despite the interdictions of the Venetian Government, Jewish courts continued to try both civil and criminal cases there and even fined Jews who took their disputes to non-Jewish courts.
>
> Opposition to Jewish self-adjudication in civil and criminal matters was motivated not only by political considerations but by religious concerns as well. Many Christian thinkers, both Protestant and Catholic, believed that Jews were to be a subjugated people and that granting Jews judicial dominion over civil and criminal matters was incompatible with their lowly status. Muslim theologians, whose influence was steadily growing in the Ottoman Empire of the seventeenth century and who were obliged to humiliate the *dhimmi* (non-Muslim subjects of the Muslim State), also kept a wary eye on Jewish legal independence.

Even in states that demonstrated a benevolent attitude towards Jewish judicial control in civil and criminal matters, such as in Mantua and Tuscany, communities continually had to urge the authorities to enforce and augment their powers. Early in the seventeenth century, the Mantuan Jewish community strove to obtain official recognition of its decisions in civil matters as well as in all matters of personal status. Although the Government eventually recognized the authority of Jewish courts, it still allowed Jews to take matters to non-Jewish courts, which they did. The demands of Jewish law that Jewish litigants come before a rabbinic court that judged matters on the basis of Jewish Law were not always enough to outweigh the temptation of exploiting a discrepancy between Jewish law and the law of the land or the ease of going to a non-Jewish court. Nevertheless, Jews continued to go to non-Jewish courts leaving the community (from 1647 with the blessing of the Duke) to threaten such people with fines and punishments. As in Poland, cases between Jews and non-Jews were judged in a special court presided over by a Government-appointed non-Jewish judge. A Jew who violated the law of the state generally fell into the hands of the state. …

Similarly, in England – which, under Oliver Cromwell, readmitted Jews to its shores in 1656, after a hiatus of 362 years – Jewish communities were completely devoid of political power, and compliance with Jewish judicial rulings, as well as membership in the Jewish community itself, was strictly voluntary. With Jews enjoying full access to state courts and, at best, tenuous connection of many English Jews to the traditional community, rabbinic courts were generally left to deal with matters of personal status. By contrast, Polish Jewry boasted local, regional, and national councils each of which enacted ordinances ranging from rules governing the marketplace to sumptuary laws. Residents were obliged to observe such laws and each organ of Government had courts to ensure that they did.

While Jews continued to enjoy judicial autonomy in eighteenth century Poland prior to the country's partition and demise as an independent nation in 1795, Jewish courts in regions owned by Polish noblemen were not independent but were part of the landowner's own court system. Jews in these areas could appeal against decisions of Jewish courts to the landowner or his representatives, although rabbis were often invited to hear the appeals together with the landowner. Landowners were also known to interfere with Jewish courts if they believed it in their best interest. While rabbis opposed this loss of sovereignty, there was little that they could do to prevent it.

> In Western Europe, the mid-eighteenth century brought with it discussion of emancipation for the Jews and the notion that they would take their place as full citizens of the state and bring their legal dispute to state courts. Yet when French Jews attained full emancipation (September 1791) they tended to guard their ritual traditions and were not immediately drawn into French society. In Austria, however, Jewish legal autonomy was abolished in 1785 as part of the emancipation of Jews.

Beginning in the last centuries of the Middle Ages, modern states were built on a judiciary that was dependent on the sovereign – either a prince or, in an ever smaller number of cases, a republican form of government in cities like Venice. However, the progress of the movement towards a state-centered judicial system was uneven. Many special courts (ecclesiastical, seigneurial, Jewish) remained active during the seventeenth and eighteenth centuries. Religious courts maintained their control of matrimonial matters and cases related to the status of persons. In the case of the Spanish Inquisition, religious courts adjudicated cases of heresy and moral offenses. In the more centralized states, such as France, these matters were dealt with by royal courts, such as seigneurial or 'patrimonial' courts. The consistorial courts in Protestant countries were able to settle minor civil matters and participate in criminal matters. Of course, all of these courts were subject to appeal or review before state courts, but the pluralism of institutions, based upon privileges, tithes paid to the Church or corporate institutions, remained relatively strong in the period 1650–1775.

4.2 *Procedural Law*

More state codification and movement towards unification of the law within national legal systems also impacted procedural law during the period 1650 to 1789. The primary trend in continental Europe was towards a simplification of the rules inherited from the Roman-canonical procedures of the previous centuries. The 1667 French ordinance, promulgated under Louis XIV at the initiative of the Minister of Finance Jean-Baptiste Colbert, was the model of a codified law with the goal of harmonizing civil procedure. As a consequence, there would be in principle a stricter subordination of judges to royal law. It provided an oral summary process next to a written procedure, with an exchange of documents between the procurators of the parties in more complicated cases. R. van Caenegem explains the situation in Germany, where, as in Italy, the resistance to the old cumbersome procedures was strong before the first reforms increasing the powers of the judge were introduced in Prussia and Austria at the end of the eighteenth century.

> *R. van Caenegem, History of European Civil Procedure, Tübingen, J.C.B. Mohr, 1973, 92*
>
> In Germany procedural reform was the result of eighteenth century enlightened despotism, French occupation and nineteenth century liberalism. The dominating *gemeiner Prozess* ('common process') was criticized ... The excessive reliance on writing rendered impossible any directness between party and court, and rendered law suits cumbersome and long; so did the possibility of interlocutory judgments at the various stages of the process (with the possibility of frequent appeals) and the reigning *Eventualmaxime*, or principle requiring all alternatives to be given ...
>
> The secrecy of procedure shielded the activity of judges and practitioners from public scrutiny and criticism; the passive attitude of the judges was full of dangers for the unskilled ...; the terminology of the courts was of foreign origin and inaccessible to the ordinary citizen ...
>
> In Prussia Frederick William I (1713–1740) tried to achieve judicial and procedural reforms ... It was under Frederick the Great (1740–1786) ... that things began to move and move fast. At first the king ... introduced certain reforms within the existing framework ... (1747 and following years), intend[ing] to replace the cumbersome written procedure in simpler causes by the principle of orality. Later this was deemed insufficient and the reforming zeal of the king and his chancellor, von Carmer († 1801), helped by Svarez († 1798) led to the introduction of an entirely new procedural system, the First Book of the *Corpus Juris Fridericanum 'Von der Processordung'*, of 26 April 1781.
>
> This most remarkable system made the *officium judicis* the central element of the lawsuit: judges were obliged to protect the parties and to investigate independently and on their own authority the merits of the case, even if the parties were passive and made mistakes.

In the period under discussion, the inquisitorial process was introduced in a significant part of continental Europe. In France, through the 1670 ordinance on criminal procedure, for example. In many parts of Europe, there was a prohibition on counsel for the accused, who was thereby in a weak position in front of the judge who was going to decide the case. Many of the written rules were quite severe, allowing, for example, the use of torture. Under the influence of Enlightenment thinkers such as Montesquieu and Beccaria, some states abolished or restricted judicial torture. At the same time, as John Langbein shows, barristers began to appear in English assize courts, which sat at intervals in each county of England and Wales to administer the civil and criminal law, first to counsel prosecutors, then for defendants, and finally the adversarial process became more and more associated with the jury.

> *J.H. Langbein, The Origins of Adversary Criminal Trial, Oxford, Oxford University Press, 2003, 93 and 292*
> The landmark reform of the Treason Trials Act of 1696 … was the grant of defense counsel at trial. The Act allowed the accused 'to make his … full Defense, by Counsel learned in the law…' The seemingly innocuous term 'full defense' would become a point of contrast with the more limited right to defense council in cases of ordinary felony that the judges began to allow in the 1730s. Parliament would have to intervene again, in the Prisoner's Counsel Act of 1836, to extend full defense of counsel to felony acts.
>
> The 1696 Act requires the trial court 'or some Judge of that Court' upon the defendant's 'Request to assign to' him 'such and so many Counsel, not exceeding Two, as the [defendant] shall desire' …
>
> Across time, as the adversary dynamic unfolded and the altercation model of trial receded, it became even more exceptional for the court or the defendant to play a direct role in cross-examination of prosecution witnesses when the defendant was represented. In a rape case in 1775 the defendant is recorded asking the court's permission to pose 'two or three questions' to the prosecutor, after the prosecutor to utter 'that my counsel have no instructions about …' By the 1780s … the court was telling the defendant that if there were 'any questions omitted that you think proper to have your counsel ask, write them down and send them over … [D]o not you put the question yourself, but hand it to your counsel'. Garrow did not need the judge to deliver that message. In a case in 1784 his client, the defendant, spoke up during Garrow's cross examination of the accused, saying 'I wish to put another question to [the prosecuting victim]'. Garrow cut him off: 'Send the question to me in writing' he said.

As an aside, in comparison English procedure remained relatively unchanged in civil cases.

4.3 *Substantive Private Law*

Private law, as far as it was concerned with the status of persons, property, and contract, was less influenced by statutory law. Customs continued to regulate a large part of the rights of persons. Marriage, however, became increasingly regulated by state legislation. The relationship between parents and children was basically not a matter of law, whereas traditional rules continued to apply to successions.

Contract law, on the other hand, evolved under the influence of the Modern School of Natural Law. James Gordley explores the break with Aristotelian philosophy under the influence of Hume's sceptical philosophy. He argues that modern theorists severed the terms traditionally used in contract law like 'essences', 'substance', and 'nature' from their Aristotelian roots. The famous *Traité des obligations* written by the French law professor Robert-Joseph Pothier in 1761–1764 was one of the first works to, inspired by Grotius and Pufendorf, develop a 'general theory' of contract. He did not try to base law on natural law, but applied rationalist methods to existing law.

> *J. Gordley, The Philosophical Origins of Modern Contract Doctrine, Oxford, Clarendon Press, 1991, 120, 121, 125, 129 and 132*
> Hume tried to free his own discussion of contract law of a virtue of fidelity however disguised. There is no reason why a contract should be binding. The problem is to explain why people feel bound anyway. …
>
> … Pufendorf and Barbeyrac preserved the doctrines of the late scholastics while rejecting Aristotle. They rejected Aristotle without genuinely embracing the philosophy of Hobbes or Locke or even coming to terms with the problem these philosophers were raising. Thus, although they claimed that their legal doctrines rested on higher philosophical principles, these doctrines lost their original moorings in Aristotelian philosophy without finding a new philosophical anchorage. …
>
> Pufendorf was sympathetic to Descartes, and, indeed, was a pupil of a Cartesian. Barbeyrac admired Locke. They both asserted their independence of Aristotle and their dislike of scholasticism. Nevertheless, the revolt against Aristotle had a different significance for them than it did to philosophers such as Descartes, Hobbes and Locke …
>
> There is no doubt that Pufendorf and Barbeyrac believed they were engaged in an intellectual revolt begun by Grotius against the scholastic tradition. …
>
> Pufendorf and Barbeyrac could speak about the virtue of fidelity or about the essence, substance, or nature of a contract without considering closely what these terms could mean in the non-Aristotelian world they thought they were inhabiting.

With Domat and his 1689 *Lois civiles dans leur ordre naturel*, and later with Pothier, French doctrine contributed to new ideas on tort law. David Ibbetson considers that Domat did not realize a complete unification of tort law under the concept of 'faute',[23] but he took part in a process of developing more general rules about liability.

Commercial law, or the 'Law Merchant' in England, was an area affected by the development of commercial contracts, legal transfers from one country to another, and new kinds of state intervention based on mercantilist economic policy designed to minimize imports and maximize exports. Jean Hilaire shows that the 1673 French Commercial Ordinance can be considered the first commercial code in Europe.

> *J. Hilaire, Introduction historique au droit commercial, Paris, PUF, 1986, 68–69 (transl. by J.-L. Halpérin)*
> As soon as in 1670 Colbert had given Jacques Savary, a former Parisian trader, the responsibility to prepare an ordinance, based on two reports he had sent to him and on investigations made of the commercial courts, Savary put quill to paper. A commission, which had members of the Royal Council and tradesmen, discussed his project under the authority of the counselor Pussort, Colbert's uncle. The 'Edict on trade, wholesale business, and retailers' was published in Versailles in March 1673; designated by the contemporaries as the 'Ordinance on trade over land', also called *Trade Code* or *Savary Code*.
>
> The novelty of the work lay in the fact that the authors tried to provide coherence and overall unity to commercial law. It was the first attempt to bring together essential rules in State legislation. … The ordinance was commented on by jurists and gave birth to legal writing, which quickly appeared in the form of rather sterile commentaries. It also had a definite effect outside France's borders, as it was used as a model, for example, in 18th century Prussia.
>
> But the value of this legislation suffered due to the economic context (the prevailing recession) and its author's narrow perspective. First, in this short text (122 articles), significant gaps could not be avoided, and it did not pretend to be exhaustive; the subject-matter only concerns the persons involved (traders, apprentices, brokers), accounting books, companies, negotiable instruments (letters and orders …), execution and bankruptcy, and finally the procedure of the commercial courts.

23 David Ibbetson, Harmonisation of the Law of Tort and Delict: A Comparative and Historical Perspective, in Reinhard Zimmermann (ed.), Grundstrukturen des Europäischen Deliktsrechts, Baden-Baden, Nomos, 2003, 83–104.

In continental Europe, feudal duties for peasants remained very burdensome. The changes in land law were limited until the first attempts of enlightened despots to improve the condition of the peasantry. In Austria, Joseph II abolished personal serfdom, in Savoy, feudal duties could be redeemed by the peasants from 1771, and, of course, the French Revolution abolished feudal duties completely without compensation for the landlords (1793).

In the period 1650–1775, there were developments in the area of property rights, which gave owners (notably, the most wealthy landowners) the freedom to dispose of their property as they wished. In England, the 1660 *Tenure Abolition Act*, introduced during the Restoration period, changed the nature of several types of feudal tenure. The Act also simplified land law. It created two categories of estates: freeholds, which depended directly on the king, and copyholds, dependent on landlords. Because of the weakening of feudal ties, conditions developed that were favourable for the creation of markets, i.e., 'capitalist' agriculture through leasehold contracts and the enclosure of common pastures. These lands were transformed into private fields for innovative agriculture practices, which benefited the wealthy landlord. This process, which started as early as the beginning of the sixteenth century, caused a significant increase in land enclosures (many sheep farms were established) between the 1760s and the 1770s.

4.4 *Criminal Law*

The criminal law of the seventeenth and eighteenth centuries has a bad reputation due to its severity and arbitrariness. There was no 'criminal code' that provided legal certainty and knowledge of offences and penalties. Besides, judges could pressure the accused, who did not have a right to a defense, with violent measures. There is a traditional view that draws a contrast between the English criminal jury process and the quasi-disappearance of torture, with the continental inquisitorial procedure from the medieval period used first by the ecclesiastical courts and then by municipal and state courts.

It is true that the inquisitorial procedure, which was well established in France during the sixteenth century, was reinforced by the 1670 criminal ordinance of Louis XIV. It prohibited counsel from assisting the accused, but did allow the use of torture.

However, this situation changed even before the reformist legislation of the second half of the eighteenth century. First, the inquisitorial procedure became less rigorous in Spain, Italy, and the Netherlands. Counsel was allowed to be present, and torture became the exception. In Germany, under the 1532 *Carolina* (an imperial ordinance promulgated by Charles V) and other similar texts, criminal procedure continued to be based on a formal accusation by the victim or his/her family. But it did give the court the power to conduct its own investigation and base its decision on the facts, not just the interests of the parties.[24] Even in France, around 75% of criminal cases were brought by victims seeking financial compensation. However, they were also discouraged by the difficulties of initiating litigation. A rigorous procedure was used only for the more severe offences, and a 'civil' procedure was put in place for lesser crimes (called *petit criminel*). In some cases, counsel was admitted to submit a written defense to the judges, and the accused could submit 'supportive facts' (for example, an alibi) before the public hearing in court.

> *F. Lopez-Lázaro, 'No Deceit Safe in Its Hiding Place': The Criminal Trial in Eighteenth-Century Spain, Law and Society Review 20/3 (2002), 452, 455–460, 462–463, 475–477*
>
> The *Sala* is ideal for our purposes. Its civil and criminal jurisdiction of ten leagues stretched over the capital of the Spanish Empire during this period and extended in serious capital cases beyond Madrid to the Kingdom of Castile. The *Sala*'s fundamental structure was typical of Spanish courts: it contained the executive governor (the court's chief senior magistrate), eight to nine judges (*alcaldes*), a prosecutor (*fiscal*), a defense lawyer for the poor (*abogado de podres*), and various ushers, policemen, jailors and administrative assistants, all appointed by the Crown's principal governing body, the Council of Castile … Appeals of *Sala* decisions were only heard by the Council of Castile in exceptional cases.
>
> The actual trial procedure of the *Sala*, which was characteristic of most royal courts in the Spanish Empire, was developed over the course of centuries and diverged substantially at times from statute, or royal law. Because Spanish legal historians, particularly the doyens of Spanish law studies, Francisco Tomás Valiente and Alfonso García Gallo, have based their analyses exclusively on published statutes and legal manuals, their descriptions of actual practice are significantly flawed. An analysis of the legal drama of Spanish courts should begin with the real world of court practice as it is revealed, for example, in the *Sala*'s extensive archival records, and not with the more readily available published material …
>
> According to this liberal view, one of the most serious indictments was that eighteenth-century criminals had been tried unfairly because

24 See https://pages.uoregon.edu/dluebke/Witches442/ConstitutioCriminalis.html (accessed in August 2022).

sumarias, or investigations, were conducted in absence of legal counsel and before formal charges were made. Furthermore, suspects were jailed during the initial process, a nefarious Inquisition-like process. Even worse than these excesses, critics held, was the fact that the next phase in a case, the *plenaria* or trial, was in their view nothing more than a formality ... How historically accurate was this portrayal of a 'secretive inquisitorial procedural style' that permeated courts in the eighteenth century?

Whatever bias judges may have had during the investigation stage of a criminal case, suspects were not presumed guilty. Both the legal theory and legal practice of the eighteenth century testified to the truth of this assertion ... Eighteenth-century Spanish court theory followed continental law in naming the initial procedural control on a trial's legality *habeas corpus*. If irregularities arose in the initial investigations, lawyers on either side could appeal to the court that errors in procedure had vitiated the trial process ... The reality in the eighteenth century was that *habeas corpus* and convincing proof of wrongdoing had to be established before a case progressed from investigation to trial. In Spanish bureaucratic terms, this transition was called changing a file from *sumaria* to a *plenaria* stage ...

The procedure circumscribing nullification of trials for lack of *habeas corpus* exemplifies the court's strict adherence to the principle of unprejudiced adjudication. The step between the two stages of prosecution hinged on correctly turning the *sumaria* into a *plenaria*, a critical part of judicial ritual that guaranteed the discovery of unprejudiced evidence ... The judge under whose orders constables and notaries accumulated evidence presented the results of the *sumaria* to a panel of three to five of his peers. The *Sala* governor ensured that the *alcaldes*, or judges, never heard capital cases without a quorum of five, the number assigned by court custom ... The officiating magistrates determined whether the prosecution's case met the requirements of *habeas corpus* and also considered other important issues at this initial stage ... If the prosecution had a case, it would proceed to the *plenaria* stage. It was at this point that minors and the poor were assigned solicitors and legal counsel, and, in any case where it was legally justified, torture was recommended.

Significantly, the Madrid's court procedure did not arise from royal statute, which fact did not stop many jurists from recommending that the monarchy adopt its customary system of judging crime throughout the empire. As in many other things, royal authority was not troubled unduly by the unlegislated nature of Madrid's court; nor were the judges. That court custom and not royal law was responsible for the 'style' (customary trial procedure) and was accepted almost unquestioningly in the seventeenth and eighteenth centuries. It only became an issue when Royalist reform in the eighteenth-century empire claimed that governmental abuses were linked to such customary judicial practices ...

Because of the effective self-governing nature of the *Sala*, political reformers and modern historians alike have been unable to find traces of its legal procedure in most of the published records. Unwritten and unlegislated style, like a micro Spanish version of the famous unwritten English constitution, was everything to the legality of eighteenth-century proceedings.

According to the *Sala*'s style, minor criminal charges, such as misdemeanors, petty theft, and pickpocketing (*raterías*), were summarily judged at this point orally in the presence of the accused's solicitor and counsel, without the presence of the crown prosecutor. Toward the end of the eighteenth century, reforming ministers argued for an extension of this practice, making oral judgment more common throughout the court in minor criminal cases. But their attempts failed and differing local court practices continued fundamentally unchanged into the nineteenth century ...

The physical layout of the courthouse and its rooms clearly indicated that trials were far from 'secretive'. Court practice did control public participation, however, and much of this control was expressed in the jargon of theatricality, a fact that is not incidental to eighteenth-century perceptions of how sin was to be punished ...

Trial length did not affect as many people as critics claimed either. The overwhelming majority of accused did not rot in dungeons awaiting their sentencing and many indeed did not even stay incarcerated after the initial arrest. Out of 3,020 individuals indicted in the sample count examined for the years 1750–1802, 432 were released during the investigation ... under bail, placed under house arrest under oath, or bound over some other fashion. The length of the defense and prosecution did not seriously affect the personal freedom of many accused.

The Madrid court's procedure from 1750 to 1898 clearly did not fit the nineteenth-century stereotype. Elaborate measures were in place to ensure judicial impartiality and the frequent use of the courts by individuals and groups to prosecute those they believed guilty of sinful crime is proof that Spaniards did not find the criminal system 'repugnant'. Trials were also clearly orchestrated in the eighteenth century to solemnize and sanctify the public punishing of crime ...

> At least one important question arises from this discussion that is, unfortunately, beyond the scope of the present study. How far did the *Sala*'s system apply in the provincial and imperial areas of the Spanish monarchy? The secondary literature indicates that it may have been exceptional to a certain degree. There is clear evidence, however, that the *Sala*'s moral-cum-legal mythology of 'fair' trial procedure applied everywhere in the monarchy, at least in theory. More and more studies of colonial legal culture stress the common cultural norms that extended far and wide. There is growing evidence of the interconnectedness of legal institutions and religio-moral codes in the Spanish empire, a link that was perpetuated in local cultural customs. A procedure not unlike the *Sala*'s, for example, was characteristic of such a distant and disparate place as the New Mexico frontier.

How does this evolution compare with the English criminal law and the institution of the jury? The English system did not truly guarantee the defendant's rights, as most criminal cases were decided in a single day. Counsel for the prosecution and accused only began to, cautiously, make an appearance in the second half of the eighteenth century. The aforementioned *Bloody Code*, a compilation of statutory laws approved by Parliament during the eighteenth century which made all kinds of thefts subject to the death penalty was also a problematic feature of English criminal law.

Historians like Douglas Hay[25] have argued that criminal law was used as an instrument of repression by the ruling class of wealthy landowners to control the working class at the beginning of the industrial revolution. Legal historians like John H. Langbein have made the case that the thesis of a 'conspiracy' by the dominant class is exaggerated. He notes that the majority of victims of crimes were members of the working class, that the jury was not only composed of landowners, and that humane verdicts were not a rarity.[26]

> *J.H. Langbein, The Criminal Trial before the Lawyers, University of Chicago Law Review 45 (1978), 273, 276–277, 284–287, 296–297 and 314*
>
> For many centuries in England until quite lately, cases of serious crimes were routinely tried before itinerant justices at semi-annual assizes (literally, 'sittings') … [In the London court, called the Old Bailey, which was the equivalent of the provincial assize courts, only a single jury] commonly

25 E.P. Thomson, D. Hay, P. Linebaugh, J.G. Rule and C. Winslow (eds), Albion's Fatal Tree, London, Verso, 1976.

26 John H. Langbein, Albion's Fatal Flaws, Past and Present 98 (1983), 96–120.

tried dozens of cases at a single session, but most of the dozen jurors who sat at any one sessions were veterans of other sessions. Cockburn's comprehensive name index to the assize file makes it easy to illustrate this point for the assize courts on the Home Circuit in Elizabethan-Jacobean times … Thus, in a good but incomplete collection of OBSP [*Old Bailey Session Papers*] for the period 1720–1727, it is reported that on the Middlesex jury William Tame and Henry Goddard served six times, John Mills and Thomas Phillips five, and Edward Percival four. Many other names recur as often. In a vast metropolis jurors were recurrently drawn from a miniscule cohort.

A cardinal assumption that underlies the law of evidence and criminal procedure today is that jurors are inexperienced, and hence require to be and can be shielded, guided and controlled. But in early modern times most juries were full of jurors who were 'old hands' at the job, and at the Old Bailey those who were not experienced at the start of sessions were veterans at the end.

The substantive criminal law probably held few mysteries for these experienced jurors, especially since the comparatively uncomplicated but still nominally capital felony of larceny in its various forms constituted the vast bulk of Old Bailey cases. A few fact patterns recur endlessly in the OBSP reports: (1) a shoplifter is observed by the proprietor or by a bystander and apprehended in the act or in flight; (2) a silver tankard is missing from a pub just after the accused has used it; he is seized with it, or observed to leave with it, or attempts to pawn or sell it, or is found to have it in his lodgings; (3) household or commercial goods are missed, and a servant or apprentice is found with them or with the supposed proceeds; (4) money, jewelry, and/or clothing is taken in highway robbery; the accused is apprehended fleeing, or with the loot, or he is identified by an accomplice who turns state's evidence; and (5) a pleasure-seeking victim loses money or jewelry in a bawdy house or a pub while intoxicated; his erstwhile companion claims to have received the goods as favours in payment for sexual services. Old Bailey jurors must have been for the most as familiar with these plots and with the simple legal issues they presented as the professional judges who presided at the trials …

Ordinary criminal trials took place with what modern observers will see as extraordinary rapidity. We have already noticed that thirty-two cases were processed to verdict in the courtroom at the Old Bailey in the two-day sessions of December 1678. Throughout the next decades an average of twelve to twenty cases per session day went to jury trial …

In the 1660s the indistinct division of responsibility within the trial court between judge and jury produced a conflict that came to a head in 1670 in one of the most famous precedents in English law, *Bushell's Case*. The decision established the principle that jurors could not be fined for returning a verdict contrary to the instructions of the trial judge. Most of what has been written about the judge-jury relationship in our period has had *Bushell's Case* as the center-piece and has celebrated the triumph of jury autonomy over judicial authoritarianism.

Like so much of the political jurisprudence of the State Trials, *Bushell's Case* presents a distorted perspective on the ordinary criminal trial. The OBSP, which commence in the decade after *Bushell's Case*, show us that the judge exercised so much influence over the jury that it is difficult to characterize the jury as functioning autonomously; and that in the rare cases where judge and jury found themselves in conflict, the judge had ways to prevail without fining jurors. We shall suggest that the routine Old Bailey practice throws some light back on *Bushell's Case* itself.

(1) *Comment and instruction*. In the years we are studying the judge dominated jury trial. We have previously mentioned how, in lieu of counsel, the judge often served in effect as examiner-in-chief of both the witnesses and the accused. Both in this capacity as examiner, and especially when instructing a jury, the judge possessed what seems to have been a wholly unrestricted power to comment on the merits of the case. The judge was certainly under no duty to comment on the evidence, and in many cases he seems not to have bothered. Further, the OBSP reporters omitted much, probably most, of what the judges were saying to the juries; these harmonious internal workings of the trial court were of no particular interest to the OBSP readership. Nevertheless, over the years enough examples were transcribed to suggest the range of judicial comment. The judges' remarks show that they did not regard the jury as an autonomous fact-finder. The jury alone rendered the verdict, but the judge had no hesitation about telling the jury how it ought to decide. We find the jury routinely following the judge's lead in these cases ...

The OBSP also report numerous directed verdicts of acquittal, and some of these appear to turn on considerations of fact that would today be regarded as strictly within the province of the jury. The judge was not always so explicit about the outcome he desired; the jury seems to have been eager for the judge's guidance, and the judge could often content itself with uttering a broad hint of his view of the merits. In the case of Henry Nowland and Thomas Westwood (1730), tried for highway robbery, '[t]he Court observed, That the Witnesses which appeared to the Prisoners' Characters seemed to stand in need of some Persons of Reputation to support their own; the Jury found them both guilty, Death'. William Harris (1729) was prosecuted for theft when he returned a purse to its owner that he claimed to have found; the purse contained £ 29 when he returned it rather than the £ 46 that the owner claimed to have lost. 'Upon the whole, it appeared to the Court, That the Prisoner might have kept all the Money, and probably have come to no Damage, and the greatest part of it being returned, the Jury acquitted him' ...

(5) *Remedying conviction-against-direction.* If the jury did convict against the wishes of the judge, the judge could still defeat the verdict. Hale says that 'if the jury will convict a man against or without evidence, and against the direction or opinion of the court, the court hath this salve, to reprieve the person convict before judgment, and to acquaint the king, and certify for his pardon'. The OBSP, which were hurried to press while the trials were fresh, would therefore appear before the pardon process had run its course. We see it in a complementary OBSP pamphlet devoted to the sensational case of Francis Charteris (1730), which was published after the royal view. Charteris, a noted rake with important political connections, was convicted of raping a servant; six weeks later, 'His Majesty, having heard severally the Opinions of the ... Judges upon the said Case, who also agreed in their Report, was pleased ... to order that' Charteris was pardoned. In the eighteenth century royal review of judicial recommendations for pardon and commutation became a regular and systematic part of ordinary criminal procedure. Juries knew of it, indeed they sometimes made use of it themselves by returning a guilty verdict to which they coupled a request that the court recommend the convict to royal mercy. For example, Jane French (1732) fell into bad company and aided a theft of her master's goods, but turned in her cohorts when she was detected. She was convicted and sentenced to death. 'But both the Jury and the Prosecutor recommended her to the Court for a favourable Report to his Majesty, and she escaped the sentence. ...'

There is a special irony in this rationale; The judge was so dominant that he could admit the lawyers as an act of grace. Perhaps it was not foreseen that the power to admit them could not be kept perpetually in judicial discretion as the precedents accreted. It was certainly to be foreseen that the lawyers could alter the dynamic of jury trial in the most fundamental way, that they could break up the ancient working relationship of judge and jury and cost one judge his mastery of the proceedings. In the Old Bailey at the end of our period in the mid-1730s there was still hardly a sign that adversary procedure and the law of evidence lay just ahead.

Even if the work of Beccaria was the beginning of an independent penal doctrine separated from Roman sources, and the point of departure for the development of imprisonment as the chief form of punishment for modern penal systems (the Penitentiary Act introduced state jails for the first time in England in 1779), this new trend did not immediately lead to the decline of state social repression. Nor did it end the use of legal instruments to control the working classes. However, it can explain how Montesquieu's appeal for less repression was praised by Blackstone, who approved of the Penitentiary Act. Beccaria's criticism of traditional criminal law, including his rejection of 'imaginary crimes' like heresy or homosexuality, was applauded by, amongst others, Jeremy Bentham (1748–1832), one of the most famous early theoreticians of utilitarianism.

O.F. Robinson, T.D. Fergus, W.M. Gordon, European Legal History: Sources and Institutions, Oxford, Oxford University Press, 2020, 410–412
In France men such as Montesquieu, Voltaire and Rousseau were also including the penal law in their analyses of society, analyses undertaken in the rational philosophical mood. Cesare Bonesana, Marchese de Beccaria (1738–94), the most notable figure in penal reform, produced his ideas under their influence … In 1764 Beccaria published his *Dei Delitti e delle Pene* (*On Crimes and Punishments*). … Beccaria accepted the theory of the social contract, and consequently the need to defend the social order thus established … The duty of the ruler was to prevent violations of the social contract; to this end he should ensure that laws were clear and simple, that all citizens had an interest in their enforcement, that all men were treated alike and that education was made widely available. Before any punishment was inflicted there must be certainty that a crime had been committed and committed by the accused. Secret accusations and the use of informers should be forbidden, and so too should the arbitrary exercise of a judge's discretion … Penalties therefore should not be inhumane; confiscation was unjust because it affected the victim's family and, above all, the death penalty was unjust and ineffective, life imprisonment, being continuing and visible, was also more of a deterrent …

C. Beccaria, An Essay on Crimes and Punishments, London, J. Almon, 1767, 7–8 and 102–105 (anonymous English translation)
Every punishment, which does not arise from absolute necessity, says the great *Montesquieu*, is tyrannical. A proposition which may be made more general, thus. Every act of authority of one man over another, for which there is not an absolute necessity, is tyrannical. It is upon this then, that the

sovereign's right to punish crimes is founded; that is, upon the necessity of defending the public liberty, entrusted to his care, from the usurpation of individuals; and punishments are just in proportion, as the liberty, preserved by the sovereign, is sacred and valuable. Let us consult the human heart, and there we shall find the foundation of the sovereign's right to punish; for no advantage in moral policy can be lasting, which is not founded on the indeliable sentiments of the heart of man. Whatever law deviates from this principle will always meet with a resistance, which will destroy it in the end; for the smallest force, continually applied, will overcome the most violent motion communicated to bodies ...

The useless profusion of punishments, which has never made men better, induces me to inquire, whether the punishment of *death* be really just or useful in a well governed state? What *right*, I ask, have men to cut the throats of their fellow-creatures? Certainly not that on which the sovereignty and laws are founded. The laws, as I have said before, are only the sum of the smallest portions of the private liberty of each individual, and represent the general will, which is the aggregate of that of each individual. Did any one ever give to others the right of taking away his life? Is it possible, that in the smallest portions of the liberty of each, sacrificed to the good of the public, can be contained the greatest of all good, life? If it were so, how shall it be reconciled to the maxim which tells us, that a man has no right to kill himself? Which he certainly must have, if he could give it away to another. But the punishment of death is not authorised by any right; for I have demonstrated that no such right exists. It is therefore a war of a whole nation against a citizen, whose destruction they consider as necessary or useful to the general good. But if I can further demonstrate, that it is neither necessary nor useful, I shall have gained the cause of humanity. The death of a citizen cannot be necessary but in one case. When, though deprived of his liberty, he has such power and connections as may endanger the security of the nation; when his existence may produce a dangerous revolution in the established form of government. But even in this case, it can only be necessary when a nation is on the verge of recovering or losing its liberty; or in times of absolute anarchy, when the disorders themselves hold the place of laws. But in a reign of tranquillity; in a form of government approved by the united wishes of the nation; in a state well fortified from enemies without, and supported by strength within, and opinion, perhaps more efficacious; where all power is lodged in the hands of a true sovereign; where riches can purchase pleasures and not authority, there can be no necessity for taking away the life of a subject.

The reduction of state repression was, undoubtedly, accelerated by the impact of Beccaria's work, which was translated into French and English. It was supported by many philosophers and reformers (the young Bentham was a great admirer of Beccaria). Torture to obtain confessions was, for example, abolished in Sweden by King Gustav III in 1774. But the Austrian grand-duke of Tuscany Leopold (Joseph II's brother and successor) in 1786 promulgated a penal law which did have the death penalty. In 1787 the Austrian Penal Code reserved the death penalty for the crime of sedition. It was, however, the next step towards the codification of crimes and penalties.

4.5 *Public Law*

Despite the fact that there are Roman texts on the notion of *ius publicum*, and many questions about public powers were dealt with in the texts of Justinian's *ius civile*, European lawyers often did not distinguish private from public law during the Middle Ages and sixteenth century. Lawyers were not yet ready to think of state authority as bound by legal norms. Works on the *ius publicum* and *ius publicum imperii* in the laws of the German Holy Empire, and on the *ius publicum universale,* which included elements of natural law and the law of nations (*ius gentium*) appeared in German countries. First in the writings of Althusius (1557–1638), then those of university professors such as Rhetius, Cocceji, Boehmer and Moser, who taught the *ius publicum* and whose students published dissertations on this matter.[27] During the eighteenth century, this scholarship spread to some parts of Italy, notably Austrian Lombardy. However, in most parts of Europe *public law* was not taught until the French Revolution. Even the wording *droit public* remained rare in France until the second half of the eighteenth century; it is scarcely used by Montesquieu (see *Esprit des lois*, X, 3). He preferred the term *droit politique* when he formulated his revolutionary ideas about making private law subject to the fundamental principles of the political regime in an important text critical of absolute monarchy and a single sovereign. He proposed that these 'fundamental laws' of the kingdom would prevent despotism and help control the royal power. In England, neither Matthew Hale nor William Blackstone used the expression 'public law' when they dealt with the 'constitution' of the monarchy.

However, it is possible to speak of public law in the period beginning in the 1650s and ending with the American and French Revolutions to characterize

---

27 Karl Härter, Ius publicum und Reichsrecht in den juristischen Dissertationen mitteleuropäischer Universitäten der Frühen Neuzeit, in Jacques Krynen and Michael Stolleis (eds), Science politique et droit public dans les facultés de droit européennes (XIIIe–XVIIIe siècle), Frankfurt am Main, Klostermann, 2008, 489.

the development of specific rules to organize the state, its administrative organs, and the control and status of public servants. The common element of some of the 'ancient constitutions' that were kept was the limitation of the prince's powers through institutions representing the 'estates', which can be understood as the first kind of public law. This emergence of a corpus of rules for defining the royal prerogative and the competences of the assembled estates or Parliament took place in England (with the evolution towards a parliamentary regime after the Glorious Revolution) as well as in some German states. James Allen Vann shows how the development of the state apparatus in seventeenth and eighteenth century Württemberg combined development of central agencies like a privy council with the reinforcement of the importance of the *Landtag*, a traditional assembly representing the lay notables and heads of Protestant religious institutions. In many German states, security became one of the main areas of state action and this led to an increase in police ordinances. In the theoretical discourse, security came to be seen as one of the central objectives of a well-ordered police state. This focus laid the foundation for the expansion of an administrative state which not only sought to provide the safety policing offered, but security for all kinds of events ranging from natural disasters to house fires and insurance. In this way, the ideal of a 'good police' (*Gute Policey*) provided the basis for a wide variety of general legislation.[28]

> *J.A. Vann, The Making of a State: Württemberg, 1593–1793, Ithaca and London, Cornell University Press, 1984 38–39, 45–46, 50–53, 58–59, 85, 87, 88–89, 118, 211, 256, 270–271 and 286–288*
> The peculiarities of historical compromise, like the geographic and economic organization of the duchy, supported in Württemberg a political system that in turn both reflected and shaped the contemporary social structure … For local institutions contributed substantially to the formation of powerful interest groups that sought in turn to exercise their influence with which ducal administration had to reckon. The *Amt*, or *Vogtei* as it was sometimes called, constituted the most basic of these local political units and around that organization crystallized a powerful domestic unit known as the *Ehrbarkeit*. It was these local leaders who in course of the sixteenth century gained control over the territorial diet and became the principal counterweight to ducal power …

28 Karl Härter, Security and 'Gute Policey' in Early Modern Europe: Concepts, Laws, and Instruments, Historical Social Research 35/4 (2010), 41–65 (https://www.jstor.org/stable/25758857; accessed in August 2022).

The fifty-eight Aemter varied widely in size and importance … Regardless of scale every Amt contained a relatively substantial urban unit where the *Amtmann*, or *Vogt*, as the ducal commissioner was called, had his seat. One can think therefore of local ducal administration as resting upon a network of market towns, within which an official appointed by the duke carried out his commands and from which they went into the surrounding countryside to provide such services and to extract such resources as had been determined by the state. In both the town and the outlying villages (*Dörfer*) the *Amtmann* dealt with established administrative structures over which he had only varying degrees of control. Towns usually maintained two elective boards to carry out the responsibilities of local government: a *Gericht* that functioned as a criminal court of first instance for the entire *Amt* and handled civil litigation in the town, as well as appeals from the village courts; and a *Rat* that advised on the task of daily municipal administration …

The Württemberg constitution, personified in the Landtag, rested on an agreement worked out in 1514 between the estates and Duke Ulrich (1530–1550) which became famous in Württemberg history as the *Tübinger Vertrag*. Its specific terms were complicated and spoke in large part to details of only immediate concern, but it also assented to principles with long-term significance for political life in the duchy. In particular, the estates agreed to accept responsibility for liquidating government debts … In exchange for this acknowledgment the estates raised some immediate cash money and set up a permanent treasury for amortizing the remaining debt … In addition Ulrich recognized the rights of the estates to levy taxes and to participate in the supervision of the territorial administration. He also promised to consult the estates prior to any declaration of war …

Tradition stipulated that two delegates represent each *Amt* at the diet. One delegate was always the *Amtmann* who, though he usually belonged to the local establishment, held his office from the duke rather than by election and was regarded at the *Landtag* as a ducal creature. The other … came from the ranks of the *Landschaften*. By law, representatives from both village and town could stand for elections as delegates, but more often than not urban oligarchs managed to exclude their rural counterparts and to elect as second delegate a man of the *Ehrbarkeit* …

The withdrawal of the knights left the Württemberg prelates as the second estate of the duchy; and this group, unlike the knights, participated in territorial politics from a base in the *Landtag* … The Reformation ended the financial autonomy of this group and radically redefined its composition. Bishops, as such, were dismissed, and the episcopal hierarchy abolished. Monastic houses suffered dissolution and the loss of all endowment and political influence. An exception was made for the fourteen largest and most influential of the male establishments. These houses continued to operate with their endowments, more or less intact, but they functioned in a quite different manner, serving the duchy now as schools and preparatory colleges for advanced theological students at Tübingen. Two officials, appointed directly by the duke, presided of each former monastery. One was a Lutheran divine who took the ancient title of prelate or abbot and supervised the spiritual and intellectual life of the establishment. By virtue of his office, he also sat in the territorial diet as an estate of the realm … As opposed to the Aemter, whose delegates constituted the first estate and whose number grew in this period from forty-five to more than sixty-five, the prelates remained constant at fourteen … On the Executive Committee (*Kleiner Ausschuss*), the governing board of the diet, the prelates occupied two seats; the burghers six. An identical ratio obtained on the larger council (*Grösserer Ausschuss*), where four prelates sat with twelve burghers …

The Stuttgart government had a structural organization similar to that of most German territories. Four central departments directed routine business: the chancellery (*Kanzlei*), the judicial council (*Oberrat*), the treasury (*Rentkammer*), and the church council (*Kirchenrat*) …

Curiously it was the territorial estates rather than the ruler who provided the final impetus for the establishment in 1629 of a permanent privy council … The bureaucracy in place in Württemberg on the eve of the Thirty Years War, one that had emerged in the previous half-century, had drawn firm lines of control between the embryonic order of bureaucratic officials and the autocratic prince … Furthermore, departmental heads had no officially constituted board on which they could work together to marshal departmental energies behind a coordinated perspective. In this sense one can think of the Württemberg government as centralized in the concentration of political responsibility but compartmentalized in the carrying of this responsibility.

Whereas the late-Renaissance princes strove to rule authoritatively and to free themselves from their territorial estates, the government of Eberhard III, who ruled as eighth duke of Württemberg from 1633 to 1674, took a different direction. Eberhard himself set the new course when he proclaimed that the prince and his estates were *correlativa*, the holders of a correlative power that bound them together indivisibly. He accompanied this emphasis upon shared sovereignty with a reluctance to promote innovative politics over the opposition of the estates, so that his reign constituted a period of efflorescence for the Württemberg Landtag ... In this way Eberhard turned the privy council into a mediating force between prince and principality and created for the first time in Württemberg a central college to which all agencies of the government reported. As with so much that Eberhard did, these reforms were not in themselves part of a larger program of state building. The council had no legislative power like that of the French *conseil d'État*. But its presence rendered the role of the monarch more effective and made possible a more systematic operation of the government.

The status of the privy council, however, now changed. Carl Alexander [1733–1737] was a convert to Roman Catholicism and was married to a Thurn and Taxis princess who shared his religious convictions ... In order to secure the succession, Eberhard Ludwig had required Carl Alexander to negotiate a religious settlement with the territorial estates known in Württemberg history as the *Reversalien* ... Carl Eugen [Carl Alexander's son] took over the government officially in 1744, at the age of sixteen, and ruled until his death in 1793. For the first decade of the reign he left the administration in the hands of his privy councillors ... Personal rule became official policy in 1758. At this time Carl Eugen created the *Staats- und Cabinettsministerium* for the direction of the government ... He allowed the privy council to continue its deliberations but turned the board into a clerical clearinghouse ... The cabinet functioned independently of the great bureaucratic offices; it was staffed entirely at the duke's pleasure and accountable only to him.

Under the auspices of the emperor and the Reichshofrat, representatives of the concerned parties negotiated the final settlement. In the winter of 1770 they forwarded the summation of their six years of labor to Stuttgart for ratification by the duke and his estates. By any standard the terms of the *Erbvergleich* constituted a defeat for the monarchy ... The settlement fixed the annual military budget at 460,000 florins, a sum that could support a standing army of no more than 3,000 soldiers ... At the level of state politics the *Erbvergleich* reaffirmed the Erberhardline principle of correlative sovereignty for the duchy. The duke was obliged to acknowledge his estates and their executive committee as the '*corpus representativum* of the whole beloved fatherland' and to promise that he would deal with them 'in the time-honored ways of negotiation' (*in altüblichen modus tractandi*). Moreover, the duke agreed to make no changes in the constitution of the legal code (*Allgemeine Landesgesetze und Ordnungen*) without the approval of the estates.

The French absolutist monarchy provided another example of the development of a substantial 'administrative law' designated as *police.* An example of this can be found in the *Traité de la police* published in 1705 by Nicolas Delamare. This was part of increased centralization and the creation of new types of royal agents. The complex organization of the *Conseil du roi* (King's Council), an institution formally deprived of the power to make decisions and given only consultative functions in the service of the king by the reforms of Louis XIV, gave birth to a set of rules for the institutional framework, process of law-making, and relations with public servants across the whole kingdom. From 1661, with the abolition of the office of 'principal minister', Louis XIV personally appointed the members for every meeting of the *Conseil d'en haut,* the most important institution for discussing political, diplomatic, and military affairs. Another governmental council presided over by the king himself, the *Conseil des dépêches*, brought together the four *Secrétaires d'État* (whose 'departments' were Foreign affairs, War, Navy, and *Maison du roi*), the *Contrôleur general des finances* and, especially during the reign of Louis XV, two State Counsellors. The role of the *Conseil royal des Finances*, a similar institution devoted to financial matters, dimished at the end of the reign of Louis XIV (1715) and declined even more dramatically during the reign of Louis XV. The *Conseil ordinaire des finances*, a large council presided over by the Chancellor and composed of the Counsellors of State, disappeared early – between 1680 and 1690. All these governmental councils provide evidence for the decline of the 'judicial monarchy', symbolized by the Chancellor's fate, whom Louis XIV excluded from the *Conseil d'en haut* in favour of an 'administrative monarchy'. That is to say, a bureaucracy directed by the *Contrôleur général des finances*, which made decisions in the form of '*arrêts en finance*' – formally decisions by the Council but in actuality made by the offices of the *Contrôleur général des finances*.[29] On the other hand, civil litigation belonged to the *Conseil du roi* by way of 'cassation' or 'evocation'. At the end of the *ancien régime*, in 1777, Necker's reforms created a *Comité contentieux des finances*, which announced the emergence of a court circuit devoted to administrative matters.[30]

A comparable evolution occurred in Austria during the periods of 'Enlightened Despotism' during the reign of Maria Theresa, Joseph II, and Leopold II. Werner Ogris discusses the relationship between centralized institutions established to curtail the estates' powers and the influence of the

29 Michel Antoine, Le Conseil du Roi sous Louis XV, Genève, Droz, 1970, 631.

30 Jean-Louis Mestre, Introduction historique au droit administratif français, Paris, PUF, 1985, 200–211.

nobility, but also the functional separation of powers between administrative and judicial organs and the emergence of a new type of state agents, and their rights and duties under public law.

> *W. Ogris, The Habsburg Monarchy in the Eighteenth Century: The Birth of the Modern Centralized State, in Antonio Padoa-Schioppa (ed.), Legislation and Justice, Oxford, Oxford University Press, 313–314, 319, 324, and 326–328*
> This process of unification and centralization which, of course, called for and, at the same time, was brought about by dramatic changes in constitutional and administrative structures (without, however, totally destroying them), was to be the achievement of mainly three rulers: of Maria Theresa (1740–80) and of her two sons and successors, Joseph II (1765/80–90) and Leopold II (1790–92). Although widely different in character and temperament and by no means identical in their ideology or their outlook on philosophy and state affairs, mother and sons aimed at one main and common goal: welding their multiple and multifarious possessions into a centralized and unified state.
>
> In doing so let us return to the crucial point of reform: the deprivation of the Estates (*Landstände*) coupled with their removal from power. This process concentrated on two main elements: the formation of a standing army of some 108,000 men and the provision of a sum of 14 million gulden for their support. This was a relatively modest demand compared to the monarchy's human and financial resources, but the heinous nature of this plan showed itself in the way these contributions to a standing army should be assessed and collected. Until the mid-eighteenth century the Estates' contribution had to be negotiated with the central government every single year. Count Haugwithz's plan called for an agreement covering a ten-year period at a time. Worse still, from the Estates' point of view, the contributions were not, as hitherto had been the case, to be collected by the administrative staff of the Estates themselves, but by the sovereign's administrative machinery. In return, the Estates were released from taxes and contributions in kind
>
> The extension of the central state's influence, authority and sphere of competence did not, in itself, procure (more) effective and relevant handling of public affairs. It had to be accompanied and supplemented by the establishment of corresponding administrative structures and administrative bodies. Clearly, in the early years of Maria Theresa's reign, the infrastructure of the official machinery left much to be desired

at least from the point of view of the Viennese centralists. At that time the internal administration was carried out (among others) by two main administrative bodies, namely by the Austrian and the Bohemian Court Chancelleries (*Österreichische und Böhmische Hofkanzlei*), both located in Vienna and both powerful and influential strongholds of the upper nobility of Bohemia (and Moravia) and the traditional Austrian territories.

Consequently, the two Court Chancelleries, the one for Bohemia and Moravia (*Böhmische Hofkanzlei*), the other for the German Hereditary lands (*Österreichische Hofkanzlei*) were first put aside, and then completely abolished. Their place was taken by two new administrative bodies, the *Oberste Justizstelle* and the *Directorium in publicis et cameralibus*. Both administrative 'superstructures' were composed of several public officials (*Kollegialbehörden*) and both were filled with newly appointed public servants, who had no or few feudal ties and obligations. As members of a relatively young and rising social group, they owed their individual loyalty to the state-sovereign and thus became the spearhead of reforms.

Both bodies, the *Oberste Justizstelle* and the *Directorium*, had territorial jurisdiction (*örtliche Zuständigkeit* = territorial competence) over the whole of the monarchy (except Hungary, and its 'satellite' territories, and the Austrian Netherlands). Thus, for the first time in the history of the monarchy, a (constitutional and administrative) entity comprising the Austrian territories and the territories of the Crown of Saint Wenceslas was brought about. In other words, the two new authorities represented the organizational point of crystallization for a unified Austro-Bohemian state.

As for material competence (*sachliche Zuständigkeit*), the two new bodies translated into reality Maria Theresa's idea of separating the judiciary from the administrative branch of government. The *Oberste Justizstelle* served as higher court of appeal and, at the same time, as the highest and central authority in all (other) matters concerning the judiciary (such as the drafting of laws and codifications and of the sovereign's mandates and patents). The *Oberste Justizstelle*, in this way, continued to exist in its original form for another century. It was abolished as late as 1848–50, when the revolution brought about a constitutional change that had been long overdue ... This again underlines the fact, that one hundred years ago it had not been the idea of a separation of powers so propagated by Montesquieu, that stood sponsor to the creation of the

Oberste Justizstelle, but quite different considerations, that had nothing to do with a system of checks and balances.

As for the *Directorium*, it was meant to be and ultimately was in fact the sovereign's stronghold in the field of internal and financial administration. Originally organized on the model of the Prussian *Generaldirectorium*, it was soon to undergo substantial changes in its scope of jurisdiction and of its internal structure and organization. These reforms, however, left the basic objective of the two governing bodies unchanged: to transform the monarch's will into practice and to weld the various territories of the monarchy into a unified and centrally governed state

All this could not have been effectuated without the purposeful employment of a 'new weapon' in the modern state's struggle against feudal structures, namely, the *Staatsdiener* or public official. Public officials, as opposed to the feudal hierarchy, were not, of course, an entirely new phenomenon in the mid-eighteenth century. They had been employed by kings and princes, by cities, and, especially, by the Church since the Middle Ages and, from then onwards, had played an important part in developing an effective and rationale public administration within the framework and in the limits of the circumstances. Now, however, in the wake of reform (and at the same time as a prerequisite for it) the number of public officials was dramatically increased and their sphere of action considerably enlarged. A massive and sometimes ruthless employment policy channelled loyal civil servants into practically all key posts in the administrative machinery. In doing so, Maria Theresa and Joseph II very rapidly succeeded in pushing aside all traditional administrative structures, especially those of the Estates, and in establishing a truly bureaucratic system of government.

Against this background it was no accident that the reign of these two rulers saw the improvement and the definition of the legal status of public servants. A great number of regulations procured something like social security for the state's servants, such as financial relief for the civil servant himself and/or his family in case of illness or death. In 1781, for instance, the *Pensionsnormale* (Retirement Decree) guaranted old age pensions to all civil servants which was more than most other comparable states at this time provided.

From the reign of Peter the Great (1682–1725), Russia clearly developed public law and institutions under the control of the monarch accompanied by an attempt to reform private law through new statutes. However, these new statutes encountered social resistance, especially within the nobility, and many of them remained ineffective – a situation comparable to the difficult process of the emergence of modern states in Western Europe during the fifteenth and sixteenth centuries.

L. Hugues, Peter the Great. A Biography, New Haven, London, Yale University Press, 1998, 211–213

Central government by and large retained its Petrine outlines, the Senate and the procurator-general surviving until 1917 and the collegiate system until the early nineteenth century, but other administrative reforms quickly withered because they had never taken root. Among the first victims was much of the paraphernalia of provincial offices and posts with Germanic names. Peter's ambitious multi-tiered system of new courts and his attempt to separate the administrative and judicial systems also proved a failure, mainly as a result of the lack of qualified personal and conflict with established local power bases. In 1727 the courts of appeal were closed and military governors resumed control in law as well as in fact. Peter may not have mastered the provinces and the periphery of his empire, but neither did his successors. They continued to experience both misconduct by local officials and widespread popular disobedience, at worst major outbreaks encompassing whole regions, of which the most devastating was the Pugachev revolt of 1773–74. Catherine II's response was the Statute on Provincial Administration (1775), which acknowledged that Russia's problem was not so much an overarching, all-powerful state as under-administration, which hampered both the government's ability to control the population and the people's access to redress and protection. This and other measures sought, with limited success, to harness the voluntary efforts of the nobility in the provinces, something which Peter tried to do but failed, mainly because his nobles were always on the move and under severe pressure.

Peter's belief that the best means of promoting the common good was to make laws, and plenty of them, proved illusory. In volume, Peter's edicts surpassed those of his Muscovite predecessors many times over, but his success in enforcing laws was patchy and his efforts to codify the laws came to nothing, so the cast body of old and new legal acts remained scattered in the archives of state departments. Often even the judges, who received no special training, did not know the laws. The Military and Naval Statutes, which at least existed in single published editions, were used for both civil and criminal cases well into the eighteenth century and Tsar Alexis's law code of 1649 continued to operate. Catherine II's attempt to codify the laws also failed, although she presented the exercise

> in a Petrine framework. A miniature portrait (1770–80) of Catherine writing her 1767 *Instruction to the Legislative Commission* features a marble bust of Peter on the desk beside her. Codification was achieved only in the 1830s.
>
> After Peter's death some of his own favourite legislation was repealed. This was the fate in 1731 of the Law on Single Inheritance of 1714, never popular with the land-owning class. The 1722 law on the succession to the throne survived to determine the accession of six monarchs – Catherine I, Peter II, Anna, Ivan VI, Peter III and Paul – while two others (Elizabeth and Catherine II) used palace coups to establish their claims, then evoked Peter's spirit. The law was repealed in 1797 by Paul, who had lived in fear of his mother disinheriting him in favour of one of his sons. Thereafter for the rest of the Romanov era primogeniture was restored, which meant, among other things, no more woman rulers.
>
> It suited both the rulers and the elite to live with amended versions of some of Peter's civil reforms, for example the Table of Ranks, which survived to the end of imperial Russia. Peter did not intend to do away with a hereditary elite in principle, nor did he do so in practice. In 1730, for example, of the 179 officials in the top four classes of the Table, nine-tenths were descended from old Muscovite families and one-third from men who recently had been boyars. After Peter's death it became harder to become a hereditary noble by being promoted within the civilian ranks. At the same time, it suited both the servitors and the state to reduce the period of compulsory service. In 1736 service was reduced to twenty-five years and in 1762 the requirement was abolished, although state service remained a way of life for most nobles.

In France, the development of specific rules governing public administration was a weapon used by the king against the traditional apparatus of state officials (*officiers de justice* or judges and *officiers de finances* or administrators of royal finances). During the sixteenth and seventeenth centuries, they had acquired various privileges (for example, the power to sell their office or transmit it to an heir) related to the patrimonial nature of those offices. There was a large group of more than 80,000 *officiers* who could only lose their office if they committed a crime. If the king wanted to replace an officeholder, he had to compensate them, which was costly. As it was difficult to discipline this large group of officeholders, the French monarchy developed a small but efficient superstructure of counselors of the state. It consisted of royal commissioners (*intendants*) and subaltern agents (*commis*) in the ministries and in the financial administration, and included the *ferme générale*, a semi-public organization directed by private persons which had the right to collect indirect taxes in exchange for an advance payment to the royal Treasury.[31] The French monarchy began to establish modern bodies of public servants with a specific public status in the second half of the eighteenth century. There were the *commis*, who were subject to strict discipline and received government pensions, as well as the engineers, recruited by public competition within the context of the *École royale des ponts et chaussées* (created in 1747) and the *École des mines* (created in 1783).

As far as American constitutional law is concerned, one has to keep in mind that one of the main causes of the conflict between the American colonists and British rulers was that the former contested the Westminster Parliament's competence to legislate for the colonies (especially when creating new taxes). They considered themselves free polities, and their citizens only a had personal allegiance to the English king.

4.6 *Informal Justice*

There is no doubt that, despite the progress of state institutions and the development of a network of judicial institutions (including seigniorial or patrimonial courts, which were a legacy of the Middle Ages, ecclesiastical courts, municipal courts, and merchant courts), a share of the criminal and civil conflicts remained outside the scope of formal justice. This matter is the subject of a debate among social historians. They focus on these informal systems of regulation, and describe them as the 'real' justice, as opposed to the 'theoretical' discourse of jurists and legal historians. The latter traditionally concentrate on legal rules and distinguish them from non-legal practice.

Recent studies have focused on what has become known as the Great Litigation Decline in Europe in the eighteenth century, a period in which demand for legal services fell sharply, and many more cases were settled.[32] Possible explanations for this phenomenon are the gradual impoverishment of sectors of society so there was less need for litigation, the development of

31 Vida Azimi, Un modèle administratif de l'Ancien Régime, Paris, Presses du CNRS, 1988.

32 See https://research.flw.ugent.be/nl/projects/explaining-great-litigation-decline-impact-social-economic-change-litigation-patterns-franc, and also https://cris.vub.be/en/projects/explaining-the-great-litigation-decline-the-impact-of-socialeconomic-change-on-litigation-patterns-in-bruges-and-the-liberty-of-bruges-16501800(915a7a53-cffd-4ddc-a2b7-449154776 9a9).html (accessed in August 2022).

'low law' as opposed to 'high law'[33] and the summary jurisdiction, especially for minor offences, of the Justices of the Peace in England.

In criminal matters, there is a large gap in the legal system of the *ancien régime* between the small number of individuals prosecuted and punished (though, the penalties were often very severe) and the significant expansion of the criminal domain. This question of a 'dark figure' (the number of unrecorded crimes) raised by P. King, is a subject of criminology or criminal sociology studies, a part of a vast area of informal justice. The seventeenth and eighteenth centuries are an important 'period of transition' between the Middle Ages and the nineteenth century, which witnessed the birth of repressive systems in prisons and social control through harsh discipline (for example, in schools and the army). Only a small number of offenders were identified and arrested, which may explain the severity of the punishment of those who were caught. Extreme penalties and torture were thought to have a deterrent effect, and to compensate for the small number of perpetrators actually convicted.

> *P. King, Crime, Justice and Discretion in England, 1740–1820, Oxford, Oxford University Press, 2000, 5–9 and 11*
>
> In reconstructing the series of often brief but interconnected dramas that each individual accused of property appropriation was forced to play a part in until he or she gained access to an appropriate exit, the historian meets a myriad of problems. As we move through the play from the initial victim/accused negotiations, through committal and trial proceedings to sentencing, pardoning, and punishment, the later acts are relatively well documented, but even here complex evidential difficulty remains … Since the legal requirements about formal record-keeping only gradually emerged as the accused got nearer to conviction and sentence, the earlier informal stages of the judicial process are far more difficult to reconstruct, although it was there that the majority of the accused made their exit. Many offenders, for example, escaped prosecution by compounding paying the victim off in exchange for the charge being dropped. However, compounding a felony was illegal and the parties to such agreements deliberately left no record of their negotiations, which means that the

33 Douglas Hay, Legislation, Magistrates and Judges. High Law and Low Law in England, in David Lemmings (ed.), The British and their Laws in the Eighteenth Century, Woodbridge, Boydell Press, 2005, 59–79.

number of accused who escaped through this particular tunnel is impossible to calculate …

Along with crimes of extreme violence, such as murder or rape, crimes against property were the chief types of offense that came to mind when contemporaries spoke about 'crime'. The main yardstick with which the eighteenth-century public measured changes in the prevalence of crime, for example, was the length of the assize calendar, which was frequently noted and commented on in newspapers, pamphlets, and judges' speeches. Since nearly 90 per cent of those awaiting trial at the assizes were property offenders, this effectively meant that property appropriation was the key element of lawbreaking on which contemporaries focused their attention.

All definitions of crime are, of course, social constructions changing over time and between societies, social groups and individuals. Thefts of tools and personal or household items were, for example, undoubtedly regarded as 'crimes' by a much higher proportion of the population than would have applied that term of smuggling, wrecking, coining, poaching or gleaning.

It is often very difficult to define precisely what constituted an illegal act of appropriation in the eighteenth century. Contemporary writers, like many recent historians, not infrequently compared the number of indictments with 'real' levels of crime (i.e. with the vastly greater number of lawbreaking acts, prosecuted or unprosecuted, committed over a given time period) in order to make sense of changing levels of property crime indictments. However, contemporary discussions of the amount of property crime that remained unprosecuted were based on very rough commonsense notions of what constituted a theft and the borderlines remained ill-defined and highly problematic. The same act was often subject to very different interpretations according to the context in which it occurred. The act of taking grain from another's field could, for example, be a summarily triable offense if the corn was still standing unharvested, an indictable larceny if it had been cut and gathered but not yet carted away, or a legal act of gleaning if carting had been completed. Since the harvest was an uneven process it was often impossible to establish in which of these contexts grain had been taken, which perhaps explains why eighteenth-century farmers so often complained about the frequency with which gleaners stole from the sheaves.

The boundary between legality and illegality also changes over time. Many new statutes involving, for example, different forms of forgery or offense committed by bank or post office employees were passed during this period in an attempt to protect new forms of property or commercial transactions. Moreover, historians continue to debate the extent to which the eighteenth and early nineteenth centuries witnessed the legal redefinition as theft both of rural customary rights such as wood-gathering and of many of the perquisites generated by industrial process.

The boundaries between the civil and the criminal law were extremely blurred in the eighteenth century. Those who considered themselves to be victims of acts of appropriation often had to decide not only whether or not to prosecute, but also whether to become plaintiffs in a civil suit or prosecutors in a criminal one. Victims of indirect forms of appropriation, such as fraud, forgery, or uttering, were frequently faced with the latter decision. In the 1780s, for example, the Essex farmer John Lambert, having paid too much for a horse after being given false information about its age, ignored the civil remedies available and indicted the horse dealer for fraud, a transportable offense. A huge variety of more direct appropriations were subject to similar borderline interpretations. Offense of dubious actions committed by those who hired horses or other goods and failed to abide by the terms of hiring; who borrowed tools and failed to return them; who mistook others' property for their own; who appropriated goods they believed had been abandoned; or who refused to return articles left temporarily in their custody are just some of the more obvious examples.

Although the vast majority of the property appropriation cases that reached a court with criminal jurisdiction were heard by magistrates in the local summary courts or tried at the quarter session or assizes, there were also other courts with limited powers to try subgroups of property offenders. In the sixteenth century the manorial courts were probably the most important. In many parts of Essex these courts were still dealing with wood thefts and other minor forms of property appropriation in 1600 but here, as elsewhere, the manorial courts had almost entirely ceased to perform such functions by 1750. The English forest courts continued to punish wood, turf, and game appropriation in the eighteenth century, using a variety of minor sanctions, and the Court of Attachments in the Essex royal forest of Waltham was no exception.

In particular it is necessary to be very clear about the size of the so-called 'dark figure' of unrecorded crime, which in the context of eighteenth-century studies is usually equated with unindicted crime. Any precise calculation of the size of the dark figure is, of course, impossible, not only because no systematic record was kept of unprosecuted crime, but also the definition of what constituted a property crime was and is

> proper to take … Colquhoum for example estimated that a maximum of one offender in ten was indicted in late eighteenth-century London and in his more pessimistic moment he seems to have thought that one in a hundred might be a more according estimate.

Many victims were reluctant to bring court action, even in systems which allowed private plaintiffs to seek compensation through criminal judges (which was possible in France but not in England), as B. Garnot shows. Women were afraid to allege sexual assaults of any kind, and people from modest backgrounds and those confronting powerful families or communities feared the revenge of the rich and powerful. Another worry for them was that judges were partial. Additionally, individuals who were not entirely blameless were reluctant to go to court because some victims exacted reprisals and revenge with violence or duels. Perpetrators of crimes could try to settle conflicts, especially with monetary compensation for the victims and their families. Small crimes were settled this way. We know, for example, of cases in France where tortfeasors who cut wood illegally made a written agreement with landowners in the presence of witnesses that established the offence and required compensation. By agreeing to this they avoided any complaint against them. In England, an important feature of this period were voluntary associations and moral leagues, which could simultaneously prosecute crimes and exercise social pressure on offenders.

In civil and commercial matters, arbiters could settle conflicts without trial. For example, traders preferred settlement over complicated and public litigation before the courts of law (even in countries like France, where special commercial courts had been established with elected merchants as judges). In England and in other European countries,[34] the decreasing number of trials during the first half of the eighteenth century is difficult to explain. One of the factors that could help elucidate this surprising phenomenon, besides demographic stagnation in England between 1650 and 1750, is the increasing cost to parties in accessing the courts and, as a consequence, the growth of mediation to solve conflicts.[35] Generally speaking, in the second half of the seventeenth century and in the eighteenth century, there seemed to be a growing separation

34 Wilfrid Prest, The Experience of Litigation in Eighteenth Century England, in David Lemmings (ed.), The British and their Laws in the Eighteenth Century, Woodbridge, Boydell Press, 2005, 153.

35 Christopher Brooks, Litigation Participation and Agency in Seventeenth- and Eighteenth Century England, in David Lemmings (ed.), The British and their Laws in the Eighteenth Century, Woodbridge, Boydell Press, 2005, 155–181.

between the 'high law' administrated by professional jurists and the 'low law' of the justices of the peace and 'informal justice'. The high law might have been difficult to access for the poorest litigants, which may be why low law was more attractive to the working classes.[36] Another factor was the uneven geographical distribution of judges and lawyers. In some territories and States there were relatively few of them. This could explain the two-tier justice system in the nineteenth and twentieth centuries, and could be seen as a confirmation of the existence of the distinction between formal law and informal justice.

> *B. Garnot, L'Infrajudiciaire du Moyen Âge à l'époque contemporaine, Dijon, Éditions Université de Dijon, 1997, 70–71 (transl. by J.-L. Halpérin)*
> In France, a great many criminal cases, probably the majority of them, were not brought before the courts, because those concerned did not want this to happen. The fact that courts were a long distance away from the rural population as they were located in cities cannot explain why the population had hardly any recourse to the judiciary. After all, seigniorial courts were nearby and could serve as a conduit to royal justice. It is also not due to ignorance about the existence of the judicial institutions: in civil matters, the population, including those from the countryside, did not hesitate to start a court case … and would continue these lawsuits for long periods. It is only in criminal matters that they preferred, often deliberately, to settle the matter without involving royal justice. They associated that type of justice with a far away, hegemonic, and tyrannical power. The fear it inspired was intensified by the violent character of some of the penalties and the perceived disproportionate severity of the penalties for some offenses. As a result, victims did not act as plaintiffs, for example, in domestic theft cases … The population basically selected the matters that should be kept within the community and matters that would be sent to court, and they did this according to three criteria. The first criterion was a social one, it concerns the question of how marginal the (supposed) culprit was … The second criterion was related to the community's cohesion, as it deals with the way the offense was committed. Here the respect of rules of comportment, particularly those concerning honor, is at stake. … The third criterion was connected to what we may call a threshold of tolerance, the level of danger a person represents to a whole community.

36 Douglas Hay, Legislation, Magistrates and Judges. High Law and Low Law in England and the Empire, in David Lemmings (ed.), The British and their Laws in the Eighteenth Century, Woodbridge, Boydell Press, 2005, 59–79.

The way the French kings used their powers to arrest individuals by way of royal letters (*lettres de cachet*) is an example of the treatment of 'troublemakers' outside the judicial channels. The king could order the arrest of anyone and keep them in prison at his pleasure. Such letters were requested by many, for example, by the relatives of the mentally ill, by husbands whose wives had committed adultery, by fathers who wanted to discipline their sons, et cetera. Honoré Gabriel Riqueti, the count of Mirabeau and future revolutionary leader, was a 'victim' of such paternal authoritarianism.

Questions

1. What was the relationship between law and religion in the period 1650–1775? What do we know about Jewish law? Why was the Spanish Inquisition created? What was its original purpose? How did it evolve?
2. How would you describe the development of the law of criminal procedure in the same period?
3. Were public and private law clearly distinguished? Why (not)?
4. What does it mean that Pothier developed a 'general theory' of contract and that, in doing so, 'he did not try to base law on natural law, but applied rationalist methods to existing law'?
5. Did judicial discretion play any significant role in the various systems of criminal law between 1650–1775?

5 Summary

In his famous *Esprit des lois* (Geneva, 1748), Montesquieu was very sensitive to the most important legal developments from 1650 to his own time. He argued for the primacy of public law. His so-called theory of the 'separation of powers' (an expression he himself did not use) was used to describe the growing separation between the legislative, executive, and judicial powers in his time. The latter had to respect the law, and the judges were nothing more than a 'mouth that pronounces the words of the law'.[37]

During the period from 1650 to 1775, the development of the modern state involved increased intervention by the legislative and judicial authorities in domains such as procedural law, commercial and tort law, the law of contract, and criminal law. However, the effectiveness of public institutions remained

37 Charles de Secondat, baron de Montesquieu, The Spirit of the Law, transl. Anne M. Cohler, Basia Carolyn Miller and Harold Samuel Stone, Cambridge, Cambridge University Press, 1989, 163, in the famous chapter 8 of book XI about 'the constitution of England'.

limited in many areas. For example, different social classes in Western societies used informal justice. Also, the gap between 'high law' (at central courts and councils) and 'low law' (administered by subordinate magistrates and officials, as well as by the arbitrary will of the heads of families) was significant. The triumph of the modern state was far from complete: the hierarchy of legal sources was more a phenomenon of the 'law in the books' than a reality of 'law in action'.

In this period, the civil and common law also spread outside the European continent, in North America, India, and Australia. This transfer of law to different regions and cultures had profound consequences. It played a part in the first of the great revolutions at the end of the eighteenth century: the war of independence in the United States of America, and the birth of its constitution, which paved the way for the French Revolution and the end of the *ancien régime*. The 1770s and 1780s were the start of a new era. However, the scope of these revolutions in the legal field remains a topic of debate. Even though lawyers mostly organized and led these revolutions, the new rulers, who were usually politicians from the bourgeoisie chosen through elections, reduced the political role of the traditional legal professions. Furthermore, the effects of the American and French Revolutions were not noticeable in all Western countries. The *ancien régime* remained in place in some legal systems until the nineteenth century. The British political system continued to evolve at its own pace.

A metamorphosis of the legal field during the period 1650–1775 certainly prepared the ground for the 'great' American and French revolutions which achieved many of the goals of the 'modern state', such as administrative centralization and legislative rationalization. They created new opportunities to strengthen the state based on constitutional law, codified statutes, and precedents.

Further Reading

Ackerman, Bruce. We the People. I. Foundations, Cambridge Mass., Cambridge University Press, 1991.

Anderson, Perry. Lineages of the Absolutist State, London, Random House Incorporated, 1974.

Antoine, Michel. Le Conseil du Roi sous Louis XV, Paris-Genève, Droz, 1970.

Azimi, Vida. Un modèle administratif de l'Ancien Régime, Paris, Presses du CNRS, 1987.

Bhattacharyya-Panda, Nandini. Appropriation and Invention of Tradition. The East India Company and Hindu Law in Early Colonial Bengal, New Delhi, Oxford University Press, 2008.

Brauneder, Wilhelm. Europäisches Privatrecht aber was its es?, Zeitschrift für Neuere Rechtsgeschichte 1993, 225–235.

Brewer, John. The Sinews of Power. War, Money and the English State 1688–1783, Cambridge Mass., Harvard University Press, 1990.

Brooks, Christopher. Litigation Participation and Agency in Seventeenth- and Eighteenth century England, in David Lemmings (ed.), The British and Their Laws in the Eighteenth Century, Woodbridge, Boydell Press, 2005, 155–181.

Castan, Nicole. Justice et repression en Languedoc à l'époque des Lumières, Paris, Flammarion, 1980.

Coing, Helmut. (ed.), Europäisches Privatrecht. I: Älteres Gemeines Recht (1500 bis 1800), München, C.H. Beck, 1985.

Coing, Helmut (ed.), Handbuch der Quellen und Literatur der neueren europäischen Privatrechtsgechichte, Vols. II/1 and II/2: 1500–1800, München, C.H. Beck, 1976–1977.

Cutter, Charles R. The Legal Culture of Northern New Spain, 1700–1810, Albuquerque, University of New Mexico Press, 1995.

Deleuze, Gilles. Foucault, London, Continuum, 1999.

Feenstra, Robert and Reinhard Zimmermann (eds), Das römisch-holländische Recht: Fortschritte des Zivilrechts im 17 and 18 Jahrhundert, Berlin, Duncker und Humblot, 1992.

Godding, Philippe. Le droit privé dans les Pays-Bas méridionaux du XIIe au XVIIIe siècle, Brussels, Académie royale de Belgique, 1987.

del Granado, Juan Javier and Alejandra Mayagoitia. Roman Law and Ratio Decidendi in Spanish Colonial Law, 16th through the 19th Centuries, in Serge Dauchy, W. Hamilton Bryson and Matthew C. Mirow (eds), Ratio Decidendi. Guiding Principles of Judicial Decisions, Vol. 2: 'Foreign' Law, Berlin, Duncker & Humblot, 2010, 107–112.

Grossi, Paolo. Assolutismo giuridico e diritto privato, Milano, Giuffrè, 1998.

Hadden, Sally S. The Fragmented Laws of Slavery in the Colonial and Revolutionary Areas, in Michael Grossberg and Christopher Tomlins (eds), The Cambridge History of Law in America, Vol. 1, Cambridge, Cambridge University Press, 2007, 259–264.

Halpérin, Jean-Louis. Five Legal Revolutions since the 17th century. An Analysis of a Global Legal History, Heidelberg, New York, Dordrecht, London, Springer, 2014.

Härter, Karl. Ius publicum und Reichsrecht in den juristischen Dissertationen mitteleuropäischer Universitäten der Frühen Neuzeit, in Jacques Krynen and Michael Stolleis (eds), Science politique et droit public dans les facultés de droit européennes (XIIIe – XVIIIe siècle), Frankfurt am Main, Klostermann, 2008, 485–528.

Hay, Douglas. Legislation, Magistrates and Judges. High Law and Low Law in England and the Empire, in David Lemmings (ed.), The British and their Laws in the Eighteenth Century, Woodbridge, Boydell Press, 2005, 59–79.

Hazard, Paul. La crise de la conscience européenne, 1680–1715, Paris, Boivin, 1935.

Hoppit, Julian. Patterns of Parliamentary Legislation, 1660–1800, The Historical Journal 39 (1996), 109–131.

Husa, Jaakko, Kimmo Nuotio and Heikki Pihlajamäki. Nordic Law – Between Tradition and Dynamism, Tilburg Institute of Comparative and Transnational Law Working Paper, 2008/10.

Ibbetson, David. A Historical Introduction to the Law of Obligations, Oxford, Oxford University Press, 1999.

Israel, Jonathan. The Dutch Republic: Its Rise, Greatness and Fall, 1477–1806, Oxford, Clarendon, 1993.

Kelsen, Hans. Pure Theory of Law, transl. Max Knight, Berkeley, University of California Press, 1967 and Clark NJ, The Law Book Exchange, 2008.

Kennedy, Duncan. The Structure of Blackstone's Commentaries, Buffalo Law Review 28 (1979), 205–382.

Landau, Norma. The Justices of the Peace, 1679–1760, Berkeley, University of California Press, 1984.

Langbein, John H. Albion's Fatal Flaws, Past and Present 98 (1983), 96–120.

Lesaffer, Randall. The Classical Law of Nations (1500–1800), in Alexander Orakhelasvill (ed.), Research Handbook on the Theory and History of International Law, Cheltenham, Edward Elgar Publishing, 2011.

Lobban, Michael. The Common Law and England Jurisprudence, 1760–1850, Oxford, Clarendon, 1991.

Lutz, Donald S. The Origins of American Constitutionalism, Baton Rouge, LSU Press, 1988.

Mannoni, Stefano. Une et indivisible. Storia dell'accentramento amministrativo in Francia, 2 vols., Milano, Giuffrè, 1994–1996.

Mestre, Jean-Louis. Introduction historique au droit administratif français, Paris, PUF, 1985.

Mirow, M.C. Latin American Law: a History of Private Law and Institutions in Spanish America, Austin, University of Texas Press, 2004.

Pérez-Perdomo, Rogelio. Latin American Lawyers: a Historical Introduction, Stanford, Stanford University Press, 2006.

Pierson, Christopher. The Modern State, London, Routledge, 1996 and 2004.

Pihlajamäki, Heikki, Markus D. Dubber and Mark Godfrey (eds), The Oxford Handbook of European Legal History, Oxford, Oxford University Press, 2018.

Pocock, J.G.A. The Ancient Constitution and the Feudal Law: a Study of English Historical Thought in the Seventeenth Century (2nd ed.), Cambridge, Cambridge University Press, 1987.

Poggi, Gianfranco. The Development of the Modern State, Stanford, Stanford University Press, 1978.

Poggi, Gianfranco. The State: Its Nature, Development and Prospects, Stanford, Stanford University Press, 1990.

Prest, Wilfrid. The Experience of Litigation in Eighteenth Century England, in David Lemmings (ed.), The British and their Laws in the Eighteenth Century, Woodbridge, Boydell Press, 2005, 132–154.

Schulze, Reiner. Die Polizeigesetzgebung der Wirtschafts- un Arbeitsordnung der Mark Brandenburg in der früheren Neuzeit, Aalen, Scientia, 1978.

de Secondat, Charles, baron de Montesquieu. The Spirit of the Law, transl. Anne M. Cohler, Basia Carolyn Miller and Harold Samuel Stone, Cambridge, Cambridge University Press, 1989.

Stolleis, Michael. Geschichte des öffentlichen Rechts in Deutschland. Erster Band: Reichspublizistik und Policeywissenschaft, München, Beck, 1988.

Thompson, E.P., D. Hay, P. Linebaugh, J.G. Rule and C. Winslow (eds), Albion's Fatal Tree, London, Verso, 1976.

Tomás y Valiente, Francisco. Manual de Historia del Derecho Español, Madrid, Tecnos, 1987.

Urofsky, Melvin I. and Paul Finkelman. A March of Liberty. A Constitutional History of the United States, New York/Oxford, Oxford University Press, 2002.

Wagner, Wolfgang (ed.), Das schwedische Reichsgesetzbuch (Sveriges Rikes Lag) von 1734, Frankfurt am Main, Klostermann, 1986.

Wood, Gordon. The Creation of the American Republic, Chapel Hill, University of North Carolina Press, 1969.

Zimmermann, Reinhard. The Law of Obligations. Roman Foundations of the Civilian Traditions, Cape Town, Juta & Co., 1990.

CHAPTER 6

Revolutionary Period and Nineteenth Century (1776–1900)

Aniceto Masferrer and Cornelis Hendrik (Remco) van Rhee

1 Introduction

In continental Europe, the French Revolution serves as a watershed between the *ancien régime* and the modern nation state. The French Revolution brought about the first European constitution in the sense of a basic law promulgating fundamental rights.

The American and French Revolutions at the end of the eighteenth century were, undoubtedly, political revolutions of a new kind: the former with the first emancipation of colonies from their mother-country, the latter with the establishment of a 'New Regime' with the Revolution of 1789 and later with the abolition of the monarchy and the institution of a Republic in 1792. Cromwell's seventeenth-century English Commonwealth was, despite the beheading of the king and the functioning of a republican authority, a less disturbing change.

The common point of reference between the two revolutions of the Age of Enlightenment and the reason why some American rules and ideas could be transplanted, or at least discussed, in revolutionary France is the phenomenon called 'modern constitutionalism': the sea change from an 'unwritten constitution' (the 'king-in-parliament' on the British Isles and the 'fundamental laws of the kingdom' of the French absolute monarchy, if one admits that these were a kind of unwritten constitution) to a written constitution contained in an homogenous act conceived to distribute and thus limit the different powers or 'departments' within the State, and to be applied as the 'fundamental law'.

The aim of modern constitutions is to set limits to the power of the sovereign, who in earlier times was identified with the state itself. Since the beginning of the modern era in the late fifteenth century this identification had given rise to the absolute states of Europe. After the French Revolution, these states were slowly replaced by what became known as 'constitutional states'.

The Declaration of the Rights of Man and of the Citizen (1789) states that the opposite of a constitutional state is '[a] society in which fundamental rights have not been assured or where the separation of powers has not been established'. Such a state is not considered to have a Constitution (Article 16).

 | DOI:10.1163/9789004687257_008

Both the guarantee of fundamental rights and the separation of powers have a common objective, i.e. to establish a space in which the individual is free from state intervention. For this to be possible, it is necessary that public power is exercised by distinct, if not completely independent, bodies subject to the 'rule of law' (the idea of the 'rule of law' finds its origins in the eighteenth century United States of America), bodies that observe the principle of legality (a term used to reflect the idea that public power is subject to the will of the people as a whole) or the related principle of legislative supremacy (the latter expression originates from France).

Apart from constitutional changes, the revolutionary period was also significant for other areas of law. On the European Continent, the French Revolution may be considered as the starting point of the modern codification period. Like the Revolution itself, the idea of codification found its origins in the period of Enlightenment of the second half of the 18th century. Important changes in the law can be seen, including particularly in respect of the legal professions and the judiciary. Venality of offices was abolished and the promulgation of a constitutional rule that judges are not allowed to refuse to administer justice on the pretext that the law is not clear, stimulated judicial interpretation. The role of court decisions as a source of law was enhanced, in part because judges thenceforth had to provide reasons in their judgments. A national court hierarchy was established and the primacy of national legislation together with a reduced role for other sources of law caused further centralization in the legal field. Since the law became more national, the role of the *ius commune* as a source of legal inspiration was relegated to the background in many parts of Europe. Legal doctrine focused on the new national codes. This gave rise to legal positivism, of which the French Exegetical School is perhaps the best-known representative. The Exegetical School was not only influential in France, but also in Belgium and, albeit to a lesser extent, in the Netherlands. In the German speaking territories, the situation was different and civil codification uniting the German states only proved to be possible after a long period of gestation during which much work was done by the representatives of the German Historical School of Law. With the introduction of the German civil code in 1900, the codification period began to draw to a close.

2 Creation

2.1 *Modern Constutionalism*

The subjection of all public power to the rule of law or the principle of legality, together with the safeguarding of fundamental rights, which in this context are to be understood as individual rights, was based on the older principle of national sovereignty. According to this principle, ultimate power does not reside in the monarch or the institution of the monarchy but in the 'nation' – even though the monarch may participate in the exercise of these powers as head of the executive. The history of the principle of sovereignty is closely linked to the evolution of the institution of the monarchy, right up until the moment when the nation itself was deemed to exercise state sovereignty and the monarch was relegated to a role of secondary importance in legislative matters. This evolution has passed through the stages of the absolute monarchy and the 'limited monarchy' up to the emergence of the constitutional monarchy.

The principle of national sovereignty was a creation of modern constitutionalism, and without it, authentic constitutions would not have been possible. The first North American constitutional texts contain the principle that all power is vested in, and consequently derived from, the people.

2.2 *Sovereignty of the People or National Sovereignty*

> *Declaration of Rights of Virginia, 12 June 1776, Section 2*
> That all power is vested in, and consequently derived from, the people; that magistrates are their trustees and servants and at all times amenable to them.

Constitutional texts like this granted the people the power to dissolve the political ties that connected them to other nations.

> *Preamble to the US Declaration of Independence, 4 July 1776*
> When in the Course of human events, it becomes necessary for one people to dissolve the political bands which have connected them with another, and to assume among the powers of the earth, the separate and equal station to which the Laws of Nature and of Nature's God entitle them, a decent respect to the opinions of mankind requires that they should declare the causes which impel them to the separation.

Constitutional texts also provided the faculty to promulgate and sanction one's own constitution.

> *Constitution of the United States of America (1787), Preamble*
> We the People of the United States, in Order to form a more perfect Union, establish Justice, insure domestic Tranquility, provide for the common defence, promote the general Welfare, and secure the Blessings of Liberty

> to ourselves and our Posterity, do ordain and establish this Constitution for the United States of America.

The same rights were conferred upon the people by the first French constitutional texts.

> *Declaration of the Rights of Man and of the Citizen (1789), Preamble*
> The representatives of the French people, organized as a National Assembly …, have determined to set forth in a solemn declaration the natural unalienable and sacred rights of man.

> *Declaration of the Rights of Man and of the Citizen (1789), Article 3*
> The principle of all sovereignty resides essentially in the nation. No body or individual may exercise any authority which does not proceed directly from the nation.

> *French Constitution of 1791, Title III, Article 1 [Of Public Powers]*
> Sovereignty is one, indivisible, inalienable, and imprescriptible. It appertains to the nation; no section of the people nor any individual may assume the exercise thereof.

Similar texts can be found in other European states, for example in Spain, Belgium and Romania.[1]

2.3 *Separation of Powers*

National sovereignty conferred legitimacy on constitutional texts by empowering the people, or their representatives, to organize the public powers, and so to divide them or separate them. The first examples of texts expressing this idea can be found in the United States of America.

> *The Virginia Declaration of Rights (1776), Section 5*
> That the legislative and executive powers of the state should be separate and distinct from the judiciary; and that the members of the two first may be restrained from oppression, by feeling and participating the burdens of the people.

1 Spanish Constitution of Cádiz (1812), Art. 3; Belgian Constitution (1831), Art. 25; Romanian Constitution (1866), Article 31.

A few years later, the Constitution of the United States of America would organize the State by separating the legislative bodies (Article I, Sections 1–10) from the executive (Article II, Sections 1–4) and the judiciary (Article III, Sections 1–3). In fact, the North American Constitution (1787) was concerned primarily with the organization and structuring of state power and omitted the express recognition of fundamental rights and liberties, a matter that was dealt with in the first ten articles of the amendment to the Constitution that was passed four years later, on 15 December 1791.

The close link between national sovereignty and the separation of powers can be appreciated in French history as well. Article 2 of the 3rd Title of the French Constitution of 1791 established the relationship between the two very clearly.

> *French Constitution of 1791, Title III, Article 2 [Of Public Powers]*
> Art. 2. The Nation, from which all power emanates, cannot exercise power except by delegation. The French Constitution is representative: the representatives are the legislative body and the King.

Among the powers that emanated from the nation were the legislative power (Article 3), the executive power (Article 4) and the judiciary (Article 5).

> *French Constitution of 1791, Title III, Article 3 [Of Public Powers]*
> Art. 3. The legislative power is delegated to a National Assembly, composed of temporary representatives freely elected by the people, to be exercised by it, with the sanction of the King, in the manner hereinafter determined.

> *French Constitution of 1791, Title III, Article 4 [Of Public Powers]*
> Art. 4. The government is monarchical; the executive power is delegated to the King, to be exercised, under his authority, by ministers and other responsible agents in the manner hereinafter determined.

> *French Constitution of 1791, Title III, Article 5 [Of Public Powers]*
> Art. 5. The judicial power is delegated to judges who are elected at stated times by the people.

Similar provisions can be found in almost all the states of continental Europe.[2] However, some states did not embrace these ideas at an early stage. An example of a rather conservative approach is Sweden, where the Constitution of 1809 did not provide for a proper separation of powers (cf. Articles 17–19 and 87).

2.4 *Recognition of Fundamental Rights*

While the recognition of national sovereignty was a sufficient title for the organization of the various state powers, as it was understood that these had been created or formed by the people of the nation, the same could not be said with respect to fundamental rights, as they were thought to be derived from nature, and not from national sovereignty. Fundamental rights could only be recognized by the state and not be created by it, as they were considered to be inherent to humanity and not susceptible to restriction or privation by the state or at the mercy of any type of pact.

> *Aniceto Masferrer, The Fragility of Fundamental Rights in the Origins of Modern Constitutionalism. Its Negative Impact in Protecting Human Rights in the 'War on Terror' Era, in Aniceto Masferrer and Clive Walker (eds), Counter-Terrorism, Human Rights and the Rule of Law: Crossing Legal Boundaries in Defence of the State, Cheltenham, Edward Elgar Publishing, 2013, 49–51*
>
> It is important not to forget that the creators of the first Declarations and Constitutional texts, both in Europe and in North America, assumed the existence of a series of rights that stemmed from nature and were intrinsic to man. These rights were pre-political in character, and it was accepted that men, once they had formed political communities, could not have them taken away by virtue of any pacts or agreements. For example, Section 1 of the Declaration of Rights of Virginia of 1776 expressed this idea in the following way:
>
> That all men are by nature equally free and independent and have certain inherent rights, of which, when they enter into a state of society, they cannot, by any compact, deprive or divest their posterity; namely, the enjoyment of life and liberty, with the means of acquiring and possessing property, and pursuing and obtaining happiness and safety.

2 E.g. Costituzione della Repubblica Napoletana (1799), Titles V, VI and VIII; Spanish Constitution of Cádiz (1812), Arts. 15–17; Norwegian Constitution (1814), Arts. 3ff (Executive power), Arts. 49ff (Legislative power), and Arts. 86ff (Judicial power); Belgian Constitution (1831), Arts. 25–31; Romanian Constitution (1866), Arts. 32, 35, 36.

The United States of America's Declaration of Independence of 1776 went even further by affirming, after having insisted on the inalienable quality of fundamental rights, that: 'To secure these rights, governments are instituted among men, deriving their just powers from the consent of the governed' (Paragraph II of the Preamble).

From this perspective, the function of governments, whose power derives from the consent of those they govern, is to guarantee and protect fundamental rights. The same idea is expressed in the Preamble to the French Declaration of the Rights of Man and of the Citizen of 1789, which explains that the purpose of the Declaration is: 'To set forth in a solemn declaration the natural, unalienable, and sacred rights of man, in order that this declaration, being constantly before all the members of the Social body, shall remind them continually of their rights and duties'.

The same document, after stating in its first article that 'Men are born and remain free and equal in rights', goes even further by declaring that: 'The aim of all political association is the preservation of the natural and imprescriptible rights of man'.

It is precisely because these rights were declared to be natural and imprescriptible that the French Constitution of 1791, when guaranteeing a number of these fundamental rights in its First Title, stated that: 'The legislative power may not make any laws which infringe upon or obstruct the exercise of the natural and civil rights recorded in the present title and guaranteed by the Constitution'.

The idea that fundamental rights, being grounded in the very nature of human beings, are not dependant on the sanction either of public powers or of the people or nation in whom or in which sovereignty is invested, is at the very heart of modern Western constitutionalism, so much so, that almost all international declarations and constitutional texts over the last two hundred years have stated this principle unambiguously. For example, the Preamble of the Universal Declaration of Human Rights (1948) affirms that: 'Recognition of the inherent dignity and of the equal and inalienable rights of all members of the human family is the foundation of freedom, justice and peace in the world.' The first article of the Declaration goes on to proclaim that: 'All human beings are born free and equal in dignity and rights. They are endowed with reason and conscience and should act towards one another in a spirit of brotherhood.'

This article recognises that rights stem from human dignity, a natural quality possessed from birth, and are not derived from citizenship. Dignity and human rights are natural, pre-political realities, and the role of the State is to recognise and protect them. The idea that declarations

> and constitutional texts can only recognize the existence of rights but not create them according to the circumstances and on the basis of current consensus constitutes another characteristic of modern constitutionalism. An example of this approach is the European Convention on Human Rights (1950) which proclaims in its 2nd Consideration that 'this Declaration aims at securing the universal and effective recognition and observance of the Rights therein declared.'

For Spain, the Constitution of Cádiz meant a decisive break with the past. This constitution did not contain a bill of rights, but it included a number of rights. The creation of the new constitution by the Assembly resulted in the regulation of citizen's rights, for example the abolition of private jurisdictions and the rights of freedom of the press and expression. The right to education was provided for (Articles 366 to 370) and the principle of legal equality was introduced. A series of unified legal codes had to be applied throughout the territory according to Article 258, the administration of law had to be unified according to Article 248, and the principle of equality in the obligation to perform military service was introduced by Article 361. Furthermore, the Constitution of Cádiz established a series of guarantees to protect citizens from arbitrary arrest and house searches. In addition, trial procedures were established.

Further examples of constitutional provisions recognising fundamental rights can be found in many other jurisdictions.[3]

2.5 *Rule of Law and Legality Principle or Principle of Legislative Supremacy*

The notion of a modern constitution also entails the subjection of the state or public power to the law. This took the form of the rule of law in the United States of America and the principle of legislative supremacy in France.

> *Aniceto Masferrer and Anna Taitslin, The Ill-Fated Union: The Constitutional Entrenchment of Rights and the 'Will Theory' from Rousseau to Waldron, in P. Barenboim, J. Hickey and J.R. Silkenat (eds), Legal Doctrines of the Rule of Law and the Legal State, Cham, Springer Verlag, 2014, 119–123*
>
> Rousseau effectively originated the dogma of supremacy of the legislature, whose laws were regarded as the expression of the general will. Rousseau presented the notions of sovereignty and legislation as being interlinked.

3 See, for example, Constitution of Bologna (1796), Arts. 1–2; Ordonnance royale grand-ducale du 16 octobre 1841 (portant promulgation de la Constitution d'États pour le Grand-Duché de Luxembourg), Art. 41; Romanian Constitution (1866), Arts. 13, 16, 18.

In this vein, legislation being the expression of the general will carried with it the force of democratic legitimacy. Rousseau defended 'a form of government that places the law *supra* man' and warned that 'liberty is impossible in a state in which the body entrusted to apply it has the right to make it speak according to its fancy, for then it could enforce its most tyrannical desires as law'. According to Rousseau, 'a free people' 'obeys nothing but the laws, and thanks to the force of laws, it does not obey men'. 'A people' 'is free, whatever form its government takes, when it sees in him who governs not a man but the organ of the law. In a word, liberty always follows the fate of the laws, it reigns or perishes with them …'

Rousseau's presumption of the subjection of all public power to the will of the people or the principle of legislative supremacy rested on Bodin's principle of sovereignty. Moreover, the same presumption underlined the idea of safeguarding fundamental rights, which in the French revolutionary context meant individual rights. According to this principle, ultimate power did not reside in the monarch or the institution of the monarchy but in the people (popular sovereignty). The evolution of the principle of sovereignty passed through various stages until the nation came to be seen as the exclusive bearer of the sovereignty of the state.

According to Rousseau, sovereignty was indivisible; only differentiation among the functions of government was possible. This idea was to have an enormous influence on posterior French thought. From a political perspective, Rousseau distinguished between the 'will' and the 'force' ['power'] of the people. While the notion of will corresponded to the functions of the legislature, whose task it was to determine the will of the nation and to enact legislation in accordance with this will, 'force' ['power'] was the province of the executive power who carried out the mandates of the law and, if necessary, forcibly executed them.

Another important contributor to the French theory of sovereignty was Abbé Sieyès (1748–1836), who distinguished between the 'constituent power' and the 'constituted power'. According to Sieyès, the constituent power was … the constitution-making power. The constitution was the first and highest juridical norm, the rule of recognition for the whole legal and political system. Thus, the constituent power was not merely about writing and enacting a constitution, but rather a power that established political community, by creating and institutionalizing its members (citizenship), the relationships among them (basic rights), and political authority bound by the requirements of constitutionalism (the constituted power).

To put it simply, whereas the assembly in charge of drafting and promulgating the constitution is the constituent power, all other powers emanating from the approved constitutional text, such as the legislative, the executive and the judiciary, were the constituted powers. However, the fact that national sovereignty resided more in the former than in the latter did not impede the legislature acquiring supremacy over the executive and the judiciary, both theoretically and in practice. Even accepting that all state powers emanated from national sovereignty, if the legislature, given its representative character, embodied sovereignty more than any other state power, it followed that once the constitution had been passed and the bodies invested with state power had been constituted, the legislature and the laws would be unequalled in authority.

Added to this, the French Constitution did not have the status of a law: its precepts were not legally binding unless they became the object of legislation. French Constitutionalism, thus, was characterized by the marked supremacy of the legislature over the executive and, above all, the judiciary.

It was the legislature as a constituted state power invested with national (not popular, as Rousseau suggested) sovereignty that assumed the role of a protagonist [of Constitutionalism]. Firstly, since the Constitution lacked the status of a supreme law, it was not subject to interpretation and application by the courts in particular cases. Thus, the courts could not regard any laws to be hierarchically inferior to the Constitution. It was therefore impossible to question their consistency with the Constitution. Secondly, since laws were seen as the expression of the general will, the courts were unable to declare any law passed by the legislature a nullity (even though, strictly speaking, the legislature was a 'constituted' rather than a 'constituent' power). Finally, at the end of the *Ancien Régime*, there was a general antipathy towards both the traditional parliaments, which had served as higher jurisdictional organs, and the judges, who had often exercised their power in an arbitrary manner (in the King's name). Unsurprisingly, 'the members of the [National] Assembly acted in the conviction ... that legislation was the complete expression of the law, that only legislation could express the aims of law and that as a consequence, only legislation could create law. The role of the judge was reduced therefore, to the servile application of legislation to each case that came before him.'

Owing to Sieyès's distinction between constituent and constitutive powers, Rousseau's doctrine of popular sovereignty had been transformed into the notion of parliamentary sovereignty with the national legislature, as a constituted power, fused with the legislative constituent power. This relation between national sovereignty, the separation of powers and the principle of legislative supremacy in French constitutionalism can be summarized as follows:

1. Parliamentary sovereignty, and therefore the supremacy of legislation, the Constitution, even when 'rigid', being no more than a text outlining the political organization of the state;
2. A strong executive power kept in check by the legislative power, not by the judiciary; and
3. The judiciary as an auxiliary to the legislature, not able to intervene in the affairs of either of the other two state powers. It could not declare the nullity of a law in case of its inconsistency with the Constitution as the Constitution did not have normative status.

Provisions on the rule of law or legislative supremacy can be found in many modern constitutions all over Europe. The following Articles are from the Declaration of the Rights of Man and of the Citizen (1789).

> *Declaration of the Rights of Man and of the Citizen* (1789)
> Art. 4. Liberty consists in the freedom to do everything which injures no one else; hence the exercise of the natural rights of each man has no limits except those which assure to the other members of the society the enjoyment of the same rights. These limits can only be determined by Law.
> Art. 5. Law can only prohibit such actions as are hurtful to society. Nothing may be prevented which is not forbidden by Law, and no one may be forced to do anything not provided for by Law.
> Art. 6. Law is the expression of the general will. Every citizen has a right to participate personally, or through his representative, in its foundation. It must be the same for all, whether it protects or punishes. All citizens, being equal in the eyes of the Law …
> Art. 7. No person shall be accused, arrested, or imprisoned except in the cases and according to the forms prescribed by Law … But any citizen summoned or arrested by virtue of the Law shall submit without delay, as resistance constitutes an offense.
> Art. 8. … no one shall suffer punishment except if it be legally inflicted by virtue of a law passed and promulgated before the commission of the offense.

Despite the fact that the French model had incorporated some aspects of American Constitutionalism (for example, the Declaration of the Rights of Man and the Citizen of 1789 had been inspired by the Declaration of Rights of Virginia of 1776), the American model contained a number of clear differences.

American Constitutionalism, in contrast to its French counterpart, recognised the Constitutional text as a law from the very beginning, and not only were public powers and individuals legally bound by its precepts, but judges were able to apply the Constitution in specific cases and declare ordinary legislation null and void when they conflicted with the Constitution, by a process known as judicial review.

To this normative character of the Constitutional text one needs to add the fact that the United States of America, which had adopted a system of common law, had never identified the law exclusively with legislation, as was the case in France. The country had rather been governed by the principle of the rule of law, and this was very different in meaning to the principle of legislative supremacy that was central in France.

While in England, the birthplace of the Anglo-American legal tradition, the Glorious Revolution of 1688 had resulted in the consecration of the sovereignty of Parliament and the rule of law in the Bill of Rights of 1689, it is important to remember that English law had long before sown the seeds of what would become one of the pillars of American Constitutionalism: the famous Bonham case presided over by judge Edward Coke in 1610. According to some scholars, this case defended the position of the common law as hierarchically superior to parliamentary legislation, which meant that judges, following judicial precedent, were able to declare the nullity of a law passed by Parliament if it was contrary to the tenets of the common law or of the natural law that was thought to form part of the common law. This case was of great significance because it presupposed the subjection of Parliament to the common law, or in other words, that the rule of law bound Parliament, and that judges were empowered to declare void any law that contravened the common law. Judge Coke could never have imagined the influence this case was to have in North American Constitutionalism.

> *Bonham's case: (1610) Hilary Term, 7 James 1, In the Court of Common Pleas, First Published in the Reports, volume 8, page 113b*
> And it appeareth in our Books, that in many Cases, the Common Law doth controll Acts of Parliament, and somtimes shall adjudge them to be void: for when an Act of Parliament is against Common right and reason, or repugnant, or impossible to be performed, the Common Law will controll it, and adjudge such Act to be void; and, therefore, in 8 E. 3.

> 30 a, b. *Thomas Tregor's Case* upon the Statute of *West* 2. Cap 38. and *Artic' Super Chartas, cap* 9. Herle saith, Some Statutes are made against Common Law and right, which those who made them, would not put them in execution.

However, other authors using contemporary evidence from English and Continental legal works contend that Bonham's Case actually rested upon then commonly accepted principles of the law of nature, and that those principles stopped short of embracing judicial review in the modern sense.

> *R.H. Helmholz, Bonham's case, Judicial Review and the Law of Nature, Journal of Legal Analysis 1(1) 2009, 345–346*
> There is little doubt that the words of Coke's opinion in Bonham's Case retain the power to impress. He said that the common law would 'control Acts of Parliament, and sometimes adjudge them to be utterly void.' After all the explanation – all the explaining away – these words still appear to endorse judicial review of legislation in something like the modern sense. I grant this.
>
> But the appearance is false all the same. Coke was merely stating an accepted doctrine of his time. It was conventional wisdom to suppose that a law contrary to fundamental legal principles was no law at all. The medieval *ius commune* had held that a statute or custom contrary to natural law 'was to be held for naught.' Later writers on the general law regularly described statutes as invalid if they offended against principles of the law of nature.
>
> [No] ... commentator ... meant to assert that judges had the power to declare legislative acts invalid because they did not conform to the law of nature. They did mean that in some (but not all) circumstances, individual men and women might make a legitimate claim to disobey statutes that ran counter to natural law. Such statutes might not bind in conscience. ... In extreme cases, they might even be justified in casting off the yoke of a tyrant.
>
> ... Coke was simply taking the approach to positive law that was characteristic of his time.

2.6 *Equality before the Law*

The idea of equality before the law, which was the logic consequence of recognising '[t]hat all men are by nature equally free and independent and have certain inherent rights' (Virginia Constitution, 1776, Section 1), was also present in many Western constitutions.[4]

This 'modern constitutionalism' has been glorified in the Western legal tradition, particularly in France and in the United States of America, with the possible exception of the British tradition of parliamentary supremacy. One has to be prudent towards these kinds of mythology, which led, for example, to nineteenth century French historians considering that 1789 was the true beginning of the 'rule of law'. Not only were revolutions violent phenomena, especially in France with the 1793–1794 Terror, but also in America where many loyalists, amongst them a large number of lawyers, were victims of the war of independence. The problems did not come to an end with the triumph of democracy. The franchise remained restricted to freeholders, i.e. owners of certain property, except in some American States and in France from 1792 to 1795 with the introduction of universal male suffrage. And, after all, slavery was maintained in the United States of America as well as in the French Caribbean colonies (except from 1794 to 1802). The American and French revolutions were bourgeois revolutions. In both countries centre stage was afforded to the right of property. Finally, the common law was maintained in the United States of America and many aspects of the French *ancien droit* were integrated in the Napoleonic Codes. Furthermore, the French Revolution failed to anchor a stable constitution, unlike America with the 1787 federal constitution and the succession of constitutions in various States. The French Revolution came to an end on 18 brumaire of year 8 (9 November 1799) with the coup d'État of Napoleon Bonaparte, establishing monarchic power that can be compared with enlightened despotism in Prussia or Austria. For these reasons, the legal impact of the American and French Revolutions cannot be compared.

2.7 *Political Organisation and Law*

It is often considered that the 1791 Constitution, influenced by theories developed by abbé Sieyès, has established the basis for modern French public law: the distinction between the constituent power (entrusted with the creation of a constitution) and the constituted powers (entrusted with its application), the principle of the supremacy of the law and the supremacy of the legislature (as well as the superiority of statutory law as the main source of the legal order), the recognition of the nation (a body of associates living under a

4 See, e.g., Constitution of Bologna (1796), Art. 3; Spanish Constitution of Cádiz (1812), Art. 248; French Constitution (1814), Arts. 1–3; Statuto Fondamentale Del Regno (1848), Art. 83; Romanian Constitution (1866), Art. 10; Constitution of Switzerland (1874), Arts. 3 and 60; Spanish Constitution (1876), Art. 75.

common legal framework and represented by the same legislature, according to Sieyès) as the source of all sovereignty, and elected representatives. Linked with the idea of a unitary nation and State, the idea of citizenship and the emergence of the idea of 'nationality' gave to the French model uniform features, different from those of the *ancien régime*.[5]

The reform of the French judiciary, initiated by the *Assemblée constituante*, was a complete break with the *ancien régime*. The venality of offices (offices being sold by the state) was suppressed and judges were elected among lawyers and former judges for a relatively short period of time (five to six years). Small claims and small offences were to be judged by justices of peace. Ordinary jurisdiction belonged to courts of five judges established in each of the more than 400 districts. There were no courts of appeal, but the decisions of the civil courts could be appealed before another district court, whereas verdicts of criminal juries were not subject to appeal at all. On top was the *Tribunal de cassation*, established in Paris in 1790–1791. Its mission was to quash judgements deemed contrary to the law. As the guardian of the laws, especially the new statutory laws, the *Tribunal de cassation* was to make sure that ordinary judges would strictly apply the rules promulgated by the legislature. The *Tribunal de cassation* succeeded in creating genuine case law in criminal and civil matters.[6]

2.8 *Legislation*

If the making of the modern state in the early modern age strongly contributed to the primacy of legislation (*lex*) over other legal sources (*ius*), i.e. custom, judicial decisions, legal doctrine and so on, modern constitutionalism started to understand legislation as the expression of the will of the people or the 'general will', as dogmatically expressed by Rousseau. The relevance of legislation increased to such an extent that it almost displaced the other sources of the law.

Legislation was regarded as the best tool for legal reform and as the instrument for shaping society. This has been called 'legal instrumentalism' and, along with the need for law reform, it led states, particularly (but not only) in continental Europe, to codify the law. However, not in all civil law jurisdictions codes were being promulgated. Exceptions are, for example, Finland, Scotland and South Africa.

The following text is on codification in France.

5 Stefano Mannoni, Une et indivisible. Storia dell'accentramento amministrativo in Francia, 2 vols, Milan, Giuffrè, 1994–1996.

6 Jean-Louis Halpérin, Le Tribunal de cassation et les pouvoirs sous la Révolution française (1790–1799), Paris, LGDJ, 1987.

J-L Halpérin, The French Civil Code (transl. by Tony Weir), London, Taylor & Francis Ltd, 2006, 5–8

The Revolution of 1789 certainly did away with some of the obstacles to the codification of private law which had existed under the *ancien régime*. [However] [t]he *Constituante* regarded it as more important to reform criminal law than to produce a civil code, so the first code to see the light of day in France was the *Code pénal* of 1791 … It was perhaps wise to be cautious in dealing with controversial [subject-matter] such as marriage and succession …

The *Montagnards* among the deputies, passionately devoted to the indivisibility of the republic as against the 'hydra' of federalism endorsed by the Girondins, now proscribed, wanted a civil law which was uniform and egalitarian, and on 9 August 1793, after the adoption of the Constitution of 1793, Cambacérès, as president of the legislative committee, put before the *Convention* and submitted for popular approval a project for a civil code. It had been prepared in two months by a committee of 12 lawyers, including specialists in private law [such] as Berlier, Oudot, Garran-Coulon and Merlin de Douai (working under Cambacérès), whose official task was to reform the law of securities, and using a library containing works by the *philosophes* of the Enlightenment as well as earlier jurists.

This, the first of Cambécérès's projects, purported to be building 'on the terra firma of the law of nature and the virgin soil of the Republic'. Lean and mean, its mere 791 articles rejected prior law almost *in toto*. It endorsed the principles of the two laws of 20 September 1792 on personal status and divorce (no grounds needed to be stated) and abolished the power of the husband and father: the administration of household property was to be shared between the spouses, whose only duty to the children was to educate and protect them until they were 21. Anyone, married or not, could adopt a minor, illegitimate children voluntarily recognized by their father were to have the same rights of succession as legitimate children, and strict equality was to be observed among children, none to be preferred to others and no gifts to be made to those already wealthy enough. The purpose of all this was to 'break up large estates'. In contrast with the radical innovations in family law, the proposals relating to property and obligations came largely from prior law, subject to the abolition of feudal rights, but ownership was defined as 'the right of the owner to enjoy and dispose of it' (as under the Declaration of Rights of 1793), and the freedom to contract, to acquire and to dispose of property, was entrenched.

In August and September 1793, the *Convention* discussed Books One and Two of the draft (personal status and property); it endorsed most of the texts but adjourned others. In October it went against the wishes of Cambacérès in deciding that the principle of equal rights on succession should be applied retrospectively to all cases arising after 14 July 1789 (the fall of the Bastille), but adoption of the text still seemed imminent when on 3 November 1793 the *Convention* deferred further discussion *sine die* and voted to remit the project to a commission of 'six philosophers'. The ostensible ground was that a civil code should be 'purged' of legalistic prejudices, but the truth was that since the members of the *Convention* had just suspended the Constitution and set up a revolutionary government, the adoption of a civil code was no longer appropriate. The only parts enacted were the two retrospective laws of 2 November 1793 and 6 January 1794 (12 *brumaire* and 17 *nivôse* year II) relating to illegitimate children and successions.

The commission of 'philosophers' never met, but the legislative committee set to work again, probably in the Spring of 1794, and produced a further draft which Cambacérès submitted to the *Convention* on 9 September 1794 (23 *fructidor* year II). This text was very laconic, only 297 articles long, not only shorter than its predecessor but also modified in the light of the reservations of the legislative committee. Cambacérès's report sought to justify this supposed 'code of nature' by a rather paradoxical reference to Lockean 'liberal' philosophy: 'All civil rights rest on freedom of liberty, property and contract'. In December 1794 the *Convention* discussed 10 of these articles but then abandoned the matter as inconsistent with its aims, for in the 'reaction to Thermidor' it was now ready to reconsider the enthusiasm of the Revolution. The *Convention* broke up in October 1795 without adopting a civil code, but only a law on mortgages and on crimes and penalties.

Cambacérès, however, was as determined as ever to have a civil code, and at the beginning of the Directory in June 1796 he and a few collaborators, including Oudot and Berlier, produced a third draft. The 1794 idea of a 'collection of maxims' was now abandoned, and the 1,104 articles of this third draft drew openly on Roman law, pre-Revolutionary law and Pothier. In his introductory remarks Cambacérès tried to give the impression that he was being true to the principles of the various laws he cited, but in fact he emphasised marriage as being 'of the first importance to society' in order to placate the many people who found the revolutionary legislation 'immoral'.

Not all the innovations of the Revolution were discarded: divorce remained available in accordance with the Law of 1792, subject to 'adjustments' proposed by Cambacérès, the adoption of minors remained possible in principle, and equality was still to be strictly observed in the succession of legitimate children. Nevertheless there were certain important differences: only persons with no children of their own could adopt, women married under the statutory matrimonial property regime were [incapacitated], testators without children were allowed to dispose of more of their estate than under the Law of 6 January 1794 (17 *nivôse* Year II), and adopted children were entitled to only half as much as legitimate children, as were illegitimate children ...

In December 1796 Cambacérès did his best to move the discussion of this draft forward, but the Council of Five Hundred temporised and in the Assembly where more reactionary proposals regarding illegitimate children and divorce were ventilated, only two of his articles were adopted. In February 1797 when Cambacérès last spoke on the subject, he conceded that the draft should be sent back for reconsideration. He was quite right to scuttle the project, for the chances of success were virtually nil: in the following Spring, indeed, he himself failed to be re-elected.

Some jurisdictions started enacting a digest of laws and later decided to promulgate a code. This was the case in Louisiana, a civil law jurisdiction in North America.

Olivier Moréteau and Agustín Parise, Recodification in Louisiana and Latin America, Tul. L. Rev. 83 (2008–2009), 1113–1115

The Act of March 31, 1808, by the Territorial Legislature, approving and putting in effect the Digest of 1808 reads: '§ 2. And be it further enacted, That whatever in the ancient civil laws of this territory, or in the territorial statute, is contrary to the dispositions contained in the said digest, or irreconcilable within them, is hereby abrogated.'

The French law of March 21, 1804, promulgating the *Code civil des français* as a whole reads: Article 7. From the day when these laws [constituting the Code] become effective, the Roman laws, the ordinances, the general and local customs, the charters and the regulations all cease to have the force either of general or of special law concerning the subjects covered by the present code ...

In 1825, Louisiana enacted a civil code. The need for a new enactment was felt because of the confusion generated by the fact that judges kept citing sources that were not easily accessible and were written in a foreign language. The Digest was meant to clarify and simplify the laws, making them more accessible, in the French language and also in the English language, since the original French was translated into English, though rather poorly. The fact that judges had to rely on ancient Spanish law and antique Roman law sources, available in only Spanish and Latin, defeated the central purpose of the Digest: there was no simplification. The situation was completely different in France where, with an energetic abrogation clause, judges understood that there was a break with the past and a fresh start. It does not mean that judges never looked back to Roman law and custom, but when they so did it was in an attempt to clarify the solutions in the Code, not to have the ancient laws survive.

The text of the Code of 1825 very much resembles that of the Digest.

Originally, legal positivism and codification were inextricably connected. However, this did not mean that other legal sources were not taken into consideration. The French civil code did not explicitly recognize the validity of other legal sources (custom, judicial decisions, legal doctrine), but this did not mean that they were not considered. Many other civil codes did contain a legal provision prescribing the validity of other legal sources, which were supposed to be applied when a solution was not found in the text of the code. It was recognized that law was not restricted to legislation, and that customs, judicial decisions and legal doctrine were also needed. The *Preliminary Address on the First Draft of the Civil Code* expresses this as follows.

Preliminary Address on the First Draft of the Civil Code, presented in the year IX by Messrs. Portalis, Tronchet, Bigot-Préameneu and Maleville, members of the government-appointed commission, 6–7 (https://www.justice.gc.ca/eng/rp-pr/csj-sjc/ilp-pji/code/civil.pdf; accessed in October 2022) © The International Cooperation Group, Department of Justice of Canada (English transl.)

A code, however complete it may seem, is no sooner finished than thousands of unexpected questions present themselves to the magistrate. For these laws, once drafted, remain as written. Men, on the other hand, never rest. They are always moving; and this movement, which never ceases and whose effects are variously modified by circumstances, continually produces some new fact, some new outcome.

Many things are therefore necessarily left to the authority of custom, to the discussion of learned men, to the arbitration of judges.

The function of the statute is to set down, in broad terms, the general maxims of the law, to establish principles rich in consequences, and not to deal with the particulars of the questions that may arise on every subject.

It is left to the magistrate and the jurisconsult, fully alive to the overall spirit of laws, to guide their application.

Hence, in all civilised nations one always sees, alongside the sanctuary of laws and under the watchful eye of the lawmaker, the formation of a body of maxims, decisions and doctrine that is refined daily by practice and by the impact of judicial deliberations; that continually grows from all the knowledge acquired; and that has constantly been regarded as the true supplement of legislation.

Many constitutions refer to codifications. The 1791 French Constitution contains an article prescribing that 'A code of civil law common to the entire kingdom shall be drafted' and the 1793 Constitution provides a similar statement: 'The civil and penal code is the same for the whole republic' (Article 85). References to codes were made also in the French Constitutions of 1804 (Article 130: 'The high imperial court can pronounce only the penalties provided by the penal code') and 1814 (Article 68: 'The civil code, and the laws actually existing which are not in conflict with the present charter, remain in force until legally abrogated'). Following the French model, the constitutions of many other jurisdictions – like those of Spain and Norway – did the same.[7]

Continental codes reflect the triumph of rationalism over historicism. This led some authors to present codes as a break with the past.

Aniceto Masferrer, Spanish Legal Traditions. A Comparative Legal History Outline (2nd ed.), Madrid, Dykinson, 2012, 22–23

One of the clearest signs of the triumph of rationalism over historicism in the European legal tradition was the codification movement. ...

What did codification consist of? The idea of a 'Legal Code' implied, in the nineteenth century, much more than a mere collection of rules gathered in a single book, edition, or volume. The introduction of a 'Code' meant a break with the past and with tradition; to dispose of the old and incorporate the new. This 'new' was not meant to be understood as a mere reform of the old, but rather as an authentic break with the past,

7 Cf. Statute of Bayonne for Spain (1808), Art. 169; Spanish Constitution of Cádiz (1812), Art. 258; Spanish Constitution (1837), Art. 4; Spanish Constitution (1845), Art. 4; Spanish Constitution (1869), Art. 91; Spanish Constitution (1876), Art. 75; Norwegian Constitution (1814), Art. 94; Norwegian Constitution (1814), Art. 95; Paris Convention of 1858, Article 35 (enacted by the European Powers in order to be the Basic Law of the Romanian Principalities).

as if the 'new' had no connection at all with what had existed up to that moment. This is how one of the protagonists of the codification movement, J.F. Pacheco, expressed it:

> a legal order in which nothing was worthy of respect, or conservation: no part of which could be saved for the ordering of a future society. All of it, absolutely all of it, needed to be left behind. ... The cart of destruction and reform had to pass through the ruined building, because in it there was scarcely an arch, scarcely a column that neither could nor should be saved. In Spanish Criminal law there was only one legitimate and viable system, the system of codification, the system of absolute change.

The system of codification, the system of absolute change, was the only legitimate and indeed, the only possible system, affirmed Pacheco, one of the most remarkable 19th century criminal law scholars and the main commentator of the Spanish Criminal Codes of 1848 and 1850. He highlighted the identification of 'codification' with 'absolute change', ideas which were antithetical to 'compilation' and 'tradition.'

According to this view, if the legislation on criminal law, contained in the compilations of the early modern age (XV–XVIII centuries), represented the law that came from tradition, and the specific history of each locality, kingdom or crown, the legislation on criminal law that constituted the Codes did not respond to tradition, but rather to reason: to that which the mentality of the time judged rational and reasonable. Considering the historical and the traditional as reactionary and unworthy of modern times, reason would erect the emblem and sign of the (new) modernity.

[Codification] was not simply another demand of liberal enlightenment, ... but was rather a postulate of the whole movement, and was brandished as a symbol of radical renovation. Codification and rationalist Natural Law Theory ... were closely linked concepts. [Codification] seemed to be the final stage in the already secular tendency toward legal unification. The eighteenth century ideologies of the Enlightenment acted as vehicles for the codification movement. Indeed, the objective of this movement was not to produce compilations, but rather, in keeping with Enlightenment thought, it was to reform and innovate. The codification movement was able to collate systematically the new ideas of the Enlightenment, which provided a doctrinal body that was extraordinarily critical of authoritarian political systems. Those political systems were finally dismantled thanks to the triumph of the liberal revolutions.

The process of codification was intended to introduce both a new law and a new legal science that had nothing to do with the *ancien régime*, that is, with history and tradition.

However, the reality was much more complex. Codes were not so revolutionary or radical and were not made out of nothing. As the main drafters of the French Civil Code recognized, codes could not ignore history, and legal tradition was seriously considered and used in drafting the Napoleonic Codes.

> *Address on the First Draft of the Civil Code, presented in the year* IX *by Messrs. Portalis, Tronchet, Bigot-Préameneu and Maleville, members of the government-appointed commission, 3–4, 16 (https://www.justice.gc.ca/eng/rp-pr/csj-sjc/ilp-pji/code/civil.pdf; accessed in October 2022) © The International Cooperation Group, Department of Justice of Canada (English transl.)*
>
> But what a great task is the drafting of a civil legislation for a great people! The endeavour would be beyond human powers, if it entailed giving this people an entirely new institution and if, forgetting that civil legislation ranks first among civilised nations, one did not deign to benefit from the experience of the past and from that tradition of good sense, rules and maxims which has come down to us and informs the spirit of centuries.
>
> Laws are not pure acts of power; they are acts of wisdom, justice and reason. The lawmaker does not exert an authority so much as a sacred function. He must not lose sight of the fact that laws are made for men, and not men for laws; that they must be adapted to the character, customs, circumstances of the people for whom they are made; that one must be sparing of the new in matters of legislation, because, while one can, in a new institution, calculate the advantages that theory offers, one cannot know all the disadvantages which practice alone can reveal … Rather than change laws, it is almost always more useful to present the citizenry with new reasons to love them; that history offers us the promulgation of no more than two or three good laws over the span of several centuries …
>
> One must not give in to blind prejudices. All that is old was once new. What is essential is to impart to the new institutions that character of permanence and stability that can guarantee them the right to grow old.
>
> We have made, if one can express it this way, a compromise between written law and customs whenever we were able to reconcile their provisions, or to modify some in light of others, without disrupting the unity of the system or offending the general spirit. It is useful to protect all

> that need not be destroyed: laws must show consideration for common practices, when such practices are not vices. Too often one reasons as though the human race ended and began at every moment, with no sort of communication between one generation and that which replaces it. Generations, in succeeding one another, mingle, intertwine and merge. A lawmaker would be isolating his institutions from all that can naturalize them on earth if he did not carefully observe the natural relationships that always, to varying degrees, bind the present to the past and the future to the present; and that cause a people, unless it is exterminated or falls into a decline worse than annihilation, to always resemble itself to some degree. We have, in our modern times, loved change and reform too much; if, when it comes to institutions and laws, centuries of ignorance have been the arena of abuses, then centuries of philosophy and knowledge have all too often been the arena of excesses.

2.9 *Custom*

Custom constituted the main legal source of the Western legal tradition throughout many centuries, particularly from the downfall of the Western Roman Empire onwards (476). Law in the Middle Ages was based upon custom, both in the civil law and common law traditions. Although in the Early Modern Age customary law went through a crisis all over Europe, being gradually displaced and replaced by other legal sources, it maintained its validity until the codification period (in the nineteenth century) and beyond.

Despite of its explicit recognition in the *Preliminary Address on the First Draft of the Civil Code* ('[M]any things are therefore necessarily left to the authority of custom, to the discussion of learned men, to the arbitration of judges') the French Civil Code did not provide for a general provision declaring custom to be a source of law, although we find a few specific references to custom throughout the text of the Code (see, for example, Articles 590, 593, 608, 663 and 671 of the Code).

The situation was different in Germany. Despite the fact that the German Historical School considered custom as an expression of the German *Volksgeist*, the German civil code did not consider custom as a source of law. The position of customary law in the Western legal tradition is ambiguous and paradoxical: the less it was discussed in doctrine, the greater its relevance. It may also be said that the relevance of custom as a source of law was inversely proportional to the extent of state power and public authority in a certain polity.

The Spanish civil code (1888/89) is the only European code which considered custom to be a source of law.

L. Neville Brown, The Sources of Spanish Civil Law, Int'l & Comp. L.Q. 5 (1956), 364–365

Article 6 of the Spanish Civil Code of 1889 consists of two paragraphs. The first states that the court which refuses to reach a decision because of the silence, obscurity or insufficiency of the laws (*las leyes*) incurs a legal liability. The second paragraph explains how the judge is to escape from this dilemma: 'When there is no statute (*ley*) exactly applicable to the issue in question, one shall apply the custom of the place (*la costumbre del lugar*) and, in default, the general principles of the law (*los principios generales de derecho*).'

The two paragraphs read in conjunction show that the primary source of law is *la ley:* in this the Code remains loyal to Spanish traditions and the principles of the modern civilians. Only in the absence of a provision of *la ley* can one turn to the two 'extra-legal' subsidiary sources indicated in the Code, namely, local custom and the general principles of the law …

In recognising local custom as a second source of legal rules the Code does not prescribe the conditions which the particular custom might satisfy before the judge may accept it as a rule of law applicable to the case before him. Rather these conditions have been evolved by the jurists and the judges themselves in the manner of the English law: it is not surprising that the list of conditions is very similar to that required by English law.

In the absence of a provision of *la ley* or of a local custom, Article 6 directs the judge to apply the general principles of the law (*los principios generales de derecho*).

A. Masferrer, Was the French Civil Code 'the Model' of the Spanish One? An Approach to the Uniqueness of the Spanish Civil Code, GLOSSAE. European Journal of Legal History 15 (2018), 113 (http://www.glossae.eu; accessed in October 2022)

In North America, [the] Louisiana codes, namely, the Digest of 1808 and the Civil Code of 1825, clearly departing from French influence, explicitly admitted custom as a legal source. In Latin America, Andrés Bello, the drafter of the Civil Code of Chile (1856) – which was used as a model by other Latin American jurisdictions – explicitly rejected custom as a legal source. The following jurisdictions followed the approach of the Civil Code of Chili: Ecuador (1858), El Salvador (1859), Panamá (1860), Uruguay (1868) and Argentina (1869). Custom was ignored as a legal source in Bolivia (1831), the Dominican Republic (1845), Mexico (1870), Guatemala (1877) and Costa Rica (1887). Custom was only recognized as a source of law in the civil codes of Colombia (1887) and Cuba (1889),

> the latter country having adopted the Spanish code. Later, some 20th-century American civil codes would admit custom: Honduras (1906), Panamá (1916), Puerto Rico (1930) and Argentina as a result of Decree/Law 17.711 of 1968.

Customary law was also relevant in the nineteenth-century Anglo-American context. In England, many areas of law were governed by custom. Sir Frederick Pollock, dealing with land law, made the following observations.

> *Frederick Pollock, The Land Laws, London, MacMillan, 1883, 42*
> ... that rights of common and all similar rights are derived *either* from the ancient use and enjoyment of undivided common land under the customary regulations imposed by the township to which the land belonged, or from use and enjoyment really granted by lords to their inferior tenants in imitation of the ancient customs.

The origins of customary law are not necessarily of a popular nature. It has, for example, been shown that the customary nature of the English Law Merchant was a product of legal reasoning and judicial decisions.

> *E.K. Braybrooke, Custom as a Source of English Law, Mich. L. Rev. 50 (1951–1952), 85–86*
> What was received into English law under the name of the custom of merchants was in fact the law which was applied to these instruments already in the courts of the Continent, though, no doubt to save the face of the common lawyers, it was as a matter of practice established by the evidence of merchants, and not (at any rate not at first) by reference to the treatises and codes of the civil lawyers. Similar remarks apply to the concept of negotiability; Holdsworth points out that the English rules as to bearer bills clearly followed the continental practice. Indeed, the whole range of mercantile customs eventually incorporated into the Common Law rests in its origin upon the practice, including the judicial practice, of a class of men who formed a community in themselves, transcending national barriers; and the so-called customs of merchants are as much a product of legal reasoning and judicial decision as of popular action.

In the United States of America, custom was used 'to reconcile opposition to legislation with the democratic spirit.'[8] In doing so, custom was presented as the best alternative to legislation in light of the ideal of popular sovereignty. Since judges – not legislators – were the main 'discoverers' and 'expositors' of custom, they were seen as the ultimate representatives of the people. This argument was used in the United States of America by James C. Carter in his fight against the codification of private law.

> *Aniceto Masferrer, Defense of the Common Law against Postbellum American Codification: Reasonable and Fallacious Argumentation, American Journal for Legal History 4/50 (2008–2010), 390–392*
> The province of public law did not unhinge this legal principle, since that branch of the law could be regulated by written laws enacted by the legislature. But as to private law, Carter found democratic legitimacy in the classic notion of common law based on custom, which the judges applied in the specific cases presented before them. By equating custom with common law, he argued that the common law is much more democratic than legislation, because, while the legislature can be dominated by biased or corrupt interests, custom is the product and reflection of popular thought and belief:
>
>> Customs ... being common modes of action, are the unerring evidence of common thought and belief, and as they are the joint product of the thoughts of all, each one has his own share in forming them. In the enforcement of a rule thus formed no one can complain, for it is the only rule which can be framed which gives equal expression to the voice of each.
>
> Carter revitalized the classical idea of custom as the main legal source of the common law, asserting that the law is, above all – with the narrow exception of legislation – custom. It is noteworthy that he used the term 'custom' in his last writings. In previous works he usually referred to a 'popular standard of justice,' a 'social standard of justice,' or a 'national standard of justice,' which ought to be applied by judges in order to pronounce a fair judgment. By equating the common law with customary standards of justice, based on popular customs, the province of the unwritten law seemed to be clearly legitimated in democratic terms. Since

8 Morton J. Horwitz, The Tranformation of American Law, 1870–1960, Oxford, Oxford University Press, 1992, 119.

> he was convinced that Anglo-American civilization was highly advanced, its legal tradition based mainly and primarily on custom, approached the ideal. From this point of view, it was clear to Carter that there was no need to codify the private law.
>
> Leaving aside the province of public law and other specific cases in which Carter recognized that legislation was needed, he erected the 'social standard of justice' as the cornerstone of his common law legal theory, bestowing upon it, at the same time, the requisite democratic legitimacy. In fact, he introduced this expression for the first time in American jurisprudence in his *Proposed Codification of our Common Law*. As previously mentioned, in his late works he tended to refer to the common law with the simpler expression 'custom,' or alternatively as the 'opinions, customs and habits of the people.'

The notion of a 'social standard of justice' flowing from custom endowed the common law, according to Carter, with the requisite democratic legitimacy, and laid the foundations of judicial activity (which – according to Carter – did not consist of making or creating law, but of simply applying it to specific cases), putting justice at the center of Carter's theory of jurisprudence, in which there are no absolute legal rules but rather provisional ones. These rules cannot be codified since they are constantly subject to change as a result of their application on a case-by-case basis.

2.10 *General Principles of Law, Natural Law, Equity and Reason*

Article 4 of Napoleon's Civil Code prescribed that '[T]he judge who shall refuse to provide justice, under the pretext of the silence, obscurity, or insufficiency of the law, shall be liable for refusal of justice.' Since the code did not foresee all possible legal disputes which might arise in the future, additional legal sources were needed to ensure that all cases could be adjudicated.

The admission of secondary legal sources such as general principles of law, equity and natural law, prevented judges from resorting to the lawmaker when they did not find a legal provision to settle the dispute at hand.

> *Preliminary Address on the First Draft of the Civil Code, presented in the year* IX *by Messrs. Portalis, Tronchet, Bigot-Préameneu and Maleville, members of the government-appointed commission, 10–11 (https://www.justice.gc.ca/eng/rp-pr/csj-sjc/ilp-pji/code/civil.pdf; accessed in October 2022) © The International Cooperation Group, Department of Justice of Canada (English transl.)*
>
> To compel the magistrate to resort to the lawmaker would be to admit the most grievous of principles; it would be to revive among us the disastrous

legislation of rescripts. For when the lawmaker steps in to rule on matters arising and heatedly debated between individuals, he is no more protected from surprises than the courts. There is less reason to dread the controlled, timid and circumspect arbitrariness of a judge who can be overturned, and who can be prosecuted for abuse of authority, than the absolute arbitrariness of an independent authority that is never accountable.

Parties who have dealings with each other in an area not defined by positive law are subject to accepted customs or to universal equity in the absence of any custom. Now, observing a point of custom and applying it to a private dispute is a judicial act, not a legislative one. The very application of this equity or this distributive justice, which follows and must follow, in each particular case, together with all the little threads that tie one litigant to the other, can never be left to the lawmaker, who is only the agent of this justice or this general equity and who, without considering any particular circumstance, embraces the universality of things and persons. Laws pronounced on private matters would, then, often become suspected of bias and always be retroactive and unjust for the parties to a dispute that preceded the pronouncement of these laws. Furthermore, resorting to the lawmaker would result in disastrous delays for litigants and, even worse, would compromise the wisdom and sanctity of the laws.

In effect, the law governs everyone: it considers men collectively, never individually; it must not involve itself in individual events or disputes that divide citizens. If it did, new laws would have to be made every day: their sheer number would stifle their dignity and compromise their observance. The jurisconsult would have no function, and the lawmaker, bogged down in the particulars, would soon be no more than a jurisconsult. The legislative power would be besieged by private interests, distracting it, at every turn, from the general interest of society.

The 1791 French Constitution was highly influenced by Rousseau's legal positivism. It provided that the judges might refer questions of interpretation to the legislature in order to resolve differences among the courts. This so-called *réferé législatif* was suppressed in 1837 because of the danger of decisions inspired by biased, political considerations and the lack of the necessary independence to resolve existing disputes. In this vein, the drafters of the French Civil Code had warned, in their *Preliminary Address*, of the danger of involving the legislature in particular disputes. Historical experience shows they were completely right.

The admission of general principles of law as a subsidiary legal source constituted a clear sign of the impossibility of getting rid of the old *ius* or *iura*, the insufficiency of *lex*, as well as of the limits of legal positivism. The majority of the nineteenth-century Western civil codes admitted the general principles of law. Many of them recognized only two legal sources, namely *lex* (provisions of the code) and the general principles of law. Examples are France, Belgium, Italy, the Netherlands, Chile, Uruguay, Guatemala, Brazil, Mexico and Argentina. Others ecognized three legal sources since – as we saw – they admitted custom as well. Examples are Austria, Spain, Cuba, Colombia and Switzerland. The Spanish Civil Code, after reproducing – almost literally – the abovementioned Article 4 of the French Civil Code, added: 'When there is no law exactly applicable to the point in controversy, local customs shall be observed, and in the absence thereof, the general principles of law.' The German Civil Code did not specifically mention the latter principles since the drafters took it for granted that judges would need to resort to the spirit of the legal order. This idea of a legal order or general principles of law is what the drafters of the Swiss Civil Code (1907) might have had in mind when they provided: 'If the law does not furnish an applicable provision, the judge shall decide in accordance with customary law, and failing that, according to the rule which he would have established as a legislator. In this he shall be guided by approved legal doctrine and judicial tradition' (Article 1).

Since codes could not cover all contingencies, and since cases of first impression must occur in common law jurisdictions as well, the prohibition of *non liquet* demanded recognition of such *rationes decidendi* as have been found in general principles of law, natural law, equity or reason. It may be argued that the nineteenth-century general principles of law were designed to replace natural law, but that is not fully accurate and was not the case in many territories. The *Preliminary Address on the First Draft of the Civil Code* stated that 'while the foresight of lawmakers is limited, nature is limitless; it applies to everything that may be of interest to men.' Furthermore, it also explicitly recognized that 'positive laws could never entirely replace the use of natural reason in life's affairs.' The way the *Preliminary Address* refers to the convenience to resort to usages, equity and natural law is most revealing.

> *Preliminary Address on the First Draft of the Civil Code, presented in the year IX by Messrs. Portalis, Tronchet, Bigot-Préameneu and Maleville, members of the government-appointed commission, 7 and 10 (https://www.justice.gc.ca/eng/rp-pr/csj-sjc/ilp-pji/code/civil.pdf; accessed in October 2022) © The International Cooperation Group, Department of Justice of Canada (English transl.)*
>
> It would doubtless be desirable for all matters to be provided for by laws. But, in the absence of a specific enactment on every subject, an

> old, consistent and well-established custom, an unbroken succession of similar rulings, a received opinion or maxim serves as law. When not guided by anything established or known, when faced with an entirely new occurrence, one returns to the principles of natural law. For while the foresight of lawmakers is limited, nature is limitless; it applies to everything that may be of interest to men. …
>
> On the basis of the maxim that judges must obey laws and are prohibited from interpreting them, the courts, in recent years, have been referring the litigants to the legislative authority, through summary procedures, every time they lacked law or found the existing law obscure. The court of cassation has continually considered this abuse as a denial of justice.
>
> There are two kinds of interpretation: one doctrinal, and the other authoritative.
>
> Doctrinal interpretation consists in grasping the true meaning of laws, in applying them judiciously and in supplementing them in cases where they do not apply. Can one conceive of fulfilling the office of judge without this type of interpretation?
>
> Authoritative interpretation consists in settling issues and doubts by means of rules or general provisions. This mode of interpretation is the only one denied the judge.
>
> When the law is clear, it must be heeded; when it is unclear, the provisions must be further elaborated. If there is no law, then custom or equity must be consulted. Equity is the return to natural law when positive laws are silent, contradictory or vague.

The natural law was indeed present in the mind of the drafters of the French Civil Code, for whom the distinction between natural law, the law of nations and positive law was clear.

> *Preliminary Address on the First Draft of the Civil Code, presented in the year IX by Messrs. Portalis, Tronchet, Bigot-Préameneu and Maleville, members of the government-appointed commission, 12 (https://www.justice.gc.ca/eng/rp-pr/csj-sjc/ilp-pji/code/civil.pdf; accessed in October 2022) © The International Cooperation Group, Department of Justice of Canada (English transl.)*
>
> Law is universal reason, supreme reason based on the very nature of things. Legislation is, or ought only to be, law reduced to positive rules, to specific precepts.

> Law is morally imperative, but in itself is not constraining. It guides; laws command. It is the map; and laws, the compasses.
>
> Diverse peoples coexist only under the rule of law; the members of a city are governed, as men, by law, and as citizens, by legislation.
>
> Natural law and the law of nations differ not at all in their substance, only in their application. Reason, as it governs all men for all time, is called natural law, and it is called the law of nations as it governs the relations among peoples.
>
> If one speaks of a natural law of nations and a positive law of nations, it is to distinguish the eternal principles of justice that peoples have had no part in making, and to which the various bodies of nations, and every individual, are subject, from the capitulations, treaties and customs that are the work of peoples.

Despite of this, the ideology of the French Civil Code precluded the admission of any reference to natural law (and custom and equity), and eventually it only admitted the law (*lex*) and the general principles of law as sources of law.

The Austrian Civil Code (1811), on the contrary, directed the judge to equity, usage and the principles of natural justice (Article 7). The Louisiana Civil Codes of 1825 and 1870 also admitted these sources. Article 21 of these Civil Codes invited the judge to proceed and decide according to equity (defined as natural law, reason and received usages) where positive law was silent: 'In all civil matters, where there is no express law, the judge is bound to proceed and decide according to equity. To decide equitably, an appeal is to be made to natural law and reason, or received usages, where positive law is silent.' Furthermore, in Louisiana in the first half of the nineteenth century judges not only regarded natural law as a source of law – as part of the *iura* – but also maintained that it could not be abrogated by the legislature.

> *Olivier Moréteau, François-Xavier Martin Revisited: Louisiana Views on Codification, Jurisprudence, Legal Education and Practice, Louisiana Bar Journal 6/60 (2013), 475–479*
>
> [François-Xavier] Martin [a Louisiana Supreme Court Justice] was in favor of a clean abrogation clause, as it is the best way to make the law predictable for the citizen to whom it is to be applied. Yet he believed that such a clause would only repeal the positive laws adopted by a legislature. In *Reynolds v. Swain*, a case decided in 1839, at a time when Martin was the Chief Judge, he said that the legislature cannot abrogate unwritten law such as natural law or the law of nations:

> The repeal spoken of in the code, and the act of 1828, cannot extend beyond the laws which the legislature itself has enacted … It cannot be extended to those unwritten laws which do not derive their authority from the positive institution of any people, as the revealed law, the natural law, the law of nations, the laws of peace and war, and those laws which are founded in those relations of justice that existed in the nature of things, antecedent to any positive precept.

> There is no clearer statement in Louisiana jurisprudence that the law is grounded on universal principles. After all, those who deny the existence of natural law nonetheless recognize the supremacy of human rights and fundamental rights, and are willing to accept that they may only be defined in the context of a case. Whatever the name and wherever such rights receive constitutional support, we accept that judges may strike down legislative provisions unreasonably denying their protection. We are willing to accept that positive civil or municipal laws, as defined by Justinian and Blackstone, are just conducive of local variations. The reference to equity and natural law in the gap filling provision of the Digest and Codes of 1825 and 1870, copied from the French *Projet* and yet abandoned in the French *Code civil*, supports Martin's view, and the omitted reference to natural law in the revised article 4 [1987 Reform] may be regretted. The reason given in comment (b), 'The term *natural law* in Article 21 of the 1870 Code has no defined meaning in Louisiana jurisprudence' is shameful and wrong.

The first judges who sat on the Louisiana Supreme Court were not positivists, and the Louisiana civil law consistently differs from the French Code in this respect. They show an open-minded view of what the law is.

> *Olivier Moréteau, De Revolutionibus: The Place of the Civil Code in Louisiana and in the Legal Universe, J. Civ. L. Stud. 5 (2012), 40–41 (available at http://digitalcommons.law.lsu.edu/jcls/vol5/iss1/4, accessed in October 2023)*
> What made a remarkable difference, however, was the judicial resistance to positivism. Louisiana judges of the first half of the 19th century did not accept that legislation (*lex*) could do away with or abrogate what Professor Pascal calls right order and may simply be called law in its broadest sense, meaning *droit* or *ius*. François-Xavier Martin, who sat on the Louisiana Supreme Court between 1812 and 1846, had been in favor of a clean abrogation clause in the Digest, and yet at the same time believed

> that such a clause could only repeal the positive laws adopted by a legislature. In *Reynolds v. Swain*, a case decided in 1839 when Martin was Chief Justice (at that time called Chief Judge), he said that the legislature cannot abrogate unwritten law such as natural law or the law of nations, proving that Louisiana law was much more than mere positive law. The Civil Code is *lex*, not *ius*, and therefore has a lower density than it may have in a positivistic system.

The link between natural law and general principles of law was present in many nineteenth-century Western jurisdictions, reaching Asia in the twentieth century.[9] The importance of natural law in the common law tradition was also undeniable. The doctrine of a law of nature controlling even the legislative power, dramatically proclaimed by Coke in Bonham's Case (1610) and partly accepted by Blackstone in his *Commentaries on the Laws of England* (1765–1769), was part of the Anglo-American legal heritage.

Whereas the meaning of natural law in both common law and civil law is the same, the notion of equity is different. Whereas in the latter judges pronounced equitable decisions when they thought it was fitting for particular cases, in the former equity became an independent jurisdiction, a competing system different to that of the common law which was deemed too rigid and thus unsuitable to solve certain cases. However, since the nineteenth century, equity has gradually become less flexible. The Judicature Act of 1873 eliminated the distinction between the two systems of courts, transferring the powers of the common law courts and courts of equity to the newly established Supreme Court of Judicature. When common law and equity were merged, Parliament laid down that where equity and law were in conflict, equity would prevail. In the United States of America, the Constitution fused equity and law, providing that 'judicial power shall extend to all cases, in Law and Equity' (Article III, Section 2), but did not tackle their hierarchy in case of conflict, or limitations on equity. Furthermore, the Field Code of Civil Procedure (1848) abolished the complex scheme of common law pleading, as well as equity procedure, and replaced them with a simplified, uniform procedural system. This procedural code, which was enacted in the state of New York, was particularly relevant in the nineteenth century because the majority of other states ultimately embraced this Code or some revised version of it.

9 Some adaptations of the Western codes used the expression natural law to refer to the general principles of law. For example, Art. 1 of the Civil Code of Egypt (1949), which influenced all Arab nations possessing modern civil codes, with the exception of Saudi Arabia and Oman, laid down that: 'In the absence of an express provision, the judge shall follow the rules of custom; if they do not exist, the principles of Islamic law, and, if they in turn do not exist, he shall follow principles of natural law and equity.'

2.11 *Judicial Decisions and Judge-Made Law*

The drafters of the French Civil Code did not disregard the relevance of previous judgments in judicial decision making, emphasizing the goodness of having 'compendia, and a continuous tradition of customs, maxims and rules, so that one must, in a sense, judge today as one judged yesterday; and that there are no variations in public judgements other than those brought about by the advance of knowledge and force of circumstance.' In fact, they seemed to trust in the judges. According to them, 'they [i.e. the judges] have a wide experience in matters; they have insight and knowledge; and they believe they have a constant duty to consult with each other. There is no telling the degree to which this habit of science and reason mitigates and regulates power. To balance the authority that we give judges to rule on matters not determined by statutes, we invoke the right of every citizen to be judged only according to a previous and constant law.'[10]

'To be judged only according to a previous and constant law' seems to mean that judicial decisions were supposed to be something else than just an authoritative source of legal interpretation. These decisions were not a main source of law, but they were nevertheless regarded as sources of law and applicable 'on matters not determined by statutes.' That was particularly clear in civil matters.

> *Preliminary Address on the First Draft of the Civil Code, presented in the year* IX *by Messrs. Portalis, Tronchet, Bigot-Préameneu and Maleville, members of the government-appointed commission, 9–10 (https://www.justice.gc.ca/eng/rp-pr/csj-sjc/ilp-pji/code/civil.pdf; accessed in October 2022) © The International Cooperation Group, Department of Justice of Canada (English transl.)*
>
> … in civil matters, the dispute is always between two or more citizens. An issue of property or any other similar issue cannot remain unresolved between them. A decision must be taken; the dispute must somehow be brought to an end. If the parties cannot themselves reach an agreement, what is the State to do? Unable to give them laws on every subject, it offers them, in the person of the public magistrate, an informed and impartial arbitrator whose decision prevents them from coming to blows, and he is certainly more beneficial to them than a prolonged dispute, neither the repercussions nor the outcome of which they could predict. The apparent arbitrariness of equity is better than the turmoil of passions.

---

10 Preliminary Address, 8.

In criminal matters, however, the dispute is between the citizen and the State. The intent of the State can only be represented by that of the law. The citizen whose actions do not contravene the law will therefore not be disturbed or accused on behalf of the State. Here, not only is there no need to judge, but there is no matter to be judged.

The law that serves as the basis for the accusation must precede the action of which one is accused. The lawmaker must not strike without warning; otherwise, the law, contrary to its fundamental purpose, would not set out to make men better, but only to make them more miserable, which would go against the very essence of things.

Thus, in criminal matters, where the judge's action can be based only on a formal, pre-existing enactment, there must be specific laws and no jurisprudence. This is not so in civil matters. Here, there must be jurisprudence, because it is impossible to regulate every civil matter by laws and because it is necessary to end disputes between individuals that cannot be left unresolved, without forcing every citizen to become the judge in his own case, and not forgetting that justice is the first debt of sovereignty.

This may explain why the drafters maintained that 'If there is one area in which excessive commentary, discussion and writing can be excused, it is, above all, in jurisprudence.'[11] According to them, whereas '[t]he lawmaker's science consists in finding, on every subject, the principles most favourable to the common good, … the magistrate's science consists in applying those principles, ramifying them, extending them, through wise and reasoned application, to private hypotheses; in analysing the spirit of the law when the letter is silent.' They never explicitly referred either to the 'binding' force of previous judgments or to judicial precedent as a 'source of law', but left no doubt about the relevance of jurisprudence as legal source.

Preliminary Address on the First Draft of the Civil Code, presented in the year IX by Messrs. Portalis, Tronchet, Bigot-Préameneu and Maleville, members of the government-appointed commission, 11–12 (https://www.justice.gc.ca/eng/rp-pr/csj-sjc/ilp-pji/code/civil.pdf; accessed in October 2022) © The International Cooperation Group, Department of Justice of Canada (English transl.)

The lawmaker must keep a watchful eye on jurisprudence; it can enlighten him, and he, for his part, can improve it; but jurisprudence there must be.

11 Preliminary Address, 7.

> In this vastness of the diverse subjects that constitute civil matters, and the judgement of which entails, in the majority of cases, less the application of a specific enactment than the combining of several enactments that lead to, rather than contain, the decision, one can no more do without jurisprudence than without laws. Now, it is to jurisprudence that we leave those rare and exceptional cases that cannot fit within the framework of a reasonable legislation, the too-volatile and too-contentious particulars that must not occupy the lawmaker, and all the subjects it would be futile to try and foresee, or whose hasty prediction could not be free of risk. It is left to experience to continually fill the voids we leave. The codes of peoples are made over time; but, strictly speaking, we do not make them.

This was not, however, the view of some late eighteenth-century political reformers and other nineteenth-century French lawyers, particularly those belonging to the exegetical school of law (see below).

Most civil law jurisdictions were reluctant to consider case law as a primary, binding source of law, viewing it – at least, theoretically – as a secondary, persuasive source of law.

> *Vincy Fon and Francesco Parisi, Judicial Precedents in Civil Law Systems: A dynamic analysis, International Review of Law and Economics 26 (2006), 522*
>
> Most civil law systems underwent quite a different evolution, relegating case law to the rank of a secondary legal source. Codes and special legislation were recognized as the only primary source of law. In 19th century Europe, the doctrine of the separation of powers was understood to imply that '[t]he role of the courts is to solve disputes that are brought before them, not to make laws or regulations'. This strict historical conception of separation of powers was due to general distrust of courts that were manipulated by the king before the French revolution. The ideals of certainty and completeness in the law implied that legislative provisions had to be formulated and interpreted as mathematical canons to avoid any room for discretion or arbitrary decisions in the judiciary.
>
> However, European jurists gradually developed a healthy skepticism concerning the ideals of certainty and completeness in the codified law. As memories of the abuses of pre-revolution regimes began to fade, ideological concerns over the judiciary's role were assuaged. In their own judicial practices, civil law jurisdictions gradually adhered to a system of informal precedent law, where a sequence of analogous cases acquired persuasive force as a source of law. ...

> This path of legal development gave rise to *jurisprudence constante*, the doctrine under which a court is required to take past decisions into account only if there is sufficient uniformity in previous case law. ...

By the end of the nineteenth century, the exegetical school had declined and was replaced by the school of free scholarly research. François Gény, in his *Méthode d'interprétation et sources en droit privé: Essay critique* (1899) (*Method of interpretation and sources of positive private law: A critical essay*) proposed a new method of interpretation to discover the origins of legal principles and rules. To put it simply, instead of worrying about consulting legislative history to know the will of a legislator who had already passed away, he maintained that judges faced with an obscurity or gap in the law should become legislators and be concerned about social needs, the ideals of the moment, comparative law and history. This theory influenced Germany and Switzerland, where the Civil Code of 1907 provided in its Article 1 that if the judge could not find an applicable provision in the Code, he should decide in accordance with customary law, and failing that, according to the rule which he as a legislator would have adopted, in line with approved legal doctrine and judicial tradition.

The principle of precedent, which started at the end of the sixteenth century, when English courts adhered to previous custom in matters of procedure and pleading, did not constitute a substantive rule of precedent until the seventeenth and eighteenth centuries. In that period, courts were supposed to 'find' the law, rather than to 'make' it. When several cases presented the same legal principle, the persuasive force of judicial findings increased. Precedents became more authoritative when they were reaffirmed by a sequence of consistent decisions over time. However, it was only during the late eighteenth and early nineteenth centuries – partly because of Bentham's positivist influence – that the doctrine of *stare decisis* gave rise to the common law principle of the binding authority of precedent. By the end of the nineteenth century, due to the reorganisation of the judicial system by the Judicature Acts of 1873 and 1875 and the new character of the Law Reports, the notion of formally binding rules of precedent was established. From then precedents were no longer viewed as persuasive evidence of the law, but as a primary source of law.

> *Geoffrey Cross and G.D.G. Hall, The English Legal System, London, Butterworths, 1964, 365–367*
> But in the nineteenth century it came gradually to be established that a principle to be extracted from a previous decision of a superior court was binding on an inferior court, and further, that the highest tribunal was bound by its own decisions. This development was aided by the

reorganisation of the judicial system by the Judicature Acts and by the contemporaneous changes in the character of the Law Reports. In the eighteenth century there were a number of separate courts which had little hesitation in differing from one another, and a supreme tribunal which was so constituted that its decisions did not command any great respect in the profession. After 1875 there were a well-regulated hierarchy of courts – High Court, Court of Appeal and House of Lords – and it was natural to conclude that decisions of the Court of Appeal should be binding on the High Court and the decisions of the House of Lords [now the Supreme Court of the UK] on the Court of Appeal. The rule that the House of Lords is bound by its own decisions [this is currently not true anymore; see Practice Statement [1966] 3 All ER 77] and that the Court of Appeal is bound by its own decisions unless they conflict with a decision of the House of Lords is perhaps unfortunate – but it is now well established. Judges of the first instance do not consider themselves to be bound by the decisions of their brother judges though they usually follow them 'out of courtesy' even if they feel doubts as to their correctness.

The decisions of the courts are now reported in a quasi-official form. Down to 1866 the publishing of reports was a matter of private enterprise, and there were great differences in their quality. A far greater respect would be accorded to a decision reported by Burrows or Campbell than to one reported by Comberbach or Espinasse, and judges were sometimes able to ignore decisions which they disliked by suggesting that they were incorrectly reported. In 1866 private reporting in the old sense of the word came to an end and the Incorporated Council of Law Reporting was established. This is indeed a private body, but has a quasi-official character, since its members are representatives of the Inns of Court and the Law Society. The Council employs an editor and a staff of reporters and produces a uniform series of reports of cases in all the superior courts. Of course only a small minority of cases heard are reported. It rests with the discretion of the reporter in court to decide whether any case seems *prima facie* to deserve a report, and with the editor to select from cases noted by the reporters those which shall in fact be reported. If it is decided to report a case the judge has an opportunity of revising the wording of his judgment. In addition to the reports published by the Council of Law Reporting, which are known as 'The Law Reports' *par excellence*, there are a number of proprietary series issued by journals and legal publishers. The great majority of cases reported in these series of reports are also published in the Law Reports. All the reporters are barristers.

Thus, in nineteenth-century common law, case law was regarded as the main source of law, despite of statutes, digests, restatements and codes. This is particularly true in the province of private law, whose development common lawyers preferred to entrust to judges over legislators. The need for private law reform and the instrumental conception of law (whereby law was regarded as a tool to change society) led some judges to what has been called judicial activism.

Daniel R. Coquillette, The Anglo-American Legal Heritage. Introductory Materials (2nd ed.), Durham, Carolina Academic Press, 2004, 502–505

[T]he American judiciary also adopted an 'instrumental conception' of law. While leaders such as Jefferson took a dim view of the judicial activism of Mansfield – whom Jefferson accused of rendering the law 'more uncertain under pretense of rendering it more reasonable' – they also failed to replace judicial reform with legislative codes.

Judicial instrumentalism can be found in many leading American courts during this period. A particularly excellent example is the famous case of *Commonwealth v. Hunt*, decided in 1842 by the Supreme Judicial Court of Massachusetts. The opinion was written by a true peer of Mansfield, the great Chief Justice of Massachusetts, Lemuel Shaw (1781–1861). Like Mansfield, Shaw was Chief Justice for more than thirty years (1830–1860), and changed the legal landscape of Massachusetts by common law adjudication.

Commonwealth v. Hunt was a pioneer 'union' case. The facts were these. One Jeremiah Horne, a boot-maker, was discharged by his employer because Horne was not willing to pay a penalty to the Boston Journeymen Bootmakers' Society, a union. Horne had been fined by the union for doing extra work without pay, a violation of union rules. His employer wished to enjoy good relations with the union and to avoid strikes. An indictment was then brought by the state against John Hunt and six other union leaders for conspiracy on three counts: (1) forming an 'unlawful ... combination' to 'extort great sums of money' by imposing a rule that members would not work for an employer who hired non-members – today called a 'closed shop' rule; (2) that Horne's employer was forced to discharge him for this reason; and (3) that the defendant thus 'wicked and unjustly intending unlawfully, and by indirect means, to impoverish one Jeremiah Horne ... and hinder him from following his trade ...'

In theory, this case was of the greatest interest. Freedom of contract was widely regarded as a fundamental right of the individual protected by the common law, closely analogous to the right to private property. Unlawful interference with the right of a person to make contracts or to follow a legal trade had long been seen by Anglo-American common law as a 'criminal conspiracy', similar to extortion. Further, as James Willard Hurst pointed out, 'contract and free private association' were seen as the cornerstones of the 'release-of-energy' principle: i.e. that the elimination of archaic, status-oriented legal doctrines would free trade to reach its most beneficial and profitable potential, to the ultimate benefit of all. According to this theory, the activities of the union not only violated Horne's common law rights as an individual, but also impeded the general public good.

But the case was even more important politically. Workers in the industrial states were discovering that any 'equality' in bargaining their services with big employers was a myth. As Hurst observed:

> Economic growth tied the lives of an increasing proportion of people to the market and the division of labor; they were either wage or salary earners, or small producers or traders in specialized ranges of goods or services. Theoretically buyers consent to the practical compulsions of the market in which they buy; if they do not consent, they stay out. But men who find their whole livelihood in the market are too vulnerable to stay out. An outstanding recognition of this simple but slowly learned truth was the legislation which limited or abolished the employer's defense of assumption of risk in industrial accident cases.

Contract law, uninformed by social policy, could be a 'pretty blunt instrument.' Again, Hurst stated the problem clearly:

> We had to learn a second major lesson about our release-of-energy principle. During the first half of the [nineteenth] century we expressed that principle chiefly through contract. But sound doctrine for so fundamental a community concern as the organization of power requires built-in points of view and procedures to take account of all important values in the situation. Contract was inherently too limited an institution to serve this need.

How would Chief Justice Shaw deal with this dilemma? First, Shaw affirmed that, in the absence of a relevant statute, the case should be decided by 'the general rules of the common law.'

> We have no doubt, that by the operation of the constitution of this Commonwealth, the general rules of the common law, making conspiracy an indictable offence, are in force here, and that this is included

> in the description of laws which had, before the adoption of the constitution, been used and approved in the Province, Colony, or State of Massachusetts Bay, and usually practised in the courts of law.

But not all common law precedents are absolutely binding on Massachusetts courts. '[A]lthough the common law in regard to conspiracy in this Commonwealth is in force, yet it will not necessarily follow that every indictment at common law is a precedent for a similar indictment in the State.' For example,

> All those laws of the parent country, whether rules of the common law, or early English statutes, which were made for the purpose of regulating the wages of laborers, the settlement of paupers, and making it penal for anyone to use a trade or handicraft to which he had not served a full apprenticeship – not being adapted to the circumstances of our colonial condition – were not adopted, used or approved, and therefore do not come within the description of the laws adopted and confirmed by the provision of the constitution already cited.

But if the common law is not to be blindly followed where inappropriate to Massachusetts, and there is no legislative authority directly on point, how are cases involving major legal and political issues to be resolved? In the end, for Shaw, it was an issue of judicial authority. For over 20 pages, a huge opinion for the day, Shaw reviewed every statutory analogy and every relevant common law doctrine. His final conclusion was that the purpose of the union was 'to induce all those engaged in the same occupation to become members of it' and that '[s]uch a purpose is not unlawful.' Nor were the means employed, withholding of labor, criminal. Therefore the damage to Horne was simply that of a legal competition, allowable in everyday economic life. As Shaw observed:

> Suppose a baker in a small village had the exclusive custom of his neighborhood, and was making large profits by the sale of his bread. Supposing a number of those neighbors, believing the price of his bread too high, should propose to him to reduce his prices, or if he did not, that they would introduce another baker; and on his refusal, such other baker should, under their encouragement, set up a rival establishment, and sell his bread at lower prices; the effect would be to diminish the profit of the former baker, and to the same extent to impoverish him. And it might be said and proved, that the purpose

> of the associates was to diminish his profits, and thus impoverish him, though the ultimate and laudable object of the combination was to reduce the cost of bread to themselves and their neighbors. The same thing may be said of all competition in every branch of trade and industry; and yet it is through that competition, that the best interests of trade and industry are promoted. It is scarcely necessary to allude to the familiar instances of opposition lines of conveyance, rival hotels, and the thousand other instances, where each strives to gain custom to himself, by ingenious improvements, by increased industry, and by all the means by which he may lessen the price of commodities, and thereby diminish the profits of others.

> Thus, as the indictment did not charge a 'criminal conspiracy punishable by law,' the judgment … was arrested. The union movement gained a landmark victory.
>
> The fundamental argument of scholars such as Morton Horwitz and others is that Shaw could have decided this case 'either way', and that it is hard to assume that he was oblivious to the great social and political issues hinging on the outcome. The need to 'adapt' a non-statutory common law tradition to new settings gave powerful judges law-making opportunities equivalent to those of the legislatures themselves. The classical common law theory of law as immemorial custom was a shallow fiction. Judges such as Shaw, boldly used judicial opinions to create a law for a new America. This was the point of 'instrumentalism'.

The notion and practice of judicial activism was contrary to the separation of powers, whereby law was supposed to be made or created by the legislature, and judges just applied it or (when the case to be resolved revolved around common law principles) followed judicial precedent. If judges made new laws instead of the legislature, these laws lacked democratic legitimacy because they had not been enacted by the institution which was composed of the representatives of the people. This was one of the main criticisms of those who favored a codification in common law jurisdictions. Some common lawyers such as James C. Carter who considered codification as a threat to the common law, fought against it by arguing that judges did not make the law, but just declared it. Other opponents of codification such as Fowler, Hoadly and Oliver Wendell Holmes had no problem in recognizing the principle of 'judge-made law'.[12]

12 On this matter, see Aniceto Masferrer, Defense of the Common Law against postbellum American Codification: Reasonable and Fallacious Argumentation, American Journal of Legal History 50/4 (2008–2010), 401–405.

2.12 *Doctrine Including Legal Science and Legal Study*

In nineteenth-century civil law jurisdictions, legal doctrine (*la doctrine* in French, *la doctrina* in Spanish, *die Lehre* in German) continued to be regarded as a relevant persuasive source of law. Whereas primary sources (e.g. enacted laws and custom) were binding on the courts *ratio imperii* (for the reason of its authority), jurisprudence and doctrine bound the courts *imperio rationis* (for the power of reason).

The drafters of the French Civil Code, faithful to the civil law tradition, highly regarded legal doctrine.

> *Preliminary Address on the First Draft of the Civil Code, presented in the year IX by Messrs. Portalis, Tronchet, Bigot-Préameneu and Maleville, members of the government-appointed commission, 8 (https://www.justice.gc.ca/eng/rp-pr/csj-sjc/ilp-pji/code/civil.pdf; accessed in October 2022) © The International Cooperation Group, Department of Justice of Canada (English transl.)*
>
> Given the present state of our societies, it is most fortunate that jurisprudence forms a science that can focus talent, flatter pride and awaken emulation. A whole class of men now devotes itself to this science, and this class, dedicated to the study of laws, provides advisers and defenders to citizens who could not find their own way and defend themselves and is becoming a kind of seminary of the magistracy.

It would be difficult to overemphasize the role of doctrine in the nineteenth-century civil law jurisdictions. Legal scholars highly contributed to the law-making process and to legal interpretation, supporting judges in the decision-making process. Codes were drafted by committees mainly composed of scholars, although some codes are particularly linked to one or two individuals (for example, Portalis in France, Anton Freiherr von Martini and Franz von Zeiller in Austria, Edward Livingston in Louisiana, Viscount Seabra in Portugal, Andrés Bello in Chile, Friedrich Carl von Savigny and Bernard Windscheid in Germany, Eugen Huber in Switzerland). Scholars also published commentaries which were highly regarded and carefully studied and followed by judges and lawyers. They commented case law. Some scholars were eventually appointed as judges of the courts of appeals or supreme courts.

In England, William Blackstone was the first Vinerian Professor of English Law and his *Commentaries on the Laws of England* (1765–1769) played a considerable role in the development of the American legal tradition. They may be considered as the first methodical treatise of the common law suitable for a lay readership since the medieval period. In the nineteenth-century common law, legal treatises were practical in nature and mainly written for practicing lawyers. In the US, the three most significant nineteenth century legal writers were James Kent (*Commentaries on American Law*, 1826–1830), Joseph Story (*Commentaries*, 1831–1845) and Oliver Wendell Holmes (*The Common Law*, 1881; *The Path of the Law*, 1898).

In the nineteenth century the role of doctrine as a persuasive source of law was notably connected to legal scholarship and legal education. Natural law came to be regarded as old-fashioned. Despite of the fact that some nineteenth-century legislators and judges admitted natural law as a source of law, the main currents of legal thought rejected it. The nineteenth century marked a decline in the popularity of natural law theories.

> *Tuğrul Ansay & Adnan Güriz, The Concept of Law, Ankara, unpublished, 1968 (revised 2005), 83–84*
> The nineteenth century marked a decline in the popularity of natural law theories. For this there were many reasons. In the first place, the existence of absolute, unchanging principles was convincingly attacked, notably by Hume … Secondly, a reaction set in against the excessive individualism, fostered by natural law theories, which had resulted in the French revolution. Thirdly, we find in the course of the century a new preoccupation with society, a collectivist outlook on life, which has been gathering strength in ever increasing measure. The natural law theories of the age immediately preceding, which were based on the social contract, were adapted to an individualist outlook. In the dawn of a collectivist epoch these theories began to fall into disrepute. Fourthly, the *a priori* methods of the natural law philosophers were unacceptable to those nurtured in the critical and inductive spirit of science. The postulates of natural law were subjected to analytical examination with disastrous results. Their bases were revealed as unsubstantiated hypotheses or else built up by means of false inferences. Where, for instance, is the foundation for the sweeping assertion that man must always seek society, or that man is necessarily selfish, etc.? Again, it is a wild inference to assume that because certain institutions in different countries are alike, that must be because they are reflecting some universal law. Fifthly, historical investigation also helped to explode many of the *a priori* assumptions of the naturalists. The social contract, in particular, came in for damaging criticism. Research into the early history of society exposed the wholly mythical nature of the social contract. *Maine* pointed out that in primitive communities the prevailing idea was that of status, not of contract, and that the progress of societies was towards the notion of contract. Moreover,

> the social contract theories did not take account of the fact that the unit in early communities was not the individual, but the family or clan. Sixth and finally, the increasingly complex problem of the nineteenth century demanded a realistic and practical approach, not the easy application of abstract *a priori* preconceptions.
>
> In the new climate of opinion natural law theories could not survive. In their place we find two currents of thought, analytical positivism [legal positivism] and the historical approach.

Legal positivism – with the French Exegetical School – and the Historical School shared their rejection of natural law theories.

2.13 *Legal Positivism*

Although legal positivism has a long history, its modern roots can be found in the conventionalist political philosophies of Hobbes and Hume, but it was particularly developed by Jeremy Bentham (1748–1832) and his disciple John Austin (1790–1857), who adopted, modified and popularized Bentham's thought. According to their views, law is the command of a sovereign backed by force, a theory which dominated legal positivism and the Western philosophical reflections on law.

Jeremy Bentham replaced the idea of 'nature' (or 'natural law') by that of 'utility,' becoming a proponent of legal utilitarianism.

> *Jeremy Bentham, An Introduction to the Principles of Morals and Legislation, J.H. Burns and H.L.A. Hart (eds), London, Methuen, 1982, nn. 6–7*
>
> 6. A great multitude of people are continually talking of the Law of Nature; and then they go on giving you their sentiments about what is right and what is wrong: and these sentiments, you are to understand, are so many chapters and sections of the Law of Nature.
>
> 7. Instead of the phrase, Law of Nature, you have sometimes, Law of Reason, Right Reason, Natural Justice, Natural Equity, Good Order. Any of them will do equally well. This latter is most used in politics. The three last are much more tolerable than the others, because they do not very explicitly claim to be anything more than phrases: they insist but feebly upon being looked upon as so many positive standards of themselves, and seem content to be taken, upon occasion, for phrases expressive of the conformity of the thing in question to the proper standard, whatever that may be. On most occasions, however, it will be better to say *utility*: *utility* is clearer, as referring more explicitly to pain and pleasure.

2.14 *The French Exegetical School*

Legal positivism constituted one of the main pillars of the French Exegetical School which dominated French nineteenth-century jurisprudence. In the second half of this century it was notably influenced by German Pandectism. For the Exegetical School, the texts of the code – once enacted – were sufficient and there was no need to look at the sources from which they were derived. In other words, once natural law understood as natural reason had been put into written form, law and legal science should get rid of the law of reason and other sources which had been used to draft the codes.

> *Aniceto Masferrer, Spanish Legal Traditions. A Comparative Legal History Outline (2nd ed.), Madrid, Dykinson, 2012, 269–271*
>
> The rational or the ideal that constitutes in itself the form of universal law needs to be formulated in written form through a method called *positivization.* Written law puts in material form the work of reason and this is opposed to the scholastic and theological fundament of natural law.
>
> The fundamental idea of positivism explains the reliance on the technique of codification. Man is a rational being and it is the work of the legislator to transform rational principles into written laws that are called to be applied equally to all men.
>
> The legal historian Bonnecase identified three stages in the work of the French School of Exegesis:
>
> - The foundation of the school (1804–1830). During this period, the jurists Proudhon and Melville stand out.
> - The apogee (1830–1880). The great commentators of this period are Duranton, Aubry, Rau, and Troplong. These authors produced extensive commentaries on the Legal Codes of the day.
> - The decline of the School (1880–1900). One of the most notable authors of this final period was Guillouard.
>
> The Historian A. Hernández Gil produced a clear summary of the main characteristics of the Exegetical School:
>
> 1. Only written law is of value and the concept of 'natural' law is rejected.
> 2. Only the recognized legislators are authorized to produce written laws. Case law is not a valid source of law and the function of judges when applying the law is simply that of searching for the intention of the legislator.

3. Analogy can only be used when the fundamental principle that inspired the legislator has been identified.
4. The identification of Law with written law means that Custom acquires a negative value within the legal system.
5. Law is entirely in the hands of the State.

These principles were well received by some but their practical realization faced many difficulties, some of them internal and others external:

a) The rationalist and positivist tendencies contained a grave flaw. The application of rationalist principles to the legal system resulted in a concept of law as the fruit of speculation and this presupposed its separation from the empirical world.
   The positivism postulated by the School of Exegesis received criticism. The most significant came from Gény, whose comments are believed to have led to the decline of the school. Gény wrote that the positivists' ideas led to legal paralysis. They imposed permanent respect for the criteria that the legislator had held at the time the law was written. They also mistook subjective and provisional considerations for ideals that had an objective and permanent nature.
b) The rationalist ideology and the positivistic conception of law would not find the same acceptance in every community within the nation. The ideology was critical, revisionist and revolutionary. It attacked the doctrine of *ius commune* and the abstract theological ideas that characterized Catholic theories of natural law. Understandably, it faced fierce opposition from those sectors of society that felt solidarity with these traditional ideas.
c) The idea of forming legal bodies with authority over the entire State and even over several States was only well received by those that were in favor of centralization.

2.15 *The German Historical School – Pandectism – Jurisprudence of Concepts (Begriffsjurisprudenz)*

The French Exegetical School rejected the scholastic conception of natural law as it only considered as valid law that was written and based on reason. It also rejected the historicism of the Historical School of Law. The Historical School in turn rejected both the scholastic and the rationalist conceptions of law. This school of thought can be placed in the tradition of the romantic historical movement of the beginning of the nineteenth century. In opposition to the rationalist school, it proclaimed the essentially historical character of law.

The Historical School originated at the Universities of Marburg (Friedrich Carl von Savigny and Jacobus Grimm) and Göttingen (Gustavus Hugo, who is credited with the foundation of the school). Eichhorn and Puchta may be mentioned alongside these famous jurists.

From the perspective of the Historical School, the law is an unconscious and spontaneous manifestation of the popular spirit (*Volksgeist*). The law is the fruit of an authentic and exclusive historical tradition; law has its deepest roots in history.

The law in Germany at the beginning of the nineteenth century was a mixture of written laws and Germanic customs; Roman law still had a supplementary function when no other legal precept could be applied. German jurists were, broadly speaking, divided into two camps: those who studied Roman law, such as Savigny and Puchta, and those who studied law of Germanic origin, such as Eichhorn, Grimm and Waitz. The primary postulates of the Historical School were the opposition to the concept of natural law and the prevalence of customs over written law. It was believed that customs did not serve to create written law, but rather that customs were the external manifestation of the law of a nation. The School also opposed codification based on natural law.

The Historical School was to occasion a divide between its own theory and practice. It was from the Historical School that the Pandectist movement was formed, a movement that aspired to unite all strands of law in a systematic and abstract fashion. The legal system was to be dogmatic and complete, and it would provide the solution to all legal problems. There were to be no gaps in the system thanks to its reliance on abstract, generic, and impersonal precepts. In this way, it was very different from Roman law with its concrete and casuist precepts.

Extreme Pandectism became known as *Begriffsjurisprudenz* (Jurisprudence of Concepts), i.e. a conceptual and mathematical orientation in jurisprudence, which was accused of being remote from reality. No jurist has ever called himself a follower of *Begriffsjurisprudenz*. The term itself was first used in 1884 by Rudolph von Jhering as a catchword against contemporary pandectism. He convincingly associated it with a breach in his own thinking.[13]

> *Tammo Wallinga, The Common History of European Legal Scholarship, Erasmus Law Review 4/1 (2011), 17-18*
> It is an ironic twist of fate that the German codification, the *Bürgerliches Gesetzbuch* (BGB) of 1900, was profoundly influenced by the works of

13 See http://www.enzyklopaedie-rechtsphilosophie.net/inhaltsverzeichnis/19-beitraege/105-jurisprudence-of-concepts (accessed in August 2022).

a man who in 1814 strongly argued against the feasibility of a codification. In that year, Professor Anton Friedrich Justus Thibaut of Heidelberg had put forward the idea of carrying out a general civil law codification (including private, penal and procedural law) for Germany, in order to promote national political unity. He made no secret of his admiration for the French *Code civil* (which at the time applied in parts of Germany west of the Rhine). That same year, a Professor of Roman and Civil law in Berlin, Friedrich Carl von Savigny (1779–1861), wrote an eloquent and famous answer, *Vom Beruf unserer Zeit für Gesetzgebung und Rechtswissenschaft*, in which he argued that Germany was not ready for codification, and that much work still needed to be done before a successful codification could be carried out in Germany. Whether the delay is entirely due to Savigny is debatable, but the fact remains that it took almost another century before the BGB came into force and Germany obtained its unified civil law.

Savigny's theory is a reaction to the pretensions of rational natural law as a product of the Enlightenment, just as Romanticism in art and literature was a reaction to the dry intellectualism of the previous era. He was, in fact, closely related to such famous German romantic figures as Von Arnim and Brentano, having married the latter's sister Kunigunde in 1804. In *Vom Beruf*, Savigny laid down most of the programme for the Historical School, which he officially founded in 1815, together with his Berlin colleague Karl Friedrich Eichhorn (1781–1854). They edited the programmatic journal of the school, the *Zeitschrift für geschichtliche Rechtswissenschaft* – the predecessor of the modern *Savigny-Zeitschrift*.

In *Vom Beruf*, Savigny opposes the idea that law can be constructed in a mathematical way, *more geometrico*. In his view, the law of a nation is as characteristic of that nation as its language. It is not made for the people, but grows organically with the people; it is a historical phenomenon – Roman law being the most eminent example. A codification, therefore, can only be successful if it builds on the historical tradition of the law of the people, and intimate knowledge of this tradition is essential for carrying out the right codification. This knowledge of the historical tradition – or rather the lack of it – is pointed out by Savigny as the great weakness in Germany and, consequently, as the main obstacle to a successful codification. His conclusion is that the only way to achieve a better law for Germany is to have a legal scholarship that proceeds organically and studies the tradition from the beginning. And this is exactly what he and his pupils did, starting with the medieval reception of Roman law in Italy. In fact, Roman law – in its Justinianic form – was found to be an important common element in the law of many German countries, especially since it had been applied by the common German Supreme Court, the *Reichskammergericht*, since its foundation in 1495.

Roman law, however, was studied not so much for its own sake, but with a view to the future. Savigny's pupils used Roman law, and especially the Digest or *Pandectae*, to develop general notions that the Romans themselves had never used, like legal act (*Rechtsgeschäft*) or legal capacity (*Geschäftsfähigkeit*). This form of legal scholarship came to be known as *Pandektenwissenschaft*. One of its most famous representatives, Bernhard Windscheid (1817–1892), wrote a manual that has still not lost its importance, and he later became a central figure in the committee that would prepare the BGB. In the German BGB (1900), we find yet another form of reception of Roman law. The BGB certainly is a codification that is much more closely related to Justinian's than, for instance, the French *Code civil*, even if it is almost a century further removed from Justinian in time. It is the most recent example of the influence of Roman law on the formation of modern private law.

The fact that the main nineteenth-century schools of jurisprudence rejected natural law does not mean that all western scholars shared this view. In many jurisdictions, natural law was highly regarded.

Harold J. Berman, Law and Revolution: The Formation of the Western Legal Tradition, Cambridge Mass., Harvard University Press, 1983, 556

Thus the Western legal tradition grew – in part – out of the structure of social and economic interrelationships within and among groups on the ground. Behavioural patterns of interrelationships acquired a normative dimension: usages were transformed into custom. Eventually custom was transformed into law. The last of these transformations – custom into law – is accounted for partly by the emergence of centralized political authorities, when a conscious restructuring at the top was needed to control and direct the slowly changing structure in the middle and at the bottom. Law, then, is custom transformed, and not merely the will or reason of the lawmaker. Law spreads upward from the bottom and not only downward from the top.

Social theory must therefore accept a broader concept of law than that which Marx and Weber adopted. Law is, as they believed, an instrument of domination, a means of effectuating the will of the lawmaker. But this theory of law, usually identified with the positivist school of jurisprudence, tells only part of the story. Law is also an expression of moral standards as understood by human reason. This view of law, which is associated with natural-law theory, is also partly true. Finally, law is an outgrowth of custom, a product of the historically rooted values and norms of the community. This third view, identified with the historical school of legal philosophy, can also claim – like each of the other two schools – one third of the truth.

By combining all three perspectives it may be possible to give better answers.

2.16 *Diffusion of Laws and Legal Institutions*

The diffusion of laws and legal institutions in the nineteenth century mainly occurred through codes of law, both in civil and common law jurisdictions.

The *ius commune*, although it highly influenced the content of new codes, lost its validity. Roman and canon law sources could not be invoked anymore by lawyers or judges. It may be said that the codes made possible the 'nationalization of law', in accordance with the rise of nationalism throughout Europe in this period and the use of national laws as a manifestation of nationalistic ideologies. Nonetheless, codes also brought about the 'de-nationalization of law', since civil law jurisdictions adopted many elements from foreign laws. In this regard, the influence of the Napoleonic codes was notable.

Common law codification generally opposed the idea of replacing the old common law with something new.

> *Mary Ann Glendon, Paolo G. Carozza and Colin B. Picker, Comparative Legal Traditions. Text, Materials and Cases on Western Law, St Paul MN, Thomson West Publishing, 2007, 68–71*
>
> France and Germany probably have been less influenced by each other's law, legal institutions and scholarship than have other countries within the civil law world. The distinctive French and German codifications and styles of thought each had far-reaching influence, and to some extent their influences overlapped. Thus, a case can be made that the 'typical' civil law systems today are not those of France or Germany, but rather those civil law systems which in modern times have undergone the combined influence of both. Nevertheless, in the post-codification era, French law and German law science have both become the principal tributaries to the modern civil law tradition.
>
> Just as ancient Roman law had been introduced into the conquered territories of a vast empire, the French Civil Code was brought by Napoleon and his armies to Belgium, the Netherlands, parts of Poland, Italy and the western regions of Germany. Then, in the colonial era,

France extended her legal influence far beyond continental Europe to parts of the Near East, Northern and sub-Saharan Africa, Indochina, Oceania, French Guiana and the French Caribbean islands. The influence of the French law both outlived and went beyond the Napoleonic conquests and French colonialism, for the Code was widely admired for its own merits. Its clarity and elegance of style and its consolidation of the results of a Revolution which had abolished the old, unequal statuses and relations of feudalism inspired imitation in many corners of the earth. Thus, one can speak of a 'reception' of the French Civil Code not only in countries which retained it after armies and colonial governments withdrew, but also in countries that were untouched by French military or colonial power.

The Civil Code remains in effect to this day, with revisions, in Belgium and Luxembourg; and was a major influence on the Netherlands Civil Code of 1838 (replaced by a new civil code which came fully into effect in 1992), the Portuguese Civil Code of 1867 (replaced in 1967), the Spanish Civil Code of 1888, some of the Swiss cantonal codes, and on the legal institutions of 19th century Italy, as well as on those of some of the Eastern European countries. French law and legal theory remained important for France's former colonies and possessions even after they gained independence in the 20th century. Furthermore, when the Spanish and Portuguese empires in Latin America dissolved in the 19th century, it was mainly to the French Civil Code that the lawmakers of the new nations of Central and South America looked for inspiration. French culture and the French revolutionary heritage were widely admired in the Latin American countries. The language and concepts of the French codes were clear, and were already familiar because of their affinities with the legal ideas and institutions that had been introduced in Latin America by the Spanish and the Portuguese. It thus was natural for them to turn to French law as a model. In North America and the Caribbean, the French Civil Code applied at first only to the French settlers, but later became an influence on the Codes of Louisiana, Quebec, Haiti and the Dominican Republic, and continues to apply in Martinique and Guadeloupe.

In Africa, the influence of the French Civil Code was more diluted. Even in the French possessions in the region, French law often only applied to French settlers, while the personal law of the native inhabitants continued in effect with regard to others. After independence from the French Empire, many of these countries mixed their colonial law with customary or Islamic law.

The German Civil Code of 1896 put before the world an entirely different model from the French and earlier codes. Though French law and legal ideas were influential in German procedural and administrative law, they had hardly any effect on the thinking that went into the late 19th century German private law codification. The German model, however, appeared too late to be as widely imitated as the French. By the end of the 19th century nearly all the more developed countries had already adopted codes. Apart from those that had been influenced in varying degrees by the French Civil Code, there was the Austrian General Civil Code of 1811, the product of several decades of drafting under an enlightened and authoritarian monarchy, which had in turn influenced the law of some parts of Eastern Europe. The Nordic countries, where the earliest national civil codes had appeared, historically had been and remained relatively far removed from the composite of influences from which the civil law tradition was forged.

Even if the German Civil Code had not appeared relatively late, its highly technical and reticulated structure in all likelihood would have discouraged its direct transplantation to foreign soil. Nevertheless, the German Civil Code did play a significant role in the preparation of the Italian Code of 1942, and was the major influence on the Greek Civil Code of 1940, effective in 1946. Although the German Code as a whole was not built to travel, the legal science that preceded and accompanied it has had an important influence on legal theory and doctrine in other countries, particularly in Austria, [former] Czechoslovakia, Greece, Hungary, Italy, Switzerland and former Yugoslavia. It was one of many influences on the eclectic Brazilian Code of 1916 (replaced by a new code in 2002). The Japanese Civil Code drew heavily upon the first draft of the German Civil Code and, as a result, German civil law scholarship has remained important in Japan. Through Japan, the German civil law influence also spread to Korea. Since the end of World War II, however, American law, too, has had a substantial impact on the law of Japan and South Korea.

Switzerland, except for certain cantons, had remained aloof from the reception of the French Civil Code, and when Switzerland achieved legal unity through its civil code of 1907, and its Law of Obligations which went into effect together with the Civil Code in 1912, it did not follow either the French or the German model. A single scholarly draftsman, Eugen Huber, fashioned for the confederation a civil code that was inspired by Swiss traditions and adapted to Swiss circumstances. He drew upon German and, to a lesser extent, French sources but did not permit them to dominate. In 1926, the Swiss Civil Code (together with the Law of Obligations) was adopted, almost word for word, as the Civil Code of the newly formed Republic of Turkey. …

A few places in the civil law world were untouched by codification. Thus, for example, in Scotland and South Africa, the Roman *ius commune* survives in uncodified form, combined in the case of Scotland with common law, and in the Union of South Africa [current Republic of South Africa] with common law and Dutch law.

Jean Limpens, Territorial Expansion of the Code, in Bernard Schwartz (ed.), The Code of Napoleon and the Common-Law World, New York, New York University Press, 1956, 93–94

On the promulgation of the Code, March 21, 1804, it was naturally introduced into areas then a part of French territory. It was thus introduced into Belgium, Luxembourg, the German territories situated on the west side of the Rhine, the Palatine, Rhenan Prussia, Hesse-Darmstadt, Geneva, Savoia, the duchies of Parma and Plaisance, Blemont, and the Principality of Monaco. The greater part of these territories, it should be noted, conserved the Code for a long time: the German territories until 1900, Geneva until 1912, Belgium, Luxembourg, and the Principality of Monaco until the present time. …

Though Napoleon did not realize his grandiose scheme of an all-European legal system, the results achieved in that direction by his Code were far from mediocre. The Code was introduced in Italy (1805–1820), in the Netherlands (March 1, 1811), in the Habseatic territories (December 13, 1820), and in the Grand Duchy of Berg (December 17, 1811).

Early 19th century Italian private law, for example, was heavily influenced by French models, as Napoleon brought his code to the Italian territories he conquered. After Napoleon's defeat and the restoration (1814) codes were often regarded as a negative legacy of the French domination. But the advantages of codification were profoundly felt as the code was seen to embody the new spirit of the time. One of the first fruits of the unification of Italy (1861) was the civil code of 1865, heavily dependent on the French model.

The diffusion of laws and legal institutions through codes was also present in common law jurisdictions. In the United Kingdom all-comprehensive codes did not succeed, but several English lawyers, who fought for codification and drafted code projects, played an important role in the enactment of codes in British colonies. That is the case of Sir James Fitzjames Stephen, whose *Digest of English Criminal Laws* (1878) was used as a model to draft the criminal codes of Canada (1892), New

Zealand (1893) and Queensland – in Australia – (1899). It has been shown that the Zanardelli Code (1889), which had also a remarkable influence on the Queensland code, was used as a model to draft the criminal codes of Western Australia and other Australian codes, of British New Guinea (1903), of New Guinea (1924) – then separate from Papua –, of the British Protectorate of Northern Nigeria (1904) and of the entire Nigeria (1916), of the model penal code by Albert Erhardt (1925) – which would be used as model for Cyprus and Israel in 1928, many African colonies (Kenya, Uganda, Tanganyika, Nyasaland in 1930; Zanzibar and Gambia in 1934), and Palestine (1936), among others.

In the US, although David Dudley Field failed in enacting his civil code project in New York, he succeeded with the Code of Civil Procedure enacted in 1848 (and 1851) and the Penal Code (drafted in 1865) that was enacted by the New York Legislature in 1881. He also succeeded in other states, where some of his codes were enacted. For example, both California (1872) and Montana (1895) enacted versions of four of the codes that Field drafted for New York: the Code of Civil Procedure, the Civil Code, the Political Code, and the Penal Code. The Dakota Territory enacted its Civil Code with almost no changes in 1865, and the Dakotas (North and South) continued to use it when they became states in 1889. Georgia enacted in 1860 the first Civil Code in the United States, being the first codification of the substantive common law. In the West of the US, many states adopted the Field Code of Civil Procedure: Missouri in 1849; California in 1851; before the Civil War, Iowa, Minnesota, Indiana, Ohio, Washington Territory, Nebraska, Wisconsin, Kansas and Nevada (1861); and after the Civil War, Dakotas, Idaho, Arizona, Montana, North Carolina, Wyoming, South Carolina, Utah, Colorado, Oklahoma and New Mexico.

Questions

1. What are the main pillars of modern constitutionalism? Is there any connection between them? What does it mean that fundamental rights were born fragile in the origins of constitutionalism?
2. What is the relationship between modern constitutions and codes approved by liberal parliaments?
3. Why did most of the codes establish that sources of law were statutes and general principles of law, neglecting custom? What codes did not follow that path? Why?
4. What was the role of judicial precedent in the 19th-century Western legal tradition?

5. What was the role of Natural law, Equity and Reason after the approval of modern codes? Was there any room left for them? If yes, where and how could they be enforced?

3 Actors

At the end of the eighteenth century and in the nineteenth century, the character and regulation of the legal professions increased considerably in both civil law and common law jurisdictions.[14] Important developments in France are discussed by H. Leuwers.

H. Leuwers, L'Invention du barreau français, 1660–1830. La construction nationale d'un groupe professional (Civilations et Sociétés, 126), Paris, Editions de l'École des hautes études et sciences sociales, 2006, 9–12, 46, 115, 219, 255, 290, 333 (transl. Cornelis Hendrik (Remco) van Rhee)

Whether a nobleman or commoner, the advocate of the modern age presents himself as a member of an 'order' conceived as a group of all individuals in the country who have the [relevant] title and share the rights to which [the order] gives access. According to a first definition – the only one used in the sixteenth and seventeenth centuries -, the 'advocates' order' brings together those individuals who share the same status and not necessarily the same occupation; the members of the ['order'] do not necessarily represent clients in court. In the second half of the eighteenth century, the terminology 'order' is given an additional meaning, referring to the locally organized bar association or professional group within the jurisdiction of a 'sovereign' court [i.e. a court administering justice in the highest instance]. [From then on] the expression 'French bar' is used to refer to all of the advocates in the [French] kingdom ...

In most states of today's Western Europe, the assistance of litigants was entrusted to two legal officers, one of whom monitored the proceedings [in court], and the other advised and provided legal counsel. In France, [but also] in the French-speaking territories of the former Low Countries and in Geneva, these officials were designated respectively as 'procurators' and 'advocates'. The same division of tasks, which stems

14 For a general overview of the development of legal professions (attorneys and notaries) in France, Italy, Germany and England in the late modern age, see Jean-Louis Halpérin (ed.), Avocats et notaires en Europe. Les professions judiciaires et juridiques dans l'histoire contemporaine, Paris, LGDJ, 1996.

from the Roman distinction between *procurator* and *advocatus*, could be found in Spain (*aboga / procurador*) and in most of the states of the Italian peninsula (*avvocato / procuratore*), but also in a number of [other] territories ranging from England (barrister / attorney, solicitor) to certain states in Germany (*Advokat / Prokurator*). However, one should not be deceived by the continued use of the same terminology and the relationship between words; in each territory, the number, training, status and field of action of each of these auxiliaries of justice had their specificities and their regional variations ... We must also be careful not to equate this terminology [of advocate and procurator] with narrowly defined [professional] activities. In France, the distinction between the powers of the two professionals became more clearly defined in the eighteenth century, without necessarily making the person designated as *avocat* an attorney or legal counsel; the word certainly [did not only] refer to a [professional] activity, which was not always exercised exclusively, but also to 'status', which allowed the [relevant individuals] to acquire a license to practise law and to take [the relevant] oath. In no way did it oblige [the avocat] to exercise a particular profession. ...

... In the last two centuries of the Ancien Régime, the profession of advocate underwent a surprising transformation which reinforced its common culture; *avocats* developed and became subject to a common set of rules regulating the bar. This [state of affairs] became an argument in their fight for the freedom to exercise their activities and the independence of their professional organizations. During the Enlightenment period, this ... was reinforced by the ... development of a common terminology (order, *bâtonnier* [i.e. head of the bar], internship, *tableau* [i.e. register of advocates allowed to practise]) ... In 1789 [i.e. at the start of the French Revolution], this development was far from complete; paradoxically, the suppression of the title of *avocat* and their professional organisations ... [during the early revolutionary period] allowed a restart [of this development] and its near completion in the first three decades of the nineteenth century. ...

Within little more than a century (1660–1789), the changes in the profession of *avocat* took place on an unprecedented scale, although they were part of a development starting in the Middle Ages. To define [these changes] in terms of 'professionalization' amounts to recognizing three dimensions in this terminology, which are partly intertwined. The terminology first evokes a growing demand for [professional] competences at the start of one's career [as an advocate], marked by the reform of university studies [in law] and the introduction of 'internships'. It also betrays the wish to see registered advocates ... exercise their profession, more or less, while residing in town, in order to demonstrate their willingness to carry out certain professional tasks. Finally, there is a strong trend towards ... specialization, marked by the growing separation of the activities of the advocate and the procurator, and the multiplication of incompatibilities. ...

Beyond individual differences, it is indeed a process of professional harmonization that is at work [from the end of the eighteenth century]. Now, in the same way that the [individual] advocates fit into a more or less structured order, the bar associations become part of a network of provincial and national professional bodies. ... [T]he terminology 'order' which, for a long time, designated only a rather diffuse group of people having the same status without necessarily exercising the same [professional] activities, now refers to a group whose existence is affirmed at three different levels: locally, 'the order' designates the bar attached to a certain jurisdiction and subject to a responsible official from the group; within a specific jurisdictional territory, the word identifies a professional community which adopts a common vocabulary (*syndic* or *bâtonnier*), maintains a spirit of solidarity and sometimes recognizes the disciplinary authority of the head of the court order; across the [French] kingdom, the notion of order, like that of the 'French bar', betrays the awareness of shared rights and the recognition of the moral authority of the Paris bar. ...

The integration of the advocate into public life does not date from the eighteenth century. Since the profession originates from a Roman-Christian tradition, which legitimizes its existence through the services rendered to litigants and to justice, it could not develop without close links with society. In court, the advocate assists the litigants and devotes himself gracefully to the defense of the poor; in public life, [the advocate] is associated with charities, municipal bodies and provincial institutions. In the last century of the *Ancien Régime*, however, this situation partly changed in form and scope. From the beginning of the eighteenth century, legal aid remained an individual duty [of the advocate] but also became the common cause of certain bars which established free [legal] consultation offices. At the same time, the advocate, individually or collectively, participated in the development of the public debate, contributing to the transformation of the political culture of his time. Somehow like the members of the high courts who, through the defense of existing interests and principles, developed a discussion with revolutionary potential – such as national sovereignty –, the advocate took the adversarial debate from the courtroom to society, helping to free thought, word and action. …

Much more than the former notaries, many of whom became public notaries [after the French Revolution], and much more than procurators, advocates were deeply affected by the constitutional reforms. When examining their career after 1790, one is above all struck by the large number of those who disappeared from legal life. The magnitude of the phenomenon has various origins; it can be understood by the hostility of some of [the advocates] to the Revolution, or by their loyalty to the old magistracy … Paradoxically, the abolition of the title of advocate facilitated unofficial judicial assistance; while the advocate of the *Ancien Régime* did not necessarily practice law, the official legal representative always provided advice and legal assistance. Without being a true professional, he was an actor in legal life. The revolutionary break also separated the former advocates to a certain extent from their colleagues, a large minority of whom continued to frequent the courthouses, as legal representatives or as judges. But not everything was erased with the same ease; when the reorganization of legal assistance was started, the practices of the *Ancien Régime* remained a model, particularly if they were in use in Paris. However, by suppressing the profession [of advocate], the Constituent Assembly allowed its possible reinvention on a new basis, but also brought about an unprecedented acceleration in the professionalization and the organization of the group on a national basis. …

Much more than under the *Ancien Régime*, the [nineteenth-century] evolution of the profession followed a common chronology, structured by official texts which defined its rights and its organization. From the re-establishment of the title of advocate (1804) to the ordinance of 1830, we can distinguish four main phases in the reorganization of the orders. In the years preceding their official re-establishment (1810), the former bars at the provincial high courts [*parliaments*] and presidential bars took the initiative to reopen their registers, to elect officials, to reintroduce internships and to ensure their financial independence while respecting the customs of their direct predecessors. The decree of 1810, by continuing to standardize the conditions of access to the bar and by allowing bars of more than twenty members to set up a disciplinary council, broke with local traditions, while allowing a large number of orders to rebuild fraternal life which was partly inspired by it. For small bars, the reorganization did not gain momentum until after the ordinance of 1822, which invited them to appoint a *bâtonnier*, and especially after that of 1830, which recognized them as competent organizations and granted them rights. …

> But in a century [i.e. the nineteenth century] when, from the … Netherlands to Italy, the professionalization of scholarly activities was progressing through the active support of a State which envisaged its responsibilities and prerogatives in a broad way, the movement was taking place largely without the [advocates'] orders. However, we know that, from one country to another, the effective role of power varied. From this point of view, France represents an intermediate case between the Prussian, Bavarian and Lombard models, on the one hand, where a 'professionalization from above' was achieved, and that of England, on the other hand, in which the bar had a very broad autonomy vis-à-vis the State. Despite public intervention, this French model, which spread to Belgium and to certain German and Italian territories …, is usually qualified as 'liberal'. …

The United States of America witnessed the rise of Bar Associations, and the creation of the American Bar Association in 1878. Roscoe Pound, Dean of the Harvard Law School from 1916 until 1936, explains this in one of his lectures.

> *Roscoe Pound, Legal Profession in America, Notre Dame L. 19 (1943–1944), 344–345*
> After the middle of the eighteenth century, as the bar became established in the wealthier communities and an increasing number of lawyers had been trained in the Inns of Court, the lawyers began to organize, either in bar associations or as the organized bar of some court, and to establish rules fixing the requirements for study and admission to the profession. They could do this under an apprentice system by agreeing not to take any students in their offices except those having certain qualifications, and not to recommend or move the admission of any students unless they had studied a specified time. For example, in 1768, the bar at Salem, Massachusetts, adopted rules and agreed that the members should not take any student to study law with them without previously obtaining the consent of the bar; that they would not recommend any one to be admitted in the inferior court as an attorney unless he had studied three years with some barrister; that they would not recommend any one to be admitted as attorney in the Superior Court unless he had studied three years in the office of a barrister and practised at least two years in the inferior court; that they would not recommend any one to be admitted as a barrister until he had been attorney in the inferior court two years and then had practised as attorney in the Superior Court two years more; and that they would not have more than three students at one time. In

> 1770, the Boston bar resolved not to consent to any one being taken on as apprentice student who had not been educated at college or had an equivalent liberal education. Thus very high standards were being set up by these organizations. Requirements of local bars or bar associations of this sort survived the Revolution, and are to be found as late as 1800. But the sweep of Jeffersonian democracy over the country and legislation hostile to lawyers led to a decay of the requirements everywhere.
>
> In Virginia, only one year's study was required; in Maryland, three years; in Delaware, three. In North and South Carolina, no time was prescribed. Contrast with this the requirements before the Revolution: In Pennsylvania in 1788, four years' study as a clerk and one year's practice in the Common Pleas; in New York, at the end of the eighteenth century, seven years – four of liberal education and three in the office of an attorney. But while one side of these associations decayed, bar associations as social organizations continued and kept a certain degree of professional organization alive until the revival of bar associations as they are today, in the last quarter of the nineteenth century. Also, in the last century, the county bars often had annual meetings, with an address and a dinner, and were sometimes called specially to pass resolutions when some scandal of jury fixing or of flagrant misconduct called for exceptional action.
>
> After the Civil War, bar associations had become social organizations, meeting for a social reunion once a year, with sometimes an address by some well known lawyer, and sometimes passing resolutions on matters of more than usual professional interest. A change began with the organization of the American Bar Association in 1878. The initiative came from the Bar Association of Connecticut at the instance of Simeon E. Baldwin, afterwards Chief Justice of that state. It is said that the idea originated with a group of lawyers who were in the habit of spending a brief summer vacation at Saratoga Springs and conceived that their annual reunion might grow into a national association of lawyers. Six hundred and seven lawyers, outstanding in their home bars, were invited, but only one hundred and eight responded, and but seventy five attended the organization meeting. The association began on August 21, 1878, with two hundred and ninety-one members from twenty-nine states and the District of Columbia. It is significant that the subjects which it took up at the outset were legal education and law reform.

In general, lawyers were well regarded, enjoying a considerable prestige. Lawyers were also proud of their professional vocation. The image of the 'true lawyer' was particularly present in the nineteenth-century US.

Philip Gaines, The 'True Lawyer' in America: Discursive Construction of the Legal Profession in the Nineteenth Century, Am. J. Legal Hist. 45/132 (2001), 152–153

Intra-professional discourse from the middle fifty years of the nineteenth century suggests that lawyers, judges, and legal educators had a relatively cohesive sense of what constituted the 'true lawyer.' Emerging from a colonial era in which the profession of the law was not highly regarded, writers and orators of the period used their opportunities for public discussion of law practice to construct a highly-idealized representation of the lawyer and his profession. While much of what was written and spoken clearly emulated the traditional perspectives of the English bar, American explications of the lawyer and his work brought a unique coloring to the subject, inasmuch as the new country was embarking on a political, social, and economic enterprise the likes of which the world had not seen and was in need of lawyers equipped with what it took to legally negotiate this brave new world. ...

The remarkable thing about this discourse is its short-lived nature. By the 1880s, published discussions of law practice focused almost exclusively on practical matters of skill, expertise, effectiveness – an emphasis in keeping with a new conception of the lawyer as technician and of legal education as the training of experts. A flood of manuals, guidelines, and other advice materials came into publication – texts whose purpose it was to broaden and deepen lawyers' knowledge of law practice and polish their skills in its application.

Questions

1. Why did the regulation of the legal professions increase considerably in both civil law and common law jurisdictions in our period?
2. Why did bar associations come into being in the 19th century?
3. Why were lawyers so well regarded and why did they enjoy such considerable prestige in the nineteenth-century US? Was this also true in Europe and England?

4 Application

Nineteenth-century codes reflect continuity in the law and moderate reform. This is true for civil and procedural law alike. Although the influence of certain codes cannot be denied, in many cases this influence only concerned notions, concepts and categories which were common to all European jurisdictions.

4.1 *Substantive Private Law*

> *Gábor Hamza, Continuity and Discontinuity of Private/Civil Law in Eastern Europe after World War II, 1/12 (2006) Fundamina, 55*
> The civil-law systems of the countries of continental Europe are frequently categorised into four major groups: Codes patterned after the French and Spanish Civil Codes; Codes following the Swiss Code of Obligations of 1881/1883 and the Swiss Civil Code of 1907/1912; Codes patterned after either the drafts or the final version of the German Civil Code of 1896/1900; and Codes drawing upon the Italian Civil Code of 1865 and the Italian Civil Code of 1942.
>
> The impact of the Austrian General Civil Code was generally limited to the territory of the Austrian Empire and later – after the Austro-Hungarian 'Compromise' (*Ausgleich*)[15] – to the Austrian-Hungarian Empire. The Austrian Civil Code consists of 1502 sections (paragraphs) and is divided into three books: I. On Personal Rights; II. On Real Rights – rights arising from things – encompassing both property and obligations (contracts and torts); and III. On Provisions Common to Personal and Real Rights. The Austrian General Civil Code also has a short Introduction consisting of fourteen sections. It was substantially modified by means of regulations (*Notverordnungen*) during World War I. The Austrian General Civil Code had a large influence on the Serbian Civil Code of 1844 which contained only 950 sections. The Serbian Civil Code of 1844 showed several divergences from the Austrian General Civil Code, mainly in family law and the law of succession.

The influence of the French Civil Code (and some other European models) was facilitated by the fact that it contained many elements from the *ius commune*. This was due to the influence of Domat and Pothier.[16] James Gordley has demonstrated that the French Code was less liberal or individualistic than traditionally depicted.

---

15 The Austro-Hungarian Compromise of 1867 established the dual monarchy of Austria-Hungary.

16 On this matter, see, for example, Rodolfo Batiza, Origins of Modern Codification of the Civil Law: The French Experience and Its Implications for Louisiana Law, Tul. L. Rev. 56 (1982), 477–601.

James Gordley, Myths of the French Civil Code, Am. J. ComL. 42 (1994), 488–489

The Code did not rebuild the law of property, contract or tort on new and individualistic principles. Indeed, it was drafted in what one can only describe as the trough between two intellectual waves: a wave of natural law theory that crested in the 16th and 17th centuries, and a wave of individualistic will-centred theory that did not emerge clearly until the 19th century. To the extent the drafters were guided by general principles at all, they used those of the natural lawyers which were already old-fashioned. The principles of the Revolution that did influence the drafters were a republican vision of law and the principle of human equality. The republican vision, however, was rejected by the drafters themselves, and the principle of equality did not lead to a reshaping of private law. Although the Code is often said to have abolished feudal property, it is hard to find much of economic consequence that changed.

Roman law influence on the French Civil Code is, for example, evident where it concerns Article 1134 *Code civil*: Agreements legally formed take the place of law for those who have made them. They can only be revoked by mutual consent or for reasons authorized by law. They must be executed in good faith. This Article finds it origins in the writings of Jean Domat.

J. Domat, Les Loix civiles dans leur ordre naturel (1713), liv. prelim. (transl. by James Gordley)

Agreements are engagements formed by the mutual consent of two or more persons who themselves make a law between themselves to do that which they promise each other. The use of agreements is a natural consequence of the order of civil society and the bonds that God forms between men. For He has made necessary for all their needs the reciprocal use of their industry and labor, and various sorts of commerce in things and it is principally by agreements that men satisfy these needs. Thus for the use of industry and labor, men form partnerships, hire each other, and act in various ways for each other. Thus, for the use of things, when they need to acquire or alienate them, they enter into commerce through sales and barter, and when they only need to have them for a time, they rent or borrow them. And so, according to other and different needs, there are different types of agreements.

In formulating the above, Domat was inspired by older materials.

> *James Gordley, Myths of the French Civil Code, Am. J. ComL. 42 (1994), 469*
> The statement that contracts take the place of law between the parties paraphrased a passage from Domat ... Domat had taken it from a collection of decretals promulgated by the medieval pope Boniface VIII [Liber Sextus V.13.85], who had taken it in turn from the *Corpus Juris Civilis*, the 6th century compilation of the Emperor Justinian [D. 50,17,23]. As Burge has observed, the passage says agreements take the place of law; it does not say anything about autonomy.[17] Yet according to many scholars, this text proclaimed the autonomy of the will ... and the freedom of contract ... – indeed, it exalted contract to the same level as law ... Some writers seem to believe that the drafters themselves discovered this principle, a possibility we shall examine shortly. Halpérin suggests that, as in the case of property law, the drafters drew upon individualistic principles already espoused by members of the natural law school such as Domat.

The former Dutch civil code also stated in Article 1374(1): 'All legally concluded agreements have the force of law for the parties to such agreements.'

> *Robert Feenstra and Margreet Ahsman, Contract. Contract and Freedom of Contract in Historical Perspective (transl. and edited by Cornelis Hendrik (Remco) van Rhee), Maastricht, unpublished, 2008, 11–12*
> J.H. Beekhuis ... believes that Article 1374(1) means 'nothing more nor less than that every citizen may, by means of a contract with a fellow citizen, act as his own lawmaker in the private sphere'. One may interpret the Article in that way, if one wishes, and many before and after Beekhuis have done so. The question remains, however, whether those who formulated this Article wished to ascribe this meaning to it. Probably such interpretation of the Article did not come about until the 19th century, when the concept of the 'socially regulating force' of private law was very much emphasised. Article 1374(1) is almost a literal translation of Article 1134 of the French Civil Code; all that is missing is an equivalent for 'any'. The Civil Code borrowed the formulation – with the addition of the element of 'legally concluded' – from the French writer on natural law from the 17th century, Jean Domat (1625–1696), who in turn simply generalised the content of a text from Roman law (D. 50,17,23) which had a very restrictive meaning: the contracting parties could, by including a special

17 A. Bürge, Das franzosische Privatrecht im 19. Jahrhundert zwischen Tradition und Pandektenwissenschaft, Liberalismus und Etatismus, Frankfurt am Main, Klostermann, 1991, 64–65.

clause, depart from the general rules regarding the degree of liability of one party (e.g. the seller or the lessor) to the other (e.g. the buyer or the lessee) for matters to which the contract related; if they did so, 'the contract established the legal position.'

Irrespective of the formulation of Article 1374(1) and its natural law antecedents, we should note that the concept of freedom of contract as regards content (the 'open system') – whether or not coupled with the freedom to conclude a contract with whoever one wishes and equally the freedom not to conclude a contract (both elements are also referred to as components of the freedom of contract in the broadest sense) – came into being long before the 19th century.

It is described by a number of writers on natural law from the 17th and 18th centuries who were more philosophers than lawyers; these in their turn had been influenced by theologians from the 16th century and the Middle Ages. A modern French legal historian and philosopher (M. Villey) wrote: 'our theory of contract is an inheritance that we lawyers received from a certain group of European philosophers from the Early Modern Age' (by which he means the 16th, 17th and 18th centuries). He adds there that it is unfortunate that on this issue 'we have to credit our legal knowledge to thinkers who were entirely unskilled in the law'. These thinkers, he argued, started off with the hypothesis of a state of nature in which mankind was a kind of Robinson Crusoe, entirely free of all legal obligations; such obligations could only be created through man's free will. Such views were later adopted by lawyers; they are mentioned, for example, by Hugo Grotius in his exposition on the history of contract.

Roscoe Pound also described the evolution of the binding force of the given word.

Roscoe Pound, The French Civil Code and the Spirit of Nineteenth Century Law, B.U. L. Rev. 35 (1955), 80–81

Hence the law as to the making and keeping of promises had been a chief part of the legal system since the classical jurists at Rome. A philosophical idea of a universal law grounded in reason and the nature of man as a rational creature rather than simply on the force of a humanly created authority, has played a great part in legal history and not the least item in this natural law has been the binding force of the given word. The classical Roman jurists used the term *lex* (statute, enacted legal precept) for terms of a contract established as binding rules by the wills of the parties to a legal transaction [Ulpian in Digest, 50, 17, 23]. Ulpian wrote that a 'contract gives law' (*lex*, an enacted rule, not *jus*) and that agreement gives to contracts the standing of a law (Digest, 16, 1, 6). Domat in the seventeenth century (citing Ulpian) said that 'when agreements are concluded, whatever has been agreed upon stands in place of a law (*loi*) to those who made them.' (Domat, *Loix civiles dans leur ordre naturel*, 1689, I, 1, 2, no. 7). Note that the word here is *loi, lex*, the word for an enacted rule of law, not *droit, jus*, what is right backed by the authority of the state. This way of putting the matter culminates in Art. 1134 of the French Civil Code: 'Agreements take the place of law (*loi*) for those who have made them.' But by this time the law making force of reason, calling on men as rational beings to make good the expectations created by their undertakings, has been replaced by the law making force of the individual free will enabling one who enters into an agreement to manifest the sovereignty of his free will by laying down a binding rule of law for the case in hand.

This idea of the sovereign will, which by its own authority could create rights and duties to be enforced by the law of the land as the precepts laid down by legislative authority were enforced, had come into French law from the canon law. In the later Middle Ages there was a standing controversy between the civilians, the teachers of Roman law, and the canonists, the teachers of the universal law of the church. The former stood for the categories of enforceable agreements they found in Justinian's Digest, which to them was the universal law of Christendom postulated as the empire of which Justinian was the lawgiver. The canonists held to a proposition of Christian morals for which in the Corpus of the Canon Law they cited a canon of a Council of Carthage dated A.D. 348 (Decretals of Gregory, i, 35, 1). The church, as Planiol puts it, 'sought to plant respect for the given word deep in human consciousness.' This was reinforced by the philosophers and the philosophical jurists of the law of nature school. Out of it all there grew a concept of the sovereign will, able by its own force to create rights and binding duties (6 Planiol et Ripert, *Traité pratique de droit civil français*, 1930, 21). To quote Planiol again, 'this concept of the creative role of the will and the all powerfulness of contract was consecrated by the legislation born of the Revolution.' (*Ibidem*). It was the era of the Social Contract and the idea of governments deriving their just powers from the consent of the governed.

After the eighteenth century the individualist liberalism of the nineteenth century carried this further. Moreover, the theory of autonomy of the will did not stop at the doctrine of sovereign law making authority. Nineteenth century legal and political theory held that the will in action

> ought not to be limited except by imperative demands of public order and that restriction on that ground ought to be reduced to the necessary minimum. It was held that private interests freely argued out by the parties conduced to the public welfare and no injustice to the parties can result from contract since the obligations are freely created. This, too, was put in a general provision of the Civil Code: 'Laws concerning public order and morals cannot be modified by any private agreement' (Art. 6).

Another important principle is *Pacta sunt servanda*. It originates in canon law.

> *Robert Feenstra and Margreet Ahsman, Contract. Contract and Freedom of Contract in Historical Perspective (transl. and edited by Cornelis Hendrik (Remco) van Rhee), Maastricht, unpublished, 2008, 12*
>
> As for the freedom of contract in its formal sense – the principle of consensualism – this is usually regarded as an 'inheritance' from the Canonists of the Middle Ages (authorities on the canon law, i.e. the law of the Catholic Church). Indeed, in a 13th century codification of canon law we find the statement that 'agreements, however naked, must be honoured' ('pacta quantumcunque nuda servanda sunt'; Decretals of Pope Gregory IX from 1234, heading of 1,35,1). One could think that such a statement – made in a legal context – would have immediately acquired great practical significance. However, this appears not to have been the case at all; for a few centuries it remained largely of theoretical importance, because the texts of Roman law that contained a contrary view stood in the way of its further application. The canon law maxim did, however, contribute to increasing efforts to find ways to remove this obstacle from Roman law. Only since the 16th century, when people in various countries began to adopt a more independent attitude towards Roman law and when natural law authors began to play a larger role, did the principle of consensualism also gain the upper hand in practice.

The law of marriage underwent influences from the past as well, although in France it was deeply changed by two laws voted on 20 September 1792: one law establishing civil marriage (before municipal officers) and the other authorising divorce. In order to set aside discrimination of illegitimate children, a 1793 law gave to those children who were recognised by their parents the same succession rights as legitimate children.

However, after the Revolution some of these changes were reversed. In the *Preliminary Address on the First Draft of the* [*French*] *Civil Code* the drafters explained the changes.

Preliminary Address on the First Draft of the Civil Code, presented in the year IX *by Messrs. Portalis, Tronchet, Bigot-Préameneu and Maleville, members of the government-appointed commission, 24–28 (https://www.justice.gc.ca/eng/rp-pr/csj-sjc/ilp-pji/code/civil.pdf; accessed in October 2022)* © *The International Cooperation Group, Department of Justice of Canada (English transl.)*

Citizens may profess diverse faiths; but laws must be for everyone.

We therefore did not think it necessary to forbid divorce among us, because our laws would too formally conflict with the various faiths that permit it, and the laws could not hope for the men who profess these faiths to make of marriage a stronger bond than religion itself.

Moreover, apart from the consideration inferred from the diversity of faiths, civil law may very well, out of fear of greater ills, not use authority and constraint to force unhappy spouses to remain together, or to live in a forced celibacy, which is as harmful to morals as it is to society.

Law that allows all citizens, without distinction, the possibility of divorce, without troubling spouses whose faith opposes divorce, is a result, a consequence of our regime, that is to say, of the political and religious situation in France.

But the desire for perpetuity in marriage being the very desire of nature, the laws must establish a salutary curb on passions; they must prevent the holiest of contracts from becoming the victim of caprice, of inconstancy, or even from becoming the object of all the shameful speculations of a base avidity.

Since our new laws, the mere allegation of incompatibility of temperament and character could bring about the dissolution of the marriage.

To allege is not to prove: incompatibility of temperament and character is not even susceptible of rigorous, legal proof. So, in the final analysis, permitting divorce on a single ground is to give each spouse the grievous right to dissolve the marriage at will. Is there a single contract in the world that only one of the parties can arbitrarily and capriciously dissolve, against the wishes of the party with whom he has contracted?

It is observed that the allegation of incompatibility of temperament and character may conceal the very real causes, public discussion of which would bring shame on families and be a scandal for society. Moreover, the shared life of two spouses can become unbearable through a multitude of hostile behaviours, bitter reproaches, daily scorns, relentless, biting and persistent clashes, in a word, by a host of acts no one of which may be thought serious, and which together are the misery and torment of the spouses who suffer them.

All that may be so; but it is also true that the mere allegation of incompatibility of temperament and character may conceal merely the absence of any reasonable motive. Who will assure us that sufficient cause to divorce does exist, in a case where none is given?

Marriage is not a situation, but a status. It must in no way resemble those brief and fleeting unions that pleasure forms, that end with pleasure, and that have been condemned by the laws of all civilised peoples.

It is said that we must come to the aid of two ill-matched spouses. We blame our morals and our customs for favouring bad marriages. The only remedy for these ills is found in the facility of divorce.

It is all too true that two spouses often form a union without knowing each other, and are condemned to live together without loving each other. It is all too true that designs of ambition and wealth, and often fantasies and easy morals, govern the formation of alliances and the fate of families. Moral and natural proprieties are usually sacrificed for civil proprieties.

But should these abuses summon others? Should the corruption of laws compound that of men? Because there are bad marriages, is one to conclude that there ought to be none that are sacred and inviolable? When the abuses are the work of passions alone, laws can remedy them; but when they are the work of laws, the ill is incurable, because it lies in the remedy itself. …

What we must fear today is that moral laxity will replace the former nuisance of marriage, and that, because of the considerable facility of divorce, a regular, as it were, libertine outlook, the product of permitted inconstancy, will replace marriage itself.

But, one might say, if the simple allegation of incompatibility of temperament and character is not allowed to stand, all the advantages of divorce are removed. Quite the contrary, we say; the abuses of divorce are merely multiplied and made worse if the means deduced from incompatibility of temperament and character are allowed to remain.

The allegation of this incompatibility will become the means of all those who have no means. The most important, the most noble, of contracts will have no substance and gain no respect; morals will continually be violated by laws. …

In ordinary partnerships, one stipulates for one's own undisclosed and private interests, and as the supreme arbiter of one's own destiny. In marriage, one does not stipulate solely for oneself, but for others. One promises to become the protector of the new family that one will bring into being. One stipulates for the State, for the general society of the human race.

The public is therefore always a party in matters of marriage; and, over and above the public, there are always third parties worthy of the utmost consideration and for whom one can have neither the desire nor the power to do harm. The conjugal partnership is like no other.

Mutual consent therefore cannot dissolve marriage, whereas it can dissolve any other partnership. ...

As a rule, divorce must not be pronounced without cause. The causes of the divorce must be obvious breaches of the contract. Hence, we allow, as legal causes, only civil death, which imitates natural death, and the crimes or offences of which one spouse may accuse the other. We did not think it tolerable to make divorce easier than separations once were.

4.2 *Substantive Commercial Law*

France would take the lead in the codification of commercial law in the early nineteenth century. That codification was, however, very conservative, and based on the royal ordinances promulgated under Louis XIV in the seventeenth century. It was also influenced by the personal concerns of Napoleon, who did not trust merchants for the reasons explained below. This code was quickly dated and not suitable to meet the requirements of the nineteenth century. As a result, various subject-matters began to be regulated outside the code, developments which later authors have termed as 'decodification'.

J. Monéger, De l'ordonnance de Colbert de 1673 sur le commerce au Code de commerce français de Septembre 2000: Réflexion sur l'aptitude du droit économique et commercial à la codification, Revue internationale de droit économique 2/18 (2004), 175–176, 179–180, 184–185 (transl. by Cornelis Hendrik (Remco) van Rhee)

Until the 18th century, commercial law was Italian. In France, Colbert would give birth to codification, not in civil matters left to the Parliaments and the Church, but in procedural law with the high quality ordinance on civil procedure published in 1667, and then in commercial law with the ordinances on trade by land of 1673 [the 'Savary code'] and on maritime matters of 1681. The second [ordinance], which was of good quality and very modern, was directly incorporated into the Napoleonic commercial code in 1807.

The 'Savary code', in spite of its weaknesses, would apply beyond the Revolution until the promulgation of the Commercial Code in 1807, after the Emperor's great anger provoked by the bankruptcies of suppliers to the armed forces and the risk of bankruptcy of the new *Banque de France*.

By a sort of paradox, while the Revolution of 1789 advocated equality, it was accepted that there would be a civil code and a commercial code. Logic would have wanted a single code for all French people. The Revolution, however, was not concerned with the creation of a new law to compensate for the patent shortcomings of the 'Savary code', but it allowed the continued disintegration of this code.

Under the Consulate [1799–1804], the return to normal business life again led to questioning the advisability of codifying commercial law which had tended over a century to develop outside the 'Savary code', which had been quickly struck down by its obsolescence. The [commercial] code, promulgated by the law of 15 September 1807, except for the incorporation of the excellent ordinance on maritime matters, was lacking in strength from its inception. It would experience a progressive decodification throughout the two centuries that followed. The question of recodification then arose.

The continuation of the past in the imperial codification of 1807 [i.e. the French Commercial Code] is patent. In 1801, a seven-member Reform Commission was established under the Interior Ministry, the Ministry on which commerce depended. This commission was not composed of great jurists, but of judges or former commercial court judges. Its chairman, Garneau, a very competent lawyer, was not a Portalis. The most prominent member was a certain Vital Roux, a brilliant autodidact who favoured the separation of commercial law and private law. The approach of these men from practice was decidedly practical. Even if some progress was made when compared to the 'Savary code', in particular with the clarification of bankruptcy law, the quality of the project was very poor. In addition, the Council of State, passionate about the final drafting of the Civil Code, ignored the work of the Commercial Law Codification Commission for five years. It was only when they were scolded by the Emperor that the Councilors of State discovered a sleeping project in their drawers. The [Commercial] Code has not benefited from the care given to the Civil Code. ... The 'new' code is a copy of the law of the *Ancien Régime* ...

The code, written by practitioners ... is mediocre. This is true of its structure and content. This is due to its objectives. ...

As for the substance and the objectives, the Napoleonic Commercial Code is exemplary of the lack of a forward-looking vision and support for the economic change that was underway. It was not meant to encourage the creativity of merchants, but to control them. Napoleon I wanted merchants who failed in their commitments to be punished. The most important part of the code was therefore devoted to bankruptcy, then to merchant books to better monitor the merchant, this potential delinquent. …

The code of 1807 would know the same fate as the 'Savary code'. It was gradually ignored because it was incapable of meeting the needs of trade or of ensuring appropriate protection against scandalous practices. When the legislator intervened, the code was emptied of its content. From 1838, Book II on bankruptcy was replaced by a special statute. Later, all company law was transferred to specific statutes. …

The first book of the Napoleonic Commercial Code is even more a 'bric-a-brac', a legislative gibberish, than that of the 'Savary Code'. …

As for Book II on Maritime Matters, it is a carbon copy of part of Colbert's Maritime Ordinance. One may recognize a small novelty with maritime insurance. However, nothing is said about insurance in general.

4.3 *Public Law*

In the area of public law, the nineteenth century witnessed the birth of modern administrative law, regulating the relations between the executive and the citizen. Although French legal historians have traced the history of administrative law back to the medieval period, modern administrative law differed from the law of earlier periods due to the rise of modern constitutionalism.

Jean-Louis Mestre, Introduction historique au droit administratif français, Paris, PUF, 1985, 9, 21 (transl. by Cornelis Hendrik (Remco) van Rhee)

While the history of each of the main branches of French private law has been the subject of critical evaluative studies, no comprehensive work has been devoted, so far, to the history of administrative law. This omission stems mainly from the widely held conviction that this branch of the law does not go back beyond the 19th century. … The existence of administrative law in France is generally presented, in fact, as a consequence of the Revolution of 1789. More precisely, as a consequence of the proclamation, by the National Constituent Assembly, of the principle dear to Montesquieu of the separation of powers. The adoption of this principle as the basis of the constitutional order, replacing the absolutist conceptions of the monarchy of the *Ancien Régime*, entailed the separation of executive and judicial powers, and the establishment in the year VIII [1799], under the Consulate, of a purely administrative court system. Responsible for ruling exclusively on disputes between the executive and individual citizens, this jurisdiction undertook the development of a new [area of the] law, administrative law, consisting of a set of rules detached from private law …

It is easy to understand why it started in 1789. Of course, the choice of this date does not mean that the activities of the executive were previously not governed by any rule. However, it is from the Declaration of the Rights of Man and of the Citizen that modern administrative law proceeds. Let us understand by this [administrative law] a set of rules based on the principle that the executive is limited, mainly, to the execution of the law, to which is reserved the power to ensure the social coexistence of individual rights. In fact, it was only at the very end of the 18th century that the expression 'administrative law' appeared, before it came in common use around the middle of the first decade of the following century.

F. Burdeau, Histoire du droit administratif (de la Révolution au début des années 1970), Paris, PUF, 1995, 29, 89, 105, 154 (transl. by Cornelis Hendrik (Remco) van Rhee)

1789 replaced the administrative law developed through centuries of monarchical history by administrative law built on entirely new foundations. …

Two circumstances, since then, would contribute to the emergence of a law specific to the executive which was more and more clearly individualized. The strengthening of an order of courts reserved for the executive, and the progressive development of the scholarship of administrative law, taking its place within the various legal disciplines. …

Before the first years of the 19th century, the almost complete absence of the teaching of administrative law, together with the idea of the absence of firm principles ensuring limits to the powers of public authorities, prevented the emergence of legal analyses of administrative activity. …

The individualization, in year VIII [1799], of authorities vested with judicial responsibilities, however imperfect their separation from the executive remained, led to the definition of the scope of their respective competences. The general principle adopted was apparently clear: administrative acts, 'pure administration' in the terminology used since the *Ancien Régime*, constituted the sphere reserved for agents of the executive; as for contentious cases, that is to say those [cases] which found their origin in a dispute and a complaint, they belonged to the courts, with the exclusion of the executive. By the Napoleonic era, however, the demarcation line between these two types of activity had become blurred.

4.4 *Criminal Law*

Far-reaching reforms were also introduced in criminal law under the influence of Enlightenment ideas, as appears from the following text by Aniceto Masferrer.

> *Aniceto Masferrer, The Principle of Legality and Codification in the 19th-century Western Criminal Law Reform, in Georges Martyn, Anthony Musson and Heikki Pihlajamäki (eds), From the Judge's Arbitrium to the Legality Principle: Legislation as a Source of Law in Criminal Trials, Berlin, Duncker & Humblot, 2013, 263–268*
>
> Montesquieu, Beccaria, Rousseau and Voltaire, among others, criticized the 18th-century criminal law, but their main ideas were applied in the 19th-century liberal state, not in the context of absolutist monarchies. Voltaire, for example, claimed that the criminal laws should be clear and precise ... The law had to express clearly the constituent elements of a crime and the punishment. Along with Voltaire, other authors criticized the system of criminal law and advocated a new system based on legality under which the punishment assigned by a judge could not cross the limits established by the law itself. ...
>
> The early codes observed ... the principle of legality without accepting all of its consequences. ... [T]he first European criminal code that established ... the principle of legality ... was the Austrian Code of 1787 (*Allgemeine Gesetz über Verbrechen und Strafen*), enacted by of Joseph II. ... [T]he [1794] Prussian *Allgemeines Landrecht* ... [was more ambiguous since it allowed] punishing offenses that violated [the] rules of natural law ... The French code of 1791 established a regime of legality that was too inflexible with a fixed punishment, and abolished any possible pardon. [This] inflexibility was corrected by the French criminal code of 1810. French criminal lawyers recognized that the legality principle did not preclude that judges may 'rely on certain pre-existing principles not contained in the code', since such immutable principles, not being proclaimed by the legislator, were 'already imprinted in the hearts of all magistrates'.
>
> The Bavarian code of 1813, inspired – if not drafted – by Feuerbach, also introduced the principle of legality with all of its consequences, thus excluding – theoretically, not in practice – any possible judicial discretion and analogy, and affirming this principle 'more strongly than ever'.
>
> From then onwards, many European criminal codes, [some of them] influenced by the criminal Codes of France (1810) and Bavaria (1813), laid down the principle of legality. ...

It is important to consider that the recognition of the principle of legality within the context of the French Revolution [was part of] ... a broader principle, namely, the recognition of the rights of man, the separation of powers and the supremacy of the legislative power ... inasmuch as any law enacted by parliament was considered to be the expression of the 'general will' ...

The new notion of the constitutional state and sovereignty, based upon the protection of human natural rights and the supremacy of law, paved the way to the recognition of the principle of legality in criminal law.

4.5 *Civil Procedure*

Civil procedure was rather traditional in its outlook in the early nineteenth century. In France, the 1806 Code of Civil Procedure copied, to a large extent, the 1667 *Ordonnance civile* of Louis XIV. Nevertheless, this 1806 Code served as an example for codification attempts in many parts of Europe. The procedural model the 1806 Code prescribed can be defined as liberal, which meant that procedure was more or less adversarial, leaving much of the initiative to the parties. This would only change at the end of the nineteenth century under the influence of the Austrian *Zivilprozessordnung* drafted by Franz Klein (1854–1926). Klein realized that civil litigation has an importance that goes beyond the individual interests of the parties to a civil lawsuit and, therefore, he advocated a social model of civil litigation, as is explained below.

C.H. (Remco) van Rhee, Introduction, in C.H. (Remco) van Rhee (ed.), European Traditions in Civil Procedure, Antwerp, Intersentia, 2005, 5–8, 10–12

It is not too bold a statement to say that the history of modern civil procedure in Continental Europe starts with the 1806 French Code of Civil Procedure, which came into force in 1807. It was this younger sister of the equally influential *Code civil* that would serve as a model for many other codifications in Europe (and beyond) in the field of civil procedure. This may come as a surprise because, taken as a whole, the French procedural Code was not very modern; it was in fact one of the least innovative of Napoleon Bonaparte's Codes since it incorporated, to a large extent, civil procedural law as it could be found in Colbert's 1667 Royal Ordinance on civil procedure (as promulgated under Louis XIV). Two reasons may nevertheless have contributed to the popularity of the French Code. First, its procedural model had become familiar to lawyers in many different parts of Europe due to the fact that it had been introduced in these territories as a result of the expansion of the French empire and its sphere of influence at the end of the eighteenth and the beginning of the nineteenth centuries. It was in many cases the first time these lawyers had come into contact with a codified system of civil procedural law and its advantages. Additionally, although the Code was rather conservative in various respects, it was also a modern Code. … The fact that its procedure reflected the liberal attitude of the nineteenth century, with its emphasis on the individual responsibility of the citizens, citizens who were deemed to be reasonable men who would litigate against each other from a position of equality, was another feature of the Code that fitted nineteenth-century Europe well. As a result, the power of the court to intervene in the litigation process for the sake of efficiency, and in order to prevent undue delay, were not very pronounced. …

As stated above, the French 1806 Code lay at the basis of reform and codification of civil procedural law in many European countries and territories. Often these countries and territories had been annexed to, or had become dependent on, the French empire in the Napoleonic era and before. … [Examples are Belgium, the Netherlands, Geneva,] and several regions on the left bank of the river Rhine that were incorporated into the French Republic from the 1790s onwards and which currently belong to modern Germany (Rheinpreussen, Rheinhessen and Rheinbayern, the Kingdom of Westphalia and the Grand Duchy of Berg). …

… [N]one of the above countries and territories reverted to its original practice and procedure in civil litigation after the defeat of the French Emperor in 1813. In all these countries and territories, the French Codes, including the Code of Civil Procedure, remained in force until a product of native soil had been drafted. …

An example of a German codification project that was influenced by the French procedural model was the 1850 Code of Civil Procedure of the Kingdom of Hanover. The advantages of the modified French model of the Code of Civil Procedure of Geneva were also recognized. … The Hanover Code has a French-Genevan outlook in that it emphasises orality and party autonomy. This does not, however, mean that features from the German tradition are absent. One may, for example, refer to the *Beweisinterlokut* of the Hanoverian Code …

… French influence was also present in the various drafts for an all-German procedural code. The first draft was presented in 1866, within the framework of the German Confederation (*Deutsche Bund*). This draft was not acceptable to Prussia. After Austria had left the German Confederation which led to the creation of the *Norddeutsche Bund* in 1867, a new draft was presented in 1870, within the framework of the latter Confederation.

Again, the French influence was evident due to the fact that this draft was mainly a revised version of the 1866 draft. The draft was, however, never introduced. An all-German procedural code would only see the light of day after the Second German Empire had been proclaimed at Versailles, in 1871. The Prussian Minister of Justice Leonhardt (1815–1880), who, inter alia, had played an important role in the drafting of the 1850 Hanover Code (Hanover having been annexed by Prussia in 1866), played a primary role in the drafting of this all-German Code as well. Therefore, it is not a surprise that the Hanover Code influenced the ensuing 1877 German Code of Civil Procedure, i.e., the *Reichscivilprozessordnung* (ZPO). In some respects, the 1877 Code was even more 'French' in its outlook than its Hanoverian predecessor; a typical German feature of the Hanoverian Code, i.e., the *Beweisinterlokut* was not, for example, present in the 1877 German Code. Other elements of 'German stock,' however, remained (such as the rules on the participation of third parties in the procedure). The procedure of the 1877 German Code can, therefore, best be qualified as a combination of French ideas on civil procedure and those of the common legal tradition of the German States (*gemeines Recht*). …

For most of the nineteenth century, the French, non-interventionist liberal model of civil litigation dominated the European legal scene. It was partly due to embryonic ideas of what may be called the 'welfare state' that things started to change. The Austrian *Zivilprozessordnung* of 1895, introduced in 1898 and drafted by Franz Klein (1854–1926), stands as landmark legislation in the field of civil procedure, reflecting the new ideas. It is this Code that, often on the basis of older procedural concepts as well as positive elements of civil procedure of other countries, changed the face of civil procedure in Austria. During the twentieth century, this Code would serve as a model for other countries, just as the 1806 French Code had done during a large part of the nineteenth century.

Franz Klein, at that time *Privatdozent*, systematically explained his ideas on civil litigation in 1890–91 in a collection of articles in the *Juristische Blätter*. They were republished in his *Pro Futuro. Betrachtungen über Probleme der Civilprocessreform in Oesterreich*. Klein's aim was the realisation of the so-called 'social function' (*Sozialfunktion*) of civil litigation. This 'social function' may be viewed as a reaction against the nineteenth-century liberal ideal of procedure. It meant that litigation should not only be considered as a means to solve individual lawsuits between private litigants, but as a phenomenon that touched upon society as a whole. Civil procedure should serve the public interest (*Wohlfahrtsfunktion*), but it had to be viewed from an economical perspective as well. The economical perspective meant that one should, for example, guard against civil procedure being used as a means to postpone payment of a debt or to obtain money at a low interest rate.

That many of Klein's ideas were modern appears from nearly all pages of his *Pro Futuro*. The modernity of his ideas may be proven by the following quote, in which he described the Austrian procedural model which he wanted to change.

> *Klein, Pro Futuro, Betrachtungen über Probleme der Civilprozessreform in Oesterreich, Leipzig and Vienna, Franz Deuticke, 1891, 39 (transl. by Cornelis Hendrik (Remco) van Rhee)*
> The youth is impressed with the moral principle that one must also help the enemy in need, but in litigation this is something completely different! Litigation is a war in which the parties, as fiercely hating enemies intent on mutual annihilation, endeavour to fight each other with all means – and have the right to do so. Not a fight, like the duel, with loyalty and nobility, without exploitation of the adverse accidents to which the opponent party is prone, no a fight, in which the striving for victory suppresses all other considerations, all noble impulses remaining silent, in which pretty much everything is allowed that is useful, and in which one can witness the opponent bleeding to death, without the legal or ethical obligation to provide assistance; a war without the Red Cross, so to speak.[18]

> *C.H. (Remco) van Rhee, Introduction, in C.H. (Remco) van Rhee (ed.), European Traditions in Civil Procedure, Antwerp, Intersentia, 2005, 12–13*
> In order to change this approach to civil procedure as a kind of 'battle' between the parties, and to create a new procedural model in which the 'social function' of civil litigation was recognised, Klein aimed at finding

18 Der Jugend wird der Moralgrundsatz eingeprägt, man müsse auch dem Feinde in der Noth helfen, aber im Processe ist das etwas ganz Anderes! Der Process ist ein Krieg, in dem sich die Parteien als ingrimmig hassende, auf gegenseitige Vernichtung bedachte Feinde mit allen Mitteln niederzuringen bemühen – und dazu das Recht haben. Nicht ein Waffengang, wie etwa das Duell, mit einem Beisatze von Loyalität und Noblesse, welcher das Ausnützen widriger Zufälligkeiten, die den Einen treffen, verschmäht, nein ein Kampf, in welchem das Streben nach dem Sieg alle anderen Rücksichten verdrängt, alle edleren Regungen schweigen dürfen, so ziemlich Alles erlaubt ist, was nur nützt, und in dem man namentlich auch den Gegner ruhig sich verbluten sehen kann, ohne juristische oder ethische Hilfeleistungspflicht; sozusagen ein Krieg ohne rothes Kreuz.

a new balance between the powers of the judge and those of the parties. More than a hundred years ago, he advocated the idea that the parties to a lawsuit should co-operate in order to facilitate a judgment. Because he viewed a legal dispute as a negative social phenomenon, he claimed that civil litigation should be quick, efficient and cheap. It should result in cases being judged on the basis of the 'substantive' or 'factual' truth, i.e., on the basis of the facts as they had occurred and not merely on the truth as fabricated by the parties to the lawsuit. Consequently, in his view the parties had to observe a so-called *Wahrheitspflicht*, meaning that they had an obligation to present 'true' facts to the court.

Apparently Klein's ideas were found appealing, since he was appointed *Ministerialsekretär* at the Austrian Ministry of Justice on 17 February 1891. There he was entrusted with the task of drafting a new procedural code in order to replace the 1781 Austrian *Allgemeine Gerichtsordnung*.

In Klein's *Zivilprozessordnung*, the judge was in charge of the duration of the lawsuit and exercised important powers in the area of fact gathering. The judge was allowed to collect evidence ex officio. Evidence was to be evaluated freely by the court. An interesting, innovative, feature of the *Zivilprozessordnung* was the division of the lawsuit into a written, preparatory stage and a (preferably single) oral hearing.

The Austrian *Zivilprozessordnung* became very influential outside Austria, first of all in the German-speaking world. … An example is the 1924 *Novelle* of the German Secretary of Justice Emminger. As a result of this *Novelle*, the powers of the German judge were extended. Now, this judge was also given a responsibility as regards time-limits. Additionally, the lawsuit was divided into a preparatory stage and a concentrated oral hearing. In 1933, the *Wahrheitspflicht* was introduced into Germany.

4.6 *Criminal Procedure*

French pre-revolutionary criminal procedure was generally regarded as cruel and secretive and thus contrary to the spirit of the Enlightenment. Along with the claim for the reform of some substantive criminal law institutions (the abolition of traditional punishments such as banishment and whipping, as well as offenses such as sorcery and blasphemy), the enlightened authors fiercely criticized the existing criminal justice system. The influence of English law was particularly clear in calls for the writ of habeas corpus and, above all, the demands for trial by jury.

> *William Savitt, Villainous Verdicts? Rethinking the Nineteenth-Century French Jury, Colum. L. Rev. 96 (1996), 1024–1026*
> The procedural reform, highly influenced by the English model, introduced the grand jury (*jury d'accusation*) into French law, and replaced the secret and inquisitorial felony trial practice of the Ordinance of 1670 with an 'oral, confrontational, public, and adversarial' procedure in which the 'public prosecutor and the accused do battle with equal arms.' In addition, the Assembly created an absolute right to defense counsel for felony defendants, providing for court appointed assistance where the defendant had not independently retained counsel.
>
> The most important innovation of these reform measures, however, was the introduction of the trial jury (*jury de jugement*) for all felony proceedings. The Law of 16–29 September provided for the establishment of *tribunaux criminels*, the highest trial courts in the country, staffed by three judges – a president, who directed the proceedings, and two assesseurs and a twelve person jury. At the close of the trial, the president presented the jury foreman with a packet of questions asking the following three questions for each charge: Was the criminal act established? If yes, was the defendant guilty? And finally, was the criminal act intentional? Although the English rule of unanimity was not adopted, decisions unfavorable to the defendant on any of these questions required ten votes. Over the objection of Robespierre and other 'democrats,' the Assembly limited jury participation to 'active citizens;' that is, those citizens who paid taxes equivalent to ten days of work and thus were qualified to serve in the departmental government.
>
> The legislation of 1791 recast not only the personnel, but also the process of fact finding in criminal law. The complex system of 'legal proofs' that dominated the old regime was replaced by 'the reliable illumination of common sense' that lay judges would bring to the court. Jurors were asked to follow their 'conscience' and their 'profound convictions;' indeed, the jury system was simply incompatible with the prior regime of legal proofs. By turning verdicts over to laypersons entrusted with a specific mandate to adjudge on grounds of conscience rather than technical proof, the National Assembly created the possibility of popular justice and set the stage for the controversial career of the nineteenth century jury.

However, Revolutionary laws lasted shortly because of the Napoleonic legislative reforms. In this regard, the 1808 *Code d'instruction criminelle* (Code of criminal procedure) and the 1810 *Code pénal* (Penal Code), which took effect together on 1 January 1811, constituted the cornerstones of French criminal justice until well after World War II.

William Savitt, Villainous Verdicts? Rethinking the Nineteenth-Century French Jury, Colum. L. Rev. 96 (1996), 1031–1033

The framers of the Codes had witnessed the jury's uncertain performance since 1792 and their handiwork shows the signs of their accumulated skepticism. At a procedural level, much of the Revolutionary model was discarded in favor of the Ordinance of 1670. At the indicting phase, the procedures of the old regime were reinstated virtually in their entirety: indicting panels would be secret, written, and staffed by professional magistrates. The grand jury was banished from French jurisprudence.

The petty jury survived, however, as the principal finder of fact at the felony trial court, rebaptized the *cour d'assises*. Procedure at the *cour d'assisses* would be oral, public and adversarial, with defense counsel still guaranteed for the accused. The Code's framers confirmed the rejection of the old system of legal proofs, as jurors were ordered to find defendants guilty only when the prosecution's evidence was sufficient to create in their 'conscience' a 'profound conviction' of culpability. Nevertheless, the Procedural Code restrained the sway of jury authority considerably. Five rather than three judges oversaw the proceedings, rendering the professional magistracy a more intimidating courtroom presence. Press and political crimes were removed from jury competence, and the government reserved the right to suspend trial by jury in emergency circumstances. Wealth and education qualifications for jurors were raised, and the government conferred upon itself an unlimited discretionary power to inscribe non qualifying citizens. More significantly, the power to designate the short list of sixty jurors, from which the trial session pool of thirty-six would be selected by the presiding judge, was accorded to the government. And as if to highlight the political subordination of the jury, the Code affirmed that 'His Imperial Majesty reserves the right to give the honorable affirmation of his satisfaction to jurors who have demonstrated praiseworthy zeal.'

The jury's responsibilities in court were altered as well. The Procedural Code suppressed the nettlesome 'intentional question'; under the new Code, the three constituent questions of guilt were pared to two: first, was a crime established, and second, did the defendant commit the crime? Jurors also affirmed or rejected any legal excuses proffered by the defendant and retained the authority to determine whether any alleged aggravating circumstances were established at trial. All of these questions would be resolved by simple majority vote. Finally, even the jury's sovereignty over questions of guilt or innocence was curbed: upon

> a conviction by a mere seven-to-five majority of the jury, the five judges were to be polled. Where four judges voted for acquittal, the defendant was released, on the theory that a majority of those voting (nine of seventeen) were unpersuaded by the evidence.

Under the influence of the Enlightenment, and following the French example, the criminal jury was created in other European jurisdictions (e.g. Belgium, Spain, Germany, Hungary, Switzerland and Denmark). Although the French type of jury served as the model for some Continental countries 'to assume an exact imitation would be misleading, for each country has made alterations more or less radical. The system has not only evolved, but has been transformed and diversified. In some countries, the assessor-system is not much more than a reformed jury-system; certainly the assessorate in Germany, Austria, and Swiss Berne, is far removed from the original jury-type.'[19]

The popularity of the jury in eighteenth-century England, where it was seen as a useful tool to curb manipulation of the law by royal despotism, was shared by the colonies with an added patriotic sense. This explains why colonial juries were preferred to royal judges. In the early nineteenth-century United States of America, for example, state juries in criminal cases decided questions of both fact and law.

> *Anon., The Changing Role of the Jury in the Nineteenth Century, Yale L.J. 74 (1964–1965), 173–174*
> Judging from the limited sources available, the right of the jury to decide questions of law was widely recognized in the colonies. In 1771, John Adams stated unequivocally that a juror should ignore a judge's instructions on the law if it violates fundamental principles:
>
>> It is not only … [the juror's] right, but his duty, in that case, to find the verdict according to his own best understanding, judgment, and conscience, though in direct opposition to the direction of the court.
>
> There is much evidence of the general acceptance of this principle in the period immediately after the Constitution was adopted. In *Georgia v. Brailsford*, a jury trial in the Supreme Court, Chief Justice Jay submitted the case to the jury on an agreed set of facts after four days of argument.

19 Francois Gorphe, Reforms of the Jury-System in Europe: France and Other Continental Countries, Am. Inst. Crim. L. & Criminology 27 (1936–1937), 155–168.

> In his charge to the jury, the Chief Justice noted the presumption 'that the courts are the best judges of law,' but stressed the jurors' right to take upon ... [themselves] to judge of both, and to determine the law as well as the fact in controversy. During the first third of the nineteenth century, other judges frequently charged juries that they were the judges of the law as well as the fact and were not bound by the judge's instructions. A charge that the jury had the right to consider the law had a corollary at the level of trial procedure: counsel had the right to argue the law – its interpretation and its validity to the jury.

At the end of the nineteenth-century, the image of the jury changed dramatically.

> *Anon., The Changing Role of the Jury in the Nineteenth Century, Yale L.J. 74 (1964–1965), 194*
> Many influential members of the bar evidently objected to the jury because it would be hostile to their clients and sympathetic to poor litigants. Francis Wharton extended the argument to criminal cases. After describing the risks of partiality in juries, he noted that the decisive issues of the future will not be race or party, but 'those which involve the relations of capital to labor, of corporations to the public.' He foresaw the possibility that juries, if they had the right to decide law as well as fact, might convict corporate officers and directors of attempting to monopolize the goods of the community.
>
> At the end of the nineteenth century the rhetoric of the jury's critics reflected the decreased importance of the jury in the trial process and in legal and political theory. The concept of a natural law accessible to the common man was alien to lawyers and judges who distrusted the common man, and who thought of the law as a set of positive rules leading to predictable results. The jury at the outset of the century had been regarded as a mainstay of liberty and an integral part of democratic government. But by the end of the century the jury had come to be seen as an outmoded and none-too-reliable institution for resolving disputed questions of fact.

Questions

1. Why do 'nineteenth-century codes reflect continuity in the law and moderate reform?'
2. Did 'Pacta sunt servanda' or provisions such as 'All legally concluded agreements have the force of law for the parties to such agreements'

reflect the liberal or individualistic character of modern civil codes? Were these provisions new or revolutionary?
3. Why did the promulgation of the French commercial code bring about so-called 'decodification'?
4. What were the two main models of civil procedure in nineteenth-century Europe?
5. To which extent did criminal codes contain notions, principles and categories of the medieval and early-modern *ius commune*?

5 Conclusion

The period discussed in this chapter starts with the great revolutions of the second half of the 18th century. These revolutions and the idea of modern constitutionalism to which they gave rise, meant a decisive break with the past. The effects of these developments were particularly important in the province of public law (e.g. constitutional law, administrative law, and procedure), although it also affected some areas of private law. It would be wrong, however, to think that this break constituted a departure from notions, concepts, categories and institutions of the previous periods. It would not be accurate to emphasize legal changes in the nineteenth century without recognizing the weight of tradition. This appears very clearly, when one considers the contents of the various codifications of the laws to which this so-called codification period gave rise. Very often, the substance of the codes reflected the laws of the previous period. Examples are the French 1806 *Code de procédure civile* and the 1807 *Code de commerce,* which codified existing laws and derived much materials from the seventeenth-century royal ordinances of Louis XIV. What was, however, new was the idea of a codification being an exclusive and exhaustive source of law, an idea that found its origins in the period of Enlightenment. Judges were given an important role in the interpretation of the codes, due to the fact that they could not excuse themselves from administering justice when they came to the conclusion that the law was unclear on the subject-matter at hand. Court decisions gained in importance since, unlike the previous period, from now on judgments needed to contain reasons.

Nineteenth-century legal development was complex and paradoxical. Laws were sometimes interpreted differently from what the legislature intended. This is what happened with the French Civil Code: whereas the drafters did not reject other sources of law, the French Exegetical School made tireless efforts to exclude other sources, interpreting the Civil Code in a way that reduced the law to *lex* (legal positivism). The same occurred where it concerns the recognition of fundamental rights: whereas modern constitutions state that the aim of all political associations is to guarantee natural rights, contemporary legal philosophers exalted the notions of social contract and sovereignty, denying the existence of any pre-political reality.

The nineteenth century, and with it the modern codification period, began to draw to a close in 1900 with the coming into force of the German civil code. Just like its French counterpart, this code is traditional, especially were it concerns content. Different from the French code, however, the German code did not allow much room for customary law: it consists mainly of Roman law as interpreted by the followers of the German Historical School and their successors. This resulted, paradoxically, in France having a civil code that is much more Germanic in character than the German civil code. However, in both codes the *ius commune* tradition lives on, albeit that the *ius commune* itself is now replaced by national codifications. This explains why the *ius commune* could become a central theme in discussions on the future of European private law at the end of the twentieth and the beginning of the twenty-first century. These matters will be discussed in the final chapter of this book.

Further Reading

Baker, John. An Introduction to English Legal History (5th ed.), Oxford, Oxford University Press, 2019.

Bellomo, M. The Common Legal Past of Europe, 1000–1800, Washington DC, The Catholic University of America Press, 1995.

Billias, George Athan. American Constitutionalism Heard Round the World, 1776–1989: a Global Perspective, New York, New York University Press, 2009.

Blaufarb, Rafe. The Great Demarcation: the French Revolution and the Invention of Modern Property, New York, Oxford University Press, 2016.

Censer, Jack R. and Lynn Hunt, Liberty, Equality, Fraternity. Exploring the French Revolution, University Park, Pennsylvania State University Press, 2001.

Coing, H. Europäisches Privatrecht, Vols. 2–5, Munich, Beck, 1977–1988.

Cook, Charles M. The American Codification Movement: a Study of Antebellum Legal Reform, Westport CT, Greenwood Press, 1981.

Cottrol, Robert J. The Long Lingering Shadow. Slavery, Race, and Law in the American Hemisphere, Athens, Unversity of Georgia Press, 2013.

Cox, Marvin R. (ed.), The Place of the French Revolution in History, Boston, Houghton Mifflin, 1998.

Dilcher, Gerhard. The Germanists and the Historical School of Law: German Legal Science between Romanticism, Realism, and Rationalization, Rechtsgeschichte – Legal History 24 (2016), 20–72.

Ecklund, John E. The Origins of Western Law from Athens to the Code of Napoleon, Clark NJ, Talbot, 2014.

Farmer, Lindsay. Reconstructing the English Codification Debate: the Criminal Law Commissioners, 1833–45, Law and History Review 18/2 (2000), 397–426.

Golove, David M. and Daniel J. Hulsebosch. A Civilized Nation: the Early American Constitution, the Law of Nations, and the Pursuit of International Recognition, NYU Law Review 85/4 (2010), 932–1066.

Gordley, James. Myths of the French Civil Code, American Journal of Comparative Law 42/3 (1994), 459–505.

Hancock, Ralph C. and L. Gary Lambert (eds), The Legacy of the French Revolution, Lanham MD, Rowman and Littlefield, 1996.

Hunt, Lynn. (ed. and trans.), The French Revolution and Human Rights: a Brief Documentary History, Boston, Bedford Books, 1996.

John, Michael. Politics and the Law in Late Nineteenth-Century Germany. The Origins of the Civil Code, Oxford, Clarendon Press, 1989.

Kelley, D.R. Historians and the Law in Post-revolutionary France, Princeton NJ, Princeton University Press, 1984.

Kelly, J.M. A Short History of Western Legal Theory, Oxford, Oxford University Press, 1992.

Kroppenberg, Inge and Nicolaus Linder. Coding the Nation: Codification History from a (Post-)Global Perspective, in Thomas Duve (ed.), Entanglements in Legal History: Conceptual Approaches, Frankfurt am Main, Max Planck Institute for European Legal History, 67–99.

Langbein, J.H., R.L Lerer and B.P Smith. History of the Common Law: the Development of Anglo-American Legal Institutions, New York, Aspen, 2009.

Lesaffer, Randall. European Legal History: a Cultural and Political Perspective (8th ed.), Cambridge, Cambridge University Press, 2014.

Levasseur, Alain A. Code Napoleon or Code Portalis?, Tulane Law Review 43/4 (1969), 762–774.

Loveman, Brian. The Constitution of Tyranny: Regimes of Exception in Spanish America, Pittsburgh, University of Pittsburgh Press, 1993.

Milsom, S.F.C. Historical Foundations of the Common Law, London, Butterworths, 1981.

Mirow, M.C. Latin American Law: a History of Private Law and Institutions in Spanish America, Austin, University of Texas Press, 2004.

Mirow, M.C. Latin American Constitutions: the Constitution of Cádiz and its Legacy in Spanish America, Cambridge, Cambridge University Press, 2015.

Mirow, M.C. and Rafael Domingo (eds.), Law and Christianity in Latin America: the Work of Great Jurists, London, Routledge, 2021.

Nelson, William E. The Common law in Colonial America, 3 vols., Oxford, Oxford University Press, 2008–2016.

Parise, Agustin. Codification of the Law in Louisiana: Early Nineteenth-Century Oscillation between Continental European and Common Law Systems, Tulane European and Civil Law Forum 27 (2012), 133–164.

Parise, Agustín. Ownership Paradigms in American Civil Law Jurisdictions: Manifestations of the Shifts in the Legislation of Louisiana, Chile, and Argentina (16th-20th Centuries), Leiden, Brill Nijhoff, 2017.

Pérez-Perdomo, Rogelio. Latin American Lawyers: a Historical Introduction, Stanford, Stanford University Press, 2006.

Plucknett, Theodore F.T. A Concise History of the Common Law (5th ed.), Boston, Little Brown and Co., 1956.

Reimann, Mathias. The Historical School Against Codification: Savigny, Carter, and the Defeat of the New York Civil Code, American Journal of Comparative Law 37/1 (1989), 95–119.

Robinson, O.F., T.D. Fergus and W.M. Gordon. European Legal History: Sources and Institutions, Oxford, Oxford University Press, 2020.

Schwartz, Bernard (ed.), The Code Napoleon and the Common Law World. The Sesquicentennial Lectures Delivered at the Law Center of New York University, December 13–15, 1954, New York, NYU Press, 1956.

Sewell, William H. A Rhetoric of Bourgeois Revolution: the Abbé Sieyès and What is the Third Estate?, Durham NC, Duke University Press, 1994.

Stein, Peter. Roman Law in European History (12th ed.), Cambridge, Cambridge University Press, 2013.

Tierney, B. Liberty and Law. The Idea of Permissive Natural Law, 1100–1800, Washington DC, The Catholic University of America Press, 2014.

Tomlins, Christopher (ed.), The Cambridge History of Law in America, Cambridge, Cambridge University Press, 2008, 144–177.

Uribe-Uran, Victor M. Honorable Lives: Lawyers, Family, and Politics in Colombia, 1780–1850, Pittsburgh, University of Pittsburgh Press, 2000.

Van Caenegem, R.C. An Historical Introduction to Private Law (translated by D.E.L Johnston), Cambridge, Cambridge University Press, 1992.

van den Berg, P.A.J. The Politics of European Codification: a History of the Unification of Law in France, Prussia, the Austrian Monarchy and the Netherlands, Groningen, Europa Law Publishing, 2007.

Watson, A. The Evolution of Western Private Law, Baltimore MD, Johns Hopkins University Press, 2001.

Weiss, Gunther A. The Enchantment of Codification in the Common Law World, Yale Journal of International Law 25/2 (2000), 435–532.

Whitman, J.O. The Legacy of Roman Law in the German Romantic Era. Historical Vision and Legal Change, Princeton NJ, Princeton University Press, 1990.

Wieacker, Franz. A History of Private Law in Europe with Particular Reference to Germany (transl. by Tony Weir), Oxford, Clarendon Press, 1995.

Wisner, D. The Cult of the Legislator in France, 1750–1830. A Study in the Political Theology of the French Enlightenment, Liverpool, Liverpool University Press, 1997.

Zimmermann, Eduardo. Judicial Institutions in Nineteenth-Century Latin America, London, Institute of Latin American Studies, 1999.

Zimmermann, R. Roman Law, Contemporary Law, European Law. The Civilian Tradition Today, Oxford, Oxford University Press, 2001.

CHAPTER 7

Contemporary Period (1900–Present)

Olivier Moréteau, Agustín Parise and Jacques Vanderlinden†

1 Introduction

The final chapter of this volume covers a number of events that continue to shape the law and society. Society encompasses everything from the smallest, simplest unit (e.g., a couple) to the largest, most complex entities (e.g., the United Nations). The interconnectedness of this complex system is woven into the fabric of the minds of the individuals who make up society. This period witnessed, among others, two World Wars. The First World War exacted a tremendous human toll on the warring parties and caused deep frustration in the losing nations. Apart from tremendous human toll, the Second World War left the world with a sword of Damocles hanging above it in the form of the use and proliferation of nuclear weapons. During the second half of the twentieth century, the Cold War took central stage. The role of supranational organizations – first in the form of the League of Nations and later the United Nations – increased, if only as a forum to discuss and encourage reforms. After that came the advent of the European Union (EU). And today, the internet has eliminated many barriers to the circulation of legal information and ideas, bridging the distance between jurisdictions and continents.

The European Convention on Human Rights of 1950 and its supplementary protocols fundamentally changed the European project with the creation of the European Court of Human Rights to ensure their enforcement within the member states. It should be noted that these days opinions about the decisions of that court vary widely from very positive to very negative. International law-making in Europe is also growing, even though there are occasional signs of political desire and will to reduce its role. These political rumblings were not so much caused by the multiplication of international conventions which are, after all, more in the nature of declarations than law that can be enforced (although they are part of the legal environment in which lawmakers operate), but by the existence of supranational institutions with real law-making power, which can be legislative, judicial or doctrinal. There is also a movement in the opposite direction in European states, where law-making is taking place at a level below that of the nineteenth-century state. Therefore, the national legislator has been deprived of its power by two forces moving in opposite

 | DOI:10.1163/9789004687257_009

directions: supranational institutions above it and provincial, regional and cultural institutions below it.

In this period, the world experienced revolutions and paradigm shifts. The effort to impose a theoretical model (i.e., socialism) on societies led to a perversion of that model. However, because of its place of origin, the model 'necessarily' contaminated (the verb is used here in a strictly neutral sense) Asia to such an extent that only the Indian sub-continent and some neighbouring and peripheral countries escaped from its influence. The World Wars were a decisive factor in the spread eastward and westward of this ideology's economic theories and legal systems. Movements and events that sought to socialize the economy and society – which were different from pure socialist ideas – would trigger changes in the law during the first decades of the period discussed here. A social function paradigm became prominent at that time. These events paved the way for changes in private and public law alike.

New approaches to law took the stage during this period, gestating in the United States of America and spilling over in much of the Western world. Legal realism (law in action) reacted to the traditional, formalistic approach to law (law in the books), offering challenging views on the role of actors within the natural environment provided by the judicial process. In addition, law and economics gained the stage in Chicago as from the 1970s, considering economic efficiency as an important factor for the life of the law. Its tenets would soon spread to Europe and the Americas at large. The period also welcomed other approaches to the study and understanding of the law (e.g., critical legal studies, gender legal studies), even having an impact on the shaping of the law and offering novel means to explore law as an important aspect of society.

If we broaden our view beyond Europe and the Americas, it becomes clear that another main feature of this period was the spread of Western legal traditions to Africa, Asia and Oceania. This was when globalization entered the stage. Increasingly, constitutions and codes became the main feature of many legal systems throughout the world. Under the banner of universality, globalization led to the spread of Western values such as the rule of law and human rights. At the same time, the constitutionalization of private law and the privatization of constitutional law took place. The efforts to harmonize law shaped the period. In recent decades, multiple harmonization projects have been undertaken, such as the effort to formulate the Principles of European Contract Law, published in 1994 and updated several times by the Lando Commission, and the Principles of European Tort Law, prepared by the European Group of Tort Law (2005). However, none of them have become law. They remain examples of doctrinal codification or restatements of the law similar to those produced by the American Law Institute on the other side of the Atlantic. The UNIDROIT

Principles of International Commercial Contracts, published in 1994, which have been updated regularly, also belong to the category of soft law. In the meantime, compilations of laws were made both at the national and supranational levels. But are they a form of codification? Compilation, consolidation and codification *à droit constant* are, in essence, a rearrangement of existing legislation making it more accessible, in line with an already existing well-known practice both in the common law and the civil law tradition. On the other hand, the more recent European Draft Common Frame of Reference for private law may actually fall between these two categories or be a *sui generis* form of codification if it is referred to as a code rather than a 'toolbox.'

Finally, this period also saw the blossoming of comparative legal studies, their evolution and their critical reappraisal. This book is a testament to that. The term 'comparative law' has often been criticized, and it has been argued that the content it supposedly covers does not exist in reality. However, it became a combination of words that had staying power. These days there seems to be a general agreement on what can be put in the basket of comparative law. However, there is an endless controversy about whether some 'odd' flowers should be part of it and even more about how the flowers in it should be arranged.

2 Creation

In this period, the narrative of what law is was challenged from several different corners. It is indisputable that during this time, a process of the legalization of societies took place. This meant that law gained an ever-increasing prominence in the regulation of social relations among all the cultural, economic, political or social regulatory mechanisms operating in social life. This phenomenon can, partly, be explained by the weakening of the role that traditional institutions such as the family and the church played in the regulation of society and by an increase of individualism. Legislation was the normal tool for the state to use in this process. However, this, in turn, caused more people to turn to judges to seek redress. The result was an increase in judicial decisions as a complementary source of law.

At the beginning of our period, the development of the theory of the formal sources of law was still in its infancy. There was unanimous agreement about the paramount position of legislation in the hierarchy of sources, which remained the case until just before the twenty-first century. This is also true for the law of England, even though it seems to contradict the general impression that this system of law is judge-made. In most other countries, the principle embodied in the French doctrine that the only source of law is legislation prevails, even if judicial decisions or customs challenge its dominance. Before examining the 'classical' formal sources of law, it is worth considering briefly the hypothesis of what could be called the theory of sources of law *à la carte*. This theory maintains that each legal person produces law ('the law is what each one says it is'). It assumes that the underlying, implicit, assumption of civil law systems is that law is only expressed in pre-formulated rules of a general nature applicable to all the situations which fall under its ambit through a deductive process, even though there could be exceptions to the rule. It implies that, for instance, contracts create law but so do the results of arbitration and mediation processes.

This is not the place to attempt to redefine the nature of law. However, the change in perspective and the challenges that resulted from the critical or radical pluralism that emerged in the last years of our period has to be mentioned as a potential part of the Western legal tradition.

> *Olivier Moréteau, The Future of Civil Codes in France and Louisiana, Journal of Civil Law Studies 2 (2009), 51–52*
> We must clarify our speech when we talk about the sources of the law. When addressing the matter from the top end of the pyramid of norms, it may be right to say that legislation and custom are the direct sources of the civil law. Both are based on the will of the people, as expressed by their representatives in the case of legislation, and as produced and evidenced by the people in their daily life in the case of custom. But when considering the matter from the people's viewpoint, turning the pyramid top down, it may be wrong to say that legislation and custom are the only sources. We must acknowledge that the law is shaped by a number of other actors or factors. In good days, our belief in higher values often referred to as 'natural law,' 'equity,' and 'general principles of the law' shapes positive rules established by legislation, influences judges when deciding cases in the absence of applicable law and also trumps positive laws when courts sanction an abuse of right or apply the maxim *fraus omnia corrumpit*, fraud corrupts everything. The teaching and publications of law professors, referred to as 'doctrine' in the civil law tradition, shape the way laws are made, applied, interpreted. The decisions of judges, referred to as 'jurisprudence' [i.e., case law], have a direct impact on the people, whether judges apply the Code, distort it or create rules *ex nihilo*. The acts and deeds of practitioners referred to as 'practice' also have a tremendous impact on the people, for the good and occasionally for the bad. All these shape the rules we apply, in such a way

that Rodolfo Sacco came to call them 'legal formants.' Acknowledging the existence and the role of all actors and factors helps us to have a better understanding of what is going on in the civil law, as in all other legal systems. The development of the law is indeed based on the interaction of such actors and factors. Making that clear would no doubt help us to have a better grasp of what the law is. This helps to identify the driving forces, which are at times customary, legislative, jurisprudential or doctrinal and very often a combination of all, including legal practice. This way we would enrich, rather than revise the doctrine of sources, being mindful of a duality of perspectives, distinguishing the law as it ought to be (the upstream lawmaker's perspective or formalistic doctrine of sources) and the law as it is applied and perceived by those subjected to the rule (the downstream citizen's perspective or pluralistic doctrine of sources). This way of looking at things may also help transcend a narrow positivist approach, the moral dimension of norms and judgments being inescapable in both perspectives.

Questions

Some dogmas should not remain uncontested.

1. Why does Moréteau speak about inverting the pyramid of norms? How does this change the understanding of what the sources of law are?

2.1 *Political Organization and Law*

The period starting in 1900 produced different fora for the creation of law beyond state borders. This multilevel environment was the result of a societal evolution. Globalization was no longer confined to economics but spread to culture, politics, science, technology, ideology, and also affected the law. As a worldwide phenomenon, it required international cooperation and the search for common ground. Some, like the Canadian philosopher Marshall McLuhan, claimed that the world was turning into a global village. To address this new reality required new perspectives, new solutions and new paradigms. In this context, different supranational entities emerged. First, the League of Nations; then, the United Nations; and finally, the European Union (EU) at the European level. A look at the EU experience can illustrate the interplay of sources of law.

EU Treaty, Consolidated versions of the Treaty on European Union and the Treaty on the Functioning of the European Union (https://curia.europa.eu; accessed June 2022)

Article 5 (ex Article 5 Treaty Establishing the European Community (TEC))

1. The limits of Union competences are governed by the principle of conferral. The use of Union competences is governed by the principles of subsidiarity and proportionality.
2. Under the principle of conferral, the Union shall act only within the limits of the competences conferred upon it by the Member States in the Treaties to attain the objectives set out therein. Competences not conferred upon the Union in the Treaties remain with the Member States.
3. Under the principle of subsidiarity, in areas which do not fall within its exclusive competence, the Union shall act only if and in so far as the objectives of the proposed action cannot be sufficiently achieved by the Member States, either at central level or at regional and local level, but can rather, by reason of the scale or effects of the proposed action, be better achieved at Union level.
The institutions of the Union shall apply the principle of subsidiarity as laid down in the Protocol on the application of the principles of subsidiarity and proportionality. National Parliaments ensure compliance with the principle of subsidiarity in accordance with the procedure set out in that Protocol.
4. Under the principle of proportionality, the content and form of Union action shall not exceed what is necessary to achieve the objectives of the Treaties.
The institutions of the Union shall apply the principle of proportionality as laid down in the Protocol on the application of the principles of subsidiarity and proportionality.

Article 6 (ex Article 6 Treaty on European Union (TEU))
1. The Union recognises the rights, freedoms and principles set out in the Charter of Fundamental Rights of the European Union of 7 December 2000, as adapted at Strasbourg, on 12 December 2007, which shall have the same legal value as the Treaties.
The provisions of the Charter shall not extend in any way the competences of the Union as defined in the Treaties.
The rights, freedoms and principles in the Charter shall be interpreted in accordance with the general provisions in Title VII of the Charter governing its interpretation and application and with due regard to the explanations referred to in the Charter, that set out the sources of those provisions.

2. The Union shall accede to the European Convention for the Protection of Human Rights and Fundamental Freedoms. Such accession shall not affect the Union's competences as defined in the Treaties.
3. Fundamental rights, as guaranteed by the European Convention for the Protection of Human Rights and Fundamental Freedoms and as they result from the constitutional traditions common to the Member States, shall constitute general principles of the Union's law.

Winston Churchill described the new context in which the law would evolve. In a speech in 1946, he sketched the challenges that lay ahead and what was at stake.

Winston Churchill, Address given by Winston Churchill (Zurich, 19 September 1946), Council of Europe (https://rm.coe.int/090000168069 81f3; accessed June 2022)

I wish to speak about the tragedy of Europe, this noble continent, the home of all the great parent races of the Western world, the foundation of Christian faith and ethics, the origin of most of the culture, arts, philosophy and science both of ancient and modern times. If Europe were once united in the sharing of its common inheritance there would be no limit to the happiness, prosperity and glory which its 300 million or 400 million people would enjoy. Yet it is from Europe that has sprung that series of frightful nationalistic quarrels, originated by the Teutonic nations in their rise to power, which we have seen in this 20th century and in our own lifetime wreck the peace and mar the prospects of all mankind.

What is this plight to which Europe has been reduced? Some of the smaller states have indeed made a good recovery, but over wide areas are a vast, quivering mass of tormented, hungry, careworn and bewildered human beings, who wait in the ruins of their cities and homes and scan the dark horizons for the approach of some new form of tyranny or terror. Among the victors there is a Babel of voices, among the vanquished the sullen silence of despair. That is all that Europeans, grouped in so many ancient states and nations, and that is all that the Germanic races have got by tearing each other to pieces and spreading havoc far and wide. Indeed, but for the fact that the great republic across the Atlantic realised that the ruin or enslavement of Europe would involve her own fate as well, and stretched out hands of succour and guidance, the Dark Ages would have returned in all their cruelty and squalor. They may still return.

Yet all the while there is a remedy which, if it were generally and spontaneously adopted by the great majority of people in many lands, would as by a miracle transform the whole scene and would in a few years make all Europe, or the greater part of it, as free and happy as Switzerland is today. What is this sovereign remedy? It is to recreate the European fabric, or as much of it as we can, and to provide it with a structure under which it can dwell in peace, safety and freedom. We must build a kind of United States of Europe. In this way only will hundreds of millions of toilers be able to regain the simple joys and hopes which make life worth living. The process is simple. All that is needed is the resolve of hundreds of millions of men and women to do right instead of wrong and to gain as their reward blessing instead of cursing.

Much work has been done upon this task by the exertions of the Pan-European Union, which owes so much to the famous French patriot and statesman Aristide Briand. There is also that immense body which was brought into being amidst high hopes after the First World War – the League of Nations. The League did not fail because of its principles or conceptions. It failed because those principles were deserted by those states which brought it into being, because the governments of those states feared to face the facts and act while time remained. This disaster must not be repeated. There is, therefore, much knowledge and material with which to build and also bitter, dearly bought experience to spur.

There is no reason why a regional organisation of Europe should in any way conflict with the world organisation of the United Nations. On the contrary, I believe that the larger synthesis can only survive if it is founded upon broad natural groupings. There is already a natural grouping in the Western Hemisphere. We British have our own Commonwealth of Nations. These do not weaken, on the contrary they strengthen, the world organisation. They are in fact its main support. And why should there not be a European group which could give a sense of enlarged patriotism and common citizenship to the distracted peoples of this mighty continent? And why should it not take its rightful place with other great groupings and help to shape the honourable destiny of man? In order that this may be accomplished there must be an act of faith in which the millions of families speaking many languages must consciously take part …

Questions

Law evolves within specific contexts. Political organization at a particular time and particular place provides an important context for the development of law.

1. What are the principles mentioned in Article 5, and how do they help explain the interaction of European law and national laws? What is the

place of universally recognized rights in the framework of the European Union according to Article 6?

Churchill referred to the context in which law was going to develop.

2. Why does he speak of a United States of Europe? Why did he think a United States of Europe would not conflict with the international context at that time?

2.2 *Legislation*

Legislation was still the paramount source of law, but it was not the only source of law during this period. The evolution of legislation can be viewed in terms of quantity. From this vantage point, the overabundance of legislation in most jurisdictions is obvious. The mass of legislation was overwhelming, whether it was in the form of statutes as such or the statutory instruments required for their practical implementation. This phenomenon did not exclusively originate in this period, but the effects were noticeable at this time, and those effects moved people to call for solutions to the issues caused.

The evolution of legislation can also be viewed in terms of quality. Within the thicket of legislation, multiple forms of codification occupied a particular place. Codification continued to be the hallmark of the continental legal system. The possibility of codification was also explored in England; it did not, however, make inroads there. Codification was also often seen as a way to increase knowledge of the law. This was certainly the case for one of its main proponents in the previous period, Jeremy Bentham. He argued that: 'the principle of justice is that law should be known by all; and for its being known, codification is absolutely essential.' It seems, however, that the period under discussion completely dispelled that illusion. Even some of what appeared to be the clearest and most admired legal formulations (e.g., Art. 1382 of the French Civil Code) could not be understood without an abundance of case law covering pages of court decisions. The idea of effective transmission of the law through codification often seemed, as it had for centuries, an illusion.

The codes, particularly the civil codes, shaped the period. A look into this phenomenon helps illustrate the value of legislation as a source of law during this period.

Olivier Moréteau, A Summary Reflection on the Future of Civil Codes in Europe, in Peter Apathy et al. (eds), Festschrift für Helmut Koziol, Vienna, Jan Sramek Verlag, 2010, 1144–1146

Codification does not put the evolution of the civil law to a standstill, as Friedrich Karl von Savigny once feared. There is much life in the law, by way of judicial interpretation but also legislative reform. The latter can take the form of revision or recodification, but may also generate decodification, as part of the life of the codes. …

Codes are sometimes decodified as a consequence of empirical legislative reform, distorting the structure of the code or reforming significant matters by way of ancillary legislation that is no longer to be found in the code. Efforts to rewrite the codes, either partly or completely, and sometimes piecemeal, are confusingly described as revision or recodification. A few doctrinal efforts have been made to clarify the concepts of decodification, revision, and recodification.

A redefinition of those terms was recently proposed, based on architectural metaphors, comparing codes with churches or temples.

Codification is the construction of a homogenous building where the spirit can be felt in every single stone, window or ornament. Where the building is expanded in such a way that the connection between the different parts is lost, one gets close to what is called decodification. This may be the addition of new chapters in the code that do not connect clearly to the original text – like the addition of the regime of contracts with tour operators, full of consumer protections, making exception to the general law of obligations. Like unconnected wings of an enlarged building, they exist next to it, and the material is sometimes of a different fabric. Decodification also occurs when extensions are totally unconnected, like separate statutes or free standing buildings.

Codes can be revised by the reform of one or several articles, chapters, or titles. It sometimes happens that the entire code is rewritten, sometimes as the consequence of a complete revision process, as happened in the Netherlands and Quebec.

Partial revision may revitalize the code, but may also trigger a decodification process where the revision causes the code to lose its coherence. Decodification also typically happens with the multiplication of ancillary statutes outside the code, dealing with matters that were once regulated by the code itself.

Recodification is sometimes the answer. The entire civil code may be rewritten, either on a new structure, or based on new doctrines or ideas. The new civil code regains the density and gravity the previous one had lost by the effect of revision and decodification. The new civil code appears like a revitalized star in the legal system, and we may describe this as 'solar recodification.'

Recodification, however, often takes place in a far less ambitious way. Decodified matters will not be returned to the civil code. They will be amalgamated into specialized codes that may be described as satellite codes, revolving around a less dense and partly emptied civil code. These satellite codes are often little more than clerical compilations, coming close to the common law idea of consolidation. They do not have the density of the civil code. Those satellite codes are generally created because those specific areas of law started to develop fragmentarily outside of the civil code, thus generating a decodification process. This process may be described as 'satellite recodification.'

Like solar recodification, satellite recodification is meant to make legal provisions more accessible for jurists and laypersons alike. However, it often appears to be more technical, and therefore, less accessible to ordinary citizens.

Recodification may generate new types of re-energized civil codes, strengthening the solar system. Examples of solar recodification are not many. Quebec and the Netherlands may to some extent pass the test.

Recodification more often results in the enactment of loose satellite codes, which would probably not pass the test of being called codes in the Napoleonic or Germanic sense. These satellites revolve, sometimes at a distant orbit, around a weakened solar civil code, which may undergo revisions and continued decodification.

For instance, France allowed substantial matters to be moved outside the Civil Code. Legislation on insurance and consumer protection grew outside the code by way of separate statutes, causing a decodification process. The enactment of an Insurance Code and a Consumer Code were meant to consolidate dispersed legislation, and this looks like recodification in the form of satellite codes. To take the most recent of those codes (the *Code de la consommation*), it was not meant to be more than a rearranged collection of existing statutes and regulations protecting consumers in various transactions, without any change in substance. The content table appears more coherent, and like the *Code des assurances*, it contains a legislative part and a regulation part. These codes are a rearranged collection of existing legislation and regulation on a given topic, to make the texts more accessible. They are a collection rather than a system, and are satellites to the Civil Code.

Other jurisdictions prefer to remedy the disorder caused by decodification with a revision process. In Germany, consumer protection was moved into the Civil Code on the occasion of the big reform of the law of obligations at the beginning of the present century. While this is technically a revision of the BGB, it may also be described as decodification, in the sense that some of the new provisions do not connect easily with the rest of the code or are of a different fabric.

How may we improve the codes, in order to keep them accessible to the citizens? Here are a few thoughts that may help improve drafting techniques. …

Questions

Codification proved to be resilient in different contexts. It remained the leading form of legislation in the world of the civil law during the period discussed in this chapter.

1. Why does Moréteau believe that codification does not bring the evolution of the civil law to a standstill? What does he mean by re-codification and de-codification?

2.3 *Judicial Decisions*

The place of judicial decisions within the hierarchy of the sources of law changed considerably during this period. Jurisprudence (case law) is important as it clarifies the understanding of the written law by showing how it is interpreted and implemented.

A major (but not a lasting) change occurred in the former Soviet Union when, after the Revolution of 1917, the ultimate decision in judicial matters was taken away from the courts and transferred to the *Praesidium* of the Supreme Soviet. This restored a type of hierarchy that had also existed in France under the *référé legislatif*. However, neither the Soviet nor the French example became part of the tradition. The former disappeared with the establishment of the Russian Federation, and the latter was abolished as early as 1837 in France.

The abolition of the *référé legislatif* in France during the previous period did not increase the status of judicial decisions in the hierarchy of sources, not even in the writings of Francois Gény, who promoted its study in the late nineteenth century. Few – if any – of the authors of classical treatises considered case law to be a source of law. At best, after Jean Carbonnier published his theoretical classification of sources, it was considered an 'authority' (*autorité*) along with legal science. The characterization of something as a 'source' was reserved for legislation and custom. Needless to say, the validity of this theory was seriously challenged. Some even declared that the issue of the classification of sources was impossible to solve.

Even if the issue was not resolved in theory, in practice there were very few cases that lawyers could argue based on the text of a statute alone. Because of this, they needed to address the great mass of decisions which, in most editions were fortunately appended to each article of the relevant code or statute. This situation prevailed, *mutatis mutandis*, in most civil law legal systems. The situation was completely different in the common law world, the far western part of Western Europe, for obvious 'traditional' reasons. However, during this century, a few major changes in the nearly immutable status of precedent in the common law, a status which was reaffirmed until the very end of the 1890s, were brought about. First, the 1966 statement of practice regarding precedent was adopted, which expressly allowed the House of Lords (now the Supreme Court of the United Kingdom) to overrule its own decisions in exceptional circumstances. Judges themselves, however, did not unanimously support this. In 1993 the possibility to reference parliamentary history as an aid to legal construction was adopted, with the intent to increase the flexibility of judicial decisions. This led to greater uniformity in the Western legal traditions.

> *Lord Gardiner's Statement in the House of Lords, 26 July 1966 (https://publications.parliament.uk/pa/ld199697/ldinfo/ld08judg/redbook/redbk45.htm; accessed June 2022)*
>
> Their Lordships regard the use of precedent as an indispensable foundation upon which to decide what is the law and its application to individual cases. It provides at least some degree of certainty upon which individuals can rely in the conduct of their affairs, as well as a basis for orderly development of legal rules.
>
> Their Lordships nevertheless recognise that too rigid adherence to precedent may lead to injustice in a particular case and also unduly restrict the proper development of the law. They propose therefore, to modify their present practice and, while treating formal decisions of this house as normally binding, to depart from a previous decision when it appears to be right to do so.
>
> In this connection they will bear in mind the danger of disturbing retrospectively the basis on which contracts, settlement of property, and fiscal arrangements have been entered into and also the especial need for certainty as to the criminal law.
>
> This announcement is not intended to affect the use of precedent elsewhere than in this House.

The judicial decision in *Pepper v. Hart* serves as an illustration of the possibility to reference parliamentary materials as an aid to construction.

> *Pepper (Inspector of Taxes) v. Hart [1992] UKHL 3 (26 November 1992), 19–28 (Judgment delivered by Lord Browne-Wilkinson), 630–631, 633–635, 637–638, 640*
>
> 1. Should the rule prohibiting references to Parliamentary material be relaxed?

Under present law, there is a general rule that references to Parliamentary material as an aid to statutory construction is not permissible ('the exclusionary rule'): Davis v. Johnson [1979] A.C. 264; Hadmor Productions Ltd v. Hamilton [1983] A.C. 191. This rule did not always apply but was judge made. Thus, in Ash v. Abdy (1678) 3 Swans. 663 Lord Nottingham took judicial notice of his own experience when introducing the Bill in the House of Lords. The exclusionary rule was probably first stated by Willes J. in Millar v. Taylor (1769) 4 Burr. 2303, 2332. However, the case of In re Mew and Thome (1862) 31 L.J. Bank. 87 shows that even in the middle of the last century the rule was not absolute: in that case Lord Westbury L.C. in construing an Act had regard to its Parliamentary history and drew an inference as to Parliament's intention in passing the legislation from the making of an amendment striking out certain words.

The exclusionary rule was later extended so as to prohibit the court from looking even at reports made by commissioners on which legislation was based: Salkeld v. Johnson (1848) 2 Exch. 256, 273. This rule has now been relaxed so as to permit reports of commissioners, including law commissioners, and white papers to be looked at for the purpose solely of ascertaining the mischief which the statute is intended to cure but not for the purpose of discovering the meaning of the words used by Parliament to effect such cure: Eastman Photographic Materials Co v. Comptroller-General of Patents, Designs and Trade-marks [1898] A.C.571; Assam Railways and Trading Co Ltd v. Commissioners of Inland Revenue [1935] A.C. 445 457–458. Indeed, in Reg. v. The Secretary of State for Transport, Ex parte Factortame Ltd. [1990] 2 A.C. 85 your Lordships' House went further than this and had regard to a Law Commission report not only for the purpose of ascertaining the mischief but also for the purpose of drawing an inference as to Parliamentary intention from the fact that Parliament had not expressly implemented one of the Law Commission's recommendations.

Although the courts' attitude to reports leading to legislation has varied, until recently there was no modern case in which the court had looked at parliamentary debates as an aid to construction. However, in Pickstone v. Freemans Plc [1989] A.C. 66 this House, in construing a statutory instrument, did have regard to what was said by the Minister who initiated the debate on the regulations. My noble and learned friend Lord Keith of Kinkel (at p. 112B) after pointing out that the draft Regulations were not capable of being amended when presented to Parliament, said that it was 'entirely legitimate for the purpose of ascertaining the intention of Parliament to take into account the terms in which the draft was presented by the responsible Minister and which formed the basis of its acceptance.' My noble and learned friend Lord Templeman (at pp. 121–122) also referred to the Minister's speech, although possibly only by way of support for a conclusion he had reached on other grounds. My noble and learned friends Lord Brandon of Oakbrook and Lord Jauncey of Tullichettle agreed with both those speeches. This case therefore represents a major inroad on the exclusionary rule: see also Owen Bank Ltd v. Bracco [1992] 2 W.L.R. 621.

Mr Lester, for the taxpayers, did not urge us to abandon the exclusionary rule completely. His submission was that where the words of a statute were ambiguous or obscure or were capable of giving rise to an absurd conclusion it should be legitimate to look at the Parliamentary history, including the debates in Parliament, for the purpose of identifying the intention of Parliament in using the words it did use. He accepted that the function of the court was to construe the actual words enacted by Parliament so that in no circumstances could the court attach to words a meaning that they were incapable of bearing. He further accepted that the court should only attach importance to clear statements showing the intention of the promoter of the Bill, whether a Minister or private member: there could be no dredging through conflicting statements of intention with a view to discovering the true intention of Parliament in using the statutory words. …

Thus the reasons put forward for the present rule are first, that it preserves the constitutional proprieties leaving Parliament to legislate in words and the courts (not Parliamentary speakers), to construe the meaning of the words finally enacted; second, the practical difficulty of the expense of researching Parliamentary material which would arise if the material could be looked at; third, the need for the citizen to have access to a known defined text which regulates his legal rights; fourth, the improbability of finding helpful guidance from Hansard. …

My Lords, I have come to the conclusion that, as a matter of law, there are sound reasons for making a limited modification to the existing rule (subject to strict safeguards) unless there are constitutional or practical reasons which outweigh them. In my judgment, subject to the questions of the privileges of the House of Commons, reference to Parliamentary material should be permitted as an aid to the construction of legislation which is ambiguous or obscure or the literal meaning of which leads to an absurdity. Even in such cases references in court to Parliamentary material should only be permitted where such material clearly discloses the mischief aimed at or the legislative intention lying behind the ambiguous or obscure words. In the case of statements made in Parliament, as at present advised I cannot foresee that any statement other than the statement of the Minister or other promoter of the Bill is likely to meet these criteria.

I accept Mr Lester's submissions, but my main reason for reaching this conclusion is based on principle. Statute law consists of the words that Parliament has enacted. It is for the courts to construe those words and it is the court's duty in so doing to give effect to the intention of Parliament in using those words. It is an inescapable fact that, despite all the care taken in passing legislation, some statutory provisions when applied to the circumstances under consideration in any specific case are found to be ambiguous. One of the reasons for such ambiguity is that the members of the legislature in enacting the statutory provision may have been told what result those words are intended to achieve. Faced with a given set of words which are capable of conveying that meaning it is not surprising if the words are accepted as having that meaning. Parliament never intends to enact an ambiguity. Contrast with that the position of the courts. The courts are faced simply with a set of words which are in fact capable of bearing two meanings. The courts are ignorant of the underlying Parliamentary purpose. Unless something in other parts of the legislation discloses such purpose, the courts are forced to adopt one of the two possible meanings using highly technical rules of construction. In many, I suspect most, cases references to Parliamentary materials will not throw any light on the matter. But in a few cases it may emerge that the very question was considered by Parliament in passing the legislation. Why in such a case should the courts blind themselves to a clear indication of what Parliament intended in using those words? The court cannot attach a meaning to words which they cannot bear, but if the words are capable of bearing more than one meaning why should not Parliament's true intention be enforced rather than thwarted?

A number of other factors support this view. As I have said, the courts can now look at white papers and official reports for the purpose of finding the 'mischief' sought to be corrected, although not at draft clauses or proposals for the remedying of such mischief. A ministerial statement made in Parliament is an equally authoritative source of such information: why should the courts be cut off from this source of information as to the mischief aimed at? In any event, the distinction between looking at reports to identify the mischief aimed at but not to find the intention of Parliament in enacting the legislation is highly artificial. Take the normal Law Commission Report which analyses the problem and then annexes a draft Bill to remedy it. It is now permissible to look at the report to find the mischief and at the draft Bill to see that a provision in the draft was not included in the legislation enacted: see Factortame [1990] 2 A.C. 85. There can be no logical distinction between that case and looking at the draft Bill to see that the statute as enacted reproduced, often in the same words, the provision in the Law Commissions's draft. Given the purposive approach to construction now adopted by the courts in order to give effect to the true intentions of the legislature, the fine distinctions between looking for the mischief and looking for the intention in using words to provide the remedy are technical and inappropriate. Clear and unambiguous statements made by Ministers in Parliament are as much the background to the enactment of legislation as white papers and Parliamentary reports. …

In sum, I do not think that the practical difficulties arising from a limited relaxation of the rule are sufficient to outweigh the basic need for the courts to give effect to the words enacted by Parliament in the sense that they were intended by Parliament to bear. Courts are frequently criticised for their failure to do that. This failure is due not to cussedness but to ignorance of what Parliament intended by the obscure words of the legislation. The courts should not deny themselves the light which Parliamentary materials may shed on the meaning of the words Parliament has used and thereby risk subjecting the individual to a law which Parliament never intended to enact. …

I therefore reach the conclusion, subject to any question of Parliamentary privilege, that the exclusionary rule should be relaxed so as to permit reference to Parliamentary materials where

a. Legislation is ambiguous or obscure, or leads to an absurdity;
b. The material relied upon consists of one or more statements by a Minister or other promoter of the Bill together if necessary with such other Parliamentary material as is necessary to understand such statements and their effect;
c. The statements relied upon are clear.

Further than this, I would not at present go.

Questions

Precedent is a fundamental doctrine in the common law.

1. What are the benefits and the limitations of precedent according to Lord Gardiner?

Parliamentary materials can be used as an aid to construct the meaning of legal provisions. Legislative history, it should be noted, is also used in the civil law to interpret law.

2. What is the main reason, according to Lord Browne-Wilkinson in *Pepper v. Hart*, to conclude that the reference to Parliamentary material in the common law should be permitted as an aid to construct the meaning of laws which are ambiguous?

2.4 *Doctrine*

During this period, doctrine consisted mainly of monographs, law review articles and commentaries on jurisprudence (or case law in common law jurisdictions) and legislation. There was a proliferation of this type of literature, partly because of the exponential growth of the number of students in higher education and the related growth of academic positions for law graduates. Furthermore, the internet and electronic databases enhanced the accessibility of this material. They assisted the interpretation of the legal texts and invited, as it were, proposals for improvement, resulting in changes in other sources of law. This era provided many opportunities for debate amongst scholars through the many symposia and debates that were organized across the different jurisdictions. Supranational entities also nurtured those exchanges through grants and financial support. The internet is a valuable tool for disseminating doctrine across jurisdictions.

Doctrine also became a source of law in the common law world and particularly in the USA. An enormous amount of literature has been developed in the common law context. Lawrence M. Friedman, in an early edition of one of his celebrated works, provides a description of the situation in the USA that offers an excellent illustration of the growth.

> *Lawrence M. Friedman, A History of American Law (2nd edition), New York, Simon and Schuster, 1985, 692–694*
>
> This was the age of great treatises. Samuel Williston built a monumental fortress (1920–22) out of the law of Contracts, volume after volume, solid, closely knit, fully armored against the intrusion of any ethical, economic, or social notions whatsoever. After 1920, the legal realist movement threw down the gauntlet and became a serious rival of the dominant school. Karl Llewellyn and Jerome Frank, among others, did battle against any jurisprudence of concepts; there were even realist treatises, like Arthur Corbin's *Contracts,* a counterpoise out of Yale to the old man of Harvard. The realist idea also had an effect on the curriculum. Administrative law and taxation entered the ranks of the courses;

and there was some attempt to change content in older courses, in line with the new temper of the times. On the whole, though, law school curricula have remained amazingly resistent to radical transformation, despite generations of manifestoes. Some schools have added 'enrichment' courses; some have tinkered with clinical training. The center seems to hold, for better or for worse. The core curriculum has proved incredibly tough and impermeable.

There has been, from time to time, a movement to bring law back into the intellectual world. There were experiments in integrating law and social science in the 1920s and 1930s at Columbia, Johns Hopkins, and Yale, and a fling or two at curricular reform. These essays failed. After the Second World War, there were more serious efforts. Now, at last, government and foundation money began to trickle into the law schools. In the 1950s, an empirical study of the jury, at the University of Chicago, showed that collaboration between legal scholars and their social science colleagues was at least possible. Mostly, law and social science was still only a promise; but the promise seemed a little less hollow and dreamlike. In a few schools – notably Wisconsin and Berkeley – there was something more than lip service to the idea. In the 1960s, law study broadened to include more social issues – law and poverty, for example, and a richer, more varied dose of foreign law. The social sciences, basically, made hardly a dent, except for economics. Here Chicago was a leader, and Richard Posner, later a federal judge, was a major contributor. The 'law and economics' school was widely attacked as right-wing and excessively narrow; but it had gained, by the 1980s, a significant place in legal teaching, thought, and research.

Of the making of books, quality aside, there was truly no end. The few university law reviews of the 19th century had grown to an incredible number by the 1980s. There were probably on the order of one hundred and fifty. Virtually every law school, no matter how marginal, published a review as a matter of local pride. Somehow, all of these thousands of pages filled up with words. The more prestigious schools put out more issues per year than the weaker schools; then, when thick volumes became commonplace, they put out two journals, or more. By law school tradition, students ran the journals; law-review editors were the student elite of their schools. They had the best grades, the best, or only, rapport with the faculty, and went to the best firms when they got their degrees. (Some schools, in a burst of 1960s egalitarianism, opened law-review competition to all students who wished to try, regardless of grades.) It was a rare and daring event when Duke University, in the early 1930s, began to publish a journal called *Law and Contemporary Problems*. Each issue was a symposium on some topical subject; and there was no section set aside for the work of students. Later, specialized and scholarly journals, for example, the *American Journal of Legal History*, began to appear. The first issue of *The Law & Society Review* was published in 1966.

On the whole, despite the baleful influence of conceptualism, legal literature was never richer than in the 20th century. During his long life, Roscoe Pound (1870–1964), a product of Nebraska who switched from the study of fungus to law, poured his enormous creative energy into many subjects, sometimes erratically, but always provocatively. Between the two world wars, Charles Warren wrote a number of seminal studies of the American legal past. Legal history emerged once more from the shadows after the Second World War, and produced at least one major figure, Willard Hurst of Wisconsin. Hurst and his followers – the so-called Wisconsin school – focused a major part of their effort on the relationship between law and the economy. In the 1970s, a group of younger historians, somewhat more radical, began questioning the work of the Hurst school, but this too was a mark of its permanent influence. Scholars from other disciplines, too, began to look *at* law with a fresh and sometimes illuminating eye. Most of these – but not all – stood outside the law school world.

Legal realism challenged previous dogmas in US legal science. A number of scholars enrolled in that movement, offering a place of preeminence to the natural environment where the law evolved. Law was deemed to be shaped within those environments, as other living creatures. Karl N. Llewellyn was one of the main advocates of legal realism. His understanding of legal realism is present in the excerpt below, taken from lectures that he held in 1929 and 1930 to introduce students at Columbia Law School (USA) to the study of law.

K.N. Llewellyn, Bramble Bush: Some Lectures on Law and Its Study, New York, s.n., 1930, 2–5
What, then, is this law business about? It is about the fact that our society is honeycombed with disputes. Disputes actual and potential; disputes to be settled and disputes to be prevented; both appealing to law, both making up the business of the law. But obviously those which most violently call for attention are the actual disputes, and to these our first attention must be directed. Actual disputes call for somebody to do something about them. First, so that there may be peace, for the disputants; for other persons whose ears and toes disputants are disturbing. And secondly, so

that the dispute may really be put at rest, which means, so that a solution may be achieved which, at least in the main, is bearable to the parties and not disgusting to the lookers-on. This doing of something about disputes, this doing of it reasonably, is the business of law. And the people who have the doing in charge, whether they be judges or sheriffs or clerks or jailers or lawyers, are officials of the law. *What these officials do about disputes is, to my mind, the law itself.* ...

The main thing is what officials are going to *do*. And so to my mind the main thing is seeing what officials do, do about disputes, or about anything else; and seeing that there is a certain regularity in their doing – a regularity which makes possible prediction of what they and other officials are about to do tomorrow. In many cases that prediction cannot be wholly certain. Then you have room for something else, another main thing for the lawyer: the study of how to make the official do what you would like to have him. At that point 'rules' do loom into importance. Great importance. For judges think that they must follow rules, and people highly approve of that thinking. So that the getting of the judge to do a thing is in considerable measure the art of finding what rules are available to urge upon him, and of how to urge them to accomplish your result. In considerable measure. Rules, too, then, and their arrangement, and their logical manipulation, make up some portion of the business of the law and of the lawyer. ...

If I am right, finding out what the judges *say* is but the beginning of your task. You will have to take what they say and compare it with what they *do*. You will have to see whether what they say matches with what they do. You will have to be distrustful of whether they themselves know (any better than other men) the ways of their own doing, and of whether they describe it accurately, even if they know it. Nor is this all. If I am right you will also have to look into the question of what difference what the judges do is going to make to you, or to your client, or to any other person who may be affected by the judges' rulings on disputes. And even that will not be all. For when you find out what difference the judges' acts will make you will then be confronted with the task of figuring what you, or your client, are to do about it. ... If I am right, in a word, the action of the judges past and prospective becomes a piece of your environment, a condition of your living – like the use of money – with which you must reckon if you want to get where you would go to. And you cannot then rest content upon their words. It will be their action and the available means of influencing their action or of arranging your affairs with reference to their action which make up the law you have to study. And *rules*, through all of this, are important so far as they help you see or predict what judges will do or so far as they help you to get judges to do something. That is their importance. That is all their importance, except as pretty playthings. But you will discover that you can no more afford to overlook them than you can afford to stop with having learned their words.

Law and economics likewise challenged traditional approaches to law. Even when precursors can be traced to earlier decades, the movement gained significant attention starting in the 1970s in Chicago, with the writings of, amongst others, Richard Posner. The law and economics approach soon spread to other parts of the globe, reaching Europe and Latin America in a short time period, and offering new testing grounds for its tenets. The excerpt below, by Posner, encapsulates one of the foundational postulations of law and economics, and has been revisited (and challenged) by numerous authors since its first publication in the early 1970s:

Richard A. Posner, Economic Analysis of Law, Boston, Little, Brown and Company, 1972, 6–8

Economics turns out to be a powerful tool of normative analysis of law and legal institutions – a source of criticism and reform. ... Since efficiency is a widely regarded value in our world of limited resources, a persuasive showing that one course of action is more efficient than the alternatives may be an important factor in shaping public choice.

The normative role of economic analysis in the law is fairly obvious. The positive role – that of explaining the rules and outcomes in the legal system as they are – is less obvious, but not less important. As we shall see, many areas of the law, especially the great common law fields of property, torts, and contracts, bear the stamp of economic reasoning. Few legal opinions, to be sure, contain explicit references to economic concepts and few judges have a substantial background in economics. But the true grounds of decision are often concealed rather than illuminated by the characteristic rhetoric of judicial opinions. Indeed, legal education consists primarily of learning to dig beneath the rhetorical surface to find those grounds. It is an advantage of economic analysis rather than a drawback that it does not analyze cases in the conceptual modes employed in the opinions themselves.

Nor is it correct that only a trained economist can behave in accordance with the predictions of economic theory. Economic theory is designed to predict the behavior not of economists but of businessmen, consumers, and others who generally know little of economics. Since judges are frequently called upon to decide cases in which economic factors are inescapable, it is not surprising that they should frequently decide in accordance with an intuitive perception of cost and efficiency.

But do not the lawyer and the economist approach the same case in such different ways as to suggest a basic incompatibility between law and economics? X is shot by a careless hunter, Y. The only question in which the parties and their lawyers are interested, the only question tendered to the judge and jury, is whether the cost of the injury should be shifted from X to Y – whether it is 'just' or 'fair' that X should receive compensation. X's lawyer will argue that it is just that X be compensated since Y was at fault and X blameless. Y's lawyer may argue that X was also careless and hence that it would be just for the loss to remain on X. Not only are justice and fairness not economic concepts, but the economist is not interested in the one question that concerns the victim and his lawyer: who should bear the costs of this accident? To the economist, the accident is a closed chapter. The costs that it inflicted are 'sunk' costs that cannot be retrieved by a transfer payment from the injurer to the victim (why?). The economist is interested in methods of preventing future accidents and thus reducing accident costs but the parties to the litigation have no interest in the future. Their concern is limited to the financial consequences of a past accident.

The dichotomy is overstated. The decision in the case will affect the future, and so should interest the economist, because it will confirm or establish a rule for the guidance of people engaged in dangerous activities. The decision is a warning that if one behaves in a certain way and an accident results, he will have to pay a judgment (or will be unable to obtain a judgment, if the victim). By thus altering the prices that confront people, the warning may affect their behavior and therefore accident costs.

Conversely, the judge (and hence the lawyer) in the case cannot ignore the future. Since any ruling of law will constitute a precedent, the judge must consider the probable impact of alternative rulings on the future behavior of people engaged in activities that give rise to the kind of accident involved in the case before him. If, for example, judgment were awarded to the defendant on the ground that he was a 'deserving,' albeit careless, fellow, the decision would encourage similar people to be careless, a type of costly behavior.

Once the frame of reference is expanded beyond the immediate parties to the case, justice and fairness assume broader meanings than what is just or fair as between this plaintiff and this defendant. The issue

> becomes what is a just and fair result for a class of activities, and cannot be resolved without at least some consideration of the impact of alternative rulings on the frequency of accidents and the cost of accident precautions. The legal and economic approaches are not so divergent after all.

Lawyers in many civil law jurisdictions regularly referred to the work of scholars when arguing before courts, and judges likewise were also not reluctant to include the opinions of scholars when rendering their own opinions. A judicial decision from the Supreme Court of the State of Louisiana (USA) shows how doctrine played a role in the decision making in the mixed legal system of that state. Besides, as can be seen in this example, doctrine can be timeless and apply across jurisdictions and languages.

> *Supreme Court of Louisiana, John Anderson and Eva Washington Anderson v. Avondale Industries, Inc., Oct. 16, 2001, 798 So.2d 93*
>
> ... However, citing Walls, plaintiffs argue that because their wrongful death cause of action arose at death (October 25, 1994), and La. C.C. art. 2315.3 was in effect when the cause of action arose, there is no retroactive application. In Walls, we were faced with the issue of whether the Workers Compensation Act, specifically La. R.S. 23:1032 as amended in 1976, which extends tort immunity to executive officers, bars a wrongful death action against the executive officers when the decedent's occupational exposures occurred entirely before the statute was amended, but his death from silicosis did not occur until years after the amendment's effective date.
>
> In Walls, we recognized that:
>
> [d]etermining whether a statute operates retroactively can be difficult when the statute must be applied to a case in which some operative facts pre-date the law while others occurred after the law's effective date. It is imperative to understand that a law may permissibly change the future consequences of an act and even the consequences of acts committed prior to the law's enactment without operating retroactively.
>
> In Walls, we adopted the formula set out by Planiol for identifying the only two situations in which a law operates retroactively:
>
> [a] law is retroactive when it goes back to the past either to evaluate the conditions of the legality of an act, or to modify or suppress the effects of a right already acquired. Outside of those conditions, there is no retroactivity.

In Walls, we held that applying the 1976 amendment of La. R.S. 23:1023 to silicosis exposure that predated the statute, resulting in death after the effective date of the statute, did not result in an impermissible retroactive application of the law. First, we held that the tort immunity for an executive officer is based upon the individual's 'status' and is an affirmative defense, not a law governing conduct. Therefore, we concluded that the 1976 amendment does not evaluate the conditions of liability or attach new legal consequences to past acts. Secondly, we held that the law did not go 'back to the past' to 'modify or suppress the effects of a right already acquired' because the wrongful death cause of action did not arise, and thus the plaintiffs could not have acquired a 'right' in their cause of action for wrongful death, until the date of the death, which occurred after the effective date of the statute. Therefore, we held that the 1976 amendment applied to the case and barred the plaintiffs from asserting a wrongful death action against the employer's executive officers and their liability insurers.

However, contrary to the court of appeal's ruling in this case, Walls does not stand for the proposition that the accrual of a cause of action during the time a law is in effect necessarily determines the law's application to the claim:

Rather, what we adopt here today is a case by case approach to determine, in cases involving facts that span enough legislative sessions to allow for the innovation of the law, whether any intervening statute, if applied to that case, would operate retroactively. If the statute would operate retroactively under Planiol's definition, then, the two-fold analysis from La. C.C. Art. 6, with which all courts are familiar, must be made. Making the determination of when the cause of action arose for the various causes of action which might be asserted merely provides the temporal guidepost from which a court may determine whether the intervening statute operates retroactively or prospectively, and the consequences that flow from that determination will differ in each case.

In a case such as Walls, where a new substantive law essentially extinguishes a cause of action, the date that the cause of action accrues is a crucial determining point in considering the second condition of retroactivity of Planiol's formula, i.e., whether the law modifies or suppresses the effects of a right already acquired. Once a cause of action accrues, a party has a vested right in the cause of action that a new substantive law cannot take away. See also Bourgeois v. A.P. Green Indus., Inc., 00–1528 (La.4/3/01), 783 So.2d 1251 (holding that the Due Process clauses of the United States and Louisiana Constitutions prohibited the Legislature from retroactively abolishing a claim for medical monitoring to causes of action that accrued before the amendment to Article 2315 because the retroactive application of the amendment would divest the injured parties of their vested rights.)

However, Planiol's analysis for retroactivity does not stop with the protection of vested rights; it also prevents retroactive evaluation of the conditions of the legality of past conduct. Under Planiol's first situation in which a law operates retroactively, when a[n] intervening new law creates a cause of action, and thus attaches new consequences to past events, the retroactivity event is the conduct or activity regulated.

Walls made this plain in its discussion of the First Circuit's decision in Pitre v. GAF Corp., 97–1024 (La.App. 1st Cir.12/29/97), 705 So.2d 1149, writ denied, 98–0723 (La.11/19/99), 749 So.2d 666, and the federal court's decision in Arledge v. S7Holnam, Inc., 957 F.Supp. 822 (M.D.La.1996). In Pitre, the First Circuit declined to apply the Louisiana Products Liability Act (the 'LPLA') in a product liability action for wrongful death from cigarette and asbestos exposures because the decedent's exposures occurred prior to the LPLA's enactment. In Walls, we specifically approved of this result, explaining that application of the LPLA in that case would have been an impermissible retroactive operation, in violation of Planiol's first test:

Unlike the exclusivity provision at issue in this case, the LPLA at issue in Pitre sets out the elements of the cause of action for product liability, the standards for evaluating the tortfeasor's conduct, and the remedies or consequences of such conduct. Therefore, it may easily be said that the LPLA evaluates the conditions of the defendant's liability for the conduct at issue and under Planiol's formula would certainly operate retroactively under the facts of that case.

Conclusion

In Walls, we adopted the formula set out by Planiol for identifying the two situations in which a law operates retroactively in violation of La. C.C. art. 6. Under that formula, a law operates retroactively when it either (1) evaluates the conditions of the legality of a past act, or (2) modifies or suppresses the effects of a right already acquired. Because former La. C.C. art. 2315.3 creates a cause of action for punitive damages for certain enumerated conduct, the application of that article to the facts of this case would be an impermissible retroactive application of the law because it would go back to the past to evaluate the conditions of the legality of the defendants' conduct, which occurred before the enactment of former La. C.C. art. 2315.3.10.

Our holdings in Walls do not demand a different result. Planiol's formula envisions two situations when a law operates retroactively. In this case, just as in Walls, the application of La. C.C. 2315.3 does not modify or suppress the effects of plaintiffs' vested right in their wrongful death cause of action because that cause of action did not arise until after the effective date of the statute. However, contrary to Walls, La. C.C. art. 2315.3 is a law governing conduct and the application of that law to evaluate the conditions of the legality of defendants' past conduct results in the retroactive application of the law, in violation of La. C.C. art. 6.

Decree

For the reasons expressed herein, the judgment of the court of appeal is reversed and defendants T & N, PLC, and Benjamin Foster Division of AmChem Products' exception of no cause of action is granted.

Questions

Doctrine became part of the world of the common law.

1. Which different fora for the development of doctrine are mentioned by Friedman?
2. As doctrine developed in the USA, what was the interplay between law and social sciences during this era?

Legal realism took the stage in the USA at the start of this period.

3. What is the law according to legal realists? And, what is the role of rules according to those that subscribe to legal realism?

Another important development was sensed by the emergence of studies in law and economics.

4. Why does Posner state that legal and economic approaches are not so divergent after all?

Doctrine can be useful for judges when rendering opinions.

5. Which work of doctrinal analysis was followed by the Louisiana court?

Research into the background and scholarly work of the author of this doctrinal analysis provides more information about his ideas and their context.

6. Why did a court in a mixed jurisdiction, like that of the state of Louisiana, use the writings from this author from across the Atlantic who wrote in a much earlier era? What does that tell the reader about the value and limitations of doctrine?

2.5 *Custom*

Custom was a source of law in this period. However, it gave up most of its ground to legislation. Much has been written about François Gény's importance for understanding custom, at least in the French legal system. However, it seems that scholars now agree that his influence was much more significant in the academic world than in legal practice. The role of custom in the common law did not increase in this period, although a noteworthy exception to this view can be found in the writings of Carleton Kemp Allen.

> *Carleton Kemp Allen, Law in the Making, Oxford, Oxford University Press, 1927, 26–27*
>
> All creatures are creatures of habit. In the lower forms of life, habit is automatic and apparently uncontrollable; we call it instinct, and beyond knowing that it exists and produces extraordinary phenomena, we are unable to explain it. … But civilized man possesses a certain degree of individual liberty of choice in the adoption of habits and customs. No more than the ant, however, can he entirely rid himself of customary conduct. The mere existence of a society, the mere plurality of individuals, gives rise to customs from which no single member of the totality can completely divorce himself. Our 'highly-developed' 'civilized' societies of the modern world are just as replete with social customs as the 'primitive' societies of the past or the 'backward' societies of today. These customs are doubtless more intelligent and for the most part less superstitious than once they were; but they are just as numerous and just as powerful. In varying degrees they all possess a sanction: to disregard them involves some kind of penalty. It may be slight and in some cases almost ineffectual; but it always exists. Society always takes a revenge for the breach of any of its conventions. No man can be compelled to be moral, as the not infrequent attempts at this kind of compulsion have shown; but the open defiance of morality involves social reprobation, a severe and often a cruel punishment, except to the few who are content to forfeit social esteem. The real punishment of our criminals lies not in the deprivation of their liberty, but in the stigma which society itself, not the Judge or the jailer, brands upon them. Many would prefer, as a matter of personal comfort, to defy the dictates of fashion, but few are prepared to face the ridicule which defiance involves. A large section of the population of England would consider themselves social outcasts if they did not provide a certain kind of funeral, far beyond their means, for their deceased relatives. The average Englishman could no more be induced to wear his hair long than the average Chinese mandarin could be induced to wear his finger-nails short.
>
> Yet none of these customs is completely obligatory. Their sanction, though in many cases powerful, is imperfect. No man is under an absolute

> compulsion to visit the barber, or to wear garments of usual design, or to be moral or polite or cleanly or amiable. Legal custom occupies a place by itself in that its sanction is more effectual than that of any other. The effect of the sanction is usually negative rather than positive: if the custom is not followed, certain desired legal consequences will not be effected. Law, backed by the opinion and at later stages by the tribunals of the community, will forbid those relationships to be effected; in some cases it will go farther, and actually punish the citizen who persists in ignoring a custom. No option, however small, is left to the individual, as in other social customs. A man may, if he chooses, argue that it is a waste of time and money to cut his hair; in consequence, he may, if he is sensitive, be made uncomfortable, but he will not lose a single right of citizenship or property. He may argue with as much, or as little, reason that the custom of signing, sealing, and delivering a deed is an absurd anachronism; but if he ignores this quaint survival in a transfer of stock – *nihil agit.*

Custom also re-emerged in the context of international trade, with the development of a new, non-national, *lex mercatoria.*

> *Bernardo M. Cremades and Stephen L. Plehn, The New Lex Mercatoria and the Harmonization of the Laws of International Commercial Transactions, Boston University International Law Journal 2 (1984), 323–327*
>
> Commercial self-regulation based on expansion of the businessman's freedom to regulate his affairs by contract is another avenue by which the laws affecting international business transactions could be harmonized. National paternalism embodied in the mandatory application of national laws to international commerce transacted within national boundaries would be limited. Instead, businessmen engaging in international commerce would, in most cases, be able to avoid national laws and courts by detailed contracting and submitting to arbitration. National law would intercede only to the extent necessary to ensure that enforcement of arbitration awards does not contradict fundamental principles of public policy.
>
> A non-national New Lex Mercatoria would be encouraged if businessmen submit their disputes to arbitration to be decided on the basis of the prevailing standards of the international business community and not national law. These standards would reflect customs as well as general principles of law. The non-national New Lex Mercatoria would be a single autonomous body of law created by the international business community.

The non-national approach toward the harmonization of international commercial law is less dependent on national action than is the national approach. However, given the world's present political structure, in particular the overwhelming power of the nation state, any so-called non-national legal system can only exist with the sponsorship, or at least tolerance, of nations. Such a legal system is therefore best described as autonomous from, rather than independent of, national control.

Non-national harmonization is a two step process: first, nations must permit businessmen to avoid the application of national law; and second, a coherent body of law (the New Lex Mercatoria) must be established as an alternative.

Parties can avoid the application of supplementary national law to the extent that they are free to contract. So long as they do not infringe upon national public policy parties may contractually establish their own arbitration tribunals, procedures and applicable non-national substantive rules of law. Greater contractual freedom and less restrictive national public policy will allow further avoidance of national law.

Businessmen can also avoid the application of national law by concerted action in the form of trade and professional associations. These associations, which facilitate market transactions, play key roles in particular industries. For example, they often bring together buyer and seller, establish quality standards, and provide arbitration services. Such associations rarely need to rely on national courts to encourage compliance with their internal norms of behavior and arbitral awards. Rather, they can exclude recalcitrant parties from the association or blacklist them, thereby causing them substantial economic harm. Nonetheless, if these actions do not conform to national public policy, the particular association may risk intervention by the state.

Once released from the application of national law the international business community must create a coherent body of non-national law. This non-national law is the New Lex Mercatoria. Like its medieval predecessor the New Lex Mercatoria will be composed of the customs and practices of the international business community. These customs and practices may take a number of forms. They may, for example, be the usages employed within a given commercial sector that, although unwritten, are common practice among the great majority of participants. Such customs and practices, on the other hand, may actually be codified, as is the case in the International Chamber of Commerce's Incoterms. An arbitrator may apply custom and practice when contractually authorized, as a means of contractual interpretation or even as independent sources of law applicable regardless of the parties' express or implicit consent.

A non-national approach to a New Lex Mercatoria has a number of advantages over a national approach. First, a non-national approach can more easily provide needed uniformity to the regulation of international transactions; a single, homogeneous law would be created by the business community. By contrast, under a national approach, model laws, and often treaties, are subject to alteration prior to adoption by individual political systems. Moreover, national courts may interpret the same provisions in different ways.

Second, because of its reliance on custom, a non-national approach is far more flexible than a national approach. The reliance of the national approach on national legislation or international conventions creates a more rigid and static law. For instance, amending national legislation requires compliance with the domestic political process. Localized interests, incompatible with international commercial requirements, may therefore affect the amendment. Furthermore, amendments would have to be coordinated on a world-wide basis to maintain uniformity of national laws. The process of writing and ratifying a treaty is similarly cumbersome.

However, the non-national approach, which involves extensive selfregulation within the international community, has certain flaws. The non-national approach is particularly weak when contracting parties deal with matters that fall within the scope of national public policy. Where contractual provisions do not correspond with a particular national public policy, a party will be unable to rely on that nation's courts to enforce the contract. Nor can the parties count on arbitration to give effect to such provisions, because the arbitration award itself will be subject to national court examination at the time of attempted enforcement. Even more disconcerting is the lack of consistency likely to be found when national public policies are not harmonized by treaty. Contracting parties may well find that their rights vary depending on the national jurisdiction.

By contrast, the national approach, as embodied in the international treaty or model law process, is particularly amenable to dealing with matters of public policy. Rather than deal with public policy on a case-by-case basis, nations may negotiate treaties or model laws that comprehend national policies and create uniform rules of conduct for the international business community. Nonetheless, such a procedure is likely to be difficult and is still subject to the inflexibility noted earlier.

Because of the practical limitations imposed on the non-national approach by national public policy, the former must necessarily be complemented by international treaties, model laws and national legislation. The national approach will be critical in defining, in a uniform manner, those areas in which a non-national New Lex Mercatoria can develop. The two approaches are best seen as complementary rather than mutually exclusive.

Questions

Customs are connected to a specific context.

1. Why does Allen claim that the sanctions of legal customs are more effective than that of any others?

The *lex mercatoria* kept expanding with the development of international commercial arbitration and the advent of soft law.

2. What was it that made it more flexible than other sources? What were the potential dangers of its non-national character? How could these dangers be mitigated?

2.6 *Soft Law*

Soft law crossed the border between the common law and civil law during the period discussed here, and became ubiquitous. Soft law refers to instruments which often have the form of legislation (black letter law) complete with a section of comments that resemble doctrine. These texts have no legally binding force, but can be persuasive.

The Restatements of the Law by the members of the American Law Institute were intended to become a new legal paradigm and the approach inspired scholars across the Western world and beyond. The excerpt below shows that this way of creating law can be traced back to the first decades of the twentieth century. The excerpt is from the first edition of a seminal selection of contract law sources by E. Allan Farnsworth and William Franklin Young. Farnsworth had served as Reporter for the preparation of the Restatement of the Law (Second) of Contracts, and the excerpt further shows that the American Law Institute integrated efforts by numerous scholars, judges, and practitioners.

E. Allan Farnsworth and William Franklin Young, Selections for Contracts: Uniform Commercial Code, Restatement Second, UN Sales Convention, UNIDROIT Principles, Forms, New York, Foundation Press, 1988, 92–95

The American Law Institute was formed in 1923 as the outgrowth of a 'Committee on the Establishment of a Permanent Organization for the

Improvement of the Law.' Its members were to be 400 practitioners, judges and law professors (there are now about 2,000). The idea of the Institute, and of 'restating' the law, was broached by Professor William Draper Lewis and fostered by Elihu Root and others. The Carnegie Corporation contributed some quarter of a million dollars toward work on the original Restatement, comprising nine subjects, which was completed by 1944.

Contracts was one of the first three subjects upon which the Institute began work, and the Restatement of Contracts was completed in 1932. Professor Samuel W. Williston acted as Reporter, with responsibility for preparing drafts. (Professor Arthur L. Corbin served as Reporter for the Chapter on Remedies.) Other experts in the subject were formed into a Committee of Advisers who conferred with the Reporter over the whole period in producing drafts for submission to the Council of the Institute. The plan was 'that the drafts of the different chapters submitted to the Council shall be the product of the committee composed of the Reporter and his advisers; that these drafts after discussion and amendment by the Council and before revision shall be submitted as tentative drafts for criticism and suggestion with a view to their improvement to the annual meetings of the Institute and to bar associations and the profession generally.' Final promulgation depended on approval of the text by both the Council and the full meeting of Institute members. The same procedure was followed in making revisions and in preparing the Restatement Second.

In 1962 the Institute initiated the preparation of the Restatement (Second) of Contracts … Professor Robert Braucher served as Reporter until his appointment to the Supreme Judicial Court of Massachusetts in 1971; he was succeeded by Professor E. Allan Farnsworth. The work was completed in 1980.

As originally conceived, the first Restatement was to be accompanied by treatises citing and discussing case authority, but experience proved that group production of such volumes was not feasible. As they stand, the Restatements consist of sections stating rules or principles (the so-called black letter), each followed by one or more comments with illustrations, and in the Restatement Second also by Reporter's Notes in which supporting authorities are collected. …

An eminent critic of the Restatement of Contracts immediately questioned the value of 'black-letter Principles' not supported by discussion and analysis. 'The Institute,' he wrote, 'seems constantly to be seeking the force of a statute without statutory enactment.' … To what measure of authority is the Restatement entitled, then, in the courts?

This general question can have only a general answer. The Supreme Court of Oregon has emphasized the difference between statutory and Restatement texts:

> Although this court frequently quotes sections of the Restatements of the American Law Institute, it does not literally 'adopt' them in the manner of a legislature enacting, for instance, a draft prepared by the Commissioners on Uniform State Laws, such as the Residential Landlord and Tenant Act. In the nature of common law, such quotations in opinions are no more than shorthand expressions of the court's view that the analysis summarized in the Restatement corresponds to Oregon law applicable to the facts of the case before the court. They do not enact the exact phrasing of the Restatement rule, complete with comments, illustrations, and caveats. Such quotations should not be relied on in briefs as if they committed his court or lower courts to track every detail of the Restatement analysis in other cases. The Restatements themselves purport to be just that, 'restatements' of law found in other sources, although at times they candidly report that the law is in flux and offer a formula preferred on policy grounds.

There is agreement among those who applaud the Restatement and those who deprecate it about the persuasiveness of an *ideal* restatement of the law. 'A restatement, then, can have no other authority than as the product of men learned in the subject who have studied and deliberated over it. It needs no other, and what could be higher?' … Judge Herbert Goodrich, for many years Director of the Institute, explained:

> If an advocate thinks the Restatement was wrong as applied to his case, he can urge the court not to follow it, but to apply some other rule. If the court agrees, it will do so, but it will so do with the knowledge that the rule which it rejects has been written by the people who by training and reputation are supposed to be eminently learned in the particular subject and that the specialist's conclusions have been discussed and defended before a body of very able critics. The presumption is in favor of the Restatement … Yet it can be overthrown and the fact leaves Restatement acceptance to persuasion. It is common law 'persuasive authority' with a high degree of persuasion. …

The Restatement Second. To a substantial extent the Restatement Second reflects the thought of two men in particular: Professor Corbin and Professor Llewellyn, both of whom shared attitudes toward law sometimes described as 'legal realism.' Professor Corbin prepared a critical review of the original Restatement, which 'has been the basis for much of the work on the revision.' He served also as consultant for the Restatement Second in its early stages. Professor Llewellyn's efforts affected the revision less directly, largely through the impact of his contributions to the Uniform Commercial Code.

In restating the law of contracts for the second half of the century, an obvious difficulty arose from the fact that large tracts of the subject had recently been occupied by legislation such as the Code and certain consumer-protection statutes. Indeed, the worth of the enterprise was questioned on the ground of an apparently diminishing importance of common law doctrine. In response, Professor Braucher made this claim: 'The effort to restate the law of contracts in modern terms highlights the reliance of private autonomy in an era of expanding government activity … Freedom of contract, refined and redefined in response to social change, has power as it always had.'

A continuing theme of controversy about the Restatements is the wisdom or unwisdom of departing from rules derived from existing precedents, in the interest of a more just and more convenient regime of law. The Oregon opinion quoted above refers to a section of the Torts Restatement as a 'bold sally.' Notwithstanding that, the section has gained widespread adherence. An example from the first Restatement of Contracts was the formulation of the doctrine of promissory estoppel, in section 90.

European scholars also welcomed the use of soft law. An emblematic example of this were the Principles of European Contract Law (PECL), which were the product of scholarly efforts from across Europe undertaken during the last decades of the twentieth century.

Ole Lando and Hugh Beale (eds), Principles of European Contract Law: Parts I and II, The Hague, London, Boston, Kluwer Law International, 2000, 2

Article 1:101: Application of the Principles

(1) These Principles are intended to be applied as general rules of contract law in the European Union.

(2) These Principles will apply when the parties have agreed to incorporate them into their contract or that their contract is to be governed by them.

(3) These Principles may be applied when the parties:

(a) have agreed that their contract is to be governed by 'general principles of law,' the 'lex mercatoria' or the like; or
(b) have not chosen any system or rules of law to govern their contract.

(4) These Principles may provide a solution to the issue raised where the system or rules of law applicable do not do so.

Questions

The Restatements and PECL are prime examples of soft law. These instruments, together with many others, proliferated during this period.

1. What are the main differences between statutes and restatements?
2. How can the text of restatements benefit the judges and lawyers?
3. What is the authority of PECL when compared with national, supranational or international law?
4. To whom is Article 1:101 of PECL addressed?

3 Actors

In past centuries, legal actors tended to belong to the social elite, and were rather homogeneous and predominantly conservative. Things changed in the twentieth century. Despite resistance from the establishment, progress has been made towards greater social, racial and gender diversity on all levels of the legal profession. With very few exceptions, there were almost no women in the legal profession, on the bench or as professors at law schools before the First World War. The feminization of actors is probably the most significant change during this period. Several jurisdictions have seen women accede to the highest position on the highest courts.

Though the period marks the advent of globalization, actors, for the most part, operated in a national or domestic framework. Though laws are, more than ever before, developed on the international level, the large majority of actors remain rooted in their domestic practice and way of thinking. Legal ideas circulate internationally more easily than they ever did in the past, but legal education remains predominantly focused on domestic practice. Legal traditions and systems proved resistant to globalization in the sense that it remained easy to identify and distinguish the US, English, French or German lawyers from one another, just to mention a few salient examples.

The dialogue between the different actors was largely interrupted during the World Wars and during the Cold War at least as far as contacts with Eastern

Europe were concerned. Communication increased later on, facilitated by European and transnational integration. Fascist and communist doctrines had a significant impact on the elimination, appointment and performance of different legal actors in many parts of the world, at least until the end of the Cold War. During the periods of such dictatorships, discrimination, persecution and distortion of open-textured rules and principles were commonplace – whether the law was changed or not. In response, actors from across Europe and beyond joined efforts to promote human rights and explored different pathways towards greater harmonization. In Europe, even when it encountered obstacles, the harmonization of private law continued on its own path at its own pace, slowly but surely, producing a new generation of European and transnational actors.

3.1 *Judges*

Judges were – as in the previous periods – of paramount importance in the world of the common law. They were also important actors in civil law systems. In these countries, the position of judge was seen as prestigious, even though they were just another type of civil servant. The process mentioned above of the legalization of society that took place during this period increased the importance of judges as fundamental actors. The judges were, more than ever before, crucial to the promotion of human rights and the comprehensive development of European law, as well as the development of international criminal courts after the Second World War.

At the same time, the US model of judicial review became prevalent across the Americas, where high courts were given the mandate to ensure the primacy of constitutional law over ordinary legislation. Europe kept living under legislative supremacy both on the continent and in the United Kingdom (parliamentary sovereignty). After the Second World War, countries which moved away from totalitarian regimes towards democratic ones, such as Germany and Italy, followed by Greece, Spain and Portugal later in the century, adopted systems that provided for the review of the constitutionality of statutes by constitutional courts. France moved more slowly in this direction. It was reluctant to acknowledge the dark side of its history after the war (a limited *a priori* abstract moral review was put in place in 1958, and an open *a posteriori* review after 2008). It did, however, develop the paradigmatic model of judicial review of administrative action. In most European countries, legislation gradually became the subject of review by domestic constitutional courts and by the two European courts (i.e., Court of Justice of the European Union, European Court of Human Rights), much in the same way as North American states or provinces are subject to the review of a federal supreme court and state or provincial supreme courts.

The influence of the USA increased in the Western world and beyond. On the one hand, because major US law firms opened branches in all major cities of the world, law schools in the USA became a paradigm for legal education, and the LL.M. degree became the key for access to international practice. On the other hand, international organizations such as the World Bank and the International Monetary Fund promoted deregulation and US-drafted statutes. Some perceived European integration as a bulwark against US hegemony and others saw it as an accelerator of a brutal liberalism that unleashed the global financial markets, which would, ultimately, rule the planet. Never before in the history of the West had the primacy of law been more pronounced, yet individuals were no longer sure where to turn to for adequate legal protection in a complex and multi-layered system that seemed to favour forum shopping, at least for those who had the means to shop around.

Lord Denning was a common law judge whose work was emblematic of this period. Not only were his decisions written in exquisite prose, they also explained and created law. One of his most seminal opinions deals with the incoming tide of EU law in England.

> *Lord Denning, HP Bulmer Ltd & Anor v. J. Bollinger SA & Ors [1974] EWCA Civ 14 (22 May 1974)*
> The Master of the Rolls: In France the name Champagne is well protected by law. It denotes a sparkling wine produced in a well favoured district of France, called the Champagne district. The vineyards are about a hundred miles east of Paris, around Rheims and Epernay. The wine has a high reputation all the world over.
>
> In England, too, the name Champagne is well protected by law when used for wine. As far back as 1956 some intruders brought into England a somewhat similar wine. It had been produced in the Costa Brava district of Spain. They marketed it under the name 'Spanish Champagne.' The French growers and shippers brought an action to stop it. They succeeded. Mr. Justice Danckwerts held that the French growers had a goodwill connected with the word Champagne: and that the Spanish intruders had been guilty of dishonest trading, see Bollinger v. Costa Brava (1960) Ch 262, 1961 1 W.L.R. 271. That case opened up a new field of English law. It gave a remedy for unfair competition. It was applied in the Sherry Case (1969) R.P.C. 1, when Mr. Justice Cross said at page 23:
>
>> The decision went beyond the well trodden paths of passing-off into the area of 'unfair trading' or 'unfair competition.'

It was followed recently by Mr. Justice Foster in the Scotch Whisky Case (1970) 1 W.L.R. 917.

That case in 1960 concerned wine – wine made from grapes – for which the French are so famous. Now we are concerned with cider and perry. Cider from apples. Perry from pears. We English do know something about these. At any rate, those who come up from Somerset or Herefordshire. …

Reference to Luxembourg

Now the French producers ask that two points of European Community Law should be referred to the European Court at Luxembourg. Shortened they are:

(A) Whether … the use of the word 'Champagne' in connection with any beverage other than Champagne is a contravention of … the provisions of European Community Law.

(B) Whether … a national court of a member state should … refer to the Court of Justice of the European Community such a question as has been raised herein.

The Judge at first instance refused to refer either question at this stage. He said that he would try the whole case out before he came to a decision on it.

The French producers appeal to this Court. …

To make the discussion easier to understand, I will speak only of the interpretation of 'the Treaty,' but this must be regarded as including the regulations and directions under it. I will make reference to the English Courts because I am specially concerned with them: but this must be regarded as including the national Courts of any Member State.

The Impact of the Treaty on English Law

The first and fundamental point is that the Treaty concerns only those matters which have a European element, that is to say, matters which affect people or property in the nine countries of the Common Market besides ourselves. The Treaty does not touch any of the matters which concern solely the mainland of England and the people in it. These are still governed by English law. They are not affected by the Treaty. But when we come to matters with a European element, the Treaty is like an incoming tide. It flows into the estuaries and up the rivers. It cannot be held back. Parliament has decreed that the Treaty is henceforward to be part of our law. It is equal in force to any statute. The governing provision is section 2(1) of the European Community Act, 1972. It says:

> All such rights, powers, liabilities, obligations and restrictions from time to time created by or arising under the Treaties, and all such remedies and procedures from time to time provided for by or under the Treaties, as in accordance with the Treaties and without further enactment to be given legal effect or used in the United Kingdom, shall be recognised and available in law, and be enforced, allowed and followed accordingly; and the expression enforceable Community right and similar expressions shall be read as referring to one to which this sub-section applies.

The statute is expressed in forthright terms which are absolute and all-embracing. Any rights or obligations created by the Treaty are to be given legal effect in England without more ado. Any remedies or procedures provided by the Treaty are to be made available here without being open to question. In future, in transactions which cross the frontiers, we must no longer speak or think of English law as something on its own. We must speak and think of Community law, of Community rights and obligations, and we must give effect to them. This means a great effort for the lawyers. We have to learn a new system. The Treaty, with the regulations and directives, covers many volumes. The case law is contained in hundreds of reported cases both in the European Court of Justice and in the national Courts of the nine. Many must be studied before the right result can be reached. We must get down to it. …

Applied to the Present Case

To return to the three questions I asked at the beginning.

First: I think these Regulations should be interpreted by the High Court and the Court of Appeal in England. But if the cases should reach the House of Lords they must be interpreted by the European Court.

Second: The task of interpretation should be done at the time of the trial or the appeal, together with the other issues in the case.

Third: The English Court should apply the same principles of interpretation as the European Court would do if it had to decide the point.

I come now to the two specific questions sought to be referred. The first question raised is: 'Whether … the use of the word 'Champagne' in connection with any beverage other than Champagne is a contravention of the provisions of European Community law.' I do not think it is necessary at this stage to decide that question. Take the claim in passing-off. If the French growers succeeded in this claim for passing-off in English law – for an injunction and damages – it would not be necessary to decide the point under the Regulations. So the facts must be found before it can be said that a reference is 'necessary.'

Next take the claim of the French growers for a declaration that the use of the expression 'Champagne cider' and 'Champagne perry' was contrary to European Community law. Mr. Sparrow, Q.C., said that it would be necessary on this issue to decide the point on the Regulations. I do not agree. It is always a matter for the discretion of the Judge whether to grant a declaration or not. He could very properly say in the present case: Whatever the true interpretation of the Regulations, it is not a case in which I would make any declaration on the point. Taking that view, it would not be necessary to decide the point.

Even if it could be said to be necessary to decide the point, I think that an English Court (short of the House of Lords) should not, as matter of discretion, refer it to the European Court. It should decide the point itself. It would take much time and money to get a ruling from the European Court. Meanwhile, the whole action would be held up. It is, no doubt, an important point, but not a difficult one to decide. I think it would be better to deal with it as part of the whole case, both by the trial Judge and by the Court of Appeal. If it could then go to the House of Lords, it will by that time have become clear whether it is a 'necessary' point or not. If it is, then the House of Lords will refer it.

The second point is: 'Whether a national Court should … refer to the Court of Justice such a question as has been raised herein.' The object of this question is to get a ruling from the European Court as to the circumstances in which a national Court should refer a question of interpretation to the European Court. I am quite clear that it is unnecessary to ask this question. The answer is clear. It is not the province of the European Court to give any guidance or advice to the national Court as to when it should, or should not, refer a question. That is a matter for the national Court itself. It is no concern of the European Court.

In my opinion Mr. Justice Whitford was right in refusing to refer either of the questions. I would dismiss the appeal.

An account of the judges' roles in Argentina offers an insight into the place these fundamental actors played in a civil law jurisdiction of the Western world during this period.

Agustín Parise, Judicial Decision-Making in Latin America: Unveiling the Dynamic Role of the Argentine Supreme Court, in J. Basedow, H. Fleischer and R. Zimmermann (eds), Legislators, Judges, and Professors, Tübingen, Mohr Siebeck, 2016, 151–156

Law is shaped by a number of actors. Those actors interact, evolve, and perform fundamental roles in society. Judges are fundamental actors for the shaping of law: they develop the law while undertaking their judicial function, and they must be clearly aware of that creative activity. They must be self-conscious of their role as operators of a system of social control within a social reality, since judges are after all active organs of society. Raoul van Caenegem asked in his seminal book – while undertaking an historical approach to the role of judges, legislators, and professors – who

> … were these judges, what did they stand for and what was their contribution to t=he political power-game that is endemic in every society? … [P]eople, pressure groups and classes will be seen struggling with each other for power: controlling the law is the way to control society.

And yet, what about the role of those actors today? In order to answer these questions a first step must be taken: a step that focuses on legal methodology and the differences and the similarities between legal systems. There is currently a need to know the way in which each actor operates, and then eventually understand the current power-struggle between them. There is a need to know how judges, legislators, and professors operate today, and only then it will be possible to understand the current impact of the activities of each actor.

Acting requires a level of commitment. Judges must know the environment in which they operate and their role, since each judge operates in a certain time and space. …

Judges play an important role in legal development. They were incorporated within the structure of modern states by democratic societies, and have the ability to create guidelines for coexistence within those structures. Judges must be equidistant, impartial, and objective; and their discussions should be shared with and by colleagues, members of the bar, political leaders, intellectuals, and members of social groups. Their discussions are to be placed within a social context, as judges offer a guarantee for the right of defence to all parties and are conductors of the different processes. They are indeed custodians of republican institutions, while they are neither only historians nor soothsayers. …

The activities of judges are undertaken before the eyes of society, and their decisions are published, analysed, discussed, and challenged. Furthermore, judges are members of society; they are not selected from an esoteric sect. [They] … state guidelines, values, and creeds that prevail in Argentine society, such as the protection of the right of property when facing economic crises. Augusto M. Morello correctly stated that judges 'offer signs and criteria that reflect changes in society.' Globalisation triggered a new regional trend in Latin America in which judges tend to fill lacunae left by the activities of legislators and of the executive. Judges have gained a more active social participation, helping to fulfil the effective protection of fundamental rights. They do not hesitate to step-in when sensing a lack of action from legislators or the executive. Currently they deal with matters that the Argentine Constitution had expressly reserved for the two other branches. Society currently expects judges eventually to revise actions of the legislature and of the executive, even though judicial review was implemented in Argentina already in the case Sojo as early as 1887, following the model of Marbury vs. Madison.

In Argentina – as in other Latin American jurisdictions and beyond – judges occupy the vertex of the procedural triangle, and their paramount role is to decide in all cases. ... The Argentine Civil and Commercial Code also welcomes the constitutionalisation of private law: a communion between constitution, public law, and private law. A harmonisation is experienced since conflicts of public interest are resolved. That harmonisation and communion can be perceived, for example, in consumer law. The new code calls for new judges who must be interested in the new paradigms of private law, and who will secure the successful implementation of the new text. New judges must consider the context when applying a code that is built on new principles, and they must look at the national and supranational legal framework. New judges must be eager to look around and to update their practices. The new code can also be considered a third generation code. It may be described as globalist, since the previous code had already been enacted after the secession from Spain. This had also entailed the carving out of the different Latin American jurisdictions. A degree of globalisation is welcomed today in Latin America.

Questions

Judges were fundamental actors in society during the period under discussion, both in common law and civil law countries.

1. Who is the audience Lord Denning addresses?
2. Why does he define the European Treaty as an incoming tide?

Parise points out other actors to whom van Caenegem assigns a paramount role.

3. Who are those actors, and why are they important?

Parise further claims that judges play an important role in legal development.

4. Explain how they play this role in a civil law system.

3.2 *Jurists*

Jurists played an important role during the period covered by this chapter. However, their role was less significant than the one described in the previous chapters of this volume, except with regard to the revision of the codes of law or law reform, and innovative areas such as new technologies and transnational activity. Comparative law studies and academic activities supported by international organizations shaped the way jurists interacted and exchanged ideas. Likewise, there was a proliferation of different platforms for dialogue. These interactions took place at conferences and in journals, and were distributed widely on the internet and by other new technologies. Due to economic and political exigencies, several jurists had to go into exile. During the Second World War, some scholars were forced to emigrate to the United Kingdom (e.g., Martin Wolff) and the USA (e.g., Karl Loewenstein, Ernst Rabel, Rudolf Schlesinger). In the aftermath of the Spanish Civil War some scholars had to emigrate to Latin America (e.g., Rafael Altamira).

The English language became the new *lingua franca*; it replaced French as the common thread that linked academics from different jurisdictions together, even beyond the Western world. Vernacular languages were part of local identities of the different peoples and helped preserve them. As scholars tried to disseminate their knowledge beyond their own local borders, language was an essential element in that dialogue.

Jurists played a crucial role in harmonization efforts and in the context created by globalization. Much human energy and financial resources were devoted to the efforts of these jurists in Europe and beyond. In the literature, parallels were drawn between jurists' roles in our period with those of jurists in, for example, the periods described in the previous chapter. Comparative law and legal history were used to advocate for the emergence of a new European legal science and a new *ius commune*.

> *Reinhard Zimmermann, Savigny's Legacy. Legal History, Comparative Law, and the Emergence of a European Legal Science, Law Quarterly Review 1996, 580–582, 584–585, 605*
>
> Our situation in Europe today is similar to that in early 19th century Germany in many respects. For, once again, we are living in a period of transition. Contrary to nearly all the other disciplines taught at a modem university, legal science in Europe has, at least for the last hundred years, been predominantly national in substance, outlook, and approach. Since the continental legal systems have been codified, there have been, in principle, as many legal systems as there are national states. This is reflected in our law curricula and examination requirements, in the conditions for

the appointment of law teachers, in the approach adopted by our courts in their decisions, and in the topics dealt with in our legal literature. ...

This national isolation of legal science is as anachronistic today as was the particularism of legal sources in early 19th century Germany. After the devastations of the Second World War, the era of political nationalism was widely perceived to have come to an end. The (three) European Communities were designed, in the second half of the 1950s as a springboard towards the eventual achievement of European unity. The preamble to the EEC treaty of 1957 asserted a determination 'to lay the foundations of an ever closer union among the peoples of Europe'. ...

In recent years, we have indeed experienced a significant process of legal harmonisation in areas as diverse as unfair competition law, antitrust law, intellectual property law, labour law and company law. Contract law and liability law have been affected, mainly, by the Product Liability, Consumer Credit and Doorstep Selling Directives. Yet, in spite of all these efforts, the present state of European legal unification is not at all reassuring; for we are dealing with no more than fragments of – more or less – uniform law, inserted rather unorganically and in a somewhat higgledy-piggledy fashion into the respective national legal systems. Rather than having gained in coherence, rationality and predictability, the law has tended to become disjointed. Its application has not been streamlined but has, instead, acquired a new dimension of complexity.

It may be possible to iron out these difficulties by way of codifying European private law. In two resolutions dating from May 1989 and May 1994 the European Parliament has, indeed, called for such a step to be taken. This is the path mapped out, in 1814, by A.F.J. Thibaut. But, as in 1814, it is highly questionable whether the enactment of a Code Civil Européen would, at the present time, be practicable, or even desirable. Moreover, we have come together today as 'public teachers' – and, I presume, researchers – of law. Our own domain is legal scholarship rather than legislation and the specific challenge with which we are faced today is the creation of a legal science 'which may be common to the whole of Europe' and which may thus inspire and sustain a European private law. This automatically raises the question of the relevance of Savigny's programme in our present situation.

That situation is characterised by a significant change of paradigm: the gradual emergence of a European (as opposed to merely national) private law. At the same time, however, our general frame of mind is still largely moulded by those national legal systems. This rather unfortunate discrepancy has only comparatively recently been recognised. ...

> A legal practice informed and sustained by legal scholarship, and an approach to legal scholarship that is always mindful of the fact that, ultimately, law serves an eminently practical function: that is what Savigny was aiming for. Unless we want to succumb to a mood of fashionable cynicism and are prepared to abandon an essential part of our cultural heritage, we will have to do the same. For law is both a constituent feature and a characteristic emanation of European culture. Not surprisingly, therefore, it exhibits a number of attributes which distinguish it from dispute regulation in other cultures. It is administered by a body of professional experts who have received a specialised training for their task. The central institution providing such training is typically a university. As a university subject, law is submitted to methodical reflection and analysis: it is the object of a 'legal science' (in the sense of *Rechtswissenschaft*). European legal science, in turn, is based on the belief that the legal material does not constitute an indigestible and arbitrary mass of individual rules and cases, but can be reduced to a rational and organised system. It aims at presenting law as a logically consistent whole. And it attempts to demonstrate how individual rules and the decisions of individual cases can be derived from general propositions, and how they can be understood and related to each other. A determined effort is made to rationalise the application of the law. ...
>
> The lesson is obvious. The essential prerequisite for the development of a European private law would appear to be the emergence of an 'organically progressive' legal science, which would have to transcend national boundaries and disciplinary divides and which would revitalise a common tradition. It would, at the very least, enable us to understand and determine the relative positions of our national legal systems *vis-à-vis* each other. It would supply a common legal 'grammar' for discussing general legal questions and evaluating possible solutions. It would provide us with a stock of systematic and conceptual tools, of rules and principles, which would reduce the existing legal systems to national variations of a common theme. This change of perception would, in turn, be reflected in the way in which the national legal systems are interpreted and developed; and it would engender a new approach to legal education and to legal writing. It would reconstitute Savigny's Historical School of Jurisprudence on a European level.

The new context offered by globalization was not free from challenges. For example, a number of comparative law scholars pointed to changes in the purposes and methods of their discipline, responding to the needs of the new environment. Critical approaches to comparative law and to other disciplines were needed, calling for studies that revisited prior understandings that could no longer be considered dogmatic or undisputed.

Horatia Muir Watt, Globalization and Comparative Law, in Mathias Reimann and Reinhard Zimmermann (eds), The Oxford Handbook of Comparative Law, Oxford, Oxford University Press, 2019, 620–623

On a practical level, the changes wrought by globalization, including new information technology, interconnectedness of national economies, and the emergence of transnational norms and practices, raise two different and apparently contradictory challenges to comparative law. On the one hand, the ever-widening access to data about foreign laws, as well as the expansion of transnational or international sources of uniform law might appear to make comparative law obsolete. What need is there for comparative scholarship if information on foreign law is readily available or if the applicable rule is a rule of substantive uniform law? On the other hand, comparative scholarship still has an important rôle to play, albeit in novel forms. An increase in the available volume of information renders all the more necessary a comparative legal grammar capable of converting bare data on a national legal system into an understandable form for the foreign user. At the same time, uniform law requires, for both its elaboration and its interpretation, a comparison of possible alternative solutions.

1. Increased Information and Interconnectedness

First and most obviously, increased access to knowledge of foreign law through new information technology has important implications for the usefulness of comparative law as a source of information about foreign laws. Traditionally, as David Gerber has pointed out, one of the main functions of comparative law was to provide information about other, different, legal cultures. Indeed, comparative studies often tended to be descriptive or 'anatomical,' concentrating on the assembling of stark data about a foreign law which was otherwise unobtainable. As access to information improves, this particular function of comparative legal scholarship is no doubt becoming redundant.

While essential in this respect, new information technologies are not the only reason for the increase in widespread knowledge about foreign legal cultures. The existence of supranational courts such as the European Court of Human Rights, for instance, inevitably feeds a common core of knowledge about the legal systems of the other contracting states. …

Available information may be increasingly dense, but it may be becoming more opaque. It may be creating a new, double problem of understanding, since bare data such as texts may be undecipherable to the uninitiated and even in the clearest form are unlikely to provide insights as to how they fit within the foreign legal system or how the latter actually works in practice. … A common conceptual language, a comparative legal grammar, will be necessary to maximize the benefits of increased information and make them significant to the foreign user. …

Legal advice and litigation involve increasingly cross-border elements – from products liability to investment choices to car accidents abroad – which may require making decisions in the light of foreign law or which call for the application of foreign law under conflict of laws principles. The easy availability of information about foreign law is obviously likely to enhance cross-border legal practice. However, comparative law as a disciplinary field is far from obsolete in this context. …

2. The Rise of Transnational Uniform Law

A second practical challenge for the comparative lawyer in a global context stems from the changes affecting the sources and nature of applicable legal rules. These will frequently be contained in international conventions bearing uniform rules … Once more, in view of this trend towards unification, the question arises as to whether comparative law is becoming redundant through the lack of national, local laws to compare. But once again, the answer appears to be that comparative law retains all of its usefulness, albeit in new ways.

First, at the outset, comparative legal scholarship can contribute to the improved content of transnational uniform rules, whether these are negotiated at a diplomatic conference or chosen by a single arbitrator invested by contract with a mission to apply a better rule. A uniform rule is always to some extent the product of competition between diverse legal rules. Preparatory comparative studies should therefore be, and frequently are, systematically undertaken in both a diplomatic and private context. At a later stage, similar comparative knowledge remains essential when courts and arbitrators are called upon to interpret uniform rules in a given case. When a given uniform rule is clearly borrowed from a given national legal culture, insights as to the difficulties it raises and its mode of functioning are certainly useful even if national case-law or doctrinal constructions can obviously have no more than persuasive authority in such a context. Quite frequently, too, international instruments appeal to common principles of national law to fill the gaps in its own provisions.

> … In all these contexts, comparative law as a way of structuring knowledge about foreign laws, and translating it into a comprehensible form for the user, retains real practical usefulness.

This period provided a fertile ground for the further development of legal theory in Western legal traditions. Jurists developed different schools of thought and doctrines and found refuge in different law schools on different continents (some of them because they were in exile). Many different authors entered the stage. However, the positivist and naturalist approaches to law dominated discussion. Versions could be found in different contexts and jurisdictions. In 1958, in the pages of the *Harvard Law Review*, a seminal debate took place between H.L.A. Hart and Lon Fuller about positivism and natural law. It should be noted that this debate occurred in the wake of the atrocities of the Second World War.

> *H.L.A. Hart, Positivism and the Separation of Law and Morals, Harvard Law Review 71 (1958), 615–620*
>
> The third criticism of the separation of law and morals is of a very different character; it certainly is less an intellectual argument against the Utilitarian distinction than a passionate appeal supported not by detailed reasoning but by reminders of a terrible experience. For it consists of the testimony of those who have descended into Hell, and, like Ulysses or Dante, brought back a message for human beings. Only in this case the Hell was not beneath or beyond earth, but on it; it was a Hell created on earth by men for other men.
>
> This appeal comes from those German thinkers who lived through the Nazi regime and reflected upon its evil manifestations in the legal system. One of these thinkers, Gustav Radbruch, had himself shared the 'positivist' doctrine until the Nazi tyranny, but he was converted by this experience and so his appeal to other men to discard the doctrine of the separation of law and morals has the special poignancy of a recantation. What is important about this criticism is that it really does confront the particular point which Bentham and Austin had in mind in urging the separation of law as it is and as it ought to be. These German thinkers put their insistence on the need to join together what the Utilitarians separated just where this separation was of most importance in the eyes of the Utilitarians; for they were concerned with the problem posed by the existence of morally evil laws.
>
> Before his conversion Radbruch held that resistance to law was a matter for the personal conscience, to be thought out by the individual as a moral problem, and the validity of a law could not be disproved by

showing that its requirements were morally evil or even by showing that the effect of compliance with the law would be more evil than the effect of disobedience. Austin, it may be recalled, was emphatic in condemning those who said that if human laws conflicted with the fundamental principles of morality then they cease to be laws, as talking 'stark nonsense.'…

Radbruch, however, had concluded from the ease with which the Nazi regime had exploited subservience to mere law – or expressed, as he thought, in the 'positivist' slogan 'law as law' (*Gesetz als Gesetz*) – and from the failure of the German legal profession to protest against the enormities which they were required to perpetrate in the name of law, that 'positivism' (meaning here the insistence on the separation of law as it is from law as it ought to be) had powerfully contributed to the horrors. His considered reflections led him to the doctrine that the fundamental principles of humanitarian morality were part of the very concept of *Recht* or Legality and that no positive enactment or statute, however clearly it was expressed and however clearly it conformed with the formal criteria of validity of a given legal system, could be valid if it contravened basic principles of morality. This doctrine can be appreciated fully only if the nuances imported by the German word *Recht* are grasped. But it is clear that the doctrine meant that every lawyer and judge should denounce statutes that transgressed the fundamental principles not as merely immoral or wrong but as having no legal character, and enactments which on this ground lack the quality of law should not be taken into account in working out the legal position of any given individual in particular circumstances …

It is impossible to read without sympathy Radbruch's passionate demand that the German legal conscience should be open to the demands of morality and his complaint that this has been too little the case in the German tradition. On the other hand there is an extraordinary naïveté in the view that insensitiveness to the demands of morality and subservience to state power in a people like the Germans should have arisen from the belief that law might be law though it failed to conform with the minimum requirements of morality. Rather this terrible history prompts inquiry into why emphasis on the slogan 'law is law,' and the distinction between law and morals, acquired a sinister character in Germany, but elsewhere, as with the Utilitarians themselves, went along with the most enlightened liberal attitudes. But something more disturbing than naïveté is latent in Radbruch's whole presentation of the issues to which the existence of morally iniquitous laws give rise. It is not, I think, uncharitable to say that we can see in his argument that he has only half digested the spiritual message of liberalism which he is seeking to convey to the legal profession. For everything that he says is really dependent upon an enormous overvaluation of the importance of the bare fact that a rule may be said to be a valid rule of law, as if this, once declared, was conclusive of the final moral question: 'Ought this rule of law to be obeyed?' Surely the truly liberal answer to any sinister use of the slogan 'law is law' or of the distinction between law and morals is, 'Very well, but that does not conclude the question. Law is not morality; do not let it supplant morality.'

However, we are not left to a mere academic discussion in order to evaluate the plea which Radbruch made for the revision of the distinction between law and morals. After the war Radbruch's conception of law as containing in itself the essential moral principle of humanitarianism was applied in practice by German courts in certain cases in which local war criminals, spies, and informers under the Nazi regime were punished. The special importance of these cases is that the persons accused of these crimes claimed that what they had done was not illegal under the laws of the regime in force at the time these actions were performed. This plea was met with the reply that the laws upon which they relied were invalid as contravening the fundamental principles of morality. Let me cite briefly one of these cases.

In 1944 a woman, wishing to be rid of her husband, denounced him to the authorities for insulting remarks he had made about Hitler while home on leave from the German army. The wife was under no legal duty to report his acts, though what he had said was apparently in violation of statutes making it illegal to make statements detrimental to the government of the Third Reich or to impair by any means the military defense of the German people. The husband was arrested and sentenced to death, apparently pursuant to these statutes, though he was not executed but was sent to the front. In 1949 the wife was prosecuted in a West German court for an offense which we would describe as illegally depriving a person of his freedom (*rechtswidrige Freiheitsberaubung*). This was punishable as a crime under the German Criminal Code of 1871 which had remained in force continuously since its enactment. The wife pleaded that her husband's imprisonment was pursuant to the Nazi statutes and hence that she had committed no crime. The court of appeal to which the case ultimately came held that the wife was guilty of procuring the deprivation of her husband's liberty by denouncing him to the German courts, even though he had been sentenced by a court for having violated a statute, since, to quote the words of the court, the statute 'was contrary to the sound conscience and sense of justice of all decent human beings.' This reasoning was followed in many cases which have been hailed as a triumph of the doctrines of natural law and as signaling the overthrow of positivism. The unqualified satisfaction with this result seems to me to be hysteria. Many of us might applaud the objective – that of punishing a woman for an outrageously immoral act – but this was secured only by declaring a statute established since 1934 not to have the force of law, and at least the wisdom of this course must be doubted. There were, of course, two other choices. One was to let the woman go unpunished; one can sympathize with and endorse the view that this might have been a bad thing to do. The other was to face the fact that if the woman were to be punished it must be pursuant to the introduction of a frankly retrospective law and with a full consciousness of what was sacrificed in securing her punishment in this way. Odious as retrospective criminal legislation and punishment may be, to have pursued it openly in this case would at least have had the merits of candour. It would have made plain that in punishing the woman a choice had to be made between two evils, that of leaving her unpunished and that of sacrificing a very precious principle of morality endorsed by most legal systems. Surely if we have learned anything from the history of morals it is that the thing to do with a moral quandary is not to hide it. Like nettles, the occasions when life forces us to choose between the lesser of two evils must be grasped with the consciousness that they are what they are. The vice of this use of the principle that, at certain limiting points, what is utterly immoral cannot be law or lawful is that it will serve to cloak the true nature of the problems with which we are faced and will encourage the romantic optimism that all the values we cherish ultimately will fit into a single system, that no one of them has to be sacrificed or compromised to accommodate another.

'All Discord Harmony not understood
All Partial Evil Universal Good'

This is surely untrue and there is an insincerity in any formulation of our problem which allows us to describe the treatment of the dilemma as if it were the disposition of the ordinary case.

Questions

Jurists form a network through which legal science can be developed and shaped. Hart indicates that the separation of law and morals is not merely an intellectual exercise.

1. What are the possible practical implications of such a separation?
2. What practical examples can you think of in the context of the Second World War?
3. What examples can you think of based on topics addressed in previous chapters of this volume?
4. What are the main tenets of Radbruch's concept of law before and after the Second World War?

Jurists tried to build the structure in which harmonization of the law could be pursued. Zimmermann points to the fact that legal science seems to be characterized by national isolation.

5. What does he think about that isolation?

He further draws a parallel between the jurists in our period with those in another chapter of this volume.

6. To which other jurists is he referring? Why does he refer to them?

Muir Watt alerts of challenges to comparative law at a practical level.

7. Which are those challenges? Why would it be possible to refer to them as seemingly challenging?

3.3 *Legislators*

The model of the *trias politica* ensured – including during the period discussed here – that the legislative branch played a role in society. However, in this period legislators could not always operate in complete freedom. Sometimes they were hampered by, for example, military interventions or a political context that suppressed or hindered the freedom of the three branches of government. Also, professional lobbyists could shape the activities of law-makers. However, there was also room for bottom-up activism as individuals could reach out to the legislators and advocate for change. A 'healthy' legislature can guarantee the rule of law in a specific jurisdiction. All other actors require a legislature that rigs the game for them. A look into the US model offers a clear illustration of the role of the legislators during our period.

> *Lawrence M. Friedman and Grant M. Hayden, American Law: An Introduction (3rd edition), New York, Oxford University Press, 2017, 85–88*
> Yet the legislative branch is a tremendous presence in society and in the legal system. It is part of the bulk and body of Leviathan. There are vast numbers of lawmaking bodies, all up and down the land. As with the courts, we can imagine them arranged in a kind of pyramid. At the base of the pyramid, in the typical state, are the lawmaking organs of local government. In California alone, there are more than five thousand local bodies with some lawmaking or rulemaking power. These included

city councils, county boards, boards of supervisors, and thousands of special-purpose bodies. There are fifty-eight counties in California (San Francisco is specially classified as a 'city-county') and 448 cities. There is also a patchwork quilt of over a thousand school districts and, as of 2012, 4,711 special districts in charge of everything, from parks, water, and power, to mosquitos, sewers, and cemeteries.

One could quibble about whether these were all really legislative bodies, but they all have one thing in common: it is part of their business to establish general rules. …

We live, of course, in a federal system. There is a national legislature, too: Congress. It, too, is divided into an upper house (the Senate) and a lower house (the House of Representatives). The House is elected on a population basis, but every state is entitled to at least one representative, no matter how tiny its population. There are 435 members, or roughly one for every 700,000 people. There are one hundred senators; each state has two, regardless of the size of the state or its population. California, with over 38 million people, has two senators; so do states with less than a million people, like Wyoming, Alaska, and Vermont. This scheme was written into the Constitution …

The legislative system, like the rest of our legal structure, is influenced by federalism and, more significantly, by the American habit of decentralization. Voters take it for granted that the people they elect represent localities and local interests. We do not elect senators or congressmen 'at large.' Members of Congress must please the people in their districts, or they will find themselves out of a job. Also, in the states, and in most cities, each lawmaker is elected from a particular district, and must be a resident of that district. …

It is easy to think of legislatures and courts as alternative lawmakers, or even as rivals. In some ways they are. But in our tradition, legislatures do many things that courts cannot do at all, or do only poorly. Legislatures can impose taxes and can spend money, which courts cannot really do, at least not directly. Courts respond to particular cases, in which John Smith sues Mary Jones, or the Acme Toothpick Company sues the city of Little Rock. In making a decision, an appeals court may lay down a general rule; but even so, the rule is supposed to be limited to the class of cases which *Smith v. Jones* represents.

Of course, it is anybody's guess how broad that category is. But in theory, anything that goes beyond the case is 'dictum' (incidental talk) and is not binding on later courts. Whatever the theory, courts do act with caution most of the time. They do not presume to lay down minute, specific,

> detailed regulations. When a court hears a zoning case that turns on whether a gas station can be lawfully opened for business on the corner of Oak and Elm, the court may think the whole zoning ordinance or plan badly needs redoing, but it will not assume it has the right or the power to redo it on its own. Nor do courts change the speed limit or adjust parking fines; they do not generate systems of traffic rules or propose a list of chemical additives that can safely be used to make chicken soup yellow. Courts, in general, do not propose specific quantitative measures. They might (for example) decide that a tax rate is, for some reason, illegal or unconstitutional; but they will not suggest what the right rate might be. That is a job for the legislature. In the opinion of some critics, courts have strayed far from their classic preserves; they are, it is said, meddling in affairs that should not concern them, and crossing the line that sets them apart from the legislature and the legislative function. The point is controversial. Nonetheless, we think it is fair to say that the basic boundary between courts and legislative bodies still, in general, remains, and holds fast.

Nearly everywhere where law was produced, the exclusive law-making power of the state was challenged. We are not referring to the law-making, which, for centuries, had been delegated by the state to various institutions or individuals. Neither are we referring to the carefully constructed hierarchy of transnational or regional laws of international and 'devolved' institutions. The real challenge came – no matter the level it appeared at – from different normative orders that could be applied by different institutions in an autonomous fashion *praeter* or *contra* the law of the State, without the latter exerting any control over it. This is the essence of the theory of critical or radical legal pluralism. It extends the sphere of law-making far beyond the semi-autonomous mechanisms through which the state controls the production of law. This theory takes direct aim at the heart of the Western legal tradition as it had developed over the centuries starting with Hobbes and directly challenges its validity. It holds that at the bottom of the scale are the couple and the family, and at the top the world of finance, with all sorts of self-regulated associations in between. The state and its well-organized pseudo-legal pluralism certainly play a role in this constantly evolving landscape. Instead of an orderly system of law, the result is a disorderly amalgam of *laws*. This presented lawyers with a completely new set of challenges when they were confronted with contemporary disorder in contrast to the orderly system law schools continued to teach.

Roderick A. Macdonald, Unitary Law Re-form, Pluralistic Law Re-Substance: Illuminating Legal Change, Louisiana Law Review 67 (2007), 1121
The burden of this article is to deploy the hypothesis of legal pluralism to provide an alternative account of legal change in contemporary official normative regimes, whether domestic or transnational. The argument proceeds in two steps.

First, I argue that the plurality of *modes* of law within any system requires us to adopt a theory of legal change that sees these *modes* of law not as pieces of a single legal order, but as each constituting a discrete normative regime. Crudely put, this means much law *reform* in modern States produces no substantive normative change; conversely, it means that much *substantive* normative change occurs without any law reform. Legal pluralism invites us to notice that, especially in multi-jurisdictional and international settings of legal change, plural law re-substance may well result from unitary law reform.

Second, I argue that the plurality of *sites* of law within any psycho-social-geographic space requires us to adopt a theory of legal change that does not see these *sites* of law as human artifacts that are separate from the world upon which law is meant to operate. Crudely put, this means that much law *reform* is based on the erroneous presumption that legal subjects are simply entities that law can apprehend, constitute, remake, or deny; conversely, it means that *substantive* legal change is based on the correct assumption that it is legal subjects who apprehend, constitute, remake, and deny law. Legal pluralism invites us to notice that, even in apparently uni-jurisdictional and national settings of legal change, it is possible to achieve unitary law re-substance through plural law reform.

Questions

Legislators are traditionally considered the prime lawmakers.

1. Why does Friedman point out that it is just as easy to think of legislatures and courts as alternative lawmakers, or even as rival lawmakers?

It may seem, at first sight, that Friedman confuses legislative and regulatory powers.

2. What justifies referring to municipalities, counties or school boards as legislators?

Legal pluralism indeed merits attention during the period covered in this chapter, as pointed out by Macdonald.

3. Which two arguments does Macdonald put forward to support the hypothesis of legal pluralism?

4. How do they challenge the view that the legislator is the exclusive lawmaker?

3.4 *Legal Education*

Mass enrolment in higher education increased sharply in Western Europe and Latin America in the period that followed the Second World War. It also impacted legal education, as it did most other disciplines, and was mainly a phenomenon of civil law countries. Legal education, like higher education in general, remained more selective in common law jurisdictions. In the USA, it was only accessible to a limited number of carefully selected candidates. Access became even more restricted when law schools decided to limit access to the legal profession for those with a bachelor's degree, by changing the Bachelor of Laws (LL.B) into a Juris Doctor (J.D). The cost of legal education in some parts of the world, particularly the USA, has become prohibitive. In the meantime, all over the Western world, the percentage of female students kept increasing, often exceeding half the number of students or graduates.

Teaching methods evolved all over the world, particularly in common law jurisdictions in the wake of the Langdell revolution at Harvard, which promoted teaching based on the case method. Lecturing, however, remained predominant in the civil law world, at least at the undergraduate level, with hundreds of students sitting together in one classroom. However, efforts have been made to improve the latter teaching method in order to develop more legal skills: this includes smaller-groups, *travaux dirigés*, and seminars, which promote problem-based learning. Another trend which began in US law schools and made its way to other parts of the world is experiential learning through the promotion of law clinics, advocacy programs, and internships.

An innovative development is the emergence of transsystemic teaching. The goal is to let students discover the law in several systems simultaneously, through a combination of civil law and common law materials. The method has been used in some advanced comparative law programs. McGill University's Faculty of Law in Canada implemented the transsystemic approach to legal education throughout the curriculum. This is, undoubtedly, an interesting step on a long road toward the promotion of comparative law teaching.

Especially in the last decades of our period, a growing number of students sought to add a comparative dimension to their education by enrolling in postgraduate programs abroad. This led to an expansion of the offering of LL.M degrees in the USA and beyond.

Rosalie Jukier, Transcending Boundaries in Legal Education: A Vehicle for Teaching Students to Think Critically, Collected Essays on Teaching and Learning 6 (2013), 23–26

Law is a discipline that has been traditionally taught in a manner defined by many boundaries. The most obvious of such boundaries is related to jurisdiction or political geography. After all, at a very basic level, the law in force in a given jurisdiction (be it a country, state, province or municipality) is seen to be the one relevant and applicable to legal practice in that jurisdiction. …

This traditional paradigm for law as a profession has had a tremendous influence on legal education, as the geographic boundaries that define law and the legal profession carry over into the academy. As a result, teaching the law in force in the particular jurisdiction in which a university is located is still the norm in most law schools, even those ranked amongst the best in the world. …

In 1999, the Faculty of Law at McGill University in Montreal, Quebec, Canada, moved away from this traditional conception of legal education as inextricably tied to a particular political geography or state normativity. Breaking the mold of legal nationalism in the classroom, McGill embarked on an ambitious and creative curricular innovation. Termed the 'transsystemic' law program, McGill's curriculum adopted a pedagogical approach based on the integrated study of multiple legal traditions (in particular, but not exclusively, the two major western legal traditions of the civil law and the common law) as well as alternative sites of law (such as aboriginal and religious conceptions of law, and interdisciplinary approaches to legal issues) within blended courses.

From a pragmatic standpoint, the result was the creation of a program in which all students graduate with both civil law and common law degrees following three to four years of study. While students take compulsory and optional courses, in English or French, that cover the full range of subjects one finds in most law faculties, the difference is that at McGill, these courses are offered from an integrated and transsystemic perspective. Upon completion of the program, students leave McGill as 'cosmopolitan jurists' prepared to take on legal practice in today's evermore transnational world.

From an academic perspective, however, the result was the creation of a uniquely comparative, multi-systemic, pluralistic, and dialogic program of studying law. This program is personified by the integration of many voices, perspectives, and lenses without jurisdictional or systemic

> boundaries, highlighting a dialogue with, and learning from, other legal cultures and jurisdictions.

Legal education developed even further during the period discussed here. A number of law schools in different jurisdictions started to leave behind a curriculum focused exclusively on the study of national laws. The trend to approach the study of law from a perspective that extends beyond the law within the national borders helps build a broader understanding of legal science. Part of that trend is the international classroom, such as the one implemented early at Maastricht University, which provides a model for European legal education.

> *Aalt-Willem Heringa, Towards a European Law School! A Proposal for a Competitive, Diversified Model of Transnational Co-operation, in Michael Faure et al. (eds), Towards a European Ius Commune in Legal Education and Research, Antwerp, Intersentia, 2002, 4–5*
>
> Next to the national studies of the law, that evidently focus primarily on national concepts and doctrines, it might be time to investigate the feasibility of a truly European curriculum. As opposed to the national law faculties the primary focus then had to be on European law and on the 'common law' of Europe. …
>
> First of all, many obstacles were noted: could it be said that there was already a coherent body of European and common law in all areas of the law, of sufficient quantity and quality so as to facilitate its own curriculum? Or, should a student be taught and immersed in a national legal system with its concepts and doctrines, before he can embark upon European and, even more difficult, upon comparative law and the search for common legal principles and doctrines.
>
> A second problem, which can easily be said to exist still, is the absence of a common perspective on what a legal study should entail: the studies in the European countries still differ significantly; as do the national requirements for the legal profession. And, a simple practical aspect, there is no European common view as to a European legal education. National faculties of law therefore have to deal with their own national requirements: to give an example: for a Dutch student to qualify for the bar, he should have studied for four years at a Dutch law faculty (240 ECTS credits), of which approximately 210 credits must have been spent in studying the various areas of the law. That does not seem to facilitate a truly European legal education.

A third problem raised was about the nature of a good lawyer: does it really matter if a lawyer has not been specifically trained in comparative law and European law, but instead is very familiar with one legal system? This familiarity with one legal system, accompanied with his legal tools, should provide him with the best expertise for becoming a good European lawyer. Moreover, how many European lawyers do we really need: isn't the major part of a lawyer's business about dismissals, divorces, tort and national administrative law?

There are, therefore, many obstacles and arguments which we have to surmount and counter.

The present state of affairs in Europe seems to me to be the following:

- increasingly law faculties have inserted European law courses into their curriculum;
- in addition some law faculties have gone even further. They have not only added extra courses on European law, but they have introduced into their national law a number of courses with European and comparative elements. They have, so to speak, Europeanized the curriculum;
- many post-graduate programmes have been developed on European law and comparative law; and seemingly attract many students;
- national legislation about the requirements of a law curriculum still shows major differences between the EU member states. It also poses an important obstacle for national law faculties to develop a truly European law curriculum;
- the expansion of European law; the ever increasing trends in harmonization, transnational co-operation and in comparative research show that what seemed a distant future perspective, has come a lot closer and seems much real and realistic.

Questions

Jukier illustrates how traditional legal education can be challenged by means of experiences that cross legal systems.

1. To what extent can the McGill model be reconciled with other law schools' efforts to make learning more experiential?
2. Does it require that a choice be made between conceptual learning and experiential learning, or should they be reconciled in the curriculum?
3. How can teaching methods have an impact on the development of critical thinking?
4. What is the relevance of critical thinking for legal education?
5. Why would students aspire to be 'cosmopolitan jurists'?

Heringa points to the challenges of offering legal education that does not focus exclusively on the national laws of one specific jurisdiction.

6. What further changes do you believe are required to deal with those challenges?
7. Why would it benefit lawyers to be trained in programs that can overcome those challenges?

4 Application

In this period, paradigm shifts in the application of law can be observed. To understand the reasons for these changes better, one has to keep in mind the fact that globalization and the international context continued to play a role in these shifts.

4.1 *Institutions*

The search for peace and the intensification of international trade made the creation of international fora necessary. The Hague Peace Conference of 1899 led to the creation of the Permanent Court of Arbitration. After the First World War, the covenant of the League of Nations allowed for the creation of a Permanent Court of International Justice, which was transformed into an International Court of Justice after the Second World War. War crimes were prosecuted during the Nuremberg Trials, which shaped the development of international criminal law. This led to other ad hoc courts such as the International Criminal Tribunal for the former Yugoslavia, and eventually to the creation of an International Criminal Court.

The intensification of international trade triggered the creation of prominent arbitration tribunals, such as the International Centre for Settlement of Investment Disputes, the London Court of International Arbitration and the International Court of Arbitration of the International Chamber of Commerce, to name but a few. After its creation in 1994, the World Trade Organization became one of the most active international dispute settlement centres.

The European Union also developed its own legal institutions, and the excerpt below offers a brief overview:

> *Court of Justice of the European Union (https://curia.europa.eu; accessed June 2022)*
> Since the establishment of the Court of Justice of the European Union in 1952, its mission has been to ensure that 'the law is observed' 'in the interpretation and application' of the Treaties.

As part of that mission, the Court of Justice of the European Union:
- reviews the legality of the acts of the institutions of the European Union,
- ensures that the Member States comply with obligations under the Treaties, and
- interprets European Union law at the request of the national courts and tribunals.

The Court thus constitutes the judicial authority of the European Union and, in cooperation with the courts and tribunals of the Member States, it ensures the uniform application and interpretation of EU law.

The Court of Justice of the European Union, which has its seat in Luxembourg, consists of two courts: the Court of Justice and the General Court (created in 1988). The Civil Service Tribunal, established in 2004, ceased to operate on 1 September 2016 after its jurisdiction was transferred to the General Court in the context of the reform of the European Union's judicial structure.

As each Member State has its own language and specific legal system, the Court of Justice of the European Union is a multilingual institution. Its language arrangements have no equivalent in any other court in the world, since each of the official languages of the European Union can be the language of a case. The Court is required to observe the principle of multilingualism in full, because of the need to communicate with the parties in the language of the proceedings and to ensure that its case-law is disseminated throughout the Member States.

Questions

Different institutions were established to deal with the new context in which law developed. That new field of play was shaped, amongst other things, by the aftermath of the armed conflicts and the globalization process that took place during the period under discussion. For example, in Europe, a Court of Justice was established.

1. What is the mission of that court, and what does it seek to ensure?
2. What is the best way to explain the interaction between the Court of Justice and the national courts?

4.2 *Civil Procedure*

In this period, the divide between the inquisitorial and adversarial systems narrowed. Furthermore, efforts to achieve more harmonization of procedural laws were undertaken on both sides of the Atlantic, for example, in Latin

America, the USA, and Europe. Some were successful, while others only paved the way for future attempts.

Courts had to cope with an enormous expansion of litigation. Civil procedure changed in Europe during our period. The two excerpts below address some of the main changes.

C.H. (Remco) van Rhee, Introduction, in C.H. (Remco) van Rhee (ed.), European Traditions in Civil Procedure, Antwerp, Intersentia, 2005, 14–16, 20–21

3. Codifications in the Second Half of the Twentieth Century: The Belgian *Code Judiciaire* and the French *Nouveau Code de Procédure Civile*

Whilst the 1806 French *Code de procédure civile* may have lost its position as the central point of reference in the international procedural debate by the end of the nineteenth century, this did not mean that the Code itself disappeared from the procedural firmament at this time. It remained in force both in France and in Belgium, although not without amendments, for a long period of time. As stated above, in Belgium it was only replaced in the second half of the twentieth century by the 1967 *Code judiciaire*, whereas France retained the 1806 Code until 1976.

In Belgium, important reforms were introduced with the promulgation of the new Judicial Code … The new Belgian Code, for example, formulates several general procedural principles and, in this respect, it may have been influenced by the French discussion on the *principes directeurs du procès* that would become part of the new French procedural Code in the 1970s. The Belgian Code also provides for a common procedural model that is applicable to all courts in each instance. Additionally, in comparison to the old Code, the rules on procedural nullities were softened. In the light of the Austrian experiences, it may come as a surprise that the new Belgian Code is also very liberal as regards the extension of the scope of the case on appeal, where new claims that have not been formulated at first instance may be introduced. It is exactly this liberal attitude that is currently recognised as one of the major flaws in the new Belgian procedural model, which was originally considered to be a success. This liberal regime has resulted in first instance proceedings not being taken seriously. Until now, the Belgian Legislature has not chosen the approach of the German Legislature, which in 2002 introduced reforms in order to mend this defect by limiting the appellate procedure to the control of the decision at first instance. Paul Van Orshoven claims that the problems caused by the 1967 Code are the result of the fact that the Belgian Legislator did not make a series of fundamental choices. Additionally, Belgian procedural culture did not change as a result of the introduction of the new Code. Consequently, the tools which the new Code provides are not necessarily used by the judge. Reform is needed. A first step in this direction has already been taken, with the creation, in 1999, of a High Council of Justice. The High Council of Justice is in charge of the organisation of several aspects of the Judiciary.

France followed Belgium in introducing a new Code of Civil Procedure in 1976, after a long period of gestation. The origins of the French Code must be sought in General De Gaulle's Constitution of 28 September 1958. This Constitution is known for the fact that it transferred many powers from Parliament to the Government, and this also occurred as regards the powers of statute-making in the area of civil procedure. Consequently, the main source for the law of civil procedure in France since 1958 has been Government Decrees. It is likely that this transfer of powers was beneficial as regards law reform in the area of civil procedure. In the 1950s and beyond, the French Parliament was dominated by lawyers and it seems that these are occasionally hesitant as regards procedural reform in order not to damage both their own vested interests and those of their brethren.

The aim of the French procedural reform was a change of procedural culture. According to French textbook writers, the new Code tries to steer a middle course between adversarial and inquisitorial procedure. In fact, … this is not the right manner to describe the procedure of the new Code, which aims at genuine co-operation between judges [and] advocates … for the benefit of the litigants. For instance, in order to enable the court to perform case-management tasks, a new type of judge was created, the *juge de la mise en état*. It was (and is) his task to ensure a comprehensive and balanced investigation of the case. The procedure envisaged by the Code is a mix of oral and written elements. Another feature of the reform was the formulation of so-called 'Guiding Procedural Principles' (*principes directeurs du procès*), contained in the first part of the new Code of Civil Procedure. The Guiding Procedural Principles serve a specific goal, in that they form the framework for the interpretation of the other parts of the new Code. In this context, the French situation may be compared with that of Switzerland, where a similar role is given to these principles … French and Swiss practice differ very much from the situation in other European countries (for example, Germany), where most of the procedural principles are considered by the majority of lawyers to be mere academic reflections on the *status quo* of civil procedure. …

4. The End of the Twentieth Century: The 1998 English Civil Procedure Rules

... Lord Woolf suggested drastic measures to change this situation. First and foremost, the adversarial character of English civil litigation had to be addressed. Before the introduction of the CPR [Civil Procedure Rules], the English judge was much more passive than his Continental counterparts due to the strict observance of this principle. This was even true if compared with countries like The Netherlands, which had refrained from introducing the Austrian active judge. As a result of Lord Woolf's proposals, this changed: 'case management' became the key word in English civil procedure. In fact, this is not as new as it seems, since a more active judge was already one of the aims of the nineteenth-century Judicature Acts. However, the means to achieve this goal are new and ... effective. It is now the judge and the auxiliary staff of the court that have to make sure that a balance is observed between the complexity of the case and the procedural techniques that are used and the costs involved. This has been facilitated, inter alia, by the creation of three different procedural tracks, to which cases are assigned according to their complexity, and the requirement that an appeal can only be lodged with permission of the court. As regards appeal, the English developments are, to some extent, in line with Continental developments. An important difference is that these restrictions apply only for third instance proceedings in Continental jurisdictions (e.g., *Zulassungsrevision* in Germany and Austria), whereas in England permission to appeal is already required at the second instance. However, currently there also seems to be a tendency on the European Continent to reflect on limitations as regards second instance litigation.

The single-joint expert is another measure which proves that, in England, the adversarial principle has been 'softened.' The court is also given the means to influence the parties' procedural attitude. Pre-action protocols have, for example, been put in place. These protocols aim at governing the parties' behaviour in many types of litigation even before the case is brought to the attention of the court. ... [T]hey are a means to achieve an early settlement of the action and, if this does not appear to be possible, to guarantee that the parties commence their lawsuit fully informed of the strengths and the weaknesses of their case. This is in line with developments on the European Continent, where in many countries the key word in procedural reform is co-operation between the parties and between judge and parties. Although one might ask whether the involvement of the judge puts into question the impartiality of the judge, who may become too involved in the lawsuit, it has been claimed that there are no risks in this respect. … Dr. Soraya Amrani-Mekki advanced the idea that 'neutralité active' is the direction the behaviour of the judge should take. The active involvement of the judge in procedural issues does not … interfere with his impartiality because, by intervening in procedural issues ex officio, the judge only performs the task he should perform. He aims at bringing the genuine truth to the table, and if this is not beneficial to one of the parties, this does not mean that the judge has become partial in the sense of being prejudiced.

C.H. (Remco) van Rhee, Harmonization of Civil Procedure: An Historical and Comparative Perspective, in X.E. Kramer and C.H. (Remco) van Rhee (eds), Civil Litigation in a Globalising World, The Hague, T.M.C. Asser Press, 2012, 60–61

Attempts to harmonise civil procedure have made the study of comparative civil procedure (including the history of this area of the law) an exciting field of study during the last few decades. Although the comparative study of civil procedure was originally the domain of national law reformers, busy with drafting new or amended codes of civil procedure in a national context, mainly focusing on nearby jurisdictions, globalisation has made it a field of study for a wider audience. It is a promising area of study, for example, where national procedural systems are seen to compete with each other for litigation business. Comparative civil procedure allows these systems to evaluate their strengths and weaknesses in the international playing field when taking into consideration the preferences of litigants who have become ever more mobile where it concerns choices of forum. … Especially businesses have certain preferences as regards the procedural model for litigation, to which jurisdictions that aim at attracting litigation before their various State courts should be aware. Additionally, attempts to approximate civil procedural law in an international context benefit tremendously from this field of study. Although successes in this field are limited, especially the Principles of Transnational Civil Procedure of the American Law Institute and UNIDROIT [and the Model European Rules of Civil Procedure of the European Law Institute and UNIDROIT] show us the way ahead. Parochial criticism in this field is of course possible, but as in other areas in today's world, it will quickly become apparent that parochialism is not the way ahead to survive in our modern times in which the world is becoming smaller and smaller. It is to be hoped that the Transnational Principles [and the Model European Rules of Civil Procedure] will trigger further in-depth studies of civil procedure, and I am convinced that in this particular area the study of comparative law, including the study of the history of civil procedure, will continue to add new insights and show the way ahead.

Questions

Procedural laws experienced a significant change during the period under discussion, both in civil law and common law systems. Van Rhee describes the most important changes during the first and the second half of the twentieth century.

1. What were the main changes in France and Belgium?
2. What was the reason behind these changes?

England also experienced change.

3. What were the principal differences between the changes in England compared to the changes on the European Continent?
4. Who was one of the main architects of the push for change in England?

Van Rhee also refers to harmonization efforts for procedural laws.

5. What are the primary harmonization efforts?
6. What is the relation between globalization and the harmonization of procedural laws?

4.3 *Private Law*

Private law changed in multiple ways during this period. Law reform accelerated considerably after the Second World War, as did legislative inflation in the last quarter of the twentieth century. Some of the main pillars of private law, such as family law, the law of obligations and property law were subject to fundamental changes.

In the area of family law, the patriarchal model was progressively abandoned and replaced by gender equality. Children were given equal rights, whether they were born from married parents or out of wedlock. Divorce was allowed or made more accessible, and marriage was no longer the unique model for family organization. Starting in the late 1990s, same-sex union and same-sex marriage were recognized in a growing number of Western jurisdictions. Those changes were implemented in civil codes or in statutes, or by court decisions as was the case in the USA. International Human Rights conventions also had a noticeable impact.

In contract law, freedom of contract was limited to protect weaker parties such as consumers and employees. The rise of the insurance industry had a strong impact on the development of tort law. It sometimes led to the adoption of strict liability, and sometimes to a multiplication of special regimes. New branches of private law boomed, such as insurance law and consumer protection. With the creation of new types of transactions, for, amongst others, the distribution of goods and services, in banking and financing and transportation, business transactions became increasingly complex and diverse. The law tried to keep pace with the technological change through legislation and jurisprudence (case law).

Property rights were significantly limited by the development of land and zoning regulations. Socialist regimes moved to collectivization of the means of production, though without entirely abandoning individual ownership, as they were seen as a necessary incentive. Intellectual property law kept expanding during the period. A general theory of abuse of rights was also developed, which brought to an end the myth of ownership as an absolute right. This paved the way for other fundamental changes in private law. The excerpts below refer to these developments in property law, but also show their effect on other sectors of private law.

> *Agustín Parise, Ownership Paradigms in American Civil Law Jurisdictions: Manifestations of the Shifts in the Legislation of Louisiana, Chile, and Argentina (16th-20th Centuries), Leiden, Brill Nijhoff, 2017, 221–222*
> The doctrine of abuse of rights (*abuso del derecho, abus de droit, Rechtsmissbrauch*) can be succinctly explained by stating that 'whoever abuses his legal rights should be held liable for the consequences of such abuse.' According to that conception, there are no absolute rights and the enjoyment of rights should be exercised according to the spirit of the law itself. The new wording in civil codes did not welcome abuses and did not refer to the absolute character of property, not being an absolute or rigid principle, and indeed being subject to limitations. The theory eventually helped to abandon the Liberal paradigm that had been encapsulated in the wording of many civil codes, because, as Yiannopoulos clarified, 'the doctrine of abuse of right[s], as applied to property relations, states that a landowner is responsible for certain intentional acts that exceed the social and economic purposes for which the law recognizes ownership in immovable property.'
>
> Abuse of rights opened the door for the new paradigm, and was sensed early in France, towards the end of the nineteenth century, though its origins could be traced back to Roman law. The theory redeveloped together with the social movements and legal innovations that followed in the nineteenth and twentieth centuries, and scholarly writing in France allowed its crystallization and eventual integration into French law. Accordingly, the postulates of the doctrine were found in early French writings by, amongst others, Claude Bufnoir, Léobon Larombière, and Auguste Sourdat. Louis Josserand, another representative of that

> doctrine – perhaps being the best exponent of it – indicated, when analyzing the abuse of rights doctrine within property law, that a 'desire to harm others is in essence antisocial; [and] it never may represent the purpose of any legal concept.' That doctrine – not defended by all scholars, and challenged by, for example, Marcel Planiol – germinated within American universities, and eventually reached the lawmakers. Abuse of rights was not circumscribed to property law … It was also welcomed broadly in other areas of private law and in public law, even reaching public international law.
>
> Abuse of rights was welcomed by civil codes in Europe and in the Americas. Most modern codes that welcomed the doctrine referred to the social or economic purposes of the law. In Europe, abuse of rights was [addressed] in, for example, the *Bürgerliches Gesetzbuch* and in the civil codes of Switzerland (1912), Italy (1942), Greece (1946), and Portugal (1967). Codes in the Americas also welcomed the doctrine. For example, the civil code of Mexico (1932) incorporated ideas of social progress and social solidarity, tending to eliminate the differences between rich and poor, employee and employer, and men and women. That text further described property as a social function, and followed the important changes implemented by the 1917 Constitution.

Changes in private law affected property law during the period discussed here. A social function paradigm entered the stage during the first decades of this period and spread across the Western legal tradition. The excerpt below describes the emergence of that new paradigm of ownership and the leading role the French jurist Léon Duguit played in its rise:

> *Agustín Parise, Ownership Paradigms in American Civil Law Jurisdictions: Manifestations of the Shifts in the Legislation of Louisiana, Chile, and Argentina (16th-20th Centuries), Leiden, Brill Nijhoff, 2017, 185–186, 188–189, 192–198*
>
> Private law experienced a socialization process in the period 1890–1930, since the Liberal paradigm had offered few limitations to the right of ownership. Gradual changes started to occur in society – as explained *infra* – regarding the extent of that right, and the Social Function paradigm started to develop across the Western Hemisphere. That approach entailed a less 'egoistic' understanding of ownership. Changes had occurred in the social and economic structures of different jurisdictions, with massive migrations into cities and the effects of the Industrial Revolution. Accordingly, the crude individualistic paradigm started to

be challenged as a reaction to the social problems that were developing across the Western Hemisphere. …

Changes in the understanding of ownership therefore started to develop in academic circles, followed by decisions by courts and by the implementation of changes in the positive laws, both in Europe and in the Americas. The idea of a social function, it should be noted, was not limited to property law, being present to different extents in other areas of the law, amongst which, family law, successions, and civil procedure. Those advocating for the adoption of a broad Social Function paradigm could aim to find in the legal provisions a replication of social reality, where law should be a product of reality. Therefore, the social function could be subject to alterations, according to the mutations in the social circumstances of different societies at different times.

Advocates for a change in paradigm soon emerged throughout Continental Europe, not limited to socialist scholars and their writings. … The need for change was also present in English-speaking jurisdictions, though not necessarily along the same lines or to the same extent as in Continental Europe. … The new paradigm was … present in the writings of the Roman Catholic Church, which did not deny the existence of both a social and an individual character for ownership.

Duguit was the paladin of the Social Function paradigm, claiming early that the Liberal paradigm was in extinction. Born in France in 1859 and deceased in 1928, Duguit held teaching positions at several universities in France, and also taught in Bucharest, Cairo, Coimbra, and New York. He was very much influenced by the writings of Comte, while he further found grounding for his works in the sociological postulates of Émile Durkheim, of whom he was an acquaintance. … Duguit claimed that ownership entailed a social function, or furthermore, ownership was a social function. A status of isolation was considered fictional, and he therefore defended that the holder of a thing should fulfill a social function, and if the holder fulfilled the mission, the activities of the holder would be protected by law. However, if the holder did not fulfill the mission, the state could intervene and assure that the holder used the thing according to its purpose and [for the] benefit of all society members. The French publicist popularized the term 'social function' (*fonction sociale*) in 1905, at a lecture in the *Congrès National de la Propriété Batie*. On that occasion he referred to a social mission, role, and function. A few years later, in August and September 1911, he delivered a series of six lectures at the University of Buenos Aires, where he advocated for the social function in private law, upon reflecting on the changes experienced in private law since the adoption of the *Code Napoléon*. Those lectures resulted from early efforts to establish cultural links between Argentina and Europe. Duguit then transcribed the Buenos Aires Lectures, and published them in Paris in 1912, making them available to French readers. … The French publicist highlighted that property had to be destined towards the collective interest. He made it clear to readers of his lectures, however, that he was against class conflict or class struggle. In the second Buenos Aires lecture, he stated that men and society did not have rights, yet 'every individual ha[d] a certain function to fulfill in society, a certain task to undertake.' In the sixth lecture, dealing mainly with the social function of property, he indicated that ownership was subject to socialization, implying two things: 'that individual ownership [was] no longer an individual right, and was transform[ed] into a social function; and second, that there [was] an increase in the number of cases of wealth allocated to collectivities, that [should] be subject to juridical protection.' Duguit also stated that owners could use things as long as they fulfilled a social function. They had to undertake three duties: (i) to enjoy things when satisfying individual or collective needs; (ii) not to leave things without use or exploitation; and (iii) to allow the use of things when aiming to fulfill social interests. The author addressed the existence of subjective rights, and defended that 'ownership [was] therefore not the subjective right of the owner, it [was] the social function of the holder of the wealth.'

The ideas and writings of Duguit triggered debate and further studies. He could have been considered an iconoclast, seen as someone breaking with the symbols of the past. Duguit was criticized because property should have a social function and not be a social function. Scholars, many being trained in the civil law, claimed that the subjective right of holders should be acknowledged and not denied. Accordingly, the argumentation of Duguit was not welcomed favorably by some scholars, because it implied a rejection of the subjective right of ownership, and the owner was therefore simply a functionary. However, his ideas did generate awareness of the need for ownership to comply both with collective and individual needs. …

The reception of the Social Function paradigm was not limited to the first decades of the twentieth century or to the European legal discourse. A series of social and ideological twentieth-century shifts (i.a., WWI, WWII, the Mexican Revolution) also had an impact on the reshaping of ownership. The paradigm was welcomed in legislation and scholarly writings throughout the entire century, entering even into the twenty-first century. A diversity of legal provisions reflected a departure from the

> Liberal paradigm. For example, at the European level, Article 1 of Protocol 1 to the Convention for the Protection of Human Rights and Fundamental Freedoms (1952) referred to limitations due to public interest. Similarly, the American Convention on Human Rights (1969) addressed a social interest for property. A diversity of authors, likewise, made manifest a departure from the traditional Liberal paradigm. For example, in the US, contemporary authors refer to the renaissance of a new and social paradigm that departs from the Liberal paradigm. Accordingly, Joseph William Singer speaks of a social relations model, which 'reconceptualizes property as a social system composed of entitlements which shape the contours of social relationships,' being able to include relations between people 'both at the level of society as a whole (the macro level) and in the context of particular relationships (the micro level).' Other US scholars also speak of a social-obligation theory. For example, Gregory S. Alexander addresses an approach to the social-obligation theory that focuses on human flourishing. He defends that 'an owner is morally obligated to provide to the society of which the individual is a member those benefits that the society reasonably regards as necessary for human flourishing.' All these notions can be traced back to the Social Function paradigm that took force during the period 1890–1930.

As mentioned before, changes also took place in other areas of private law, such as the law of obligations. The excerpt below depicts the legal solution that prevailed during the period discussed to deal with the compensation for accidents.

> *Michael G. Faure, Accident Compensation, in Jan Smits (ed.), Elgar Encyclopedia of Comparative Law (2nd ed.), Cheltenham, Edward Elgar, 2012, 1–3, 14–15*
>
> The issue of how victims of accidents can receive compensation has been addressed for a long time in many legal systems and of course also in comparative law. The complicated issue of the topic 'accident compensation' is of course that a variety of legal instruments come to mind that can be used by victims to receive compensation after an accident has happened. … This is more particularly the case for tort and for insurance, both of which are important instruments. There is also an extensive literature describing the ways in which victims can achieve compensation for their damage not only in different countries, but also from a comparative perspective. It seems as if recently the number of publications in this domain has been on the increase.

One reason for the interest in accident compensation may simply be increasing interest in the harmonization of law and more particularly of private law in Europe. This has given rise to many volumes which usually are based on country reports describing the situation in the author's home country and which usually contain a comparative analysis as well. Many of these books have as their goal to examine whether there is a common core in the (European) legal systems which could be used as a basis for a possible harmonization of the law with respect to accident compensation. Hence, a lot of material is available today, much of which has emerged in recent years. To a large extent we can therefore simply discuss this material for further reference.

A second reason for the increasing interest in accident compensation from a comparative perspective is probably the sad fact that, although technological progress has undoubtedly largely added to the quality of life of mankind, at the same time mankind also seems to be exposed (increasingly) to various (new) risks which raise the question of compensation for the victims. And even in cases where the risks are not new (as with earthquakes, flooding, hurricanes or, more recently, tsunamis) the question of which legal instruments can provide adequate compensation to victims is increasingly being asked. Many specific studies address specific risks, many of which are also 'man made' and a particularly undesirable side-effect of technological progress. In this respect we can of course refer to environmental risks, medical malpractice, but especially after 9/11 also to the terrorism risk. For all of these risks (and many others, such as traffic-related risks), specific comparative studies exist, all devoted in some way or another to the question of how in different countries victims can receive compensation. There have even been specialized institutes that have set themselves the goal of promoting research with respect to the various instruments that can provide accident compensation to victims. In this respect, for instance, the European Centre of Tort and Insurance Law (ECTIL), founded in 1999 and located in Vienna, should be mentioned. In the various studies that ECTIL initiated, ... research is undertaken on similarities and differences with respect to accident compensation in various legal systems in Europe, but also in non-European countries like Israel, South Africa and the United States.

A third reason for the increasing body of literature addressing accident compensation is the growth of the field known as law and economics or the economic analysis of law. Starting from the concept of efficiency, law and economics scholars examine the types of legal rules in various legal systems and how they can be used to prevent accidents in an efficient way and to compensate victims without negative effects on prevention. The focus of law and economics scholars is indeed on prevention of accidents rather than on accident compensation. The premise of a law and economics scholar is usually that the best way to protect the victims is to prevent accidents. Hence a law and economics scholar will always be interested in the question of what the influence of a chosen compensation mechanism is on the incentives of the parties involved to prevent accidents or, more generally, whether the different instruments presented lead in an optimal way to cost reduction. The domain of law and economics has certainly reached comparative law. In this respect we can simply refer to the domain of 'comparative law and economics' which more particularly addresses inter alia the question whether differences between legal systems can also be explained on efficiency grounds. Also this interest in the economic analysis of law, more particularly among lawyers interested in accident compensation, can explain the increasing body of literature in this domain. …

[T]he way accident compensation has been dealt with in legal doctrine, legislation and practice in various legal systems in recent years has shown a number of trends. The traditional debates between, on the one hand, those who favour regulation with public compensation systems and, on the other hand, the (often private) lawyers who favour tort law and insurance is still of importance today. This debate apparently influences the legislator in many countries as well, since in various domains legislators seem to be moving away from the mere use of tort and insurance towards alternative compensation mechanisms, for instance in the areas of medical malpractice, environmental pollution and traffic accidents. Nevertheless, this tendency away from tort towards alternative mechanisms is certainly not generalized and moreover definitely not free from criticism. Many, indeed, hold that this trend away from individual responsibility towards collective compensation mechanisms may reduce essential incentives towards the prevention of accidents, which is still the primary way of victim protection.

Whether public or private instruments are best suited to providing accident compensation is, as we have shown, often an empirical matter having to do with the way in which the various systems are able to provide speedy compensation at low cost and depending upon the influence on the incentives for prevention of the different systems. However, the empirical material available seems to be limited and even its interpretation highly debated.

Although we have noticed many harmonization attempts, some in conventions and European directives, but mostly in legal doctrine, we can also observe that, especially as far as specific compensation mechanisms are concerned (compulsory insurance or compensation funds), there is still a lot of variety between the different legal systems and even between the different categories of accidents. There seems in this respect to be no general way in which different accidents such as traffic accidents, medical malpractice or environmental pollution are handled. Moreover, accident compensation is an area which today is still evolving. Ever new accidents and disasters (natural disasters, but especially terrorism) constitute new challenges for the various legal systems and new solutions are still being developed in the various legal systems today. This is therefore undoubtedly a domain that deserves to be followed carefully in the near future.

Questions

Private law experienced paradigm shifts during this period. For example, a new social function was introduced into various areas of law, such as concepts of abuse of rights and property. Parise indicates that the doctrine of abuse of rights involved a break with a previous understanding.

1. What was that previous understanding?
2. How was the new doctrine incorporated into legislation?

Parise also indicates that ownership was affected.

3. What were the goals of the new property paradigm and who was one of its main proponents?
4. What did he say were the duties of owners?

Shifts also took place, for example, in the area of obligations. Faure refers to developments in the area of accident compensation.

5. List some of the new accidents and disasters that require such compensation.
6. How do they compare to accidents or disasters that may have occurred in other periods?
7. Which are the main explanations that Faure presents for the increase in the need to attend to accident compensation?

4.4 *Public Law*

The new context also made changes in public law necessary. There were developments across the Western world and beyond that recognized a number of rights as being fundamental. These rights were phrased in broad and open-ended formulations in constitutional law. They were thereby given the strongest possible legal protection, which was a way to reconcile the promotion of natural rights with legal positivism. As soon as these fundamental rights are recognized as constitutional they transcend the whole legal system, as it were, and the traditional division of law into private and public fades away. This phenomenon has long been known in the USA, where the division between public and private law was never that sharp. It is called the constitutionalization of private law in other jurisdictions, except the UK, where it is seen as a foreign influence coming from Europe. In the UK, because of the absence of a written British constitution, the fundamental rights were reshaped by the European Convention on Human Rights. In legal systems based on codification, constitutional law elements are present in civil and commercial codes. Besides, laws that were made precisely to achieve this goal also merged private and public law components, providing an integrated approach for the challenges of everyday life for the members of the society. Private and public law are no longer separated into watertight compartments. Sectors like energy, construction and environmental protection combine public law and private law elements.

> *Thomas Buergenthal, The Evolving International Human Rights System, American Journal of International Law 100 (2006), 783–784, 787–788, 791–792, 794–799*
>
> The end of World War I and the establishment of the League of Nations produced the postwar treaties for the protection of minorities, whose application was limited to certain countries. The Covenant of the League of Nations provided for a mandates system, consisting of rudimentary normative and institutional processes for the protection of the indigenous populations of some former colonies. These developments, however, did not result in a comprehensive body of law that could be denominated international human rights law, although a few legal scholars promoted the concept. ... That the subject of human rights was still very much in its infancy is apparent from an Editorial Comment by Philip Marshall Brown that appeared in the American Journal of International Law in 1930, reporting on the 1929 meeting of the Institute and the adoption of its Declaration. The author noted that the Declaration 'aims not merely to assure individuals their international rights, but it aims also to impose on all nations a standard of conduct towards all men, including their own nationals.' Noting that the Declaration 'thus repudiates the classic doctrine that states alone are subjects of international law,' Brown continued: 'Such a revolutionary document, while open to criticism in terminology and to the objection that it has no juridical value, cannot fail, however, to exert an influence on the evolution of international law.'...

UN human rights law has evolved over the past sixty years along two parallel paths, one based on the UN Charter, the other on the human rights treaties adopted by the Organization. The Charter-based system comprises the human rights principles and institutional mechanisms that different UN organs have developed in the exercise of their Charter powers. The treaty-based system consists of a large number of human rights treaties drafted under UN auspices that codify much of the international human rights law in existence today. Some of these treaties also establish institutional mechanisms to monitor compliance by the states parties with the obligations imposed by these instruments. …

The European Convention on Human Rights ushered in the first regional system for the protection of human rights. It was followed by the inter-American and African systems. All three of the existing systems seek in one form or another to supplement the human rights efforts of the United Nations by providing protective mechanisms suited to their regions. In addition to guaranteeing many of the human rights that various UN instruments proclaim, each regional system also codifies those rights to which the region attaches particular importance because of its political and legal traditions, its history and culture.

The European Human Rights System

The European Convention for the Protection of Human Rights and Fundamental Freedoms established what has become the most effective international system for the protection of individual human rights to date. It has also served as a model for the two other regional human rights systems. The Convention traces its origin to the late 1940s, when the states constituting the Council of Europe, then a grouping of Western European states only, concluded that UN efforts to produce a treaty transforming the lofty principles proclaimed in the Universal Declaration of Human Rights into a binding international bill of rights would take many years to come to fruition. Rather than wait, they decided that the Council of Europe should proceed on its own …

By 1953, the ten ratifications necessary to bring the Convention into force had been deposited, and a total of forty-six states are now parties to it. This dramatic increase in its membership is due in large measure to the geopolitical transformation of Europe that resulted from the demise of the Soviet Union and the end of the Cold War. Today most European states are members of the Council of Europe and states parties to the Convention, including … some former Soviet Republics [the Russian Federation left in the wake of the 2022 war waged by this country against

Ukraine, a member state of the Council of Europe], as well as the United Kingdom, France, and Germany. In the meantime, the Convention itself and the system it established have also been significantly transformed. …

The Inter-American Human Rights System

When the Charter of the Organization of American States (OAS) was adopted in Bogotá, Colombia, in 1948, it made only general references to human rights. But the same Bogotá conference also proclaimed the American Declaration of the Rights and Duties of Man, though merely in the form of a nonbinding conference resolution. Before the American Convention on Human Rights entered into force in 1978, the human rights provisions of the OAS Charter, read together with the American Declaration, provided the sole, albeit rather weak, legal basis for the protection of human rights by the OAS.

Until 1960, the OAS made no serious effort to create a mechanism for the enforcement of these rights. That year the Inter-American Commission on Human Rights was established. Composed of seven independent experts elected by the General Assembly of the OAS, the Commission was charged with the promotion of the rights proclaimed in the American Declaration. It was to perform this task by preparing country studies and by adopting resolutions of a general character only. Six years later, the Commission was authorized to establish a limited petition system that allowed it to receive individual communications, charging large-scale violations of a selected number of basic rights set out in the American Declaration, including the right to life, equality before the law, freedom of religion, freedom from arbitrary arrest, and the right to due process of law …

The American Convention on Human Rights was concluded in San José, Costa Rica, in 1969 and came into force in 1978. Like the European Convention, the American Convention guarantees only civil and political rights. While the list of rights the European Convention guarantees has grown with the adoption of further protocols, the drafters of the American Convention opted for a comprehensive instrument that drew heavily on the much more extensive catalog of rights enumerated in the International Covenant on Civil and Political Rights. However, not all the rights guaranteed in the American Convention are derived from the Civil and Political Covenant. Some of them reflect the historical and cultural traditions of the Americas, such as the provision that guarantees the right to life …

The African Human Rights System

The African human rights system evolved in two distinct stages in a manner somewhat similar to that of its inter-American counterpart. The first stage consisted of the adoption in 1981 by the Organization of African Unity, now the African Union, of the African Charter on Human and Peoples' Rights. It entered into force in 1986 and in the meantime has been ratified by all fifty-three member states of the African Union. The Charter created an African Commission on Human and Peoples' Rights, but not a court. The African Court of Human and Peoples' Rights was established later by means of a separate protocol that came into force in 2004. The Court was formally inaugurated only in 2006.

The catalog of rights that the African Charter guarantees differs from its European and inter-American counterparts in several important respects. The Charter proclaims not only rights but also duties, and it guarantees both individual and peoples' rights. In addition to civil and political rights, the African Charter sets out a series of economic and social rights. The Charter permits the states parties to impose more extensive restrictions and limitations on the exercise of the rights it proclaims than the European and inter-American human rights instruments. It also does not contain a derogation clause, which leaves the question open whether all rights in the African Charter are derogable. The Charter's catalog of rights was heavily influenced by the rights proclaimed in the Universal Declaration of Human Rights and the two International Covenants on Human Rights. African historical traditions and customs are also reflected in some provisions of the Charter, particularly those dealing with duties of individuals and family matters. …

The powers of the African Commission to deal with interstate and individual communications are much more limited than those conferred by the European and inter-American human rights treaties. The Commission is so constrained in part because its findings with regard to the communications it receives cannot be made public without the permission of the African Union's Assembly of Heads of State and Government, a political body that has traditionally not been inclined to take strong action against serious violators of human rights. The Commission's power to deal with individual petitions is limited, furthermore, to 'cases which reveal the existence of a series of serious or massive violations of human and peoples' rights.' Thus, what we have here is not really a mechanism for individual petitions as it exists in the two other regional human rights systems. It is, rather, a procedure that permits individuals to file petitions charging massive or persistent violations of human rights, but not individual violations of one or the other right guaranteed by the African Charter. It is worth noting, though, that in the past the African Commission found ways around this problem by hearing claims that on their face may not have met the strict requirements of the above provision.

Important parts of the different constitutions were also changed as a reflection of the influence of the social movements that entered the stage during the first decades of the period. Because of this, our period saw the emergence of social constitutionalism. The passage below describes its spread across the Western world.

Agustín Parise, Ownership Paradigms in American Civil Law Jurisdictions: Manifestations of the Shifts in the Legislation of Louisiana, Chile, and Argentina (16th-20th Centuries), Leiden, Brill Nijhoff, 2017, 199–205
The new Social Function paradigm was encapsulated early within the constitutions of different jurisdictions. These new ideas were first welcomed in the Mexican Constitution of 1917 and in the social ideas included in the Weimar Constitution of 1919. These constitutions included references to the responsibility that derived from the ownership and control of property. The reception of the paradigm was ignited by those two constitutions; and starting with the 1917 Mexican Constitution, the Duguitian idea was soon welcomed by other constitutions of Europe and of American Civil Law Jurisdictions. The reception of the new paradigm within the text of constitutions increased during the inter-war period, yet it continued throughout the entire century. The new paradigm ultimately represented a mentality and ideal that soon predominated across the Western Hemisphere.

American Origins: Social Constitutionalism in Mexico
Mexico provided the first social constitution. The 1917 Constitution defended the democratic means of government presented in the 1857 Constitution, yet it modified individual rights by including a shift in social rights and state obligations. Those shifts contemplated the adoption of land reform, together with education and labor reforms. The new Mexican text was drafted within the context of the Revolution, aiming to achieve a radical subversion of the preexisting agrarian regime and achieving a new social structure. It has also been claimed that the 1917 Constitution was the 'first coherent expression of ideology emerging from the 1910 Revolution.' Changes in property law were mainly included in article 27 of the new Constitution, which resembled a codified text by providing solutions for single practical problems. The third paragraph of that article read in part:

> The Nation shall have at all times the right to impose on private property the modalities that the public interest may demand, as well as the right to regulate the use of natural elements subject to appropriation, to undertake an equitable distribution of public wealth and to secure their conservation. According to that objective, the necessary measures will be dictated for the fragmentation of the *latifundios* ... and [to] avoid the destruction of natural elements and damages that property may suffer in detriment of society.

The new wording converted private property into a privilege instead of a right. That idea was further present in the first and fourth paragraphs of article 27, which read that 'ownership of land and water corresponded originally to the Nation, who had and has the right to transfer dominium to individuals, creating therefore private property' and that 'direct ownership of all natural resources [was] vested [in] the Nation.' That new privilege enabled state relocation of goods in defense of public interests. In addition, the expression 'direct ownership' resembled the decomposition of ownership in *directum* and *utile*, returning to the Allocation paradigm. The Mexican government aimed therefore to project an image of being the legitimate owner, inspired in the *señorío* that the Castilian Crown had had over American territories before the independence movements. That new *señorío* would give ample power for the government to protect the public interest and introduce the Social Function paradigm. The 1917 text, after numerous modifications, is still the constitution of Mexico.

European Origins: Social Constitutionalism in Germany

Germany provided another early and influential constitutional text that welcomed the new paradigm of ownership. After WWI, Germany opted for a social democracy, and as its 1917 Mexican predecessor, the 1919 Constitution of the Weimar Republic resulted from a consolidation period that followed the downfall of a government. The 1919 text introduced the social function dimension, defending that owners should fulfill certain obligations and accept a number of limitations to their rights. Accordingly, individual ownership was preserved, yet it lost its absolute character, welcoming a more social conception of law. The tenets of this new paradigm were present mainly in two articles: on the one hand, in paragraph 3 of article 153, which in an overt form stated that 'property obliges' (*Eigentum verpflichtet*), and then declared that property should also be used for the common good; on the other hand, in paragraph 1 of article 155, which read in part that the 'distribution and use of land

[was] controlled by the Nation in a manner that prevent[ed] the abuse and secure[ed] healthy housing for all German families,' and in paragraph 3 of the same article, which read that the 'exploitation and use of the land [was] an obligation of the landowner with the community.' The German text characterized the social content of ownership. The new text fell within the creeds of the social state under the rule of law (*Sozialer Rechtsstaat*) understanding, which assumed the development of a collective responsibility for the moral, economic, and social existence of citizens, yet guaranteeing private rights. Even though not fully developed, the Social Function paradigm was encapsulated in the Weimar Constitution, preparing the ground for its development in other constitutions around the globe.

Global Contagion of Constitutions

Several European jurisdictions adopted the new paradigm in their constitutions. In the inter-war period, for example, Estonia (1919), Poland (1921), Danzig (1922), and Lithuania (1928) imposed limitations on individual property in their fundamental laws. Spain also received influences from the Weimar text. Article 44 of the 1931 Constitution stated that property could be socialized and that all wealth was subject to the interests of the national economy. The new paradigm was likewise adopted in common law jurisdictions, when the Republic of Ireland adopted a constitution in 1937. That text is of special interest, due to the place of the Church in Irish society, welcoming parallels with American Civil Law Jurisdictions. Other European jurisdictions incorporated the new paradigm into their post-WWII texts, when the social function of property was revamped in the different constitutions. Examples of these last texts are found in the constitutions of Yugoslavia (1953) and Portugal (1953). Earlier examples are found in the Italian Constitution (1947) and in the Basic Law for the Federal Republic of Germany (*Grundgesetz für die Bundesrepublik Deutschland*) (1949). Article 42 of the Italian text expressly referred to [the] social function, and aimed at the equitable division of land and the establishment of proper social relations. The German text, in paragraph 2 of article 14, also stated that 'property obliges,' as the Weimar precedent had done in 1919.

American Civil Law Jurisdictions were not immune to the reception of the new paradigm within the texts of their constitutions. Most constitutions there incorporated explicitly the Social Function paradigm during the first half of the twentieth century. Drafters in the Americas found grounding in the writings of Duguit for the changes in their constitutions, and they benefited from the texts that had been drafted in other parts of the Western Hemisphere. A contagion of constitutions developed in the region, and increased during the post-WWII period. Examples of constitutions that resulted from that contagion and that incorporated the Social Function paradigm are found in the texts of Bolivia (1938 and 1947), Colombia (1936 and 1945), Nicaragua (1939), Paraguay (1940), Guatemala (1946), Ecuador (1946), Panama (1941 and 1946), Peru (1947), Venezuela (1947), El Salvador (1950), and Honduras (1957). For example, the 1946 Constitution of Panama read in article 45 that private property implied obligations for the owner due to the social function it should fulfill; while the 1940 Constitution of Paraguay read in article 21 that the contents and limitations of private property would be established by law dealing with the social function.

Questions

Fundamental rights entered the stage during our period. Buergenthal traces the origins of the internationalization of human rights.

1. What are those origins?

The author also points to differences between the approaches to these fundamental rights in Europe, Africa and the Americas.

2. What are the main differences and similarities in the approaches? It is possible to speak about social constitutionalism during the period discussed here.

It is possible to speak about social constitutionalism during the period discussed here.

3. Which were the two main precursors for that movement according to Parise?
4. What does Parise mean when he refers to a contagion of constitutions?

5 Summary

The study of the law is a social science, and the comparative and historical approach followed in this chapter shows that law evolves over time. This chapter discusses several significant changes in law in the Western world. Those changes resulted from the different contexts in which the law evolved: for instance, early fragmentation due to wars and political divisions, followed later by harmonization due to globalization. International instruments and organizations also developed during the period under discussion. It should be stressed that this period experienced revolutions and paradigm shifts in different areas of law, which affected various aspects of life in society, including fundamental changes in, for example, property law, the law of obligations, family law, gender, equality and human rights.

In this period, law was in a constantly, sometimes rapidly, changing state of flux. It was also created in different fora by various actors. As mentioned before, legislation played a paramount role, but it was not the only source of law during this period. Judicial decisions became prominent, and doctrine, custom and soft law also entered the stage, both in civil and common law systems.

Actors shaped the law in different ways during this period. Judges conquered new ground with the development of constitutional and international courts, while jurists played a less visible role when compared with their activities described in previous chapters of this volume. Legislators had to compete more and more with influence groups and individual activists advocating for bottom-up change. Legal education was impacted by mass enrolment in higher education and by changes in teaching methods. There was a notable increase in women entering the legal profession.

The application of law was subject to a paradigm shift. The movement towards international fora and courts gained momentum, which created alternatives for the application of law beyond national borders. Important divides were bridged. For instance, the dividing line between inquisitorial and adversarial systems in civil procedure became blurred. Another major divide between private and public law was crossed. The broader context made it possible for the laws and provisions of the different areas to interact. Because of this private and public law are no longer separated into watertight compartments.

Further Reading

Abásolo, Ezequiel et al. La cultura jurídica latinoamericana y la circulación de ideas durante la primera mitad del siglo XX: Aproximaciones teóricas y análisis de experiencias, Buenos Aires, Instituto de Investigaciones de Historia del Derecho, 2014.

Basedow, Jürgen et al. (eds), Legislators, Judges, and Professors, Tübingen, Mohr Siebeck, 2016.

Bergel, Jean-Louis. Les phénomènes de codification, de décodification et de recodification, in Louis Perret and Alain-François Bisson (eds), Evolution des Systemes Juridiques, Bijuridisme et Commerce International, Montreal, Wilson et Lafleur, 2003, 31–42.

Cottrol, Robert J. The Long Lingering Shadow: Slavery, Race, and Law in the American Hemisphere, Athens, University of Georgia Press, 2013.

Dezalay, Yves and Bryant G. Garth. The Internationalization of Palace Wars: Lawyers, Economists, and the Contest to Transform Latin American States, Chicago, University of Chicago Press, 2002.

Duguit, Léon. Les transformations générales du droit privé depuis le Code Napoléon, Paris, Félix Alcan, 1912.

Faure, Michael et al. (eds), Towards a European Ius Commune in Legal Education and Research, Antwerp, Intersentia, 2002.

Frankenberg, Günter. Comparative Law as Critique, Cheltenham, Edward Elgar Publishing, 2016.

Gerber, David J. Globalization and Legal Knowledge: Implications for Comparative Law, Tulane Law Review 75 (2001), 949–975.

Gómez, Manuel and Rogelio Pérez-Perdomo (eds), Big Law in Latin America and Spain: Globalization and Adjustments in the Provision of High-End Legal Services, Cham, Palgrave Macmillan, 2018.

Guzmán Brito, Alejandro. La codificación civil en Iberoamérica. Siglos XIX y XX, Santiago, Editorial Jurídica de Chile, 2000.

Halpérin, Jean-Louis. Histoire du droit privé français depuis 1804, Paris, Presses Universitaires de France, 1996.

Hartkamp, Arthur S. et al. (eds), Towards a European Civil Code (4th revised and expanded ed.), Alphen aan den Rijn, Kluwer Law International, 2011.

Kennedy, Duncan. Three Globalizations of Law and Legal Thought: 1850–2000, in David Trubek and Alvaro Santos (eds), The New Law and Economic Development. A Critical Appraisal, Cambridge and New York, Cambridge University Press, 2006, 19–73.

Lambert, Édouard. La fonction du droit civil comparé, Vol. I, Paris, V. Giard & E. Brière, 1903.

Llewellyn, Karl N. Some Realism About Realism – Responding to Dean Pound, Harvard Law Review 44 (1931), 1222–1264.

Lundmark, Thomas. Charting the Divide between Common and Civil Law, New York, Oxford University Press, 2012.

Merryman, John H. and Rogelio Pérez-Perdomo. The Civil Law Tradition: an Introduction to the Legal Systems of Europe and Latin America, 4th edition, Stanford, Stanford University Press, 2018.

Milward, Alan S. The Reconstruction of Western Europe, 1945–1951, London, Methuen, 1984.

Mirow, M.C. Latin American Law: a History of Private Law and Institutions in Spanish America, Austin, University of Texas Press, 2004.

Mirow, M.C. and Rafael Domingo (eds.), Law and Christianity in Latin America: the Work of Great Jurists, London, Routledge, 2021.

Moréteau, Olivier and Agustín Parise. Recodification in Louisiana and Latin America, Tulane Law Review 83 (2009), 1103–1162.

Reimann, Mathias and Reinhard Zimmermann. The Oxford Handbook of Comparative Law (2nd ed.), Oxford, Oxford University Press, 2019.

Smits, Jan (ed.), Elgar Encyclopedia of Comparative Law (2nd ed.), Cheltenham, Edward Elgar, 2012.

Uzelac, Alan and C.H. (Remco) van Rhee. Transformation of Civil Justice. Unity and Diversity, Cham, Springer, 2018.

van Middelaar, Luuk. The Passage to Europe: How a Continent became a Union, Newhaven, Yale University Press, 2014.

Zimmermann, Reinhard. Roman Law, Contemporary Law, European Law: the Civilian Tradition Today, Oxford, Oxford University Press, 2001.

Zweigert, Konrad and Hein Kötz. An Introduction to Comparative Law (transl. by Tony Weir) (3rd ed.), Oxford, Clarendon Press, 1998.

Index